Lecture Notes in Computer Science 13541

More information about this series at https://link.springer.com/bookseries/558

Gianmaria Silvello · Oscar Corcho ·
Paolo Manghi · Giorgio Maria Di Nunzio ·
Koraljka Golub · Nicola Ferro ·
Antonella Poggi (Eds.)

Linking Theory and Practice of Digital Libraries

26th International Conference on Theory and Practice
of Digital Libraries, TPDL 2022
Padua, Italy, September 20–23, 2022
Proceedings

Springer

Editors
Gianmaria Silvello 🔟
University of Padua
Padua, Italy

Oscar Corcho 🔟
Universidad Politécnica de Madrid
Madrid, Spain

Paolo Manghi 🔟
CNR-ISTI – National Research Council
Pisa, Italy

Giorgio Maria Di Nunzio
University of Padua
Padua, Italy

Koraljka Golub
Linnaeus University
Växjö, Sweden

Nicola Ferro 🔟
University of Padua
Padua, Italy

Antonella Poggi
Sapienza University of Rome
Rome, Italy

ISSN 0302-9743   ISSN 1611-3349 (electronic)
Lecture Notes in Computer Science
ISBN 978-3-031-16801-7   ISBN 978-3-031-16802-4 (eBook)
https://doi.org/10.1007/978-3-031-16802-4

Preface

These proceedings contain the full papers, short papers, and accelerating innovation papers selected for presentation at the 26th International Conference on Theory and Practice of Digital Libraries (TPDL 2022)[1]. The event was organized by the Information Management Systems (IMS) research group[2] of the Department of Information Engineering[3] of the University of Padua[4], Italy. The conference was held from September 20 to September 23, 2022, in Padua, Italy.

Over the years TPDL has established an important international forum focused on digital libraries and associated technical, practical, and social issues. TPDL encompasses the many meanings of the term digital libraries, including new forms of information institutions; operational information systems with all manner of digital content; new means of selecting, collecting, organizing, and distributing digital content; and theoretical models of information media, including document genres and electronic publishing. Digital libraries may be viewed as a new form of information institution or as an extension of the services libraries currently provide.

TPDL historically approached digital libraries embracing the field at large, and also recognizing three key areas of interest that can be synthesized as scholarly communication (e.g., research data, research software, digital experiments, digital libraries), e-science/computationally-intense research (e.g., scientific workflows, virtual research environments, reproducibility) and library, archive, and information science (e.g., governance, policies, open access, open science).

TPDL 2022 received a total of 107 submissions in three categories: 51 full papers, 50 short papers, and 6 accelerating innovation papers.

Full papers present high quality, original research of relevance to the TPDL community. Submissions should detail their methods and techniques in sufficient detail to enable replication and reuse. The accepted papers are published in these conference proceedings and were presented as long conference talks.

Short papers present high quality, original research or tools or applications that are of relevance to the TPDL community. The accepted papers are published in these conference proceedings and were presented as short conference talks.

Finally, the newly introduced "accelerating innovation" papers aim to speed up the transfer and exchange of new ideas and late-breaking results in order to accelerate and drive innovation. The accepted papers were presented in a gong show-style and with a poster at the conference.

The geographical distribution of the authors of the submitted papers was as follows: 81.3% were from Europe (38.5% from Germany, 18% from Italy, and 15% from Greece),

---

[1] http://tpdl2022.dei.unipd.it/.

[2] http://ims.dei.unipd.it/.

[3] http://www.dei.unipd.it/.

[4] http://www.unipd.it/en/.

8.3% from Asia, 8% from North and South America, 1.2% from Africa, and 0.6% from Australasia.

All submissions were reviewed by at least three members of an international Program Committee and by one senior meta-reviewer. Of the full papers submitted to the conference, 18 were accepted for oral presentation (35%), nine were accepted as short papers (17.6%), and two as accelerating innovation papers (0.04%). Of the short papers, 18 were accepted for oral presentation (36%) and 10 were accepted as accelerating innovation papers (20%). Finally, TPDL 2022 accepted four out of the six submitted accelerating innovation papers.

We thank all Program Committee members for their time and effort in ensuring the high quality of the TPDL 2022 program.

Additionally, TPDL 2022 hosted two workshops covering a range of digital library topics. These were selected by the workshop committee.

The workshops were

- The 1st International Workshop on Digital Platforms and Resources for Access to Literary Heritage (DIPRAL 2022); and
- The 2nd International Workshop on Archives and Linked Data (Linked Archives 2022).

We would like to thank our invited speakers for their contributions to the program: Roberto Di Cosmo (Inria - National Institute for Research in Digital Science and Technology, France) and Georgia Koutrika (Athena Research Center, Greece). Short descriptions of these talks are included in the proceedings.

TPDL 2022 was held under the patronage of the University of Padua, and the Department of Information Engineering.

Finally, we would like to thank our sponsors: ExaMode and the Universidad Politecnica de Madrid (gold level); the Department of Information Engineering of the University of Padua (silver level); and MDPI and Springer (bronze level). The conference was supported by the Coalition for Networked Information.

August 2022

Gianmaria Silvello
Oscar Corcho
Paolo Manghi
Giorgio Maria Di Nunzio
Koraljka Golub
Nicola Ferro
Antonella Poggi

Organization

General Chair

Gianmaria Silvello   University of Padua, Italy

Program Chairs

Oscar Corcho   Universidad Politcnica de Madrid, Spain
Paolo Manghi   ISTI-CNR, Italy

Short Program Chairs

Giorgio Maria Di Nunzio   University of Padua, Italy
Koraljka Golub   Linnaeus University, Sweden

Accelerating Innovation Program Chairs

Nicola Ferro   University of Padua, Italy
Antonella Poggi   Sapienza University of Rome, Italy

Workshop Chair

Leonardo Candela   ISTI-CNR, Italy

Doctoral Consortium Chairs

Gerd Berget   Oslo Metropolitan University, Norway
Trond Aalberg   Norwegian University of Science and Technology, Norway

Organization Chair

Fabio Giachelle   University of Padua, Italy

Senior Program Committee

Trond Aalborg   Norwegian University of Science and Technology, Norway
Maristella Agosti   University of Padua, Italy

Omar Alonso	Amazon, USA
Amir Aryani	Swinburne University of Technology, Australia
Sören Auer	Leibniz Universität Hannover, Germany
José Borbinha	Universidade de Lisboa, Portugal
George Buchanan	University of Melbourne, Australia
Donatella Castelli	ISTI-CNR, Italy
Fabien Duchateau	Université Claude Bernard Lyon 1 - LIRIS, France
Edward Fox	Virginia Tech, USA
Norbert Fuhr	University of Duisburg-Essen, Germany
Carole Goble	University of Manchester, UK
Mark Michael Hall	The Open University, UK
Martin Klein	Los Alamos National Laboratory, USA
Michael Nelson	Old Dominion University, USA
Christos Papatheodorou	University of Athens, Greece
Gabriella Pasi	University of Milano-Bicocca, Italy
Thomas Risse	University of Frankfurt, Germany
Herbert Van de Sompel	Data Archiving Networked Services, The Netherlands
Ludo Waltman	Leiden University, The Netherlands

Program Committee

Sawood Alam	Internet Archive, USA
Marco Angelini	Sapienza University of Rome, Italy
Carlos Badenes-Olmedo	Universidad Politcnica de Madrid, Spain
Miriam Baglioni	ISTI-CNR, Italy
Wolf-Tilo Balke	TU Braunschweig, Germany
Alessia Bardi	ISTI-CNR, Italy
Carlos Bobed	University of Zaragoza, Spain
José Borbinha	University of Melbourne, Australia
Ricardo Campos	Polytechnic Institute of Tomar, Portugal
Annalina Caputo	Dublin City University, Ireland
Michelangelo Ceci	University of Bari, Italy
Yinlin Chen	Virginia Tech, USA
Marilena Daquino	University of Bologna, Italy
Boris Dobrov	Moscow State University, Russia
Dennis Dosso	University of Padua, Italy
Guglielmo Faggioli	University of Padua, Italy
Stefano Ferilli	University of Bari, Italy
Nuno Freire	INESC-ID, Portugal
Yannis Foufoulas	University of Athens, Greece
Fabio Giachelle	University of Padua, Italy
Jose Manuel Gomez-Perez	expert.ai, Spain

Short Program Committee

Hamed Alhoori	Northern Illinois University, USA
Robert Allen	Independent, USA
Vangelis Banos	Aristotle University of Thessaloniki, Greece
Gerd Berget	Oslo Metropolitan University, Norway
José Borbinha	Universidade de Lisboa, Portugal
Maria Manuel Borges	University of Coimbra, Portugal
Vittore Casarosa	ISTI-CNR, Italy
Songphan Choemprayong	Chulalongkorn University, Thailand
Mickal Coustaty	Laboratoire L3i - La Rochelle Université, France
Theodore Dalamagas	Athena Research Center, Greece
Tahereh Dehdarirad	Chalmers University of Technology, Sweden
Boris Dobrov	Moscow State University, Russia
Shyamala Doraisamy	Universiti Putra Malaysia, Malaysia
Fabien Duchateau	Université Claude Bernard Lyon 1 - LIRIS, France
Ralph Ewerth	L3S Research Center, Leibniz Universität Hannover, Germany
Edward Fox	Virginia Tech, USA
Nuno Freire	INESC-ID, Portugal
Maria Gaede	Humboldt-Universität zu Berlin, Germany
Manolis Gergatsoulis	Ionian University, Greece
C. Lee Giles	Pennsylvania State University, USA
Matthias Hagen	Martin-Luther-Universität Halle-Wittenberg, Germany
Mark Hall	The Open University, UK
Morgan Harvey	University of Sheffield, UK
Andreas Henrich	University of Bamberg, Germany
Nikos Housos	University of Patras, Greece
Antoine Isaac	Europeana and VU Amsterdam, The Netherlands
Robert Jäschke	Humboldt-Universität zu Berlin, Germany
Roman Kern	Graz University of Technology, Austria
Martin Klein	Los Alamos National Laboratory, USA
Petr Knoth	The Open University, UK
Stefanos Kollias	National Technical University of Athens, Greece
Marijn Koolen	Royal Netherlands Academy of Arts and Sciences, The Netherlands
Laszlo Kovacs	Institute for Computer Science and Control (SZTAKI), Hungary
Suzanne Little	Dublin City University, Ireland
Ying-Hsang Liu	Oslo Metropolitan University, Norway
Clifford Lynch	CNI, USA
Elena Maceviciute	University of Boras, Sweden

Yannis Manolopoulos	Open University of Cyprus, Cyprus
Bruno Martins	INESC-ID and University of Lisbon, Portugal
Philipp Mayr	GESIS, Germany
Robert H. McDonald	University of Colorado Boulder, USA
Dana Mckay	RMIT University, Australia
Tanja Merun	University of Ljubljana, Slovenia
Andrs Micsik	Institute for Computer Science and Control (SZTAKI), Hungary
Agnieszka Mykowiecka	Institute of Computer Science, Polish Academy of Sciences, Poland
Michael Nelson	Old Dominion University, USA
Erich Neuhold	University of Vienna, Austria
David Nichols	University of Waikato, New Zealand
Kjetil Nørvåg	Norwegian University of Science and Technology, Norway
Christos Papatheodorou	National and Kapodistrian University of Athens, Greece
Vivien Petras	Humboldt-Universität zu Berlin, Germany
Dimitris Plexousakis	FORTH-ICS, Greece
Edie Rasmussen	University of British Columbia, Canada
Cristina Ribeiro	University of Porto, Portugal
Thomas Risse	University of Frankfurt, Germany
Irene Rodrigues	Universidade de Evora, Portugal
Heiko Schuldt	University of Basel, Switzerland
Michalis Sfakakis	Ionian University, Greece
Marc Spaniol	Université de Caen Normandie, France
Cyrille Suire	Université Paris-Saclay and UVSQ, France
Chrisa Tsinaraki	European Commission - Joint Research Center, Italy
Douglas Tudhope	University of South Wales, UK
Yannis Tzitzikas	University of Crete and FORTH-ICS, Greece
Pertti Vakkari	Tampere University, Finland
Stefanos Vrochidis	ITI-CERTH, Greece
Michele Weigle	Old Dominion University, USA
Maja Žumer	University of Ljubljana, Slovenia

Additional Reviewers

Christian Otto	Aman Ahuja
David Pride	Michalis Mountantonakis
Satvik Chekuri	Eleftherios Kalogeros
Filip Kovacevic	Prashant Chandrasekar
Alexandros Vassiliades	Junaid Ghauri

Democratizing Data Access: What if We Could Just Talk to Our Data?

Georgia Koutrika
Athena Research Center, Greece

georgia@athenarc.gr

Abstract. Data is considered the 21st century's most valuable commodity. Analysts exploring data sets for insight, scientists looking for patterns, and consumers looking for information are just a few examples of user groups that need to access and dig into data. However, existing data access and exploration systems are still following two classical paradigms: they are either form-based interfaces that allow users to easily query the data but with limited query capabilities, or they are low-level programmatic tools that allow the users to write their own queries using programming or query languages such as Python or SQL, but they are intended for CS experts.

On the other hand, enabling users to query data in a database using natural language has been considered the holy grail of the database community. In 1974, E. F. Codd was underlining this need: "If we are to satisfy the needs of casual users of databases, we must break the barriers that presently prevent these users from freely employing their native language" [2]. Several natural language interfaces for databases emerged since then; recent approaches are using deep learning techniques with promising results but also important limitations [1, 3].

While these systems are taking us closer to the holy grail of "talking to data", to bridge the gap between data and humans, we envision a system that allows users to dig into data and find answers by conversing and collaborating with the system, as if it were a human. This system would enable interaction using natural language, would understand the data as well as the user intent, would guide the user, and make suggestions, and help the user find answers to questions over data in a more natural way.

These *intelligent data assistants* are much more complex than any "digital assistant" we know of today, which are based on pre-specified dialogues and can answer simple questions. They require the synergy of several technologies and innovation in all these fronts, including natural language interfaces, data exploration, conversational AI, and data management.

The intention of this talk is to give a flavor of an exciting research territory, discuss where we stand today, opportunities and challenges.

Short Bio

Georgia Koutrika is a Research Director at Athena Research Center in Greece. She has more than 15 years of experience in multiple roles at HP Labs, IBM Almaden, and Stanford. Her work emerges at the intersection of data management, natural language processing and deep learning, and focuses on intelligent and interactive data exploration, conversational data systems, and user-driven data management.

Her work has been incorporated in commercial products, described in 14 granted patents and 26 patent applications in the US and worldwide, and published in more than 100 papers in top-tier conferences and journals. Georgia is an ACM Senior Member and IEEE Senior Member.

She is a member of the VLDB Endowment Board of Trustees, member of the PVLDB Advisory Board, member of the ACM-RAISE Working Group, co-Editor-in-chief for VLDB Journal, PC co-chair for VLDB 2023, co-EiC of Proceedings of VLDB (PVLDB). She has been associate editor in top-tier conferences (such as ACM SIGMOD, VLDB) and journals (VLDB Journal, IEEE TKDE), and she has been in the organizing committee of several conferences including SIGMOD, ICDE, EDBT, among others. She has received a PhD and a diploma in Computer Science from the Department of Informatics and Telecommunications, University of Athens, Greece.

References

1. Affolter, K., Stockinger, K., Bernstein, A.: A comparative survey of recent natural language interfaces for databases. VLDB J. **28**(5), 793–819 (2019). https://doi.org/10.1007/s00778-019-00567-8
2. Codd, E.F.: Seven steps to rendezvous with the casual user. In: Klimbie, J.W., Koffeman, K.L. (eds.) Data Base Management, Proceeding of the IFIP Working Conference Data Base Management, Cargèse, Corsica, France, April 1–5, 1974, pp. 179–200. North-Holland, Jan. (1974)
3. Katsogiannis-Meimarakis, G., Koutrika, G.: A deep dive into deep learning approaches for Text-to-SQL systems. In: Proceedings of the 2021 International Conference on Management of Data, SIGMOD 2021, pp. 2846–2851. Association for Computing Machinery, New York (2021)

Contents

Short Papers

Keynote Talks

Should We Preserve the World's Software History, And Can We?

Roberto Di Cosmo$^{(\boxtimes)}$ iD

Software Heritage, Inria and Université Paris Cité, Paris, France
roberto@dicosmo.org

Abstract. Cultural heritage is the legacy of physical artifacts and intangible attributes of a group or society that a re inherited from past generations, maintained in the present and bestowed for the benefit of future generations.

What role does software play in it? We claim that software source code is an important product of human creativity, and embodies a growing part of our scientific, organisational and technological knowledge: it is a part of our cultural heritage, and it is our collective responsibility to ensure that it is not lost.

Preserving the history of software is also a key enabler for reproducibility of research, and as a means to foster better and more secure software for society. This is the mission of Software Heritage, a non-profit organization dedicated to building the universal archive of software source code, catering to the needs of science, industry and culture, for the benefit of society as a whole.

In this keynote talk we survey the principles and key technology used in the archive that contains over 12 billion unique source code files from some 180 millions projects worldwide.

1 Introduction

Software is incorporating an important part of our scientific, technical and industrial heritage.

If one looks closely, it is easy to see that the real knowledge that is contained in software is not in the executable programs, but in the "source code", which according to the definition used in the GPL, is *"the preferred form for a developer to make a change to a program"*[1]. Source code is a special form of knowledge: it is made to be understood by a human being, the developer, and can be mechanically translated into a form to be executed directly on a machine. The very terminology used by the computing community is telling: "programming languages" are used to "write" software. As Harold Habelson wrote as early as 1985, "programs must be written for humans to read, and only accessorily for machines to execute"[2]

---

[1] Gnu general public license, version 2, 1991. Retrieved September 2015.

[2] Preface to Abelson, H., and Sussman, G. J. S. (1985). Structure and Interpretation of Computer Programs. The MIT Press.

© The Author(s) 2022
G. Silvello et al. (Eds.): TPDL 2022, LNCS 13541, pp. 3–7, 2022.
https://doi.org/10.1007/978-3-031-16802-4_1

The *source code* of software is therefore a human creation in the same way as other written documents, and software developers deserve the same respect as other creators [5].

Software source code is therefore a valuable heritage, and it is essential to work on its preservation.

This is one of the missions of Software Heritage, an initiative launched in 2015 with the support of Inria and in partnership with UNESCO, to *collect, organize, preserve* and *make easily accessible* all publicly available source code on the planet, regardless of where and how it was developed or distributed.

2 A Complex Task

Archiving all available source code is a complex task: as detailed in the article [1], different strategies are needed depending on whether one seeks to collect open or proprietary source code, and one does not treat source code that is readily available online in the same way as source code that resides on older physical media.

For open source code that is readily available online, the most appropriate approach is to build a harvester that automatically collects content from a wide variety of collaborative development platforms, such as GitHub, GitLab.com, or BitBucket, or from software package distribution platforms, such as Debian, NPM. CRAN or Pypi.

For the source code of old software, a real process of computer archaeology must be set up, and we have already started this work in a collaboration with the University of Pisa and UNESCO that has resulted in the SWHAP process that has been used to find, document and archive software that is important in the history of computing in Italy (see https://www.softwareheritage.org/swhap), and which has recently been extended with the Software Stories project, which aims to highlight all the historical elements around a software whose source code has been found (see https://stories.softwareheritage.org).

3 A Universal Mission

The founding principles of Software Heritage are [1]: systematic use of open source software to build the Software Heritage infrastructure, so that its operation can be understood, and replicated if necessary; construction of a global network of independent mirrors of the archive, because a large number of copies is the best protection against loss and attack; choice of a non-profit, international, multi-stakeholder structure, to minimize the risk of having single points of failure, and to ensure that Software Heritage will indeed serve all.

For such a mission, institutional legitimacy is required, as well as openness to federate a broad consensus. This is why the framework agreement signed between Inria and UNESCO on April 3, 2017, and renewed in November 2021, is essential.

4   Past, Present, Future: Much More Than an Archive

Software Heritage is now an infrastructure that grows day by day: the bulk of the archive's content is the result of automatic harvesting, but pearls are beginning to be introduced through the patient work of recovering significant historical software, following the SWHAP acquisition process that has been developed in collaboration with the University of Pisa and UNESCO.

Exhaustiveness is still far from being achieved, but the archive already contains the largest corpus of source code available on the planet, with more than 180 million archived origins, for over 12 billion unique source files, each equipped with an intrinsic identifier based on cryptographic hashes [2,3] (Fig. 1).

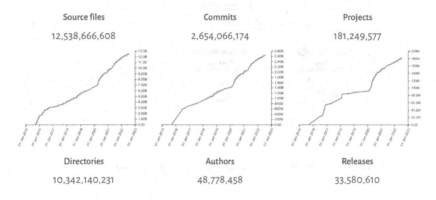

Fig. 1. Number of projects, source files, and versions archived in Sofware Heritage as of June 2022 (see `https://www.softwareheritate.org/archive`)

This unique infrastructure has a multiple mission: of course, it is about preserving for future generations the source codes of the past that made the history of Computer Science and the Information Society, but also, and above all, we are trying to build a very large telescope that will allow us to explore the present evolution of the software development galaxy, in order to better understand it, and to improve it, in order to build a better technological future.

5   A Peek Under the Hood

In Fig. 2 one can find a high level overview of the architecture of the Software Heritage crawler, and of the key data structure that is used to store all the source code with its development history. Software development and distribution platforms abound, and there is no single standard protocol to interact with them, so Software Heritage is building, with the help of a growing community, a large set of connectors, called *listers*, to identify the available software projects. There is no single standard for keeping track of versions of software either, nor for distributing packaged software, so we are also building a large set of converters, called *loaders*, that are able to encode all these different formats in a single, universal data structure, that is based on the Merkle tree construction [4]. This uniform data structure contains today over 30 billion nodes and 350 billion edges, one of the largest public graphs available.

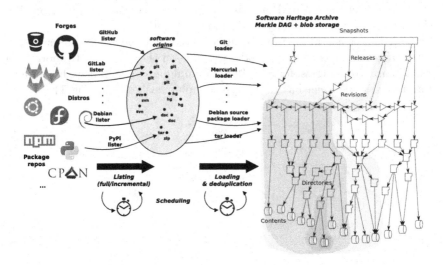

Fig. 2. The Software Heritage architecture: crawling and data structure

In this giant Merkle graph, every software artefact is identified by a cryptographic intrinsic persistent identifier, called SWHID, that can be used to check integrity of the artifact without relying on any central registry. A key side effect is the fact that duplicate artifacts can be immediately spotted (they have the same identifier!), and the Software Heritage archive only keeps one copy of each of them, while keeping track of all their occurrences.

6   Beyond Preservation, A Strategic Issue

The Software Heritage archive is already the most important source code collection in the world, but there is still a long way to go: a wide range of players, from cultural heritage to industry, from research to public administration, must be brought together around it. To do this, we are counting on a growing network of ambassadors (see https://softwareheritage.org/ambassadors/). It is clear that software has become an essential component of all human activity, and therefore unrestricted access to publicly available software source codes is becoming a digital sovereignty issue for all nations. The unique infrastructure that Software Heritage is building, and its universal approach, is an essential element to meet this challenge of digital sovereignty while preserving the common good dimension of the archive. It is therefore of the utmost importance that institutional, industrial, academic and civil society actors grasp the importance of these issues, providing the necessary resources to make Software Heritage grow and last, by taking their place alongside other international actors who are already committed, and by supporting the creation of an international non-profit institution that will carry out this mission over the long term.

7   For More Information

You can learn more about the project by visiting www.softwareheritage.org, annex.softwareheritage.org and docs.softwareheritage.org. It is possible to easily explore the source codes contained in Software Heritage on archive.softwareheritage.org.

References

1. Abramatic, J.-F., Di Cosmo, R., Zacchiroli, S.: Building the universal archive of source code. Commun. ACM **61**(10), 29–31 (2018)
2. Di Cosmo, R.: Archiving and referencing source code with software heritage. In: Bigatti, A.M., Carette, J., Davenport, J.H., Joswig, M., de Wolff, T. (eds.) ICMS 2020. LNCS, vol. 12097, pp. 362–373. Springer, Cham (2020). https://doi.org/10. 1007/978-3-030-52200-1_36
3. Di Cosmo, R., Gruenpeter, M., Zacchiroli, S.: Referencing source code artifacts: a separate concern in software citation. Comput. Sci. Eng. **22**(2), 33–43 (2020)
4. Merkle, R.C.: A digital signature based on a conventional encryption function. In: Pomerance, C. (ed.) CRYPTO 1987. LNCS, vol. 293, pp. 369–378. Springer, Heidelberg (1988). https://doi.org/10.1007/3-540-48184-2_32
5. Shustek, L.J.: What should we collect to preserve the history of software? IEEE Ann. Hist. Comput. **28**(4), 110–112 (2006)

Full Papers

Analyzing the Web: Are Top Websites Lists a Good Choice for Research?

Tom Alby$^{(\boxtimes)}$ and Robert Jäschke

Humboldt-Universität zu Berlin, Berlin, Germany
{thomas.alby,robert.jaeschke}@hu-berlin.de

Abstract. The web has been a subject of research since its beginning, but it is difficult if not impossible to analyze the whole web, even if a database of all URLs would be freely accessible. Hundreds of studies have used commercial top websites lists as a shortcut, in particular the Alexa One Million Top Sites list. However, apart from the fact that Amazon decided to terminate Alexa, we question the usefulness of such lists for research as they have several shortcomings. Our analysis shows that top sites lists miss frequently visited websites and offer only little value for language-specific research. We present a heuristic-driven alternative based on the Common Crawl host-level web graph while also taking language-specific requirements into account.

1 Introduction

The web provides an almost endless reservoir of data, but at the same time, it is virtually impossible to get a complete picture of the web due to its size and its continuous changes. As a consequence, researchers that want to leverage web resources for their research have to define how to create a valid data set to answer their questions. This can be easy if a study focuses on a data source itself such as a search engine ("What is the quality of health information in Google's search results?") but becomes more difficult if a more general question needs to be answered ("What are the most common trackers on the web?"). In absence of a database of all currently active hosts of the web, the Alexa Top Sites lists and similar offers have attracted researchers as these lists seem to provide an easy answer to a complex question [12,27,39]. In December 2021, Amazon announced that alexa.com would be retired in May 2022 [3].

However, several dimensions should be taken into account when a selection is made:

Completeness: Does the selection represent the web or the topic that is analyzed? If it is a sample, is it a random sample of all available hosts?

Freshness: In how far does the selection represent the web at the current state? Are new hosts included? Have dead hosts been removed?

Language: Is it possible to include only pages in a specific language?

G. Silvello et al. (Eds.): TPDL 2022, LNCS 13541, pp. 11–25, 2022.
https://doi.org/10.1007/978-3-031-16802-4_2

Locale: Is it possible to retrieve pages that are relevant to a specific locale? A pizza delivery website in Austria is not relevant to a German user but a pizza recipe site from Austria is.

Topic distinction: Is it possible to restrict a selection to a topic?

User-facing versus embedded resources: Some sites embed resources from other websites, for example, Google Fonts, and these sites are not intended to be seen by human users. Are these resources required for an analysis or could they distort the results?

Quality and spam prevention: Some web pages are excluded from search engines and other repositories because they include spam.

Our goal is to help researchers understand the disadvantages of each approach with respect to the points above and to provide a heuristic-driven solution. Therefore, we review several data sources that can be grouped into three categories:

- search engines (e.g., Google and Bing),
- top sites lists (e.g., Alexa and Majestic),
- other repositories that include URLs and that are freely accessible to researchers (e.g., Twitter, Wikipedia, and Common Crawl).

We only review data sources that are still being updated, excluding historical data sets that are not refreshed anymore such as the dmoz database or del.icio.us data. For comparison reasons, one example of an Alexa list is included despite its shutdown. In addition to a general look at the data sources, we will also analyze the appropriateness of sources for the German locale as an example of a language-specific subset that shares only the language with other locales.

This paper is organized as follows: In Sect. 2, an overview of related work is provided. In Sect. 3, different data sources, acquisition approaches and processing methods are described. The results of the analysis of these data sets are provided in Sect. 4. Finally, in Sect. 5, we propose our solution and close with a recommendation for further research.

2   Related Work

While no comparison between the aforementioned data sets exists to the best of our knowledge, each data source has been extensively reviewed for itself. Approaches using search results from both Google and Bing have been analyzed with respect to their limited coverage of different countries and languages [43, 46] and spam, that is, web pages of low quality [13]. The use of search engine results for linguistic research has been criticized due to the lack of transparency about linguistic processing and fluctuation of results [23]. Search engine freshness was critically viewed [25].

Internet top lists are widely used in research [4, 10, 30, 40] but their quality and stability is questionable and subject to manipulation [35, 36, 39] which also has an impact on the results of research [38]. In order to protect research from manipulated lists, top lists provided by Alexa, Cisco Umbrella, Majestic, and QuantCast have been combined in TRANCO, using either a Borda count or Dowdall's rule to let lists rank the inclusion of a site in an output list [36]. A combination of an Alexa top list with topic categories combined with crawls of the Internet Archive, restricted to .de domains emphasized the pace of changes in the web, stating however that crawling strategies of different indices are biased and will thus result in biased results [20]. A bias in terms of language and country distribution has also been detected in the Internet Archive [5,17,44]. Finally, Lo and Sedhain reviewed different website rankings of which none is available anymore [28].

Wikipedia is regarded as a stepping stone between search engines and other websites [34]. Spamming approaches that try to add links of low quality to Wikipedia articles perform poorly, resulting in a rather clean repository of URLs [49]. However, the quality of information on web sites that is being linked to by Wikipedia is inferior to the information provided by official sites [24].

Finally, undesirable content has been found in the Common Crawl corpus and challenges the language models based on this data [29]. Another quality problem in Common Crawl data is caused by near-duplicates [14].

3 Experiments and Data

3.1 Experimental Setup

Data was collected in the first half of 2021. Each dataset has been processed before it was compared to the other sets. Some datasets contain complete *URLs* such as https://www.hu-berlin.de/index.html, other include *hosts* (www.ibi.hu-berlin.de), and Alexa only offers second-level *domains* (hu-berlin.de)[1]. Our study focuses on hosts and not on second-level domains since different hosts on the same domain can have different content. As a first step, malformed URLs were removed from the datasets, host names were extracted from URLs and stripped off "www.", since some sources do not include it. The reverse domain name notation of the Common Crawl host web graph has been transformed to the notation of the other datasets. Finally, duplicates were removed from each list, and hosts were matched between the lists. The details of the acquisition and specifics for each dataset are described in the next sections. Research data is available for download [2].

3.2 Search

Search results have been analyzed in various papers, for example in order to analyze the information that users see for specific queries [1,9,19,22,24,47]. Using queries allows for topic selection and the identification of relevant hosts to that topic, while a full list of all sites in Google's and Bing's indices is not available.

---

[1] The term *sites* will be used as a synonym for *hosts*. A *page* is regarded as a single web page document on a *host*.

Query selection thus plays an important role, involving either the creation of a keyword cluster around a topic including the search volumes[2], or creating a sample of general queries. In addition, search engines offer language and locale selection, that is, search engines determine a user's locale and language preference and rank results accordingly.

For our study, we use two different data sets:

- A random sample of 1,000 English search queries of the Million Query Track Overview [8] that accounts for 101,001,690 average monthly search volume on the US version of Google. The most popular query in the data set, *google maps*, has an average monthly search volume of 24,900,000 alone.
- Three sets of German language queries that each cover a topic of different popularity level according to the Google Keyword Planner:
  - Federal Election ("Bundestagswahl") as this was a "hot" topic in Germany in summer 2021 with 614 queries that account for 939,730 average monthly search volume
  - iMac M1 (same in German) with 90 queries and an average monthly search volume of 12,180 as these new iMacs were announced in April 2021
  - Minimalism ("Minimalismus" in German, can be interpreted as an art direction, a music style or a lifestyle approach) with 86 queries and an average monthly search volume of 34,510.

Queries were sent to both Bing and Google, the first data set to the en-US versions of the search engines, the second to the de-DE versions. Only the first results page was considered as less than 1% of clicks go on a result on the second results page [6].

3.3   Top Sites

Top lists have been used in many studies [18,20,21,45], in particular the Alexa Top Sites list. Different methods are used by providers to generate each list. Alexa ranks sites based on the number of visits measured by a browser-based panel. While Cisco Umbrella also leverages user behaviour, this list is based on the number of DNS requests for hosts, including those that receive requests from other device types[3]. Looking at Table 1, the Cisco top 10 includes hosts such as Netflix delivery nodes that are typically not visited by user browsers. The main advantage of monitoring user behavior, however, is the freshness of the data.

Majestic provides a list of top sites based on a link graph that is based on links discovered in Majestic's own crawls[4], that is, it is not created based on user behavior but on the number of links of pages pointing to other pages.

---

[2] Relevant queries and their search volume can be identified using tools such as the Google Keyword Planner that provides historical data about search volume of specific queries.

[3] https://s3-us-west-1.amazonaws.com/umbrella-static/index.html.

[4] https://majestic.com/reports/majestic-million.

Table 1. Top 10 sites across different lists.

Alexa	Cisco Umbrella	Majestic	Common Crawl
google.com	google.com	google.com	facebook.com
youtube.com	netflix.com	facebook.com	fonts.googleapis.com
baidu.com	microsoft.com	youtube.com	twitter.com
facebook.com	www.google.com	twitter.com	google.com
instagram.com	ftl.netflix.com	instagram.com	youtube.com
bilibili.com	prod.ftl.netflix.com	linkedin.com	s.w.org
yahoo.com	api-global.netflix.com	microsoft.com	instagram.com
qq.com	data.microsoft.com	apple.com	goo...tagmanager.com
wikipedia.org	ichnaea.netflix.com	wikipedia.org	linkedin.com
amazon.com	eve...data.microsoft.com	goo...tagmanager.com	ajax.googleapis.com

Common Crawl (see Sect. 3.4) follows a similar approach in their web graphs. The assumption behind link-based approaches is that sites with a high link popularity are also more popular for users. Since web sites also embed resources from other hosts that count as a link, the top sites include services such as the Google Tag Manager (see Table 1). The link popularity approach has several disadvantages as it is prone to spam, links in the graph may point to dead sites, and not every active site has an incoming link, especially new sites, so that completeness could be a problem as well.

TRANCO offered a combination of Alexa, Quantcast (based on traffic measured by a toolbar and an internet service provider), Cisco, and Majestic data but two of their initial data sources, Alexa and Quantcast, are not available anymore today. We use the Tranco list generated on 31 July 2021, including a combination of ranks provided by Alexa, Umbrella, and Majestic from May 1st, 2021 to May 31st, 2021[5].

These different ways to compile a *top* list lead to the question why most lists include exactly *one million* sites. For Alexa and Cisco, no information about the frequency or length of user visits to the hosts or any other key performance indicator is included. In other words, we do not know if a top one million sites list represents 80%, 50%, or only 2% of overall web traffic, time spent on these sites, or numbers of visits. In Sect. 4.2, we will approach popularity in terms of whether a host is found for a Google search and, in Sect. 4.3 with respect to the search volume.

Cisco, Majestic, and TRANCO offer a selection based on TLDs. In Sect. 4.4, we will review in how far TLDs are suitable for representing a locale or a language. None of the data sources above provides a topic detection.

3.4 Common Crawl

The Common Crawl project's data has been widely used for research in different areas [15,16,37,41,42,48]. Seed URLs for Common Crawl are collected from

---

[5] Available at https://tranco-list.eu/list/3X4L.

outlinks or sitemaps [33]. Crawls usually take place on a monthly basis, updating known pages but also crawling new pages. The focus is set on broadness rather than depth of hosts, that is, Common Crawl tries to get a broad sample of hosts and more pages from higher ranking domains.

Common Crawl's June 2021 crawl includes 2.45 billion web pages, the host web graph of the crawls of February/March, April and May 2021 had 514,570,180 nodes[6]. The graph data includes a column with a ranked position based on harmonic centrality [7] and another one based on PageRank. Harmonic centrality takes the distance of a node into account whereas PageRank considers the importance of the neighbourhood of a node. We have used harmonic centrality due to it being less influenced by spam [31].

Common Crawl also offers domain, host, and URL information with detected languages. Language is identified and annotated by Common Crawl using the Common Language Detector 2[7]. Up to three languages can be associated with a page, cascading up to the host. We have downloaded all known hosts that were detected to include German content since the start of the Common Crawl project (10,057,081 hosts), using the Amazon Web Services Athena interface [32].

3.5 Wikipedia

Wikipedia includes one of the last manually collected and reviewed URL repositories after the closures of Yahoo's directory in 2010 and the Open Directory in 2017. For this study, data dumps of external links with 3,707,420 unique hosts of the English and 1,159,179 unique hosts of the German version of Wikipedia, published in July 2021, have been analyzed[8].

The dump of external links does not contain any topics for each URL. These could be extracted from the Wikipedia page that includes such links, requiring additional processing steps. Not all of the links included in the German external links dump refer to German-language content hosts, that is, we cannot conclude that this is a German-language dataset or specific to a locale. Wikipedia has its own link rot detection method to ensure freshness. Resources embedded from other hosts are not included in the Wikipedia links.

3.6 Twitter

Twitter offers a sampled stream that covers approximately 1% of all publicly available tweets [11]. A collection of this data with tweets from February 1st, 2021 to July 31st, 2021, has been analyzed for this study, resulting in 21,031,785 discovered unique hosts in tweets. A subset of 3,505,629 tweets in German language as detected by Twitter's own language detection engine resulted in 25,881

---

[6] Data available at https://commoncrawl.org/2021/05/host-and-domain-level-web-graphs-feb-apr-may-2021/.

[7] https://github.com/CLD2Owners/cld2.

[8] Data dumps of Wikipedia External links are available at https://dumps.wikimedia.org/backup-index.html.

unique hosts. However, while the text of a tweet is detected to be in German language, this does not mean that the URL in the same tweet will link to a German language website or that it is specific to the German locale.

Twitter does not offer topics. However, hashtags that annotate tweets could act as a proxy for topic identification. For the German language tweets subset, hashtags were extracted to search for hosts containing the topics that were used for the search data set. In order to identify URLs that could be relevant for the same topics but that are not present in search, we first looked at the URL overlap for each topic between tweets and search engines and then extracted the hashtags for those URLs present in both datasets. Of these tweets, we also extracted their other hashtags in order to broaden the recall.

4 Results

4.1 Completeness: Overlap of Data Sets

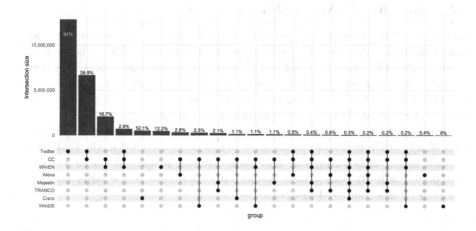

Fig. 1. UpSet diagram displaying the overlap of the data sources. Each bar shows the overlap or uniqueness of one or more data sources with a percentage of hosts unknown to the other hosts. The diagram includes only hosts from Common Crawl (CC) that are present in at least one other data source. The graph is built based on a minimum intersection size of 50,000 hosts.

Figure 1 shows the small overlap between the different data sets in an UpSet diagram [26]; the low number of overlapping unique hosts has also been described by Pochat et al. [36]. Each bar shows the number of overlapping hosts in the data sources, displayed as dots in the matrix below and a percentage of the hosts exclusive to this intersection relative to its potential size. The diagram does not include all hosts of the Common Crawl graph due to 94.9% of hosts in the Common Crawl graph being unknown to the other data sources. Instead, only those Common Crawl hosts were included that were also present in at least one other data source, resulting in 26,059,931 unique hosts.

Twitter surprisingly has 61% hosts that are unknown to the other data sources while it still has the biggest overlap with the Common Crawl Web graph. However, more than 71% of these hosts found in Twitter occur only once in the data set and their quality needs further review. Without a filter in terms of traffic, link popularity, or visits and no review by other humans as in Wikipedia, Twitter may include hosts that cannot pass the filters of the other data sources. Similarly, the majority of sites in the Cisco list is unknown to the other data sets (52.1%), which may be the result of the inclusion of hosts that are embedded by other services.

Not only is the overlap of the top lists low, they also hardly correlate in terms of ranking as pointed out by Pochat et al. [36]. To illustrate this point, for Alexa and Majestic, less than 50% of their hosts appear within the first million hosts of the Common Crawl host-level web graph; about 95% are found within the first 50 million.

4.2   Search Results Versus Other Data Sets

Given that both Common Crawl and Twitter have large amounts of hosts unknown to the other lists, the question is whether these additional hosts are of minor quality and thus excluded for good reasons by the top lists. As the overlap between the other top lists is small, search results will be leveraged as an additional signal: If a host is regarded as good enough to be included by search engines, we assume that its quality does not indicate its exclusion.

Comparing the two search engines against each other, Bing and Google have surprisingly different result with respect to the hosts included in the ranking as detailed in Fig. 2; however, this may be a result of looking at the first results page only. For both locales, Bing includes results from a larger variety of hosts in search results compared to Google.

Table 2. Coverage of search result hosts in data sources.

Search	CC Graph	WikiEN	WikiDE	TRANCO	Alexa	Majestic	Twitter
Bing DE	96.92%	48.92%	63.39%	48.00%	39.45%	51.54%	31.58%
Bing US	95.57%	63.84%	35.05%	61.46%	53.15%	56.91%	31.87%
Google DE	98.95%	57.12%	71.36%	57.57%	46.18%	62.07%	23.92%
Google US	98.45%	70.40%	39.67%	66.49%	57.83%	63.17%	24.85%

While the link-based approach was expected to perform worse in terms of completeness (see Sec. 3.3), the Common Crawl host web graph is by far the most comprehensive data set with respect to the hosts discovered in the search engines as detailed in Table 2. All other data sources perform far worse, also Majestic

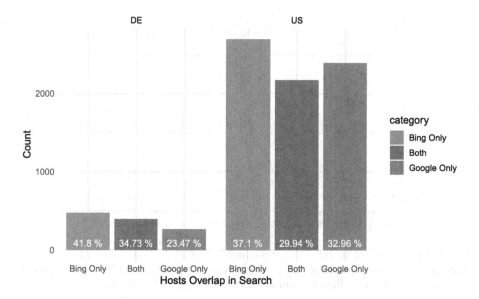

Fig. 2. Overlap of unique hosts in search engine results, divided by locale.

that also relies on a link-based approach. TRANCO is stronger than Majestic for the hosts of the US search engines, indicating that the other data sets combined in TRANCO push German language hosts out of the list as it performs worse for this subset. Given that only the first results page of the search engines was used for the host lists and that search engines leverage web graphs as well, it is assumable that the restriction to 1 million sites in the Majestic and TRANCO lists is responsible for the mediocre coverage.

Twitter has the lowest coverage for the hosts found in search, and for a focus on a topic, URLs in tweets have not added considerable value. For the minimalism and the iMac M1 topics, no tweets in German language and thus no hashtags were found at all. While tweets about these topics do exist, they seem to be so rare in the German Twitter community that they probably did not occur in the 1% sample. For the German Federal Election topic, about 100 hosts were identified that were not in the first page search results hosts, mostly regional news websites but also NGOs and alternative media. All of them were found in the Common Crawl web graph.

Hosts in search results are distributed over the Common Crawl host-level web graph, shown in Fig. 3. Web graph position data has been logarithmized in order to accommodate for the large scale. Slightly more than 50% of the hosts found in the US versions of Google and Bing come from the first one million hosts in the web graph (first vertical line on the left), more than 80% come from the first 10 million hosts (second vertical line, but even with 50 million hosts (third vertical line), we have not covered 100% of the search results. Google seems to prefer hosts with a higher link popularity with around 60% of hosts coming from the

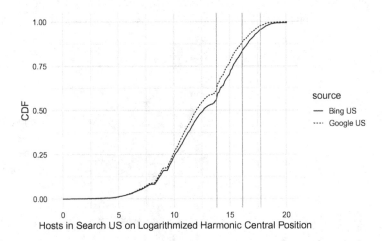

Fig. 3. Distribution of hosts found in US search engine results in the logarithmized harmonic central position displayed in a cumulative density function (CDF) plot, vertical lines at 1, 10, and 50 million computed to the logarithmized number.

first million hosts, compared to Bing where around 55% of the hosts are in the same segment.

The German language query set with three different topics shows even more differentiated results. A popular local topic (in terms of search volume) such as the German Federal Election brings up hosts that are found in the first 50% of the Common Crawl web graph, whereas the Apple iMac M1 topic benefits from globally linked sites such as apple.com that also serves German language pages. For a less popular topic such as minimalism, both search engines go beyond the 1st million as only 25%, respectively 30%, of the results were found in the top sites of the graph. While the Common Crawl host-level web graph is the most complete data source, are hosts not included in the top lists unpopular?

4.3   Is a List of 1 Million Popular Sites Enough?

A standard definition of *popular* and *less popular* does not exist, and different top sites lists have different ways to compute their flavour of popularity that is not completely transparent as discussed in Sect. 3.3. Search, however, offers a transparent currency for popularity, the number of searches for a query. If a host appears in a search engine's results for a popular search query or appears more frequently, it is more likely to be seen by a user. In Fig. 4, each host is displayed as a point with reference to the highest search volume query it is found for and its rank in the Common Crawl Web Graph, differentiated according to whether it is in the TRANCO list or not[9]. The darker a point is, the more often this host appears in search results.

---

[9] Only search volume data from Google has been taken into account, and, as a consequence, only the hosts found in Google Search.

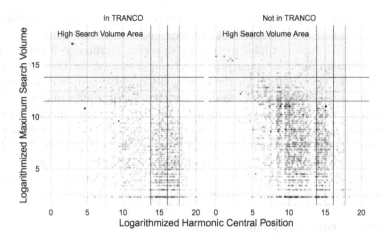

Fig. 4. Highest search volume for which a host is found versus its rank in the harmonic central web graph, differentiated by (non)-occurrence in TRANCO. Vertical lines at 1, 10, and 50 million, horizontal lines at 100 000 and 1 million monthly search volume.

The grey-shaded area includes high-volume search queries, beginning with 100 000 monthly search queries at the lower vertical line and the upper line mirroring a threshold of 1 million monthly search queries. Not only does the TRANCO list contain less hosts that are found for high-volume search queries, it also includes less hosts with a more frequent occurrence in search results. At the same time, most TRANCO hosts found in search come from the lower positions of the Common Crawl Web Graph, even from the area of position 10 million and above (second vertical line), missing more frequent hosts that are in the upper area of the graph.

4.4 TLDs are Neither a Good Proxy for a Language nor for a Locale

Using the results of the German search query dataset, we look at the distribution of TLDs of those hosts that contain German-language content. Search results differ in TLD distribution, depending on the topic as detailed in Table 3.

Table 3. Distribution of the top 5 TLDs in German-language search results.

Google	Election	Minimalism	iMac M1
.de	83.6%	75.6%	68.8%
.com	8.0%	13.6%	27.3%
.ch	1.5%	6.0%	1.4%
.net	0.7%	1.5%	0.1%
.org	5.4%	1.2%	0.1%

Bing	Election	Minimalism	iMac M1
.de	85.6%	71.8%	63.5%
.com	5.1%	14.0%	34.3%
.ch	0.0%	6.1%	0.0%
.net	1.2%	2.0%	0.3%
.blog	0.0%	1.2%	0.0%

The German Federal Election content is served from more .de domains than other content such as minimalism, the lowest number of .de domains is found for the iMac M1 topic. Apple, for example, serves German content from its apple.com domain and has unsurprisingly been dominant for the iMac search results. The TLD distribution for the Common Crawl German-language dataset includes an even lower share of .de domains, but these results may have to be taken with a grain of salt as Common Crawl does not only include German external links. As a further step, we analyzed how many hosts we would lose if we used the TLD selection provided in TRANCO: 151 out of 667 hosts (22.6%) of the Google results were not included, apart from the fact that Alexa and the other providers did not have all hosts anyway. Using the language detection of Common Crawl, only 62 out of 667 hosts (9.3%) were not included.

5   Discussion and Conclusion

Our findings challenge the value of research that uses top sites lists or TLDs for a focus on a country. Apart from the fact that there is no generally accepted definition of popularity and different sources have different ways of defining it, our results show that by cutting at 1 million, hosts are missing that are displayed in Google and Bing for popular queries and also hosts that more frequently occur in search results. As a consequence, a sampling strategy using the Common Crawl host web graph will provide more robust results for research than the use of top sites lists. The Common Crawl host-level web graph contains 95% all hosts that were present in other data sources within the top 50 million threshold. We provide sample code and a test tool to leverage this massive data set[10].

Instead of using TLDs for language/locale restriction, language detection should be used as the TLD approach prevents local sites from being included. The Common Crawl language identification approach is far from perfect, and it does not solve the problem of identifying relevant sites for a locale, but we see more than twice as many better results using the Common Crawl language detection compared to using TLDs.

The approach described in this paper has several drawbacks that require further research. The amount of spam and dead hosts in the host-level web graph has not been analyzed on a larger scale yet, and web graphs based on link popularity are not a perfect mirror of usage. Depending on the intended use, the inclusion of technical hosts and spam has to be configurable as some studies will be interested in these hosts. Topic identification is unsolved for most data sources. Finally, locale affiliation may be identifiable by using link networks of sites within a locale.

References

1. Alby, A., Bauknecht, H., Weidinger, S., Mempel, M., Alby, T.: Muster und Limitationen der Internet-basierten Selbstdiagnose bei häufigen Dermatosen. JDDG: Journal der Deutschen Dermatologischen Gesellschaft **19** (2021)

---

[10] https://alby.link/ccsample.

2. Alby, T.: Analyzing the web: are top websites lists a good choice for research? (0.1) [data set] (2022). https://doi.org/10.5281/zenodo.6821240
3. Alexa Internet, I.: We will be retiring alexa.com on 1 May 2022 (2021). https:// support.alexa.com/hc/en-us/articles/4410503838999
4. Allen, G., et al.: BiGBERT: classifying educational web resources for kindergarten- 12th grades. In: Hiemstra, D., et al. (eds.) ECIR 2021. LNCS, vol. 12657, pp. 176–184. Springer, Cham (2021). https://doi.org/10.1007/978-3-030-72240-1_13
5. AlSum, A., Weigle, M.C., Nelson, M.L., Van de Sompel, H.: Profiling web archive coverage for top-level domain and content language. Int. J. Digital Lib. **14**(3), 149–166 (2014). https://doi.org/10.1007/s00799-014-0118-y
6. Backlinko: We analyzed 5 million Google search results (2021). https://backlinko. com/google-ctr-stats
7. Boldi, P., Vigna, S.: Axioms for centrality. CoRR abs/1308.2140 (2013). http:// arxiv.org/abs/1308.2140
8. Carterette, B., Pavluy, V., Fang, H., Kanoulas, E.: Million query track 2009 overview. In: TREC (2009)
9. Craigie, M., Loader, B., Burrows, R., Muncer, S.: Reliability of health information on the internet: an examination of expert's ratings. J. Med. Internet Res. **4**, e856 (2002). https://www.ncbi.nlm.nih.gov/pmc/articles/PMC1761929/
10. Englehardt, S., Narayanan, A.: Online tracking: a 1-million-site measurement and analysis. In: Proceedings of the 2016 ACM SIGSAC Conference on Computer and Communications Security, pp. 1388–1401. CCS '16, Association for Computing Machinery, New York, NY, USA (2016). https://doi.org/10.1145/2976749.2978313
11. Fafalios, P., Iosifidis, V., Ntoutsi, E., Dietze, S.: TweetsKB: a public and large-scale RDF corpus of annotated tweets. In: Gangemi, A., et al. (eds.) ESWC 2018. LNCS, vol. 10843, pp. 177–190. Springer, Cham (2018). https://doi.org/10.1007/ 978-3-319-93417-4_12
12. Felt, A.P., Barnes, R., King, A., Palmer, C., Bentzel, C., Tabriz, P.: Measuring HTTPS adoption on the web. In: 26th USENIX Security Symposium (USENIX Security 2017), pp. 1323–1338. USENIX Association, Vancouver, BC (2017). https://www.usenix.org/conference/usenixsecurity17/technical-sessions/presentation/felt
13. Fetterly, D., Manasse, M., Najork, M.: Spam, damn spam, and statistics: using statistical analysis to locate spam web pages. In: Proceedings of the 7th International Workshop on the Web and Databases: Colocated with ACM SIGMOD/PODS 2004, pp. 1–6. WebDB 2004, Association for Computing Machinery, New York, NY, USA (2004). https://doi.org/10.1145/1017074.1017077
14. Fröbe, M., et al.: CopyCat: near-duplicates within and between the clueweb and the common crawl, pp. 2398–2404. Association for Computing Machinery, New York, NY, USA (2021). https://doi.org/10.1145/3404835.3463246
15. Funel, A.: Analysis of the web graph aggregated by host and pay-level domain. CoRR abs/1802.05435 (2018). http://arxiv.org/abs/1802.05435
16. Giannakoulopoulos, A., Pergantis, M., Konstantinou, N., Lamprogeorgos, A., Limniati, L., Varlamis, I.: Exploring the dominance of the English language on the websites of EU countries. Future Internet **12**(4) (2020). https://doi.org/10. 3390/fi12040076, https://www.mdpi.com/1999-5903/12/4/76
17. Hale, S.A., Blank, G., Alexander, V.D.: Live versus archive: comparing a web archive to a population of web pages, pp. 45–61. UCL Press (2017). http://www. jstor.org/stable/j.ctt1mtz55k.8
18. He, K., Fisher, A., Wang, L., Gember, A., Akella, A., Ristenpart, T.: Next stop, the cloud: Understanding modern web service deployment in ec2 and azure. In:

Proceedings of the 2013 Conference on Internet Measurement Conference, pp. 177–190. IMC 2013, Association for Computing Machinery, New York, NY, USA (2013). https://doi.org/10.1145/2504730.2504740

19. Höchstötter, N., Lewandowski, D.: What users see – structures in search engine results pages. Information Sciences **179**(12), 1796–1812 (2009). https://doi.org/10.1016/j.ins.2009.01.028, special Section: Web Search

20. Holzmann, H., Nejdl, W., Anand, A.: The dawn of today's popular domains: a study of the archived german web over 18 years. CoRR abs/1702.01151 (2017). http://arxiv.org/abs/1702.01151

21. Iqbal, U., Shafiq, Z., Qian, Z.: The ad wars: Retrospective measurement and analysis of anti-adblock filter lists. In: Proceedings of the 2017 Internet Measurement Conference, pp. 171–183. IMC 2017, Association for Computing Machinery, New York, NY, USA (2017). https://doi.org/10.1145/3131365.3131387

22. Kakos, A.B., Lovejoy, D.A., Whiteside, J.L.: Quality of information on pelvic organ prolapse on the Internet. Int. Urogynecol. J. **26**(4), 551–555 (2014). https://doi.org/10.1007/s00192-014-2538-z

23. Kilgarriff, A.: Googleology is bad science. Comput. Linguist. **33**(1), 147–151 (2007). https://doi.org/10.1162/coli.2007.33.1.147

24. Leithner, A., Maurer-Ertl, W., Glehr, M., Friesenbichler, J., Leithner, K., Windhager, R.: Wikipedia and osteosarcoma: a trustworthy patients' information? J. Am. Med. Infor. Assoc. **17**(4), 373–374 (2010). https://doi.org/10.1136/jamia.2010.004507

25. Lewandowski, D.: A three-year study on the freshness of web search engine databases. J. Inf. Sci. **34**(6), 817–831 (2008). https://doi.org/10.1177/0165551508089396

26. Lex, A., Gehlenborg, N., Strobelt, H., Vuillemot, R., Pfister, H.: Upset: visualization of intersecting sets. IEEE Trans. Visual. Comput. Graph. (InfoVis) **20**(12), 1983–1992 (2014). https://doi.org/10.1109/TVCG.2014.2346248

27. Libert, T.: Exposing the hidden web: An analysis of third-party HTTP requests on 1 million websites. CoRR abs/1511.00619 (2015). http://arxiv.org/abs/1511.00619

28. Lo, B., Sedhain, R.: How reliable are website rankings? implications for e-business advertising and internet search. Issues Inf. Syst. **7**, 233–238 (2006)

29. Luccioni, A.S., Viviano, J.D.: What's in the box? an analysis of undesirable content in the common crawl corpus. CoRR abs/2105.02732 (2021). https://arxiv.org/abs/2105.02732

30. Mason, A.M., Compton, J., Bhati, S.: Disabilities and the digital divide: assessing web accessibility, readability, and mobility of popular health websites. J. Health Commun. **26**(10), 667–674 (2021). https://doi.org/10.1080/10810730.2021.1987591, pMID: 34657585

31. Nagel, S.: Common crawl's first in-house web graph (2017). https://commoncrawl.org/2017/05/hostgraph-2017-feb-mar-apr-crawls/

32. Nagel, S.: Index to WARC files and URLs in columnar format (2018). https://commoncrawl.org/2018/03/index-to-warc-files-and-urls-in-columnar-format/

33. Nagel, S.: August 2019 crawl archive now available (2019). https://commoncrawl.org/2019/08/august-2019-crawl-archive-now-available/

34. Piccardi, T., Redi, M., Colavizza, G., West, R.: On the value of Wikipedia as a gateway to the web. In: Proceedings of the Web Conference 2021, pp. 249–260. WWW 2021, Association for Computing Machinery, New York, NY, USA (2021). https://doi.org/10.1145/3442381.3450136

35. Pochat, V.L., van Goethem, T., Joosen, W.: Rigging research results by manipulating top websites rankings. CoRR abs/1806.01156 (2018). http://arxiv.org/abs/1806.01156

36. Pochat, V.L., Van Goethem, T., Tajalizadehkhoob, S., Korczyński, M., Joosen, W.: Tranco: a research-oriented top sites ranking hardened against manipulation. arXiv preprint arXiv:1806.01156 (2018)

37. Robertson, F., Lagus, J., Kajava, K.: A COVID-19 news coverage mood map of Europe. In: Proceedings of the EACL Hackashop on News Media Content Analysis and Automated Report Generation, pp. 110–115. Association for Computational Linguistics (2021), https://aclanthology.org/2021.hackashop-1.15

38. Rweyemamu, W., Lauinger, T., Wilson, C., Robertson, W., Kirda, E.: Clustering and the weekend effect: recommendations for the use of top domain lists in security research. In: Choffnes, D., Barcellos, M. (eds.) Passive and Active Measurement, pp. 161–177. Springer International Publishing, Cham (2019). https://doi.org/10.1007/978-3-030-98785-5

39. Scheitle, Q., et al.: A long way to the top: significance, structure, and stability of internet top lists. In: Proceedings of the Internet Measurement Conference 2018, pp. 478–493. IMC 2018, Association for Computing Machinery, New York, NY, USA (2018). https://doi.org/10.1145/3278532.3278574

40. Silva, C.E., Campos, J.C.: Characterizing the control logic of web applications' user interfaces. In: Murgante, B., et al. (eds.) Computational Science and Its Applications - ICCSA 2014, pp. 263–276. Springer International Publishing, Cham (2014). https://doi.org/10.1007/978-3-319-09147-1

41. Srinath, M., Wilson, S., Giles, C.L.: Privacy at scale: Introducing the Privaseer corpus of web privacy policies. CoRR abs/2004.11131 (2020). https://arxiv.org/abs/2004.11131

42. Tahir, B., Mehmood, M.A.: Corpulyzer: a novel framework for building low resource language corpora. IEEE Access 9, 8546–8563 (2021). https://doi.org/10.1109/ACCESS.2021.3049793

43. Thelwall, M.: Web impact factors and search engine coverage. J. Documentation (2000). https://doi.org/10.1108/00220410010803801

44. Thelwall, M.: A fair history of the web? examining country balance in the internet archive. Lib. Inf. Sci. Res. 26, 162–176 (2004). https://doi.org/10.1016/S0740-8188(04)00024-6

45. Varvello, M., Schomp, K., Naylor, D., Blackburn, J., Finamore, A., Papagiannaki, K.: Is the web HTTP/2 yet? In: Karagiannis, T., Dimitropoulos, X. (eds.) PAM 2016. LNCS, vol. 9631, pp. 218–232. Springer, Cham (2016). https://doi.org/10.1007/978-3-319-30505-9_17

46. Vaughan, L., Thelwall, M.: Search engine coverage bias: evidence and possible causes. Inf. Process. Manag. 40(4), 693–707 (2004). https://doi.org/10.1016/S0306-4573(03)00063-3

47. Wang, L., Wang, J., Wang, M., Li, Y., Liang, Y., Xu, D.: Using internet search engines to obtain medical information: a comparative study. J. Med. Internet Res. 14(3), e74 (2012). https://doi.org/10.2196/jmir.1943

48. Wenzek, G., et al.: Ccnet: extracting high quality monolingual datasets from web crawl data. CoRR abs/1911.00359 (2019). http://arxiv.org/abs/1911.00359

49. West, A.G., Chang, J., Venkatasubramanian, K., Sokolsky, O., Lee, I.: Link spamming Wikipedia for profit. In: Proceedings of the 8th Annual Collaboration, Electronic Messaging, Anti-Abuse and Spam Conference, pp. 152–161. CEAS 2011, Association for Computing Machinery, New York, NY, USA (2011). https://doi.org/10.1145/2030376.2030394

RDFtex: Knowledge Exchange Between LaTeX-Based Research Publications and Scientific Knowledge Graphs

Leon Martin$^{(\boxtimes)}$ (ID) and Andreas Henrich (ID)

Media Informatics, University of Bamberg, Bamberg, Germany
{leon.martin,andreas.henrich}@uni-bamberg.de

Abstract. Scientific Knowledge Graphs (SciKGs) aim to integrate scientific knowledge in a machine-readable manner. For populating SciKGs, research publications pose a central source of knowledge. The goal is to represent both contextual information, i.e., metadata, and contentual information, i.e., original contributions like definitions and experimental results, of research publications in SciKGs. However, typical forms of research publications like traditional papers do not provide means of integrating contributions into SciKGs. Furthermore, they do not support making direct use of the rich information SciKGs provide. To tackle this, the present paper proposes *RDFtex*, a framework enabling (1) the import of contributions represented in SciKGs to facilitate the preparation of LaTeX-based research publications and (2) the export of original contributions to facilitate their integration into SciKGs. As a proof of concept, an RDFtex implementation is provided. We demonstrate the framework's functionality using the example of the present paper itself since it was prepared using this implementation.

Keywords: Research data management · Data and research infrastructure · LaTeX research publications

1 Introduction

Between 2008 and 2018, i.e., in one mere decade, the number of research publications published each year grew from about 1.8 million to about 2.6 million[1]. The resulting flood of publications and scientific data poses different challenges for researchers. For instance, keeping track of relevant related work and state-of-the-art experimental results has become increasingly difficult. Hence, the need for new means of organizing publications and scientific data has risen, eventually leading to the proposal of Scientific Knowledge Graphs (SciKGs) [1,6,9] that aim to integrate scientific information into a knowledge base. SciKGs have the potential to fundamentally transform the way researchers acquire information for

---

[1] https://ncses.nsf.gov/pubs/nsb20206 (accessed 2022/07/19).

© Springer Nature Switzerland AG 2022
G. Silvello et al. (Eds.): TPDL 2022, LNCS 13541, pp. 26–38, 2022.
https://doi.org/10.1007/978-3-031-16802-4_3

preparing their publications and share their contributions. However, the envisaged shift towards what is herein called *knowledge graph augmented research* raises questions about the form of research publications, i.e., their suitability for this new research paradigm. In a previous paper [10], we discussed three publication forms (including the predominant *document-based publications*) regarding their utility with respect to knowledge graph augmented research. The investigation has shown that all of them are flawed in this context. Therefore, based on the identified advantages and disadvantages, a set of requirements (cf. Sect. 2) for a publication form that is specifically designed for knowledge graph augmented research was compiled.

Building upon this, the present paper proposes RDFtex as an attempt to bridge the gap between LaTeX research publications and SciKGs. RDFtex is a framework enabling a bidirectional knowledge exchange between LaTeX research publications and a scientific knowledge graph. To implement the said knowledge exchange, RDFtex comprises two main functionalities:

1. The import functionality allows the import of research contributions from a SciKG in LaTeX documents via custom import commands.
2. The export functionality allows the export of original research contributions from LaTeX documents to a SciKG via custom export commands.

To showcase RDFtex's functionalities, we provide an implementation of RDFtex[2] serving as a proof of concept. This paper gives an impression of RDFtex since it has been produced using the implementation and a makeshift SciKG called *MinSKG* (cf. Sect. 3).

The remainder of this paper is structured as follows: Sect. 2 describes relevant foundations including related work, followed by a thorough introduction of RDFtex's functionalities in Sect. 3. The discussion in Sect. 4 investigates advantages and limitations of the framework. Finally, Sect. 5 draws a conclusion.

2 Foundations

The Resource Description Framework (RDF) [2] provides a generic approach for representing knowledge in the form of triples, where Internationalised Resource Identifiers (IRIs), a generalization of Uniform Resource Identifiers (URIs), are used as identifiers. Each triple comprises a subject (an IRI or a blank node), a predicate (an IRI), and an object (an IRI, a literal, or a blank node). The predicate represents a property, i.e., a binary relation between subject and object. Collections of such RDF triples constitute so called knowledge graphs.

Typically, triplestores [12] are employed to handle and interact with RDF-based knowledge graphs. To retrieve information from knowledge graphs, they usually provide an interface that accepts queries written in the SPARQL Protocol And RDF Query Language (SPARQL) [13]. To exchange and archive knowledge graphs, serialization formats such as Turtle, RDF/XML, and N3 exist [2].

---

[2] The implementation is written in Python 3.9. The code and other used resources are available at https://github.com/uniba-mi/rdftex (accessed 2022/07/19).

In contrast to more general knowledge graphs that gather information across domains like Wikidata[3] and DBpedia[4], SciKGs, i.e., knowledge graphs that are tailored to a (certain) scientific domain, such as the Open Research Knowledge Graph (ORKG) [6] and KnowLife [3] represent rich knowledge bases specifically for scientific information. To acquire this knowledge, research publications pose a central resource. Hence, SciKGs typically do not only aim to capture *contextual* information, i.e., metadata, of research publications but also *contentual* information, i.e., the original contributions the publications provide[5]. Figure 1 gives an example of the difference between the two types of information[6].

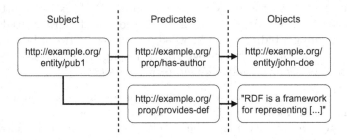

Fig. 1. A simple exemplary knowledge graph consisting of two RDF triples. The upper triple provides contextual information, the lower triple contentual information of the publication *pub1*. All non-literal triple members are identified using IRIs. (Figure and caption adopted from [10].)

To facilitate building high-quality and complete SciKGs, the process of integrating scientific information from research publications should be as simple as possible and at best be performed automatically with only little human intervention for quality assurance. From the authors' perspective, SciKGs provide the opportunity to facilitate the preparation of new publications if the rich information they provide is leveraged. However, an investigation of three different available publication forms in [10] shows that all of them have disadvantages regarding knowledge graph augmented research. *Document-based publications*, commonly called papers, pose the problem that authors have to introduce the same concepts across multiple publications to the readers even if this information is readily available in SciKGs. This results in redundant passages—typically found in a paper's introductory sections—that provide no added value while consuming valuable preparation time and effort. Furthermore, keywords and other classification systems are not sufficient to allow a direct integration of a publication into a SciKG since they are usually not formatted in an RDF-compatible

---

[3] https://www.wikidata.org (accessed 2022/07/19).

[4] https://www.dbpedia.org (accessed 2022/07/19).

[5] We use this terminology to make the distinction between metadata and the actual content more clear since both comprise semantic information but at different levels of abstraction.

[6] The use of available vocabularies for the predicates was omitted here.

way. *RDF-transformed publications* aim to close the gap between document-based publications and RDF by applying techniques like *SciIE* [9] to generate RDF graphs based on document-based publications. Nevertheless, the problems regarding the redundant passages continue to exist since authors still have to prepare regular papers in the first place.

Finally, *nanopublications* [8] (cf. Definition 1) focus on the integration with RDF by directly encoding the contributions as RDF triples. This, however, implies additional training effort for authors while readers will have to get accustomed to this publication form. As long as nanopublications are not well-established in the scientific community, the need for an interim solution for integrating the predominant form of publications, i.e., document-based publications, with SciKGs arises, to which RDFtex is our answer.

Definition 1. *Nanopublications [provide] a granular and principled way of publishing scientific (and other types of) data in a provenance-centric manner. Such a nanopublication consists of an atomic snippet of a formal statement [...] that comes with information about where this knowledge came from [...] and with metadata about the nanopublication as a whole [...]. All these three parts are represented as Linked Data (in RDF) [...]. [8]*

Based on the discussed advantages and disadvantages, five requirements for a publication form tailored for the use in SciKGs were proposed in [10]. RDFtex addresses four of them[7]. The first requirement states that authors shall still be able to prepare their main contributions in natural language. RDFtex can meet this requirement only partially since the underlying LATEX documents require non-natural language statements by design. The import and export commands introduced by RDFtex also do not use natural language. Hence, RDFtex permits the usage of natural language to the same degree regular LATEX documents do. The second requirement prescribes a means of importing knowledge from SciKGs with the goal of avoiding the need to prepare redundant passages across publications. RDFtex allows importing contributions from a SciKG via import commands. In RDFtex's preprocessing step, actual content based on the contributions' information is inserted. Vice versa, the third requirement demands means of exporting knowledge from publications to a SciKG to facilitate the integration of research publications. For this purpose, RDFtex allows marking up original contributions in publications via export commands that are then parsed in the preprocessing step to generate RDF documents based on the publications and their contributions. The final requirement states that readers shall receive a version of the publication that is enriched using information imported from the SciKG. In the preprocessing step, the import commands are replaced by templates that are populated with information retrieved from the SciKG. Compiling the preprocessed LATEX documents to PDF afterwards results in one coherent document that is enriched using the information from the SciKG.

---

[7] The remaining requirement addressing the need for additional tooling to obtain relevant URIs from a SciKG lies beyond the scope of the present paper (cf. Sect. 4).

2.1   Related Work

In the past, different approaches for linking parts of resources or documents in other documents have been proposed. One early example, Project Xanadu [11], introduced so called *xanadocs*. Essentially, a xanadoc is a so called Edit Decision List (EDL) file that consists of a set of links—typically URIs—referring to other documents with numerical start and length information for identifying spans of text in the linked resources. Special xanadoc viewers generate one coherent document by retrieving and composing the texts spans from the linked documents at the specified start positions with the specified lengths. Similar to xanadocs and with compliance to RDF, RDFtex makes use of URIs to reference content/entities, which correspond to scientific contributions in our case.

Another approach that is related to RDFtex is the so called Resource Description Framework in Attributes (RDFa) [5], which is a technique that provides a set of special attributes for XML-based languages to mark up elements with machine readable RDF information. Listing 2.1 demonstrates its core functionality using the example of an HTML snippet.

Listing 2.1. RDFa's core functionality using the example of an HTML snippet. The code was adopted from [5]. Note the tree structure of XML-based languages, which is exploited by RDFa.

```
<body prefix="dc:http://purl.org/dc/terms/">
  <div resource="/alice/posts/trouble_with_bob">
    <h2 property="dc:title">The trouble with Bob</h2>
    ...
    <h3 property="dc:creator" resource="#me">Alice</h3>
    ...
  </div>
</body>
```

By exploiting HTML's tree structure, the RDFa information in the example can be transformed into a knowledge graph featuring one blog post entity that acts as the subject of two triples, where the **property** attributes of the nested elements specify the predicates and the element contents correspond to the objects. RDFtex's export functionality follows RDFa's idea of marking up content with RDF information to provide machine readability. In RDFtex's preprocessing step, an RDF document is generated based on the marked up information that can then be used as a basis for integrating the publication into a SciKG.

Furthermore, there are projects that investigate means of annotating the contents of LaTeX documents with additional semantic information for further processing. For instance, *sTeX* [7] allows annotating mathematical knowledge in LaTeX documents. The annotations can then be transformed into mathematical knowledge management representation formats. As another example, *SALT* [4] is a comprehensive framework that aims to capture the semantic content of LaTeX documents using a federation of three interlinked ontologies. Compared to these projects, RDFtex provides the novelty that knowledge cannot only be marked up and exported but also imported. Another key difference is that the described projects do not aim to interoperate with a SciKG.

3   Concept

Introducing the framework, Fig. 2 shows that RDFtex operates on files with the `.rdf.tex` file extension and adds a composite preprocessing step to the basic workflow for producing a PDF document from `.tex` files. The preprocessing step includes the export and the import of contributions, which will be explained below. As indicated by the dashed arrow, the RDF document resulting from the export can be integrated into the SciKG later on. Syntactically, `.rdf.tex` files are regular `.tex` files that moreover permit the usage of custom RDFtex commands. The custom file extension facilitates identifying the source files with the custom commands for preprocessing. Apart from the occasional usage of the custom RDFtex commands, authors can prepare their publication using `.rdf.tex` files as they are used to; the usage of LaTeX templates is also supported. In the preprocessing step, a regular `.tex` document is generated for each `.rdf.tex` document by replacing the custom commands with actual content or removing them. The resulting `.tex` files can then be compiled as usual. Note that the framework can also be integrated into a fully automated workflow[8].

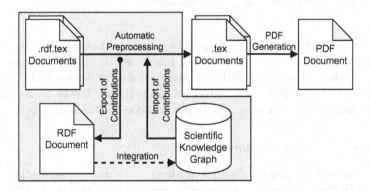

Fig. 2. The process for producing a PDF file using RDFtex. The gray box indicates additional steps and resources introduced or used by RDFtex. (Color figure online)

The present paper has been prepared using RDFtex. Thus, examples originating from this paper will be used in the following to explain the import and export functionality. As said before, preparing a LaTeX publication using RDFtex

---

[8] Our proof-of-concept preprocessor implementation can be configured to be executed whenever a `.rdf.tex` file changes. Similarly, tools like *latexmk* (https://ctan.org/pkg/latexmk, accessed 2022/07/19) provide the option to compile LaTeX projects whenever a `.tex` file changes. Combining the two, the PDF is compiled fully automatically whenever changes are made to any `.rdf.tex` file.

requires a suitable SciKG with which the knowledge exchange can be practiced. However, available SciKGs do not yet contain the papers and contributions referenced in this paper. Hence, we created the so called *MinSKG*. The MinSKG is a minimal scientific knowledge graph populated with all publications that are used as references for the present paper. The contextual information of the publications, i.e., the metadata, was added automatically by parsing their entries from the `bibtex` file. The contentual information, i.e., their contributions, was added manually. Note that only the contributions that are actually imported in the present paper have been added. The script for building the MinSKG and the MinSKG itself is also provided in RDFtex's repository (see Footnote 2).

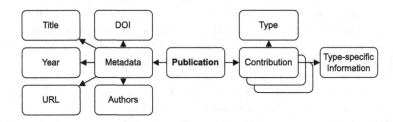

Fig. 3. The information available for each publication represented in the MinSKG. The type-specific information of a contribution depends on its type. Note that edge labels, i.e., predicates, and URIs are omitted for readability.

Figure 3 shows the structure of the information for publications represented in the MinSKG. The structure is loosely based on the ORKG to ensure that RDFtex operates on a SciKG with a realistic structure. However, the MinSKG just serves as a small makeshift SciKG (cf. Sect. 4) that has to be replaced by an actual SciKG in a comprehensive implementation of the framework.

3.1   Import of Contributions

RDFtex's import command enables authors to import contributions from a SciKG. During the preprocessing step, the import commands within the `.rdf.tex` files are parsed and snippets of actual content are produced based on the contribution information retrieved from the MinSKG. The snippets are added to the `.tex` files in place of the import commands. To identify the contributions to be imported, URIs are used. Hence, the import commands use this syntax:

```
\rdfimport{<label>}{<citation-key>}{<contrib-url>}
```

As depicted, the `rdfimport` command expects three parameters. The first parameter `<label>` corresponds to the label the authors want to assign to the generated content for future reference in their paper. Second, `<citation-key>` is a placeholder for the `bibtex` citation key of the publication from which the imported contribution originates. The final parameter `<contrib-url>` denotes

the URI of the contribution to be imported. The paragraphs to follow will build
on the example of Fig. 1, which we imported in our .rdf.tex file as follows[9]:

```
\rdfimport{fig:contentual-contextual} \
  {Martin21} \
  {https://example.org/scikg/publications/Martin21/contrib2}
```

The example shows that the import commands are agnostic regarding the
type of the imported contribution preventing the need for learning different
syntaxes.

To obtain the contribution's information, a SPARQL query of the form

```
SELECT ?p ?o WHERE {<contrib-url> ?p ?o .}
```

is performed on the MinSKG. With respect to the MinSKG's structure
(cf. Fig. 3), this query yields all predicates and objects of triples where
<contrib-url> is the subject. This information as well as the remaining two
parameters are used in the next step to generate the content snippets. The number of triples available depends on the type of the contribution. In the case of
the imported figure from the example above, the MinSKG provides information about the figure's MIME type, the URL at which the actual figure can be
found, a description, and the contribution type itself, which in this case would
be **Figure**.

The type of the contribution to be imported also determines the template
that is applied to generate the content. The templates are written in LaTeX to
allow for a direct injection in the .tex files and they incorporate the respective
information that the different contribution types in the MinSKG provide. The
template that is applied for importing figures looks as follows:

```
\begin{figure}[htb!]
  \centering
  \includegraphics[max width=0.7\columnwidth]{<figure-url>}
  \caption{<figure-desc> \
    (Figure and caption adopted from~\cite{<citation-key>}.)}
  \label{spslabelsps}
\end{figure}
```

As shown, the example uses the placeholders <figure-url> and
<figure-desc>, which correspond to the location of the figure and its descrip-
tion. All placeholders within the import templates are filled with information
retrieved from the MinSKG. Thus, it is important to ensure that no contributions are added to the MinSKG without the necessary predicates and objects.
Otherwise, they cannot be imported successfully. In such cases, the preprocessor shows meaningful error messages. For some of the supported contribution
types, templates with custom LaTeX environments are used whose definitions
are automatically inserted into the .tex files if necessary.

---

[9] In the following, single "\"-symbols indicate lines that are too long. In reality, there
are no line breaks.

3.2   Export and Integration of Contributions

For the export of original contributions, RDFtex enables authors to mark up relevant text passages in their .rdf.tex files. In the following, the export of our proof-of-concept preprocessor implementation serves as the running example for demonstrating RDFtex's export functionality. The export functionality leverages two custom LaTeX commands. The first command is used to declare the export of a certain contribution. The rationale for introducing a declaration statement is that the exact string specifying the contribution type in the MinSKG, e.g., ExpResult (indicating an experimental result), might not be explicitly mentioned in the text. At the same time, the type information is mandatory since it determines the templates to be applied in the import process as explained above. The same holds for other predicates and objects that denote the MIME type of a figure, for example. To tackle this, the export declaration command

```
\rdfexport{<contrib-name>}{<type>}{<predicate-uri=object>,...}
```

is introduced. <contrib-name> corresponds to the name of the contribution. The specified name serves as a local identifier for the contribution. When the actual export takes place, a generated preliminary URI will be used as an identifier instead to comply with the RDF standard. The second parameter <type> denotes the contribution's type and the third parameter accommodates optional <predicate-uri=object> statements, which are placeholders for predicate object combinations that are required for a valid export but cannot be included appropriately in the text. For example, to add the MIME type information for a figure to be exported, the third parameter could be set to:

```
https://example.org/scikg/terms/figure_mime=image/png
```

Applied to the running example, the following snippet declares the export of the RDFtex software:

```
\rdfexport{RDFtex Implementation}{Software}{}
```

Note that the third parameter was omitted here since all information required for a valid software export are stated explicitly in the text such that they can be marked up directly using the second export command.

The second command is similar to the property attributes of RDFa (cf. Listing 2.1) for marking up predicates. While RDFa can exploit the nested element structures of XML-based languages to associate subjects with predicates and objects, the triple components are potentially spread across sections, in our case. Therefore, each RDFtex property command has to explicitly reference the contribution they belong to via the <contrib-name> used in the export declaration command, resulting in the following syntax:

```
\rdfproperty{<contrib-name>}{<predicate-uri>}{<object>}
```

The parameter <predicate-uri> denotes a predicate used for describing contributions in the MinSKG and <object> encloses the part of the content that is to be used as the triple's object. For instance, to add a description of the RDFtex software to the MinSKG, we modified the line from Sect. 1 to the following:

```
\rdfproperty{RDFtex Implementation} \
  {https://example.org/scikg/terms/software_description} \
  {RDFtex is a framework enabling a bidirectional...}
```

When lines with `rdfexport` or `rdfproperty` commands are encountered during preprocessing, their arguments are collected for the respective contributions identified via `<contrib-name>`. For the `.tex` file generation, lines with `rdfexport` commands are omitted and `rdfproperty` commands are replaced with only their `<object>` argument, thus removing the custom commands.

Theoretically, the export of a contribution could be performed using only the `rdfexport` command due to the power of its third parameter. However, the usage of the `rdfproperty` command offers the possibility to use parts of the text in the publication directly as objects for the predicates. Among others, this serves the objective of avoiding redundant text passages.

When all files have been processed, the collected information is checked for completeness to ensure that the exported contributions can be imported again. At this point, the validated exports could be directly integrated into the Min-SKG. However, some information about the publication might not be obtainable yet, e.g., the DOI has to be assigned by publishers first, or has to adhere to certain criteria such as IRI naming schemes, which can only be verified by the maintainers of a SciKG. Hence, to avoid adding information to the SciKG that is incomplete or does not meet the quality standards, a preliminary RDF document that complies with the MinSKG's structure (cf. Fig. 3) is generated based on the exported contributions instead. For this purpose, a placeholder IRI is assigned to the paper's entity, which should later be replaced with a persistent identifier. We suggest passing the RDF document alongside the camera-ready publication to the publishers. The publishers should then add the missing information before submitting the document to the SciKG maintainers who finally adjust the IRI and perform the integration.

3.3 Prefix Syntax

To mitigate the readability problems arising from lengthy URIs, many RDF-related technologies including RDFa allow defining prefixes that can then be used to abbreviate full URIs. Following this approach, RDFtex provides another command for registering prefixes:

```
\rdfprefix{<prefix>}{<url>}
```

The parameter `<prefix>` states the prefix to be used in place of `<url>` in the `.rdf.tex` files. For this, the `rdfprefix` commands have to be placed above the lines that use the prefixes in each `.rdf.tex` file. Using the prefix command, the `rdfproperty` command for adding the software description from above can be rewritten as follows:

```
\rdfprefix{mskg}{https://example.org/scikg/terms/}
\rdfproperty{RDFtex Implementation} \
  {mskg:software_description} \
  {RDFtex is a framework enabling a bidirectional...}
```

Table 1. An overview of the custom RDFtex LaTeX commands.

Command	Purpose	Parameters
`rdfimport`	Denotes the import of a contribution from the SciKG	A label that will be assigned to the generated content snippet, the citation key, and the URI pointing to the contribution
`rdfexport`	Registers an original contribution for export	A contribution name to reference the export locally, the type of the original contribution, and an optional set of other predicates and objects that are assigned to the contribution entity if applicable
`rdfproperty`	Marks up an attribute of an original contribution to be exported	The contribution name of the export, the predicate, and the text representing the object
`rdfprefix`	Sets a prefix for abbreviating the terms of a vocabulary	The prefix and the written out form of the vocabulary URI

Summarizing Sect. 3, Table 1 provides an overview of the custom RDFtex commands, their purpose, and their parameters.

4   Discussion

RDFtex and the underlying concept of exchanging knowledge between research publications and SciKGs represent one option to facilitate the move towards knowledge graph augmented research. Our goal was to provide an extension to a well-established publication form that feels natural while providing compatibility to the SciKG world. Using RDFtex, authors gain the ability to make direct use of contributions that are already represented in SciKGs. They can also facilitate the integration of their publications using RDFtex's export functionality, which is vital for being visible in the new research paradigm. At the same time, RDFtex makes only minor changes to the familiar way of preparing a LaTeX contribution.

From the authors' perspective, using the custom RDFtex commands requires some training and somewhat impairs the readability of the LaTeX code. However, the concise syntax and the introduced prefix mechanism alleviate this problem to a certain degree. Speaking of URIs, authors also have to obtain the relevant URIs from the SciKG to use the import functionality—a topic that is not covered in the present paper because SciKG maintainers and search engines are better suited to provide tools for this task[10]. Also, tools for collaboratively preparing

---

[10] For example, Semantic Scholar (https://www.semanticscholar.org; accessed 2022/07/19) and similar search engines could provide the URIs to a publication's contributions alongside the links to the publication itself, in the future.

publications like Overleaf[11] do not support RDFtex yet. Implementation-wise, including RDFtex in such tools is feasible, though. Furthermore, one can already set up an automatic build pipeline as described in Footnote 8 and use a version control system to enable collaboration.

Runtime Evaluation. Our proof-of-concept implementation demonstrates that it is feasible to scan the `.rdf.tex` files for custom commands line by line and only once, while the lines of the `.tex` files are written simultaneously, thus requiring linear time. Since the present paper has been prepared using our proof-of-concept implementation, it was possible to monitor its runtime. Overall, this paper comprises two imports, namely Fig. 1 and Definition 1. Also, RDFtex as a software artifact, Fig. 2, Fig. 3, the MinSKG as a dataset, and the experimental results that are stated next have been exported as original contributions. Given these imports and exports, the preprocessing took only 1.15 s on a standard desktop PC across 100 runs on average, even though the MinSKG was deployed on a server in order to take into account the network overhead for the tests. At the same time, the MinSKG is still a small makeshift which results in faster than normal SPARQL answering, thus limiting the results. That being said, retrieving all predicates and objects of the entity *RDFa* from Wikidata via its SPARQL endpoint[12], i.e., a query that is comparable to the one used by RDFtex (cf. Sect. 3.1), takes just about 0.25 s. Also, caching could be used to prevent retrieving the same contribution data multiple times.

Initial User Feedback. To get initial user feedback, we asked three computer scientists and one astrophysicist who are familiar with LaTeX to perform imports and exports by means of our implementation on a blank `.rdf.tex` file using the think-aloud method. The test persons had access to the documentation of the provided repository (see Footnote 2). As expected, there is a strong need for tooling to obtain the necessary URIs because the test persons had problems finding the correct URIs in the MinSKG. RDFtex's concept, however, was received well, especially the import functionality due to its simplicity. The export functionality proved to be more complex due to the larger number of involved commands. Understandably, two test persons mentioned that they would use the framework only when the benefits of knowledge graph augmented research become noticeable.

5   Conclusion

The present paper proposed RDFtex, a framework for producing LaTeX research publications using imports and exports to and from a SciKG. For this purpose, RDFtex introduces four custom LaTeX commands. The envisaged shift towards knowledge graph augmented research, which motivated this work, poses a significant change for the research culture. It depends on the scientific community

---

[11] https://www.overleaf.com (accessed 2022/07/19).
[12] https://query.wikidata.org (accessed 2022/07/19).

if this change will actually take place, though. If so, we think that RDFtex is a promising approach to facilitate the move towards the new research paradigm since it only introduces minor differences compared to the preparation of traditional LATEX publications while narrowing the gap between papers and RDF.

References

1. Auer, S., Kovtun, V., Prinz, M., Kasprzik, A., Stocker, M., Vidal, M.: Towards a knowledge graph for science. In: Proceedings of the 8th International Conference on Web Intelligence, Mining and Semantics, WIMS 2018, Novi Sad, Serbia, 25–27 June 2018, pp. 1:1–1:6. ACM (2018). https://doi.org/10.1145/3227609.3227689
2. Cyganiak, R., Hyland-Wood, D., Lanthaler, M.: RDF 1.1 concepts and abstract syntax (2014). https://www.w3.org/TR/rdf11-concepts. Accessed 19 July 2022
3. Ernst, P., Siu, A., Weikum, G.: KnowLife: a versatile approach for constructing a large knowledge graph for biomedical sciences. BMC Bioinform. **16**, 157:1–157:13 (2015). https://doi.org/10.1186/s12859-015-0549-5
4. Groza, T., Handschuh, S., Möller, K., Decker, S.: SALT - semantically annotated latex for scientific publications. In: Franconi, E., Kifer, M., May, W. (eds.) ESWC 2007. LNCS, vol. 4519, pp. 518–532. Springer, Heidelberg (2007). https://doi.org/10.1007/978-3-540-72667-8_37
5. Herman, I., Adida, B., Sporny, M., Birbeck, M.: RDFa 1.1 primer (2015). https://www.w3.org/TR/rdfa-primer. Accessed 19 July 2022
6. Jaradeh, M.Y., et al.: Open research knowledge graph: next generation infrastructure for semantic scholarly knowledge. In: Proceedings of the 10th International Conference on Knowledge Capture, K-CAP 2019, Marina Del Rey, CA, USA, 19–21 November 2019, pp. 243–246. ACM (2019). https://doi.org/10.1145/3360901.3364435
7. Kohlhase, A., Kohlhase, M., Lange, C.: $S^t e^x$+: a system for flexible formalization of linked data. In: I-SEMANTICS. ACM (2010)
8. Kuhn, T., et al.: Nanopublications: a growing resource of provenance-centric scientific linked data. CoRR (2018). https://arxiv.org/abs/1809.06532
9. Luan, Y., He, L., Ostendorf, M., Hajishirzi, H.: Multi-task identification of entities, relations, and coreference for scientific knowledge graph construction. In: Proceedings of the 2018 Conference on Empirical Methods in Natural Language Processing, Brussels, Belgium, 31 October–4 November 2018, pp. 3219–3232. Association for Computational Linguistics (2018). https://doi.org/10.18653/v1/d18-1360
10. Martin, L., Jegan, R., Henrich, A.: On the form of research publications for use in scientific knowledge graphs. In: Wissensorganisation 2021: 16. Tagung der Deutschen Sektion der Internationalen Gesellschaft für Wissensorganisation (ISKO) (WissOrg 2021) (2021, accepted)
11. Project Xanadu: Project Xanadu (2021). https://www.xanadu.net. Accessed 19 July 2022
12. Saleem, M., Szárnyas, G., Conrads, F., Bukhari, S.A.C., Mehmood, Q., Ngomo, A.N.: How representative is a SPARQL benchmark? An analysis of RDF triplestore benchmarks. In: Liu, L., et al. (eds.) The World Wide Web Conference, WWW 2019, San Francisco, CA, USA, 13–17 May 2019, pp. 1623–1633. ACM (2019). https://doi.org/10.1145/3308558.3313556
13. W3C SPARQL Working Group: SPARQL 1.1 overview (2013). https://www.w3.org/TR/sparql11-overview. Accessed 19 July 2022

Enriching the Greek National Cultural Aggregator with Key Figures in Greek History and Culture: Challenges, Methodology, Tools and Outputs

Haris Georgiadis ⓘ, Agathi Papanoti[✉] ⓘ, Elena Lagoudi ⓘ, Georgia Angelaki ⓘ, Nikos Vasilogamvrakis ⓘ, Alexia Panagopoulou ⓘ, and Evi Sachini

National Documentation Centre, Athens, Greece
apapano@ekt.gr

Abstract. Since 2015, SearchCulture.gr, the Greek cross-domain Cultural Data Aggregator, a service developed by the National Documentation Centre in Greece (EKT), has collected a growing number of 800.000 digitised Cultural Heritage Objects (CHOs) from 73 cultural institutions. Addressing metadata heterogeneity in order to be able to provide advanced search, browsing and filtering options to users has been a key target from the start. Controlled linked data vocabularies for item types, historical periods and themes were developed over the course of the past years and are being used for the semantic enrichment of the CHOs' metadata. In the current paper we present the challenges, the methodology and tools used over the past 2 years for the process of enriching the aggregated CHOs' metadata with person entities from a Linked Data vocabulary comprising over 8.200 entries concerning Greek persons that left some mark in history, society, science, letters and art that we created for that purpose. This latest development allows all the works relating to a person to be interlinked and semantically enriched, adds significant browse and search functionalities to the portal and, therefore, opens new horizons for Greek SSH research.

Keywords: LOD vocabularies · Digital cultural heritage · Data repositories and archives · Semantic enrichment · Content aggregators

1 Introduction

SearchCulture.gr (https://www.searchculture.gr) is the Greek National Aggregator for Cultural Data. It is being developed by the National Documentation Center of Greece (EKT), a public sector organization supervised by the Ministry of Digital Governance. Since its launch in 2015, it kept growing in numbers and expanding its functionalities. Today, SearchCulture.gr has amassed more than 800,000 records from 76 providers such as libraries, museums, archives and generally, any type of institution that is custodian of cultural collections. Data ingested come from a variety of collections of archeology, folklore, history, arts and crafts and span more than 7,000 years of Greek history. SearchCulture.gr is the national accredited aggregator to Europeana.

G. Silvello et al. (Eds.): TPDL 2022, LNCS 13541, pp. 39–51, 2022.
https://doi.org/10.1007/978-3-031-16802-4_4

With the goal to address metadata heterogeneity - the biggest challenge a large cross-domain aggregator faces – and in order to provide efficient search and browsing functionalities, SearchCulture.gr's technical and operational strategy has relied heavily on semantic enrichments. We have developed an innovative metadata enrichment and homogenization scheme for types, subjects and temporal information and we embedded it in the ingestion workflow of SearchCulture.gr [1]. A key component of the enrichment scheme is Semantics.gr, a platform for publishing vocabularies as LOD. It also incorporates a Mapping Tool for enriching content en masse. We created and published three bilingual and hierarchical vocabularies for types, subjects and historical periods and we enrich and homogenize each collection we aggregate with terms from these vocabularies. This allowed us to develop advanced multilingual search and browsing features.

Our next step was to extend our enrichment scheme to persons, both creators and referred persons (i.e. a person depicted in a photograph, cast of a film, a recipient of a letter or the subject of a biography). Similar to the other enrichments, this would involve identifying person entities in metadata and mapping them to entries from a structured vocabulary, this time a catalogue of persons. The end goal was common to previous enrichments: to improve searchability and discoverability in SearchCulture,gr, by developing innovative person-driven search, browsing and faceting functionalities. This is important for the end user because with simple keyword-based search by personal names, the results are fuzzy: missing results because of the many different ways personal names are expressed (paronyms, given name diminutives, different languages, nicknames, the use of initials instead of full given names etc.) as well as false results that are related to synonimities. However, creating a vocabulary of persons and also, identifying, mining and disambiguating person entities in metadata was a much more complicated task which forced us to revise our enrichment scheme and strategy and to extend our tools in order to meet the new requirements.

2   Background: The Enrichment Scheme in SearchCulture.gr

The enrichment scheme in SearchCulture.gr is based on adding links stored in separate 'EKT' fields in *Cultural Heritage Objects'* (CHOs') metadata to terms from *Linked Open Data* (LOD) Vocabularies. These links are produced from explicit and curated mappings from distinct, aggregated metadata values to Vocabulary terms.

The scheme is based on Semantics.gr [2], a platform developed in-house by EKT for the development, curation and interlinking of vocabularies, thesauri, classification schemes and authority files- collectively hereby called *Vocabularies*- of any schema and their publication as LOD.

Semantics.gr also contains a *Mapping Tool* used to set *Enrichment Mapping Rules* (*EMRs*) in order to perform bulk data enrichment in aggregator databases and repositories. The GUI environment includes advanced automated functionalities that help the curator easily define *EMRs* from source datasets (resources/terms from other vocabularies, metadata records or aggregated metadata values or phrases) to terms from a target vocabulary. For each dataset and target vocabulary a dedicated *Mapping Form* is created. The mapping form incorporates a self-improving automatic suggestion mechanism, though, a curator always validates the produced mappings. Moreover, the curator can correct, refine or create new mappings manually. In the context of SearchCulture.gr, the source dataset is always a set of aggregated metadata values or phrases, i.e. distinct metadata field values or distinct words/phrases contained in field values of a collection. These values are produced from metadata fields harvested via OAI-PMH. Validated mappings are served on request via a RESTful API in JSON format which can be used by the aggregator or repository to enrich the collection easily and en masse. The tool is thoroughly described in [1].

We started developing vocabularies and applying semantic enrichments to our collections in 2016. First, we enriched the original metadata using a Vocabulary of Item Types[1] that we created and published in Semantics.gr [1]. It is a SKOS-based LOD original vocabulary consisting of 193 terms that cover different types of cultural artifacts. Metadata records were enriched with a separate field "EKT type" that holds references to the vocabulary's terms.

The next step of the enrichment workflow was to homogenize and normalize chronologies and historical periods. The vocabulary Greek historical periods[2] was developed in 2017 and it is constructed according to the semantic class edm:Timespan of Europeana's EDM[3]. It contains 94 terms that cover Greek history from 8000 BC to today. It is hierarchical and bilingual. Original metadata records were enriched with two distinct fields, "EKT chronology" and "EKT historical period". Depending on whether the original temporal documentation was based on period labels or chronologies, we adopted two fundamentally different enrichment strategies [1].

The last iteration of enrichments was thematic, with a new field "EKT Subject" that includes references to terms of a bilingual and hierarchical vocabulary of subjects that is interlinked to the UNESCO Thesaurus[4] (1,389 terms) and of a bilingual vocabulary of thematic tags[5] that covers more specific topics (607 terms).

3 Adapting the Enrichment Scheme for Person Entities

The enrichments we conducted in the past and those of person entities vastly differ. The former were a type of classification using hierarchical vocabularies, allowing the curator some assumptions or generalization. The latter has the element of disambiguation and is much more demanding for the curator since each EMR potentially must be double checked and in some cases researched.

3.1 Two Kinds of Enrichments: Creators and Referred Persons

The relation of a person with a CHO varies a lot. It could be the author or the subject of a book, the director, the screenwriter or the actor of a play, the sculptor, the model or the photographer of an antiquity, the sender, the receiver or the subject of a letter etc.

---

[1] https://www.semantics.gr/authorities/vocabularies/ekt-item-types.

[2] https://www.semantics.gr/authorities/vocabularies/historical-periods.

[3] https://pro.europeana.eu/page/edm-documentation.

[4] https://www.semantics.gr/authorities/vocabularies/ekt-unesco.

[5] https://www.semantics.gr/authorities/vocabularies/thematic_tags.

The main problem is that many institutions do not clarify the role of a person and most importantly, even if they did in their repositories, most of them provide their metadata in aggregation schemata that are based on Dublin Core (such as EDM), which lack the required expressiveness to distinguish these roles. As a result, whichever is the specific relation of a person with a given CHO, the personal name will either appear in one of the two *agent fields*, "dc:creator" or "dc:contributor", or it will appear in "dc:subject" or even in more descriptive fields such as "dc:title" and "dc:description". Moreover, while the creator in most cases is given in "dc:creator", persons that appear in photographs or are the subject of a book, sometimes appear in "dc:subject", some other times in "dc:contributor" or "dc:title" or "dc:description".

Ultimately, we decided that the enrichment on persons should improve SearchCulture.gr by allowing users to easily find all works of a creator (regardless of its specific role in the creation) and all the CHOs referring a person (regardless of the kind of reference). We opted for creating two separate fields, "EKT creator" and "EKT referred person" thus conducting those two kinds of person enrichments. These would be the basic fields that will be used for person-driven search, browsing and faceting.

3.2 The Disambiguation Problem

Disambiguation derived from synonymities is much harder when it comes to personal names. In the vast majority of our collections, references to persons are done with their names without any explicit identifying information (such as a link to an authority record) or explicit biographical information (such as the profession or the date of birth). It became quite obvious from the very beginning that implicit contextual information from other metadata (for example the type, the description or the date of a CHO) and sometimes the digital item itself (for example a portrait) should be taken into account by the curator in order to narrow down the options and make valid choices. Naturally, the vocabulary of persons that would be used should contain identifying and biographical information, not only for providing the end-user of SearchCulture.gr with useful information about a person, but mainly to be considered by the curator while making EMRs. The distinction between individuals with the same name is even harder when it comes to synonymities in distinguished political and economic families, where apart from the names, individuals may have common biographical information, such as a father's name, occupation/profession or place of birth.

Another problem was the different forms of a personal name due to paronyms, given name diminutives, artistic nicknames (noms de plume), the use of initials instead of full given names, etc. Those issues made the following enrichment steps more difficult to be performed: i) string similarity-based comparison that is used for automatic mapping suggestions ii) mining of personal names from descriptive fields and iii) EMR curation. To solve these problems, on one hand we tried adding well-known paronyms, diminutives and nicknames in person entries as alternative labels, and, on the other hand, we extended appropriately both the string similarity-based matching and the mining algorithms used in the Mapping Tool.

3.3 The Scope

Given that SearchCulture.gr had already reached some 700K items at the beginning of this project, the number of personal names that appeared in the aggregated metadata was quite large. A decision needed to me made at the start as to the scope of the person enrichment project, for instance, whether it should include ancient creators or non-Greek important figures, etc.

For the first iteration of the enrichment project, it was decided to focus on Greek persons of importance, from antiquity to today. Some non-Greeks were included, because of their contribution and relevance to Greek history. It was also deemed right to focus on real people and not mythological figures and characters. Corporate bodies were also out of scope as were ensembles, artists' workshops etc.

It was also important to set some realistic targets about the coverage of the enrichments. In particular, we decided to focus mainly on persons who left some mark in Greek history, arts, science, politics and social life and whose biographical information would be reasonably easy to access. This was crucial not only for the time management of the project but also because a vocabulary without basic biographical information would prove useless in the disambiguation process.

3.4 Developing a Vocabulary of Persons in Greek History and Culture

Unlike types and subjects, where the chosen level of granularity (how specialized the terms will be) can counterpoise the required number of terms in the respective vocabularies (since mappings can be done in broader concepts), a catalogue of personal names was expected to be much larger, if it was to achieve a broader enrichment coverage. Therefore, a big challenge was to come up with a vocabulary of persons with a critical mass of entries before the mapping processes started, although it was clear from the beginning that, as the mappings proceeded collection by collection, the vocabulary would be augmented with additional person entities.

One of the collections aggregated in SearchCulture.gr is "Pandektis: Modern Greek Visual Prosopography"[6]. It is a collection of more than 12,000 digitized portraits of Greek men and women who have attained distinction in different sphere of life, from the fall of Constantinople (1453) to the present day. Each record has metadata for the person's name (title and alternative title), place of birth and death, date of birth and death, and keywords that include information about the person's occupation or role in Hellenic history. Among those 12,000 records there are many duplicates, triplicates or more since the collection is not a catalogue of persons but a dataset of portraits and there can be multiple portraits of an individual.

After deduplication, we ended up with approximately 6,000 persons' records with basic metadata and (often multiple) thumbnails/portraits. These records became the core of our catalogue "Persons in Greek History and Culture"[7], (from now on referred as *Vocabulary of Persons*). After evaluating the authorities that had been amassed and due to the nature of our content, we decided to also add in our records authorities of

---

[6] http://pandektis.ekt.gr/pandektis/handle/10442/14056.

[7] https://www.semantics.gr/authorities/vocabularies/searchculture-persons.

acclaimed art galleries' databases such as the National Gallery – Alexandros Soutsos Museum and the archive of Contemporary Greek Art Institute.

The Vocabulary of Persons is a LOD vocabulary conforming to the edm:Agent class of Europena's EDM. It was created and published in Semantics.gr. Each entry was enriched when possible, with metadata regarding place of birth and death, date of birth and death, sex, occupation, bibliographic references and links to established resources, such as the Virtual International Authority File (VIAF), Wikipedia and IMDB Fig. 1, illustrates an example of a person entity in view mode and as RDF.

Fig. 1. A person entity in the catalogue, and its RDF representation (in RDF/XML).

The catalogue initially consisted of approximately 6,500 entries. During the enrichment process we continued to add new entries. Today, it consists of 8,230 persons. The number keeps growing with every collection added in SearchCulture.gr.

In the Pandektis collection the field for occupation or role in Hellenic history is more or less homogenous. We decided to isolate and build on this information introducing a second vocabulary "Professions/Occupations"[8]. Use of this vocabulary facilitated various search and navigation functionalities. The "Professions/Occupations" is a LOD vocabulary conforming to the skos:Concept semantic class and consists of 366 terms. It is hierarchical and bilingual and its terms refer to occupations such as merchants, doctors and military officers, clergy positions, noble titles, different social movements affiliates like feminists or socialists or types of artists and literary creators. The terms of this vocabulary were used to classify entries in the Vocabulary of Persons.

3.5   The Strategy for Enriching Aggregated Collections En Masse

As mentioned in Sect. 3.1, we conducted two kinds of enrichments, creators and referred persons. For each collection, we inspected the documentation particularities to decide the metadata fields on which we would conduct mappings. For most collections, the creators' enrichments were done using one mapping form on the "dc:creator" field. However, for few collections creators' enrichments were based on "dc:contributor". Regarding the referred persons' enrichments, we had to work on multiple mapping forms, usually for "dc:subject", "dc:title" and "dc:contributor". After we created all the mapping forms for every collection, we proceeded with the mapping processes.

---

[8] https://www.semantics.gr/authorities/vocabularies/professions-occupations.

Extending the Matching Algorithm Used for Automatic EMR Suggestions. The mapping tool supports automatic suggestion of EMRs which by default is based on string similarity matching between metadata field values and indexed labels of vocabulary entries (preferable and alternative labels). The automatic mapping suggestion is based on a matching algorithm which is very effective and efficient leveraging the indexing system of semantics.gr search engine, namely Apache Solr. However, due to the different forms in which personal names are given (for example, the use of initials instead of full given names, use of patronymics – either in full form or as initials - between given names and surnames), it was necessary to adapt the matching algorithm in order to be as effective as possible. For example, when a personal name value includes initials, either for the given name or for the patronymic, these are used as patterns that match words that start with that initial. Moreover, since patronymics are usually optional and perhaps not included in the person entity record in the vocabulary, their existence in a personal name value should not filter our person entities lacking that patronymic. For example, values "Eleutherios Venizelos", "E. Venizelos" and "Venizelos Eleftherios" will all match the personal entity "Eleutherios Venizelos", but "Lefteris Venizelos", "S. Venizelos" and "Sofoklis Venizelos" will not.

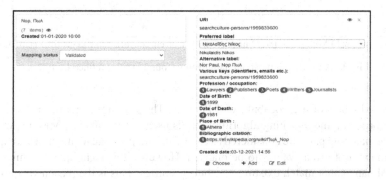

Fig. 2. An EMR set in creator mapping form.

Mapping Forms on Agent Fields. Mapping forms in "dc:creator" and "dc:contributor" were easier to handle since their values are usually personal names. Figure 2, shows an EMR in a creator mapping form where the original value "Νορ Πωλ" is mapped to person entity "Nikolaidis Nikos". Note that this EMR is automatically suggested since the "Νορ Πωλ" (Nor Paul in English) is an alternative label in Greek.

Mapping forms on Non-agent Fields. Field "dc:subject" is used for various kinds of thematic concepts including persons. More descriptive fields, such as "dc:title" and "dc:decription", are highly selective (the number of its distinct values approaches the number of all items). A mapping form for non-agent fields can be specially configured in order to search inside the values for specific words or phrases. The tool scans all distinct values of the field (e.g. all titles) and searches for inclusion matches against all

(a)   The curators click the "See items" link to inspect items with this value in SearchCulture.gr portal

(b)   The final EMR assigns the 23 items to two person entities, according to the filter configuration

Fig. 3. An EMR on personal name value (found in title) refined by filters.

the indexed labels of the Vocabulary of Persons. The search for inclusion matching is heavily based on the matching algorithm that is used for automatic EMR suggestions. Only the matching parts are considered as candidates for personal names and are exposed in the mapping form as values to be mapped. However, this technique will mine only personal names that match existing vocabulary entries. This is the reason why we first completed all mapping forms for "dc:creator" and "dc:contributor" for all collections, so as to add as many persons as possible in the vocabulary. Indeed, after all those mapping forms were processed, the vocabulary was enhanced by aprox. 1,700 entries, which significantly increased the possibility that a personal name will be mined and given a chance to be mapped in non-agent fields in consecutive enrichments.

Due to the fact that the Vocabulary of Persons expanded in tandem to the enrichment process, it forced us to return often to several collections, re-harvesting new values in mapping forms and triggering new automatic suggestions in the hopes of mining new personal names and setting more EMRs.

Dealing with Disambiguation. The mapping form provides tools that help curator in the disambiguation process. First of all, person entities from the vocabulary that appear in EMRs are presented in a panel which shows useful biographical information from the vocabulary record (see Fig. 2). The curator has immediate access to all this information that will help them in making the correct decision, without having to access the full person's record.

Moreover, for each metadata value or phrase which is subject to mapping, there is a "see items" hyperlink that curators use to search SearchCulture.gr for items having the specific values in the metadata field in the specific collection. This way, the curator can easily preview all items that would be enriched according to the EMR (Fig. 3 (a)) [1].

If the curator discovers synonimities, they can use filters (values or phrases from the same or other metadata fields) and create logical expressions in order to fine-tune the EMR and avoid false positives [1]. For instance, they can use the logical NOT operator for setting exceptions. An example of this procedure is illustrated in Fig. 3 (b). The name "Theodoros Pagkalos" belongs to a military officer/ dictator (1878–1952) and to a politician (1938-). In order to disambiguate the two persons, we used as filter a phrase from the dc:title field. Only when a CHO has the phrase "Minister of Commerce" in the title it is enriched with the latter person.

3.6 Effort

We have enriched 77 collections of SearchCulture.gr with respect to person entities. For each collection, we created multiple mapping forms on various metadata fields, mainly "dc:creator", "dc:contributor", "dc:subject" and "dc:title" (167 forms in total). Table 1 shows the number of person names occurrances identified and mapped in original metadata as well as the number of validated EMRs per metadata field. The mappings took approximately 18 person months to complete, resulting in enriching a total of 177,986 CHOs out of the aggregated >836,000. 20% of SearchCulture.gr content was enriched, a considerable percentage given that the majority of our collections are archeological or folklore thus with few person references.

Table 1. Number of person names occurrances captured and number of validated EMRs

	Number of person names occurrances identified and mapped in original metadata	Number of validated EMRs
dc:creator/dc:contributor	229,156	10,325
dc:subject	39,633	982
dc:title/dc:description	59,946	5,845
Total	328,735	17,152

4 Person-Driven Search and Browsing Functionality

All our enrichments, are used as search and browsing criteria, thus facilitating access to the items via different pathways and producing targeted search results. The new search box allows users to retrieve CHOs based on creators or referred persons, using a drop-down autocomplete list that presents entity name, a portrait and biographical information (Fig. 4 (a)). Another search field, using a drop-down autocomplete hierarchical list, allows users to retrieve CHOs created by or referring persons of a selected profession or occupation (Fig. 4(b)).

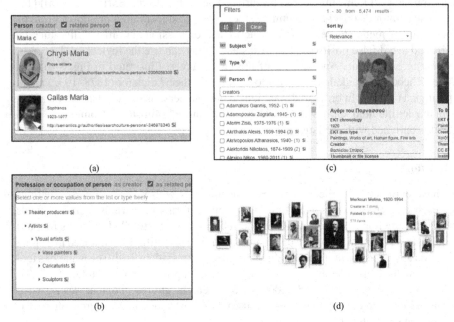

(a)   (b)   (c)   (d)

Fig. 4. New person-driven fields in the search-box (a, b), a person facet (c) and a tag cloud (d)

In the results' page, the enrichments are used as facets and serve to further narrow down the results. The newly-developed "persons" facet, showcases persons (either creators, referred persons or both) who appear in the results (Fig. 4 (c)). The facets can be used in combination, so one can search, for example, for "letters" exchanged between two persons by combining two different filters. On the homepage, an interactive navigation window displays a fraction of the persons as "tag cloud" of portraits (Fig. 4 (d)).

We also created a new search engine that targets the person entities in the aggregated content. The page is shown in Fig. 5. Browsing can be done by alphabetical order or by occurrence. Within this page one can also search for a name while autocomplete is enabled. In parallel, one can browse and select a value from the controlled list of occupations/professions and browse persons from that list. Alternatively, one can search by birth year or range of years, either in the search-box or in facets.

The resulting person entries include a thumbnail depicting the person, the name, key biographical information, the link to the person's entity in Semantics.gr and external links (VIAF, Wikipedia etc.). On the right-hand side we see the number of CHOs the person has created, those that depict/refer to him/her and the total number of CHOs relative to this person. Numbers are clickable and direct to the relevant results' page.

Fig. 5. A dedicated page for persons (https://www.searchculture.gr/aggregator/persons/search)

5 Related Work

Focusing in particular on the domain and thematic aggregators that form the Europeana Aggregators' Forum, some demand the data is enriched prior to ingestion, transferring the responsibility to the providers [3], others undertake semantic enrichment post-ingestion [7], while the majority just indexes string data without applying any semantic enrichment before delivering data to Europeana.

Europeana enriches aggregated CHOs by automatically linking text strings found in the metadata to controlled terms from LOD vocabularies [8, 9]. DBpedia is used for the enrichment of personal names in agent fields. Recently, Europeana curated an Entity Collection, a set of named entities harvested by controlled vocabularies, such as Dbpedia and Wikidata. Via this process source metadata are augmented with additional resources. This underpins some more controlled multilingual person-search functionality via the search-box.

Many EU-funded projects deal with the complexities of fully automatic or crowd-sourced enrichments such as Enrich+[9], St George on a Bike[10], Europeana XX[11] and more. Other tools used in aggregation projects, such as MoRe [10] and MINT[12] cover mainly concepts, agents and places. However automated enrichment approaches on structured fields adopt an "enrich-if-you-can" strategy, horizontally, resulting in low enrichment coverage and high percentage of mistakes [4] therefore unable to be exploited

---

[9] https://pro.europeana.eu/project/enricheuropeana.

[10] https://saintgeorgeonabike.eu/.

[11] https://pro.europeana.eu/project/europeana-xx.

[12] http://mint-wordpress.image.ntua.gr/.

for building advanced search functionalities [11]. Our semantic enrichment scheme achieves high coverage and effective disambiguation because i) it can be adjusted to the documentation particularities of the individual collections ii) it combines self-improving automatic and fuzzy-based suggestions with a suit of tools that support the curation process and iii) uses a smaller and more compact target vocabulary.

Among other cross domain aggregators, the German Digital Library provides an advanced disambiguation and search functionality for persons, using the GND thesaurus as the source vocabulary[13] and the OpenRefine tool for enriching person-values. Each person has a landing page with basic biographical information and the list of works of which one is the author or in which one is a referenced entity. Another worth mentioning tool developed by NTUA is SAGE[14], which, similarly to the Mapping Tool of semenatics.gr, combines named entity recognition and string matching techniques with a human in the loop approach.

Finally, more targeted and narrow-focused in terms of metadata heterogeneity projects adopt a mixed higher curation strategy in which domain experts validate results provided with the use of AI tools [5, 6].

6 Conclusions

The persons' enrichment scheme along with the resulting search and browsing functionalities are quite unique for a large cross-domain cultural data aggregator as shown in the related work. Although the strategy and the methodology followed depended on human curation and was quite resource-demanding, the high quality and accuracy of the results justifies the effort.

Enabling person-driven search can be a crucial wayfinding strategy for widening access to the CHOs aggregated for communities such as teachers, students, researchers etc. Our ultimate goal is using contemporary semantic technologies in order to increase the content discoverability and to provide the means to extracting new leads, connections or insights.

Acknowledgments. The work presented in this article has been supported by the project "National Research Information and Technology System: Digital Content Aggregation, Documentation and Dissemination Infrastructure ensuring interoperability, long-term preservation and open access" of the Operational Programme "Reform of the Public Sector" (NSFR), co-funded by Greece and the European Union.

References

1. Georgiadis, H., Papanoti, A., Paschou, M., Roubani, A., Chardouveli, D., Sachini, E.: Using type and temporal semantic enrichment to boost content discoverability and multilingualism in the Greek cultural aggregator SearchCulture.gr. Int. J. Metadata Semant. Ontol. **13**(1), 75–92 (2018)

---

[13] https://www.youtube.com/watch?v=thK5ZjQbUR4.
[14] https://pro.europeana.eu/page/sage.

2. Georgiadis, H., et al.: Publishing LOD vocabularies in any schema with Semantics.gr. In: Garoufallou, E., Ovalle-Perandones, M.-A., Vlachidis, A. (eds.) MTSR 2021. CCIS, vol. 1537, pp. 280–291. Springer, Cham (2022). https://doi.org/10.1007/978-3-030-98876-0_25
3. Smith, M.: Linked open data and aggregation infrastructure in the cultural heritage sector, A case study of SOCH, a linked data aggregator for Swedish open cultural heritage, In: Information and Knowledge Organisation in Digital Humanities, Routledge. https://www.taylorfrancis.com/chapters/oa-edit/10.4324/9781003131816-4/linked-open-data-aggregation-infrastructure-cultural-heritage-sector-marcus-smith (2021)
4. Manguinhas, H., et al.: Exploring comparative evaluation of semantic enrichment tools for cultural heritage metadata. In: Fuhr, N., Kovács, L., Risse, T., Nejdl, W. (eds.) TPDL 2016. LNCS, vol. 9819, pp. 266–278. Springer, Cham (2016). https://doi.org/10.1007/978-3-319-43997-6_21
5. Koho, M., Ikkala, E., Hyvönen, E.: Reassembling the lives of Finnish prisoners of the second world war on the semantic Web. In: Proceedings of the Third Conference on Biographical Data in a Digital World (BD 2019), CEUR Workshop Proceedings, p. 9. bib pdf https://seco.cs.aalto.fi/publications/2019/koho-et-al-reassembling-prisoner-biographies-2019.pdf (2022)
6. Koho, M., Leskinen, P., Hyvönen, E.: Integrating historical person registers as linked open data in the WarSampo knowledge graph. Semantic Systems. In the Era of Knowledge Graphs. SEMANTiCS 2020. In: Blomqvist, E., Groth, P., de Boer, V., Pellegrini, T., Talam, M., Käfer, T., Kieseberg, P., Kirrane, S., Meroño-Peñuela, A., Pandit, H.J. (eds.) Lecture Notes in Computer Science, vol. 12378, pp. 118–126. Springer, Cham, Amsterdam, The Netherlands (October 2020)
7. Linked Open Data for Libraries: Archives and Museums, EuropeanaTech Insight, Issue 7. Available at https://pro.europeana.eu/page/issue-7-lodlam
8. Manguinhas, H., et al.: Europeana semantic enrichment framework. Technical Documentation. Available at https://docs.google.com/document/d/1JvjrWMTpMIH7WnuieNqcT0zpJA XUPo6x4uMBj1pEx0Y
9. Stiller, J., Petras, V., Gäde, M., Isaac, A.: Automatic enrichments with controlled vocabularies in europeana: challenges and consequences. In: Ioannides, M., Magnenat-Thalmann, N., Fink, E., Žarnić, R., Yen, A.-Y., Quak, E. (eds.) Digital Heritage. Progress in Cultural Heritage: Documentation, Preservation, and Protection EuroMed 2014. LNCS, vol. 8740, pp. 238–247. Springer, Cham (2014). https://doi.org/10.1007/978-3-319-13695-0_23
10. Gavrilis, D., Ioannides, M., Theofanous, E.: Cultural heritage content re-use: an Aggregators's point of view. ISPRS. II-5/W3, 83–87 (2015)
11. Agirre, E., Barrena, A., Lopez de Lacalle, O., Soroa, A., Fernando S., Stevenson, M.: Matching cultural heritage terms to wikipedia. In: Proc. LREC 2012. Istanbul, Turkey (2012)

Figure and Figure Caption Extraction for Mixed Raster and Vector PDFs: Digitization of Astronomical Literature with OCR Features

J. P. Naiman[1]([✉])(iD), Peter K. G. Williams[2](iD), and Alyssa Goodman[2](iD)

[1] School of Information Sciences, University of Illinois, Urbana-Champaign, Champaign 61820, USA
jnaiman@illinois.edu
[2] Harvard-Smithsonian Center for Astrophysics, Cambridge 02138, USA
{pwilliams,agoodman}@cfa.harvard.edu

Abstract. Scientific articles published prior to the "age of digitization" in the late 1990s contain figures which are "trapped" within their scanned pages. While progress to extract figures and their captions has been made, there is currently no robust method for this process. We present a YOLO-based method for use on scanned pages, post-Optical Character Recognition (OCR), which uses both grayscale and OCR-features. When applied to the astrophysics literature holdings of the Astrophysics Data System (ADS), we find F1 scores of 90.9% (92.2%) for figures (figure captions) with the intersection-over-union (IOU) cut-off of 0.9 which is a significant improvement over other state-of-the-art methods.

Keywords: Scholarly document processing · Document layout analysis · Astronomy

1 Introduction

With the rise of larger datasets and the ever increasing rate of scientific publication, scientists require the use of automated methods to parse these growing data products, including the academic literature itself. In addition to being a vital component of open science [35,40], easily accessed and well curated data products are strongly encouraged as part of the submission process to most major scientific journals [28]. However, data products in the form of figures, tables and formulas which are stored in the academic literature, especially from the "pre-digital" era, published prior to ~1997, are not accessible for curation unless methods are developed to extract this important information.

The extraction of different layout elements of articles is an important component of scientific data curation, with the accuracy of extraction of the elements such as tables, figures and their captions increasing significantly over the past several years [4,15,25,50]. A large field of study within document layout analysis

© Springer Nature Switzerland AG 2022
G. Silvello et al. (Eds.): TPDL 2022, LNCS 13541, pp. 52–67, 2022.
https://doi.org/10.1007/978-3-031-16802-4_5

is the "mining" of PDFs as newer PDFs are generally in "vector" format – the document is rendered from a set of instructions instead of pixel-by-pixel as in a raster format, and, in theory, the set of instructions can be parsed to determine the locations of figures, captions and tables [3,9,23].

However, this parsing is non-trivial and many methods have been developed to complete this task. If the PDF's vector format is well structured, then text and images can be extracted by parsing this known PDF format. Several packages exist which output text and/or images from such PDF files [1]. Historically, some of the most popular include heuristic methods where blocks of text are classified as figure or table captions based on keywords (like "Fig." or "Figure") [8,11].

Deep learning methods have become popular recently for vector and raster documents [5,37], including those that use methods of semantic segmentation [45] and object detection [34]. While these methods are vital to the extraction of data products from recent academic literature, pre-digital literature is often included in digital platforms with older articles scanned at varying resolutions and deep learning methods developed with newer article training sets often perform poorly on this pre-digital literature [46]. Additionally, layouts, fonts, and article styles are typically different for historical documents when compared to "born-digital" scientific literature [46]. In these cases, text extraction must be performed with optical character recognition (OCR), and figures and tables are extracted from the raw OCR results. When applied to raster-PDF's with text generated from OCR, deep learning document layout analysis methods trained with newer or vector-based PDFs are often not as robust [45,46]. While progress has been made in augmenting these methods for OCR'd pages, especially for electronic theses and dissertations (ETDs) [46], much work can still be done to extract layout elements from these older, raster-based documents.

In what follows, we outline a new methodology for extracting figures and figure captions from a data set that includes both vector and raster based PDF's from the pre-digital scientific literature holdings of the Astrophysics Data System (ADS)[1]. Our model applies deep learning object detection methods in combination with heuristic techniques to scans of article pages as well as the text features generated from processing scans through the Tesseract OCR engine [39] and combines the results from mining any vector based PDF's for their captions with pdffigures2 [11] in a post-processing step.

While the focus of our model is the digitization of astronomical literature – one of the original "big data" sciences [38,41] – because our method relies heavily on features generated with OCR, our methodology is extendable to other scientific literature. Additionally, the design of our pipeline is heavily motivated by both the data (astronomical literature) and the expected users of our model (scientists and digital librarians). Thus, we rely on open-source software (e.g. Tesseract) and programming languages used by both communities (e.g. Python). All code is available on GitHub[2].

---

[1] https://ui.adsabs.harvard.edu/.

[2] https://github.com/ReadingTimeMachine/figure_and_caption_extraction.

2   The Data

The dataset used in this work is a subset of the English-language literature archived on ADS including pre-digital articles published between ≈1850–1997. Chosen for this work are scanned article pages that are thought to contain images of the sky derived from heuristic determinations based on color distributions [31].

We begin by defining the classes of figure and figure caption as there is often disagreement in the literature and occasionally between annotators of the same dataset [15,48]. In this work, we define a figure as the collection of one or more panels on a single page which would be referred to as a single figure in a scientific article (i.e. "Fig. 3"). This is different than other works which often treat each "sub-figure" as a separate figure [48]. Additionally, figures are defined to include all axis labels and titles as well as the area above their associated captions (or are extended on the side facing the caption if the caption is not below the figure). Finally, if a figure caption extends horizontally further than its associated figure, the figure is extended horizontally to the edges of the figure caption (see magenta lines in Fig. 3). These definitions retain the uniformity of other definitions (e.g. [50]) while defining figure and caption regions by non-overlapping boxes.

Using these definitions, we hand-annotate images to create ground-truth boxes using the MakeSense.ai[3] annotation tool for a total of 5515 pages which contain 5010 figures and 4925 figure captions.

There are 553 pages without figures or captions. Details about the annotation processing is the subject of an upcoming paper [29].

Each annotated page is also processed with Tesseract's OCR engine and outputs are stored in the hOCR format. Additionally, we process the PDF version of the article associated with each scanned page through the PDF-mining software pdffigures2 [11] and store any found figures and figure captions for combination with our model's results in a post-processing step (see Step 3 in Sect. 3.3).

In what follows, we develop a pipeline that relies heavily on features derived from the OCR results of raster-PDF's to make use of the preponderance of these types of PDFs in our dataset.

3   Model Pipeline Development

Our final goal for this dataset is the hosting of figure-caption pairs on the Astronomy Image Explorer (AIE) database[4]. Currently, a subset of the born-digital ADS holdings (articles housed in under the American Astronomical Society Journals (AAS)) automatically populate AIE with their figure-caption pairs. The Python-based pipeline developed working toward this goal is shown in Fig. 1.

3.1   Deep Learning Model and Feature Selection

Typical modern methods rely on deep learning techniques to detect layout elements on pages [5], often in combination with heuristics [37]. Methods span the

---

[3] makesense.ai.

[4] http://www.astroexplorer.org/.

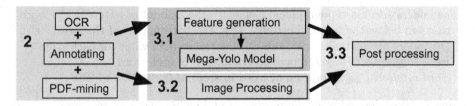

Fig. 1. Our overall pipeline is shown as four main steps. Data processing and annotating is discussed in Sect. 2, feature selection and deep learning model description is housed in Sect. 3.1, image processing techniques for heuristic figure-finding in Sect. 3.2, and post-processing techniques are discussed in Sect. 3.3.

range of object detection using models like YOLO [32,37,46] to, more recently, Faster R-CNN [16,33,36,42,48] and Mask-CNN [2,18,26]. Additionally, several pixel-by-pixel segmentation models have been proposed using semantic segmentation [45] and fully convolutional networks [22,24], including "fully convolutional instance segmentation" [13,14,27].

Often these models employ a variety of features derived from article pages as inputs along side or in place of the unprocessed page. Some of the more popular recent methods leverage image processing and computer vision techniques [48] including connected component analysis [7,10,12,17] and the distance transform [16] or some combinations thereof [49].

While the aim of many methods is to detect page objects before any OCR process, here we implement methods that can be applied after. In what follows, we use a Tensorflow implementation of YOLO-v5[5] [20,32] and focus our efforts on feature exploration by utilizing a set of features derived from the OCR outputs themselves with the goal to choose the smallest number of the "best" features on which to build our model. In addition to the raw grayscale page, there are several possible features derived primarily from the hOCR outputs of Tesseract. To minimize storage, each feature is scaled as an unsigned-integer, 8-bit "color" channel in a 512×512 (pixels), multi-layer image which is fed into a "mega-YOLO" model capable of processing more than three color channels.

Features explored which are output from Tesseract in hOCR format include:

- *fontsize (fs)*: the fontsize for each word bounding box is normalized by subtraction of the median page fontsize and division by the standard deviation. Bounding boxes with fonts outside five standard deviations are ignored.
- *carea (c_b)*: the "content area" from automatic page segmentation includes large blocks of text and sometimes encapsulates figures into separate "content areas", but not consistently.
- *paragraphs (p_b)*: automatically segmented groups of words as likely paragraphs. Often overlaps with "carea".
- *ascenders (asc)*: from typography definitions – the amount of letters in the word that are above the letter "caps" (e.g. the top of the letter "h"). Ascenders are normalized by subtracting the median value for each page.

---

[5] https://github.com/jahongir7174/YOLOv5-tf
https://github.com/jmpap/YOLOV2-Tensorflow-2.0.

- *decenders (dec)*: a typographical element – the amount of letters in the word that are below the letter "bottoms" (e.g. the bottom curl of the letter "g"). Decenders are normalized by subtracting the median value for each page.
- *word confidences (wc)*: the percent confidence of each word
- *word rotation (t_{ang})*: rotation of word in steps of 0°, 180°, and 270°.

Other features derived from the page scan and OCR-generated text are:

- *grayscale (gs)*: the image is collapsed into grayscale using the page's luminance. The majority of images are already in grayscale and those few that are in color are transformed to grayscale.
- *fraction of letters in a word (%l)*: the percentage of characters in a word that are letters (scaled 125–255 in order to preserve a "true zero" for spaces in the scanned page that contain no words).
- *fraction of numbers in a word (%n)*: the percentage of numbers in a word that are letters (scaled 125–255).
- *punctuation (p)*: punctuation marks are tagged as 250, non-punctuation characters are tagged as 125 (saving 0 for empty, non-word space).
- *spaCy POS (SP)*: spaCy's [19] 19 entries for "part of speech" (noun, verb, etc.) in the English language
- *spaCy TAG (ST)*: more detailed part of speech tag with 57 values
- *spaCy DEP (SD)*: the 51 "syntactic dependency" tags which specify how different words are related to each other.

Figure 2 shows an example of a selection of these features (grayscale (*gs*), fontsize (*fs*), and spaCy DEP (*SD*)) for a single page and their distributions across all pages in our annotated dataset. The example features of grayscale and fontsize show differences in distributions in the three categories of figure, figure caption and the "rest" of the page – grayscale distributions are more uniform inside figures (left plot of Fig. 2) and figure captions show a peak in the fontsize distributions toward higher values when compared to the fontsize distributions of figures (middle plot of Fig. 2). Trends in other features are harder to determine, as illustrated in the bottom right panel of Fig. 2 which shows a less clear distinction between figures, figure captions, and the rest of the page for the feature of spaCy DEP.

In Sect. 4 we discuss our best model which includes (grayscale, ascenders, decenders, word confidences, fraction of numbers in a word, fraction of letters in a word, punctuation, word rotation and spaCy POS) as the set of input features.

3.2   Image Processing

In addition to the deep learning model described in Sect. 3.1, we use image processing techniques to heuristically find potential figure boxes to combine with those found with the mega-YOLO model. The locations of the OCR'd words (see Sect. 2) are used to mask out text and the modified pages are processed through a basic shape finder built with OpenCV, tuned to look for rectangles (four corners and sides comprised of approximately parallel lines). This "rectangle finder"

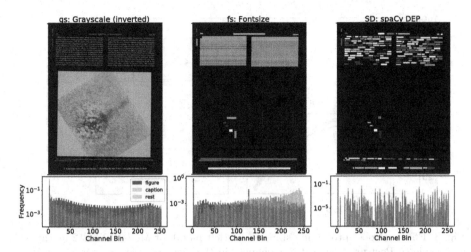

Fig. 2. Examples of selected features for a single page (top row) and the distribution across all pages in the annotated dataset (bottom row). All features have been rescaled into 8-bit color bins (see Sect. 3.1). Here, "rest" refers to rest of the page that does not include figures or captions. Several features show clear differences in distributions (e.g. grayscale and fontsize) while others do not (e.g. spaCy DEP).

is applied to several filtered versions of the page (histogram of oriented gradients, dilation, and color-reversal, and various levels of thresholding). The list of rectangles is culled with K-Means clustering on the locations of square corners, checking for artifact-rectangles which are small in size, and rectangles that are likely colorbars and not figures due to their aspect ratio.

OCR'ing a page and shape-finding with OpenCV takes approximately 20–25 seconds per page (tested on six cores of an Apple M1 Max with 64 Gb of RAM).

3.3 Post-processing Pipeline

After features are selected and the model is trained we modify the final found boxes by merging them with OCR word and paragraph boxes and any heuristically found captions and figures at the fractional-pixel level (results are rounded to nearest pixel for intersection-over-union (IOU) calculations to match precision of ground truth boxes). Post-processing is a common practice in document layout analysis [47,49], however it often differs between implementations and is occasionally not incorporated into a final pipeline [44]. Figure 3 depicts how found boxes and F1 score changes with each post-processing step in our pipeline when we compare ground-truth (true) boxes to model-found boxes at various post-processing steps:

- Step 1: "raw" found boxes are those culled with non-maximum suppression
- Step 2: if two found boxes overlap with an IOU ≥ 0.25 the box with the lowest score is removed, decreasing false positives (FP)

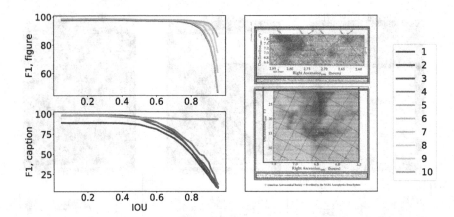

Fig. 3. Effects of post-processing steps on F1 (left plots) for Model 12 (m12 in Table 1 and Table 2). Post-processing drives changes in the metrics at larger IOU's – IOU $\gtrsim$ 0.8 and IOU $\gtrsim$ 0.6 for figures and captions, respectively. Changes are depicted for a single page (right plot) showing initial found boxes (Step 1, dark blue) and final (Step 10, orange) in comparison to true boxes (thick magenta). (Color figure online)

- Step 3: pdffigures2-found figure caption boxes replace those found with the deep learning model when they overlap which increases caption true positive (TP) rate and decreases FP and false negative (FN) at large IOU thresholds.
- Step 4: Caption boxes are found heuristically by first applying a gaussian blur filter on an image of drawn OCR text boxes. Contours of this image that overlap with text boxes that match with a fuzzy-search of words such as "Fig.", "Figure" and "Plate" are labeled as heuristically-found. If a heuristically-found caption box overlaps with a mega-YOLO-found box, we take the top of the heuristic box (which tends to be more accurate) and the minimum (maximum) of the left (right, bottom) of the two boxes. This results in an overall increase in TP while FN and FP drop.
- Step 5: found captions are expanded by their overlap with OCR word and paragraph boxes, allowing for multiple "grow" iterations in the horizontal direction. Found boxes are only expanded by paragraph and word boxes if the centers of paragraph and word boxes overlap with the found box.
- Step 6: if found figure boxes overlap with rectangles that are found through image processing (as described in Sect. 3.2), the found box is expanded to include the image processing rectangle. This increases the TP rate at larger IOU thresholds for figures.
- Step 7: any found captions that have areas larger than 75% of the page area are discarded leading to a slight drop in FP for captions.
- Step 8: Captions are paired to figures by minimizing the distance between caption center and bottom of a specific figure. Rotational information from the page and overall rotation of the OCR words is used to determine the "bottom" of the figure. Any captions without an associated figure on a page are dropped, leading to a drop in FP.

- Step 9: found figure boxes are extended down to the tops of their associated captions increasing TP for figures and captions at high IOU thresholds.
- Step 10: if a figure caption extends horizontally further than its associated figure, the figure is extended horizontally to the edges of the figure caption. This leads to an increase in TP rates for figures at high IOU thresholds.

Steps 9 and 10 are similar to the steps described for annotated boxes in Sect. 2. The effects to the metrics shown in Fig. 3 are modest and predominately affect the results at high IOU thresholds (IOU $\gtrsim 0.9$) for figures.

3.4 Feature Selection Ablation Experiments

To determine the set of features which produce the most accurate model while minimizing the feature memory footprint, we conduct a series of ablation experiments, summarized in Table 1 and Table 2. In all feature selection runs we use 75% of our data in the training set, 15% in validation, and 10% in the test dataset. Results in Table 2 are shown for this feature selection test dataset.

Table 1. Ablation experiments with the features discussed in Sect. 3.1. All models include post-processing (Sect. 3.3). Our "best" model, as determined by metrics in Sect. 2 and the discussion of Sect. 3.4, is Model 12 (m12) highlighted in bold.

Model	Description
m1	gs
m2	gs + fs
m3	gs + fs + asc + dec
m4	gs + fs + asc + dec + wc
m5	gs + fs + asc + dec + wc + %n + %l + p
m6	gs + fs + asc + dec + wc + %n + %l + p + t_{ang}
m7	gs + fs + asc + dec + wc + %n + %l + p + t_{ang} + SP
m8	gs + fs + asc + dec + wc + %n + %l + p + t_{ang} + SP + ST + SD
m9	gs + fs + asc + dec + wc + %n + %l + p + t_{ang} + SP + ST + SD + p_b
m10	gs + fs + asc + dec + wc + %n + %l + p + t_{ang} + SP + ST + SD + p_b + c_b
m11	gs + fs + wc + %n + %l + p + t_{ang} + SP
m12	**gs + asc + dec + wc + %n + %l + p + t_{ang} + SP**
m13	gs + asc + dec + wc + %n + p + t_{ang} + SP
m14	gs + asc + dec + wc + %n + %l + t_{ang} + SP
m15	gs + asc + dec + wc + %n + %l + p + t_{ang}

As it is computationally prohibitive to test all combination of all fourteen different features, we first adopt the strategy of including sets of one or two groups of features at a time until we have a model containing all fourteen features, as shown above the thick horizontal line in Table 1. From these ten models, we select the most accurate, defined here as having a high F1 score for both figures and their captions, while maintaining a low false positive score (FP). Model 7 is the "best" model out of these first ten models in Table 2. We then subtract one or two features from this model in combinations shown below the thick horizontal line in Table 1. Using the same selection criteria leads us to choose Model 12 as our overall "best" model which includes the features of (grayscale, ascenders, decenders, word confidences, fraction of numbers in a word, fraction of letters in a word, punctuation, word rotation and spaCy POS) as highlighted in Table 2.

The implemented optimizer is Adam with a $\beta_1 = 0.937$ $\beta_2 = 0.999$. Learning rate is scheduled using a cosine scheduler which depends on initial learning rate, number of epochs and batch size. Practically, when applied to our model this results in a linear increase in learning rate by a factor of ∼1.6 in the initial epoch (flat after). Our optimal initial learning rate of 0.004 was chosen from a small set of learning rates (0.008, 0.004, 0.0004, 0.0002). All experiments are run for 150 epochs and converge within this time (tracked by validation losses). No data augmentation is applied. Training is performed on a Tesla V100-SXM2 GPU with an average time of ∼6.5 min per epoch.

Table 2. Metrics for models described in Table 1. There are 497 figures (fig) and 488 figure captions (cap) used in the feature selection test dataset. IOU is 0.9 for both figures and captions. TP, FP and FN are shown as percentages of the total instances.

	TP		FP		FN		Prec		Rec		F1	
	fig	cap	fig	cap	fig	cap	fig	cap	fig	cap	fig	cap
m1	90.3	88.3	11.3	10.0	1.8	4.3	88.9	89.8	98.0	95.4	93.3	92.5
m2	89.5	86.9	10.9	8.6	2.6	6.4	89.2	91.0	97.2	93.2	93.0	92.1
m3	85.9	86.9	17.9	12.5	1.8	5.1	82.8	87.4	97.9	94.4	89.7	90.8
m4	90.5	88.7	10.1	8.8	2.0	3.7	90.0	91.0	97.8	96.0	93.7	93.4
m5	84.5	87.3	15.7	7.2	2.2	7.0	84.3	92.4	97.4	92.6	90.4	92.5
m6	89.5	89.1	11.9	9.0	2.0	4.3	88.3	90.8	97.8	95.4	92.8	93.0
m7	92.8	88.1	8.0	9.0	1.4	4.1	92.0	90.7	98.5	95.6	95.1	93.1
m8	90.5	90.0	9.1	7.2	2.0	3.9	90.9	92.6	97.8	95.9	94.2	94.2
m9	84.3	84.2	13.5	7.4	4.0	9.4	86.2	91.9	95.4	89.9	90.6	90.9
m10	88.7	87.5	11.5	9.6	1.8	4.3	88.6	90.1	98.0	95.3	93.0	92.6
m11	90.5	92.4	10.5	6.8	0.8	1.8	89.6	93.2	99.1	98.0	94.1	95.6
m12	**92.2**	**89.1**	**6.4**	**6.6**	**2.4**	**4.9**	**93.5**	**93.1**	**97.4**	**94.8**	**95.4**	**94.0**
m13	92.8	88.7	7.8	8.4	2.0	4.3	92.2	91.4	97.9	95.4	95.0	93.3
m14	87.3	88.7	15.9	8.4	1.2	6.4	84.6	91.4	98.6	93.3	91.1	92.3
m15	89.9	89.5	8.7	5.9	2.4	5.1	91.2	93.8	97.4	94.6	94.2	94.2

4 Results

To quantify the results of our "best" model (Model 12) on un-seen data we annotate an additional ≈600 pages as a "final test dataset" of ≈500 figure and figure caption ground-truths (490 and 487, respectively). We find F1 scores of

90.9% (92.2%) for figure (caption) detections at an intersection-over-union cut off (IOU) of 0.9 as shown in the last row and column of Table 3. Including post-processing, evaluation takes on average 1.8 s per page on a single core of an Apple M1 Max with 64 Gb of RAM.

4.1   Benchmarks at High Levels of Localization (IOU = 0.9)

As the ultimate goal of our method is the extraction of figures and their captions from scanned pages, we quantify how well our model performs on our dataset for a high degree of localization with an IOU cut-off of 0.9.

Table 3 shows how other deep learning models fair on our final test dataset. Here, we use ScanBank [21, 46] (based on DeepFigures [37] and trained on a corpus of pre-digital electronic thesis and dissertations (ETDs)) and a version of detectron2 [44] trained on the PubLayNet dataset [50]. ScanBank and detectron2 are used for comparison as they are applied to raster-formatted articles (as opposed to vector-based methods like pdffigures2 [11] which, applied to our data, results in F1 scores of <15% in feature and final test splits). Both ScanBank and detectron2 do not share our definitions of figures and figure captions exactly, thus to facilitate comparison we make some approximations and assumptions.

As discussed in [21], ScanBank's figure's are defined as encompassing the figure caption, while our figure definitions exclude the caption. In order to compare with our results, we initially performed metric calculations by re-defining our true figure boxes as the combination of figure and figure caption boxes when figure captions are associated with a figure. However, we found that if we instead use our definitions of figures and captions, metrics from detections made with ScanBank are optimized, thus we use our definitions of figures and captions for all comparisons with this model. As detectron2 does not find caption boxes specifically, but rather localizes generic "text" boxes, we define detectron2-detected figure captions as those boxes with centers which are closest to a found figure's center. To test the effects of our post-processing methods alone, we apply a subset of our post-processing steps to the results generated from both ScanBank and detectron2 which we show for comparison to our method with and without post-processing in Table 3. When applying post-processing to these other models' results, we use only up to the "Step 5" described in Sect. 3.3 as we found this optimized the metrics for ScanBank and detectron2 reported in Table 3.

As shown in Table 3, ScanBank does not perform well on our final test dataset with or without post-processing. In particular, ScanBank does not detect captions reliably as the false negative rate (FN) is high. Additionally, there is a large portion of both figures and figure captions which are either erroneously detected, or not well localized as shown by the high false positive (FP) rate. This is somewhat expected as the ETD format is visually distinct from the articles in our dataset, including different fonts and caption placements. When post-processing is applied the metrics for figure captions improve significantly with an increase of ≈30% in true positive (TP) rate and decrease of ≈20% in FP.

For the detectron2 model without post-processing, TP rates are slightly higher than ScanBank's, however FP rates remain comparable to ScanBank's.

FN rates are lower than our model (both with and without post-processing) by a few percentage points, likely due in part to the known differences in error profiles between YOLO-based (ours) and Mask-RCNN-based (detectron2) object detection models [32]. Post-processing makes a large improvement on the TP rate for captions, increasing it by ≈35% and decreasing FP by ≈40%. There is a modest increase in TP of ≈10% for figures as well when post-processing is applied.

Post-processing (using all steps) has the largest effect on our model's results – increasing TP rates of figures and captions by ≈25% and ≈60%, respectively. This is not surprising as our post-processing method was developed using our scanned page training data. Additionally, we employ a YOLO-based model which is used for detecting bounding boxes, not a segmentation method that would tend to produce larger TP rates at higher IOU thresholds – the post-processing pipeline "mimics" segmentation by changing box sizes to closer fit precise locations of caption words and figures, increasing overlap IOU.

Taken together, the results of Table 3 suggest that other models generalize to our dataset at best moderately at high IOU, and only with application of our post-processing pipeline. Because our post-processing steps require not only grayscale scanned pages, but their OCR outputs, this additional overhead (of both producing the OCR and post-processing steps) greatly reduces the gains in page processing speeds achieved with these other methods.

Table 3. Performance metrics for ScanBank [21,46] and detectron2 [44] for our final test dataset. IOU is 0.9. TP, FP, FN are in percentages of total true instances. Models with post-processing ("w/PP") and those without ("No PP") are shown for comparison. No retraining or transfer learning of ScanBank or detectron2 have been done with our dataset. Errors from a 5-fold cross validation on all metrics are ∼1–2%.

| | ScanBank | | ScanBank | | detectron2* | | detectron2* | | Ours | | Ours | |
| | No PP | | w/PP | | No PP | | w/PP | | No PP | | w/PP | |
	fig	cap	fig	cap	fig	cap†	fig	cap†	fig	cap	fig	cap
TP	69.9	29.0	69.3	52.8	72.0	46.4	81.0	80.9	58.2	23.2	85.7	86.7
FP	71.4	28.8	43.6	8.7	41.8	68.2	27.1	22.4	45.3	82.3	13.7	8.6
FN	1.7	42.8	2.5	40.7	0.6	1.6	1.2	4.9	3.1	5.1	3.5	6.0
Prec	49.5	50.2	61.4	85.9	63.3	40.5	74.9	78.3	56.2	22.0	86.2	90.9
Rec	97.6	40.4	96.5	56.5	99.2	96.6	98.5	94.3	95.0	81.9	96.1	93.6
F1	65.7	44.8	75.0	68.1	77.2	57.1	85.1	85.6	70.6	34.7	90.9	92.2

* The tested version of detectron2 is trained on the PubLayNet dataset [44].
† Here, captions are the "text" classified box closest to the center of a figure.

This lack of generalizability is a known problem in the field of document layout analysis [5] and our model is no exception. For example, when our model is applied to a selection of PubLayNet's non-commercial article pages [50][6] we find F1 scores lower than those produced by detectron2 for figures – 65.7% (ours) vs. 85.8% (detectron2) for 207 figures. Using the definitions of captions from Table 3 for 201 captions the results are more promising with F1 scores of 65.6% (ours) to 65.5% (detectron2). Results for our (ScanBank's) model applied to the ScanBank collection of "gold-standard" ETDs [21,46] are lower overall with F1 scores of 25.5% (38.4%) for 197 figures and 16.3% (1.4%) for 140 captions. While these results suggest that our model may be more generalizable than other models for figure captions, tests on larger datasets are necessary for a firmer conclusion.

5   Discussion and Future Work

This paper has focused on the localization of figures and figure captions in astronomical scientific literature. We present results of a YOLO-based deep learning model trained on features extracted from the scanned page, hOCR outputs of the Tesseract OCR engine [39], and the text processing outputs from spaCy [19].

Through ablation experiments we find the combination of the page and hOCR properties of (grayscale, ascenders, decenders, word confidences, fraction of numbers in a word, fraction of letters in a word, punctuation, word rotation and spaCy POS) maximize our model's performance. When compared to other deep learning models popular for document layout analysis (ScanBank [21,46] and detectron2 [44]) we find our model performs better on our dataset, particularly at the high IOU thresholds (IOU = 0.9) and especially for figure captions. In particular, in line with our extraction goals, our model has relatively low false positive rates, minimizing the extraction of erroneous page objects. For figures, our model does not perform well on other datasets (e.g. PubLayNet [50], ScanBank[46]), however is as accurate or more accurate than others for figure captions.

Our work relies on a relatively small set of scanned pages (~6000). While the results here for figures and captions surpass the estimates of ~2000 instances per class required for training YOLO-based models [6,43] our data contains many edge cases of complex layouts and we expect more data to improve results for these pages. As our model relies on more than three feature channels, transfer learning on pre-trained YOLO-based models is less straight forward, but nonetheless could be a way to make use of our small dataset in future work.

Additionally, our current methodology does not make use of popular image processing features (e.g. connected components [48]) or loss functions/processing techniques that are "non-standard" for YOLO-based methods [30]. Future testing with the inclusion of these features may increase our model performance.

While all of our models converge within 150 training epochs, this is without the inclusion of any data augmentation. As our model uses not only grayscale but hOCR properties, typical data augmentation procedures (e.g. flipping, changes in saturation) are not appropriate for all feature layers. However, it is likely that

---

[6] Non-commercial articles are necessary to access the high resolution scans and perform the OCR needed for our method.

correctly-applied data augmentation will increase our model's performance. Our work would further benefit from a future large hyperparameter tuning study beyond the several values of learning rate tested in this paper.

Finally, given the difference in error profiles between the YOLO-based method presented here and other Mask-RCNN/Faster-RCNN based [32] document layout analysis models (e.g. detectron2), it is likely that an ensemble model using both methods would further increase model performance.

This work is supported by a Fiddler Fellowship and a NASA Astrophysics Data Analysis Program Grant (20-ADAP20-0225). The authors thank the referees for their insightful input on this paper.

References

1. Grobid (2008-2021). https://github.com/kermitt2/grobid
2. Agarwal, M., Mondal, A., Jawahar, C.V.: CDeC-Net: composite deformable cascade network for table detection in document images. arXiv e-prints arXiv:2008.10831 (2020)
3. Bai, K., Mitra, P., Giles, C.L., Liu, Y.: Automatic extraction of table metadata from digital documents. In: Proceedings of the 6th ACM/IEEE-CS Joint Conference on Digital Libraries (JCDL 2006), pp. 339–340. IEEE (2006)
4. Bhatt, J., Hashmi, K.A., Afzal, M.Z., Stricker, D.: A survey of graphical page object detection with deep neural networks. Appl. Sci. **11**(12) (2021). https://doi. org/10.3390/app11125344, https://www.mdpi.com/2076-3417/11/12/5344
5. Bhatt, J., Hashmi, K.A., Afzal, M.Z., Stricker, D.: A survey of graphical page object detection with deep neural networks. Appl. Sci. **11**(12) (2021). https://doi. org/10.3390/app11125344, https://www.mdpi.com/2076-3417/11/12/5344
6. Bochkovskiy, A., Wang, C.Y., Liao, H.Y.M.: YOLOv4: optimal speed and accuracy of object detection (2020)
7. Bukhari, S.S., Al Azawi, M.I.A., Shafait, F., Breuel, T.M.: Document image segmentation using discriminative learning over connected components. In: Proceedings of the 9th IAPR International Workshop on Document Analysis Systems, DAS 2010, pp. 183–190. Association for Computing Machinery, New York (2010). https://doi.org/10.1145/1815330.1815354
8. Choudhury, S.R., et al.: Figure metadata extraction from digital documents. In: 2013 12th International Conference on Document Analysis and Recognition, pp. 135–139 (2013). https://doi.org/10.1109/ICDAR.2013.34
9. Choudhury, S.R., et al.: A figure search engine architecture for a chemistry digital library. In: Proceedings of the 13th ACM/IEEE-CS Joint Conference on Digital Libraries, pp. 369–370 (2013)
10. Chowdhury, S., Mandal, S., Das, A., Chanda, B.: Automated segmentation of math-zones from document images. In: 2003 Proceedings of Seventh International Conference on Document Analysis and Recognition, pp. 755–759 (2003). https:// doi.org/10.1109/ICDAR.2003.1227763
11. Clark, C., Divvala, S.: PDFFigures 2.0: mining figures from research papers. In: 2016 IEEE/ACM Joint Conference on Digital Libraries (JCDL), pp. 143–152 (2016)
12. Cronje, J.: Figure detection and part label extraction from patent drawing images. In: 23rd Annual Symposium of the Pattern Recognition Association of South Africa. PRASA (2012)

13. Dai, J., He, K., Li, Y., Ren, S., Sun, J.: Instance-sensitive fully convolutional networks. arXiv e-prints arXiv:1603.08678 (2016)
14. Dai, J., Li, Y., He, K., Sun, J.: R-FCN: object detection via region-based fully convolutional networks. arXiv e-prints arXiv:1605.06409 (2016)
15. Gao, L., Yi, X., Jiang, Z., Hao, L., Tang, Z.: ICDAR 2017 competition on page object detection. In: 2017 14th IAPR International Conference on Document Analysis and Recognition (ICDAR), vol. 01, pp. 1417–1422 (2017). https://doi.org/10.1109/ICDAR.2017.231
16. Gilani, A., Qasim, S.R., Malik, I., Shafait, F.: Table detection using deep learning. In: 2017 14th IAPR International Conference on Document Analysis and Recognition (ICDAR), vol. 01, pp. 771–776 (2017). https://doi.org/10.1109/ICDAR.2017.131
17. Ha, J., Haralick, R., Phillips, I.: Recursive X-Y cut using bounding boxes of connected components. In: Proceedings of 3rd International Conference on Document Analysis and Recognition, vol. 2, pp. 952–955 vol 2 (1995). https://doi.org/10.1109/ICDAR.1995.602059
18. He, K., Gkioxari, G., Dollár, P., Girshick, R.: Mask R-CNN. arXiv e-prints arXiv:1703.06870 (2017)
19. Honnibal, M., Montani, I.: spaCy 2: natural language understanding with Bloom embeddings, convolutional neural networks and incremental parsing (2017, to appear)
20. Jocher, G., et al.: ultralytics/YOLOv5: v3.1 - bug fixes and performance improvements (2020). https://doi.org/10.5281/zenodo.4154370
21. Kahu, S.Y.: Figure extraction from scanned electronic theses and dissertations. Master's thesis, Virginia Tech (2020)
22. Kavasidis, I., et al.: A saliency-based convolutional neural network for table and chart detection in digitized documents. arXiv e-prints arXiv:1804.06236 (2018)
23. Klampfl, S., Kern, R.: An unsupervised machine learning approach to body text and table of contents extraction from digital scientific articles. In: Aalberg, T., Papatheodorou, C., Dobreva, M., Tsakonas, G., Farrugia, C.J. (eds.) TPDL 2013. LNCS, vol. 8092, pp. 144–155. Springer, Heidelberg (2013). https://doi.org/10.1007/978-3-642-40501-3_15
24. Krähenbühl, P., Koltun, V.: Efficient inference in fully connected CRFs with Gaussian edge potentials. arXiv e-prints arXiv:1210.5644 (2012)
25. Lehenmeier, C., Burghardt, M., Mischka, B.: Layout detection and table recognition – recent challenges in digitizing historical documents and handwritten tabular data. In: Hall, M., Merčun, T., Risse, T., Duchateau, F. (eds.) TPDL 2020. LNCS, vol. 12246, pp. 229–242. Springer, Cham (2020). https://doi.org/10.1007/978-3-030-54956-5_17
26. Li, M., Xu, Y., Cui, L., Huang, S., Wei, F., Li, Z., Zhou, M.: DocBank: a benchmark dataset for document layout analysis. arXiv e-prints arXiv:2006.01038 (2020)
27. Li, Y., Qi, H., Dai, J., Ji, X., Wei, Y.: Fully convolutional instance-aware semantic segmentation. arXiv e-prints arXiv:1611.07709 (2016)
28. Mayernik, M.S., Hart, D.L., Maull, K.E., Weber, N.M.: Assessing and tracing the outcomes and impact of research infrastructures. J. Assoc. Inf. Sci. Technol. 68(6), 1341–1359 (2017). https://doi.org/10.1002/asi.23721, https://asistdl.onlinelibrary.wiley.com/doi/abs/10.1002/asi.23721
29. Naiman, J.P., Williams, P.K.G., Goodman, A.: The reading time machine figure localization dataset (2022). Unpublished paper

30. Neubeck, A., Van Gool, L.: Efficient non-maximum suppression. In: 18th International Conference on Pattern Recognition (ICPR 2006), vol. 3, pp. 850–855 (2006). https://doi.org/10.1109/ICPR.2006.479
31. Pepe, A., Goodman, A., Muench, A.: The ADS all-sky survey. In: Ballester, P., Egret, D., Lorente, N.P.F. (eds.) Astronomical Data Analysis Software and Systems XXI. Astronomical Society of the Pacific Conference Series, vol. 461, p. 275 (2012)
32. Redmon, J., Divvala, S., Girshick, R., Farhadi, A.: You only look once: unified, real-time object detection. arXiv e-prints arXiv:1506.02640 (Jun 2015)
33. Ren, S., He, K., Girshick, R., Sun, J.: Faster R-CNN: towards real-time object detection with region proposal networks. arXiv e-prints arXiv:1506.01497 (2015)
34. Saha, R., Mondal, A., Jawahar, C.V.: Graphical object detection in document images. In: 2019 International Conference on Document Analysis and Recognition (ICDAR), pp. 51–58 (2019). https://doi.org/10.1109/ICDAR.2019.00018
35. Sandy, H.M., et al.: Making a case for open research: implications for reproducibility and transparency. Proc. Assoc. Inf. Sci. Technol. **54**(1), 583–586 (2017). https://doi.org/10.1002/pra2.2017.14505401079, https://asistdl.onlinelibrary.wiley.com/doi/abs/10.1002/pra2.2017.14505401079
36. Schreiber, S., Agne, S., Wolf, I., Dengel, A., Ahmed, S.: DeepDeSRT: deep learning for detection and structure recognition of tables in document images. In: 2017 14th IAPR International Conference on Document Analysis and Recognition (ICDAR), vol. 01, pp. 1162–1167 (2017). https://doi.org/10.1109/ICDAR.2017.192
37. Siegel, N., Lourie, N., Power, R., Ammar, W.: Extracting scientific figures with distantly supervised neural networks. arXiv e-prints arXiv:1804.02445 (2018)
38. Smith, L., Arcand, K., Smith, R., Bookbinder, J., Smith, J.: Capturing the many faces of an exploded star: communicating complex and evolving astronomical data. JCOM J. Sci. Commun. **16**, 16050202 (2017). https://doi.org/10.22323/2.16050202
39. Smith, R.: An overview of the tesseract OCR engine. In: Proceedings of the Ninth International Conference on Document Analysis and Recognition, ICDAR 2007, vol. 02, pp. 629–633. IEEE Computer Society, USA (2007)
40. Sohmen, L., Charbonnier, J., Blümel, I., Wartena, C., Heller, L.: Figures in scientific open access publications. In: Méndez, E., Crestani, F., Ribeiro, C., David, G., Lopes, J.C. (eds.) TPDL 2018. LNCS, vol. 11057, pp. 220–226. Springer, Cham (2018). https://doi.org/10.1007/978-3-030-00066-0_19
41. Stephens, Z.D., et al.: Big data: astronomical or genomical? PLOS Biol. **13**(7), 1–11 (2015). https://doi.org/10.1371/journal.pbio.1002195
42. Vo, N.D., Nguyen, K., Nguyen, T.V., Nguyen, K.: Ensemble of deep object detectors for page object detection. In: Proceedings of the 12th International Conference on Ubiquitous Information Management and Communication, IMCOM 2018. Association for Computing Machinery, New York (2018). https://doi.org/10.1145/3164541.3164644
43. Wang, C.Y., Bochkovskiy, A., Liao, H.Y.M.: Scaled-YOLOv4: scaling cross stage partial network. In: Proceedings of the IEEE/CVF Conference on Computer Vision and Pattern Recognition (CVPR), pp. 13029–13038 (2021)
44. Wu, Y., Kirillov, A., Massa, F., Lo, W.Y., Girshick, R.: Detectron2 (2019). https://github.com/facebookresearch/detectron2
45. Yang, X., Yumer, E., Asente, P., Kraley, M., Kifer, D., Giles, C.L.: Learning to extract semantic structure from documents using multimodal fully convolutional neural networks. In: 2017 IEEE Conference on Computer Vision and Pattern Recognition (CVPR), pp. 4342–4351 (2017). https://doi.org/10.1109/CVPR.2017.462

46. Yashwant Kahu, S., Ingram, W.A., Fox, E.A., Wu, J.: ScanBank: a benchmark dataset for figure extraction from scanned electronic theses and dissertations. arXiv e-prints arXiv:2106.15320 (2021)

47. Yi, X., Gao, L., Liao, Y., Zhang, X., Liu, R., Jiang, Z.: CNN based page object detection in document images. In: 2017 14th IAPR International Conference on Document Analysis and Recognition (ICDAR), vol. 01, pp. 230–235 (2017). https://doi.org/10.1109/ICDAR.2017.46

48. Younas, J., Rizvi, S.T.R., Malik, M.I., Shafait, F., Lukowicz, P., Ahmed, S.: FFD: figure and formula detection from document images. In: 2019 Digital Image Computing: Techniques and Applications (DICTA), pp. 1–7 (2019). https://doi.org/10.1109/DICTA47822.2019.8945972

49. Younas, J., et al.: Fi-Fo detector: figure and formula detection using deformable networks. Appl. Sci. **10**(18) (2020). https://doi.org/10.3390/app10186460, https://www.mdpi.com/2076-3417/10/18/6460

50. Zhong, X., Tang, J., Jimeno Yepes, A.: PubLayNet: largest dataset ever for document layout analysis. arXiv e-prints arXiv:1908.07836 (2019)

FAIROs: Towards FAIR Assessment in Research Objects

Esteban González[✉][iD], Alejandro Benítez, and Daniel Garijo[iD]

Universidad Politécnica de Madrid, Madrid, Spain
{esteban.gonzalez,daniel.garijo}@upm.es,
guillermoalejandro.benitez@alumnos.upm.es

Abstract. The FAIR principles have become a popular means to guide researchers when publishing their research outputs (i.e., data, software, etc.) in a Findable, Accessible, Interoperable and Reusable manner. In order to ease compliance with FAIR, different frameworks have been developed by the scientific community, offering guidance and suggestions to researchers. However, scientific outputs are rarely published in isolation. Research Objects have been proposed as a framework to capture the relationships and context of all constituents of an investigation. In this paper we present FAIROs, a framework for assessing the compliance of a Research Object (and its constituents) against the FAIR principles. FAIROs reuses existing FAIR validators for individual resources and proposes i) two scoring methods for assessing the fairness of Research Objects, ii) an initial implementation of the scoring methods in the FAIROs framework, and iii) an explanation-based approach designed to visualize the obtained scores. We validate FAIROs against 165 Research Objects, and discuss the advantages and limitations of different scoring systems.

Keywords: FAIR assessment · Research object · Aggregation methods

1 Introduction

The Findable, Accessible, Interoperable and Reusable principles (FAIR) introduce a set of best practices to share data, make data more reusable and support the reproducibility of results in research [22]. FAIR addresses using persistent identifiers for resources, rich metadata to favour discovery, explicit licenses to understand usage terms and using well established vocabularies to facilitate interoperability.

Although FAIR was originally proposed for datasets, additional initiatives are appearing to apply these principles to other research outputs, such as software [15,16], ontologies [19], virtual research environments[1] or digital objects [4] among others.

---

[1] https://rd-alliance.org/group/fair-virtual-research-environments-wg/case-statement/fair-virtual-research-environments-vres.

© Springer Nature Switzerland AG 2022
G. Silvello et al. (Eds.): TPDL 2022, LNCS 13541, pp. 68–80, 2022.
https://doi.org/10.1007/978-3-031-16802-4_6

Since research outputs are rarely produced in isolation, the scientific community has proposed Research Objects [2,20] to capture the context around a scientific investigation. Research Objects also provide the means to pack all the resources within some research, easing its understandability and facilitating its dissemination. However, assessing the compliance of a Research Object against the FAIR principles (i.e., their FAIRness) is challenging, as Research Objects aggregate multiple resources which may be prompt to individual assessment.

In this work we describe FAIROs, a framework for assessing the FAIRness of a research investigation, modeled as Research Object. Our contributions include i) an approach to integrate the FAIRness scores of all resources in a Research Object, ii) an implementation of our approach in an executable tool, and iii) a visualization of the scoring system for helping users understand how to improve the FAIRness of their resources.

FAIROs integrates existing efforts developed to assess the FAIRness of individual datasets, software projects and ontologies. We have tested our framework by calculating the FAIRness scores of over 160 Research Objects available in public repositories, comparing two different aggregation metrics. Based on our results, we discuss the advantages and disadvantages of different scoring methods for Research Object FAIRness. Our results show that the score is severely affected by i) the number of tests associated to each category and ii) the number of resources of each RO.

The rest of the paper is structured as follows. Section 2 describes existing efforts for assessing FAIR in different domains. Section 3 describes our approach, while Sect. 4 compares differences when using two scoring methods. Section 5 discusses our results, and Sect. 6 concludes the paper.

2 Related Work

There are two main areas of related work: community efforts for guiding users when adopting FAIR, and quality assessment in Research Objects.

2.1 Adopting the FAIR Principles

Checking whether a resource follows the FAIR principles has been a subject of discussion in the last years. For instance, in [23], the authors propose a community-driven framework to assess the FAIRness of digital objects. This framework is based on: i) a collection of maturity indicators, ii) principle compliance tests, and iii) a module to apply those tests to digital resources. The proposed indicators are a starting point to define which tests are needed for each type of resource [18].

Community groups like FAIRassist.org[2] have compiled lists of guidelines and tools for assessing the FAIRness of digital resources. These range from self-assessment tools like questionnaires and checklists to semi-automated validators [8]. Examples of automated validation tools include the F-UJI Automated FAIR Data Assessment Tool[3] [7], FAIR Evaluator[4] and FAIR Checker[5] for datasets or digital objects; HowFairIs[6] [21] for code repositories; and FOOPS [11] to assess ontologies. In our work, we build and incorporate some of these validators when calculating the FAIRness of all resources contained within a Research Object.

However, different assessment tools may have different interpretations for each principle. In [9] the authors compare different FAIRness evaluation tools (F-UJI, FAIR Evaluator and FAIR Checker), obtaining different scores and different level of detail when assessing resources. The study highlights the importance of transparency in the evaluation, making each metric and score explainable. Hence, we follow this principle in our work.

2.2 Quality Assessment Models for Research Objects

Research Object are semantically rich aggregations of research resources designed to facilitate the publication, sharing and reuse of such entities [1]. In order to evaluate Research Objects, [10] proposes ROHUB[7], a platform with metadata checklists to assess Research Object *completeness*. This indicator is calculated by checking the inclusion of metadata such as title, description, creator, publisher information, etc.; as well as the inclusion of certain resources like datasets, software or publications. However, this approach only takes into account the presence of general metadata, implementing only a subset of the FAIR principles. Our work builds on this approach, taking into account every resource in a Research Object and assessing their compliance against all FAIR principles.

Lastly, FAIR Digital Objects (FDO) have been recently proposed as a self-contained, typed, machine-actionable data package [6]. FDOs should be FAIR by definition but, to the best of our knowledge, there are no existing works measuring the degree of compliance with FAIR in FDOs.

---

[2] https://fairassist.org/.
[3] https://www.fairsfair.eu/f-uji-automated-fair-data-assessment-tool.
[4] https://fairsharing.github.io/FAIR-Evaluator-FrontEnd.
[5] https://github.com/IFB-ElixirFr/fair-checker.
[6] https://github.com/fair-software/howfairis/.
[7] https://www.rohub.org.

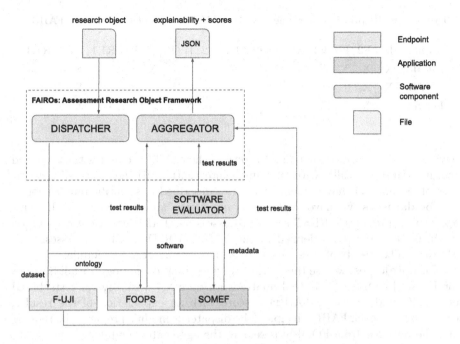

Fig. 1. FAIROs architecture

3   FAIROs: A Research Object FAIR Assessment Framework

Figure 1 shows an overview of the architecture of FAIROs. Our framework has two main components:

- **Dispatcher.** This component analyzes the Research Object metadata file and detects the different resources of the research object (datasets, software and ontologies). Once the resources are analyzed, the information is sent to the specific tool, as described in Sect. 3.1.
- **Aggregator.** This component collects the results from the tests executed and aggregates the information to calculate a FAIR score for the Research Object. Tests depend of resource's type and the FAIR principle, as described in Sect. 3.2.

FAIROs is open source and available on GitHub[8]. The source code of the version presented in this paper can be found in Zenodo [3].

3.1   Modules for Individual Resource FAIR Assessment

In order to measure the FAIRness of Research Objects, FAIROs integrates existing tools to assess individual datasets, software and ontologies. These tools

---

[8] https://github.com/oeg-upm/FAIR-Research-Object.

Table 1. FAIR principles coverage by the FAIR assessment tools used in FAIROs

Service	F1	F2	F3	F4	A1	A1.1	A1.2	A2	I1	I2	I3	R1	R1.1	R1.2	R1.3
F-UJI	X	X	X	X	X			X		X	X	X	X		X
SOMEF	X	X											X	X	
FOOPS	X	X	X	X	X	X		X	X	X		X	X	X	

have been selected for four main reasons: i) their ability to assess the analyzed resources automatically, without human intervention, ii) their accessibility, iii) ease of use and iv) they implement metrics described in scientific publications.

For **datasets**, we have deployed in our server an instance of F-UJI. This application provides a REST service to assess the FAIRness of datasets based on 16 of the 17 metrics defined in the FAIRsFAIR Data Objects Assessment Metrics.[9] The results of these tests are sent to the aggregator module.

For **ontologies**, we use the service provided by the Ontology Pitfall Scanner for FAIR (FOOPS!). This tool analyzes an ontology with several tests based on [12,19] and returns a FAIRness score with an explanation of the results, categorized by each FAIR principle. The dispatcher module prepares the request and the response from FOOPS! is sent to the aggregator module.

Regarding **software** assessment, we have created a prototype validator based on the principles identified in [16].

In order to extract metadata associated with a given code repository, we use the Software Metadata Extraction Framework (SOMEF) [17], which analyzes repository documentation to retrieve the license, description, installation instructions, requirements, versions, citation text or provenance information (authors, creation date). These metadata fields are particularly relevant for reusability and are checked by our tests.

As shown in Fig. 1, an additional component has been developed to execute SOMEF, run a set of tests to validate the extracted metadata and send the results to the aggregator component. Table 1 summarizes the FAIR principles [22] covered by the different components of our framework.

The last component of the aggregator is in charge of evaluating the metadata of **Research Objects** themselves, by using the RO-Crate specification [20] and the ro-crate-py library [5]. We run the following tests:

- F1: We verify if the RO has a persistent identifier ['w3id.org', 'doi.org', 'purl.org', 'www.w3.org'].
- F2: We verify if the following minimum metadata ['author', 'license', 'description'] are present in the RO-crate.
- F3: We verify that the hasPart elements exists and are described in the RO, as ROs aggregate resources.

---

[9] https://www.fairsfair.eu/fairsfair-data-object-assessment-metrics-request-comments.

- R1.1: We verify if there is at least one author, a datePublished and a citation in the root element.
- R1.2: We verify that all elements of the RO have the following fields: ['author', 'datePublished', 'citation']

3.2 Scoring Aggregations of Resources in Research Objects

A RO is composed by resources, including the metadata of the RO itself. Each resource is evaluated against the FAIR principles, and each principle is evaluated by a set of tests (which depend on the type of the resource and the FAIR assessment tool used). The final FAIRness score associated with a Research Object may vary depending on the percentage of tests passed by each resource and on the design decisions used to aggregate the FAIR scores.

To illustrate this difference, we have defined two aggregation metrics in our framework to calculate the final FAIRness score of a Research Object. Note that the metrics are based on the tests defined for each principle and resource. Metrics do not change the tests executed, only how test results are dealt with in the aggregation formula. Our proposed metrics are:

- **Global metric:** calculated by formula (1). It represents the percentage of total passed tests. It doesn't take into account the principle to which a test belongs.
- **FAIR average metric:** calculated by formula (2). It represents the average of the passed tests ratios for each principle plus the ratio of passed tests used to evaluate the Research Object itself.

Both metrics are agnostic to the kind of resource analyzed. The score they produce ranges from [0–100].

$$total\_score_{global} = \frac{\#tests\_passed}{\#tests} \qquad (1)$$

$$total\_score_{FAIR\_average} = \frac{\sum_{i \in G} \frac{\#test\_passed_i}{\#tests_i}}{\#G}, \qquad (2)$$

where G represents the group of tests from the categories Findable (F), Accesible (A), Interoperable (I), Reusable (R) and Research Objects (RO).

3.3 Result Format and Visualization

FAIROs generates two outputs:

- A JSON file with the executed tests and the final/intermediate scores generated by a specific metric. The final score is calculated based on the selected metric. Each resource is analyzed based on the tests defined for each FAIR principle. Also, the different tests executed for each principle are described.
- A visual diagram explaining the scores and each test. The diagram is generated in the Graphviz format.[10] An example can be seen in Fig. 2. In this diagram, the first-level boxes represent the different digital objects that make up the research object. We can find information such as identifier, type, tool used and the score. In a second level box, the partial scores for each FAIR principle (Findable, Accesible, Interoperable, Reusable) can be found. Finally, we can find the final aggregation score calculated according with the metrics selected.

The output JSON file format is composed by a list of components (resources of the RO), which describes the executed tests and includes an explanation of the obtained scores. Listing 1.1 shows an example, showing some of the tests run for the Findable principle.

```
1  {"principle_id": "F3",
2      "category_id": "Findable",
3      "title": "Metadata clearly and explicitly include the identifier of
            ↪ the data they describe",
4      "description": "This check verifies that the hasPart elements
            ↪ exists and are describe in the ro",
5      "total_passed_tests": 1,
6      "total_tests_run": 1,
7      "status": "ok",
8      "explanation": "All element identifiers exists"
9  }
```

Listing 1.1. Test execution with explanation

For each component, we include a summary of the tests categorized by principle. The final score calculated by the formula defined by the selected metric is included under the key *overall_score*, as shown in Listing 1.2.

---

[10] https://graphviz.org/doc/info/lang.html.

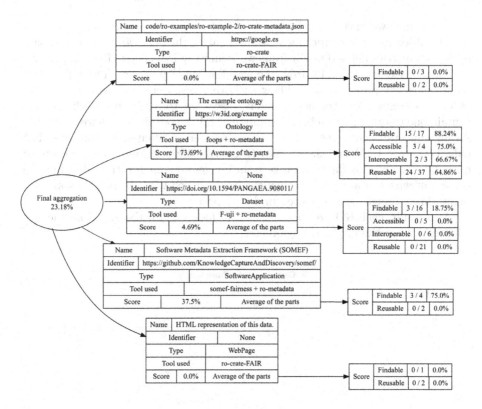

Fig. 2. Scores visualization diagram

```
1   "overall_score": {
2       "description": "The␣score␣is␣calculated␣by␣adding␣all␣the␣scores␣
        ↪ of␣the␣different␣components␣together.␣All␣passed␣tests␣
        ↪ and␣all␣total␣tests␣are␣added␣together␣and␣then␣the␣
        ↪ percentage␣is␣calculated",
3       "score": 37.5,
4       "total_sum": {
5           "total_passed_tests": 3,
6           "total_run_tests": 8
7       }
8   }
```

Listing 1.2. Total score obtained for a sample Research Object

The output file format is the same for both of our proposed metrics.

4   Comparing FAIR Research Object Assessment Metrics

We have run a small experiment comparing the effect of our proposed metrics when assessing the FAIRness of more than 160 worflow-centric Research Objects (i.e., ROs containing at least a scientific workflow).

In all runs, we have used the release v0.0.1 of our framework [3].

The objective of our experiment was to analyze the behaviour and the impact of the two metrics defined in our framework on workflow-centric ROs. Therefore, we downloaded 168 ROs [13] from the workflowhub[11] platform. These Research Objects are composed by a workflow and other resources such as datasets and other files (images of sketches in many cases). In total, 74 Research Objects contain one resource, 75 contain 2 resources, and 16 contain 3 or more resources. As an important note, 92% of the resources were evaluated as Datasets, but only 17% were CSV and JSON files (i.e., typically considered data inputs or outputs). The rest of the files range from images to configuration files, but are consistent with our analysis, as they can be described with metadata. Note that many times, images are deposited in data repositories.

As a result, each RO produces two JSON files, one for the global metric and another one for the FAIR_average metric.

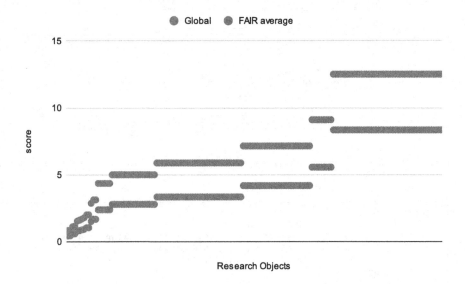

Fig. 3. Distribution of FAIR RO scores in over 160 Research Objects

The distribution of scores is depicted in Fig. 3. The x-axis, shows the different Research Objects ordered by score. Both scores are different, but consistent, i.e., when the score of a metric is increased, the scores of the other metric increase too. We also detect regular patterns in the results, influenced by the number of resources and the publication of the Research Objects in the same platform.

Figure 4 shows a histogram with the distribution and frequency of the scores obtained by each metric on the corpus of analyzed ROs. In summary:

---

[11] https://www.workflowhub.eu.

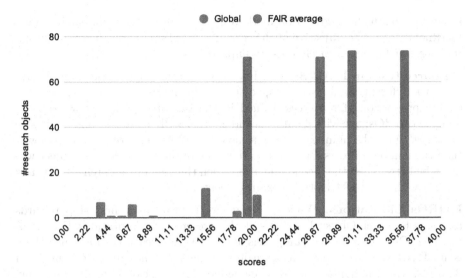

Fig. 4. Distribution of the number of ROs with a given score.

- There are four clusters of scores among the analyzed Research Objects, due to their common number of resources.
- When the value of the score is low, data from the global metric are more dispersed than the FAIR average metric. That is, the first metric generates scores with more variance. In general, the standard deviation of the global metric (6.31) is higher than the standard deviation of the FAIR average metric (5.59).

All the files used and produced in our experiment are available online [14].

5   Discussion

Based on our initial results, we discuss several points we consider key for addressing the compliance of Research Objects against the FAIR principles:

Research Object Resource Metadata. As shown in Fig. 3, many of the FAIRness scores obtained for the Research Objects analyzed are not high (scores are below 40 out of 100 for the best metric). This is due, in part, to the lack of metadata for the resources included in a Research Object. However, additional work is needed to identify whether this behavior is commonplace in ROs belonging to other common platforms or not.

Research Object FAIRness as a Proxy of RO Quality? Figure 3 shows how by using different aggregation metrics, the FAIRness score of a RO can change significantly (even if scores are consistent with each other). This has two main implications: 1) scores may be used as a guideline to improve the quality of a Research Object, but should not act as a replacement for its quality; and 2) it is key to explain the aggregation method used to produce any Research Object FAIRness score. The objective of the scoring system should not be to produce a ranking, but become a mechanism to improve the FAIRness of ROs.

Resource tests in FAIR Scores. Each type of resource (datasets, ontologies, etc.) has different number of tests, so the weight in the final score will depend on the proportion of resources defined in the Research Object. For example, imagine two ROs; one with 4 datasets and another with 6 datasets and 5 software packages. Since the number of tests to assess the FAIRness of software is lower than the number of tests for datasets, the score of the first Research Object will likely be better than the second one, even when the second Research Object may comply with more FAIR principles, in percentage.

FAIROs Limitations. While our framework provides a first step towards assessing Research Object FAIRness, it also present some limitations. For example, FAIROs makes some assumptions about concrete resources for which there is no FAIR validator (e.g., instance images and sketches may be considered datasets, which may miss metadata embedded in the files). This approach may introduce bias, but the tests defined for each resource category/principle are quite similar. For example, the process of testing the presence of a persistent identifier is the same, independently the type of the resource. Our study focused on workflow-centric ROs present in one platform, so it does not represent a total overview of the ROs domain. Nevertheless, these results can be used as a starting point and extended when applied to other categories of ROs.

6   Conclusions and Future Work

In this work we have presented FAIROs, a framework for assessing the compliance of Research Objects against the FAIR principles. FAIROs integrates existing tools for assessing the FAIRness of datasets, software and ontologies; and provides two different aggregation metrics for calculating Research Object FAIRness scores.

Our results show a potential imbalance in the FAIRness score obtained depending on the number of tests run by each principle and resource. For example, if a dataset assessment runs more tests than software, or if more tests are run for the findable principle than for interoperability. Transforming our platform in a plug-in architecture where new assessment tools can be easily incorporated would make it easier to reduce this imbalance.

As for future work, we plan to increment the number of tests run in the Research Object to get a more detailed impression of the Research Object FAIRness. These tests will be accompanied with a collection of recommendations to improve the FAIRness of the target resource. In addition, we plan include partial results from each FAIR principle (Findable, Accesible, Interoperable and Reusable) into our final reports.

Also, we aim to open the aggregation metrics to users. This way, users may define their own metrics based on their preferences. For example, assigning more weight to some resources/principles than others, according to their use cases.

From the architecture point of view, we are in the process of transforming our framework into a service, providing support to the community. We are integrating FAIROs in the RELIANCE Research Object platform,[12] in order to test our work against hundreds of Research Objects in the Geosciences domain.

Acknowledgements. This work has been funded by the European Commission within the H2020 Programme in the context of the project RELIANCE under grant agreement no. 101017501 and by the Madrid Government (Comunidad de Madrid-Spain) under the Multiannual Agreement with Universidad Politécnica de Madrid (UPM) in the line Support for R&D projects for Beatriz Galindo researchers, in the context of the V PRICIT (Regional Programme of Research and Technological Innovation), and through the call Research Grants for Young Investigators from UPM.

References

1. Bechhofer, S., De Roure, D., Gamble, M., Goble, C., Buchan, I.: Research objects: towards exchange and reuse of digital knowledge. Nat. Precedings **1** (2010). https://doi.org/10.1038/npre.2010.4626.1
2. Belhajjame, K., et al.: Using a suite of ontologies for preserving workflow-centric research objects. J. Web Semant. **32**, 16–42 (2015). https://doi.org/10.1016/j.websem.2015.01.003
3. Benitez, A., González, E., Garijo, D.: FAIROs: a framework to assess FAIR principles in research objects (2022). https://doi.org/10.5281/zenodo.6599423
4. Collins, S., et al.: Turning fair into reality: final report and action plan from the European commission expert group on fair data (2018)
5. De Geest, P., et al.: RO-crate-py (2022). https://doi.org/10.5281/zenodo.3956493
6. De Smedt, K., Koureas, D., Wittenburg, P.: Fair digital objects for science: from data pieces to actionable knowledge units. Publications **8**(2) (2020). https://doi.org/10.3390/publications8020021
7. Devaraju, A., Huber, R.: F-UJI - an automated fair data assessment tool (2020). https://doi.org/10.5281/zenodo.4063720
8. Devaraju, A., et al.: From conceptualization to implementation: fair assessment of research data objects. Data Sci. J. **20**(1), 1–14 (2021)
9. Dumontier, M.: A comprehensive comparison of automated fairness evaluation tools (2022). http://ceur-ws.org/Vol-3127/paper-6.pdf
10. Garcia-Silva, A., et al.: Enabling fair research in earth science through research objects. Futur. Gener. Comput. Syst. **98**, 550–564 (2019). https://doi.org/10.1016/j.future.2019.03.046
11. Garijo, D., Corcho, O., Poveda-Villalón, M.: FOOPS!: An ontology pitfall scanner for the fair principles. International Semantic Web Conference (ISWC) 2021: Posters, Demos, and Industry Tracks 2980 (2021). http://ceur-ws.org/Vol-2980/paper321.pdf
12. Garijo, D., Poveda-Villalón, M.: Best practices for implementing fair vocabularies and ontologies on the web. In: Giuseppe Cota, M.D., Pozzato, G.L. (eds.) Applications and Practices in Ontology Design, Extraction, and Reasoning. IOS Press, Netherlands (2020). https://doi.org/10.3233/SSW200034

---

[12] https://reliance.rohub.org/.

13. Gonzalez, E., Benitez, A., Garijo, D.: TPDL 2022 - experiment - research objects data (2022). https://doi.org/10.5281/zenodo.6595409
14. Gonzalez, E., Benitez, A., Garijo, D.: TPDL 2022 - experiment - results (2022). https://doi.org/10.5281/zenodo.6595466
15. Katz, D.S., Gruenpeter, M., Honeyman, T.: Taking a fresh look at fair for research software. Patterns **2**(3), 100222 (2021). https://doi.org/10.1016/j.patter.2021.100222
16. Lamprecht, A.L., et al.: Towards fair principles for research software. Data Sci. **3**(1), 37–59 (2020)
17. Mao, A., Garijo, D., Fakhraei, S.: SoMEF: a framework for capturing scientific software metadata from its documentation. In: 2019 IEEE International Conference on Big Data (Big Data), pp. 3032–3037 (2019). https://doi.org/10.1109/BigData47090.2019.9006447, http://dgarijo.com/papers/SoMEF.pdf
18. de Miranda Azevedo, R., Dumontier, M.: Considerations for the conduction and interpretation of fairness evaluations. Data Intell. **2**(1–2), 285–292 (2020)
19. Poveda-Villalón, M., Espinoza-Arias, P., Garijo, D., Corcho, O.: Coming to terms with FAIR ontologies: a position paper. In: Keet, C.M., Dumontier, M. (eds.) EKAW 2020. LNCS (LNAI), vol. 12387, pp. 255–270. Springer, Cham (2020). https://doi.org/10.1007/978-3-030-61244-3_18
20. Soiland-Reyes, S., et al.: Packaging research artefacts with RO-crate. Data Sci. 1–42 (2022). https://doi.org/10.3233/DS-210053
21. Spaaks, J.H., Kuzak, M., et al.: howfairis (2021). https://doi.org/10.5281/zenodo.4591110
22. Wilkinson, M.D., et al.: The fair guiding principles for scientific data management and stewardship. Sci. Data **3**(1), 1–9 (2016)
23. Wilkinson, M.D., et al.: Evaluating fair maturity through a scalable, automated, community-governed framework. Sci. Data **6**(1), 1–12 (2019)

Searching Wartime Photograph Archive
for Serious Leisure Purposes

Sanna Kumpulainen[✉][iD] and Hille Ruotsalainen[iD]

Tampere University, 33014 Tampere, Finland
{sanna.kumpulainen,hille.ruotsalainen}@tuni.fi

Abstract. A survey of image information search goals, search tactics and what was looked at in the images was circulated among serious-leisure war historians. Also, we used the user engagement scale (UES), and a user success score were measured. Search goals included general and more specific goals. It is shown that despite the lack of full coverage of descriptions and metadata, users preferred mostly keyword searching. Surprisingly, general targets were popularly looked at the images, such as milieu or scenery. Participants gave high UES and varying success scores, but they were, in general, satisfied with their interactions. Serious leisure users are very engaged with their activities, which makes them tolerant to the possible system and indexing shortages. We discuss the findings and suggest research implications based on them.

Keywords: Image searching · Photograph archive · User studies

1 Introduction

Historical photograph archives have been created to preserve the past. Digitalization has increased possibilities to access the contents. However, retrieving an image from a digital image archive may be difficult since it is relying on existing textual descriptions and metadata which may be impartial, or their usage may require special skills due to the historical context of the descriptions. We may learn from historical images something that applies also to the present. In newspaper context, the suitability of using image captions for searching have been questioned. Captions are of varying quality, often short and present only one interpretation of the image subject (e.g. [1]). Further, interpretations of images are polysemic and the same image may have multiple interpretations at the same time and the interpretations vary between viewers, which makes indexing them challenging [16].

Context of activity affect the information needs that trigger search behaviours [4]. Further, serious leisure activities are based on information acquisition and shaped as information-rich social worlds [8]. Different browsing and interaction mechanisms of image search make the search process rather different from general Web search engines [25]. Specifically, information needs related to historical images are expected to be different from a typical web image search and this may affect the interactions. We present a survey study about the users of a wartime photographic archive, who present

© Springer Nature Switzerland AG 2022
G. Silvello et al. (Eds.): TPDL 2022, LNCS 13541, pp. 81–92, 2022.
https://doi.org/10.1007/978-3-031-16802-4_7

a specific user group with possibly specific information needs. Further, the contents of the photographic archive are accessed via textual representations of the contents and metadata, but these may be impartial and inconsistent.

To find out how the collection descriptions and search functionalities match with the users' search practices, we examined searching at different stages or activities [12]: (i) what were the information needs behind searching the images (search goals), (ii) how these needs are approached (search tactics) and (iii) what was looked at in the retrieved images when selecting suitable items for further use (target of looking). We surveyed the user engagement and search success associated with them. The study was conducted in the context of a historical digitized image collection, the Finnish Wartime Photograph Archive (FWPA). The collection is publicly available via Internet (http://sa-kuva.fi/) and it provides search interface in three languages, Finnish, Swedish and English.

Development of content-based image retrieval has been popular lately, but user needs and search practices are not widely examined. Further, there were not any research about serious leisure use of images. Therefore, we analysed the users' search goals, search tactics and what they look in the images. This knowledge may be used in designing better content-based methods and in informing algorithm development. Further, given that the descriptions are often the only way how to access the photographs, also the archival profession would benefit from user studies that explore interactions with visual materials.

1.1 Image Searching in the History Domain

Although much research has been done on contents of various collections, there has been little research into how people search and use historical images. Chassanoff [5] studied historians' image selection in digital information environments in their research activities. In interview research of fifteen self-identified historians, the difficulty in describing visual materials is discussed. In the research, sixteen broad themes about experiences using digitized archival photographs were found. In locating potential material, broad visual browsing was used. Assessing the relevance of the images was a cycle of iterative events and selection included criteria such as "anything interesting and unusual". Images were also used to corroborate earlier findings and as verification [5].

In another research about querying American history images, subject contents of queries into a photo archive were analysed [6]. In the research wide range of aspects were studied, including search needs and subject contents of need statements. The search needs were categorized into four different types: specific, general/nameable, general/abstract, and subjective. Subject contents were also typified. The types included: names (person/animals/thing/; names of events/action; place names); temporal (linear/cyclical) kind of a person/thing/event/action/condition/place; emotions etc [6].

Outside the history domain in a related field of archaeology, the use of images and visual materials in work context are discussed in [9]. In examining the information resources of archaeologists with varying work roles (academic teaching, field archaeology, antiquarian, cultural heritage administration, public dissemination, academic research and infrastructural development), it was found that the archaeologists sought texts and various forms of imagery. The most extensive use of visual information, consisting of diagrams, videos, photographs and objects themselves, was involved in teaching [9].

1.2 Search Goals and Image Searching

Search behaviours vary with search goals, which vary with search tasks that are driven by task-specific needs [4]. Due to the visual nature of images, aspects surrounding use are markedly different than those of purely textual materials. The subject of a representational picture is simultaneously generic and specific, it may be of objects, but it may also be about intangibles [23]. The images may be reached out for different purposes and for various informational needs.

Image searching may include different types of search goals, i.e., the informational aspects that are expected to be obtained from the images, such as image content, identification/attribution/provenance checking, accessibility of image [1]. Image needs have been studied in the context of web search engine logs [e.g., [11, 25] and these include needs such as Explore/Learn, Entertain, and Locate/Acquire [25]. However, image needs on the general web search are substantially different from domain-specific collections and image use varies by profession [2, 3]. In the context of history research, the searchers of the historical contents have been interested in various classes of named entities, such as organizations and locations [8] and they search for combinations of locations, period of times and person names. However, this study did not study image needs *per se*, but focused on textual materials.

Image need context has shown impact the attributes used in image seeking [7]. However, the image needs in [7] were on high conceptual level and are close to "purpose of use", or underlying task than actual "information need" (c.f. [4]). The image needs included illustration, generation of ideas, aesthetic value, and learning, among others. Image use in work tasks of historians and journalists has been studied by McCay-Peet and Toms [18]. Their findings suggest that the stage of the work task process has a significant impact on how the image is used.

Research topics about searching include query formulation and modification, search strategies (e.g., keyword searching and browsing), evaluation of search results, query language and contextual factors [3, 17]. Markkula and Sormunen [16] found that journalists converted general information needs into tangible queries, e.g., searching with proper names. They considered that key word selection was difficult in general topics. Further, browsing was an essential strategy used by journalists and was found as an effortless activity. The journalists searched for named entities and concrete objects, events, but also conducted thematic searches [16].

Search success in querying was measured by downloading or browsing the thumbnails in a web search log analysis study [13]. They found also, in web searching thematic and descriptive queries are used more frequently than in expert searching [13].

Search tactics are behaviours aiming at accessing the image contents. The targets people look at may be different from the searching. The image may include some informational contents that are not searchable by the system. One approach to capture images' information contents is Shatford's [23] faceted classification of image attributes. According to Shatford, an image can be viewed within four facets, namely, Objects (Who),

Activities and Events (What), Place (Where) and Time and Space (When). Images may be interpreted to represent both concrete and objective entities called "ofness" (e.g., objects, places, actions) and abstract and subjective entities called "aboutness" (e.g., feelings, concepts manifested or symbolised by objects). Images are rich in elements and that fundamentally there are many possible attributes and levels of meanings to index, and capturing all possible user goals is difficult.

1.3 User Engagement

User engagement has been a subject of growing interest in human-computer interaction [20]. According to O'Brien [19], user engagement (UE) is a quality of user experience. It is about the depth of the user's investment when interacting with a digital system and it is more than just user satisfaction. The User Engagement Scale (UES), which has been used for various purposes in research, consisted of 31-items and was constructed to measure six dimensions of engagement: focused attention, perceived usability, aesthetic appeal, endurability, novelty and felt involvement. Further development of the scale appeared in a form of a four-factor scale referred to as the UES Short Form (SF) [20]. The factors of the SF scale are focused attention (FA), perceived usability (PU), aesthetic appeal (AE) and a reward factor (RW). UES SF has been found applicable to several domains, including digital cultural heritage [24] and search behaviour [21]. In the present study we utilize the UES to measure engagement with a historical photograph collection.

2 Research Setting

This research is descriptive in nature. Descriptive research is an appropriate choice when the research aim is to identify characteristics, frequencies, trends, and categories. It is useful when not much is known yet about the topic or problem [22]. We conducted questionnaire research, which was aimed at the users of the historical photographic archive. Questionnaires are well suited for collecting opinions in descriptive research settings [15], and selecting it we were able to handle the restrictions caused by the COVID-19 situation that took place during the research. Further, UES measure was selected due its popularity in user engagement studies to ensure robustness and comparability of findings across different digital applications. The questionnaire results would later serve as basis for interviews to gather more detailed data. We first describe the photograph archive, then data collection procedure and the questionnaire that was used.

2.1 The Photograph Archive

This research surveyed the user practices and experiences with FWPA. The collection was published on the Internet in 2013 and is open to public (http://sa-kuva.fi/). The photograph archive studied is a unique digital collection of Finnish wartime photographs containing around 160,000 pictures from the Second World War during 1939–1945.

The images portray life on the home front, events and operations at the front, the war industry, leisure time at the front (see Fig. 1), damages in bombings and the evacuation of Finnish Carelia. The pictures were mainly taken by wartime Information Company

Fig. 1. "The Punt 'swims' first time on lake Kananainen", 25.7.1941. Photographer Vilho Uomala.
SA-kuva.

photographers. Most of the photographs are in black and white, and a small number in
colour or video material.

Typically, the images appear with some metadata attached (e.g., the location, date,
photographer, some information on what's in the picture) and these metadata are visible
to the users. However, part of the collection lacks all descriptive texts and metadata.
The photographers were instructed to write annotations describing the name of the
photographer, the subject or event in the picture, and the location. Nevertheless, the
annotations were not always this precise during the chaotic times.

Further, in the existing metadata there are some obscurities of describing the locations
and dates, spelling mistakes, and possibly wrong information. In some cases, this means
that the search, based on temporal period, single date, or any textual content, may not be
reliable. The caption texts and metadata are typically in Finnish, some in Swedish. The
language and terms of the caption texts present wartime Finnish language containing
military abbreviations. The caption texts have not been edited nor proofread at any time.

The interface includes a word search and an advanced search with Boolean operators. The search indices are based on the textual descriptions and metadata. Users can
choose a pull-down menu to browse images by predefined stages of the war (Winter
War, Continuation War, Lapland War). Temporal searches can be done based on date
information. the searchers can select to search only videos, or pictures in color. It is also
possible to combine these search elements in the search.

The result page provides a set of browsable 15 thumbnail pictures. The user can click
on a thumbnail to open a larger image and to read its captions and metadata in case there
are some. The larger image can be downloaded. Help is provided in the search page and
all the functionalities are described in it.

2.2   The Questionnaire and Data Collection

The data were collected between June and August in 2021 through an anonymous on-line questionnaire. The participants were recruited by inviting members of several Facebook groups. Most of the respondents were members of an active group concentrating on the photographs in FWPA. The link to the questionnaire was shared with three other Facebook groups concerning genealogy, old photographs, and wartime experiences. After piloting the survey, the questionnaire was revised accordingly.

The questionnaire started with general information about the research setting. The respondents were informed that filling in the form would take approximately 10 min and that responses were collected anonymously. The questionnaire was built on five factors: 1) Background information and previous experience, 2) Search tactics, 3) Search goals, 4) Target of looking, and 5) User engagement and success. We also provided an opportunity to report any perceived difficulties and desired improvements. Factor 1) included asking the respondents' year of birth, municipality of residence, profession, education, how often they usually use search services, whether they have used other historical web image archives, and if so, which, how often they use FWPA and with which device, and for which purposes (multiple selection options: research, other work activities, studying, genealogy, hobby, other). Factors 2–4) were about what they were primarily aiming for when searching the FWPA (information or pictures on wartime or of their own relatives, pictures by a certain photographer, a certain organization, certain military rank or unit, on events, on leisure time, on equipment, other), what they were looking at in the pictures (milieu or scenery, details, atmosphere, expressions, composition), and how they did the search (keyword search, browsing, filtering with different options, combination).

Questions about search tactics were based on the functionalities of the FWPA. These included querying and browsing options, temporal search, and specific filtering option for stages of the war. The service also provided filtering for colour photographs and videos, and Boolean operators for combining search keys and the available search functions. Options provided for search goals were applied from [14]. Target of gaze were based on interviews with subject experts and with the research group.

Factor 5) was about user experience and engagement. We utilized the UES short form (UES-SF) to measure the user engagement [20] and translated the UES-SF into Finnish. In this section of the questionnaire the respondents agreed or disagreed with 15 sentences of UES-SF, such as "I lost myself in this experience.", "I was absorbed in this experience.", "I found this application confusing to use", "This application appealed to my senses.", "Using this application was taxing.", and "I consider my experience a success." We used a Likert scale (strongly agree, agree, neither agree nor disagree, disagree, strongly disagree) to measure engagement. Some of the questions were negative and some positive. Therefore the scores were reversed if needed so that the higher scores indicated higher value on agreement. The scores ranged from 1–5. The perceived difficulties and desired improvements were collected with open questions.

3   Results

3.1   Respondents

The total number of respondents in the survey was 114. After removing partial answers, we selected for further analysis 53 full answers in which the reported purpose of use was related to serious leisure activities. These included genealogy research, interest in war history (e.g., as authors in books for general audience/public) and for other leisure related purposes, such as being active in sharing historical information in social media (e.g., Facebook interest groups). Number of partial answers were 55 which is typical for surveys shared in social media. People tend to click links but not continue filling in. Overall, all the respondents had interest particularly for historical issues and none of the participants reported any other use.

The participants' age ranged from 25 to 88 years. The mean age was 60.2 years, median age was 61 years. The background of the respondents was divided between retired and those still being in the work life: 41.2% were retired, rest were working either as entrepreneurs or as employees. Seven reported being managers or executives.

They mostly accessed the collection by using personal computers (67.9%), the rest used mobile devices or both mobile and personal computers. 64,2% used daily some search engines and 28.3% weekly. 26.4 did not use any other historic photographic collection, but most of them reported using several other image collections.

The respondents were very frequent users of the FWPA; 54.7% used it weekly or more often, only 3.8% reported using it infrequently. All the respondents used the FWPA in Finnish.

3.2   Search Goals

We examined what were the search goals of the respondents when they last time interacted with the collection (Table 1). Respondents were able to select and report several options. The most popular search goal was to find images about wartime (60.4%). These were prompted by, e.g., in overall interest in wartime, or in general understanding about the times. Some classes of named entities were searched. These included events, military units, people, and organizations. Wartime equipment was searched by 41.5%.

Searching with leisure time goals got the highest UES score, 4.15 and events second highest, 4.13. These are surprising since these types of photos are not necessarily easy to search with the current description in the photographs. The highest success score was in searching for photographers. This information, however, is missing in a relatively large portion of the collection. Searching for people or military unit search goals were associated with poor success rate. Searchers may assume that these are searchable, e.g., querying by names, but this information may be missing from the descriptions.

3.3   Search Tactics

There were several search functionalities that allowed accessing the contents. Search tactics and associated UES and success scores are shown in Table 2. The most popular tactic was to use keyword search, which matched the query with the textual descriptions

Table 1. Search goals and user engagement (n = 53).

Search goals	Percentage	UES	Success
War time	60.4	3.92	3.48
Events	49.1	4.13	3.79
Military unit or organization	49.1	4.03	3.46
Objects or equipment	41.5	4.03	3.73
People	35.8	4.09	3.39
Activities	32.1	3.95	3.62
Leisure time	15.1	4.15	3.56
Photographers	11.3	4.05	4.33
Other	5.7	3.64	4.00

(if available), and the metadata fields. Stages of war was made searchable as a drop-down menu. It enables browsing through photographs from the Winter War, Continuation War and Lapland War in their entirety as separate categories. Searchers can also limit their search to a particular period of their choice. Of these types of temporal search functionalities, the possibility to select the stages war more popular (41.5% and 26.6%). Slightly over a third reported using browsing and only 24.5% used combinations the provided functionalities. Videos or colour images were searched only by 11.5%. This in line with the content types of the collection, since most of the material is black and white.

Used search tactics were all associated with high UES scores, ranging from 3.87 to 4.09. The highest UES score was associated with stage of war. This is an inbuild functionality that supported facet searching and therefore it worked very well. Surprisingly, stage of war was not associated with high success score. Highest success scores were associated with combining several search tactics. Browsing was associated with low success score, indicating that the layout of images as thumbnails or their ordering in the result display did not support searching. The lowest success score was related with videos or colour photographs. This can be explained by the small number of them in the collection.

3.4 Looking at the Photographs

We asked the participant to report what did they look at in the photographs to find out what was used as a cue to informational contents. The distributions are reported in Table 3. Respondents were able to select several options and provide their own targets that were not included in the predefined list. The most popular target of looking was Milieu or scenery in the photos. This was reported by 73.6% of the respondents. Over a half of them looked at details. Atmosphere was looked at by 41.4%. This target is a very abstract concept, subjectively inferred and not necessarily described in detail in the descriptions that were available. Accordingly, the success rate associated with the atmosphere is the lowest (3.25) The most successful in the listed were details (3.78)

Table 2. Search tactics (n = 53).

Search tactic	Percentage	UES	Success
Keyword search	69.8	4.04	3.68
Stage of war	41.5	4.09	3.57
Browsing	34.0	3.87	3.28
Temporal search	26.4	3.99	3.96
Combination	24.5	3.91	4.08
Videos or colour	11.5	4.00	3.17

and other (9.91). The latter included, e.g., buildings, distance between the objects and postures of people. Facial expression was looked by 30.2 and compositions by 11.3%.

The UES Scores indicated strong engagement ranging from 3.94 to 4.08. They seemed to be engaged with all the targets they were looking at. However, success rates were lower ranging from 3.25 to 3.91. This may indicate that if they succeeded accessing the contents they were expecting to see in the photos, they were engaged with them. At the same time, finding the desired contents may have been difficult.

Table 3. Target of looking (n = 53).

Looking at	Percentage	UES	Success
Milieu or scenery	73.6	4.07	3.64
Details	51.9	3.94	3.78
Atmosphere	41.5	4.15	3.25
Expressions	30.2	4.08	3.44
Composition	11.3	3.98	3.50
Other	11.3	3.96	3.91

4 Discussion

This research analysed a survey from users of a war time image collection. Users' image searching tactics and experiences has not been widely studied even though images are increasingly important in sharing and searching information. This research studied historic photograph collection users' search goals, used search tactics and the desired image contents.

Firstly, users were mainly interested in general search goals (wartime and leisure time), but the most used tactic was keyword searching. This indicates that the general topics are searched with tangible queries, which is in line with the findings of [16]. Secondly, searching with predefined stages was also a popular search tactic. More faceted search functionalities, that present search goals that are meaningful to the users, could be built-in to better support the users' goals. Thirdly, the users were interested in general topics presented in the photographs, such as milieu or scenery and atmosphere. These are difficult to predefine since they are open to different interpretations derived from the users' context and activity [4]. However, their search goals included also informational nuggets about people, events, organizations etc., which are typical classes for named entities. Identifying these from the image contents would make them more easily searchable. Named entity recognition has been tried for the textual descriptions included in the collection [10]. This, however, does not solve the problem that a large proportion of the collection has no description texts at all. Therefore, image content-based recognition methods would be more suitable in solving the findability problem to cover all the photographic contents.

The popularity of keyword searching also suggest that searchers prefer searching to browsing. This was also supported by the UES and success scores. However, typically, image collections are browsed to get large overviews [4]. The large proportion of keyword searching may be due the fact that the users in our survey were serious leisure users, meaning they were very frequent users, and they already knew what to expect from the collection. It would be interesting also to include more first-timers or more casual users to compare their search tactics to the expert users. Further, this is only one information source available, and several information sources are used in conjunction to fulfil needs. However, FWPA is a unique historical collection that has been preserved from past and digitized for future uses. All participants were members of an active Facebook group that focused solely on the collection and its photos. They follow actively the group and its discussions and share the information to others they have acquired by searching and investigating the collection [c.f., 10]. This emphasizes the meaning of this collection to its users.

There were some limitations. The method used was a survey with only a small sample invited from a social media enthusiast group. Also, the UES has been developed and tested with Western adult populations in studies that evaluate digital technologies [20] which was expected to fit our purposes. However, some of our participants reported being uncomfortable with some of the "overly emotional" questions in the scale. The reception of the UES scale by using user groups of varying cultural background or varying domains of image collections would be useful.

Few efforts have been made towards understanding the intents of image searchers. In image search, the information items are images instead of texts or textual documents. Nevertheless, the contents are accessed via textual representations of the contents, and metadata. The searchability of the photographs according to the users' needs could be improved by using automatic means. In the next steps of our research project, we will aim at testing recognizing objects and people from the photographs.

5   Conclusion

We studied the users' search goals, search tactics and what they were looking at in historical photographs. The current state of the examined digital photograph library shows that the image contents are not fully searchable. Although the participants were quite engaged with the photograph archive, supporting searching by exploring the contents in more detail would yield to improved search experiences. Content-based image search supported with modern techniques should be incorporated into photograph archives as the users prefer keyword searching in reaching their search goals. Also, browsing could be supported by faceted search beyond the period-of-time approach presented here. Researching how and why people use images will help developing photograph archives that properly support their larger activities that require visual information.

References

1. Armitage, L.H., Enser, P.G.B.: Analysis of user need in image archives. J. Inf. Sci. **23**(4), 287–299 (1997). https://doi.org/10.1177/016555159702300403
2. Beaudoin, J.: An investigation of image users across disciplines: a model of image needs, retrieval and use. Proc. Am. Soc. Inf. Sci. Technol. **45**(1), 1–5 (2008). https://doi.org/10.1002/MEET.2008.14504503118
3. Beaudoin, J.E.: A framework of image use among archaeologists, architects, art historians and artists. J. Doc. **70**(1), 119–147 (2014). https://doi.org/10.1108/JD-12-2012-0157/FULL/XML
4. Byström, K., Kumpulainen, S.: Vertical and horizontal relationships amongst task-based information needs. Inf. Process. Manag. **57**, 2 (2020). https://doi.org/10.1016/j.ipm.2019.102065
5. Chassanoff, A.M.: Historians' experiences using digitized archival photographs as evidence, Am. Arch. **81**(1), 135–164 (2018). https://doi.org/10.17723/0360-9081-81.1.135
6. Choi, Y., Rasmussen, E.M.: Searching for images: the analysis of users' queries for image retrieval in American history. J. Am. Soc. Inf. Sci. Technol. **54**(6), 498–511 (2003). https://doi.org/10.1002/ASI.10237
7. Chung, E., Yoon, J.: Image needs in the context of image use: an exploratory study. J. Inf. Sci. **37**(2), 163–177 (2011). https://doi.org/10.1177/0165551511400951
8. Hartel, J., et al.: Information activity in serious leisure. Inf. Res. **21**(4), paper 728. http://InformationR.net/ir/21-4/paper728.html
9. Huvila, I.: Analytical information horizon maps. Libr. Inf. Sci. Res. **31**(1), 18–28 (2009). https://doi.org/10.1016/j.lisr.2008.06.005
10. Hyvönen, E., et al.: WarSampo data service and semantic portal for publishing linked open data about the second world war history. In: Sack, H., Blomqvist, E., d'Aquin, M., Ghidini, C., Ponzetto, S.P., Lange, C. (eds.) ESWC 2016. LNCS, vol. 9678, pp. 758–773. Springer, Cham (2016). https://doi.org/10.1007/978-3-319-34129-3_46
11. Jansen, B.J.: Searching for digital images on the web. J. Doc. **64**(1), 81–101 (2008). https://doi.org/10.1108/00220410810844169/FULL/PDF
12. Järvelin, K., et al.: Task-based information interaction evaluation: the viewpoint of program theory. ACM Trans. Inf. Syst. **33**(1), 1–30 (2015). https://doi.org/10.1145/2699660
13. Jörgensen, C., Jörgensen, P.: Image querying by image professionals. J. Am. Soc. Inf. Sci. Technol. **56**(12), 1346–1359 (2005). https://doi.org/10.1002/ASI.20229
14. Kumpulainen, S., et al.: Historical reasoning in authentic research tasks: mapping cognitive and document spaces. J. Assoc. Inf. Sci. Technol. (2019). https://doi.org/10.1002/asi.24216
15. Kumpulainen, S.: Task-based information searching. In: McDonald, J.D., Levine-Clark, M. (eds.) Encyclopedia of Library and Information Sciences, 4th edn. CRC Press (2017)
16. Markkula, M., Sormunen, E.: End-user searching challenges indexing practices in the digital newspaper photo archive. Inf. Retr. **14.1**(4), 259–285 (2000). https://doi.org/10.1023/A:1009995816485

17. Matusiak, K.K.: Studying information behavior of image users: an overview of research methodology in LIS literature, 2004–2015. Libr. Inf. Sci. Res. **39**(1), 53–60 (2017). https://doi.org/10.1016/j.lisr.2017.01.008

18. McCay-Peet, L., Toms, E.: Image use within the work task model: images as information and illustration. J. Am. Soc. Inf. Sci. Technol. **60**(12), 2416–2429 (2009). https://doi.org/10.1002/ASI.21202

19. O'Brien, H.: Theoretical perspectives on user engagement. In: O'Brien, H., Cairns, P. (eds.) Why Engagement Matters, pp. 1–26. Springer, Cham (2016). https://doi.org/10.1007/978-3-319-27446-1_1

20. O'Brien, H.L., et al.: A practical approach to measuring user engagement with the refined user engagement scale (UES) and new UES short form. Int. J. Hum. Comput. Stud. **112**, 28–39 (2018). https://doi.org/10.1016/J.IJHCS.2018.01.004

21. O'Brien, H.L., et al.: An empirical study of interest, task complexity, and search behaviour on user engagement. Inf. Process. Manag. **57**, 3 (2020). https://doi.org/10.1016/J.IPM.2020.102226

22. Salkind, N.: Encyclopedia of Measurement and Statistics. Sage, Thousand Oaks, CA (2007). https://doi.org/10.4135/9781412952644

23. Shatford, S.: Analyzing the subject of a picture: a theoretical approach. Cat. Classif. Q. **6**(3), 39–62 (1986). https://doi.org/10.1300/J104V06N03_04

24. Speakman, R., et al.: User engagement with generous interfaces for digital cultural heritage. Lect. Notes Comput. Sci. 11057 LNCS, 186–191 (2018). https://doi.org/10.1007/978-3-030-00066-0_16/TABLES/1

25. Xie, X., et al.: Why people search for images using web search engines. In Proceedings of the Eleventh ACM International Conference on Web Search and Data Mining (WSDM '18), pp. 655–663. ACM, New York, NY, USA (2018). https://doi.org/10.1145/3159652.3159686

Implementation and Evaluation of a Multilingual Search Pilot in the Europeana Digital Library

Mónica Marrero[1(✉)] and Antoine Isaac[1,2(✉)]

[1] Europeana Foundation, The Hague, The Netherlands
{monica.marrero,antoine.isaac}@europeana.eu
[2] Vrije Universiteit Amsterdam, Amsterdam, The Netherlands

Abstract. Europeana, a digital library that aggregates content from libraries, archives and museums from all around Europe, offers search functionality using the metadata of more than 62 million objects. However, in most cases, this data is only available in one language, while users come from countries with different languages. Europeana's strategy for the improvement of multilingual experiences includes the design and implementation of a multilingual information retrieval system based on the translation of queries and metadata to English. As a first development in this context, we have implemented a pilot applying query translation to English for the Spanish version of the website in order to surface results that have English metadata associated with them. We conducted an evaluation to assess the performance of this pilot and identify issues. The good performance rates observed allowed us to take the pilot to production, and the issues identified led to a list of specific actions, which should be addressed to the extent possible before the application of a wider multilingual information retrieval system.

Keywords: Information retrieval · Multilinguality · Cultural Heritage

1 Introduction

Using metadata about Cultural Heritage (CH) content, Europeana gives access to more than 62 million objects from libraries, archives and museums from all around Europe. However, while our users come from many countries, the metadata is often in one language—the one of the institution providing it. Europeana has defined a strategy [13] for the improvement of multilingual experiences, which includes the implementation of a multilingual information retrieval (MLIR) system using English as pivot language. This approach is breaking new ground for the CH sector, so significant experimentation is necessary to find the best ways of addressing the work. With that purpose, we have implemented a prototype called *Spanish pilot* that allows users of the Spanish version of our website (*Spanish portal*)[1] to seamlessly search in any language (more probably Spanish) and

---

[1] https://europeana.eu/es.

© Springer Nature Switzerland AG 2022
G. Silvello et al. (Eds.): TPDL 2022, LNCS 13541, pp. 93–106, 2022.
https://doi.org/10.1007/978-3-031-16802-4_8

get results associated with English metadata. The pilot uses a query translation approach where the queries from the Spanish portal are translated to English. This step is part of the use of English as a pivot language, and it can be already implemented given that part of the Europeana metadata contains English data (provided by CH institutions or resulting from enrichment).

This paper reports on the methodology followed and the evaluation we carried out regarding the effectiveness of the identification of the language of the query and its translation. We compared two translation services, the Google Cloud Translation API [7] (Google Translation in the following) and the CEF Translation service (eTranslation) [2], as the latter is intended as a free, secure service for public bodies, which can be appealing for CH institutions, especially in Europe. We also compared the relevance of the results obtained with the monolingual approach, analyzed the impact of typos, ambiguity and non-translatable entities in the queries, and further identified other elements negatively affecting retrieval in the multilingual system. The work done will contribute directly to our multilingual strategy, and the evaluation results will help us focus on the main issues to solve. The query sample and the results of the evaluation are publicly available [9] and the prototype is now live at https://www.europeana.eu/es.

2   State of the Art

MLIR is still a challenge in the area of Information Retrieval, and it is one of the most relevant topics addressed in academia that has a big impact in digital libraries [1]. However, in practice, the descriptions of digital objects in the collections, as well as the tools for their access and retrieval, remain largely monolingual [12]. This is also supported by Stiller et al. [18], who observed that MLIR is rarely implemented beyond the interface. Only a few practical cases have been reported in the literature (see extensive reviews in Vassilakaki and Garoufallou [21], Diekema [4], and Chen [3]), and most of them use human translations and specialized CH vocabularies. This is the case for example of the World Digital Library [14], which provides metadata manually translated into seven languages, or the International Children's Digital Library[2], where interface and contents are translated by volunteers. Matusiak et al. [12] reports an experiment using Google to translate to English a collection of Chinese artworks, but they finally opted for human translation given the limitations found with that approach. Also in the CH domain, Kools et al. [8] obtained satisfactory results with the machine translation of queries in/to English, German and French.

A more recent experiment in Europeana shows the risks of adopting such systems [10], and confirmed some of the main problems already identified in the literature [6,15,17]: the ambiguity of the queries given the lack of context, and the issues of the translation system when dealing with named entities. These issues are especially relevant in digital libraries, where queries and metadata are usually very limited in terms of context—which also makes language detection,

---

[2] http://en.childrenslibrary.org.

when required, harder. The CH domain is also very specific to apply general translation tools, and it has limited capacity to create the appropriate language resources required. As noted by Stiller and Petras [19], machine translations should be used with care especially for highly specialized and curated content.

In other domains though, machine translation seems to work well. It has been reported that when the pair of languages includes English and one of the most widely spoken languages (such as Spanish, German, or French), currently available machine-translation systems offer high effectiveness in Information Retrieval [5]. An analysis of the multilingual ad-hoc retrieval task at CLEF (Conference and Labs of the Evaluation Forum) between 2000 and 2009 shows that there is only a decrease of performance of 5–12% compared to the monolingual setting when using machine translation in such circumstances [16]. España-Bonet et al. [6] obtained good results in an academic search engine in psychology using specialized dictionaries to automatically translate the queries, but the experiments showed that machine translation applied to the documents obtained better results in retrieval [20]. Regarding the best strategy to adopt, - document translation, query translation or both -, the literature shows that document translation is consistently more effective [15,16,20], however Savoy and Braschler [16] report that the performance differences between query translation and document translation approaches vary greatly depending on the query. They suggest taking advantage of both translation models in a hybrid approach: in an experiment run using English as a pivot language, the results obtained outperformed other strategies. This strategy is also more scalable than document translation when the number of different languages is considerable, as is the case in Europeana.

3 Approach

As a first development for the Europeana Multilingual Strategy, the Spanish pilot implements only some of the tasks described there: real-time detection of the query language, real-time translation of the query, and construction of the multilingual query and retrieval of results (see Fig. 1). We do not apply document translation, and we use instead the existing collection, where a significant portion of the metadata is in English or contains English translations (see below). We also skip the process related to identification and translation of entities in the query—we have instead analyzed the impact of this feature in the results.

Following this approach, when a query is issued in the Spanish portal, it is first parsed using an ad-hoc parser based on regular expressions to distinguish sequences with textual content as opposed to query operators. Each of these sequences are then sent separately to the Google Translation service to get their translation using the option of automatic identification of the source language. The service then returns the translations, together with the source language. The English translation of the query is then used in the construction of the multilingual query that is going to be used to retrieve the search results. For the pilot we have implemented a simple approach that consists in connecting the original and the translation using the logical operator OR. As an example, the

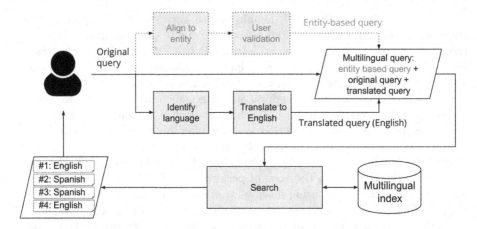

Fig. 1. Cross-lingual search using English as pivot language as described in the Europeana Multilingual Strategy. In the Spanish pilot the multilingual index does not contain all the English translations and some processes (greyed out) are not included.

query *carteles de la guerra civil NOT "National Library of Spain"* is converted in the multilingual system to *(carteles de la guerra civil NOT "National Library of Spain") OR (civil war posters NOT "National Library of Spain")*. One of the benefits of this approach is that the results retrieved with each query are already automatically merged according to the score obtained.

The search engine used is Apache Solr v7.7 and the scores are obtained using the out-of-the-box BM25 function. The queries are parsed with the default query parser (which supports boolean operators) and issued against a single collection that indexes the main elements of the 62 million metadata records currently held by Europeana, which follow the Europeana Data Model[3]. A significant part of this data is already in English: 39.8% of the records contain at least one "core" descriptive metadata field in English, while only 0.8% have at least one field in Spanish[4]. The numbers increase to 78.8% and 61.8% respectively when including metadata elements for contextual resources (i.e., concepts, places, and agents) coming from the more consistently labelled vocabularies used in the data enrichment steps.

4   Evaluation and Results

Before the deployment of the pilot in production, we conducted an evaluation in order to answer the following research questions on the quality and impact of multilingual search:

---

[3] https://pro.europeana.eu/page/edm-documentation.

[4] This reflects a quality issue in the metadata received by Europeana, which is often not labelled with language information. We know that the language of the data provider is Spanish for 5.5% of the records, while it is English for 17.5%.

- Q1. Can we assume that the language of the query is Spanish when using the Spanish portal? What is the effectiveness of the language identification service offered by Google compared to this assumption?
- Q2. Do we obtain better translations by assuming Spanish as source language, or by using the automatic identification provided by Google?
- Q3. What is the most effective translation system, Google Translation or eTranslation?
- Q4. Do we retrieve more documents in total?
- Q5. Do we retrieve more documents in English in the top ten positions?
- Q6. Is the relevance affected in the top ten positions?
- Q7. What is the impact of typos, ambiguity, and non-translatable entities?
- Q8. Are there other elements affecting relevance in the top ten positions?

We collected the queries issued from the Europeana Spanish portal from 1 December 2020 to 28 February 2021[5]. From the 34,902 different query strings obtained, we created a stratified sample of 300 queries: we took the 100 most frequent queries, a random sample of 100 queries from the long-tail with frequency 1, and a sample of 100 queries from the remaining ones using the frequency as weight. We used as collection a snapshot of the Europeana metadata collection, with 62 million records. The schema and configuration of the search engine used for the evaluation is the one that was in production when the evaluation took place (except that we disabled the "elevation" function that allows selected documents to appear in the top positions for certain queries[6]) and it is publicly available in Github[7]. The annotation of the results of the different tasks was done by the authors following a collaborative process, where the annotations done by one author were reviewed by the other, and the discrepancies were solved.

4.1 Real-Time Detection of the Query Language

We analyzed the effectiveness of the language identification service provided by Google (eTranslation did not include this service by the time the evaluation was done), and compared it with what we obtain if we consider the language of the query to be that of the portal, that is, Spanish (Q1). In order to do this, we applied the Google Translation service to the sample of queries, and from the list of languages returned, we kept only the most probable one. For example, for the query *carteles de la guerra civil NOT "National Library of Spain"* we send to the service *carteles de la guerra civil* and *National Library of Spain* separately, and we receive Spanish and English respectively as the most probable languages. We then manually annotated the accuracy of the identification with the following values: *All languages were correctly identified, Part of the languages were correctly identified (or unclear), None of the languages were correctly identified, N/A:operator or symbol, N/A:language hard to identify.*

---

[5] The period considered seeks to reduce the automatic sampling of sessions done by Google Analytics, from which we have collected the queries.

[6] https://solr.apache.org/guide/7_7/the-query-elevation-component.html.

[7] https://github.com/europeana/search/tree/12a2d78/solr_confs/metadata.

Table 1. Language identification effectiveness obtained with Google Translation and when assuming Spanish on a sample of 300 queries from the Europeana Spanish portal.

Annotation	Google (%)	Spanish (%)
All languages were correctly identified	58.3	33.3
N/A: language hard to identify (e.g., named entity)	35.3	35.3
None of the languages were correctly identified	3.0	20.7
N/A: operator or symbol	2.3	2.3
Part of the languages were correctly identified or unclear	1.0	8.3

We observed that in a significant proportion of the queries (37.7%) there is no clear language to be identified (see Table 1). This can happen because the query is made of operators (e.g., *:*) or because it is not clear what the correct language is, for example for named entities (e.g., Mozart). The latter is the most frequent reason. In those cases, it is interesting to note that Google assigns the language fitting most the entity's real-world context to the entity. For example, *Coruña* is identified as a query in Galician, *Barcelona* as a query in Catalan, *Amsterdam* as a query in Dutch, and *Mozart* as a query in German. Removing these cases, Google correctly identifies the language in 93.6% of the language-specific queries (that is, 58.3% of all queries), and only fails totally or partially in 6.4% of them (that is, 4.0 % of all queries). The results also show that if we assume Spanish to be the source language, we correctly identify 53.5% of the language-specific queries (that is, 33.3% of all queries), and it is not clear or we fail completely or partially in 46.5% of them (that is, 29% of all the queries). The percentage of wrong identifications in the latter case is in line with a previous experiment where we used a sample of queries from different web portals [10].

4.2   Real-time Translation of the Query

To evaluate the quality of the translation, we applied Google Translation and eTranslation to the sample of queries, using Spanish or the language identified by Google as source language (Q2, Q3). We then annotated each translation with *Not translated, Only change in letter case, Not clear, Translation error, None of the meaning was transferred, Part of the meaning was transferred* or *All meaning was transferred*, and answered the questions *Is the query ambiguous and could generate different translations?* and *Should the text in the query be translated?*. The combination of these leads to classifying translations into *correct, wrong, unclear* and *error*. Lexically ambiguous queries where multiple translations could be valid (e.g., *historia* can refer to *history* or *story*; *granada* could be a place or an explosive artefact) are considered *unclear*, while queries where none or only part of the meaning was transferred were considered *wrong*. Untranslated queries (or queries where the service only changed the letter case), were considered *correct* if the query was not expected to be translated.

Table 2 shows that Google Translation is approximately 20% more effective than eTranslation, reaching 72.6% accuracy when the source language is set to Spanish, and being slightly better when using automatic language identification.

Table 2. Translation effectiveness obtained with Google Translation and eTranslation using as source language Spanish (es) or automatic identification (auto) when applied on a sample of 300 queries issued in the Europeana Spanish portal.

Service	Correct	Wrong	Unclear	Error	%Correct
Google auto	220	47	33	-	**73.3**
Google es	218	49	33	-	**72.6**
eTranslation auto	159	80	23	38	**53.0**
eTranslation es	160	107	33	-	**53.3**

The lack of impact of the language identification service can be explained by the fact that most of the queries that are clearly not written in Spanish are either in English or in languages closer to Spanish, like Catalan. Translating them as if they were Spanish has a negative impact of only 7 percentage points with Google and 3 percentage points with eTranslation. Finally, we could also see that the use of automatic identification with eTranslation is not straightforward, as it raises an error when the language is not supported (for example, Latin), which happened in 12.6% of the queries.

4.3   Construction of the Multilingual Query

Finally, we evaluated the effectiveness of the multilingual system by comparing the number of results retrieved (Q4), their language (Q5), and how the relevance is affected in the top ten positions (Q6). For the latter, we calculated the difference of Precision at 10 (P@10)[8] by manually assessing the (binary) relevance of the documents that are retrieved by one system but not by the other in their top ten. That resulted in the manual assessment of 1213 documents retrieved for 297 queries (three were removed as they were not valid or intelligible).

The results show that the total number of documents retrieved in the multilingual system increases in 35.7% of the queries in our sample, with an average of 17,015 new documents found. We also observed an increase from 1.43 to 1.84 English documents in the top ten results on average. The number of queries for which we have at least one document in English also increases from 97 to 128. As a counterpart, the precision is not affected when using the multilingual system in 78.1% of the cases, while in 13.5% of the cases the documents retrieved in the top ten positions are worse, and in 8.4% of the cases the documents are more relevant. As we can see in Fig. 2, in many cases the difference in P@10 is small: on average it is −0.026, that is, we lose on average one document that is relevant in the top ten results for one query out of four.

4.4   Impact of Typos, Ambiguity, and Non-translatable Entities (Q7)

We observed that only 5.3% of the queries in the sample contain typos (e.g., *womens*), but as expected, the quality of translations is negatively affected by

---

[8] We used trec_eval v9.0, accessible at https://github.com/usnistgov/trec_eval.

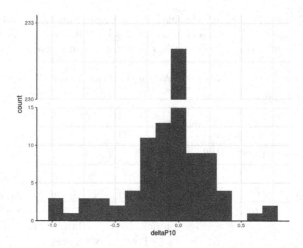

Fig. 2. Difference in Precision at 10 for the sample of queries when comparing the monolingual and multilingual version.

Table 3. Percentage of correct translation for queries with or without typos. The higher impact of typos in the case of eTranslation with language detection is due to unsupported source languages identified by Google.

Service	%correct for queries with typos	%correct for queries w/o typos
Google auto	31.3	75.7
Google es	31.3	75.0
eTranslation auto	18.8	54.9
eTranslation es	31.3	54.6

them (see Table 3). However, we observed that the precision in the top ten results does not change: usually the query with typos is not translated, meaning that no new results will be retrieved; a regression analysis using ANOVA confirms that the effect is not significant (F-value = 0.3035, P-value = 0.5821).

Regarding ambiguity, we indicated for each query if it is lexically ambiguous with different possible translations, that is, if it can have different translations depending on the intention of the user. Ambiguous queries account for 9.3% of the queries and, as expected, the translations obtained from them are annotated as *not clear*, and only in a few cases as *wrong*. This indicates that this is not a feature that affects the quality of the translation itself, but the relevance of the results retrieved with it: none of the queries increased P@10, and in one third of them it decreased. A regression analysis using ANOVA and linear models, indicates that this feature has a significant effect on the difference in P@10 (F-value = 8.7324, P-value = 0.003378).

Table 4. Percentage of correct translation for queries with or without entities that should not be translated, or where this is not clear.

Service	%correct for queries with entities	%correct when unclear	%correct for queries w/o entities
Google auto	71.7	10.0	85.2
Google es	72.4	10.0	82.8
eTranslation auto	50.7	10.0	62.5
eTranslation es	55.9	5.0	57.8

Finally, we manually annotated the queries containing entities, but only those that should not be translated (e.g., *Juan Gris* can not be translated as *John Gray*, nor *Antonio Sordi* as *Antonio Deaf*). We discovered that 50.7% of the queries contain them, while in 6.7% of the cases it is not clear. The latter usually happens with work titles with no clear English translation, but also with ambiguous queries like *granada*, which is valid as a city in Spanish and English, but could also be a common noun. In table 4 we see that this feature has an impact on the quality of the translation, and the regression analylsis indicates that it also has a significant effect on the difference in P@10 (F-value = 3.0714, P-value = 0.04785). We further observed that for queries with entities, only in one case the relevance in the top ten documents was improved (0.58%), while this happened in 23.76% of the cases when no entities were involved. The precision is also negatively affected when the existence of entities is not clear, however there is a dependency between these cases and the ambiguity in the queries.

4.5 Other Elements Affecting Relevance in the Top ten Positions (Q8)

We have manually analyzed the queries with a notable negative difference in precision at 10 (difference in P@10 <= −0.5). We removed those queries which were ambiguous, contained typos or non-translatable entities, or were wrongly translated. We analyzed the resulting 6 queries and discovered that for some of them the cause of bad results is linked to the lack of context. For example, *guerra civil* in the context of the Spanish portal probably refers to the Spanish civil war (and this is how it was annotated for the evaluation). In other cases, the problem is the lack of filters or use in search of specific fields. For example, the query *organista* (organist) matches photographs that are not relevant but they were taken by Pavel Svoboda, who happens to be also an organist (its role appears in the field for the creator's name). Finally, bad metadata as a consequence of wrong enrichments or vague descriptions could also lead to bad results. This is the case of the queries *futbol* (football), *deporte* (sport) or *alpinismo* (alpinism), where for the first one we found documents enriched correctly as sport but wrongly as football due to issues in the vocabulary used (i.e., football and sport being labels for the same thesaurus entry), for the second one we found documents wrongly enriched with sport, and for the third one we found documents talking about pilgrimages that include *mountain climbing* (as generic translation of *alpinismo*), but not in the sportive sense that would be expected today. During the relevance assessment we also observed two additional issues that affect negatively the search results: queries containing cross-language homonyms (e.g., *home* is *man* in Catalan, but it will be identified with higher probability as English by the language identification service), and translations to phrases with common keywords (e.g., *ludoterapia* is correctly translated as *play therapy*, which are two very common nouns that can appear in documents related to therapies in general).

5   Discussion

The evaluation conducted shows that Google is more effective than eTranslation in terms of translation quality and that it has high accuracy for language identification as opposed to considering that all queries are in the language of the portal. Although assuming Spanish does not have a big negative impact in the quality of the translations obtained, and could even have benefits in the case of cross-lingual homonyms in the queries, high accuracy in language detection is relevant for the display (which is not covered here, but still part of the pilot). Detecting the language also poses less potential risks in the case of other Europeana language-specific portals where users may use even less the expected language. In terms of retrieval, the evaluation shows that the number of documents retrieved increases considerably in the multilingual approach, as well as the number of English documents retrieved in the top ten positions, while the relevance in those positions is not affected significantly.

Table 5 compiles the main issues we found to negatively affect the multilingual version. Especially, the evaluation confirmed two main issues already covered in the literature, as well as in a previous experiment with different Europeana data [10]: the lexical ambiguity of the queries has a bad impact on the search results, and the queries with entities that should not be translated lead to bad translations and hence, bad search results. Note that the existence of typos was not found to be more harmful than in the monolingual approach.

Table 5 also presents possible remedial actions. To address the issues related to the ambiguity of the queries we could: a) be more transparent with portal users regarding the multilingual query generated so that they can detect and maybe correct wrong translations, b) extend and adapt the existing facets to the multilingual interface, so users can further filter the search results (e.g., by topic, creator), c) offer an advanced search functionality, so users can use specific fields in the search, and d) include a popularity criteria in the ranking, which may also include criteria based on the language/portal in order to address the lack of context in queries vaguely formulated.

Table 5. Issues observed and possible remedial actions. The first four issues are specific to the multilingual approach, and the top three have a significant effect on the results.

- **Issue:** Lexical ambiguity. E.g., *Granada* as place, explosive artifact, or fruit
- **Explanation:** The intention of the user is not clear and multiple translations are possible. E.g., *Granada*, and not *grenade* or *pomegranate*
- **Specific Multilingual:** Yes
- **Solution:** Transparency (user can see /edit the multilingual query), Topic/Author filter, Search by field, Ranking by popularity.

- **Issue:** Entities that should not be translated. E.g., *Antonio Sordi* is not *Antonio Deaf*
- **Explanation:** The name of the entity is already valid in English
- **Specific Multilingual:** Yes
- **Solution:** Use of knowledge graphs

- **Issue:** Entities that should not be translated. E.g., some titles like *glossa ordinaria*
- **Explanation:** Translation to English does not exist
- **Specific Multilingual:** Yes
- **Solution:** Use of knowledge graphs

- **Issue:** Entities that should be translated in a very specific way. E.g., the official translation of the title *Dos metros lejos de ti* is *five feet apart*
- **Explanation:** Translation to English is not literal
- **Specific Multilingual:** Yes
- **Solution:** Use of knowledge graphs

- **Issue:** Lexical ambiguity. E.g., *Granada* as region in Latin America or a city in Spain
- **Explanation:** The intention of the user is not clear but the translation is the same
- **Specific Multilingual:** No, but translations may also have this issue
- **Solution:** Transparency, Topic/Author filter, Search by field, Ranking by popularity

---

- **Issue:** Handling of phrases. E.g., *ludoterapia* is correctly translated as *play therapy*, which are two very common nouns that can appear in documents related to therapies in general
- **Explanation:** The translation is not a single term anymore and may lose specificity
- **Specific Multilingual:** No, but the translated query may have this issue even though the original does not
- **Solution:** Account in the rank for closeness in the search keywords

---

- **Issue:** Vagueness. E.g., *civil war* is probably referring to the Spanish civil war if queried in Spanish or from the Spanish portal
- **Explanation:** The translation is more generic, or the implicit information given by the user context is lost with it
- **Specific Multilingual:** No, but the issue is worse when retrieving information in other languages
- **Solution:** Topic/Author filter, Ranking by popularity (popularity depending on the language/portal)

- **Issue:** Cross-language homonyms. E.g., *home* is man in Catalan
- **Explanation:** Same or similar words with different meanings in different languages
- **Specific Multilingual:** No, but the issue may be worse when all the metadata is translated to English
- **Solution:** Filter by language, Topic/Author filter, Route queries to fields in that specific language

---

- **Issue:** Wrong enrichments. E.g., metadata related to water sports is tagged as *football*
- **Explanation:** Enrichments can be wrong due to issues in the vocabulary or the enrichment process
- **Specific Multilingual:** No, but the issue becomes more visible because most enrichments contain English tags
- **Solution:** Improvement in the enrichment process, Validation of enrichments

---

Regarding the entities, knowledge graphs (in the wider sense, i.e., including CH controlled vocabularies) like the Europeana Entity Collection[9] can help identify entities and obtain the specific translations for those when they exists. This process is already contemplated in the Europeana multilingual strategy, while it is partially implemented (no disambiguation) in the metadata collection as part of the enrichment process.

Finally, we would also benefit from taking general measures to reduce noise, like improving the precision of the current enrichment process, and improving phrase matching by boosting documents where the keywords of the query appear (quasi) contiguously (work already in progress).

6   Conclusions and Future Work

In our Spanish pilot we have prototyped processes envisioned in the Europeana strategy for multilingual search: query translation to English, and construction and use of a multilingual query. The pilot has been applied to the full Europeana collection. It has shown the feasibility of applying a multilingual information retrieval system in Europeana, given our current data and technical possibilities. The evaluation conducted shows a reasonable performance (also in terms of efficiency, although that has not been included in this paper) when using Google Translation API for the language identification and translation of the queries in real-time. This has convinced Europeana to deploy it in production for the Spanish portal. This is done since late 2021, with the idea of getting feedback that can guide the following steps.

The evaluation was also useful for the identification of issues and possible solutions to address them. One of the main issues is the poor quality of the translations obtained for the entities that should not be translated, given that they represent a big portion of the queries at Europeana, and often occur in our data. In the short term, we will probably disable the translation for queries that directly match entities contained in our Entity Collection, while in the medium term we will see the feasibility of identifying more general queries, and adopting from our knowledge graph (or others) the required translations.

The rest of the solutions proposed, many of which are already included in a more general strategy for improving search at Europeana [11], should be addressed to the extent possible before adopting multilingual search at a wider scale, when the probability of getting more noisy results will be higher given a) the planned translation of more metadata to English (which is currently worked on by the project Europeana Translate[10]), and b) other portals targeting not so common languages. Once we have more metadata translated to English, we will be able to test different approaches in the construction of the multilingual query, as for example using only language-specific fields, which will help to prevent matching keywords with different meanings in other languages.

---

[9] https://pro.europeana.eu/page/entity#entity-collection.

[10] https://pro.europeana.eu/project/europeana-translate.

In the short term we plan to experiment with the translation of the search results page. Eventually we will extend multilingual search to the Europeana portals for all 24 official languages of the European Union. Given that the evaluation presented here for Spanish cannot be extrapolated to other languages, we have to find a balance between the resources available to run such evaluations and the risk of obtaining a poor performance for some portals/languages. We could log appropriate user behaviour data and run A/B tests to alleviate the issue of the lack of in-house resources. This would also help to further evaluate future improvements for our current search process, and closely follow the impact of the planned translation of metadata to English.

References

1. Agosti, M., Fabris, E., Silvello, G.: On synergies between information retrieval and digital libraries. In: Manghi, P., Candela, L., Silvello, G. (eds.) IRCDL 2019. CCIS, vol. 988, pp. 3–17. Springer, Cham (2019). https://doi.org/10.1007/978-3-030-11226-4_1
2. CEF Automated Translation Service: eTranslation. https://ec.europa.eu/cefdigital/wiki/display/CEFDIGITAL/eTranslation
3. Chen, H.: Digital library research in the US: an overview with a knowledge management perspective. Program: Electron. Lib. Inf. Syst. **38**(3), 157–167 (2004)
4. Diekema, A.R.: Multilinguality in the digital library: a review. Electron. Libr. **30**(2), 165–181 (2012)
5. Dolamic, L., Savoy, J.: Retrieval effectiveness of machine translated queries. J. Am. Soc. Inf. Sci. Technol. **61**, 2266–2273 (2010)
6. España-Bonet, C., Stiller, J., Ramthun, R., van Genabith, J., Petras, V.: Query translation for cross-lingual search in the academic search engine PubPsych. In: Garoufallou, E., Sartori, F., Siatri, R., Zervas, M. (eds.) MTSR 2018. CCIS, vol. 846, pp. 37–49. Springer, Cham (2019). https://doi.org/10.1007/978-3-030-14401-2_4
7. Google Cloud Translation API. https://cloud.google.com/translate, Java client library (com.google.cloud:libraries-bom:4.0.0)
8. Kools, J., Lagos, N., Petras, V., Stiller, J., Vald, E.: GALATEAS project (Generalized Analysis of Logs for Automatic Translation and Episodic Analysis of Searches). D7.4 Final Evaluation of Query Translation (2013). version 2.0
9. Marrero, M., Isaac, A.: Implementation and evaluation of a multilingual search pilot in the Europeana digital library (dataset) (2022). https://doi.org/10.5281/zenodo.6861293
10. Marrero, M., Isaac, A., Freire, N.: Automatic translation and multilingual cultural heritage retrieval: a case study with transcriptions in Europeana. In: Berget, G., Hall, M.M., Brenn, D., Kumpulainen, S. (eds.) TPDL 2021. LNCS, vol. 12866, pp. 133–138. Springer, Cham (2021). https://doi.org/10.1007/978-3-030-86324-1_17
11. Marrero, M., Isaac, A., Manguinas, H., Neale, A.: Europeana DSI-4 search improvement strategy. Technical report, Europeana (2021). https://pro.europeana.eu/post/europeana-search-strategy
12. Matusiak, K.K., Meng, L., Barczyk, E., Shih, C.J.: Multilingual metadata for cultural heritage materials: the case of the Tse-Tsung chow collection of Chinese scrolls and fan paintings. Electron. Libr. **33**(1), 136–51 (2015)

13. Neale, A., Isaac, A., Manguinas, H., Moskalenko, D., Marrero, M.: Europeana DSI-4 multilingual strategy. Technical report, Europeana (2020). https://pro. europeana.eu/post/europeana-dsi-4-multilingual-strategy
14. Oudenaren, J.V.: The world digital library. Uncommon Culture **3**(5/6), 65–71 (2012)
15. Peters, C., Braschler, M., Clough, P.: Multilingual Information Retrieval: From Research to Practice. Springer, Heidelberg, Germany (2012). https://doi.org/10. 1007/978-3-642-23008-0
16. Savoy, J., Braschler, M.: Lessons learnt from experiments on the Ad Hoc multilingual test collections at CLEF. In: Information Retrieval Evaluation in a Changing World. TIRS, vol. 41, pp. 177–200. Springer, Cham (2019). https://doi.org/10. 1007/978-3-030-22948-1_7
17. Stiller, J., Gäde, M., Petras, V.: Ambiguity of queries and the challenges for query language detection. In: CLEF 2010 LABs and Workshops (2010). Padua, Italy (2010)
18. Stiller, J., Gäde, M., Petras, V.: Multilingual access to digital libraries: the Europeana use case. Inf. Wiss. Prax. **64**(2–3), 86–95 (2013)
19. Stiller, J., Petras, V.: Best practices for multilingual access. Technical report, Europeana (2016). https://pro.europeana.eu/post/best-practices-for-multilingual-access
20. Stiller, J., Petras, V., Lüschow, A.: CLUBS Project (Cross-Lingual Bibliographic Search). M5.3 Final Evaluation (2019). version 1.0
21. Vassilakaki, E., Garoufallou, E.: Multilingual digital libraries: a review of issues in system-centered and user-centered studies, information retrieval and user behavior. Int. Inf. Lib. Rev. **45**, 3–19 (2013)

DETEXA: Declarative Extensible Text Exploration and Analysis

Yannis Foufoulas[1,2]($\boxtimes$) (iD), Eleni Zacharia[1,2] (iD), Harry Dimitropoulos[1,2] (iD),
Natalia Manola[1,2] (iD), and Yannis Ioannidis[1,2] (iD)

[1] National and Kapodistrian University of Athens, Athens, Greece
johnfouf@di.uoa.gr
[2] Athena Research Center, Athens, Greece

Abstract. Metadata enrichment through text mining techniques is becoming one of the most significant tasks in digital libraries. Due to the pandemic increase of open access publications, several new challenges have emerged. Raw data are usually big, unstructured, and come from heterogeneous data sources. In this paper, we introduce a text analysis framework which is implemented in extended SQL and exploits the scalability characteristics of modern database management systems. The purpose of this framework is to provide the opportunity to build performant end-to-end text mining pipelines which includes data harvesting, cleaning, processing, and text analysis at once. SQL is selected due to its declarative nature which offers fast experimentation and the ability to build APIs, so that domain experts can edit text mining workflows via easy-to-use graphical interfaces. Our experimental analysis demonstrates that the proposed framework is very effective and achieves significant speedup in common use cases compared to other popular approaches.

Keywords: Text analytics · YeSQL · User-defined functions

1 Introduction

The exponential growth of published articles opens up new challenges and research opportunities. Text mining has gained significant attention across a broad range of applications. The researchers implement text mining workflows to enhance the understanding of academic literature and generate new knowledge. With text mining on scientific literature it is possible to identify and classify the key themes of an academic field, explore trends, assess impact and popularity of topics over a period of time, help authors to find published literature related to their research, and so on.

Python is the language that many data scientists prefer for text analysis as it is easy to learn and enhances their productivity, given its modules for text and data mining tasks (e.g., NLTK [1]). However, NLTK is usually sub-optimal in terms of performance, as Python is designed to be an easy to use high-level dynamic language. Scalable analytical frameworks that support Python are often used to make Python text analytics run faster (e.g., PySpark [2], Dask [3]).

© Springer Nature Switzerland AG 2022
G. Silvello et al. (Eds.): TPDL 2022, LNCS 13541, pp. 107–119, 2022.
https://doi.org/10.1007/978-3-031-16802-4_9

DataBase Management Systems (DBMSs) also support the execution of User-Defined Functions (UDFs) written in Python [4–6]. However, these works come with several limitations, especially for text processing. For example, in PySpark and PostgreSQL, Python functions run in a separate process, introducing big inter-process communication overheads, which is a deterrent factor for text mining that usually involves large texts. Dask targets mainly data analysis on numeric data, as it is based mainly on NumPy and Pandas. Furthermore, UDFs in DBMSs are often sub-optimal in terms of expressiveness, i.e., they are statically typed which contradicts Python's nature, stateless and without side effects. Thus, many data scientists do not integrate their text analysis workflows into DBMSs, but prefer to use simpler tools like NLTK and PySpark.

In this paper, we present a scalable text analysis framework, DETEXA [7], built on top of YeSQL [8]. Specifically, we have implemented a rich set of text mining functionalities as polymorphic scalar, aggregate, and table UDFs that can work in synergy with various database systems through YeSQL.

We consider YeSQL a perfect match for text analysis tasks as it supports polymorphic and dynamically typed functions which are critical for dealing with various data schemas (i.e., heterogeneous data input JSON, XML, etc.), as is usually the case when harvesting text data from various repositories. Moreover, its performance characteristics fit well with text mining since: 1) it supports stateful UDFs that allow data scientists to run costly operations once at global scope and reuse them through multiple functions – such operations are usual in text mining (e.g., pattern compilation, external package imports and setups, etc.) – and 2) in-process UDF execution and tracing JIT compilation of Python UDFs enhance scalability of text mining workflows. Furthermore, the declarative interface of the presented framework, which is inherited by YeSQL, allows quick experimentation concerning data analysis tasks and rapid development of data processing workflows. Finally, it allows the easy implementation of application interfaces, using the most common architecture of the web that consists of a portal frontend and a backend that produces SQL queries and submits them to the DBMS. In OpenAIRE [9], such an interface has been implemented and used by community experts to implement and tune their own information extraction algorithms without requiring any programming knowledge.

The following query illustrates the data intensive part of a classification algorithm, written using the text analysis library of the presented framework.

```
SELECT docid, class, sum(p)
FROM   (SELECT docid,
               Strsplitv(
               Stem(Keywords(Filterstopwords(Lower(text)))), 2)
               AS ngram
        FROM   documents),
        taxonomies
WHERE  ngram = taxonomies.term
GROUP  BY docid, class;
```

This query reads data from a table with documents, and first applies several standard preprocessing steps (i.e., convert to lower case, stopword removal, tokenization with punctuation removal, stemming). With dynamic function *str-splitv*, the input string with tokens is transformed into a database column with ngrams of length up to 2, which is joined against the taxonomies table that consists of the classes, terms, and weights. The latter have already been produced during the offline training phase. Finally, using relational operators the sum-of-term weights per class is calculated. That is, according to the presented framework, the heavy relational parts (i.e., join, group by, and aggregate operations) are executed by the DBMS, whereas the procedural text processing tasks (preprocessing, pattern matching, etc.) are done with a rich set of Python text analysis functions.

In more detail, the contributions of this work are the following:

Text Analysis Library. A rich library of functions for text mining implemented as scalar, aggregate and table functions, and executed inside a DBMS.

Extensibility. Data scientists are allowed to implement their own custom functions as scalar, aggregate, or table UDFs, and use them in synergy with the already-supported operations.

Moreover, contributions of YeSQL, which is our underlying system, allows our text analysis framework to support the following features:

Declarative Language for Text Mining. Complex text mining algorithms are supported using a declarative language which makes easy the implementation of interactive application interfaces. Such an interface is shown in Sect. 3.3.

Performance. As the experiments show, the proposed framework outperforms other popular libraries in important text analysis tasks. The text mining field fits well with database UDFs as they are defined in YeSQL, and reaps all its performance benefits.

The structure of the paper is as follows. Section 2 reviews popular works in the field, their advantages and limitations. Section 3 presents an overview of the DETEXA framework and its applicability. Section 4 demonstrates the potential of the presented framework through experiments on well-established algorithms against several popular text mining libraries and systems. Finally, Sect. 5 concludes the paper and discusses potential future directions.

2   Related Work

In this section, we discuss prior work on text mining with Python, divided into two main categories: 1) Python text mining libraries, and 2) Scalable data management systems with Python support.

2.1   Text Analysis Tools

The most popular text mining library in Python is NLTK. It is used for tokenization, lemmatization, stemming, parsing, etc. Thanks to its many third party extensions, it supports many approaches for almost any text mining task. However, it is based on CPython's interpreter and does not scale well with big data. Other Python libraries for text mining include scikit-learn [10], spaCy [11], Gensim [12] and more. Scikit-learn is a generic tool for machine learning with support for several text analysis tasks. However, since it is built on NumPy it is fast mostly in numeric operations but sub-optimal when processing strings. SpaCy is considered to be faster than NLTK, however it lacks flexibility as it is not customizable. Gensim was originally developed for topic modelling, and is not a complete NLP toolkit like NLTK and SpaCy, thus it should be used in synergy with other libraries. Our work differentiates from these libraries as: 1) it is more efficient in terms of performance since it is based on DBMSs, 2) it is simpler to implement new pipelines due to its declarative interface, and 3) it is customizable and extensible.

2.2   Data Management Systems with Text Mining Opportunities

Several prior efforts have focused in making Python run faster. PySpark is a Python interface to Spark which supports the definition of UDFs written in Python. This is one of the most popular systems for scalable Python among data scientists, which achieves efficiency through parallelization. However, it runs Python UDFs on the interpreter in separate processes, introducing several inter-process communication overheads. Dask is a distributed analytical tool written in Python with Pandas and NumPy. It targets mainly numeric operations and is usually suboptimal when processing strings: Pandas and NumPy natively support only a few operations on strings, so more complex string analysis is possible only outside NumPy/Pandas which requires string copy transformations into Python Objects. Moreover, several DBMSs support Python UDFs (e.g., PostgreSQL, MonetDB, Vertica, and more). However, they come with several limitations in expressiveness and performance, and thus are rarely a first option for text mining. Specifically, they require UDFs with statically defined schemata which contradicts Python's dynamic typing, they run Python in separate process, or they support NumPy which is not designed for string processing. The presented text analysis framework avoids these performance and expressiveness issues due to the polymorphic and dynamic nature of its functions and the performance characteristics introduced by YeSQL.

3   The DETEXA Framework

In this section, we analyze the presented framework and its functionalities. Specifically, we present the library of the supported functions, we explain why we selected YeSQL and the opportunities to extend the supported functionalities with fully fledged Python, and finally we present a graphical interface deployed in OpenAIRE which is used by domain experts to run simple information extraction tasks using the presented framework.

3.1   Function Library

In order to support end-to-end text analysis pipelines, the framework includes functions in several categories:

- *Data input functions*: polymorphic functions used to process data from heterogeneous sources (i.e., CSV, JSON, XML, PDF and HTML parsers, Web tables, Rest APIs, files in HDFS and storage devices, external database connectors, etc.)
- *Data processing functions*: functions which apply typical text mining steps on input data (i.e., tokenization, stopword removal, etc.)
- *Pattern matching functions*: a variety of functions for parameterised pattern matching (i.e., pattern extraction, updating, weighted patterns, etc.)
- *Bag-of-words functions*: several functions to support bag-of-words functionalities using JSON ordered or unordered arrays and dictionaries. A JSON array with terms can be converted into a database column and vice versa. A JSON dictionary can be converted into a nested table and used in SQL as any other table.
- *Distance functions*: several functions that calculate distance among JSON arrays (e.g., Jaccard, cosine, edit_distance, and more).
- *Language functions*: statistical functions that process documents to extract language information (e.g., detectlang), or functions that are language specific (e.g., stem).
- *Text filtering functions*: functions which scan a document and return text snippets according to specific patterns or document sections (e.g., textreferences, textabstract, textacknowledgements, textwindow, etc.)
- *Data output functions*: functions which return the result of a text analysis workflow to a permanent location or to standard output in various formats (JSON, CSV, SQLite database, etc.)
- *General purpose functions*: functions that are used for various data handling tasks including sampling, random generators, date functions, mathematical operations, statistics, and more.

Note that the purpose of the framework is not to implement text analysis pipelines using only Python UDFs. This would be sub-optimal as UDFs are considered black boxes for a database optimiser, thus in this case, we could not reap the benefits of in-database execution. However, according to the design of the framework, the relational parts (e.g., join, scan, filter, sort, etc.) of a pipeline are not implemented as part of procedural Python UDFs but are still expressed in the SQL part of a query so that they are executed efficiently by the DBMS, whereas the procedural parts of a pipeline are written in Python UDFs.

All the implemented functions are mapped into scalar, aggregate, or polymorphic table database UDFs according to their scope. Specifically, *data input functions* are implemented as polymorphic table UDFs, as they process external sources and return the input data as database tables. *Data processing, pattern matching*, and *language functions* process one row at a time so they are defined as scalars. *Bag-of-words functions* are divided either in aggregates or in scalars returning dynamic schemas, i.e., *jgroup* function processes a group and creates a json dictionary or array with all the elements in the group, *jsplit* processes a json dictionary or array and splits it into multiple columns, whereas *jsplitv* processes a json dictionary or array and splits it vertically into multiple rows. *Distance functions* are implemented as dynamic scalar UDFs which process json arrays or plain strings and return their distance. These functions are also implemented as aggregates in case the target data is stored in multiple rows. *Text filtering functions* process one document at a time and return dynamic schemas so they are defined as scalar UDFs. Finally, *data output functions* are implemented as polymorphic table UDFs with side effects, as they export their result table at a user defined location.

In total, the function library offers more than 150 operators for text analysis. The presented framework and its function library is deployed as a third party library of OpenAIRE's Inference Information Service, and used by OpenAIRE's data scientists every day to extract several knowledge from OpenAIRE's publication texts and abstracts, including funding information, bio-entities, software links, data citations, document classifications, and more.

3.2   Why YeSQL?

Despite that this work could be integrated in almost any DBMS with Python UDF support, we selected YeSQL as its modularity and expressiveness characteristics make it a perfect fit for the proposed text analysis framework. Specifically, as described in the previous section, YeSQL's polymorphic and dynamic functions allow the implementation of our reusable data input functions since those functions return dynamic schemata according to the input data. YeSQL's scalar UDFs returning arbitrary table forms enable the implementation of bag-of-words functions as these functions take one row in their input and return a column or a nested table. YeSQL also allows for UDFs with side effects which fit to the nature of data output functions. As for performance, YeSQL's seamless data transfer of strings between the DBMS and the procedural language which runs in-process is critical for applications on texts. YeSQL's UDF fusion is a perfect fit with text mining scenarios, as in this context, pipelines of operations are very common (e.g., specifically during preprocessing and data harvesting/transforming). Stateful UDFs also allow for performant pattern matching and data processing functions: external packages are imported and setup at global layer, and patterns are also precompiled at global layer and not once per row.

The following query illustrates some of the hallmark functionalities of the proposed framework:

```
output 'similarpairs.json'
SELECT arxivid,  pubmedid, top(similarity,5) as s
FROM (
    SELECT arxivid, pubmedid,
           Jaccard(arxivterms, pubmedterms) AS similarity _
```

```
FROM (
        SELECT arxivid,
            Jpack(Frequentterms(Stem(Filterstopwords(
            Tokenize(Textabstract(text)))), 10))
            AS arxivterms
        FROM file('arxiv.csv')
        ) ,
        (
        SELECT pubmedid,
            Jpack(Frequentterms(Stem(Filterstopwords(
            Tokenize(Textabstract(text)))), 10))
            AS pubmedterms
        FROM file('pubmed.json')
        ))
GROUP BY arxivid;
```

The above query reads raw files containing publication full-texts from arXiv and PubMed (in CSV and JSON with two keys containing the *id* and *text*), runs various processing steps (i.e., abstract extraction, tokenization, stopword removal, stemming), creates a JSON array with the top 10% frequent terms, and then calculates the Jaccard similarity. Finally, for each arXiv document it returns up to 5 PubMed documents (aggregate UDF *top* is similar to native SQL function *max*, however it returns multiple top N rows) with the highest Jaccard similarity. The analysis result is exported to an external JSON file as follows:

```
{"arxivid": "1304.2323", "pubmedid": "PMC2985735", "s": 0.5323}
{"arxivid": "1304.2323", "pubmedid": "PMC5464362", "s": 0.4932}
```

Note, that this is not considered to be the best way to calculate document similarity; this could be better based on TF-IDF calculation, but we show this as it covers well some of the main characteristics of the presented framework.

Extensibility. Although the presented framework comes with a large number of predefined operators, the data scientist is allowed to extend its functionalities by submitting her own custom functions categorized in scalars, aggregates and polymorphic table functions, according to their scope. These functions are written in Python files with support for external packages. If a function processes one row at a time then this is defined as a scalar. Aggregate functions process a group of rows at a time, and polymorphic table functions process a whole table.

3.3 Interfaces

As already mentioned in the introduction, having a fully-fledged text mining framework written in a declarative language (SQL) allows for easy implementation of application interfaces. An interactive information extraction interface on top of the presented library is deployed in OpenAIRE. Figure 1 depicts a screenshot of the interface. The purpose of the interface is to allow the users to implement and tune simple information extraction tasks. Specifically, they upload their documents in plain text format, and a CSV containing the entity titles/names for information extraction (i.e., in this example terms *clarin* and *clariah*[1]). Through this interface they select preprocessing tasks (e.g., stopword removal, punctuation removal, and more), text extraction tasks (i.e., extract acknowledgement section, citation section), positive and negative terms and phrases to disambiguate false positives, and finally the length of the text snippet before and after an occurrence of the searched concept. The user selects the functions and mining rules using a graphical interface, and the SQL query is built in the backend and runs online returning the highlighted results to the domain expert to update her algorithm accordingly and rerun. Using the rules as shown in the screenshot, the following query is automatically produced:

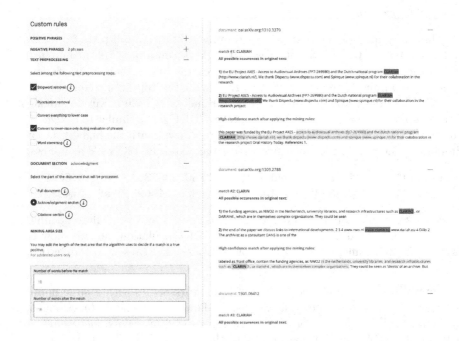

Fig. 1. Information extraction interface

```
SELECT docid, prev||middle||next as context, middle as match FROM
   (SELECT docid, textwindow(
      lower(filterstopwords(
      textaknowledgements(text))), 10,1,10, "CLARIAH|CLARIN")
   FROM file('arxivdocs.tsv')
   ),
WHERE NOT regexprmatches("gene|cofund-clarin", prev||middle||next);
```

---

[1] https://www.clarin.eu/.

4 Evaluation

4.1 Experimental Setup

Several experiments were conducted to compare the performance of end-to-end text analysis pipelines. We compared our framework against NLTK (v3.7), Scikit-learn v(1.1) on CPython (v.3.8.10), and PySpark(v2.4.7). Our framework (DETEXA) is implemented on top of YeSQL's integration with SQLite (v.3.31.11) and PyPy(v.7.3.6 with GCC 7.3.1) tracing JIT compiler. In our experiments, we selected two real word tasks of fundamental importance that have been gaining traction thanks to recent developments in the fields of text mining and Natural Language Processing (NLP). The experiments ran on real publication abstracts from OpenAIRE. We ran all experiments on an Intel(R) Core i7-4790 processor with 3.60 GHz and 4 cores/8 CPUs. The server has 16 GB main memory and runs Ubuntu 20.04. We executed all experiments with cold caches, and we report the average of 5 executions.

4.2 Experiments

Document Classification. The first task is a text classification task [13], defined as assigning pre-defined category labels to new papers based on the likelihood suggested by a training set of labelled papers. Input data for text classification consist of raw, unstructured text. Before feeding input data to any classifier, it is projected into an appropriate feature space by applying preprocessing procedures which transform plain texts into lists of terms (keywords, metadata). Terms may be single words or n-grams. Since text classification is a supervised learning task, it has two main phases: i) the training phase in which a global list of unique terms is updated, along with the respective term frequencies for each paper; and ii) the prediction phase in which the classifier predicts the labels of a given paper based on its content (list of terms).

In our experiments, we assume that the training phase has already been executed. The prediction phase of the algorithm involves three preprocessing operators running sequentially. These are tokenization, stopword removal, and stemming. Terms may be single words or 2-grams. We have implemented the classification sub-module in the presented DETEXA framework which is hand optimized with Python code as well as in NLTK. The DETEXA query implementing the classification sub-module is shown in the introduction.

We ran this experiment using 10K, 50K, 100K and 1M text abstracts. Figure 2 shows the execution times for the classification sub-module using our presented framework compared with NTKL for the different sizes of input data. In all cases, the time needed for the execution using DETEXA falls in half. This happens for 2 reasons: 1) the design of the framework which effectively maps text analysis tasks in database UDFs and lets the DBMS to handle the heavy relational tasks (e.g., joins, group by's), and 2) the performance characteristics which are inherited by YeSQL.

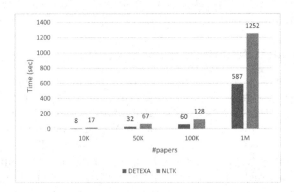

Fig. 2. Execution times of DETEXA and NLTK for the document classification task

Term Frequency-Inverse Document Frequency (TF-IDF). The second task is the implementation of the TF-IDF algorithm. TF-IDF is a predominant feature vectorization method widely used in many NLP applications, as well as in text classification and text mining systems. For example, search engines use TF-IDF to rank the relevance of a document for a query. TF-IDF is also used to recommend papers to authors or to detect similarities amongst papers. TF-IDF is divided into two parts: computation of TF (Term Frequency), and computation of IDF (Inverse Document Frequency). TF is the number of times a term appears in a document divided by the total number of words in the document. IDF of a term reflects the proportion of documents in the corpus that contain the term: it is defined as the logarithmic fraction obtained by dividing the total number of documents in the corpus by the number of documents in the corpus containing the term. TF-IDF of a term is computed by multiplying TF and IDF scores.

We have implemented the TF-IDF algorithm in the presented DETEXA framework, as well as in a hand optimised Python implementation using NLTK. We have also used the implementation of scikit-learn from [14] that uses the native *TfidfVectorizer* sklearn package. The DETEXA query implementing the TF-IDF task is the following:

```
SELECT docid, term, tf *log10(1000000.0/(1 + jgcount)) as tfidf
FROM (jgroupordered groupby:term count:docid SELECT term, docid, tf
      FROM ( SELECT c1 as term, docid, count(*)/(1.0*c2) AS tf
             FROM ( SELECT docid, strsplitv(abstract)
                    FROM ( SELECT docid, stem(filterstopwords(
                                  keywords(lower(abstract))))
                           AS abstract
                        FROM metadata LIMIT 1000000
                   ) )
             GROUP BY term, docid
      ) )
```

This query reads data from a table that contains publication abstracts. First, it executes three pre-processing operators running one after another. These are tokenization with punctuation removal (UDF *keywords*), stopword removal, and stemming. With dynamic function *strsplitv*, the input string with stemmed words is split vertically into a database column, and a new column containing the number of stemmed words in each abstract is added. Then, using relational operations, TF score is calculated. Since the heavy data processing task (i.e., *group by*) has been processed by the DBMS, *jgroupordered* UDF joins consecutive rows of the table having the same term and counts the number of documents in the corpus containing the term at hand. That is of high importance, as we do not need to execute another database *group by* operator with an aggregate function, which is a heavy data processing task; we exploit the fact that the intermediate data is already sorted by 'term' column during the previous group by. Finally, the query calculates *tfidf* score.

We ran the experiment using 10K, 50K, 100K and 1M text abstracts. Figure 3 shows the execution times for the TF-IDF task using our framework, as well as NLTK and scikit-learn. The results compared to NLTK reveal very similar trends to the previous experiment. Furthermore, using the proposed framework the *tfidf* algorithm runs much faster than the native implementation of scikit-learn.

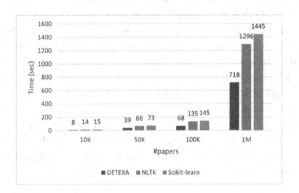

Fig. 3. Execution times of DETEXA, NLTK, Scikit-learn for TF-IDF

Finally, we ran a separate experiment on *tfidf* to compare the DETEXA framework with PySpark and its native implementation of *tfidf* (*HashingTF*, *IDF* packages). We selected PySpark, since it is a popular distributed analytical system which achieves efficient execution of algorithms through parallelization. YeSQL's implementation on top of SQLite runs only single-threaded. However, we compared it against PySpark with different configurations (i.e., single CPU execution, 2 CPUs, 4 CPUs, and 8 CPUs). As shown in Fig. 4, implementing *tfidf* with the proposed UDF library runs faster than Spark, not only in single-threaded mode but also if Spark runs using 2 CPUs in all data sizes. Spark achieves its best performance with 4 CPUs, where it runs faster than our single-core solution in 100K and 1M abstracts. This result indicates a potentially interesting future direction and testing as well: deployment of the proposed framework with multi-threaded DBMSs (e.g., MonetDB is also supported by YeSQL) will reap the benefits of parallel execution.

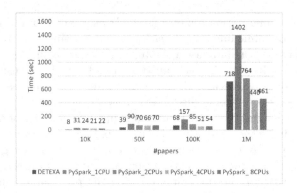

Fig. 4. Execution times of DETEXA and Spark (various parallelism) for TF-IDF

5   Conclusions

YeWe presented an efficient and extensible text analysis framework built on top of YeSQL. The DETEXA framework maps several text mining functionalities to reusable scalar, aggregate, and polymorphic table UDFs written in Python. Due to the performance characteristics of YeSQL and its design, the presented framework is able to execute faster than other popular solutions critical text mining analytical tasks. The declarative language of the DETEXA framework allows fast experimentation and implementation, as well as easy development of application interfaces. We actively concentrate on various future directions, including integration of the framework with other DBMSs that are supported by YeSQL in order to reap the benefits of multi-threaded/parallel execution, and richer interfaces to offer the opportunity to users without programming knowledge to implement and tune complex text analysis tasks.

Acknowledgements. This work is funded by EU projects OpenAIRE-Nexus (101017452) and HBP (945539). The authors would like to acknowledge Lefteris Stamatogiannakis, Mei Li Triantafillidi, Tasos Giannakopoulos and Lampros Smyrnaios for their valuable contributions in the design and implementation of the presented library.

References

1. NLTK. https://www.nltk.org
2. PySpark. https://spark.apache.org/docs/latest/api/python/
3. Dask. https://dask.org
4. Raasveldt, M., Mühleisen, H.: Vectorized UDFs in column-stores. In: Proceedings of the 28th International Conference on Scientific and Statistical Database Management (2016)
5. https://www.postgresql.org/docs/current/xfunc.html
6. https://www.vertica.com/docs/9.2.x/HTML/Content/Authoring/ ExtendingVertica/UDF-SQLFunctions/CreatingUser-DefinedSQLFunctions. htm

7. Declarative Extensible Text EXploration and Analysis (DETEXA). https://github.com/madgik/detexa
8. Foufoulas, Y., Simitsis, A., Stamatogiannakis, L., Ioannidis, Y.: YeSQL: "You extend SQL" with rich and highly per formant user-defined functions in relational databases. PVLDB (2022)
9. OpenAIRE. https://www.openaire.eu
10. Varoquaux, G., et al.: Scikit-learn: machine learning without learning the machinery. GetMob.: Mob. Comput. Commun. **19**(1), 29–33 (2015)
11. Vasiliev, Y.: Natural Language Processing with Python and SpaCy: A Practical Introduction. No Starch Press (2020)
12. Gensim text processing library. https://radimrehurek.com/gensim
13. Giannakopoulos, T., Stamatogiannakis, E., Foufoulas, I., Dimitropoulos, H., Manola, N., Ioannidis, Y.: Content visualization of scientific corpora using an extensible relational database implementation. In: Bolikowski, Ł, Casarosa, V., Goodale, P., Houssos, N., Manghi, P., Schirrwagen, J. (eds.) TPDL 2013. CCIS, vol. 416, pp. 101–112. Springer, Cham (2014). https://doi.org/10.1007/978-3-319-08425-1_10
14. tfidf algorithm. https://www.kaggle.com/code/xfffrank/tfidf-stemming/notebook

The Way We Cite: Common Metadata Used Across Disciplines for Defining Bibliographic References

Erika Alves dos Santos[1] ⓘ, Silvio Peroni[2,3(✉)] ⓘ, and Marcos Luiz Mucheroni[4] ⓘ

[1] Fundação Jorge Duprat Figueiredo de Segurança e Medicina do
Trabalho (Fundacentro), São Paulo, Brazil
erika.santos@fundacentro.gov.br
[2] Research Centre for Open Scholarly Metadata, Department of Classical Philology and Italian
Studies, University of Bologna, Bologna, Italy
silvio.peroni@unibo.it
[3] Digital Humanities Advanced Research Centre (/DH.arc), Department of Classical Philology
and Italian Studies, University of Bologna, Bologna, Italy
[4] School of Communication and Arts (ECA), Department of Information and Culture (CBD),
University of São Paulo, São Paulo, Brazil

Abstract. Current citation practices observed in articles are very noisy, confusing, and not standardised, making identifying the cited works problematic for humans and any reference extraction software. In this work, we want to investigate such citation practices for referencing different types of entities and, in particular, to understand the most used metadata in bibliographic references. We identified 36 types of cited entities (the most cited ones were articles, books, and proceeding papers) within the 34,140 bibliographic references extracted from a vast set of journal articles on 27 different subject areas. The analysis of such bibliographic references, grouped by the particular type of cited entities, enabled us to highlight the most used metadata for defining bibliographic references across the subject areas. However, we also noticed that, in some cases, bibliographic references did not provide the essential elements to identify the work they refer to easily.

Keywords: Bibliographic references · Citations · Publication metadata · Publication types · Citation behaviours

1 Introduction

Citations are fundamental tools to track how science evolves over time [1]. Indeed, citation networks are the instruments that link scientific thinking, forming a complex chain of documents related to each other that enables the highlighting of research trends within the various scholarly disciplines. The creation of such a network is possible thanks to the effort that authors and publishers invest in preparing particular elements of their articles: the bibliographic references. Bibliographic references are the means for creating conceptual citation links between a citing and cited entities and carry an

G. Silvello et al. (Eds.): TPDL 2022, LNCS 13541, pp. 120–132, 2022.
https://doi.org/10.1007/978-3-031-16802-4_10

important function: providing enough metadata to facilitate an agent (whether a human or a machine) to identify the cited works. Thus, providing precise bibliographic metadata of cited works is crucial for enabling citation networks to satisfactorily and efficiently contribute to the intellectual exchange among researchers.

Despite the massive number of citation style manuals released in the past years that have had the goal of providing standardised approaches to the definition of bibliographic references (and, in particular, their metadata), some prior studies, such as [12] and [7], have shown how the current citation practices are very noisy, confusing, and not standardised at all. For instance, several disciplinary journals often avoid adopting standardised citation style manuals and define their own (yet another) citation style [3]. This considerable heterogeneity in the adoption of citation guidelines, combined with the variability of the types of cited works (and, thus, of related metadata) that may include articles, datasets, software, images, green literature, etc., makes the identification of the cited works problematic for humans and also (and in particular) for any reference extraction software used for building bibliographic metadata repositories and citation indexes.

In this work, following prior studies we run on similar topics [7, 8], we want to investigate existing citation practices by analysing a huge set of articles to measure which metadata are used across the various scholarly disciplines, independently from the particular citation style adopted, for defining bibliographic references. In particular, we want to answer the following research questions (RQ1–RQ3):

1. Which entities are cited by articles published in journals of different disciplines?
2. What is the standard metadata set used across such disciplines for describing cited works within bibliographic references?
3. Is there any mechanism in place (i.e. hypertextual links) to facilitate the algorithmic recognition of where a bibliographic reference is cited in the text?

The rest of the paper is organised as follows. In Sect. 2, we introduce some related works concerning our research. In Sect. 3, we present the material and methods we have used for performing our analysis. Section 4 introduces the results of our analysis, which are discussed in Sect. 5. Finally, in Sect. 6, we conclude the paper by sketching out some future works.

2 Related Works

In the past, several works addressed studies and analyses of bibliographic references from different perspectives. One of the essential works in the area is authored by Sweetland [12]. In his work, he highlighted the functions conveyed by bibliographic references and citation style manuals and the errors in the reference lists and in-text citations that represent a crucial issue for accomplishing such functions. In particular, he identified the use of a great variety of formats for referencing cited articles that increased the chances of misunderstanding referencing guidelines proposed by the journals, which, consequently, contributes to the high errors in bibliographic metadata description. A recent study we performed [7], run against a larger corpus of journal articles and bibliographic references and used as starting point of the work presented in this paper, confirmed that many of the concerns highlighted by Sweetland are in place still today, thus showing that the situation has not changed in the past 32 years.

Some mistakes identified in bibliographic references may be conveyed by limited clarity in describing particular publication types cited in articles. Indeed, depending on the type of the cited works, metadata of bibliographic references may change a lot: from *author(s), year of publication, article title, journal name, volume, issue, page numbers*, typical of journal articles, to *author(s), year of publication, article title, complete title proper of proceedings volume in which it occurs, statements of responsibility for the proceedings, series statement, place, publisher* and *page numbers*, typical of conferences [11]. However, sometimes, journal citation styles fail to address all the possible publication types cited by the authors of a citing article [7].

One study introduced by Heneberg [2], among the most relevant ones focussing on the analysis of specific disciplines, analysed the percentage of uncited publications that were not journal original research articles or reviews authored by scientists in Mathematics, Physiology and Medicine who either received Fields medals or were Nobel laureates. He discovered that the most significant part of these uncited publications listed in Web of Science (WoS) was mainly editorial material, progress reports (e.g. abstracts presented at conferences), and discussion-related publications (e.g. letters to the editor). Only a small number of research articles and reviews in journals were left uncited, thus highlighting how the types of the publications seemed to be a relevant characteristic which explained, at least to a certain extent, why part of the works of even influential authors are not cited at all.

In another work, Kratochvíl et al. [3] analysed the declared referencing practices of 1,100 journals in the biomedical domain. They discovered that, even if there exist still today several citation guidelines for biomedical research, a considerable number of biomedical journals preferred to adopt their own style and that the most essential metadata used when referencing cited works were *author(s), cited work title*, and *year of publication*. However, helpful metadata (e.g. *DOI*), recognised from the answers to more than 100 surveys the authors performed, were not included in several of the citation styles adopted by the journals in the corpus analysed.

Other studies have concerned the analysis of citations to specific kinds of publications, e.g. data (in a broader sense, i.e. including datasets and software). For instance, Park *et al.* [5] analysed hundreds of biomedical journals to measure the number of *formal* citations to data (i.e. specified by including a bibliographic reference describing them) against the *informal* citations (i.e. mentions contained within the text of an article, e.g. by simply adding their URL). They highlighted how informal citations to data were the most adopted approach due mainly to the absence of explicit requirements by the publisher to correctly add them as bibliographic references (showing an inadequate citation type coverage in the citation styles adopted) and, in part, to the limited familiarity of the authors when dealing with formal citations to data. Indeed, several studies, such as [4], stressed that mastering citation styles is a complex activity and that there is a need to reflect on (and even redesign) citation styles to address current citation habits.

3   Materials and Methods

The articles from which we have extracted the bibliographic references to analyse for this study were obtained from a selection of the journals included in the SCImago Journal & Country Rank (https://www.scimagojr.com/). Following a methodology we defined, which is introduced with more details in [10] and that has been already success-fully adopted in previous studies [7, 8], we first selected the most cited journals in each of the 27 subject areas listed in SCImago in the 2015–2017 triennium according to the SCImago total cites ranking. We grouped these subject areas in five macro categories: *Health Sciences* [H] (including the subject areas *Medicine* [S1], *Nursing* [S2], *Veteri-nary* [S3], *Dentistry* [S4], *Health Professions* [S5]), *Social Sciences and Humanities* [S] (including *Arts and Humanities* [S6], *Business, Management and Accounting* [S7], *Decision Sciences* [S8], *Economics, Econometrics and Finance* [S9], *Psychology* [S10] and *Social Sciences* [S11]), *Life Sciences* [L] (including *Agricultural and Biological Sciences* [S12], *Biochemistry, Genetics and Molecular Biology* [S13], *Immunology and Microbiology* [S14], *Neuroscience* [S15], *Pharmacology, Toxicology and Pharmaceutics* [S16]), *Physical Sciences* [P] (including *Chemical Engineering* [S17], *Chemistry* [S18], *Computer Science* [S19], *Earth and Planetary Sciences* [S20], *Energy* [S21], *Engineer-ing* [S22], *Environmental Science* [S23], *Materials Science* [S24], *Mathematics* [S25], and *Physics and Astronomy* [S26]), and *Multidisciplinary* [M] (including the subject area *Multidisciplinary* [S27] mainly involving big magazine and journals). The sample we obtained was the proportional representation of each subject area at SCImago Rank-ing in terms of dimension. We included only one journal from each publisher under the same subject area to avoid having, under the same subject area, journals sharing similar editorial policies.

Each journal in the sample was represented by five articles (in PDF format) published in the most recent issue (excluding special issues that sometimes adopt diversified journal policies for referencing) published between October 1st and October 31st, 2019. For journals not releasing any issue in this period, the sample considered the immediately previous issue published before October 1st. For issues containing more than five articles, the selection adopted a probabilistic systematic random sampling technique based on the average number of articles published by the journal in the period mentioned above. As for the journals containing less than five articles, the sample considered all those attending the selection criteria described in detail in [10].

Starting from such sample, we considered the total of 34,140 bibliographic references composing the bibliographic references lists of the selected 729 articles (172 in Health Sciences, 191 Social Sciences and Humanities, 114 in Life Sciences, 232 in Physical Sciences, and 20 in Multidisciplinary) which were analysed to detect the types of the cited works in each discipline and the structure of bibliographic references for each type of cited work, considering different reference styles' formatting guidelines. In particular, we identified the descriptive elements (introduced in Table 1) adopted for the bibliographic references for each type of cited work.

Table 1. Kinds of metadata retrieved in the bibliographic references analysed.

Title	Series statement
1. Chapter title	34. Conference date
2. Chapter title in English (when original title is in another language)	Identifier for manifestation
3. Conferences' title	35. Abstract number
4. Journals' title (abridged format)	36. Article ID within publisher's webpage
5. Journals's title (full format)	37. Article number part note
6. Journals's title in English (for titles in other languages)	38. Chapter number
7. Newspaper/magazine title	39. ISBN number
8. Proceedings' title	40. Paper number
9. Session title	41. Patent number
10. Works' subtitle in original language	42. Technical report number
11. Works' title in original language	43. Work number
12. Works's title in English (when original title is in another language)	44. Work number within the conference
Statement of responsibility	45. Working paper number
13. Author full name	**Carrier type**
14. Chapter author	46. Content type/media type/carrier type (general material designation in AACR2)
15. Proceedings' editor	**Extent**
16. Translator	47. Abridged work pagination length (e.g. 80–9)
17. Work's author or editor	48. Mentioned excerpts pages range (e.g. 80–89)
Edition statement	49. Work's first page number (e.g. 80)
18. Edition number	50. Work full pagination length (e.g. 80–89)
19. Issue number	51. Work's total number of pages (e.g. 80 p.)
20. Revision number	**General notes**
21. Version number	52. Work's language note
22. Volume number	53. Supplemental issue note
Numbering of serials	54. Special issue note
23. Series number	55. Supplementary content note
Publication statement	56. General notes
24. Conference date	57. Unpublished note

(*continued*)

Table 1. (*continued*)

25. Conference place	58. In press note
26. Date of citation (date of access)	59. Database system number
27. Date of last update/revision	**Online availability notes**
28. Day of publication	60. Hypertext hyperlink (URL)
29. Month of publication	61. DOI string or DOI URL
30. Place of publication	62. Online availability note
31. Proceedings date of publication	63. Institutional link (university department)
32. Publisher (or granting institutions for thesis and dissertations)	**Miscellaneous**
33. Year or date of publication	64. Latin expression "in" (i.e. for book chapters or conference papers in a proceedings)

Such descriptive elements were classified according to the Resource Description & Access (RDA) core elements (https://www.librarianshipstudies.com/2016/03/rda-core-elements.html). In addition, we also analysed all the in-text reference pointers – e.g. "(Doe et al., 2022)" and "[3]" – denoting all the bibliographic references in our sample to see how many of them are accompanied by a link pointing to the related bibliographic reference they denote.

4 Results

All the data gathered in our analysis are available in [9]. In the first stage of the analysis we considered all the 34,140 bibliographic references composing our sample, that we used to identify the following different kinds of publications (RQ1): articles [a], books and related chapters [b], manuscripts [c], technical reports and related chapters [d], web-pages [e], proceeding papers [f], conference papers [g], grey literature [h], data sheets [i], forthcoming chapters [j], forthcoming articles [k], unpublished material [l], standards [m], working papers and preprints [n], e-books and related chapters [o], newspapers [p], online databases [q], web videos [r], patents [s], software [t], manuals/guides/toolkits [u], personal communications [v], book series [w], other kinds of publications (includ-ing memorandum, governmental official publications, legislation, informative materi-als, audio records, motion pictures, speeches, photographs, slide presentation, podcasts, engravings, lithography and television shows) [y], and unrecognised publications [z].

As summarised in Table 2, articles, books (and their chapters), and proceeding papers were the first, second and third most cited types of publications across all the sub-ject areas. The same seven types of publications corresponded to at least 50% of the total bibliographic references in each subject area, namely articles (83.55%), books and their chapters (7.93%), proceeding papers (2.53%), webpages (1.30%), technical reports (1.17%), working papers and preprints (0.67%) and conference papers (0.51%). However, these types did not comprise some other publication kinds cited by specific disciplines. For instance, grey literature is the eighth most cited type of work across all subject areas (0.47% of total bibliographic references). Still, it is the third most cited type of publication in arts and humanities articles (S6) and the fourth most cited type in chemical engineering (S17), decision sciences (S8) and mathematics (S25) articles. Thus, considering only the most cited types of publications overall does not properly represent the actual citing habits across the subject areas since some subject areas (e.g. social sciences – S11) tend to cite a greater variety of types of publications while others (e.g. dentistry – S4) only a few types. In addition, as highlighted in Table 2, the types of publications supporting discussions across subject areas may vary.

To understand the variability of the metadata for defining bibliographic references across the macro areas, we decided to select the seven most cited types of publications in each subject area to assure that the analysis coverage includes the most cited types of publications from the subject areas' perspective. After this selection, all the types of publications in Table 1 were considered except manuscripts (c), forthcoming chapters (j), web videos (r), other kinds (y) and unidentified types of publications (z).

The 33,786 bibliographic references concerning such most significant types of publications were individually analysed to identify their descriptive elements (i.e. metadata) according to those introduced in Table 1. We have tracked all the bibliographic elements appearing in the bibliographic references of our sample, and we marked all the elements specified in at least one bibliographic reference of at least 50% of the articles composing each subject category. Finally, we have computed the most used descriptive elements for each type of publication mentioned above by considering each macro area's most used descriptive elements. In practice, a descriptive element was selected if it was one of the most used in all the macro areas. The result of this analysis is summarised in Table 3 (RQ2).

In the last part of our analysis, we identified if the in-text reference pointers – e.g. "(Doe et al., 2022)" or "[3]" – included in all the articles of our sample are hypertextually linked to the respective bibliographic references they denote (RQ3). The result of such analysis is shown in Fig. 1.

5   Discussion and Lessons Learnt

The data in Table 2 suggest that articles are the most used channel to communicate scientific findings across all the subject areas. However, books were observed among the three most cited types of publications in all disciplines considered in our sample. In addition, we observed considerable variability in the types of publications cited by the articles composing our sample – we found 36 different types of publications within disciplines. Such variety suggests and reveals some citing habits across disciplines. For instance, we noticed a considerable portion of bibliographic references for which we could not identify which type of publication is referred to (columns "z" in Table 2), considering the data provided in the bibliographic references. This suggests that either reference styles adopted by the journal were unclear or did not provide enough instructions on describing certain types of publications. We could also speculate that part of these issues derived from the lack of attention that authors and publishers sometimes put when writing/revising bibliographic references; however, this aspect should be investigated in more detail.

Table 2. All the different kinds of publications (a–z, as defined in the text) cited by the various subject areas (column S, S1–S27 as defined in Sect. 3) grouped in macro areas (column A, values as defined in Sect. 3). The colours of the squares represent the proportion of citations from the citing articles of S1–S27 to the a–z publication kinds, described as follows:

■ >80%, ■ >60%, ■ >40%, >20%, >10%, ■ >5%, >1%, >0%

A	S	a	b	c	d	e	f	g	h	i	j	k	l	m	n	o	p	q	r	s	t	u	v	w	y	z
	S1																									
	S2																										
H	S3																										
	S4																										
	S5																										
	S6																										
	S7																										
S	S8																										
	S9																										
	S10																										
	S11																										
	S12																										
	S13																										
L	S14																										
	S15																										
	S16																										
	S17																										
	S18																										
	S19																										
	S20																										
P	S21																										
	S22																										
	S23																										
	S24																										
	S25																										
	S26																										
M	S27																										

Still looking at the results in Table 2, it seemed that some disciplines, e.g. the humanities and social sciences, cited many publication types. This suggests that the discussions on such disciplines demand more comprehensive approaches. Second, reference styles adopted by such disciplines should provide more extensive guidelines for describing citing and referencing data, i.e. they should provide instructions on describing a greater variety of publications. The lack of specific guidelines for describing uncommon types of publications across disciplines, such as lithographs and engravings (which appeared in some social sciences articles), contributes to the number of unidentifiable bibliographic references mentioned above.

Despite the existence of thousands of reference styles and standards to guide the use and interpretation of bibliographic metadata uniformly, we observed (Table 3) that the representation of the information is approached differently across subject areas and, in general, macro areas: the same type of publication may have different descriptions in

Table 3. Most used metadata in bibliographic references – the numbers identify the kinds of metadata as introduced in Table 1. H: Health Sciences, S: Social Sciences and Humanities, L: Life Sciences, P: Physical Sciences, M: Multidisciplinary, A: average.

Articles	Books	Book chapters	
H 4,11,17,22,33,50	H 11,17,18,30,32,33	H 1,11,14,17,30,32,33,48,64	
S 5,11,17,19,22,33,50	S 11,17,30,32,33	S 1,11,14,17,30,32,33,48,64	
L 4,11,17,22,33,36,50	L 11,17,30,32,33	L 1,11,14,17,30,32,33,48,64	
P 4,11,17,22,33,50	P 11,17,30,32,33	P 1,11,14,17,30,32,33,48,64	
M 4,11,17,22,33,36 50	M 11,17,32,33	M 1,11,14,17,30,32,33,38,48,64	
A 11,17,22,33,50	**A 11,17,32,33**	**A 1,11,14,17,30,32,33,48,64**	

Technical reports	Webpages	Proceeding papers	
H 4,11,17,22,33,50	H 11,17,26,60	H 3,11,17,33,48,64	
S 5,11,17,19,22,33,50	S 11,17,33,60	S 8,11,17,30,32,33,48,64	
L 4,11,17,22,33,36,50	L 11,17,33,60	L 8,11,17,32,33,48,64	
P 4,11,17,22,33,50	P 11,17,33,60	P 8,11,17,32,33,48,64	
M 4,11,17,22,33,36,50	M 11,17,60	M 3,8,11,17,32,33,48,64	
A 11,17,22,33,50	**A 11,17,60**	**A 11,17,33,48,64**	

Conference papers	Grey literature	Data sheets	Technical rep. chapters
H 3,11,17,33	H 11,17,30,32,33,46	H No citations	H 1,11,14,22,30,32,33,60
S 3,11,17,25,33	S 11,17,32,33,46	S No citations	S 1,11,14,30,32,33
L 3,11,17,25,33	L 11,17,30,32,33,46	L No citations	L No citations
P 3,11,17,25,33	P 11,17,30,32,33,46	P 11,32,33	P No citations
M No citations	M No citations	M No citations	M No citations
A 3,11,17,33	**A 11,17,32,33,46**	**A 11,32,33**	**A 1,11,14,30,32,33**

Forthcoming articles	Unpublished	Standards	Working papers
H 4,11,17,33,58,61	H No citations	H No citations	H 11,17,26,30,32,33,60
S 5,11,17,58	S 11,17,33,57	S 11,17,33	S 11,17,33,45,60
L 4,11,17,22,29,33,58,60	L No citations	L 11,17,30,33	L 11,17,26,33,61
P 4,11,17,33,58	P 11,17,32,33,57	P 11,17,18,33,51	P 11,17,33,60
M No citations	M No citations	M No citations	M 11,17,32,33,60
A 11,17,58	**A 11,17,33,57**	**A 11,17,33**	**A 11,17,33**

E-books	Newspapers	Online databases	
H 11,17,30,32,33	H No citations	H 11,17,21,26,33,60	
S 11,17,30,32,33	S 7,11,17,28,33,60	S 11,17,32,33,60	
L 11,17,26,30,32,33,60	L No citations	L 11,17,21,33	
P 11,17,18,26,33,39,60,61	P No citations	P 11,17,21,32,33,46,60,61	
M No citations	M No citations	M No citations	
A 11,17,33	**A 7,11,17,28,33,60**	**A 11,17,33**	

E-books chapters	Patents	Software	
H 1,11,14,17,30,32,33,48	H 11,17,33,41	H 11,17,30,32,33	
S 1,11,17,30,32,33,64	S No citations	S 11,17,30,32,33,46	
L No citations	L 11,17,33,41,46	L 11,17,21,26,30,32,33,60	
P 1,11,14,17,26,33,60,64	P 11,17,30,33,41,48	P 11,17,21,33,60	
M No citations	M 11,17,33,41,60	M No citations	
A 1,11,17,33	**A 11,17,33,41**	**A 11,17,33**	

Manual/guides/toolkits	Personal communications	Book series	
H 11,17,30,32,33,60	H 11,17,30,32,33,60	H 1,14,19,22,32,33,34,47,49,61	
S 11,17,30,32,33	S 11,17,28,33,46,60	S No citations	
L 11,17,32,33	L No citations	L No citations	
P 11,17,21,32,33	P No citations	P 1,14,19,22,32,33,34,49,61	
M No citations	M No citations	M No citations	
A 11,17,32,33	**A 11,17 33,60**	**A 1,14,19,22,32,33,34,49,61**	

different disciplines. This may suggest a failure of reference styles' purposes concerning their role in standardising bibliographic references on a large scale.

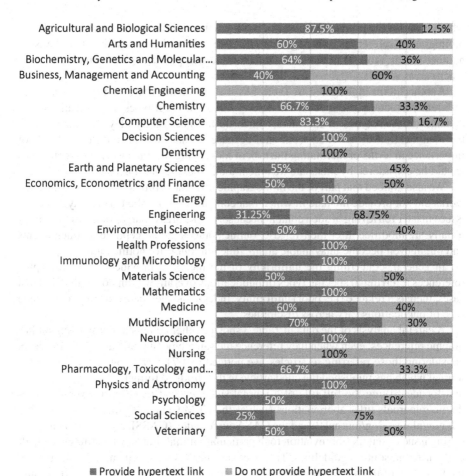

Fig. 1. Distribution of articles per subject area providing in-text reference pointers – e.g. "(Doe et al., 2022)" and "[3]" – hypertextually linked to the bibliographic references denoted.

For instance, among their various purposes, bibliographic references act like sources of information and, from this perspective, the efforts to provide (at least) the necessary metadata for the proper identification of the referred publications are worthwhile and essential as a means for retrieving the cited works in external sources, such as bibliographic catalogues and bibliographic databases. However, we noticed that such kinds of metadata were not always provided. Even if the title of the cited works (11 in Table 3) is one of the most used metadata across all the macro areas, we observed that bibliographic references in some articles did not always provide it. For instance, in 27% of articles from Physical Sciences, we noticed that bibliographic references pointing to web pages did not provide the title of the cited work. At the same time, they include a URL or a persistent identifier (e.g. DOI) to enable accessing the cited publication. Indeed, in some cases, the article's title itself is not a mandatory element for allowing its retrieval (e.g. if a DOI is present). However, it is a crucial element to correctly identify the cited work, which is one of the primary purposes of bibliographic references. Similarly, considering bibliographic references referring to articles, we observed that metadata like the issue number (19 in Table 3) in which the cited article was published were omitted in most macro areas.

Another point highlighted in Table 3 is that different publication types may have different characteristics. Indeed, the description of different types of publications may demand different types of metadata, which do not necessarily play the same role in the identification of the cited work and, because of that, may have different levels of importance in terms of facilitating the task of identifying the cited work and such issues should be considered by metadata treatment tools, like the ontologies.

We also noticed that part of the bibliographic references providing URLs to the cited works did not provide the date in which that content was consulted. This may represent issues in later retrieving of such content because, unlike press sources of information that usually are modified after their release, online sources are susceptible to amendments and might even become unavailable at any time without prior notification.

In general, concerning the uniformity of the metadata provided by bibliographic references referring to specific types of publications overall, we can notice that, in most cases, there is a relative (i.e. poor) uniformity. Indeed, the metadata referring to the same type of publications vary across disciplines.

A careful analysis of the data in Table 3 showed other deficits in normalising bibliographic references, even when they reference the same type of publication. For instance, considering those referring to articles, we noticed that 71.59% provide the title of the journal which has published the cited article in the abridged format. This may be a problem for identifying the full title of a journal since, even if there exist several sources defining journals titles abbreviations such as the NLM Catalog (https://www.ncbi.nlm.nih.gov/nlmcatalog/journals/) and the CAS Source Index (CASSI, https://cassi.cas.org), the big issue is that the abbreviation for a particular journal title may be different considering different sources guidelines. This may have negative consequences for the precise identification of the referred journal and, consequently, for its retrieval. Thus, to ensure the correct interpretation (also in the context of computational approaches), the journal title abbreviation should be accompanied by the indication of the source on which it was based.

By analysing the most used metadata (rows "A" in Table 3), we can observe that bibliographic references usually dismiss important elements that help readers identify the cited works. For instance, the DOI is not included in the most used metadata in the bibliographic references referring to articles, as the ISBN is not part of the most used metadata in the bibliographic references referring to books and book chapters.

Overall, the most used metadata gathered are enough, in general, to identify the publications the bibliographic references refer to. We did notice some peculiar situations, however. The most used metadata for proceedings do not comprise the title of the proceedings in which the cited work was published nor the title of the conference in which the cited work was presented, even if these kinds of metadata were indeed used in the macro areas: Health Sciences and Multidisciplinary included the title of the conference (3), while Social Sciences, Life Sciences, Physical Sciences and, again, Multidisciplinary included the title of the proceedings (8).

For some publication types – i.e. software (t); manual, guides and toolkits (u), data sheets (i), standards (m) and personal communications (v) – we noted that bibliographic references do not provide any information concerning the nature of the document (i.e. the "general material designation in AACR2", carrier type, point 46, in Table 1). The description of less-traditional types of publications – i.e. those except articles, books, and other similar textual publications – requires a clear indication of the type of publication being cited for allowing its immediate identification from the metadata provided in bibliographic references. For instance, grey literature usually provides a short note like "master thesis" or "doctoral thesis", which enables the reader to understand the format of the cited work immediately.

The links between in-text reference pointers and the bibliographic references they denote (RQ3) are helpful tools to formalise the connections between the text of the citing article (i.e. the sentences including the in-text reference pointers, the related paragraphs and sections) and the correspondent cited works referenced by the bibliographic references. Around 49% of the articles in our sample provide such a feature (Fig. 1). Indeed, having such mechanisms in place simplifies, in principle, the development of computational tools to track where cited works are referred to in the text of the citing articles, thus facilitate the computational recognition of citation sentences [6] and, by analysing these, of citation functions [13], i.e. the reason an author cites a cited work – because it reuses a method defined in the cited work, because it either agrees or disagrees with concepts and ideas introduced in the cited works, etc.

However, 51% of the articles did not specify such links, which is a barrier to identifying the position where a citation is defined in the text. Of course, one could use natural language processing tools and other techniques to retrieve the in-text reference pointers referring to bibliographic references in the text, but this is made complex by the heterogeneity of the formats used to write bibliographic references and in-text reference pointers, as highlighted in [7].

Finally, it is worth mentioning that our analysis is not free from limitations. For instance, we considered only one type of publication for the citing entities, i.e. journal articles. Indeed, since they represent the main types of publication cited across all the subject areas, at least according to our analysis, they should be a reasonable sample acting as a proxy of the entire population of the citing publications in all the subject areas considered. However, it would be possible that different publication types of citing articles may convey different citation behaviours. We leave this analysis to future studies.

6   Conclusions

This work has focussed on presenting the results of an analysis of 34,140 bibliographic references in articles of different subject areas to understand the citing habits across disciplines and identify the most used metadata in bibliographic references depending on the particular type of cited entities. In our analysis, we observed that the bibliographic references in our sample referenced 36 different types of cited works. Such a considerable variety of publications revealed the existence of particular citing behaviours in scientific articles that varied from subject area to subject area. In the future, further investigation should be performed to understand, for instance, why software was not listed among the most cited type of works in Computer Science while being one of the main topics discussed in several areas of Computer Science research.

Acknowledgements. This work was partly conducted when Erika Alves dos Santos was visiting the Department of Classical Philology and Italian Studies, University of Bologna. The work of Silvio Peroni has been partially funded by the European Union's Horizon 2020 research and innovation program under grant agreement No 101017452 (OpenAIRE-Nexus).

References

1. Fortunato, S., et al.: Science of science. Science **359**(6379), eaao0185 (2018). https://doi.org/10.1126/science.aao0185
2. Heneberg, P.: Supposedly uncited articles of Nobel laureates and fields medalists can be prevalently attributed to the errors of omission and commission. J. the Am. Soc. Inf. Sci. Technol. **64**(3), 448–454 (2013). https://doi.org/10.1002/asi.22788
3. Kratochvíl, J., Abrahámová, H., Fialová, M., Stodůlková, M.: Citation rules through the eyes of biomedical journal editors. Learn. Publ. **35**(2), 105–117 (2022). https://doi.org/10.1002/leap.1425
4. Lanning, S.: A modern, simplified citation style and student response. Ref. Serv. Rev. **44**(1), 21–37 (2016). https://doi.org/10.1108/RSR-10-2015-0045
5. Park, H., You, S., Wolfram, D.: Informal data citation for data sharing and reuse is more common than formal data citation in biomedical fields. J. Am. Soc. Inform. Sci. Technol. **69**(11), 1346–1354 (2018). https://doi.org/10.1002/asi.24049
6. Rotondi, A., Di Iorio, A., Limpens, F.: Identifying citation contexts: a review of strategies and goals. In: Cabrio, E., Mazzei, A., Tamburini, F.: In Proceedings of the Fifth Italian Conference on Computational Linguistics (CLiC-It 2018), CEUR Workshop Proceedings, vol. 2253. CEUR-WS, Aachen, Germany. http://ceur-ws.org/Vol-2253/paper11.pdf (2018)
7. Santos, E.A.d., Peroni, S., Mucheroni, M.L.: An analysis of citing and referencing habits across all scholarly disciplines: approaches and trends in bibliographic metadata errors (2022). https://doi.org/10.48550/arxiv.2202.08469
8. dos Santos, E.A., Peroni, S., Mucheroni, M.L.: Citing and referencing habits in medicine and social sciences journals in 2019. J. Doc. **77**(6), 1321–1342 (2021). https://doi.org/10.1108/JD-08-2020-0144
9. Santos, E.A.d., Peroni, S., Mucheroni, M.L.: Raw and aggregated data for the study introduced in the paper "The way we cite: common metadata used across disciplines for defining bibliographic references" (2022). https://doi.org/10.5281/zenodo.6586859
10. Santos, E.A.d., Peroni, S., Mucheroni, M.L.: Workflow for retrieving all the data of the analysis introduced in the article "Citing and referencing habits in Medicine and Social Sciences journals in 2019" (2020). https://doi.org/10.17504/protocols.io.bbifikbn
11. Smiraglia, R.: Referencing as evidentiary: an editorial. Knowl. Organ. **47**(1), 4–12 (2020). https://doi.org/10.5771/0943-7444-2020-1-4
12. Sweetland, J.H.: Errors in bibliographic citations: a continuing problem. Libr. Q. **59**(4), 291–304 (1989). https://doi.org/10.1086/602160
13. Teufel, S., Siddharthan, A., Tidhar, D.: Automatic classification of citation function. In: Proceedings of the 2006 Conference on Empirical Methods in Natural Language Processing (EMNLP '06), vol. 103. Association for Computational Linguistics, Sydney, Australia (2006). https://doi.org/10.3115/1610075.1610091

Event Notifications in Value-Adding Networks

Patrick Hochstenbach[1,2]([✉]) [iD], Herbert Van de Sompel[2,3] [iD],
Miel Vander Sande[4,5] [iD], Ruben Dedecker[2] [iD], and Ruben Verborgh[2] [iD]

[1] Ghent University Library, Ghent University, Ghent, Belgium
[2] IDLab, ELIS, Ghent University - IMEC, Ghent, Belgium
{Patrick.Hochstenbach,Herbert.VandeSompel,Ruben.Dedecker,
Ruben.Verborgh}@UGent.be
[3] DANS, Data Archiving and Networked Services, The Hague, The Netherlands
[4] Meemoo, Vlaams Instituut voor het Archief, Ghent, Belgium
Miel.VanderSande@meemoo.be
[5] Dutch Digital Heritage Network, The Hague, The Netherlands

Abstract. Linkages between research outputs are crucial in the scholarly knowledge graph. They include online citations, but also links between versions that differ according to various dimensions and links to resources that were used to arrive at research results. In current scholarly communication systems this information is only made available post factum and is obtained via elaborate batch processing. In this paper we report on work aimed at making linkages available in real-time, in which an alternative, decentralised scholarly communication network is considered that consists of interacting data nodes that host artifacts and service nodes that add value to artifacts. The first result of this work, the "Event Notifications in Value-Adding Networks" specification, details interoperability requirements for the exchange real-time life-cycle information pertaining to artifacts using Linked Data Notifications. In an experiment, we applied our specification to one particular use-case: distributing Scholix data-literature links to a network of Belgian institutional repositories by a national service node. The results of our experiment confirm the potential of our approach and provide a framework to create a network of interacting nodes implementing the core scholarly functions (registration, certification, awareness and archiving) in a decentralized and decoupled way.

Keywords: Scholarly communication · Digital libraries · Open science

1 Introduction

In the 2004 paper "Rethinking Scholarly Communication" [1], Van de Sompel et al. introduced the perspective of an open scholarly communication system in which decentralized service hubs add value to research outputs hosted in repositories by fulfilling the core functions of scholarly communication - registration, certification, awareness, archiving [2] - in a decoupled manner and in

© Springer Nature Switzerland AG 2022
G. Silvello et al. (Eds.): TPDL 2022, LNCS 13541, pp. 133–146, 2022.
https://doi.org/10.1007/978-3-031-16802-4_11

ways they see fit. The fact that value of a certain kind was added was intended to be openly exposed and, as such, would support creating bidirectional linkages between resources jointly involved in a life-cycle event, such as a preprint and a review thereof, an article and a copy of it in a long-term archive, etc. The authors understood that, in order for such an environment to be feasible, "the service hubs needed to be interconnected, as if they were part of a global scholarly communication workflow system".

A similar perspective is at the basis of the more recent "Linked Research on the Decentralized Web" [3] and COAR's "Next Generation Repositories report" [4] but remains in sharp contrast with the status quo. The scholarly communication system does not provide real-time life-cycle information. To a large extent, linkages between related research outputs are revealed by means of post-factum, heuristic-bound mining processes across research output corpora (e.g., Cabernac et al. efforts to discover preprint/publication links [5]), that are so laborious that only the happy few can consider providing them as production services.

This paper introduces the "Event Notifications in Value-Adding Networks" [6] specification, which is a first step towards realizing the ability to expose life-cycle information for research outputs in real-time and hence to reveal linkages as they become known. In the network (see Fig. 1) considered by the specification, service nodes add value to artifacts hosted by data nodes and the nodes exchange messages with that regard: a data nodes asks a service node to add value to one of its artifacts, and the service node responds with information about the service result; a service node volunteers information about value it unilaterally added to an artifact hosted by a data node. For example, a researcher can request that a research output be peer-reviewed via a certification service or directly by selected peers; she can request that a search engine include

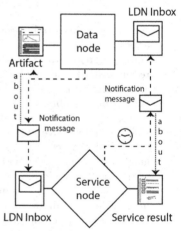

Fig. 1. Data nodes and service node exchanging notification messages.

the research output in its index; she can ask an archive to collect the output and store it for posterity; a service can inform the researcher that her research output was leveraged by another endeavor; a peer can inform the researcher about a new annotation made to the research output. In the scholarly realm, the nature of the added value crucially includes fulfilling the core functions of scholarly communication. But, while scholarly communication was the main driver for the specification, it is conceived in a generic way and allows for a wide range of added-value as well as applications in other domains such as cultural heritage.

The messages between the autonomous systems that operate on the network are point-to-point, owing to its decentralized nature. The "Event Notifications in Value-Adding Networks" specification details interoperability regarding the messaging protocol and the communication payloads that are essential to allow the envisioned network to be functional.

Our specification effort is generally motivated by the Decentralized Web [7] movement that emerged in reaction to the disconcerting evolution of the Web towards an environment in which a limited number of portals have become dominant, control personal data, and monetize online presence information as a product. Similar concerns exist in scholarly communication (e.g. [8–10]), with consolidation of services that cover the entire research life-cycle and publishers turning into data analytics companies. Decoupling content hosting from service provision yields a separation between ownership, control, and storage of data on the one hand, and the functionality that can provided on top of it, on the other. It levels the playing field to allow for new entrants and creativity.

The remainder of this paper is structured as follows. Section 2 discusses related work. Our ongoing standards-based specification work is discussed in Sect. 3. Section 4 reports on an experiment in which data-literature links are pushed towards the repositories that host the resources involved in such links in a manner that complies with the specification. Section 5 provides a summary and an outlook for future work.

2   Related Work

With dokie.li [11], Capadisli introduced the use of Linked Data Notifications [12] (LDN) with ActivityStreams2 [13] (AS2) payloads as a push-oriented interoperability glue for communication among researchers that publish research outputs in personal data pods and with services that add value to these outputs. His approach provided inspiration for the Researcher Pod [14] and COAR Notify [15] projects.

The Researcher Pod project, funded by the Andrew W. Mellon Foundation, explores a scholarly communication system based on the Decentralized Web vision of Tim Berners-Lee [16] as was envisioned by Capadisli [3] and Van de Sompel [17]. A Researcher Pod network is highly decentralized: each researcher publishes research outputs in a personal data pod [18,19] that is hosted in a personal web domain. Value is added to these research outputs through interaction with appropriate decoupled services and/or peers. The Researcher Pod network uses LDN and AS2 as core interoperability ingredients, but the AS2 payloads are strictly profiled in order to avoid ambiguous interpretation of notifications. Our "Event Notifications in Value-Adding Networks" specification is one of the outcomes of this project.

In COAR Notify, the network consists of repositories and providers of overlay review services. A core goal of the project is establishing bidirectional links between preprints and certifications thereof (e.g., stand-alone reviews, endorsements, peer-reviewed articles) as soon as the latter get published. Our specification work is closely aligned with COAR Notify to which we actively contribute, uses the same interoperability ingredients, but has a broader scope regarding what constitutes added value and in which communities the specification can be used.

ScholeXplorer [20], based on the Scholix framework [21,22], is a centralized approach to exchange life-cycle information about research outputs, focused on the discovery of research data-literature links. Scholix was partly motivated by the lack of interoperability among various approaches for the point-to-point exchange of data-literature links that had resulted from numerous bilateral agreements [23]. It introduced an approach in which a limited number of hubs, including Crossref, DataCite, and OpenAIRE collect and mine linkage information from a variety of scholarly and web corpora. The hubs support retrieving the link information, which is uniformly expressed according to a link information package schema [24]; no specific protocol for transporting these packages is selected. ScholeXplorer collects the link information from the hubs and makes it available by means of a query-oriented API allowing, for example, a repository to recurrently poll ScholeXplorer in search of linkages in which its resources are involved. Our specification details an approach that allows expressing and exchanging data-literature (and other) links in a push-oriented, point-to-point manner that leverages W3C standards. Conceptually, it aims to provide the capability to broadcast linkage information directly between the systems that host the artifacts as soon as a link is established. This in contrast with the Scholix framework that needs to wait for scholarly artifacts to be published, harvested and released in batches, months after the artifact creation date.[1]

3   The Value-Adding Network

3.1   Design and Technology Considerations

The Value-Adding Network approach utilizes a *point-to-point* communication style, avoiding the need for centralized hubs that can eventually become too powerful to remain trustworthy and too big to fail. The approach is *push-oriented*, with only the relevant nodes being updated about new information as soon at it becomes available. In the highly distributed Value-Adding Network set-up, a pull-oriented approach would introduce a hardly tractable "which node to pull" challenge in addition to the well-known "when to poll" conundrum. Interactions are necessarily *asynchronous* owing to the fact that the time between requesting a service and providing a service is unpredictable and could range between almost immediate (e.g., provide a trusted timestamp) to months (e.g., provide a peer-review report).

The communication patterns in the Value-Adding network are *action-oriented*. The patterns express *when* an activity was initiated, acknowledged, or yielded a result (See Sect. 3.3). The internal workflow of *how* the activity was executed is treated as a black box. As such, message payloads contain only core information (in most cases URL identifiers) to convey in which value-adding activities data nodes, service nodes, and artifacts are involved and what the service results are. The assumption is that further information about the entities involved is available by using their identifiers in auto-discovery mechanisms supported by protocols such as Signposting [25], WebID [26], Solid [27], and Hydra [28]. As such, message payloads can be expressed in a *by reference* rather than *by value* style.

---

[1] See for example https://scholexplorer.openaire.eu/#/statistics for an overview of ScholeXplorer batch frequencies.

Several candidate protocols exist that could meet the point-to-point, push-oriented, and asynchronous design choices, including WebHooks [29], Webmention [30], and Linked Data Notifications [12]. Webhooks, while commonly used, is not formally standardized and does not have a natural tie-in with specific serializations and/or vocabularies. Webmention is uni-directional and, as such, can't be used off-the-shelf for a request-response communication style. Moreover, it does not actually allow transmitting messages and rather merely informs the target resource that the sender resource mentions (links to) it. We chose for Linked Data Notifications in combination with the ActivityStreams 2.0 vocabulary, both W3C standards. That combination was successfully used in the dokie.li work, and has proven to work at scale with ActivityPub [31] implementations that provide a communication channel for millions of users on social networks such as Mastodon [32].

3.2 A Network of Data Nodes and Service Nodes

In a scholarly Value-Adding Network, artifacts are research outputs hosted by Data Nodes, while Service Nodes are systems that add value to these research outputs. Both types of node are essentially web servers that host one or more LDN Inboxes where Notifications can be received. An LDN Inbox is an HTTP endpoint associated with a web server to which notifications can be POSTed. Our specification describes how a value-added service can be triggered by sending an appropriate notification to LDN Inbox of a service node. And it describes how the outcome of providing a value-adding service for an artifact, the Service Result, can be communicated to a data node's LDN Inbox by means of a notification. The notification patterns and payload are discussed in Sect. 3.3 and Sect. 3.4, respectively.

The manner in which value-added services are provided is not in scope of our specification. The internal workflows of a service node is considered as a black box yet could be openly exposed on the basis of other specifications. How nodes, or better the agents that operate on behalf of the nodes, act upon receipt of a notification is also out of scope of our specification. For instance, the notifications could be added to a queue for further processing, e.g., to update the metadata of an artifact, or to write life-cycle information in an Event Log [33] that is made accessible to support the creation of scholarly knowledge graphs that cover artifacts across data nodes.

3.3 Network Communication Patterns

At this point, our Value-Adding Network specification details two communication patterns: a one-way pattern and a request-response pattern.

One-Way Pattern. This pattern is used when the agent that operates on behalf of a node sends an unsolicited message about an artifact. One-way patterns are used for sending informational messages pertaining to an artifact to another node in the network. These messages can originate from a data node or a service node. Examples of one-way patterns are:

- A repository (data node) informs a subject index (service node) about a new artifact.
- A linkage service (service node) informs a repository (data node) about a discovered linkage between a hosted data set artifact and a publication.

Request-Response Pattern. This pattern allows agents that act on behalf of a data node to ask a service node to apply a value-added service to one of its artifacts. There is no expectation of an immediate response but definitely the expectation of an eventual response. The pattern doesn't assume there is only one response (or request) but introduces a communication thread (similar to email threads) which will be used to relate notifications to each other. An example of a request-response pattern is:

- A repository (data node) would like a peer review for one of the artifacts and therefore contacts a peer review service (service node) to provide this service. The peer review service can first evaluate the request and acknowledge or reject it. When acknowledged, a peer review can be made available at a later date, and a reference to this peer review can be sent back in a notification to the repository.

3.4   Anatomy of a Notification Message

Notifications are exchanged in order to inform agents about added-value that is requested or was provided for artifacts. Network agents send and receive the notifications, data and service nodes provide LDN Inboxes to accept incoming messages. Value-Adding Networks uses a subset of the ActivityStreams 2.0 vocabulary [13] serialized as JSON-LD [34] payloads. The LDN protocol requires all the payloads to be expressed by default as JSON-LD, but other RDF serializations are allowed. For brevity, all examples in this paper use Turtle syntax [35]. We refer to our specification for further JSON-LD examples.

Every notification has at least one AS2 type that is a subset of the `as:Activity` types. The subtypes are limited to those that express facts about artifacts and currently exclude types related to typical social activities (such as `as:Like`, `as:Follow`). The subtypes used are:

- Activities to request or receive notifications about value adding services: `as:Announce`, `as:Offer`, `as:Accept`, `as:Reject`, and `as:Undo`
- Activities that express CRUD (*Create,Update,Delete*) life-cycle event on data nodes: `as:Create`, `as:Update`, and `as:Remove`.

In addition to the activity types listed above, an activity may have additional subtypes that are specific to an application domain. For instance, when a service node would like to use `as:Announce` for the endorsement of a publication an extra `schema:EndorseAction` could be added as activity type.

Table 1 shows the mapping between AS2 entities and the Value-Adding Network entities that are used for the notification shown in Listing 1, which illustrates a typical notification that uses the **one-way pattern** from a service node to a data node. In it, an agent at the end of the service node uses the `as:Announce` activity type to inform an agent at the end of a data node about the result of adding value to one of the latter's hosted artifacts. In human language, the notification expresses the following: "Fairfield Archive (service node) announces to Springfield Library (data node) a service result concerning Springfield's artifact https://springfield.library.net/artifact/13-02.html. For this artifact, the https://fairfield.org/archive/version/317831-13210 is a memento".

Table 1. One-way AS2 pattern for notification messages from a service node to a data node.

AS2 element	Description
id	Message identifier
type	Activity type
as:actor	Agent that performed the activity
as:origin	Agent responsible for sending the notification
as:context	The artifact on the data node for which an value-added service was provided
as:object	The result of the value-added service provided for an artifact on the data node
as:target	The agent at the data node that is the addressee of the notification

```
@prefix as: <https://www.w3.org/ns/activitystreams#> .
@prefix ldp: <http://www.w3.org/ns/ldp#> .

<urn:uuid:239FD510-03F4-4B56-B3A0-0D3B92F3826D> a as:Announce ;
   as:actor    <https://fairfield.org/about#us> ;
   as:origin   <https://fairfield.org/system> ;
   as:context  <https://springfield.library.net/artifact/13-02.html> ;
   as:object   <urn:uuid:CF21A499-1BDD-4B59-984A-FC94CF6FBA86> ;
   as:target   <https://springfield.library.net/about#us> .

<https://fairfield.org/about#us> a as:Organization ;
   ldp:inbox <https://fairfield.org/inbox> ;
   as:name "Fairfield Archive" .

<https://fairfield.org/system> a as:Service;
   as:name "Fairfield Archive System".

<urn:uuid:CF21A499-1BDD-4B59-984A-FC94CF6FBA86> a as:Relationship ;
   as:object <https://fairfield.org/archive/version/317831-13210> ;
   as:relationship <https://www.iana.org/memento> ;
   as:subject <https://springfield.library.net/artifact/13-02.html> .

<https://springfield.library.net/about#us> a as:Organization;
   ldp:inbox <https://springfield.library.net/inbox/> ;
   as:name "Springfield Library" .
```

Listing 1. A value-adding Activity Streams 2.0 notification using Turtle syntax

4   Experimental Investigation

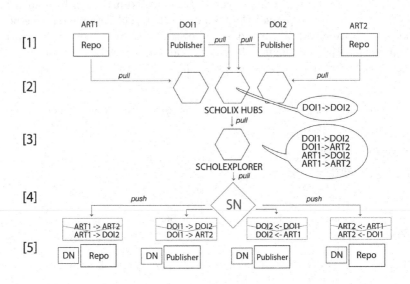

Fig. 2. Scholix network with an added national service node.

The COAR Notify project has already illustrated the feasibility of real-world use of profiled LDN/AS2 notifications in a request-response pattern between repositories and certification services. We set up an experiment to investigate the one-way pattern where a service node informs a network of data nodes about the *linkages* its artifacts are involved in. We leverage the existing Scholix link base which provides an extensive collection of such linkage information.

In the Scholix network, data-literature linkages are provided via a limited number of hubs such as DataCite, CrossRef and OpenAIRE ([2] in Fig. 2). that obtain information from systems that host research outputs ([1] in Fig. 2). ScholeXplorer ([3] in Fig. 2) is an aggregation service that collects link information from the hubs and makes the result linkages available as a dataset at an irregular frequency. ScholeXplorer can be polled to discover data-literature links between research outputs hosted in the systems covered by the hubs. For our experiment, we prototype a national service NatServ ([4] in Fig. 2) that queries ScholeXplorer for data-literature links in which artifacts hosted by Belgian institutional repositories are involved, and that pushes the link information to the relevant repository according to the Value-Adding Network approach. Using the terminology of that specification, NatServ is a service node that pushes link information to data nodes associated with the institutional repositories ([5] in Fig. 2). Figure 2 also shows the research outputs identified by ART1, DOI1, DOI2, ART2 hosted by a variety of repositories. The hubs pull information about these artifacts, and as a result of data processing, determine that DOI1 is related to DOI2. ScholeXplorer pulls such linkage information from all hubs and further discovers that DOI1 is a manifestation of ART1 and DOI2 is a manifestation of ART2. Finally, our prototype NatServ (SN) pulls data-literature links pertaining to selected repositories from ScholeXplorer and pushes the information using profiled LDN/AS2 notifications to the LDN Inboxes of data nodes associated with the pertinent repositories, e,g, the data node at the left bottom receives information that its ART1 is related to ART2 and DOI2.

4.1   Experiment

We downloaded Scholix data for the following Belgian repositories: *Institutional Repository Universiteit Antwerpen* (Antwerpen), *Ghent University Academic Bibliography* (Biblio) and *Open Repository and Bibliography - University of Liège* (Orbi). These downloads resulted in 711 records for Antwerpen, 1056 for Biblio, and 669 for Orbi. Between May 10 and May 25 2022, we also tried to download Scholix data for the KU Leuven *Lirias* repository and the Vrije Universiteit Brussel *Vrije Universiteit Brussel Research Portal* repository. Although hundreds of Scholix records are available that indicate linkages in which their research outputs are involved, none contained actual URLs of those artifacts.[2] Since these URLs are needed for the remainder of the experiment, we excluded the Scholix records for these repositories. At the time of writing, our communication with ScholeXplorer representatives have not led to an explanation for this problem.

Discovery of LDN Inboxes. With NatServ in possession of the linkages in which artifacts of the three repositories are involved, its next step is to discover the data nodes and associated LDN Inboxes to which linkage information needs to be pushed. The goal is to push the information to the systems that host source as well as target of the links. Since we assume auto-discovery mechanisms for the discovery of pertinent Inboxes, this requires dereferencing the URLs of the all artifacts (expressed in Scholix as PID-URLs, e.g. DOI[3], HANDLE[4], PMID[5], PMC[6] and ARXIV[7] up to their landing pages and extracting the link with http://www.w3.org/ns/ldp#inbox Link relation from its HTTP header.[8] The URL derferencing process is less trivial than it may seem [36] and we employed the simplest possible algorithm by following for each link identifier all the HTTP redirects until a page with a HTTP 200 response was found. Obviously, no LDN Inboxes were found because none of the systems involved in linkages currently support Value-Adding Networks, but the excercise remains important as a means to understand the effort that would be involved if they did.

---

[2] see e.g. https://gist.github.com/phochste/4d6ed7f7748c5d74417ac45d38480540.
[3] Digital Object Identifier https://doi.org.
[4] Handle identifier http://hdl.handle.net.
[5] PubMed Identifier https://pubmed.ncbi.nlm.nih.gov.
[6] PubMed Central https://www.ncbi.nlm.nih.gov/pmc/.
[7] arXiv Identifier https://arxiv.org).
[8] See https://www.w3.org/TR/ldn/#discovery.

Table 2 provides an overview of the complete resolved data-literature link network for each Belgian institution: this is the network of all data-literature links involving artifacts hosted by the institutional repositories. For instance, if one institutional artifact references ten datasets, then this is a network of 10+1 artifact URLs.

Table 2. Number of artifact URLs resolved for the data-literature network of each Belgian institution and time required to resolve PID-URLs to their landing page.

Scholix link provider	#Records	# Artifact URLs	#Resolve time (sec)	Time/req
Antwerpen	711	4335	695	0.978 ± 0.01 s
Biblio	1056	7189	3651	3.457 ± 0.02 s
Orbi	669	3375	367	0.549 ± 0.02 s

To proceed with the experiment, we created LDN Inboxes for all systems that host artifacts involved in the linkages, using a Solid CSS server as proxy of LDN Inboxes.[9] We created the inboxes at addresses generated as follows `https://{data.host}/inbox` where `data.host` is the base url of the landing page. For example, the LDN Inbox URL: https://arxiv.org/inbox will be hosted at: `http://solidpod-baseurl/arxiv.org/inbox` where `solidpod-baseurl` is the base URL of the Solid CSS server.

With Solid CSS, the implementation of LDN Inboxes doesn't require any fundamental changes in institutional repositories to add read-write capabilities to an existing network. In our experiment effortless created hundreds of LDN Inboxes given the fact that: 1) LDN is a subset of the Solid protocol stack [18], and, 2) an LDN Inbox can be put on any node as long at it can be discovered from the artifact landing page.

In total, 197 [Antwerpen], 245 [Biblio], and 193 [Orbi] LDN Inboxes were created to cover the data-literature network of the institutions.

Generating Notification Messages. Next, we use the guidelines from our specification for sending data about a linking event to transform a ScholeXplorer data-literature link into a profiled LDN/AS2 payload.[10] The generated payloads are nimble (see snippet in Listing 2) because we assume that further information pertaining to entities involved can be obtained via auto-discovery mechanisms. The ActivityStreams 2.0 Activity `as:Relationship` is used to express a relationship between two artifacts and the mapping that was used is shown in Table 3.[11]

---

[9] https://github.com/CommunitySolidServer/CommunitySolidServer.

[10] https://www.eventnotifications.net/#pattern-5-a-service-node-notifies-a-data-node-about-linking-event.

[11] The full Turtle representation of the notification message is available online https://gist.github.com/phochste/afdc7bc5d6a09cec2b12c60755ef1c82.

Table 3. One-way AS2 mappings for notification messages in the Scholix experiment.

AS2 element	Description
as:actor	We minted the WebID https://scholexplorer.openaire.eu/#about
as:origin	We minted the WebID https://mellonscholarlycommunication.github.io/about#us
as:context	Points to the artifact URL on the target data node the data-literature link is about
as:object	Contains the description data-literature link. An example such a data-literature link description is shown in Listing 2
as:target	This contains the generated (or discovered) LDN Inbox for each data-literature link

```
1    <urn:uuid:240c0091-b271-4e44-87f7-5598da5b24ad>
2      a as:Relationship ;
3      as:object <https://dx.doi.org/10.5061/dryad.10hq7> ;
4      as:relationship <http://www.scholix.org/References> ;
5      as:subject <https://biblio.ugent.be/publication/8646849> .
```

Listing 2. Snippet of the **as:object** of data-literature notification.

Sending Notifications to LDN Inboxes. For each institution, we sent the generated notifications to the simulated LDN Inboxes of all systems for which artifacts are involved in links either as source and target. This doubles the number of messages that is provided in Table 2. For instance, if one artifact A references two data sets B and C, then we send two messages for A: A references B, A references C. To B we can send: A references B. To C we can send A references C. In total four messages.

Table 4 shows the number of messages that were posted and the typical throughput that is not dependent on the payload of the message.

The generated inboxes and the notifications that were sent to them can be downloaded at Zenodo[12]. The software to download and transform Scholix into AS2 notifications and to publish notifications to LDN Inboxes is available at GitHub.[13] All experiments were run on a 2 CPU, 1 GB, Linux host connected to the Belnet research network.

Table 4. Sending LDN Notifications for the complete network of three Belgian institutions. The mean posting time for these networks have a constant rate of about 80 notifications per second.

Scholix link provider	# Sent notifications	#Post time (sec) & Time/req
Antwerpen	8670	108 s, 80 req/s
Biblio	14378	183 s, 78 req/s
Orbi	6720	86 s, 78 req/s

---

[12] https://zenodo.org/record/6555821.

[13] https://github.com/MellonScholarlyCommunication/scholix-client.

5   Summary and Outlook

Our work demonstrated how the introduction of decentralized read-write technology on top of existing research networks provides a push-based mechanism to provide up-to-date information of life-cycle events pertaining to artifacts that are stored in the network. In our case, the network was applied to the distribution of data-literature links by an experimental national NatSev service node (built on top of ScholeXplorer) to data nodes in the network. These experiments demonstrate how the service node could be able to inform a network of institutional repositories about data-literature links using push-based LDN Notifications.

The scalability of the distribution of data-literature links in the Scholix experimental network is dependent the time it takes to resolve PID-URLs to the landing pages of the artifact. Even with our naive resolve algorithm, which doesn't employ any optimization strategies, the complete Belgian national data-literature network for all known linkages could be distributed within two hours on a small Linux host.

Our Scholix experiment was dependent on data mining capabilities of centralized Scholix hubs. The real goal of a distributed Value-Added Network is for linkages to be mined (or cataloged), and sent from the repository that hosts an artifact that is the source of a link to a repository that hosts the artifact of is the target of that link. Research in our Researcher Pod project has already been started to explore how data-mining capabilities can be added to Value-Added networks via orchestration [37].

With our small sample of Scholix providers, we could already create for three Belgian institutions a network with $197 + 245 + 193$ data nodes. It would be a bright future for the decentralisation of scholarly communication when all linkage information could be made available in real-time (instead of months after a long publication and review process) and point-to-point instead of requiring a few massive central hubs and gateways. The question how this can be accomplished in a repository landscape that has hardly invested in interoperability affordances since the broad adoption of OAI-PMH [38] in the early 2000s.

Our hope is that COAR's "Next Generation Repositories" vision will get a broader uptake. Important steps are taken in the COAR Notify project with the first concrete implementations that make profiled LDN/AS2 notifications a reality for communication between repositories and review services. Arcadia has recently recommended a 4 year, US\$4 million grant [39] to accelerate COAR Notify enhancing the role of repositories, thereby transforming scholarly communications, making it more research-centric, community-governed, and responsive to the diverse needs across the globe.

Acknowledgements. This work is funded by the Andrew W. Mellon Foundation (grant number: 1903-06675) and supported by SolidLab Vlaanderen (Flemish Government, EWI and RRF project VV023/10). The authors would like to thank the COAR Notify (Kathleen Shearer, Paul Walk, Martin Klein) for involving them from the outset, allowing them to provide input and gain valuable insights for their generic specification effort.

References

1. Van de Sompel, H., Payette, S., Erickson, J., Lagoze, C., Warner, S. : Rethinking scholarly communication. D-Lib Mag. **10**(9) (2004). https://www.dlib.org/dlib/september04/vandesompel/09vandesompel.html
2. Roosendaal, H., Geurt, P.: Forces and functions in scientific communication: an analysis of their interplay (1998) https://perma.cc/5HYM-BEKF. Accessed 3 June 2019
3. Capadisli, S.: Linked research on the decentralised web (2020) https://csarven.ca/linked-research-decentralised-web
4. Rodrigues, E., et al.: Next generation repositories: behaviours and technical recommendations of the COAR next generation repositories working group. Zenodo (2017). https://doi.org/10.5281/zenodo.1215014
5. Cabanac, G., Oikonomidi, T., Boutron, I.: Day-to-day discovery of preprint-publication links. Scientometrics **126**(6), 5285–5304 (2021). https://doi.org/10.1007/s11192-021-03900-7
6. Hochstenbach, P., Vander Sande, M., Dedecker, R., Walk, P., Klein, M., Van de Sompel, H.: Event notifications in value-adding networks (2020). https://www.eventnotifications.net. Accessed 14 July 2022
7. Berners-Lee, T : Socially aware cloud storage (2009). https://www.w3.org/DesignIssues/CloudStorage.html
8. Pooley, J.: Surveillance publishing. Elephant in the Lab (2022). https://doi.org/10.5281/zenodo.6384605
9. Siems, R.: Das Lesen der Anderen: die auswirkungen von user tracking auf bibliotheken. O-Bib. Das Offene Bibliotheksjournal/Herausgeber VDB **9**(1), 1–25 (2022) https://doi.org/10.5282/o-bib/5797
10. Posada, A., Chen, G.: Inequality in knowledge production: the integration of academic infrastructure by big publishers. In: ELPUB 2018, Toronto, Canada, June 2018. https://dx.doi.org/10.4000/proceedings.elpub.2018.30
11. Capasidli, S.: Dokieli. https://dokie.li
12. Capadisli, S., Guy, A.: Linked data notifications. W3C recommendation (2017) https://www.w3.org/TR/ldn/
13. Snell, J., Prodromou, E.: Activity streams 2.0. W3C recommendation (2017) https://www.w3.org/TR/activitystreams-core/
14. Scholarly Communications in the Decentralized Web. https://mellon.org/grants/grants-database/grants/ghent-university/1903-06675/. Accessed 20 May 2022
15. The Notify Project. https://www.coar-repositories.org/notify/. Accessed 20 May 2022
16. Berners-Lee, T.: https://www.w3.org/DesignIssues/Principles.html
17. Van de Sompel, H.: Scholarly communication: deconstruct & decentralize? https://www.youtube.com/watch?v=o4nUe-6Ln-8
18. Sambra, A.V., et al.: Solid: a platform for decentralized social applications based on linked data. Technical report, MIT CSAIL & Qatar Computing Research Institute (2016). http://emansour.com/research/lusail/solid_protocols.pdf
19. Mansour, E., et al.: A demonstration of the solid platform for social web applications. In: Proceedings of the 25th International Conference Companion on World Wide Web, pp. 223–226 (2016). https://dl.acm.org/doi/10.1145/2872518.2890529
20. La Bruzzo, S., Manghi, P. : OpenAIRE ScholeXplorer service: Scholix JSON dump (5.0) [data set]. Zenodo (2022) https://doi.org/10.5281/zenodo.6338616

21. Burton, A., et al. : The Scholix framework for interoperability in data-literature information exchange. D-Lib Mag. **23**(1/2) (2017) http://www.dlib.org/dlib/january17/burton/01burton.html

22. Burton, A., et al.: On bridging data centers and publishers: the data-literature interlinking service. In: Garoufallou, E., Hartley, R.J., Gaitanou, P. (eds.) MTSR 2015. CCIS, vol. 544, pp. 324–335. Springer, Cham (2015). https://doi.org/10.1007/978-3-319-24129-6_28

23. Callaghan, S., Tedds, J., Lawrence, R., Murphy, F., Roberts, T., Wilcox, W.: Cross-linking between journal publications and data repositories: a selection of examples. Int. J. Digit. Curation (2014). https://doi.org/10.2218/ijdc.v9i1.310

24. Scholix metadata schema for exchange of scholarly links. http://www.scholix.org/schema. Accessed 24 May 2022

25. Signposting the Scholarly Web. https://signposting.org. Accessed 20 May 2022

26. W3C. WebID. https://www.w3.org/wiki/WebID. Accessed 25 May 2022

27. Capadisli, S., Berners-Lee, T., Verborgh, R., Kjensmo, K. : Solid protocol version 0.9.0, 17 December 2021. https://solidproject.org/TR/protocol. Accessed 25 May 2022

28. Lanthaler, M.: Hydra core vocabulary. W3C Unofficial Draft (2021). https://www.hydra-cg.com/spec/latest/core/

29. Webhooks - The Definitive Guide (2022). https://webhook.net. Accessed 20 May 2022

30. Parecki, A. : Webmention. W3C recommendation (2017). https://www.w3.org/TR/webmention/

31. Lemmer-Webber, C., Tallon, J., Shepherd, E., Guy, A., Prodromou, E.: Activity-Pub. W3C recommendation (2019). https://www.w3.org/TR/activitypub/

32. Giving social networking back to you - Mastodon. https://joinmastodon.org. Accessed 20 May 2022

33. Vander Sande, M., Hochstenbach, P., Dedecker, R., Werbrouck, J.: Artefact lifecycle event log (2022). https://mellonscholarlycommunication.github.io/spec-eventlog/

34. Sporny, M., Longley, D., Kellogg, G., Lanthaler, M., Champin, P.A., Lindström, N.: JSON-LD 1.0. W3C recommendation (2014). https://www.w3.org/TR/json-ld/

35. Beckett, D., Berners-Lee, T., Prud'hommeaux, E., Carothers, G. : RDF 1.1 turtle. W3C recommendation (2014). https://www.w3.org/TR/turtle/

36. Klein, M., Balakireva, L.: On the persistence of persistent identifiers of the scholarly web. In: Hall, M., Merčun, T., Risse, T., Duchateau, F. (eds.) TPDL 2020. LNCS, vol. 12246, pp. 102–115. Springer, Cham (2020). https://doi.org/10.1007/978-3-030-54956-5_8

37. Vander Sande, M., Hochstenbach, P., Dedecker, R., Werbrouck, J.: Orchestrator for a decentralized Web network. Working Draft, 26 November 2021 (2021). https://mellonscholarlycommunication.github.io/spec-orchestrator/

38. Lagoze, C., Van de Sompel H., Nelson, M., Warner, S.: The open archives initiative protocol for metadata harvesting. Protocol Version 2.0 of 2002-06-14 (2015). http://www.openarchives.org/OAI/openarchivesprotocol.html

39. COAR. COAR welcomes significant funding for the Notify Project. https://www.coar-repositories.org/news-updates/coar-welcomes-significant-funding-for-the-notify-project/. Accessed 25 May 2022

A Chromium-Based Memento-Aware Web Browser

Abby Mabe, Michael L. Nelson(iD), and Michele C. Weigle[✉](iD)

Old Dominion University, Norfolk, VA 23529, USA
amabe002@odu.edu, {mln,mweigle}@cs.odu.edu

Abstract. Current web browsers do not differentiate between the live Web and the past Web. If a user loads an archived webpage, or *memento*, they have to rely on elements in the page itself to be aware that they are not viewing a live webpage. Another problem is that browser bookmarks only save the URL of a webpage. But if the webpage is deleted or changed, the user may have lost access to the very information that they had wanted to save. We present a proof-of-concept Memento-aware Browser, built on Google's Chromium open-source web browser. We add native memento detection that displays an icon when the user is visiting an archived webpage and a "bookmark as archive" feature that allows users to request archiving of individual webpages when they are bookmarked.

Keywords: Web browser · Web archiving · Memento · Bookmarks

1 Introduction

Archiving the Web has become increasingly important. Archived webpages, or *mementos* [37], allow users to go back in time on the Web and view webpages as they used to appear. One way to view mementos is by using a web browser to visit a web archive, such as the Internet Archive [12] or Archive.today [5]. We rely on web browsers to allow us to safely and securely navigate the Web. Web browsers process information about a webpage as it loads and present us with appropriate user interface (UI) cues and messages, keeping us aware of important information about the webpages we are viewing. For example, browsers can detect if a connection is secure and warn us when a website is potentially unsafe. However, unlike displaying HTTP status or blocking web trackers, web browsers do not have native support for indicating that a displayed webpage is a memento. Because of this, the user has to look for visual cues on the page itself or inspect the browser's address bar to see if the webpage they are viewing is from the past or live Web. As web archiving becomes more known by the general public, web browsers should natively provide mechanisms for users to be aware of and interact with archived webpages.

We have built a *proof-of-concept* Memento-aware Web Browser, based on Google's Chromium open-source browser [29]. Prior work has focused on building browser extensions [14,27], but extensions depend on the user choosing to install

© Springer Nature Switzerland AG 2022
G. Silvello et al. (Eds.): TPDL 2022, LNCS 13541, pp. 147–160, 2022.
https://doi.org/10.1007/978-3-031-16802-4_12

and activate the extension. Only users who already know about web archives would be likely to install a browser extension related to web archiving. With this work we wanted to demonstrate the feasibility of native browser support, in the same idiom that browsers currently convey significant metadata about what they display. With such a capability in browsers, web archives could gain even more visibility with the general public. We are not advocating that users switch to a new browser, but exploring what could be enabled if current popular browsers included such capabilities. We have added memento detection with UI additions to notify the user when they are viewing an archived webpage. We have also added a "bookmark as archive" feature that allows users to request that the page they are bookmarking be archived by a public web archive. This proof-of-concept browser is available for download in a GitHub repo [20] and more details on the implementation are available in a tech report [19].

2   Background

Memento [37] is an HTTP protocol extension that allows for content-negotiation in the time dimension, essentially providing HTTP-level mechanisms for accessing archived webpages. A web archive that is Memento-compliant will return Memento headers in the HTTP response. For our purposes, the key header is Memento-Datetime (e.g., `Memento-Datetime: Mon, 12 Apr 2010 12:50:57 GMT`), which indicates the datetime when the resource was captured. Web archives only return this header for archived resources.

In the Memento framework, the identifier of an original resource from the live Web is a *URI-R* and the identifier of an archived version of that resource at a particular point in time is a *URI-M*. Many web archives construct URI-Ms that include the Memento-Datetime and the URI-R, such as https://web.archive.org/web/20100412125057/http://www.mitre.org/. In this example, the Memento-Datetime is represented by the 14-digit date string 20100412125057 and the URI-R is http://www.mitre.org/. Not all web archives use this type of URI-M construction, so we will use the presence of the Memento-Datetime HTTP header as an indication that the resource is a memento.

Within the Chromium browser, HTTP response header information for all resources on a page makes up the Security State for that page. Included in the Security State is information about whether the page contains any insecure (HTTP) content and if the user should be presented with the HTTPS secure lock icon or the "Not Secure" warning. We used the method for displaying the security icon as a template for adding a Memento icon to Chromium.

3   Related Work

There have been several browser extensions developed for interacting with web archives. Sanderson et al. [27] describe the MementoFox Firefox plugin that allowed users to navigate in the past Web, an Internet Explorer plugin providing the same functionality, and Memento Browser app for Android mobile devices that allowed users to view only mementos, but not the live Web. Nelson et al. [22,23] describe a Google Chrome extension for navigating to mementos. Mink [14] is another Chrome extension that allowed users to survey all of the available mementos for a web page and provided a feature to add live web pages to public web archives. Tweedy et al. [33] developed a Memento Web Browser for iOS mobile devices. The Internet Archive has developed extensions [9,13] for Chrome, Firefox, Edge, and Safari, but these only provide mementos from the Internet Archive. All of these tools provide valuable features and demonstrate the usefulness of being able to interact with the past Web, but they all require the user to install an extension to a browser or install a separate app from the user's standard mobile web browser. Our goal is to demonstrate how memento-aware UI elements could be integrated into a standard web browser, without having to use an extension. The Internet Archive has collaborated with Brave to integrate automatic links to the Wayback Machine on 404 pages [10], but this is not a fully Memento-aware browser implementation.

In addition to providing navigation in the past Web, some of the extensions also allow users to submit webpages for archiving from the browser [13,14]. This feature is also something that we support, but again, our goal is to show how this could be integrated into a standard browser without an extension.

4   Memento Detection and Icon Display

The first step to creating a Memento-aware Browser is to be able to reliably detect archived resources. As mentioned in Sect. 2, we use the presence of the Memento-Datetime HTTP header to indicate that a resource is a memento. For most web archives, this is trivial as the root HTML page is a memento and includes the Memento-Datetime HTTP header. But some archives include the root memento as an iframe inside a live webpage. In addition, we want to also detect when root mementos load resources from the live Web. Here we discuss these three scenarios.

4.1   Detection of Root Page Memento

The first memento detection possibility to consider is when the entire root webpage is archived and considered to be a memento. In this case, we want the browser to classify the webpage as a memento and alert the user that the page is archived and not live. We cannot accomplish this by looking at the URI of the webpage alone since, as mentioned in Sect. 2, there is no single defined format for a URI-M. Instead, we parse the HTTP response headers and look for the Memento-Datetime HTTP header to determine if the webpage is a memento.

When the browser detects that a root webpage is a memento, the Memento icon plus the datetime in YYYY-MM-DD format will appear to the left of the HTTPS secure lock icon, as shown in Fig. 1.

Fig. 1. If the root page is considered to be an archived page, the Memento icon will display along with the Memento-Datetime in YYYY-MM-DD format.

The user can click on the Memento icon for more information about the archived page as shown in Fig. 2, similar to the operation of the HTTPS secure lock icon to bring up the connection popup for more connection security information.

4.2 Detection of Mementos Embedded in a Live Page

It is possible that a live root webpage could contain one or more embedded frames with archived content. Most commonly this occurs when the root webpage contains an iframe that loads an archived webpage. There are two different scenarios where this may occur.

First, the iframe memento may be intended to make up the whole webpage. In this case, the root page should be considered a memento even though the HTTP response for the root page does not contain the Memento-Datetime header. Web archives such as Trove [32] and Perma.cc [25] display archived web-

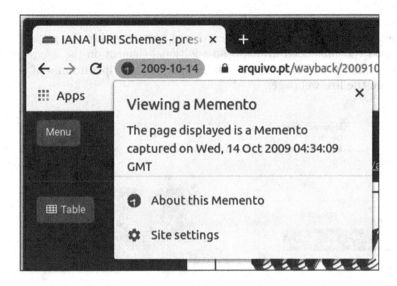

Fig. 2. The user can click the memento icon to view the exact memento datetime.

pages in this manner. Figure 3 shows this case translated into a tree structure where the root webpage is the root node and the memento iframe is the child node. The Memento-aware Browser will detect the datetime from the headers of the archived content in the iframe, detect that the iframe is formatted to make up the entire page, and then promote the frame's Memento-Datetime to the root. In this case, the Memento icon and Memento-Datetime will display in the browser just as in the root page memento case.

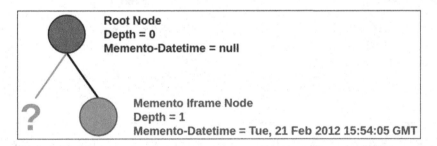

Fig. 3. Tree structure of a live root webpage from Trove containing an iframe Memento

The second case involves a live webpage that is simply displaying a memento without intending for the memento to make up the whole page. This possibility is shown in Fig. 4, where a live page has included a memento for https://www.aerogard.com.au/products/ in an iframe. This can be translated into a tree structure similar to the structure of the memento from Trove shown in Fig. 3. In this case, the browser will detect the archived content within the page, but also detect that the embedded iframe is an additional element on the live page. The browser similarly handles the case where there are multiple iframes of archived content on the live webpage.

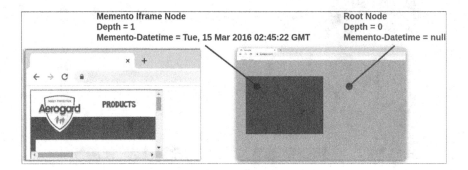

Fig. 4. Memento displayed within an iframe as an additional page element on a live webpage

When the user visits such pages, the Memento-aware Browser will display the Memento icon and show the message "Mixed archival content" instead of a YYYY-MM-DD datetime. All Memento-Datetimes will be listed in the popup that appears when the Memento icon is clicked (Fig. 5, right).

Fig. 5. The browser shows a message if the archived page contains live content (left). If the page is live and contains archived content, the browser will indicate this (right).

4.3   Detection of Live Content Embedded in a Memento

An archived iframe could contain one or more embedded elements that are displaying content from the live Web. This is a rare yet undesirable occurrence since the archived webpage is intended to present content from the past. When this occurs, it is not obvious to the user that the live Web is leaking into the archived page. Such occurrences have been called "zombies" [8] and "archive escapes" [16]. If frames within the archived content do not return the Memento-Datetime header, the user should be alerted that the archived content they are viewing contains elements from the live Web. When live content is detected in the archived page, the browser will display the message "Memento + live content" and the popup will include information for the containing archived page (Fig. 5, left).

5   Bookmark as Archive

In addition to making users aware of any archived content they are viewing, users should also be able to easily archive any live content that they want to save [38]. Since bookmarking only saves the URI of the page, if the page were to be taken down, resolving the URI would result in an HTTP 404 Not Found status. Additionally, if page remained available but the content on the webpage were to change, the content that the user originally saw and wanted to save would no longer be present. A way to make these bookmarked pages constant is through the use of public web archives. In addition to the standard bookmark functionality, the Memento-aware Browser submits the webpage for capture by a user-selected public web archive. In this way, the user has access to both the traditional live Web bookmark and a bookmark to archived content. This feature incorporates archiving into the standard bookmarking process.

To implement the "bookmark as archive" feature, we added a dropdown to Chromium's edit bookmark popup, shown in Fig. 6. The user selects the desired archive, and the browser uses ArchiveNow [6,7] to submit the request to the web archive.

When the user clicks the bookmark star icon, a standard bookmark node for the URI is created. If the user selects an archive in the edit bookmark popup, then when they exit the popup, a request will be submitted to the selected archive and a bookmark node for the archived version will be created. Processing the archiving request at the web archive can take between a few seconds to several minutes to complete. All bookmark actions run on the UI thread, and we have implemented the archiving process on the background thread since it can take several minutes to complete. Because of this, when the archiving is complete, the bookmark node cannot be updated without crashing the browser with an invalid sequence error. Instead of creating a placeholder bookmark node that links to the URI-R, a bookmark node is created that links to a special URI-M with the datetime of the time of submission. The Internet Archive's Wayback Machine and Archive.today both support URI-Ms with 14-digit date strings, as described in Sect. 2. For example, https://web.archive.org/web/20100412125057/http://www.mitre.org/ is a URI-M for an archived webpage in the Wayback Machine. If you change the date string to one for which the Wayback Machine does not have a memento, it will redirect to the memento with the closest datetime that they do have. The same is true for Archive.today. But Megalodon.jp does not

Fig. 6. The "bookmark as archive" option appears in the edit bookmark popup.

redirect to the nearest datetime, so this method cannot be used. However, once the archiving process completes, the actual URI-M is returned and added to the file `archive-urls.txt` so that it can be accessed later.

To keep bookmarks for the live Web version and archived versions together (a user may create multiple archived versions for the same URI-R), we create a bookmark folder titled with the URI-R. The original bookmark node will be placed into this folder alongside the archive bookmark node. This way, the user will see their single bookmark folder on the bookmarks bar and when they click it they will see a dropdown showing all the versions of that page they saved (Fig. 7).

Fig. 7. When the user archives a page they have bookmarked, a folder gets created to hold all the bookmark nodes that lead to that webpage, either live or archived.

To walk through the example shown in Fig. 8, say the user wanted to use the "bookmark as archive" feature to submit example.com to Archive.today on

March 10, 2021 at 4:18pm. The browser will immediately create a bookmark node folder for the webpage and place two bookmark nodes in the folder, the first being the standard bookmark that leads to the live webpage and the second bookmark node being the one for the archived version of the page. The URI-M for the archive bookmark node would be constructed using the method described above and would initially redirect to Archive.today's latest memento of example.com, which at that time would be from February 28, 2021. When the archiving process completes a few minutes later, the archive bookmark node URI-M will redirect to the newly added URI-M of example.com that was archived a few minutes after the user submitted it.

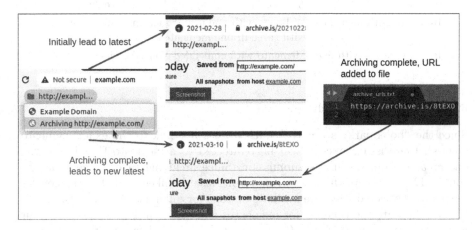

Fig. 8. The archive bookmark node will redirect to the memento in the archive that is closest to the given datetime.

6   Evaluation

6.1   Memento Detection

Memento detection was tested with the web archives and webpages shown in Table 1. Each of the tested web archives was navigated to with the browser so that memento detection could be tested. The Memento icon does not display until an actual archived page was selected, meaning the memento detection was working as expected by not displaying the icon while selecting a memento from the archive. Figure 1 shows examples of testing with four different web archives. Three of the tested archives display the root memento in an iframe meant to make up the whole webpage (Sect. 4.2), and we verified that those displayed the YYYY-MM-DD datetime along with the Memento icon. We also tested live webpages with one and three iframe mementos, and these properly displayed the "Mixed archival content" message. Finally, we tested with a memento that contained an embedded YouTube video, and the browser displayed the "Memento + live content" message.

Table 1. Memento detection evaluation

Cases	Archives/webpages tested
Root memento	Archive-It [4], Archive.today [5], Icelandic Web Archive [11], Internet Archive [12], Library and Archives Canada [17], Library of Congress [18], National Records of Scotland [21], Portuguese Web Archive [26], Stanford Web Archive [28], UK National Archives Web Archive [34], UK Parliament Web Archive [35]
Root memento in iframe	Perma Archive (Perma.cc) [25], Australian Web Archive (Trove) [32], UK Web Archive [36]
Root live with memento	Webpage with one iframe memento, webpage with three iframe mementos
Root memento with live	Memento with embedded YouTube video

6.2   Bookmark as Archive

Since the "bookmark as archive" URI-M does not link to the exact memento created, there is a chance it will be redirected to a memento that is not the one created from the user's submission. Since archiving takes some time, we could add an offset to the date string to increase the likelihood that the correct memento is selected. Here we evaluate options for different offset values.

We illustrate the timeline for mementos and offsets in Fig. 9. We show four cases, two that are successful (Case 1 and Case 3) and two that result in an incorrect memento being selected (Case 2 and Case 4). In the figure, M1 is the latest memento before the bookmark is created, t1 is the time the bookmark request is made, t1+x is the datetime used in the bookmark URI-M, with x being the offset value we are testing, and MC is when the bookmark memento is actually created. The difference between Case 1 and Case 2 is how long it takes for the archive to create the new memento. Just looking at Cases 1 and 2, we might think it best to set the offset x to be large. But we also have to consider the cases where another memento, M2, is created in the archive (by some other process) after the bookmarking process has started (Cases 3 and 4). If the offset results in the bookmark URI-M being too close to M2 (Case 4), then the incorrect memento will be selected. The archive will redirect the URI-M to the closest existing datetime, so we want to set t1+x so that in most cases, it is closer to MC than any other mementos, without knowing exactly how long the archive will take to capture the page or what other mementos exist.

To determine an appropriate offset for popular websites, we analyzed 17 TimeMaps to see how well different offsets would return the correct memento. The 17 TimeMaps were of popular news websites [24] likely to have been archived frequently. For each TimeMap, a datetime for each second between January 1, 2021 and April 16, 2021 was generated and the memento closest to that datetime was found, representing MC. Then, an offset was added to the datetime (t1+x)

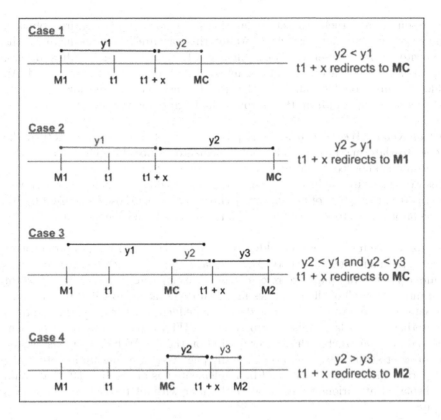

Fig. 9. Four cases of timelines for mementos and offsets for "bookmark as archive".

and the memento closest to that new datetime was found. If the memento closest to the original datetime was the same as the memento closest to the datetime plus the offset, this was counted as the offset leading to the correct memento. In this evaluation, only seconds were considered since the Memento-Datetimes have only second granularity. We tested offsets of {30, 60, 120} seconds for each of the 9 million seconds in our test period over all 17 TimeMaps. We obtained an accuracy of 99.1% with a 30-s offset, 98.4% with a 60-s offset, and 96.9% with a 120-s offset.

7   Future Enhancements

We see several features and enhancements that could be built on top of the existing features, specifically the memento detection feature since it stores the Memento-Datetimes for all resources but is currently only considering the datetime returned by the main URI.

"About This Memento" Popup. Our current implementation has a placeholder for an "About This Memento" popup that could list all the archived embed-

ded resources and their respective datetimes that make up the entire webpage, similar to the Internet Archive's "About this capture" drop-down. Since the Memento-aware Browser stores the Memento-Datetime values for all resources, implementing this feature would mainly consist of completing the front-end. An added feature would be allowing the user to click on a listing for a resource within the popup and have that resource highlighted on the page.

List of Known Web Archives. It is possible for a live webpage to return the Memento-Datetime header and spoof a memento. A possible guard against this is to only acknowledge the header if its iframe is from a known web archive. This would require the browser to have a hard-coded list of known web archives. There are existing lists of known web archives, including those recognized by the MemGator memento aggregator [3], TimeTravel [31], and Webrecorder [15].

Temporal Coherence. Another addition would be to consider the temporal coherence of the memento [2]. An HTML webpage and all the embedded resources required for the full page are referred to as a *composite memento* [1]. It is not guaranteed that all of the resources in a composite memento will be archived at the same time, or even on the same day. If embedded resources are replayed from a datetime with a large offset from the main HTML page, composite mementos could be constructed that never existed on the live Web. When this occurs, the browser should alert the user that the page they are viewing is potentially temporally incoherent. This could be implemented as an infobar [30] that could be displayed at various times to alert the user without the obtrusiveness of a popup.

8   Conclusion

We have created a proof-of-concept Memento-aware Browser by extending Google's Chromium open source web browser. We added memento detection, notification of mementos in the UI, and a "bookmark as archive" feature. We accounted for complex memento detection, such as iframe mementos and mementos that contain live web resources. For "bookmark as archive", we found that since all bookmark actions run on the UI thread, bookmarks could not be updated after archiving was completed. We implemented a workaround taking advantage of Internet Archive and Archive.today redirecting links that contain datetimes they do not have to mementos closest to that datetime. The Memento-aware Browser source code [20] can be built and run on Linux and Windows. Additionally, there are release builds for Linux and Windows attached to the GitHub repository.

References

1. Ainsworth, S.G., Nelson, M.L., Van de Sompel, H.: A framework for evaluation of composite memento temporal coherence. Technical report arXiv:1402.0928, arXiv (2014)
2. Ainsworth, S.G., Nelson, M.L., Van de Sompel, H.: Only one out of five archived web pages existed as presented. In: Proceedings of ACM Hypertext, pp. 257–266 (2015)
3. Alam, S., Nelson, M.L.: MemGator - a portable concurrent Memento aggregator: Cross-platform CLI and server binaries in Go. In: JCDL 2016: Proceedings of the 16th ACM/IEEE-CS Joint Conference on Digital Libraries, pp. 243–244 (2016)
4. Archive-It. http://www.archive-it.org
5. Archive.today. http://archive.vn/
6. Aturban, M.: ArchiveNow. https://github.com/oduwsdl/archivenow
7. Aturban, M., Kelly, M., Alam, S., Berlin, J.A., Nelson, M.L., Weigle, M.C.: ArchiveNow: simplified, extensible, multi-archive preservation. In: JCDL 2018: Proceedings of the 17th ACM/IEEE-CS Joint Conference on Digital Libraries, pp. 321–322 (2018)
8. Brunelle, J.F.: Zombies in the archives, October 2012. https://ws-dl.blogspot.com/2012/10/2012-10-10-zombies-in-archives.html
9. Graham, M.: Wayback machine chrome extension now available, January 2017. http://blog.archive.org/2017/01/13/wayback-machine-chrome-extension-now-available/
10. Graham, M.: Brave browser and the Wayback machine: working together to help make the web more useful and reliable, February 2020. http://blog.archive.org/2020/02/25/brave-browser-and-the-wayback-machine-working-together-to-help-make-the-web-more-useful-and-reliable/
11. Icelandic Web Archive. https://wayback.vefsafn.is/
12. Internet Archive. http://www.archive.org
13. Internet Archive: Wayback Machine web browser extension. https://github.com/internetarchive/wayback-machine-webextension
14. Kelly, M., Nelson, M.L., Weigle, M.C.: Mink: integrating the live and archived web viewing experience using web browsers and memento. In: JCDL 2014: Proceedings of the 14th ACM/IEEE-CS Joint Conference on Digital Libraries, pp. 469–470 (2014)
15. Kreymer, I.: Public web archives (2021). https://github.com/webrecorder/public-web-archives
16. Lerner, A., Kohno, T., Roesner, F.: Rewriting history: changing the archived web from the present. In: Proceedings of the 2017 ACM SIGSAC Conference on Computer and Communications Security, pp. 1741–1755 (2017). https://doi.org/10.1145/3133956.3134042
17. Library and Archives Canada. https://webarchive.bac-lac.gc.ca/
18. Library of Congress. https://webarchive.loc.gov/
19. Mabe, A.: A chromium-based memento-aware web browser. Technical report arXiv:2104.13361, arXiv (2021)
20. Mabe, A.: Memento-aware browser (2021). https://github.com/oduwsdl/Memento-aware-Browser
21. National Records of Scotland. https://webarchive.nrscotland.gov.uk/
22. Nelson, M.L.: Right-click to the past - memento for chrome, October 2013. https://ws-dl.blogspot.com/2013/10/2013-10-14-right-click-to-past-memento.html

23. Nelson, M.L., Van de Sompel, H.: Adding the dimension of time to HTTP. In: Brügger, N., Milligan, I. (eds.) The SAGE Handbook of Web History, chap. 14, pp. 189–214. SAGE Publishing (2018)
24. Nwala, A.C., Weigle, M.C., Nelson, M.L.: 365 dots in 2019: quantifying attention of news sources. Technical report arXiv:2003.09989, arXiv (2020)
25. Perma.cc. https://perma.cc/
26. Portuguese Web Archive. https://arquivo.pt/
27. Sanderson, R., Shankar, H., Ainsworth, S., McCown, F., Adams, S.: Implementing time travel for the web. Code4Lib J. (13) (2011)
28. Stanford Web Archive. https://swap.stanford.edu/
29. The Chromium Projects: Download Chromium. https://www.chromium.org/getting-involved/download-chromium. Accessed 02 June 2021
30. The Chromium Projects: Infobars. http://www.chromium.org/for-testers/enable-logging. Accessed 02 Feb 2021
31. TimeTravel: Time travel archive registry (2021). http://labs.mementoweb.org/aggregator_config/archivelist.xml
32. Trove. https://trove.nla.gov.au/
33. Tweedy, H., McCown, F., Nelson, M.L.: A memento web browser for iOS. In: Proceedings of the ACM/IEEE Joint Conference on Digital Libraries (JCDL), pp. 371–372 (2013). https://doi.org/10.1145/2467696.2467764
34. UK National Archives Web Archive. https://webarchive.nationalarchives.gov/
35. UK Parliament Web Archive. https://webarchive.parliament.uk/
36. UK Web Archive. https://webarchive.org.uk/
37. Van de Sompel, H., Nelson, M., Sanderson, R.: HTTP framework for time-based access to resource states - memento. Internet RFC 7089, December 2013
38. Weigle, M.C.: Enabling personal use of web archives. Keynote talk presented at Web Archiving and Digital Libraries (WADL), June 2018. https://www.slideshare.net/mweigle/enabling-personal-use-of-web-archives

Analysis of the Deletions of DOIs

What Factors Undermine Their Persistence and to What Extent?

Jiro Kikkawa(✉) , Masao Takaku , and Fuyuki Yoshikane

University of Tsukuba, Tsukuba, Ibaraki, Japan
{jiro,masao,fuyuki}@slis.tsukuba.ac.jp

Abstract. Digital Object Identifiers (DOIs) are regarded as persistent; however, they are sometimes deleted. Deleted DOIs are an important issue not only for persistent access to scholarly content but also for bibliometrics, because they may cause problems in correctly identifying scholarly articles. However, little is known about how much of deleted DOIs and what causes them. We identified deleted DOIs by comparing the datasets of all Crossref DOIs on two different dates, investigated the number of deleted DOIs in the scholarly content along with the corresponding document types, and analyzed the factors that cause deleted DOIs. Using the proposed method, 708,282 deleted DOIs were identified. The majority corresponded to individual scholarly articles such as journal articles, proceedings articles, and book chapters. There were cases of many DOIs assigned to the same content, e.g., retracted journal articles and abstracts of international conferences. We show the publishers and academic societies which are the most common in deleted DOIs. In addition, the top cases of single scholarly content with a large number of deleted DOIs were revealed. The findings of this study are useful for citation analysis and altmetrics, as well as for avoiding deleted DOIs.

Keywords: Digital Object Identifier (DOI) · Scholarly communication · Bibliometrics · Altmetrics

1 Introduction

It is important to ensure persistent access to scholarly articles because many scholarly articles have been distributed on the Web. Digital Object Identifier (DOI) is the best-known persistent identifier of scholarly content and is an international standard. As of May 2022, 130 million DOIs have been registered by Crossref [5].

In the DOI system, a single and unique DOI is registered for each content item. A DOI name consists of a prefix, slash (/), and suffix. A prefix is assigned to a particular DOI registrant, such as publishing companies or academic societies. DOI registrants assign suffixes to their content and register DOIs through DOI registration agencies (hereinafter referred to as "RAs"). DOIs also provide hyperlinks (hereinafter referred to as "DOI links") by adding DOI name after

© Springer Nature Switzerland AG 2022
G. Silvello et al. (Eds.): TPDL 2022, LNCS 13541, pp. 161–174, 2022.
https://doi.org/10.1007/978-3-031-16802-4_13

"https://doi.org/". Content holders, such as publishers and academic societies, maintain the relationship between the DOI and the original content's URI. Through these functions, scholarly content can be consistently accessed using DOI links. Once registered, the DOIs are regarded as persistent and are not deleted.

Because of these characteristics of DOIs, citation indexes and altmetrics depend on them to identify unique scholarly articles. With the rapid increase in the number of scholarly articles, DOIs are playing an increasingly significant role in scholarly communication. However, in practice, DOIs and their artifacts (e.g., identifiers, metadata, and redirected URIs) may be deleted by content holders, such as publishers and academic societies, if something wrong happens, e.g., multiple DOIs were assigned to the same content item. These deletions cause problems not only for persistent access to scholarly content but also for bibliometric analysis, including citation analysis and altmetrics. In this study, we focus on the deletion of identifiers and metadata, and define DOIs for which identifiers and associated metadata cannot be retrieved as "Deleted DOIs".

Deleted DOIs are an important issue in bibliometrics; however, little is known about their quantity and causes. Thus, we developed a methodology to identify deleted DOIs and analyze not only their quantity but also their causes, with a focus on the content holders and their patterns of DOI assignment.

The following research questions were addressed in this study:

RQ1 How many deleted DOIs exist?
  – We present the total number of deleted DOIs and classify deleted DOIs according to the redirect URIs and Crossref metadata.
RQ2 Which document types are the most common in deleted DOIs?
  – We investigate which document types have large numbers of deleted DOIs; i.e., we clarify whether these content items are single scholarly articles (such as a journal article, conference proceedings paper, or book chapter) or non-single scholarly articles (such as an entire book or a specific volume or issue of a journal). If a large number of deleted DOIs were registered for a single scholarly article, we analyze them in detail according to their metadata.
RQ3 Which prefixes are the most common in deleted DOIs?
  – We find publishers and academic societies with large numbers of deleted DOIs.
RQ4 What are the most common changes in the suffixes of deleted DOIs?
  – We investigate the pattern of changes in the suffixes of DOIs for the same scholarly content to determine the relationship between DOI assignment patterns and deleted DOIs.

The contributions of this study are twofold. (1) We present the overall picture of deleted DOIs by clarifying the number of deleted DOIs and the characteristics of their content. The potential impact of deleted DOIs for citation analysis and altmetrics is demonstrated. (2) By identifying the factors that cause deleted DOIs, we provide guidance for avoiding deleted DOIs and making the DOI system more stable.

2   Related Work

Crossref DOI Statistics. Hendricks et al. [8] reported the statistics of Crossref DOIs in June 2019. More than 106 million Crossref DOIs had been registered, and the number of DOIs had increased by 11% on average over the past 10 years. As for the types of contents, 73% are journals, 13% are books, and 5.5% are conference papers and proceedings.

Investigation of Duplicated Crossref DOIs. Tkaczyk [18] investigated Crossref DOIs not marked as an alias to other DOIs to consider their quantity and impact on citation-based metrics. Among DOIs randomly sampled from 590 publishers and academic societies with $\geq 5,000$ DOIs, 0.8% were duplicated, i.e., different DOI names but their metadata were the same or highly similar. The majority of them were caused by the re-registration of DOIs by the same publishers and academic societies. As for duplicated DOIs among different publishers and academic societies, one of the most frequent cases was content with DOIs initially registered by JSTOR and re-registered by new content holders.

Incorrect DOIs Indexed by Scholarly Bibliographic Databases. Several studies have revealed errors in DOIs indexed by scholarly bibliographic databases. Franceschini et al. [7] analyzed DOIs in the records of Scopus and found that multiple DOIs were incorrectly assigned to the same record as rare cases. Zhu et al. [19] analyzed DOIs in the Web of Science records. They reported not only "wrong DOI names" but also "one paper with two different DOI names". The former are similar errors, as reported by Franceschini et al. [7]. The latter are classified into the following two cases: (1) there were both correct and incorrect DOIs in the records; (2) multiple correct DOIs were assigned to the same scholarly article.

Analysis of Persistence of Crossref DOIs. Klein and Balakireva [12,13] examined the persistence of Crossref DOIs by analyzing their HTTP status codes. They randomly extracted 10,000 Crossref DOIs and examined the final status codes for each DOI link by using multiple HTTP request methods. More than half of the DOI links did not redirect to the content when an external network from academic institutions was used. However, the errors of all the DOI links were reduced to one-third when an internal network from academic institutions was used. These results indicate that the responses for the same DOI can differ according to conditions such as the HTTP request methods and network locations, which implies a lack of persistence of DOIs.

Analysis of the Usage of DOI Links in Scholarly Articles. Regarding the usage of DOI links in the references of scholarly references, Van de Sompel et al. [16] examined references from 1.8 million papers published between 1997 and 2012. Consequently, they identified a problem that numerous scholarly articles were referenced using their location URIs instead of their DOI links.

As described previously, researchers have reported duplicated Crossref DOIs [18,19], and some Crossref DOIs cause errors and are unable to lead to the contents [12, 13]. It has also been reported that DOIs included in the records of scholarly bibliographic databases contain errors [7, 19]. However, these studies were based on relatively small samples because a methodology to identify duplicated or deleted DOIs at a large scale has not been proposed. Thus, we propose a methodology for identifying deleted DOIs and conducting a large-scale analysis to determine how many deleted DOIs exist and what factors cause them.

3   Materials and Methods

3.1   Identifying Deleted DOIs

In this section, we describe the proposed method for identifying deleted DOIs, i.e., DOIs whose identifiers and metadata cannot be retrieved. Specifically, we extracted the DOIs that existed at a point in time and did not exist later by comparing the dump files of Crossref DOIs on two different dates. We then treated these DOIs as a candidate set of deleted DOIs.

First, we obtained the two datasets of all Crossref DOIs on different dates: March 2017 [9] and January 2021 [2, 10]. We unescaped and downcased to remove duplicates. The total numbers of unique DOIs were 87,542,203 and 120,684,617, respectively.

Next, we obtained the differences and product sets between the two datasets, as shown in Table 1. There were 711,198 Crossref DOIs that existed as of March 2017 but did not exist as of January 2021. Then, for the 711,198 DOIs, we (1) identified the RA, (2) examined the redirected URI of DOI links, and (3) obtained the Crossref metadata. For (1), we used a web API called "Which RA?" [17], which returns the RA name if the DOI exists and returns an error if it does not exist. For (2), we examined the HTTP header of each DOI link. For (3), we used the Crossref REST API [3, 4].

Table 1. Basic statistics of the datasets

	Dataset as of March 2017		Dataset as of January 2021	
	# of DOIs	%	# of DOIs	%
Difference set	**711,198**	**0.81**	33,853,612	28.05
Product set	86,831,005	99.19	86,831,005	71.95
Overall	87,542,203	100.00	120,684,617	100.00

According to the results for (1) to (3), we classified the DOIs into the groups shown in Fig. 1. First, we classified them into "Non-existing DOIs", "Crossref DOIs", and "Non-Crossref DOIs" according to the results of "Which RA?"; these groups were derived from the results of "DOI does not exist," "Crossref," and RA names other than Crossref, respectively. Among these groups, Non-existing DOIs corresponded to deleted DOIs. In contrast, Non-Crossref DOIs were not deleted, because they were not included in the dataset as of March 2021, owing to the transfer of the RAs.

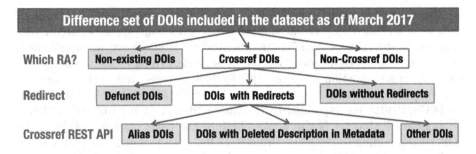

Fig. 1. Classification of the DOIs that existed as of March 2017 but no longer existed as of January 2021. Items with a red box correspond to deleted DOIs. (Color figure online)

Next, we classified the Crossref DOIs into the groups "Defunct DOIs", "DOIs without Redirects", and "DOIs with Redirects" according to the results of each HTTP header for the DOI links. "Defunct DOIs" were the DOIs that redirected to the specific URI (https://www.crossref.org/_deleted-doi/) for the deleted content [15]. "DOIs without Redirects" were the DOIs without redirects when we accessed DOI links; thus, we could not reach the content via these DOIs. We treated defunct DOIs and DOIs without redirects as deleted DOIs.

Finally, the DOIs were classified into three groups according to the results of the Crossref REST API. They were all deleted DOIs, because they were unable to retrieve the Crossref metadata.

- **Alias DOI:** When multiple Crossref DOIs were assigned to the same content item, one was set as the Primary DOI, and the others were set as the Alias DOIs [6]. The Crossref REST API returned the error "Resource not found" for the Alias DOIs.
- **DOI with Deleted Description in Metadata:** Crossref metadata for a particular DOI or the corresponding Alias DOI contains the word "delete" in the value of "title" or "container title". Moreover, the first author manually confirmed that the content was deleted by accessing the landing page.
- **Other DOI:** These DOIs had redirects that were not applicable to any of the conditions above.

When the DOIs were applicable to both the "Alias DOI" and "DOI with Deleted Description in Metadata" groups, we assigned them to the latter group.

3.2 Analysis Methods

The following four analyses were performed on the deleted DOIs identified by the method described in Sect. 3.1. Each analysis corresponds to an RQ.

(1) Basic Statistics of Deleted DOIs. We investigated the number of deleted DOIs and their distributions using the groups presented in Sect. 3.1.

(2) Content Analysis Based on Crossref Metadata and DOI Links.
First, we determined which content types were common among the deleted DOIs
according to the value of "type" in the Crossref metadata. Next, we investigated
the number of alias DOIs corresponding to a single Primary DOI to clarify the
characteristics of deletion when multiple DOIs were registered to the same content. For example, when Alias DOIs "10.14359/15303", "10.14359/15304", and
"10.14359/15305" corresponded to the same Primary DOI "10.14359/15306",
the number of Alias DOIs was 3. We obtained the basic statistics of the Alias
DOIs corresponding to the same Primary DOIs. We examined articles for cases
in which many Alias DOIs were associated with a single Primary DOI.

(3) Prefix Analysis. We compared the prefixes of deleted DOIs and identified
which publishers or academic societies had large numbers of deleted DOIs. In
addition, we calculated the ratios P_1 and P_2 for each prefix, as follows.

$$P_1(X) = \frac{total\ number\ of\ the\ Deleted\ DOIs\ whose\ Prefix\ was\ X}{total\ number\ of\ all\ Deleted\ DOIs} * 100$$

$$P_2(X) = \frac{total\ number\ of\ the\ Deleted\ DOIs\ whose\ Prefix\ was\ X}{total\ number\ of\ all\ DOIs\ whose\ Prefix\ was\ X\ as\ of\ March\ 2017} * 100$$

When both P_1 and P_2 are high in a prefix, it indicates not only that the
percentage of deleted DOIs for this prefix in the total deleted DOIs is high but
also that a large percentage of the DOIs registered by the registrant with this
prefix are deleted. On the other hand, when P_1 is high and P_2 is low in a prefix,
the percentage of deleted DOIs in the total deleted DOIs is high but a small
percentage of the DOIs registered by the registrant with that prefix are deleted.

(4) Suffix Analysis. We analyzed the suffixes of the deleted DOIs when multiple DOIs were registered for the same content. Here, we set the target to the pairs
of Alias DOIs and Primary DOIs. First, we classified the patterns of the pairs of
Alias DOI and Primary DOI suffixes into the following categories: (A) only the
suffix changed (B) both the prefix and the suffix changed, and (C) only the prefix
changed. Next, for (A) and (B), we analyzed the similarity of strings between
the suffixes of the Alias DOI and Primary DOI. The Levenshtein distance [14]
normalized by the string length of the suffixes was used as the similarity score.
The following formula was used:

$$Sim(str1, str2) = 1 - \frac{Levenshtein(str1, str2)}{Max(|str1|, |str2|)},$$

where Sim takes values between 0 and 1, with higher values indicating a higher
degree of similarity between the two strings. We observed the distributions for
the similarity score in groups (A) and (B). When the similarity scores of the
majority in a group are high, it can be interpreted that there are many cases
where slightly changed suffixes of Alias DOIs are set as those of Primary DOIs.
In contrast, when the similarity score of the majority in a group is low, it can
be interpreted that there are many cases where strings that differ significantly
from the Alias DOI suffixes are set as the suffixes of Primary DOIs.

Finally, we analyzed the character-level differences between each pair of Alias and Primary DOIs to determine what types of changes were common. We used the package "diff-lcs" [20] from RubyGems to obtain the diffs of the Primary and Alias DOIs using the Diff::LCS.diff method. We retrieved the changes between each Primary DOI and Alias DOI as actions of adding or deleting the position and the corresponding characters. We analyzed which characters were added, deleted, or replaced (when both "delete" and "add" were present in the same position) for each pair. For example, in the case of the Alias DOI "10.14359/15303" and Primary DOI "10.14359/15306", the change was to replace "3" with "6" once.

4 Results and Discussion

4.1 Basic Statistics of Deleted DOIs

RQ1 How many deleted DOIs exist?

Table 2 presents the number of deleted DOIs in each group. We identified 708,282 deleted DOIs by applying the method described in Sect. 3.1. Most deleted DOIs were Alias DOIs, accounting for 94.29% of the total. Therefore, the majority of the deleted DOIs were caused by the deletion of multiple DOI assignments for the same content. The percentage of deleted DOIs relative to all DOIs in 2021 was 0.59% ($= 708,282/120,684,617 * 100$).

Table 2. Number of deleted DOIs in each group (n = 708,282)

#	Group	Count	%
1	Non-existing DOIs	240	0.03
2	Defunct DOIs	388	0.05
3	DOIs without redirects	693	0.10
4	Alias DOIs	667,869	94.29
5	DOIs with deleted description on metadata	1,144	0.16
6	Other DOIs	37,948	5.36

4.2 Content Analysis Based on Crossref Metadata and DOI Links

RQ2 Which document types are the most common in deleted DOIs?

Table 3 presents the document types of the deleted DOIs based on Crossref metadata. The top three types were journal articles (78.35%), proceedings articles (8.48%), and book chapters (6.77%). Thus, most of the deleted DOIs were individual scholarly articles rather than books or journals.

The minimum value, maximum value, median, and standard deviation of the number of alias DOIs corresponding to each primary DOI were 1, 1,474,

Table 3. Document types of deleted DOIs (n = 708,282)

#	Type	Count	%	#	Type	Count	%
1	Journal-article	554,948	78.35	10	Standard	70	0.01
2	Proceedings-article	60,092	8.48	11	Book-series	48	0.01
3	Book-chapter	47,974	6.77	12	Report	40	0.01
4	Dataset	23,784	3.36	13	Journal-issue	37	0.01
5	Component	8,419	1.19	14	Proceedings	23	0.00
6	Reference-entry	6,611	0.93	15	Reference-book	21	0.00
7	Book	3,094	0.44	16	Journal	15	0.00
8	Monograph	2,340	0.33	17	Dissertation	10	0.00
9	Other	754	0.11	18	Book-section	2	0.00

1, and 2.49, respectively. The majority of cases were those in which two DOIs were registered for the same content, and one of them was deleted because the median value was 1. On the other hand, focusing on the maximum value, there were cases where a large number of DOIs were assigned to a single content item.

Table 4 presents the 10 Primary DOIs with the largest numbers of associated Alias DOIs. The content item with the largest number of associated Alias DOIs was Volume 13 of the journal *Energy Procedia* (#1 in Table 4). This entire volume was retracted. These articles are different scholarly articles, and it is considered that the withdrawn information should be applied to the respective DOIs, rather than applying them as alias DOIs to a single primary DOI. In case #2, all articles published in Volume 11 of *Energy Procedia* were withdrawn. Case #3 involved abstracts of an international conference, where DOIs were registered to the abstracts of the presentations, but the publisher appeared to change the policy for registering DOIs to a set of abstracts. Cases #4–#9 were similar to #3 and all involved the *Journal of the American College of Cardiology*. Case #10 involved an abstract of an international conference published in another journal. According to these results, the Primary DOIs with large numbers of Alias DOIs corresponded to content such as retracted journal articles and abstracts of international conferences. This content would not be the target of citation analysis and altmetrics and did not have a critical impact on them. The Primary DOIs with large numbers of Alias DOIs were caused by the activities of publishers and academic societies rather than by the deletion of multiple DOIs mistakenly registered to the same scholarly articles.

4.3 Prefix Analysis

RQ3 Which prefixes are the most common in deleted DOIs?

Table 5 presents the top 10 prefixes of the deleted DOIs. P_1 and P_2 in Table 5 are the two ratios defined in Sect. 3.2. For example, the publisher

Table 4. Ten Primary DOIs with the largest numbers of associated Alias DOIs

# Count	Primary DOI Volume (Issue), Page	Title Container title
1	10.1016/s1876-6102(14)00454-8	Volume Removed - Publisher's Disclaimer
1,474	13, pp. 1–10380	Energy Procedia
2	10.1016/s1876-6102(14)00453-6	Volume Removed - Publisher's Disclaimer
748	11, pp. 1–5156	Energy Procedia
3	10.1016/j.fueleneab.2006.10.002	Abstracts
486	47 (6), pp. 384–446	Fuel and Energy Abstracts
4	10.1016/s0735-1097(01)80004-8	Hypertension, vascular disease, and prevention
399	37 (2), pp. A220–A304	Journal of the American College of Cardiology
5	10.1016/s0735-1097(01)80001-2	ACCIS2001 angiography & interventional...
394	37 (2), pp. A1–A86	Journal of the American College of Cardiology
6	10.1016/s0735-1097(01)80003-6	Cardiac function and heart failure
356	37 (2), pp. A142–A219	Journal of the American College of Cardiology
7	10.1016/s0735-1097(01)80005-x	Myocardial ischemia and infarction
333	37 (2), pp. A305–A378	Journal of the American College of Cardiology
8	10.1016/s0735-1097(01)80006-1	Noninvasive imaging
321	37 (2), pp. A379–A452	Journal of the American College of Cardiology
9	10.1016/s0735-1097(01)80002-4	Cardiac arrhythmias
254	37 (2), pp. A87–A141	Journal of the American College of Cardiology
10	10.1037/h0099051	Forty-Third Annual Meeting of the American...
162	36 (2), pp. 195–373	American Journal of Orthopsychiatry

Wiley registered 4,718,360 Crossref DOIs with the prefix "10.1002" as of March 2017, and 94,471 of them were Deleted DOIs. In this case, P_1 was 13.34% (= 94,471/708,282 * 100), and P_2 was 2.00% (= 94,471/4,718,360 * 100). As indicated by Table 5, the registrants with the largest numbers of deleted DOIs were major international commercial publishers, such as Wiley, Elsevier BV, and Springer Science and Business Media LLC (#1, #2, #9, and #10). These publishers registered numerous DOIs, but few of them were deleted, as the P_2 values for these publishers were low. In contrast, the "Society of Petroleum Engineers" (#5) had a remarkably high P_2 value of 87.62%; thus, most of the DOIs registered by this registrant with this prefix were deleted. IGI Global and the American Psychological Association (#7 and #4) had relatively high P_2 values of 17.51% and 6.74%, respectively. JSTOR (#3)—a digital library platform—was a registrant with many deleted DOIs. Regarding JSTOR, the deletions of DOI seem to be caused by the re-registration of DOIs to the same article published by content holders other than JSTOR. For these cases, it is necessary to assign a single DOI to the initial version of the article and avoid re-registration of the DOIs to the other versions. This problem would be caused by the registration agency improperly managing their content.

Table 5. Top 10 prefixes of deleted DOIs (n = 708,282)

#	Prefix	Registrant	Count	P_1 (%)	P_2 (%)
1	10.1002	Wiley	94,471	13.34	2.00
2	10.1016	Elsevier BV	85,643	12.09	0.58
3	10.2307	JSTOR	66,232	9.35	2.82
4	10.1037	American Psychological Association	51,846	7.32	6.74
5	10.2523	Society of Petroleum Engineers	35,499	5.01	87.62
6	10.1163	Brill	23,962	3.38	2.68
7	10.4018	IGI Global	23,440	3.31	17.51
8	10.1080	Informa UK Limited	21,134	2.98	0.75
9	10.1007	Springer Science and Business Media LLC	19,807	2.80	0.21
10	10.1111	Wiley	18,743	2.65	0.64

4.4 Suffix Analysis

RQ4 What are the most common changes in the suffixes of deleted DOIs?

Table 6. DOI name change patterns (n = 667,869)

Pattern	Count	%
Only the suffix changed	465,789	69.74
Both the prefix and the suffix changed	156,650	23.46
Only the prefix changed	45,430	6.80

Table 6 presents the DOI name change patterns for each pair of Alias and Primary DOIs. The most common pattern was "only the suffix changed" (69.74%), indicating that many DOIs registered under the same prefix were deleted when multiple DOIs were registered to the same content by the same registrant. In contrast, "both the prefix and the suffix changed" and "only the prefix changed" were cases of deletions in which the DOIs were re-registered with the content holder's prefix when the content holder changed. For the prefixes "10.4018 (IGI Global)" and "10.1037 (American Psychological Association)" (#7 and #4, respectively, in Table 5), almost all the patterns were "only the suffix changes."

Of the 156,650 cases in which both the prefix and the suffix changed, 56,491 were caused by the prefix "10.2307 (JSTOR)". The prefix "10.2307" was changed to "10.1090 (American Mathematical Society)" and "10.1080 (Informa UK Limited)" in 22,198 and 10,010 cases, respectively. These results match those of Tkaczyk [18] and indicate that a large amount of scholarly content provided by JSTOR was transferred to other registrants, and their DOIs were re-registered with the prefixes of new registrants, which is why the prefix "10.2307" is listed as #3 in Table 5.

Of the 45,430 cases of "only the prefix changed," 35,176 involved the prefix "10.2523" of Alias DOIs and the prefix "10.2118" of Primary DOIs, and the corresponding registrant was the Society of Petroleum Engineers. This is why the prefix "10.2523" is listed as #5 in Table 5, and these cases were due to DOIs being re-registered by the same publisher.

Table 7. Distribution of similarity scores between Alias DOI and Primary DOI suffixes

	Only the suffix changed		Both the prefix and the suffix changed	
	Count	%	Count	%
$0 \leqq sim \leqq 0.1$	9,033	1.94	**15,942**	**10.18**
$0.1 < sim \leqq 0.2$	35,253	7.57	**80,420**	**51.34**
$0.2 < sim \leqq 0.3$	20,058	4.31	**34,385**	**21.95**
$0.3 < sim \leqq 0.4$	9,539	2.05	13,278	8.48
$0.4 < sim \leqq 0.5$	27,074	5.81	6,493	4.14
$0.5 < sim \leqq 0.6$	27,783	5.96	2,243	1.43
$0.6 < sim \leqq 0.7$	26,331	5.65	878	0.56
$0.7 < sim \leqq 0.8$	**57,866**	**12.42**	536	0.34
$0.8 < sim \leqq 0.9$	**82,647**	**17.74**	2,361	1.51
$0.9 < sim < 1.0$	**170,205**	**36.54**	114	0.07
Overall	465,789	100.00	156,650	100.00

Table 7 presents the distribution of similarity scores among suffixes for "only the suffix changed" and "both the prefix and the suffix changed." The group "only the suffix changed" had a large percentage of cases with Sim values of >0.7, indicating that most of the cases had a high degree of similarity among suffixes. In contrast, the group "both the prefix and the suffix changed" had a large percentage of cases with Sim values of $\leqq 0.3$, indicating that the degree of similarity among the suffixes was low. This suggests that a slightly changed version of the suffix of the Alias DOI tended to be set as the suffix of the Primary DOI for the group "only the suffix changed". In contrast, the group "both the prefix and the suffix changed" have a tendency that a significantly different suffix from the Alias DOI was set as the suffix of the Primary DOI.

Table 8 presents frequent patterns for "only the suffix changed." The most frequent pattern was the correction of "//" to "/" as a separator between the prefix and the suffix (10.56%). The second most frequent pattern was the correction of the ISBN in the suffix by adding hyphens as separators (4.71%). The third most frequent pattern was the replacement of the ISSN in the suffix with a new one (3.99%). According to these results, we must be careful not to set double slashes between the prefix and the suffix. When we apply other identifiers such as the ISBN and ISSN to suffixes, we may need to format or update them owing to changes in the ISBN or ISSN.

Table 8. Three most frequent patterns for "only the suffix changed" (n = 465,789). Red, blue, and purple text corresponds to deletion, addition, and replacement, respectively.

#	Pattern of changes in the suffix Example	Count	%
1	Delete a slash (/) once /s12445-012-0033-7 ⟶ s12445-012-0033-7	49,169	10.56
2	Add a hyphen (-) four times 9781591401087.ch001 ⟶ 978 -1 -59140 -108 -7.ch001	21,918	4.71
3	Delete "2" twice, add "5" once, add "7" once, replace "8" with "9" once, and replace "6" with "3" once 2214- 8647_dnp_e1000010 ⟶ 1 574- 9347_dnp_e1000010	18,607	3.99

5   Conclusion

We identified and analyzed the deleted DOIs. As a result, we identified 708,282 deleted DOIs that existed in March 2017 and did not exist in January 2021 using the proposed method. The majority of these DOIs were individual scholarly articles such as journal articles, proceedings articles, and book chapters. The cases where many DOIs were assigned to the same content were retracted papers in a specific volume of a journal or abstracts of international conference proceedings. We revealed the factors that caused a large number of deleted DOIs. The findings of this study are useful for both considering the problems caused by deleted DOIs in citation analysis and altmetrics and assigning DOIs in a better way to avoid deleted DOIs.

The limitations of this study are outlined below, and directions for future work are suggested. First, we were unable to identify deleted DOIs that existed before March 2017, i.e., DOIs that had been deleted as of March 2017. We were also unable to capture the deleted DOIs after March 2021. Other DOIs whose contents were not reachable were beyond the scope of this study. The deleted DOIs in this study were defined only as deletions of identifiers and metadata. Therefore, we will expand the scope of the deleted DOIs and develop a methodology for identifying them beyond this definition. Second, we were unable and classify all the factors that caused deleted DOIs and classify them, because we only focused on the most frequent cases. Moreover, it is unclear whether the observed factors represented exceptional cases. Third, a quantitative analysis of the effects of deleted DOIs on citation analysis and altmetrics is important, e.g., examining whether Alias/Primary DOIs are included in the citation indexes and altmetrics. Recently, DOI assignments to the contents on preprint servers such as arXiv have been actively conducted [1], and there is a concern that the numbers of duplicated DOIs and deleted DOIs will increase. Analyzing these DOIs is beyond the scope of this study. However, it is important to understand the stability and persistence of the DOI system in the future. The dataset used in this study is available at Zenodo [11].

Acknowledgments. This work was partially supported by JSPS KAKENHI Grant Numbers JP21K21303, JP22K18147, JP20K12543, and JP21K12592. We would like to thank Editage (https://www.editage.com/) for the English language editing.

References

1. Cornell University: New arXiv articles are now automatically assigned DOIs | arXiv.org blog (2022). https://blog.arxiv.org/2022/02/17/new-arxiv-articles-are-now-automatically-assigned-dois/
2. Crossref: January 2021 Public Data File from Crossref. Academic Torrents. https://doi.org/10.13003/gu3dqmjvg4
3. Crossref: Crossref Metadata API JSON Format (2021). https://github.com/CrossRef/rest-api-doc/blob/master/api_format.md
4. Crossref: Crossref REST API (2021). https://api.crossref.org/
5. Crossref: crossref.org : : crossref stats (2022). https://www.crossref.org/06members/53status.html
6. Farley, I.: Conflict report - Crossref (2020). https://www.crossref.org/documentation/reports/conflict-report/
7. Franceschini, F., Maisano, D., Mastrogiacomo, L.: Errors in DOI indexing by bibliometric databases. Scientometrics **102**(3), 2181–2186 (2014). https://doi.org/10.1007/s11192-014-1503-4
8. Hendricks, G., Tkaczyk, D., Lin, J., Feeney, P.: Crossref: the sustainable source of community-owned scholarly metadata. Quantit. Sci. Stud. **1**(1), 414–427 (2020). https://doi.org/10.1162/qss_a_00022
9. Himmelstein, D., Wheeler, K., Greene, C.: Metadata for all DOIs in Crossref: JSON MongoDB exports of all works from the Crossref API. figshare (2017). https://doi.org/10.6084/m9.figshare.4816720.v1
10. Kemp, J.: New public data file: 120+ million metadata records (2021). https://www.crossref.org/blog/new-public-data-file-120-million-metadata-records/
11. Kikkawa, J., Takaku, M., Yoshikane, F.: Dataset of the deleted DOIs extracted from the difference set between Crossref DOIs as of March 2017 and January 2021. Zenodo (2022). https://doi.org/10.5281/zenodo.6841257
12. Klein, M., Balakireva, L.: On the persistence of persistent identifiers of the scholarly web. In: Hall, M., Merčun, T., Risse, T., Duchateau, F. (eds.) TPDL 2020. LNCS, vol. 12246, pp. 102–115. Springer, Cham (2020). https://doi.org/10.1007/978-3-030-54956-5_8
13. Klein, M., Balakireva, L.: An extended analysis of the persistence of persistent identifiers of the scholarly web. Int. J. Digit. Libr. **23**(1), 5–17 (2021). https://doi.org/10.1007/s00799-021-00315-w
14. Levenshtein, V.I.: Binary codes capable of correcting deletions, insertions, and reversals. Sov. Phys.-Dokl. **10**(8), 707–710 (1966)
15. Smulyan, S.: Defunct DOI - Crossref (2020). https://www.crossref.org/_deleted-doi/
16. Van de Sompel, H., Klein, M., Jones, S.M.: Persistent URIs must be used to be persistent. In: Proceedings of the 25th International Conference Companion on World Wide Web, WWW 2016 Companion, pp. 119–120. International World Wide Web Conferences Steering Committee (2016). https://doi.org/10.1145/2872518.2889352
17. The International DOI Foundation: Factsheet DOI Resolution Documentation - 4. Which RA? (2020). https://www.doi.org/factsheets/DOIProxy.html#whichra

18. Tkaczyk, D.: Double trouble with DOIs - Crossref (2020). https://www.crossref. org/blog/double-trouble-with-dois/
19. Zhu, J., Hu, G., Liu, W.: DOI errors and possible solutions for web of science. Scientometrics **118**(2), 709–718 (2018). https://doi.org/10.1007/s11192-018-2980-7
20. Ziegler, A.: halostatue/diff-lcs: generate difference sets between Ruby sequences (2022). https://github.com/halostatue/diff-lcs

Analysing User Involvement in Open Government Data Initiatives

Dagoberto Jose Herrera-Murillo⬛, Abdul Aziz(✉)⬛, Javier Nogueras-Iso⬛, and Francisco J. Lopez-Pellicer⬛

Aragon Institute of Engineering Research (I3A), Universidad de Zaragoza, Zaragoza, Spain
{dherrera,abdul.aziz,jnog,fjlopez}@unizar.es
https://www.iaaa.es

Abstract. Over the last decade, many Open Data initiatives have been launched by public administrations to promote transparency and reuse of data. However, it is not easy to assess the impact of data availability from the perspective of user communities. Although some Open Data portals provide mechanisms for user feedback through dedicated discussion forums, web forms, and some of the user experiences are listed as use cases in their portals, there is no consistent way to compare user feedback in different data initiatives. To overcome the difficulty of assessing user impact, this paper examines the activity generated by Open Data initiatives through the social network Twitter: a forum used by all types of stakeholders and publicly available for consistent analysis. We propose a methodology to compile a set of variables that describe both the main characteristics of Open Data initiatives and the associated Twitter activity. The collected data is then analysed using factor analysis and clustering techniques to derive possible relationships between the variables. Finally, the initiatives are classified according to their activity on social networks and the values that characterise some of their features. The methodology was evaluated by analysing 27 European Open Government Data portals and their activity on Twitter in 2021.

Keywords: Open Government Data · Open Data Portals · Metadata Quality · User engagement · Social media

1 Introduction

In the current digital world, the movement of Open Data (OD) is expanding at a breakneck speed, and the ever-increasing availability of data at Open Data Portals is fuelling the expansion of this movement [6,19]. Governments are increasingly implementing open data projects and setting up open data portals to facilitate the distribution of this data in open and reusable formats. As a result, a vast number of open data repositories, catalogues, and websites have sprouted up. The philosophy of openness in Open Data is to use, share and access the data freely in any format. Open Data portals are online catalogues that contain

© Springer Nature Switzerland AG 2022
G. Silvello et al. (Eds.): TPDL 2022, LNCS 13541, pp. 175–186, 2022.
https://doi.org/10.1007/978-3-031-16802-4_14

dataset descriptions, i.e. they are a type of digital library. Such catalogues allow the discovery and management of metadata records describing datasets which maybe available for access or download in one or more distribution formats. Governments acquire and generate massive volumes of data. In addition, metadata records describe datasets in terms of authorship, provenance, and licensing, among many other aspects [13].

According to the European Commission [5], Open Government Data (OGD) portals play a vital role in opening the data and the continuous publication of open data in OGD portals raises the demand for high-quality data and the quality of the portal itself. In this respect, the use and reuse of public sector data is a significant factor in driving the current trend of opening government data through the EU portal [5, 20].

Most of the current OD ecosystems are not user-driven and do not adequately match supply and demand. It is generally accepted that the role of users is critical for the development of OD ecosystems, but the current ecosystems are driven by providers [22]. Engagement is a critical success factor to make current open OGD initiatives more user-centric. The lack of mature feedback and interaction mechanisms to engage users, however, can be seen as a major limitation. Focusing directly on receiving feedback from users, the portals of some Open Data initiatives have proposed communication channels with users through dedicated discussion forums or web forms where different communities of users can report on their experiences of reusing data made available through the portals. Some of these initiatives even provide specialised tools to access the data and offer storytelling features to users [1]. However, this kind of user feedback is very heterogeneous and feedback from different initiatives cannot be compared automatically.

This is the main reason for our decision to study user feedback in social networks: social networks are a general forum where different stakeholders express their opinions about any kind of activity or organisation. Moreover, social media can play a strategic role in improving visibility by encouraging users to visit the portal and engaging them by presenting the available data and portal features [18].

Twitter is the most attractive social platform when it comes to measuring user engagement of open data portals. Among the many reasons why this platform is useful are the following: Twitter is one of the social media platforms with the largest audience; it is used to discuss topics ranging from personal to professional interests; and, at least in Europe, it is the most widely used social media channel by open government data initiatives [18]. In contrast to other digital social networks, it has a greater tendency to circulate academic content and knowledge [9].

The purpose of this work is to analyse user involvement in Open Government Data initiatives. To this end, we have compiled a set of variables that describe both the main characteristics of the Open Data initiatives and the associated Twitter activities. These are later analysed through factor analysis and clustering techniques to derive possible relationships between the variables and the classification of the initiatives according to their activity on the social networks, as well as the values that characterise some of their features.

The rest of the paper is as follows. Section 2 provides a review of the relevant literature, where we also discuss the methodologies used in the past for Open Data initiatives. The methodology that includes the analytic framework of the working model is presented in Sect. 3. Section 4 presents the findings and results of this research. Section 5 compares our findings with the Open Data Maturity Report for 2021. We conclude with a summary of the contributions and future work.

2 Related Work

There are several research works in the literature about the monitoring of the quality of Open Data Portals [11,15], which are relevant to have an overall perspective of the current status of Open Data initiatives, their maturity or their commitment to FAIR principles [23], but they did not take into account any insights of the direct opinion of user engagement [24]. Likewise, Begany and Gil-Garcia [3] monitored the levels of user engagement by analysing web analytic behavioural data taken from the New York State open health data portal. In addition, they emphasised the actual use of open data and more specifically how users of Open Data Portals interact with open datasets.

Concerning the study of influence in social networks, several research works in the literature have investigated how to measure the impact of organisations and Twitter profiles. For instance, Berrocal et al. [4] studied the influence of University Libraries on Twitter using an influence index based on Klout [7]. Furthermore, Khan et al. [10] explored data citation and reuse practices in 43,802 openly available biodiversity datasets. The altmetrics sourced from blogs, Twitter, Facebook, and Wikipedia suggest that social activity is driven by data publishers and data creators. Authors made a hypothesis that such activities are promotion-related and may lead to more reuse of open datasets.

Concerning user-centric Open Government Data Initiatives, Nikiforova and McBrid [14] analysed and compared the various contexts regarding the employment of Open Government Data Portals by users and emphasising the most often disregarded user-centred aspects. They used the questionnaire technique to verify the user-centric usability of Open Government Data Portals. Notably, Zhu and Freeman [24] evaluated different methods of user interactions with Open Government Data Initiatives and developed a framework called user interaction framework where they evaluated the U.S. Municipal Open Data Portals and provided the findings regarding user understanding and engagement with the data portals.

For several years the Open Data Maturity Report [18] has benchmarked the development of European countries in the field of open data. The document mentions four dimensions: policy, impact, portal, and quality. In the portal dimension, it includes a sustainability variable that identifies actions conducted to ensure the portal visibility, including social media presence. According to the Open Data maturity report, Twitter is the most widely used social media channel in 16 of the analysed countries.

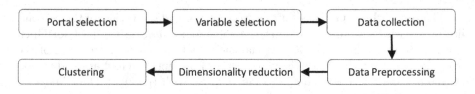

Fig. 1. Proposed methodology for data processing

3   Methodology

This research utilises a quantitative approach for analysing multiple metrics related to the national Open Data Portals of EU member countries. As shown in Fig. 1, the proposed methodology consists of 6 steps, which are described below:

Portal Selection: The first step of the methodology is to find appropriate resources to identify the location of portals and the documents describing their features. The list of platforms studied comes from two sources: the national catalogues of the European Data Portal (EDP) [16], and the compilation made by Juana-Espinosa and Lujan-Mora [6]. Both sources showed a high degree of concordance.

Variable Selection: This refers to the process of choosing relevant variables describing the features of the Open Data portal to include in our model. The relevant variables and their sources are shown in Table 1. In our experimental design, we make a choice of variables taking advantage of the sources of information available through the national portals under observation and through the European Data Portal. Therefore, some of the most representative operational attributes are gathered from the EDP (ND, ODM, MQA, URL), some of them are Twitter activity metrics (NT, TFP, UT, NI), and there are other variables (NU, GS) that help us understand the magnitude of data reuse around each portal. It must be noted that the variables present in Table 1 are the final selection of variables: our experiment included some other variables and combinations of them, but they were discarded due to their negative effect on the feasibility of indicators obtained during experiment in the last two phases of the methodology (Dimensionality Reduction and Clustering). Variables present in Table 1 are by no means intended as a complete and exhaustive list. In fact, later steps help us to explore the underlying structure that may be useful for refining the variable selection in the future.

Data Collection: This refers to the process of gathering data from reliable sources mentioned in Table 1 that guarantee the reproducibility of the measurements. We assume that the values obtained are valid and representative as they are gathered from recognized sources such as the European Data Portal and the academic Twitter API. The variables representative of the EDP can be collected through the EDP API (MQA, ND, URL) [17] or manually (ODM). The variables measuring the conversation on Twitter related to portals for the year 2021 (NT, TFP, UT, NI) can be collected using the Twitter API for Academic

Table 1. Description of the variables

Variable	Description	Source
ND	Number of datasets available for consultation	Automatic from data.europa.eu
ODM	Open Data Maturity score (0–100)	Manual from data.europa.eu
MQA	Metadata Quality Assurance rating (0–405)	Automatic from data.europa.eu
URL	% of accessible URLs	Automatic from data.europa.eu
NU	Number of data use cases listed in the portal	Manual from portals
GS	Number of items in Google Scholar citing the portal	Manual from Google Scholar
NT	Number of relevant Tweets	Automatic, derived from Twitter API
TFP	Number of Tweets by portal account	Automatic Twitter API
UT	Number of users posting Tweets	Automatic Twitter API
NI	Number of interactions generated by Tweets. This corresponds to the sum of retweets, replies, quotes and likes	Automatic Twitter API

Research [21]. This API allows the retrieval of tweets whose text mentions the URL of portals or their Twitter accounts. Finally, the number of use cases listed in a data portal (NU) and the number of mentions in Google Scholar (GS) must be collected manually for each data portal.

Data Processing: This consists of preparing the raw data and making it suitable for the analytical models. First, we must compute the correlations between the metrics using the Spearman coefficient. This coefficient can range from -1 to 1, with -1 or 1 indicating a perfect monotonic relationship: when the value of one variable increases, the other variable value also increases or decreases. After that, we must normalise the variables by removing the mean and scaling them to unit variance.

Dimensionality Reduction: This step involves exploring the underlying variable structure and reducing the data to a smaller number of explainable factors. For this purpose, we propose the use of factor analysis to reduce the dimensions of the original dataset [8]. Likewise, Bartlett test ($X^2 = 166.56$, $p < 0.0001$) and the Kaiser-Mayer-Olkin test ($KMO = 0.67$) are employed to verify the feasibility of the overall factor analysis. We take into account the Kaiser-Guttman criterion (*eigenvalue* > 1.0) to decide the optimal number of factors and, for each factor, only variables with loading greater than 0.4 after applying Varimax rotation are considered to influence the factor.

Clustering: Clustering consists of grouping portals into groups based on the dimensions that describe them. For this step, we propose to apply three common clustering methods: hierarchical clustering, K-means clustering, and K-medians clustering [12] (less sensitive to outliers). Combining these clustering techniques is a common way to improve the robustness of the final results [2]. The ideal number of clusters for K-means is defined by plotting the explained variation as a function of the number of clusters and identifying the inflection point at which adding another cluster does not improve much better intra-cluster variation, a procedure also known as the "elbow method".

4   Results

This section displays the outcomes of applying the proposed methodology on the national Open Data Portals of 27 EU member countries and their Twitter activity in 2021. We selected 2021 as this is the last year with complete information on Twitter activity. In addition, the values obtained from the Open Data Maturity report or from available APIs also reflect the situation after year 2021 had finished (when the experiment was performed).

Table 2 shows the results about the values of variables for the 27 portals under observation with the mean and coefficient of variation (CV) corresponding to each of them. The variables describing Twitter activity (NT, TFP, UT, NI) and the number of use cases (NU) are the ones with the greatest relative variability. Similarly, in terms of relevance to portals, France, Spain, and Austria have the highest nominal values for the parameters of Twitter conversation, number of use cases, and Google Scholar mentions. The Hungarian platform is the only one that does not follow a catalogue structure and does not have values for most of the indicators under observation.

Furthermore, the Spearman rank correlation coefficient is used to measure the strength and direction of association between pairs of variables, which is shown in Table 3. While looking at the Twitter metrics (except for the number of tweets by the portal account itself), the number of use cases and mentions in Google Scholar are strongly and positively correlated with each other. Moreover, the Metadata Quality Assurance rating correlates positively and moderately with the number of datasets (0.54) and the percentage of accessible URLs (0.54). The remaining correlations are weak.

Given the high correlation between the Twitter conversation variables, we removed UT and NI before factor analysis to reduce the effect of multicollinearity. The outcome for a three-factor solution accounting for 72% of the variance is shown in Table 4. The number of use cases, mentions in Google Scholar, and tweets are the variables that best explain factor 1. The number of datasets, MQA rating, and the percentage of accessible URLs are the most representative variables for factor 2. Finally, the number of tweets by portal account is considered the best variable for factor 3, with a small contribution of the number of tweets. The ODM score did not load in any of the three factors. From the factor loadings, factor scores are computed for each portal.

Observing high factor loadings associated with particular variables implies that these variables contribute more to this component. Therefore, portals with high values on these variables tend to have higher factor scores on this particular dimension and vice versa for low values.

Table 2. Values of variables for Open Government Data portals of the EU countries and their Twitter activity in 2021

Country*	Portal URL	ND	ODM	MQA	URL	NU	GS	NT	TFP	UT	NI
FR	data.gouv.fr	41,881	98	172	67	3,099	556	1,843	45	921	33,750
ES	datos.gob.es	60,102	95	196	46	400	137	1,384	448	294	9,974
AT	data.gv.at	38,586	92	199	93	689	158	258	110	85	3,696
IT	dati.gov.it	53,490	92	152	54	0	31	214	44	35	1,041
IE	data.gov.ie	13,815	95	185	42	23	73	173	3	46	1,377
LV	data.gov.lv	612	77	165	49	0	19	144	0	30	1,914
PL	dane.gov.pl	26,180	95	166	99	45	104	116	0	57	1,481
LU	data.public.lu	1,613	66	131	97	150	24	104	37	25	319
NL	data.overheid.nl	21,259	92	192	89	118	53	95	40	40	363
DE	govdata.de	51,275	89	240	56	24	118	85	9	55	1,502
CZ	data.gov.cz	142,554	74	276	99	0	19	62	43	11	702
GR	data.gov.gr	10,446	82	106	29	0	36	44	0	37	303
BG	data.egov.bg	10,680	78	47	0	0	6	37	15	12	119
FI	avoindata.fi	2,058	86	203	4	77	60	28	3	17	571
RO	data.gov.ro	2,753	76	98	7	10	15	28	0	18	24
DK	opendata.dk	823	91	164	42	0	22	27	14	12	137
PT	dados.gov.pt	4,928	66	183	81	51	43	25	0	14	242
CY	data.gov.cy	1,210	91	226	12	47	9	8	3	6	52
SE	www.dataportal.se	7,825	84	170	30	0	15	8	0	6	153
HR	data.gov.hr	1,141	84	96	52	6	22	6	0	3	23
BE	data.gov.be	13,056	55	218	31	81	12	3	0	3	15
SI	podatki.gov.si	5,098	92	120	61	14	17	2	0	2	12
EE	avaandmed.eesti.ee	879	94	0	0	150	5	0	0	0	0
LT	data.gov.lt	1,721	89	99	56	28	3	0	0	0	0
MT	open.data.gov.mt	205	51	0	0	0	2	0	0	0	0
SK	data.gov.sk	2,862	50	124	0	11	12	0	0	0	0
HU	kozadat.hu	0	58	0	0	0	0	0	0	0	0
Mean		19150.1	81.2	145.5	44.3	186.0	58.2	173.9	30.1	64.0	2139.6
CV		1.6	0.2	0.5	0.8	3.2	1.9	2.4	2.9	2.8	3.1

*We are using the two letter-code of ISO-639 to refer to the country of the Open Data initiatives that have been analysed.

Table 3. Spearman correlation

	ND	ODM	MQA	URL	NU	GS	NT	TFP	UT	NI
ND	1									
ODM	0.19	1								
MQA	0.54**	0.30	1							
URL	0.49*	0.32	0.54**	1						
NU	0.19	0.29	0.12	0.21	1					
GS	0.28	0.39*	0.26	0.30	0.96**	1				
NT	0.33	0.36	0.20	0.20	0.84**	0.87**	1			
TFP	0.39*	0.26	0.23	0.17	0.19	0.26	0.63**	1		
UT	0.25	0.33	0.16	0.19	0.97**	0.96**	0.94**	0.33	1	
NI	0.26	0.32	0.16	0.19	0.97**	0.96**	0.93**	0.32	1.00**	1

$**p < 0.01$ and $*p < 0.05$ indicate significant correlation.

Table 4. Rotated matrix for factor analysis

Variable	Factor		
	1	2	3
ND		0.64	
ODM			
MQA		0.78	
URL		0.72	
NU	0.97		
GS	0.96		
NT	0.84		0.52
TFP			0.94
Eigenvalues	2.70	1.80	1.30
Variance	0.34	0.22	0.16
Cum. Variance	0.34	0.56	0.72

Note: Loadings with absolute values below 0.40 are omitted from the table

The next stage of the research process involved clustering methods to group the EU data portals. Figure 2 shows the clustering dendrogram, which is the result of the hierarchical clustering algorithm. In addition, Fig. 3 shows the best clustering solution for k-means (k = 5) using a cluster profiling plot in parallel coordinates (the clustering profiling plot obtained with K-medians is almost identical). Parallel coordinates are a frequent way of visualising how the Open Government Data Initiatives differ from each other across factors.

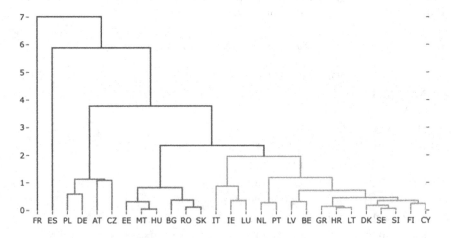

Fig. 2. Cluster dendrogram.

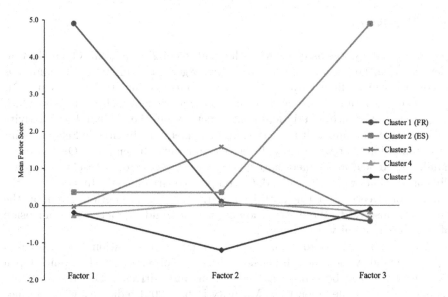

Fig. 3. Cluster profile plot for mean factor score of the clusters obtained with K-means.

Moreover, the composition of Open Data initiatives that form each cluster for K-means, K-medians and hierarchical clustering is shown in Table 5. In general, the techniques converge for the identification of 5 groups that are clearly distinguished from each other based on their behaviour through the factors. The resulting assignments of hierarchical clustering (with a cutoff distance equal to 2) and K-medians were identical. K-means reallocated one member (NL).

The first cluster is determined by the preeminent performance of France in factor 1. In the second cluster, Spain stands out for its score in factor 3, and has a slightly higher value for factor 1. Cluster 4 is the most numerous and shows an intermediate behaviour in the three factors. Cluster 3 and cluster 5 are characterised respectively by high and low values of the variables in factor 2.

Table 5. Cluster membership

Cluster	K-means	K-medians	Hierarchical clustering
1	FR	FR	FR
2	ES	ES	ES
3	AT, PL, NL, DE, CZ	AT, PL, DE, CZ	AT, PL, DE, CZ
4	IT, IE, LV, LU, GR, FI, DK, PT, CY, SE, HR, BE, SI, LT	IT, IE, LV, LU, NL, GR, FI, DK, PT, CY, SE, HR, BE, SI, LT	IT, IE, LV, LU, NL, GR, FI, DK, PT, CY, SE, HR, BE, SI, LT
5	BG, RO, EE, MT, SK, HU	BG, RO, EE, MT, SK, HU	BG, RO, EE, MT, SK, HU

5 Discussion

Our methodology was assessed with the analysis of 27 European Open Government Data initiatives and the Twitter activity generated in 2021. This allows us to compare our findings with the Open Data Maturity Report for the year 2021.

For our experiment, we used correlation analysis and factor analysis, which indicate the existence of a dimensional structure. On the one hand, the activity on Twitter, the number of use cases, and the mentions in Google Scholar point to a dimension that we could call "user community drivenness". On the other hand, the indicators of metadata quality and quantity of datasets describe a dimension that we could call "data compliance drivenness". In addition, the number of tweets from the portal suggests that the promotion given by the portals themselves to the distribution of content could characterise a dimension of "portal community drivenness".

The cluster analysis allows us to profile the European national portals based on the previously identified dimensions. First, we observe how the French Open Data initiative can be defined as "user community driven". This result is consistent with what the Open Data Maturity Report 2021 indicates, where France is the best-positioned country and is described as user-centric. The main reason for this can be the efforts paid by the French Open Data initiative that monitors the user feedback through multiple functionalities, including discussion forums on the individual datasets. Second, we see that the Spanish Open Government Data initiative has a high Twitter activity but this activity is mainly ruled by the public body coordinating the initiative. The Open Data Maturity Report highlights the efforts of this portal to create editorial content, optimise the search and discoverability of content, and use actively Facebook, LinkedIn, YouTube, and Flickr. Spain also reports using social listening tools, web analytics, and SEO positioning. Third, there are some initiatives with remarkable quality and size of published datasets, which do not hold a direct impact on Twitter activity, probably because the bodies coordinating the initiatives are not so active in disseminating their work in social networks. In general, these countries are positioned in the best performing categories of the Open Data Maturity Report. Fourth, we can observe that most initiatives report a medium-low level of quality and social network activity. Last, there are also some initiatives with the lowest level of quality and almost no presence on Twitter, which probably denotes that they have been started recently and are not mature enough to generate the interest of users. The members of this cluster correspond to the lagging categories of the Open Data Maturity Report.

Given the exploratory nature of the study, we would like to reflect on a series of issues that could serve to improve and deepen the measurement of user involvement in Open Government Data Initiatives. One of these issues is the effect of using absolute values of variables instead of relative values. In this regard, the population of the countries or the number of published datasets could be used as weighting factors of the involved variables. However, in the experiment carried out, these variables were poorly correlated with all the others. For instance, while populous countries like France and Spain nominally lead the interactions, we can see at the same time cases like Germany performing modestly for its large population. At this point, we can only formulate hypotheses to explain this lack of direct correlation between the population of the reference country and the volume of interactions around its national open data portal. Open data could not be considered a mainstream phenomenon and be limited to very compact community niches where the size of the national reference population has a secondary effect.

6 Conclusion

To conclude, this paper has proposed a methodology for measuring user involvement in Open Data initiatives by analysing the activity generated on Twitter and trying to understand the relationship between the social network activity and the main features characterising the size, quality, and maturity of Open Data initiatives. Moreover, apart from compiling the values of the different selected variables for these initiatives, there are relevant conclusions that can be derived from the results obtained through factor analysis and clustering techniques. Overall, policy makers can use findings to benchmark Open Data initiatives according to their interaction with the user community.

As future work, we would like to perform additional experiments validating the methodology and include a temporal analysis of the evolution of Twitter activity generated by Open Data initiatives since the year of their launch. Moreover, we would also like to explore the potential of making a qualitative analysis of the content through the use of techniques for sentiment analysis and semantic analysis of the tweets mentioning the Open Government Data Initiatives.

Last, in line with the growing interest in monitoring and measuring the open data re-use and the impact it generates, we hope that our work stimulates the discussion on the development of quantitative and qualitative alternative metrics for the evaluation of the impact of Open Data initiatives.

Acknowledgements. This paper is partially supported by the Aragon Regional Government through the project T59_20R. The work of Dagoberto José Herrera-Murillo and Abdul Aziz is supported by the ODECO project. This project has received funding from the European Union's Horizon 2020 research and innovation programme under the Marie Skłodowska-Curie grant agreement No. 955569.

References

1. Escribano, L.A., Collado, J.M.: Contar historias con los datos: Aragón Open Data Focus, una experiencia innovadora de reutilización de los datos del sector público. Scire: representación y organización del conocimiento **27**(1), 31–43 (2021)
2. Argüelles, M., del Carmen Benavides, M., Fernández, I.: A new approach to the identification of regional clusters: hierarchical clustering on principal components. Appl. Econ. **46**(21), 2511–2519 (2014)
3. Begany, G.M., Ramon Gil-Garcia, J.: Understanding the actual use of open data: levels of engagement and how they are related. Telemat. Inform. **63**, 101673 (2021)
4. Berrocal, J.L.A., Figuerola, C.G., Rodriguez, Á.F.Z.: Propuesta de índice de influencia de contenidos (Influ@ RT) en Twitter. Scire: representación y organización del conocimiento 21–26 (2015)

5. Carrara, W., Chan, W.-S., Fischer, S., Van-Steenbergen, E.: Creating value through open data: study on the impact of re-use of public data resources. European Commission (2015)
6. de Juana-Espinosa, S., Luján-Mora, S.: Open government data portals in the European Union: a dataset from 2015 to 2017. Data Brief **29**, 105156 (2020)
7. Edwards, C., Spence, P.R., Gentile, C.J., Edwards, A., Edwards, A.: How much Klout do you have... A test of system generated cues on source credibility. Comput. Hum. Behav. **29**(5), A12–A16 (2013)
8. Hair, J., Balbin, B., Black, W., Anderson, R.: Multivariate Data Analysis. Cengage Learning EMEA (2019)
9. Haustein, S., Costas, R., Larivière, V.: Characterizing social media metrics of scholarly papers: the effect of document properties and collaboration patterns. PLoS ONE **10**(3), e0120495 (2015)
10. Khan, N., Thelwall, M., Kousha, K.: Measuring the impact of biodiversity datasets: data reuse, citations and altmetrics. Scientometrics **126**(4), 3621–3639 (2021). https://doi.org/10.1007/s11192-021-03890-6
11. Kubler, S., Robert, J., Neumaier, S., Umbrich, J., Le Traon, Y.: Comparison of metadata quality in open data portals using the Analytic Hierarchy Process. Gov. Inf. Q. **35**(1), 13–29 (2018)
12. Moshkovitz, M., Dasgupta, S., Rashtchian, C., Frost, N.: Explainable k-means and k-medians clustering. In: International Conference on Machine Learning, pp. 7055–7065. PMLR (2020)
13. Neumaier, S., Umbrich, J., Polleres, A.: Automated quality assessment of metadata across open data portals. J. Data Inf. Qual. (JDIQ) **8**(1), 1–29 (2016)
14. Nikiforova, A., McBride, K.: Open government data portal usability: a user-centred usability analysis of 41 open government data portals. Telemat. Inform. **58**, 101539 (2021)
15. Nogueras-Iso, J., Lacasta, J., Ureña-Cámara, M.A., Ariza-López, F.J.: Quality of metadata in open data portals. IEEE Access **9**, 60364–60382 (2021)
16. Publications Office of the European Union. European Data Portal. https://data.europa.eu/en. Accessed 27 May 2022
17. Publications Office of the European Union. European Data Portal SPARQL Endpoint. https://data.europa.eu/sparql. Accessed 30 May 2022
18. Publications Office of the European Union. Open data maturity report 2021. Publications Office, LU (2022)
19. Reggi, L., Dawes, S.S.: Creating Open Government Data ecosystems: network relations among governments, user communities, NGOs and the media. Gov. Inf. Q. 101675 (2022)
20. Simonofski, A., Zuiderwijk, A., Clarinval, A., Hammedi, W.: Tailoring open government data portals for lay citizens: a gamification theory approach. Int. J. Inf. Manag. **65**, 102511 (2022)
21. Twitter, Inc., Twitter API v2. https://developer.twitter.com/en/docs/api-reference-index#twitter-api-v2. Accessed 30 May 2022
22. Van Loenen, B., et al.: Towards value-creating and sustainable open data ecosystems: a comparative case study and a research agenda. JeDEM-eJournal of eDemocracy Open Gov. **13**(2), 1–27 (2021)
23. Wilkinson, M.D., et al.: The FAIR Guiding Principles for scientific data management and stewardship. Sci. Data **3**(1), 160018 (2016)
24. Zhu, X., Freeman, M.A.: An evaluation of US municipal open data portals: a user interaction framework. J. Am. Soc. Inf. Sci. **70**(1), 27–37 (2019)

The Rise of GitHub in Scholarly Publications

Emily Escamilla[1]([✉])[iD], Martin Klein[2][iD], Talya Cooper[3][iD], Vicky Rampin[3][iD], Michele C. Weigle[1][iD], and Michael L. Nelson[1][iD]

[1] Old Dominion University, Norfolk, VA, USA
evogt001@odu.edu, {mweigle,mln}@cs.odu.edu
[2] Los Alamos National Laboratory, Los Alamos, NM, USA
mklein@lanl.gov
[3] New York University, New York, NY, USA
{tc3602,vs77}@nyu.edu

Abstract. The definition of scholarly content has expanded to include the data and source code that contribute to a publication. While major archiving efforts to preserve conventional scholarly content, typically in PDFs (e.g., LOCKSS, CLOCKSS, Portico), are underway, no analogous effort has yet emerged to preserve the data and code referenced in those PDFs, particularly the scholarly code hosted online on Git Hosting Platforms (GHPs). Similarly, the Software Heritage Foundation is working to archive public source code, but there is value in archiving the issue threads, pull requests, and wikis that provide important context to the code while maintaining their original URLs. In current implementations, source code and its ephemera are not preserved, which presents a problem for scholarly projects where reproducibility matters. To understand and quantify the scope of this issue, we analyzed the use of GHP URIs in the arXiv and PMC corpora from January 2007 to December 2021. In total, there were 253,590 URIs to GitHub, SourceForge, Bitbucket, and GitLab repositories across the 2.66 million publications in the corpora. We found that GitHub, GitLab, SourceForge, and Bitbucket were collectively linked to 160 times in 2007 and 76,746 times in 2021. In 2021, one out of five publications in the arXiv corpus included a URI to GitHub. The complexity of GHPs like GitHub is not amenable to conventional Web archiving techniques. Therefore, the growing use of GHPs in scholarly publications points to an urgent and growing need for dedicated efforts to archive their holdings in order to preserve research code and its scholarly ephemera.

Keywords: Web archiving · GitHub · arXiv · Digital preservation · Memento · Open source software

1 Introduction

Researchers increasingly use and create open source software as a part of their scholarship, making software a vital element of our scholarly record. A 2014 sur-

Supported by the Alfred P. Sloan Foundation.

G. Silvello et al. (Eds.): TPDL 2022, LNCS 13541, pp. 187–200, 2022.
https://doi.org/10.1007/978-3-031-16802-4_15

vey by the Software Sustainability Institute found that 92% of academic respondents use research software and 56% developed their own software [15]. These researchers rely on tools such as version control systems and repository hosting platforms to develop, reuse, version, and share software. A version control system (VCS) is a tool that helps users manage changes to a repository over time. A typical code repository contains a set of files, such as program and configuration files. Web-based repository hosting platform services let users host their code projects remotely. Repository hosting platforms also provide collaborative features, including discussion threads, and allow for edits and contributions by outside collaborators.

A study by Fäber [9] found that GitHub[1], a Git Hosting Platform (GHP), was the most popular repository hosting platform. A GHP is a type of repository hosting platform made specifically for Git VCS. These include platforms such as GitHub, GitLab, and SourceForge. The increased use of Git and GHPs in academia represents a victory for open access scholarship and for computational reproducibility. We believe that when people share code openly and receive credit for it (for example, through citations), potentially leading to novel collaboration and funding endeavors, open science benefits. These platforms allow for a number of scholarly activities like peer review; however, most lack a preservation plan. The fact that some VCSs have already been discontinued – Gitorious (2014), Google Code (2016), among others [25] – points to the urgency of the need for a more concerted preservation effort. In addition to sustainability concerns with the platforms themselves, few workflows, tools, and processes exist for preservation of research code, as they do for other scholarly materials such as papers, data, and media [7, 13, 23, 24]. As the use of Git and GHPs rises amongst researchers, it becomes more important to preserve research code in order to prevent gaps in this part of the scholarly record. Often these repositories represent the bulk of a scholar's time and efforts in their research. As such, these materials are key for verifying, reproducing, and building on each others' scholarly contributions.

In this paper, we present work that finds research software as it is represented in literature, quantifies its impact in the scholarly record, and provides a stronger basis for addressing the long-term sustainability of scholarly code and its contextual, scholarly ephemera. While source code repositories are not always included in the references of a publication, links to repositories appear throughout scholarly manuscripts as part of the evidence and support for the work being presented. We analyzed the arXiv and PubMed Central (PMC) corpora to determine the extent to which publications reference the Web at large and reference GHPs, specifically GitHub, GitLab, SourceForge, and Bitbucket. In both arXiv and PubMed Central, we found that the average number of URIs in a publication has steadily increased, as has the number of links to GHPs. In the arXiv corpus, one out of five publications contains a reference to GitHub, the most popular GHP in arXiv and PMC.

---

[1] https://github.com.

2   Related Work

This is one of few studies that looks at the representation of links *to* scholarly source code in scholarly literature. Previous works have investigated the opposite: representation of links *to* scholarly literature *from* scholarly source code repositories. Wattanakriengkrai et al. [28] studied the extent to which scholarly papers are cited in public GitHub repositories to gain key insights into the landscape of scholarly source code production, and uncovered potential problems with long-term access, tracing, and evolution of these repositories. Färber [9] analyzed data from Microsoft Academic Graph, which attempts to map publications to their source code repositories, in order to look at the content and popularity of academic source code related to published work. Färber's work focuses on the content of the GitHub repositories referenced in scholarly publications, while our work looks at how scholarly publications link to GHPs. Other related work addresses finding scholarly source code repositories hosted on GHP, either by looking through the content of the repository or by searching for links to scholarly literature in the repositories themselves. Hasselbring et al. [12] investigated public repositories on GitHub and estimated that it contained over 5,000 repositories of specifically research software – a similar estimation to Färber.

Understanding the extent to which scholarly articles reference source code is important because scholarly materials that are hosted on the Web are vulnerable to decay in the same manner as Web resources in general. In 2014, Klein et al. [19] analyzed the use of URIs to the Web at large in the arXiv, Elsevier, and PMC corpora from 1997 to 2012. They found that the number of general URIs used in scholarly publications rapidly increased from 1997 to 2012. However, they also found that reference rot affects nearly 20% of Science, Technology, and Medicine (STM) publications. When looking specifically at publications with a Web reference, seven out of ten publications are affected by reference rot. Reference rot is a general term that indicates that either link rot or content drift has altered the content of the Web page to be different than the content to which the author was originally referring [27]. Link rot occurs when the URI that was originally referenced is completely inaccessible. Link rot can cause the "404: Page not found" error that most Web users have experienced. Reference rot is caused by the dynamic and ephemeral nature of the Web. Content drift occurs when the content that was originally referenced by a URI is different from the content currently available at the URI. Jones et al. [16] found that 75% of references suffer from content drift. Additionally, they found that the occurrence and impact of content drift increases over time. In 2015, only 25% of referenced resources from 2012 publications were unchanged and, worse yet, only 10% of publications from 2006 were unchanged.

Understanding the scope of how scholarly source code is represented in scholarly literature is vital to strengthening efforts to preserve and make this code available for the long-term, as a part of the scholarly record. Some researchers attempt to make their code available for the long-term by self-archiving: depositing their own materials into a repository or archive. However, of academics who write source code, only 47.2% self-archive that code [22]. While self-archiving can help safeguard research software, it has not yet become part of scholars' routines.

Zenodo[2], a non-profit repository maintained by CERN that supports open data and open access to digital scholarly resources, is one example of a repository with specific functionality to support researchers who wish to self-archiving their code for long-term access. Zenodo provides a webhook that allows users to deposit new releases from GitHub repositories. Zenodo makes a copy of the code, rather than simply linking out to the GitHub page, creates relationships to previous and subsequent versions of the code, and mints a DOI for the record with software-specific metadata attached.

Other approaches aim to ensure long-term access to scholarly code without relying on researchers doing preservation work themselves. The non-profit Software Heritage[3] conducts programmatic captures of public source code on the web with the goal "to collect, preserve, and share all software that is publicly available in source code form". As part of this goal, the content of Google Code, which was phased out in 2016, is contained in Software Heritage [5].

However, software and code are not sufficient as stand-alone products, especially in a scholarly context where reproducibility matters. For instance, documentation about installation and dependencies are crucial for secondary users who want to reproduce and build on research. In addition, many projects maintain discussions, wikis, and other contextual items that make the source code more comprehensible and reusable for others. When referring to scholarly source code, we call these materials *scholarly ephemera* [10]. Scholarly ephemera housed with a repository on a GHP (e.g., Issues on GitHub) include useful, preservation-worthy information, such as peer review, discussion of important implementation details, and questions from secondary users of the scholarly code.

Presently, neither self-archived code nor programmatically captured code incorporates the scholarly ephemera that can help secondary readers understand and evaluate the source code being cited. This is where Web archiving may be beneficial. Web archiving's goal lies in preserving the Web so that users can see a Web page as it existed at a certain point in time, which is helpful for archiving source code and the accompanying scholarly ephemera. However, because of the resources it takes to archive the Web, automated Web archiving services like the Internet Archive will crawl the most visited Web pages frequently, while the least visited Web pages, including scholarly content, may never be fully captured. Although the Internet Archive includes some GHP sites, it cannot be depended upon to preserve any given page in its entirety. Other Web archiving tools like the Webrecorder suite [20] provide higher quality captures of source code and ephemera, but take more time, resulting in decreased scalability for archiving the Web at large. Also, while current Web archiving implementations are well-suited for archiving the scholarly ephemera around scholarly code, they are less effective with the source code itself, which has different metadata and reuse needs than a typical Web page.

---

[2] https://zenodo.org.

[3] https://softwareheritage.org/.

We know that: a) materials hosted on the Web and cited in scholarly literature are subject to reference rot, b) source code and its important scholarly ephemera are particularly at risk because of a lack of holistic archiving, and c) source code is being cited more in our scholarly literature. To understand the scope of source code citations and quantify the risk of loss, we analyzed a corpus of scholarly publications and the URIs to GHPs that the publications contain.

3   Methodology

We decided to analyze the arXiv and PubMed Central corpora as a representative sample of scholarly publications across Science, Technology, Engineering, and Math (STEM) disciplines, in order to understand how scholarly code is being referenced over time and, therefore, both woven into the fabric of our scholarly conversation and worthy of preservation. arXiv is one of the largest and most popular pre-print services, and the corpus contains over 2 million submissions [8] from eight disciplines: physics, mathematics, computer science, quantitative biology, quantitative finance, statistics, electrical engineering and systems science, and economics. The arXiv corpus does not allow for anonymous submissions, is publicly available, and is accessible for programmatic acquisition and analysis. The PubMed Central (PMC) corpus contains publicly available full-text articles from a wide range of biomedical and life sciences journals. Only peer-reviewed journals are eligible for inclusion.[4] The most prevalent journals in the corpus are listed in Table 1 along with the number of articles in the corpus, the date of the first article available, and the date of the latest article. The size and availability of the arXiv and PMC corpora make them suitable for the purposes of our study.

Table 1. Five most popular journals in the PMC corpus

Journal	Articles	Earliest	Latest
The Indian Medical Gazelle	29,143	1866	1955
The Journal of Cell Biology	24,349	1962	2022
The Journal of Experimental Medicine	24,207	1896	2022
BMJ Open	21,565	2011	2022
Edinburg Medical Journal	20,160	1855	1954

In April 2007, the arXiv identifier scheme changed to accommodate a larger number of submissions and to address other categorization issues.[5] We decided that beginning our arXiv corpus in April 2007 would suit our analysis, because three of the four repository platforms that we analyzed began after 2007. Each pre-print in arXiv can have multiple versions. When an author uploads a new version of the pre-print to the service, the version number increments by one.

---

[4] https://www.ncbi.nlm.nih.gov/pmc/pub/addjournal/.

[5] https://arxiv.org/help/arxiv_identifier.

All versions of a pre-print are accessible in arXiv via a version-specific URI. For our analysis, we considered only the latest version of each submission, assuming that the final submission was the most complete and most representative of the author's intentions. With only the latest version of each submission, our arXiv corpus contained 1.56 million publications in PDF format from April 2007 to December 2021.

The PMC corpus includes articles from the late 1700s to present. In order to more easily compare the corpora and because, as previously noted, three of the four repository platforms we analyzed began after 2007, we decided that beginning our PMC corpus in January 2007 was appropriate for our analysis. Additionally, the PMC corpus separates articles that are available for commercial use from those that are only available for non-commercial use. We chose to analyze the articles that were only available for non-commercial use. Our PMC corpus contained 1.08 million publications in PDF format from 2007 to 2021. Between the arXiv and PMC corpora, we analyzed 2,641,041 publications.

A study by Milliken [10] conducted initial testing of GitHub, GitLab, Source-Forge, and Bitbucket to understand the archival quality available through Brozzler (Archive-It's crawler), a Standard crawler (Heritrix and Umbra), and Memento Tracer. Our project is a continuation of that study and, as a result, we chose to analyze the use of those four GHPs in the arXiv and PMC corpora. The GHPs are summarized in Table 2.

Table 2. Repository platforms

Name	Start date	Protocol	URI
SourceForge	1999	git and SVN	https://sourceforge.net
Bitbucket	2008	git	https://bitbucket.org
GitHub	2008	git	https://github.com
GitLab	2014	git	https://gitlab.com

URIs are not exclusively found in the References section of a publication; they also commonly appear in footnotes and the body of the text. To extract all of the URIs in each publication, regardless of location, we leveraged two Python libraries: PyPDF2[6] and PyPDFium2.[7] We used PyPDF2 to extract annotated URIs and PyPDFium2 to extract URIs from the PDF text. We followed a similar URI characterization method as that done by Klein et al. [19] who identified URIs to "Web at large" resources in-scope for their study. Since we are investigating links to GHPs, our primary goal with extraction was to identify URIs to one of the four GHPs. However, we also identified URIs to the Web at large to provide context for the frequency and use of URIs to the GHPs. To do this, we filtered out a number of URIs that were out of scope for this study. We dismissed URIs with a scheme other than HTTP or HTTPS, including localhost

---

[6] https://pypi.org/project/PyPDF2/.
[7] https://pypi.org/project/pypdfium2/.

and private/protected IP ranges. We also dismissed URIs to arXiv, Elsevier RefHub,[8] CrossRef Crossmark [14], and HTTP DOIs and, as such, follow the definition of URIs to "Web at large" resources that are in-scope for our work. DOIs resolve to artifacts, most commonly papers but increasingly also to data (e.g., via Dryad) and source code (e.g., via Zenodo). Links to Elsevier RefHub and CrossRef Crossmark function similarly to DOIs and are often added by the publisher. We decided to exclude DOI and DOI-like references following Klein et al.'s assumption that, for the most part, such artifacts are in-scope for existing archiving and preservation efforts such as LOCKSS [23], CLOCKSS [24], and Portico [7]. Our source code is available on GitHub [6].

After extracting URIs from the PDFs in our corpora, we found 7,746,682 in-scope URIs: 4,039,772 URIs from the arXiv corpus and 3,706,910 URIs from the PMC corpus. Out of 2.64 million files, 1,439,177 files (54.06%) contained a URI. Once we had collected all of the URIs from the PDFs, we used regular expressions to filter and categorize the URIs that referenced one of the four GHPs. As a result, URIs to repository pages with custom domain names [11] were not captured. We found a total of 253,590 URIs to one of the four GHPs: 231,206 URIs from the arXiv corpus and 22,384 URIs from the PMC corpus. Additionally, we found that 92.56% of the GHP URIs were still available on the live Web. All GHP URIs in a publication have been deemed by the authors to be important enough for inclusion in the publication. As a result, we do not differentiate links to GHPs regardless of link depth or location in the publication. Inclusion of a GHP URI does not indicate an authorship or ownership claim. GHP URIs in a publication indicate that a resource either 1) impacted the work presented in the publications or 2) was a product of the study. Both cases communicate the importance of the repository and need for preservation. The number of URIs for each GHP are shown in Table 3. The URIs to GitHub account for 92.3% of the URIs to one of the four GHPs.

Table 3. Number of references to each GHP in the arXiv and PMC corpora

Repository platform	arXiv	PMC
GitHub	215,621	18,471
SourceForge	9,412	3,309
Bitbucket	3,525	437
GitLab	2,648	167

4 Results

By extracting URIs for the four repository platforms, we made a number of interesting observations. As shown in Fig. 1, we found a continuation of the significant increase in the prevalence of URIs in publications that Klein et al.

---

[8] https://refhub.elsevier.com.

[19] found in 2014. Figure 1 shows the average number of in-scope URIs and the average number of URIs to one of the four GHPs in each publication by month of submission for both the arXiv and PMC corpora. The URIs to one of the four GHPs are a subset of in-scope URIs extracted from the publications. From 2007 to 2021, the average number of URIs per publications has steadily risen. In 2007, publications contained an average of 1.02 URIs. In 2021, publications contained an average of 5.06 URIs. The average number of in-scope URIs in each publication is indicated by the red and orange lines in Fig. 1.

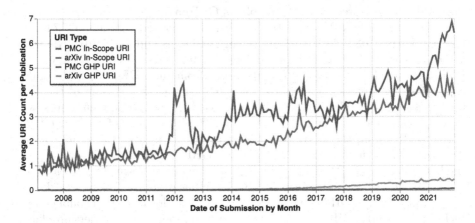

Fig. 1. The average number of in-scope URIs and URIs to repository platforms per publication over time (Color figure online)

While the prevalence of URIs in general has increased, the number of URIs to repository platforms has also grown from 2007 to 2021. Just as there was a shift from not including Web resources in scholarly publications to including Web resources, there has also been a shift to referencing repository platforms in scholarly publications. Figure 2 shows that references to GitHub have steadily risen from 2014 to 2021 while the frequency of references to the other three platforms have remained low during that time period. In the arXiv corpus shown in Fig. 2a, less than 1% of publications contain a URI to GitLab, Bitbucket, or SourceForge in any given year from 2007 to 2021. However, an average of 20% of publications contained a URI to GitHub in 2021. The PMC corpus in Fig. 2b shows an initial prevalence of SourceForge beginning in 2007, but it is replaced by GitHub in 2015. Both graphs show a steady increase in the use of GitHub URIs in scholarly publications. Like URIs to the Web at large, URIs to repositories contribute to the context and argument of the publication. As the prevalence of GitHub URIs in publications increases, so does the importance of archiving source code repositories with its scholarly ephemera.

Additionally, while 67% of publications only reference a given repository once, 45,780 publications reference a given platform's holding more than once. Figure 3 shows the frequency of GHP URIs in publications that contain one or

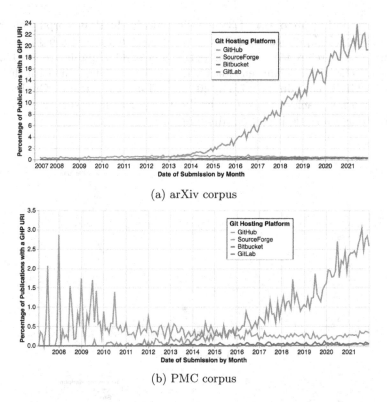

(a) arXiv corpus

(b) PMC corpus

Fig. 2. The percentage of publications with a URI to a repository platform over time. Please note that the graphs are not on the same y-axis scale.

more GHP URI. For example, as shown in Fig. 3a, of the 125,711 publications in the arXiv corpus that reference GitHub, 83,328 publications (66.3%) reference GitHub once, 42,383 publications (33.7%) reference GitHub more than once, and 863 publications (0.687%) reference GitHub more than ten times. We manually inspected a sample of the publications with the most URIs to one of the four GHPs and found these publications tend to detail a software product or provide an overview of a topic, such as survey paper. The top three publications containing the most URIs to a GHP include 153 [4], 160 [1], and 896 [26] URIs to GitHub. Dhole et al. [4] developed a software product and included URIs to the implementation of the features listed in the publication. Agol et al. [1] created an open-source package and linked to the implementation of the algorithms and processes described in the publication. Truyen et al. [26] wrote a survey paper comparing frameworks. A majority of the frameworks surveyed are documented in GitHub, so the survey contains numerous URIs to the documentation. The publication by Truyen et al. with 896 URIs to GitHub is not included in Fig. 3, because it represents such a large outlier compared to the other publications in the corpus.

As shown in Fig. 3b, of the 11,386 publications in the PMC corpus that reference GitHub, 7,983 publications (70.1%) reference GitHub once, but 3,403 publications (29.9%) reference GitHub more than once and 60 publications (0.527%) reference GitHub more than ten times. The top four publications with the most URIs to a GHPs contain 39 [17,21], 40 [3], and 45 [29] URIs to GitHub. Like the arXiv corpus, each of these four publications provides a survey of the computation tools available in a given discipline.

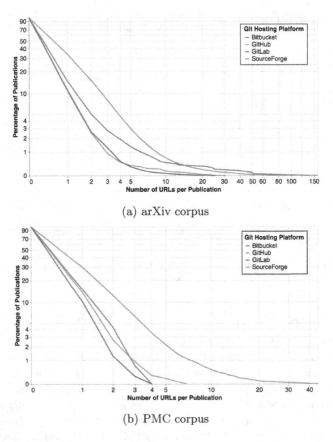

(a) arXiv corpus

(b) PMC corpus

Fig. 3. If a publication links to GHP, how many links does it have? This figure is a Complementary Cumulative Distribution Function (CCDF) graphing the frequency of GHP URIs in publications with 1 or more GHP URI

Publications with multiple references to GitHub imply the repositories have significant value and relevance for the authors, indicating that they deemed the repository contents important to the content of the publication. As a result, these repositories should be preserved in archives to guarantee that future readers can access the publication's full context.

We also analyzed the use of URIs to GHPs by discipline for the arXiv corpus. When submitting an article to arXiv, authors are prompted to select the primary discipline of the article. We used the metadata associated with each article to map each discipline to the four GHPs based on the number of URIs to each GHP. Figure 4 shows a visualization of the relationship between GHPs and STEM disciplines. Computer Science and Physics contain the highest number of URIs to a GHP. Considering the prevalence of software products and models in the Computer Science and Physics disciplines, these results are not surprising.

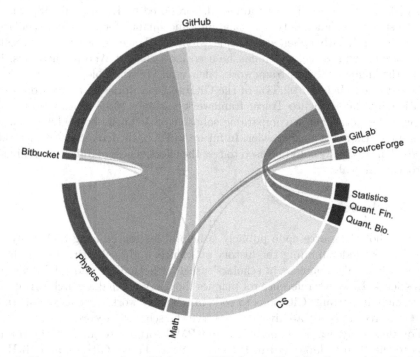

Fig. 4. Mapping the number of links to a GHP (top half of the diagram) by discipline (bottom half) for the arXiv corpus

5   Discussion

We analyzed the holdings of the arXiv and PMC corpora, but other corpora that service a wider variety of disciplines could provide additional perspectives. Additionally, authors must submit their paper to the arXiv corpus. This could create another source of bias in that authors must be able to navigate the submission process and must choose to submit their publication. Authors who intentionally submit their paper to arXiv are proving that they value open source and resource sharing, so this may be one reason that links to GHPs are more prevalent in the arXiv corpus. The PMC corpus is an example of a corpus that does not require action by the authors. Journals apply to be included in the PMC archive and all articles from the journal are automatically included. In future work, we will look at aggregating additional corpora to obtain a more representative sample of disciplines.

This analysis can also be used to supplement software preservation efforts. Curators and archivists could use these extraction methods to identify potential software of interest for their collections. Using different methods, these URIs can then be used to seed the archiving process. For instance, these URIs could be used with the Memento Tracer framework[9] proposed by Klein et al. [18], which aims to strike a balance between scalability and quality for archiving scholarly code with its scholarly ephemera at scale. Memento Tracer allows users to create a heuristic called a trace, which can be used for a class of Web publications. In testing the Memento Tracer framework, Klein et al. [18] was able to capture 100% of the expected URIs for 92.83% of the GitHub repositories in a given dataset. Additionally, the Memento Tracer framework was only 10.17 times slower than a typical crawler, while a comparable solution by Brunelle et al. [2] was 38.9 times slower than a typical crawler. In future work, URIs derived using methods proposed in this study could be used to test the effectiveness of different archiving approaches at scale.

6   Conclusions

Sharing scholarly source code publicly is helpful for reproducing and verifying others' work, understanding the history of science, and facilitating far-reaching collaborations. The increase in scholars' usage of both VCS and GHP will aid open science. However, reference rot plagues the live Web, making archival efforts increasingly important. Citations to code in scholarly work serve as signals that these resources must be archived to preserve the scholarly record.

For this study, we used the arXiv and PMC corpora to analyze the use of URIs to the Web at large and to Bitbucket, SourceForge, GitLab, and GitHub in scholarly publications. Our research found that scholarly publications increasingly reference the Web and software repository platforms. On average, a publication contains five URIs. Additionally, one out of five publications contains a reference to GitHub in the arXiv corpus. Each reference to a GHP's URI illustrates that content on these platforms constitutes an essential part of the context of the scholarly publication, and highlights the need to archive source code and accompanying scholarly ephemera hosted on GHPs.

References

1. Agol, E., Hernandez, D.M., Langford, Z.: A differentiable N-body code for transit timing and dynamical modeling. I. Algorithm and derivatives. Technical report arXiv:2106.02188, arXiv (2021). https://doi.org/10.1093/mnras/stab2044

---

[9] http://tracer.mementoweb.org.

2. Brunelle, J.F., Weigle, M.C., Nelson, M.L.: Archival crawlers and JavaScript: discover more stuff but crawl more slowly. In: Proceedings of the 2017 ACM/IEEE Joint Conference on Digital Libraries (JCDL), pp. 1–10. IEEE (2017). https://doi.org/10.1109/JCDL.2017.7991554

3. Chen, L., et al.: The bioinformatics toolbox for circRNA discovery and analysis. Brief. Bioinform. **22**(2), 1706–1728 (2021). https://doi.org/10.1093/bib/bbaa001

4. Dhole, K.D., et al.: NL-augmenter: a framework for task-sensitive natural language augmentation. Technical report. arXiv:2112.02721 [cs], arXiv (2021)

5. Di Cosmo, R., Zacchiroli, S.: Software heritage: why and how to preserve software source code. In: Proceedings of the iPRES 2017–14th International Conference on Digital Preservation, pp. 1–10 (2017). https://hal.archives-ouvertes.fr/hal-01590958

6. Escamilla, E.: Extract-URLs (2021). https://github.com/elescamilla/Extract-URLs

7. Fenton, E.G.: An overview of portico: an electronic archiving service. Ser. Rev. **32**(2), 81–86 (2006). https://doi.org/10.1080/00987913.2006.10765036

8. Fromme, A.: arXiv hits 2M submissions (2022). https://news.cornell.edu/stories/2022/01/arxiv-hits-2m-submissions

9. Färber, M.: Analyzing the GitHub repositories of research papers. In: Proceedings of the ACM/IEEE Joint Conference on Digital Libraries in 2020, pp. 491–492. ACM (2020). https://doi.org/10.1145/3383583.3398578

10. Milliken, G.: Archiving the scholarly git experience: an environmental scan. Technical report, arXiv (2021). https://osf.io/ku24q/

11. GitHub Docs: Managing a custom domain for your GitHub Pages site (2022). https://docs.github.com/en/pages/configuring-a-custom-domain-for-your-github-pages-site/managing-a-custom-domain-for-your-github-pages-site

12. Hasselbring, W., Carr, L., Hettrick, S., Packer, H., Tiropanis, T.: FAIR and open computer science research software. Technical report. 1908.05986, arXiv (2019). https://doi.org/10.48550/arXiv.1908.05986

13. He, L., Nahar, V.: Reuse of scientific data in academic publications: an investigation of Dryad Digital Repository. Aslib J. Inf. Manag. **68**(4), 478–494 (2016). https://doi.org/10.1108/AJIM-01-2016-0008

14. Hendricks, G., Tkaczyk, D., Lin, J., Feeney, P.: Crossref: the sustainable source of community-owned scholarly metadata. Quant. Sci. Stud. **1**(1), 414–427 (2020). https://doi.org/10.1162/qss_a_00022

15. Hettrick, S.: It's impossible to conduct research without software, say 7 out of 10 UK researchers (2014). https://www.software.ac.uk/blog/2014-12-04-its-impossible-conduct-research-without-software-say-7-out-10-uk-researchers

16. Jones, S.M., Van de Sompel, H., Shankar, H., Klein, M., Tobin, R., Grover, C.: Scholarly context adrift: three out of four URI references lead to changed content. PLoS ONE **11**, 1–32 (2016). https://doi.org/10.1371/journal.pone.0167475

17. Kayani, M., Huang, W., Feng, R., Chen, L.: Genome-resolved metagenomics using environmental and clinical samples. Briefings Bioinform. **22**(5) (2021). https://doi.org/10.1093/bib/bbab030

18. Klein, M., Shankar, H., Balakireva, L., Van de Sompel, H.: The memento tracer framework: balancing quality and scalability for web archiving. In: Doucet, A., Isaac, A., Golub, K., Aalberg, T., Jatowt, A. (eds.) TPDL 2019. LNCS, vol. 11799, pp. 163–176. Springer, Cham (2019). https://doi.org/10.1007/978-3-030-30760-8_15

19. Klein, M., et al.: Scholarly context not found: one in five articles suffers from reference rot. PLoS ONE **9**, 1–39 (2014). https://doi.org/10.1371/journal.pone.0115253

20. Kreymer, I.: A New Phase for Webrecorder Project, Conifer and ReplayWeb.page (2020). https://webrecorder.net/2020/06/11/webrecorder-conifer-and-replayweb-page.html

21. Kuo, T., Zavaleta Rojas, H., Ohno-Machado, L.: Comparison of blockchain platforms: a systematic review and healthcare examples. J. Am. Med. Inform. Assoc. **26**(5), 462–478 (2019). https://doi.org/10.1093/jamia/ocy185

22. Milliken, G., Nguyen, S., Steeves, V.: A behavioral approach to understanding the git experience. In: Proceedings of the HICSS-54, p. 7239 (2021). https://doi.org/10.24251/HICSS.2021.872

23. Reich, V., Rosenthal, D.S.H.: LOCKSS: a permanent web publishing and access system. D-Lib Mag. **7**(6) (2001). https://doi.org/10.1045/june2001-reich

24. Reich, V.: CLOCKSS-It takes a community. Ser. Libr. **54**(1–2), 135–139 (2008). https://doi.org/10.1080/03615260801973968

25. Squire, M.: Forge++: the changing landscape of development. In: Proceedings of the HICSS (2014). https://doi.org/10.1109/HICSS.2014.405

26. Truyen, E., Van Landuyt, D., Preuveneers, D., Lagaisse, B., Joosen, W.: A comprehensive feature comparison study of open-source container orchestration frameworks. Technical report, arXiv (2021). https://doi.org/10.48550/arXiv.2002.02806

27. Van de Sompel, H., Klein, M., Shankar, H.: Towards robust hyperlinks for web-based scholarly communication. In: Watt, S.M., Davenport, J.H., Sexton, A.P., Sojka, P., Urban, J. (eds.) CICM 2014. LNCS (LNAI), vol. 8543, pp. 12–25. Springer, Cham (2014). https://doi.org/10.1007/978-3-319-08434-3_2

28. Wattanakriengkrai, S., et al.: GitHub repositories with links to academic papers: public access, traceability, and evolution. J. Syst. Softw. **183** (2022). https://doi.org/10.1016/j.jss.2021.111117

29. Yang, C., et al.: A review of computational tools for generating metagenome-assembled genomes from metagenomic sequencing data. Comput. Struct. Biotechnol. J. **19**, 6301–6314 (2021). https://doi.org/10.1016/j.csbj.2021.11.028

Whois? Deep Author Name Disambiguation Using Bibliographic Data

Zeyd Boukhers[1,2](✉) and Nagaraj Bahubali Asundi[1]

[1] Institute for Web Science and Technologies (WeST), University of Koblenz-Landau,
Koblenz, Germany
{boukhers,nagarajbahubali}@uni-koblenz.de
[2] Fraunhofer Institute for Applied Information Technology,
Sankt Augustin, Germany

Abstract. As the number of authors is increasing exponentially over years, the number of authors sharing the same names is increasing proportionally. This makes it challenging to assign newly published papers to their adequate authors. Therefore, Author Name Ambiguity (ANA) is considered a critical open problem in digital libraries. This paper proposes an Author Name Disambiguation (AND) approach that links author names to their real-world entities by leveraging their co-authors and domain of research. To this end, we use a collection from the DBLP repository that contains more than 5 million bibliographic records authored by around 2.6 million co-authors. Our approach first groups authors who share the same last names and same first name initials. The author within each group is identified by capturing the relation with his/her co-authors and area of research, which is represented by the titles of the validated publications of the corresponding author. To this end, we train a neural network model that learns from the representations of the co-authors and titles. We validated the effectiveness of our approach by conducting extensive experiments on a large dataset.

Keywords: Author name disambiguation · Entity linkage · Bibliographic data · Neural networks · Classification

1 Introduction

Author name disambiguation is an important task in digital libraries to ensure that each publication is properly linked to its corresponding co-authors. Consequently, author-level metrics can be accurately calculated and authors' publications can be easily found. However, this task is extremely challenging due to the high number of authors sharing the same names. In this paper, *author name* denotes a sequence of characters referring to one or several authors[1], whereas *author* refers to a unique person authoring at least one publication and cannot be identified only by his/her *author name*[2] but rather with the support of other

---

[1] It is estimated that about 114 million people share 300 common names.

[2] In the DBLP database, there are 27 exact matches of 'Chen Li', 23 reverse matches and more than 1000 partial matches.

© Springer Nature Switzerland AG 2022
G. Silvello et al. (Eds.): TPDL 2022, LNCS 13541, pp. 201–215, 2022.
https://doi.org/10.1007/978-3-031-16802-4_16

identifiers such as ORCID, ResearchGate ID and Semantic Scholar author ID. Although relying on these identifiers almost eliminates any chance of mislinking a publication to its appropriate author, most bibliographic sources do not include such identifiers. This is because not all of the authors are keen to use these identifiers and if they are, there is no procedure or policy to include their identifiers when they are cited. Therefore, in bibliographic data (e.g. references), authors are commonly referred to by their names only. Considering the high number of authors sharing the same names (i.e. homonymy), it is difficult to link the names in bibliographic sources to their real-world authors especially when the source of the reference is not available or does not provide indicators of the author's identity. The problem is more critical when names are substituted by their initials to save space, and when they are erroneous due to wrong manual editing. Disciplines like social sciences and humanities suffer more from this problem as most of the publishers are small and mid-sized and cannot ensure the continuous integrity of the bibliographic data.

Since these problems are known for decades, several studies [2,7,9,16–18, 20,24,27,36] have been conducted using different machine learning approaches. This problem is often tackled using supervised approaches such as Support Vector Machine (SVM) [11], Bayesian Classification [36] and Neural networks [31]. These approaches rely on the matching between publications and authors which are verified either manually or automatically. Unsupervised approaches [6,19,22] have also been used to assess the similarity between a pair of papers. Other unsupervised approaches are also used to estimate the number of co-authors sharing the same name [37] and decide whether new records can be assigned to an existing author or a new one [27]. Due to the continuous increase of publications, each of which cites tens of other publications and the difficulty to label this streaming data, semi-supervised approaches [23,38] were also employed. Recent approaches [33,35] leveraged the outstanding efficiency of deep learning on different domains to exploit the relationship among publications using network embedding. All these approaches use the available publication data about authors such as titles, venues, year of publication and affiliation. Some of these approaches are currently integrated into different bibliographic systems. However, all of them require an exhausting manual correction to reach an acceptable accuracy. In addition, most of these approaches rely on the metadata extracted from the papers which are supposed to be correct and complete. In real scenarios, the source of the paper is not always easy to find and only the reference is available.

In this paper, we aim to employ bibliographic data consisting of publication records to link each author's name in unseen records to their appropriate real-world authors (i.e. DBLP identifiers) by leveraging their co-authors and area of research embedded in the publication title and source. Note that the goal of this paper is to disambiguate author names in newly published papers that are not recorded in any bibliographic database. Therefore, all records that are considered unseen are discarded from the bibliographic data and used only for testing the approach. The assumption is that any author is most likely to publish articles in specific fields of research. Therefore, we employ articles' titles and sources (i.e. Journal, Booktitle, etc.) to bring authors close to their fields of research represented by the titles and sources of publications. We also assume that authors who already published together are more likely to continue collaborating and publishing other papers.

For the goal mentioned above, our proposed model is trained on a bibliographic collection obtained from DBLP, where a sample consists of a target author, pair of co-authors, title and source. For co-authors, the input is a vector representation obtained by applying Char2Vec which returns character-level embedding of words. For title and source, the BERT model is used to capture the semantic representations of the sequence of words. Our model is trained and tested on a challenging dataset, where thousands of authors share the same atomic name variate. The main contributions of this paper are:

- We proposed a novel approach for author name disambiguation using semantic and symbolic representations of titles, sources, and co-authors.
- We provided a statistical overview of the problem of author name ambiguity.
- We conducted experiments on challenging datasets simulating a critical scenario.
- The obtained results and the comparison against baseline approaches demonstrate the effectiveness of our model in disambiguating author names.

The rest of the paper is organized as follows. Section 2 briefly presents related work. Section 3 describes the proposed framework. Section 4 presents the dataset, implementation details and the obtained results of the proposed model. Finally, Sect. 5 concludes the paper and gives insights into future work.

2   Related Work

In this section, we discuss recent approaches softly categorized into three categories, namely unsupervised-, supervised- and graph-based.

2.1   Unsupervised-Based

Most of the studies treat the problem of author name ambiguity as an unsupervised task [18,19,27,37] using algorithms like DBSCAN [18] and agglomerative clustering [32]. Liu et al. [22] and Kim et al. [19] rely on the similarity between a pair of records with the same name to disambiguate author names on the PubMed dataset. Zhang et al. [37] used Recurrent Neural Network to estimate the number of unique authors in the Aminer dataset. This process is followed by manual annotation. In this direction, Ferreira et al. [8] have proposed a two-phases approach applied to the DBLP dataset, where the first one is obtaining clusters of authorship records and then disambiguation is applied to each cluster. Wu et al. [32] fused features such as affiliation and content of papers using Shannon's entropy to obtain a matrix representing pairwise correlations of papers which is in return used by hierarchical agglomerative clustering to disambiguate author names on Arnetminer dataset. Similar features have been employed by other approaches [1,34].

2.2   Supervised-Based

Supervised approaches [11,26,28,31,36] are also widely used but mainly only after applying blocking that gathers authors sharing the same names together. Han et al. [11] present two supervised learning approaches to disambiguate authors in cited references. Given a reference, the first approach uses the naive Bayes model to find the author class with the maximal posterior probability of being the author of the cited reference. The second approach uses SVM to classify references from DBLP to their appropriate authors. Sun et al. [28] employ heuristic features like the percentage of citations gathered by the top name variations for an author to disambiguate common author names. Neural networks are also used [31] to verify if two references are close enough to be authored by the same target author or not. Hourrane et al. [15] propose a corpus-based approach that uses word embeddings to compute the similarity between cited references. In [5], an Entity Resolution system called the DEEPER is proposed. It uses a combination of bi-directional recurrent neural networks along with Long Short Term Memory (LSTM) as the hidden units to generate a distributed representation for each tuple to capture the similarities between them. Zhang et al. [36] proposed an online Bayesian approach to identify authors with ambiguous names and as a case study, bibliographic data in a temporal stream format is used and the disambiguation is resolved by partitioning the papers into homogeneous groups.

2.3   Graph-Based

As bibliographic data can be viewed as a graph of citations, several approaches have leveraged this property to overcome the problem of author name ambiguation [12,14,33,35]. Hoffart et al. [14] present a method for collective disambiguation of author names, which harnesses the context from a knowledge base and uses a new form of coherence graph. Their method generates a weighted graph of the candidate entities and mentions to compute a dense sub-graph that approximates the best entity-mention mapping. Xianpei et al. [12] aim to improve the traditional entity linking method by proposing a graph-based collective entity linking approach that can model and exploit the global interdependence, i.e., the mutual dependence between the entities. In [35], the problem of author name ambiguity is overcome using relational information considering three graphs: person-person, person-document and document-document. The task becomes then a graph clustering task with the goal that each cluster contains documents authored by a unique real-world author. For each ambiguous name, Xu et al. [33] build a network of papers with multiple relationships. A network-embedding method is proposed to learn paper representations, where the gap between positive and negative edges is optimized. Further, HDBSCAN is used to cluster paper representations into disjoint sets such that each set contains all papers of a unique real-world author.

3   Approach: *WhoIs*

In this paper, author name disambiguation is designed using a bibliographic dataset $\mathcal{D} = \{d_i\}_{i=1}^N$, consisting of N bibliographic records, where each record d_i refers to a unique publication such that $d_i = \{t_i, s_i, \langle a_{i,u}, \delta_{i,u} \rangle_{u=1}^{\omega_i}\}$. Here, t_i and s_i denote the *title* and *source* of the record, respectively. $a_{i,u}$ and $\delta_{i,u}$ refer to the uth author and its corresponding name, respectively, among ω_i co-authors of d_i. Let $\Delta = \{\delta(m)\}_{m=1}^M$ be a set of M unique author names in D shared by a set of L unique authors $\mathcal{A} = \{a(l)\}_{l=1}^L$ co-authoring all records in D, where $L >> M$. Note that each author name $\delta(m)$ might refer to one or more authors in $\mathcal{A}$ and each author $a(l)$ might be referred to by one or two author names in Δ. This is because we consider two variates for each author as it might occur differently in different papers. For example the author *"Rachid Deriche"* is assigned to two elements in Δ, namely *"Rachid Deriche"* and *"R. Deriche"*.

Given a reference record $d^* \notin \mathcal{D}$, the goal of our approach is to link each author name $\delta_u^* \in \Delta$ that occurs in d^* to the appropriate author in $\mathcal{A}$ by leveraging t^*, s^* and $\{\delta_u^*\}_{u=1}^{\omega^*}$. Figure 1 illustrates an overview of our proposed approach. First, the approach computes the correspondence frequency $\delta_u^* \mathbf{R} \mathcal{A}$ that returns the number of authors in $\mathcal{A}$ corresponding to δ_u^*. $\delta_u^* \mathbf{R} \mathcal{A} = 0$ indicates that δ_u^* corresponds to a new author $a(\text{new}) \notin \mathcal{A}$. $\delta_u^* \mathbf{R} \mathcal{A} = 1$ indicates that δ_u^* corresponds to only one author $a(l) \in \mathcal{A}$. In this case, we directly assign δ_u^* to $a(l)$ and no further processing is necessary. Note that in this case, δ_u^* might also refer to a new author $a(\text{new}) \notin \mathcal{A}$ who have the same name as an existing author $a(l) \in \mathcal{A}$. However, our approach does not handle this situation. Please refer to Sect. 4.3 that lists the limitation of the proposed approach.

The goal of this paper is to handle the case of $\delta_u^* \mathbf{R} \mathcal{A} > 1$ which indicates that δ_u^* can refer to more than one author. To this end, the approach extracts the atomic name variate from the author name δ_u^*. For example, for the author name $\delta_u^* = $ *"Lei Wang"*, the atomic name variate is $\overline{\delta_u^*} = $ *"L Wang"*. Let $\overline{\delta_u^*}$ correspond to $\overline{\delta_\mu}$ which denotes the μth atomic name variate among K possible name variates. Afterwards, the corresponding Neural Network model $\theta_\mu \in \Theta = \{\theta_k\}_{k=1}^K$ is picked to distinguish between all authors $\mathcal{A}_\mu = \{a(l_\mu)\}_{l_\mu=1}^{L_\mu}$ who share the same name variate $\overline{\delta_\mu}$.

3.1   Model Architecture

The Neural Network model θ_μ takes as input the attributes of d^*, namely the first name of the target author $\delta_u^{*\text{first-name}}$, full names of two co-authors δ_p^* and δ_j^*, title t^* and source s^*. Figure 2 illustrates the architecture of θ_μ, with an output layer of length L_k corresponding to the number of unique authors in $\mathcal{A}_\mu$ who have the same atomic name variate δ_k. As shown in Fig. 2, θ_μ takes two inputs $\mathbf{x}_{\mu,1}$ and $\mathbf{x}_{\mu,2}$, such that:

$$\mathbf{x}_{\mu,1} = \text{char2vec}(\delta_u^{*\text{first-name}}) \bigoplus \frac{1}{2}\left(\text{char2vec}(\delta_p^*) + \text{char2vec}(\delta_j^*)\right),$$
$$\mathbf{x}_{\mu,2} = \frac{1}{2}\left(\text{bert}(t^*) + \text{bert}(s^*)\right), \tag{1}$$

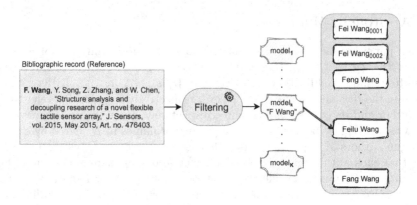

Fig. 1. An illustration of the task for linking a name mentioned in the reference string with the corresponding DBLP author entity.

where char2vec($\mathbf{w}$) returns a vector representation of length 200 generated using *Char2Vec* [3], which provides a symbolic representation of w. bert($\mathbf{w}$) returns a vector representation of each token in $\mathbf{w}$ w.r.t its context in the sentence. This representation of length 786 is generated using BERT [4]. The goal of separating the two inputs is to overcome the sparseness of content embedding and force the model to emphasise more on target author representation.

All the hidden layers possess a ReLU activation function, whereas the output is a Softmax classifier. Since the model has to classify thousands of classes, each of which is represented with very few samples, 50% of the units in the last hidden layers are dropped out during training to avoid over-fitting. Furthermore, the number of publications significantly differs from one author to another. Therefore, each class (i.e. the author) is weighted according to its number of samples (i.e. publications). The model is trained with *adam* optimizer and sparse categorical cross-entropy loss function. This architecture and these parameters achieved the best performance in our empirical analysis.

3.2   Author Name Representation

The names of authors do not hold any specific semantic nature as they are simply a specific sequence of characters referring to one or more persons. Therefore, we need a model that can encode words based on the order and distribution of characters such that author names with a similar name spellings are encoded closely, assuming possible manual editing errors of cited papers.

Chars2vec is a powerful Neural Network-based language model that is preferred when the text consists of abbreviations, typos, etc. It captures the non - vocabulary words and places words with similar spelling closer in the vector space. This model uses a fixed list of characters for word vectorization, where a one-hot encoding represents each character.

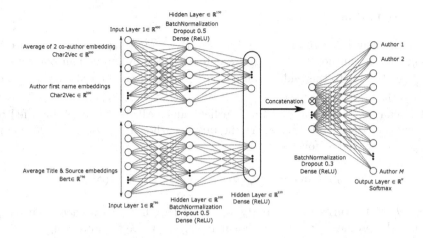

Fig. 2. The architecture of *WhoIs* model.

3.3   Source and Title Embedding

The source (e.g. journal names and book titles) of reference can provide a hint about the area of research of the given reference. In addition, the title is a meaningful sentence that embeds the specific topic of the reference. Therefore, we used these two features to capture the research area of the author. Contrary to the author's name, the goal here is to capture the context of the sequences of words forming the title and source. Therefore, we employed the pre-trained BERT model [4] to obtain sentence embeddings of both the title and source.

3.4   Model Training

Given the training set $\mathcal{D}_\mu \subset \mathcal{D}$ that corresponds to the subset of bibliographic records authored by authors having the atomic name variate $\overline{\delta_\mu}$, $d_{i_\mu} \in \mathcal{D}_\mu$ generates ω_{i_μ} training samples $\langle \delta_\mu, \delta_{i_\mu,p}, \delta_{i_\mu,j}, t_{i_\mu}, s_{i_\mu} \rangle_{p=1}^{\omega_{i_\mu}}$, where $\delta_{i_\mu,j}$ is a random co-author of d_{i_μ} and might be also the same author name as $\delta_{i_\mu,p}$ and/or δ_μ. Note also that we consider one combination where $\delta_{i_\mu,p} = \delta_\mu$. In order to train the model with the other common name variate where the first name is substituted with its initial, for each sample, we generate another version with name variates $\langle \overline{\delta_\mu}, \overline{\delta_{i_\mu,p}}, \overline{\delta_{i_\mu,j}}, t_{i_\mu}, s_{i_\mu} \rangle$. Consequently, each bibliographic record is fed into the model $2 \times \omega_{i_\mu}$ times.

Since the third co-author $\delta_{i_\mu,p}$ is randomly assigned to the training sample among ω_{i_μ} co-authors d_{i_μ}, we randomly reassign it after Y epochs. In addition to lower training complexity, this has shown in the conducted experiments a slightly better result than training the model at each epoch with samples of all possible co-author pairs p and j.

3.5   Prediction

Given the new bibliographic record $d^* = \{t^*, s^*, \langle\delta^*_u\rangle^{\omega^*}_{u=1}\}$, the goal is to disambiguate the author name δ^*_{target} which is shared by more than one author ($\delta^*_{\text{target}}\mathbf{R}\mathcal{A} > 1$). To this end, Y samples $S^Y_{y=1}$ are generated for all possible pairs of co-author names p and j: $\langle\delta^*_{\text{target}}, \delta^*_p, \delta^*_j, t^*, s^*\rangle^{\omega^*,\omega^*}_{p=1,j=1}$, where $Y = \omega^* + 1C2$ and δ^*_u can be a full or abbreviated author name. All the Y samples are fed to the corresponding model θ_μ, where the target author a_{target} of the target name δ^*_{target} is predicted as follows:

$$a_{target} = \underset{1\cdots L_\mu}{argmax}\left(\theta_\mu(S_1) \oplus \theta_\mu(S_2) \oplus \cdots \oplus \theta_\mu(S_Y)\right), \tag{2}$$

where $\theta_\mu(S_y)$ returns a probability vector of length L_μ with each element l_μ denotes the probability of the author name δ^*_{target} to be the author a_{l_μ}.

4   Experiments

This section presents the experimental results of the proposed approach to the DBLP dataset.

4.1   Dataset

In this work, we collected our dataset from the DBLP bibliographic repository[3]. As stated by the maintainers of DBLP[4], the accuracy of the data is not guaranteed. However, a lot of effort is put into manually disambiguating homonym cases when reported by other users. Consequently, we are aware of possible homonym cases that are not resolved yet. From the repository, we collected only records of publications published in journals and proceedings. Each record in this collection represents metadata information of a publication with one or more authors, title, journal, year of publication and a few other attributes. The availability of these attributes differs from one reference to another. Also, the authors in DBLP who share the same name have a suffix number to differentiate them. For instance, the authors with the same name 'Bing Li' are given suffixes such as 'Bing Li 0001', and 'Bing Li 0002'. The statistical details of the used DBLP collection are as follows:

# of records	5258623
# of unique authors	2665634
# of unique author names	2613577
# of unique atomic name variates	1555517

---

[3] https://dblp.uni-trier.de/xml/ (July 2020).
[4] https://dblp.org/faq/How+accurate+is+the+data+in+dblp.html.

Since our approach gathers authors with the same name variates, 261464 models are required to disambiguate all author names in our collection. Therefore, we present in this paper the experimental results on 5 models corresponding to the highest number of authors sharing the same name variates. Table 1 presents statistical details of the five sub-collections which demonstrates the challenges inherent in author name disambiguation in real-world scenarios. # **R2A** for example shows that in some publications two co-authors have the same exact names. This makes the disambiguation more difficult as these authors share not only their names but also co-authors and papers.

Table 1. Statistical details of the top 5 sub-collections of authors sharing the same atomic name variates, where # **ANV** is the corresponding atomic name variate, # **UTA** is the number of unique target authors, # **RCD** is the number of bibliographic records, # **UCA** is the number of unique co-author full names, # **UAN** is the number of unique target author full names, # **R2A** is the number of records with two co-authors of the same record having the same names or the same atomic name variates and # **R3A** is the number of records with three co-authors of the same record having the same names or the same atomic name variates. For # **R2A** and # **R3A**, it is not necessary that the authors have the same name/atomic name variate as the target author but most probably.

	'Y Wang'	'Y Zhang'	'Y Chen'	'Y Li'	'Y Liu'
# **UTA**	2601	2285	2260	2166	2142
# **RCD**	37409	33639	26155	29154	27691
# **UCA**	43199	39389	33461	35765	33754
# **UAN**	2005	1667	2034	1734	1606
# **R2A**	582	598	316	372	338
# **R3A**	13	12	4	4	3

To ensure a credible evaluation and result reproducibility in real scenarios, we split the records in each sub-collection into a training set ($\sim$70%), validation set ($\sim$15%) and training set ($\sim$15%) in terms of records/target author. Specifically, for each target author, we randomly split the corresponding records. If the target author did not author enough publications for the split, we prioritize the training set, then validation and finally the test set. Consequently, the number of samples is not necessarily split according to 70 : 15 : 15 as the number of co-authors differs among publications. Moreover, it is highly likely that the records of a unique target author are completely different among the three sets. Consequently, it is difficult for the model to recognize the appropriate author only from his/her co-authors and research area. However, we believe that this is more realistic and a perfect simulation of the real scenario.

To account for possible name variates, each input sample of full names is duplicated, where the duplicate down sample full names of all co-authors to atomic name variates. Note that this is applied to training, validation and test sets. The goal is to let the model capture all name variates for each author and his/her co-authors. In none of the sets, the variates are mixed in a single sample as we assume that this case is very less likely to occur in the real world.

4.2   Results

The existing Author Name Disambiguation approaches use different datasets to design and evaluate their models. This lead to different assumptions and challenge disparity. Unfortunately, the codes to reproduce the results of these approaches are not available or easily accessed [16]. Therefore, it is not possible to fairly compare *WhoIs* against baseline approaches. For future work, our code and the used datasets are publicly available[5].

Table 2 presents the result of *WhoIs* on the sub-collections presented in Table 1. The label *All* in the table denotes that all samples were predicted twice, one with full names of the target author and its co-authors and another time with only their atomic name variates, whereas the label *ANV* denotes that only samples with atomic names are predicted. The obtained results show that an important number of publications are not properly assigned to their appropriate authors. This is due to the properties of the sub-collections which were discussed above and statistically presented in Table 1. For example, 1) two authors with the same common name authoring a single publication. 2) more than one author with the same common atomic name variate authoring a single publication, 3) number of authors with the same full name, 4) the uncertainty of the accuracy of the dataset, etc.

Table 2. Detailed results of *WhoIs* on the sub-collections corresponding to the top five of authors sharing the same atomic name variates in the DBLP repository. The results are presented in terms of Micro average precision (**MiAP**), Macro average precision (**MaAP**), Micro average recall (**MiAR**), Macro average recall (**MaAR**), Micro average F1-score (**MiAF1**) and Macro average F1-score (**MaAF1**). **ANV** denotes that only atomic name variates were used for all target authors and all their co-authors.

	'Y Wang'	'Y Zhang'	'Y Chen'	'Y Li'	'Y Liu'
MaAP(ANV)	0.226	0.212	0.255	0.193	0.218
MaAP(All)	0.387	0.351	0.404	0.342	0.347
MaAR(ANV)	0.299	0.276	0.301	0.229	0.267
MaAR(All)	0.433	0.383	0.409	0.339	0.361
MaAF1(ANV)	0.239	0.220	0.258	0.195	0.223
MaAF1(All)	0.385	0.342	0.383	0.321	0.332
MiAF1(ANV)	0.274	0.278	0.366	0.260	0.322
MiAF1(All)	0.501	0.482	0.561	0.492	0.504

---

[5] https://whois.ai-research.net.

Although the comparison is difficult and cannot be completely fair, we compare *WhoIs* to other state-of-the-art approaches, whose results are reported in [35]. These results are obtained on a collection from CiteSeerX[6] that contains records of authors with the name/atomic name variate '*Y Chen*'. This collection consists of 848 complete documents authored by 71 distinct authors. We picked this name for comparison because of two reasons; 1) the number of authors sharing this name is among the top five as shown in Table 1 and 2) All methods cited in [35] could not achieve a good result. We applied *WhoIs* on this collection by randomly splitting the records into 70% for training, 15% for validation and 15% for testing. The results are shown in Table 3. Note that in our collection, we consider way more records and distinct authors (see Table 1) and we use only reference attributes (i.e. co-authors, title and source).

As the results presented in Table 3 show, *WhoIs* outperforms other methods in resolving the disambiguation of the author name '*Y Chen*' on the CiteSeerX dataset, which is a relatively small dataset and does not really reflect the performance of all presented approaches in real scenarios. The disparity between the results shown in Table 2 and Table 3 demonstrates that the existing benchmark datasets are manually prepared for the sake of accuracy. However, this leads to covering a very small portion of records whose authors share similar names. This disparity confirms that author name disambiguation is still an open problem in digital libraries and far from being solved.

Table 3. Comparison between *WhoIs* and other baseline methods on CiteSeerX dataset in terms of Macro F1 score as reported in [35]. **ANV** denotes that only atomic name variates were used for all target authors and all their co-authors.

	Macro ALL/ANV	Micro ALL/ANV
WhoIs	**0.713/0.702**	0.873/0.861
NDAG [35]	0.367	N/A
GF [21]	0.439	N/A
DeepWalk [25]	0.118	N/A
LINE [30]	0.193	N/A
Node2Vec [10]	0.058	N/A
PTE [29]	0.199	N/A
GL4 [13]	0.385	N/A
Rand [35]	0.069	N/A
AuthorList [35]	0.325	N/A
AuthorList-NNMF [35]	0.355	N/A

The obtained results of *WhoIs* illustrate the importance of relying on the research area of target authors and their co-authors to disambiguate their names.

---

[6] http://clgiles.ist.psu.edu/data/.

However, they trigger the need to encourage all authors to use different author identifiers such as ORCID in their publications as the automatic approaches are not able to provide a perfect result mainly due to the complexity of the problem.

4.3 Limitations and Obstacles of *WhoIs*

WhoIs demonstrated a satisfactory result and outperformed state-of-the-art approaches on a challenging dataset. However, the approach faces several obstacles that will be addressed in our future works. In the following, we list the limitations of the proposed approach:

- New authors cannot be properly handled by our approach, where a confidence threshold is set to decide whether the input corresponds to a new author or an existing one. To our knowledge, none of the existing supervised approaches is capable to handle this situation.
- Commonly, authors found new collaborations which lead to new co-authorship. Our approach cannot benefit from the occurrence of new co-combinations of co-authors as they were never seen during training.
  Planned solution: We will train an independent model to embed the author's discipline using his/her known publications. With this, we assume that authors working in the same area of research will be put close to each other even if they did not publish a paper together, the model would be able to capture the potential co-authorship between a pair of authors in terms of their area of research.
- Authors continuously extend their research expertise by co-authoring new publications in relatively different disciplines. This means that the titles and journals are not discriminative anymore. Consequently, it is hard for our approach to disambiguate authors holding common names.
  Planned solution: we plan to determine the author's areas of research by mining domain-specific keywords from the entire paper instead of its title assuming that the author uses similar keywords/writing styles even in different research areas with gradual changes which can be captured by the model.
- There are a lot of models that have to be trained to disambiguate all authors in the DBLP repository.
- Commonly, the number of samples is very small compared to the number of classes (i.e. authors sharing the same atomic name variate) which leads to overfitting the model.
  Planned solution: we plan to follow a reverse strategy of disambiguation. Instead of employing the co-authors of the target author, we will employ their co-authors aiming to find the target author among them. We aim also to learn co-author representation by employing their co-authors to help resolve the disambiguation of the target author's name.
- As mentioned earlier and stated by the maintainers of the platform (See footnote 4), the accuracy of the DBLP repository is not guaranteed.

5   Conclusion

We presented in this paper a comprehensive overview of the problem of Author Name Disambiguation. To overcome this problem, we proposed a novel framework that consists of a lot of supervised models. Each of these models is dedicated to distinguishing among authors who share the same atomic name variate (i.e. first name initial and last name) by leveraging the co-authors and the titles and sources of their known publications. The experiments on challenging and real-scenario datasets have shown promising and satisfactory results on author name disambiguation. We also demonstrated the limitations and challenges that are inherent in this process.

To overcome some of these limitations and challenges, we plan for future work to exploit citation graphs so that author names can be linked to real-world entities by employing the co-authors of their co-authors. We assume that using this reverse process, the identity of the target author can be found among the co-authors of his/her co-authors. We plan also to learn the research area of co-authors in order to overcome the issue of new co-authorships.

References

1. Arif, T., Ali, R., Asger, M.: Author name disambiguation using vector space model and hybrid similarity measures. In: 2014 Seventh International Conference on Contemporary Computing (IC3), pp. 135–140. IEEE (2014)
2. Boukhers, Z., Bahubali, N., Chandrasekaran, A.T., Anand, A., Prasadand, S.M.G., Aralappa, S.: Bib2auth: deep learning approach for author disambiguation using bibliographic data. In: The 1st Workshop on Bibliographic Data Analysis and Processing at SIGKDD (2021)
3. Cao, K., Rei, M.: A joint model for word embedding and word morphology. arXiv preprint arXiv:1606.02601 (2016)
4. Devlin, J., Chang, M.W., Lee, K., Toutanova, K.: BERT: pre-training of deep bidirectional transformers for language understanding. arXiv preprint arXiv:1810.04805 (2018)
5. Ebraheem, M., Thirumuruganathan, S., Joty, S., Ouzzani, M., Tang, N.: Distributed representations of tuples for entity resolution. Proc. VLDB Endow. **11**(11), 1454–1467 (2018)
6. Fan, X., Wang, J., Pu, X., Zhou, L., Lv, B.: On graph-based name disambiguation. J. Data Inf. Qual. (JDIQ) **2**(2), 1–23 (2011)
7. Ferreira, A.A., Gonçalves, M.A., Laender, A.H.: A brief survey of automatic methods for author name disambiguation. ACM SIGMOD Rec. **41**(2), 15–26 (2012)
8. Ferreira, A.A., Veloso, A., Gonçalves, M.A., Laender, A.H.: Effective self-training author name disambiguation in scholarly digital libraries. In: Proceedings of the 10th Annual Joint Conference on Digital Libraries, pp. 39–48 (2010)
9. Foxcroft, J., d'Alessandro, A., Antonie, L.: Name2Vec: personal names embeddings. In: Meurs, M.-J., Rudzicz, F. (eds.) Canadian AI 2019. LNCS (LNAI), vol. 11489, pp. 505–510. Springer, Cham (2019). https://doi.org/10.1007/978-3-030-18305-9_52

10. Grover, A., Leskovec, J.: Node2vec: scalable feature learning for networks. In: Proceedings of the 22nd ACM SIGKDD International Conference on Knowledge Discovery and Data Mining, pp. 855–864 (2016)
11. Han, H., Giles, L., Zha, H., Li, C., Tsioutsiouliklis, K.: Two supervised learning approaches for name disambiguation in author citations. In: Proceedings of the 2004 Joint ACM/IEEE Conference on Digital Libraries, pp. 296–305. IEEE (2004)
12. Han, X., Sun, L., Zhao, J.: Collective entity linking in web text: a graph-based method. In: Proceedings of the 34th International ACM SIGIR Conference on Research and Development in Information Retrieval, pp. 765–774 (2011)
13. Hermansson, L., Kerola, T., Johansson, F., Jethava, V., Dubhashi, D.: Entity disambiguation in anonymized graphs using graph kernels. In: Proceedings of the 22nd ACM International Conference on Information & Knowledge Management, pp. 1037–1046 (2013)
14. Hoffart, J., et al.: Robust disambiguation of named entities in text. In: Proceedings of the 2011 Conference on Empirical Methods in Natural Language Processing, pp. 782–792 (2011)
15. Hourrane, O., Mifrah, S., Benlahmar, E.H., Bouhriz, N., Rachdi, M.: Using deep learning word embeddings for citations similarity in academic papers. In: Tabii, Y., Lazaar, M., Al Achhab, M., Enneya, N. (eds.) BDCA 2018. CCIS, vol. 872, pp. 185–196. Springer, Cham (2018). https://doi.org/10.1007/978-3-319-96292-4_15
16. Hussain, I., Asghar, S.: A survey of author name disambiguation techniques: 2010–2016. Knowl. Eng. Rev. **32**, e22 (2017)
17. Khabsa, M., Treeratpituk, P., Giles, C.L.: Large scale author name disambiguation in digital libraries. In: 2014 IEEE International Conference on Big Data (Big Data), pp. 41–42. IEEE (2014)
18. Khabsa, M., Treeratpituk, P., Giles, C.L.: Online person name disambiguation with constraints. In: Proceedings of the 15th ACM/IEEE-CS Joint Conference on Digital Libraries, pp. 37–46 (2015)
19. Kim, K., Sefid, A., Giles, C.L.: Learning CNF blocking for large-scale author name disambiguation. In: Proceedings of the First Workshop on Scholarly Document Processing, pp. 72–80 (2020)
20. Kim, K., Sefid, A., Weinberg, B.A., Giles, C.L.: A web service for author name disambiguation in scholarly databases. In: 2018 IEEE International Conference on Web Services (ICWS), pp. 265–273. IEEE (2018)
21. Kuang, D., Ding, C., Park, H.: Symmetric nonnegative matrix factorization for graph clustering. In: Proceedings of the 2012 SIAM International Conference on Data Mining, pp. 106–117. SIAM (2012)
22. Liu, W., et al.: Author name disambiguation for PubMed. J. Assoc. Inf. Sci. Technol. **65**(4), 765–781 (2014)
23. Louppe, G., Al-Natsheh, H.T., Susik, M., Maguire, E.J.: Ethnicity sensitive author disambiguation using semi-supervised learning. In: Ngonga Ngomo, A.-C., Křemen, P. (eds.) KESW 2016. CCIS, vol. 649, pp. 272–287. Springer, Cham (2016). https://doi.org/10.1007/978-3-319-45880-9_21
24. Müller, M.-C.: Semantic author name disambiguation with word embeddings. In: Kamps, J., Tsakonas, G., Manolopoulos, Y., Iliadis, L., Karydis, I. (eds.) TPDL 2017. LNCS, vol. 10450, pp. 300–311. Springer, Cham (2017). https://doi.org/10.1007/978-3-319-67008-9_24
25. Perozzi, B., Al-Rfou, R., Skiena, S.: DeepWalk: online learning of social representations. In: Proceedings of the 20th ACM SIGKDD International Conference on Knowledge Discovery and Data Mining, pp. 701–710 (2014)

26. Qian, Y., Hu, Y., Cui, J., Zheng, Q., Nie, Z.: Combining machine learning and human judgment in author disambiguation. In: Proceedings of the 20th ACM International Conference on Information and Knowledge Management, pp. 1241–1246 (2011)
27. Qian, Y., Zheng, Q., Sakai, T., Ye, J., Liu, J.: Dynamic author name disambiguation for growing digital libraries. Inf. Retrieval J. **18**(5), 379–412 (2015). https://doi.org/10.1007/s10791-015-9261-3
28. Sun, X., Kaur, J., Possamai, L., Menczer, F.: Detecting ambiguous author names in crowdsourced scholarly data. In: 2011 IEEE Third International Conference on Privacy, Security, Risk and Trust and 2011 IEEE Third International Conference on Social Computing, pp. 568–571. IEEE (2011)
29. Tang, J., Qu, M., Mei, Q.: PTE: predictive text embedding through large-scale heterogeneous text networks. In: Proceedings of the 21th ACM SIGKDD International Conference on Knowledge Discovery and Data Mining, pp. 1165–1174 (2015)
30. Tang, J., Qu, M., Wang, M., Zhang, M., Yan, J., Mei, Q.: Line: large-scale information network embedding. In: Proceedings of the 24th International Conference on World Wide Web, pp. 1067–1077 (2015)
31. Tran, H.N., Huynh, T., Do, T.: Author name disambiguation by using deep neural network. In: Nguyen, N.T., Attachoo, B., Trawiński, B., Somboonviwat, K. (eds.) ACIIDS 2014. LNCS (LNAI), vol. 8397, pp. 123–132. Springer, Cham (2014). https://doi.org/10.1007/978-3-319-05476-6_13
32. Wu, H., Li, B., Pei, Y., He, J.: Unsupervised author disambiguation using Dempster-Shafer theory. Scientometrics **101**(3), 1955–1972 (2014)
33. Xu, J., Shen, S., Li, D., Fu, Y.: A network-embedding based method for author disambiguation. In: Proceedings of the 27th ACM International Conference on Information and Knowledge Management, pp. 1735–1738 (2018)
34. Yang, K.H., Wu, Y.H.: Author name disambiguation in citations. In: 2011 IEEE/WIC/ACM International Conferences on Web Intelligence and Intelligent Agent Technology, vol. 3, pp. 335–338. IEEE (2011)
35. Zhang, B., Al Hasan, M.: Name disambiguation in anonymized graphs using network embedding. In: Proceedings of the 2017 ACM on Conference on Information and Knowledge Management, pp. 1239–1248 (2017)
36. Zhang, B., Dundar, M., Al Hasan, M.: Bayesian non-exhaustive classification a case study: online name disambiguation using temporal record streams. In: Proceedings of the 25th ACM International on Conference on Information and Knowledge Management, pp. 1341–1350 (2016)
37. Zhang, Y., Zhang, F., Yao, P., Tang, J.: Name disambiguation in AMiner: clustering, maintenance, and human in the loop. In: Proceedings of the 24th ACM SIGKDD International Conference on Knowledge Discovery & Data Mining, pp. 1002–1011 (2018)
38. Zhao, J., Wang, P., Huang, K.: A semi-supervised approach for author disambiguation in KDD cup 2013. In: Proceedings of the 2013 KDD CUP 2013 Workshop, pp. 1–8 (2013)

Investigations on Meta Review Generation from Peer Review Texts Leveraging Relevant Sub-tasks in the Peer Review Pipeline

Asheesh Kumar[1], Tirthankar Ghosal[2], Saprativa Bhattacharjee[3(✉)],
and Asif Ekbal[1]

[1] Department of Computer Science and Engineering, Indian Institute of Technology
Patna, Bihta, India
asif@iitp.ac.in
[2] Faculty of Mathematics and Physics, Institute of Formal and Applied Linguistics,
Charles University, Prague, Czech Republic
ghosal@ufal.mff.cuni.cz
[3] Department of Information Technology, Government Polytechnic Daman,
Varkund, Dadra and Nagar Haveli and Daman and Diu, India
saprativa.bhatt@gov.in

Abstract. With the ever-increasing number of submissions in top-tier conferences and journals, finding good reviewers and meta-reviewers is becoming increasingly difficult. Writing a meta-review is not straightforward as it involves a series of sub-tasks, including making a decision on the paper based on the reviewer's recommendation and their confidence in the recommendation, mitigating disagreements among the reviewers, etc. In this work, we develop a novel approach to automatically generate meta-reviews that are decision-aware and which also take into account a set of relevant sub-tasks in the peer-review process. Our initial pipelined approach for automatic decision-aware meta-review generation achieves significant performance improvement over the standard summarization baselines and relevant prior works on this problem. We make our codes available at https://github.com/saprativa/seq-to-seq-decision-aware-mrg.

Keywords: Meta-review generation · Peer-review · Decision-aware

1 Introduction

Peer reviews are central for research validation, where multiple experts review the paper independently and then provide their opinion in the form of reviews. Sometimes the reviewers are required to provide their 'recommendation score' to reflect their assessment of the work. They are also sometimes required to

---

A. Kumar and T. Ghosal—Equal contribution.

© Springer Nature Switzerland AG 2022
G. Silvello et al. (Eds.): TPDL 2022, LNCS 13541, pp. 216–229, 2022.
https://doi.org/10.1007/978-3-031-16802-4_17

provide their 'confidence score' to exhibit how familiar is the related literature to the reviewer or how confident the reviewer is about their evaluation. Not only the review text but also additional signals like recommendation and confidence scores from multiple reviewers help the chairs/editors to get a better feel of the merit of the paper and assist them in reaching their decision on the acceptance or rejection of the article to the concerned venue. The chair/editor then writes a meta-review cumulating the reviewers' views while justifying the decision on the paper's fate, finally communicating the same to the authors.

With the growing number of scientific paper submissions to top-tier conferences, having AI interventions [9] to counter the information overload seems justified. An AI assistant to generate an initial meta-review draft would help the chair to craft a meaningful meta-review quickly. Here in our initial investigation, we set out to investigate if we can leverage all the available signals to a human meta-reviewer (e.g., review-text, reviewer's recommendation, reviewer's conviction, reviewer's confidence [2], final judgment [4], etc.) to automatically write a decision-aware meta-review. We design a deep neural architecture pipeline that performs the relevant sub-tasks at different stages in the pipeline to generate a decision-aware meta-review finally. Our primary motivation in this work is to replicate the stages in a human peer-review process while assisting the chairs in making informed decisions and writing good quality meta-reviews.

Specifically, we present a decision-aware transformer-based multi-encoder deep neural architecture to generate a meta-review while also predicting the final acceptance decision, which is again fueled by predicting the reviewer's sentiment, recommendation, conviction/uncertainty [11], and confidence in the intermediate steps. The multi-encoder gives three separate representations to the three peer-reviews for further input to the decoder. We use the review text and the reviewer's sentiment in our pipeline to predict the recommendation score [13]. Then we use the predicted recommendation score along with the uncertainty of the reviewer (which we predict via a separate model [6]) to predict the confidence score. For each paper, we use the predicted recommendation score, uncertainty score, confidence score, sentiment, and representations of the three reviews to arrive at the final decision [19]. Finally, we use the decision to generate a decision-aware meta-review. We evaluate our generated meta-reviews, both qualitatively and quantitatively. Although we achieved encouraging results, we emphasize that the current investigation is in its initial phase. We would require further fine-tuning and a deeper probe to justify our findings. Nevertheless, our approach to meta-review generation is novel and encompasses almost all the human factors in the peer review process.

2   Related Work

Although the problem is ambitious and new, there are a handful of investigations in the recent literature. The most relevant one is the decision-aware meta-review generation [18]. Here the authors mapped the three reviews to a high-level encoder representation and used the last hidden states to predict decisions while using a decoder to generate the meta-review automatically. In MetaGen [5], authors first generate the extractive draft and then use a fine-tuned UniLM [8] (Unified Language Model) for the final decision prediction and abstractive meta-review generation. In [3], the authors investigate the role of summarization models and how far we are from meta-review generation with those large pre-trained models. We attempt a similar task, but we go one step further to perform multiple relevant subtasks in various stages of the peer-review process to automatically generate the meta-review, simulating the human peer-review process to a greater extent.

We also discuss some relevant works (decision prediction in peer reviews) that can add further context to the problem. The PeerRead [16] dataset is the first publicly available peer-review resource that encouraged Natural Language Processing (NLP)/ Machine Learning (ML) research on peer review problems. The authors defined two novel NLP tasks, *viz.* decision and aspect-score prediction [20]. Another work on conference paper acceptance prediction [15] extracted features from the paper such as title length, number of references, number of tables and figures, etc., to predict the final decisions using machine learning algorithms. Authors of DeepSentiPeer [12] used three channels of information: paper, corresponding review, and the review polarity to predict the overall recommendation and final decision. There are a few other works on NLP/ML for peer review problems [1,10] like aspect extraction [28], sentiment analysis, etc. which are worthy of exploring to understand the related NLP/ML investigations in this domain.

3   Methodology

Figure 1 shows our proposed architecture. Peer-review decision is the central component of a meta-review. The chair writes the meta-review once they have already decided on the paper's fate. Hence, meta-reviews are decision-aware. We briefly discuss the sub-tasks in our pipeline in the subsequent sections.

3.1   The Various Prediction Sub-tasks

Recommendation Score Prediction. In Table 1, we show examples of review sentences and their corresponding sentiment encoding (via VADER [14]) with the final recommendation made by the corresponding reviewers. We can see that reviewer's sentiment (positive/negative/neutral) correlates to the recommendation; we take the reviews along with sentence-level sentiment encoding to predict recommendations. We fine-tune a transformer-based pre-trained Bidirectional Encoder Representation from Transformer (BERT) [7] model for the given task. The BERT is a bidirectional transformer that is pre-trained using a combination of masked language modeling objective and next sentence prediction on a large corpus comprising the Toronto Book Corpus and Wikipedia.

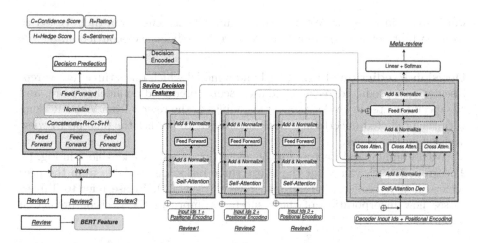

Fig. 1. Overall architecture of decision prediction (left) and seq-to-seq decision-aware meta-review generation (at the center: three encoders for the three reviews and at the right: a decoder to generate the meta-review)

Table 1. Example of sentiment encoding from VADER for review sentences with corresponding recommendation scores.

Review sentence	Sentiment ['comp', 'neg', 'neu', 'pos']	Rec-scores
Finally, the paper stops abruptly without any final discussion and/or conclusion	$[-0.15, 0.14, 0.86, 0]$	1
However, the results are not convincing and there is a crucial issue in the assumptions of the algorithm	$[-0.31, 0.12, 0.88, 0]$	1
[After author feedback] I would suggest that the authors revise the literature study and contributions to more accurately reflect prior work	$[0, 0, 1, 0]$	2
The paper sometimes uses L1 and sometimes L_1, it should be L_1 in all cases	$[0, 0, 1, 0]$	3
I find this paper both very interesting and important	$[0.62, 0, 0.54, 0.46]$	4
The paper is well written, the method is easy to implement, and the algorithm seems to have clear positive impact on the presented experiments	$[0.88, 0, 0.64, 0.36]$	4

Confidence Prediction. For confidence score prediction, we take the review's BERT representation, the predicted recommendation score, and the uncertainty score to predict the confidence score. For generating the uncertainty score, we use a pre-trained hedge-detection model [6] which uses XLNet [29] trained on BioScope Corpus [27] and SFU Review Corpus [17] to predict uncertain words. We use these predicted uncertain words and define an uncertainty score which is the ratio of the total number of uncertain word tokens in a review to the total words token in a review. We deem uncertainty/hedge cues from the reviewer as an important vertical to predict the reviewer's confidence or conviction.

Decision Prediction. Finally, we build a model which takes three review representations, predicted recommendation score, predicted confidence score, and the specific sentence-level sentiment encodings of the review from VADER along with the predicted uncertainty score [6] as input to predict the final peer review decision on the paper.

We use similar architecture for the above three tasks (see left-block in Fig. 1). The ground-truth values for the above three tasks are available from the peer review data we collected from open review (Sect. 4.1). Please refer to Table 5 to see how incorporation of these sub-tasks improves the decision-prediction performance.

3.2   Seq-to-Seq Meta-Review Generation: Main Task

Since our final problem is a generation one, we use transformer-based sequence-to-sequence encoder-decoder architecture for the generation task. As most papers have three reviews in our data, we use a transformer-based three encoders and a decoder model to automatically generate the meta-review. To make our multi-source transformer decision-aware, we use the former decision models' last encoding as input and pass it into decoder layers to provide the decision context (refer to Fig. 1).

Three encoders act as feature extractors that map the input vector to a high-level representation. With this representation, the decoder recursively predicts the sequence one at a time auto-regressively. The encoder consists of N layers of multi-head self-attention, feed-forward network, and residual connections. The decoder consists of M layers with sub-layers of multi-head self-attention, feed-forward, and extra cross attention, also known as multi-head encoder-decoder attention. In a multi-source transformer, cross attention with three past key-value pairs can be modeled in several ways [22]. We use a parallel strategy for our approach to produce a rich representation from the three encoders in the task.

In addition, we choose to train a Byte-pair encoding tokenizer with the same special tokens as RoBERTa [24] and pick its vocab size to be 52,000.

4   Evaluation

To evaluate multi-class prediction (recommendation and confidence score) and binary prediction tasks (final decision), we use metrics such as accuracy, F1 score, and Root Mean Squared Error (RMSE) from sci-kit-learn. We use some popular automatic evaluation metrics for text generation and summarization tasks for automatically generated meta-review. Since a single metric does not give the best evaluation for a generated summary, we use ROUGE-1, ROUGE-2, ROUGE-3 [23], BERTScore [31], S3 [26] and BLEU [25] metrics (Table 4).

Our seq to seq meta-review generation model outperforms all the baseline models for ROUGE precision and BLUE scores. We achieve comparable results with the BART-based summarization model for all other scores. However, we argue that the evaluation is unfair as MRG and summarization are not the same tasks.

We also evaluated the previous decision-aware model for meta-review generation [18] and found that our model outperforms all quantitative metric scores. In Table 5, we can see that the final decision module also improves by 21%.

4.1   Dataset

Research in the peer review system has been limited because of data privacy, confidentiality, and a closed system; however, in the last few years new open review system where reviews and comments along with the decision are posted publicly. This new process of review system has led to the availability of the data for studying the process.

Data Collection. We collect the required peer review data (reviews, meta-reviews, recommendations, and confidence score) from the OpenReview[1] platform along with the decision of acceptance/rejection in the top-tier ML conference ICLR for the years 2018, 2019, 2020, and 2021. After pre-processing and eliminating some unusable reviews/meta-reviews, we arrive at 7,072 instances for our experiments. We use 15% of the data as the test set (1060), 75% as the training set (5304), and the remaining 10% as the validation set (708). Our proposed model treats each review individually (does not concatenate), so for training, we create a permutation in ordering the three reviews to have a training set of 31,824 reviews. We provide the total number of reviews, meta-reviews, and length in Table 2. Table 3 shows the distribution of reviews across paper-categories (Accepted or Rejected).

Table 2. Details of the reviews and meta-review in our dataset across ICLR editions. Length is in the number of words. Each value in the row corresponds to statistics for review/meta-review.

Year	# data	Max length	Min length	Avg length
2018	2802/934	2557/458	23/8	~372.73/29.53
2019	4239/1413	4540/839	14/7	~403.32/41.29
2020	6390/2130	3970/810	15/5	~408.55/37.46
2021	7785/2595	4110/1102	14/5	~455.65/52.25

---

[1] https://openreview.net/.

Table 3. Paper distribution for decision prediction task.

Decision	Train	Test	Validation
Accept	1969	221	273
Reject	3688	415	506

Data Pre-processing. For recommendation and confidence labels, we normalize the values on the Likert scale of 0 to 5 and remove the label category when the data is less than 0.01%(rare class). Recommendation score of 0 means a strong reject, and five means a strong accept. A confidence score of 1 indicates that the reviewer's evaluation is an educated guess either the paper is not in the reviewer's area or was complicated to understand. A confidence of 5 indicates the reviewer is absolutely sure that their evaluation is correct and that they are very familiar with the relevant literature. From Fig. 2, we can see that 85% of labels for recommendation score belong to only two classes and the rest three classes are only 15%, confidence score distribution is also 78 % for two classes, and the rest classes belong to 22% only.

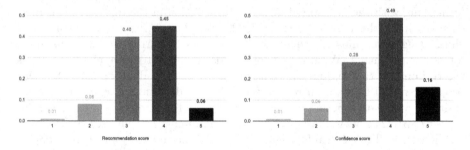

Fig. 2. Recommendation and confidence score normalized data distribution across labels.

A meta-review should contain key/deciding features along with the final decision. We remove the paper if the meta-review or review word token size is less than 10.

4.2   Baselines and Comparing System

Our initial experiments include PEGASUS, a BART-based summarizer which we treat as the baseline for comparison, and two variants of our proposed model. We also use a pre-trained decision-aware MRG model and predict our test data.

We keep the learning rate for experiments as 5e−05, the number of beams for beam search = 4, loss = cross entropy, and optimizer = Adam. We train different models for 100 epochs with learning rate scheduler = linear and choose the best variant in terms of validation loss.

Table 4. Model scores for automatic evaluation metrics. The output is the average of all the scores in the test set. R and P refers to recall and precision.

Model	ROUGE-1 (R/P)	ROUGE-2 (R/P)	ROUGE-3 (R/P)	S3(pyr/resp)	BERTScore(f1)	BLEU
Pegasus [30]	0.19/0.38	0.04/0.08	0.01/0.01	0.10/0.31	0.54	2.14
BART [21]	0.32/0.41	0.08/0.10	0.02/0.03	0.24/ 0.39	0.57	2.85
S-MRG	0.27/0.35	0.05/0.06	0.01/0.01	0.16/0.33	0.55	1.50
MRG decision [18]	0.30/0.36	0.06/0.07	0.01/0.01	0.19/0.35	0.55	1.75
Proposed approach: S2S$_{MRG}$	0.31/0.43	0.06/0.09	0.01/0.02	0.20/0.35	0.56	2.90

Table 5. Results with respect to F1 score and overall accuracy for decision prediction, where S → sentiment and H → uncertainty score.

Model	Accept	Reject	Accuracy
Review Text	0.43	0.79	0.69
Review+recommendation+conf	0.75	0.83	0.82
DeepsentiPeer [12]	0.71	0.74	0.73
MRG Decision [18]	0.29	0.75	0.63
Review+recommendation+confidence+S+H	**0.76**	**0.88**	**0.84**

PEGASUS [30] is an abstractive summarization algorithm which uses self-supervised objective Gap Sentences Generation (GSG) to train a transformer-based encoder-decoder model. In PEGASUS, important sentences are removed/masked from an input document and are generated together as one output sequence from the remaining sentences, similar to an extractive summary. The best PEGASUS model is evaluated on 12 downstream summarization tasks spanning news, science, stories, instructions, emails, patents, and legislative bills. Experiments demonstrate that it achieves state-of-the-art performance on all 12 downstream datasets measured by ROUGE scores.

BART [21] uses a standard transformer-based seq2seq architecture with a bidirectional encoder and a unidirectional decoder. The pre-training task involves randomly shuffling the order of the original sentences and a novel in-filling scheme, where text spans are replaced with a single mask token. BART is particularly effective when fine-tuned for text generation and works well for comprehension tasks. We use the Hugging Face implementation of 12 encoder layers and 12 decoder layers with pre-trained weights[2] and fine-tune them on our dataset to generate the meta-review.

Simple Meta-Review Generator (S-MRG). This is a simple transformer-based architecture with only three encoders, each with two encoder layers to map inputs to a high-level representation and a decoder of two decoder layers with softmax normalization applied on the last hidden state in decoder for generating the sequence probability distribution over whole target vocabulary recursively, one at a time auto-regressively.

---

[2] https://huggingface.co/transformers/model_doc/bart.html.

Decision-Aware MRG [18]. *MRG Decision* predicts the decision from encoders' hidden states and carries the decision vector encoded from the encoder-hidden state output to the decoder layer, to provide the context to the generator module. The decoder's last hidden state after the softmax layer predicts the sequence recursively.

Proposed Approach/Model: Seq to Seq Decision Aware Meta-Review Generation: $S2S_{MRG}$. We improve the decision prediction model by using various input features as we notice that *MRG Decision* lacks in decision making *(accuracy of 63%)*. In Fig. 1 our model $S2S_{MRG}$ Uses the decision encoded vectors in all decoder layers where vectors are concatenated before the feed-forward sub-layer to provide the context to the generator module.

Our proposed approach takes input from the decision-prediction module (hence *decision-aware* just as human chairs do) to generate the meta-reviews.

5   Results and Analysis

5.1   Quantitative and Qualitative Analysis

Our decision prediction model accuracy improves by 15% when we use several input features such as the recommendation, confidence, hedge score, sentiment encodings, and three reviews.

The Root Mean Squared Error (*RMSE*) for the recommendation prediction when we use only review is 0.76. When we use sentence-level sentiment encoding and reviews, our RMSE error reduces to 0.75. For sentence-level sentiment encoding example, refer to Table 1. When we predict only using review for the confidence prediction, we obtain an RMSE error of 0.86. In our model, when we use recommendation and uncertainty scores along with a review, we obtain the RMSE to be 0.82.

Table 6 shows the MRG output of the different techniques. We use the pre-trained models for PEGASUS and BART from HuggingFace[3] but fine-tune on our review dataset. Our custom architectures with two different setups are entirely trained on our dataset. We find that although PEGASUS generated meta-review manifests sentences with polarity, the output is not detailed. The significant aspects of concern in the human-generated review are not prominent in the generated meta-review. The overall polarity and the decision do not match with the original meta-review. On the other hand, BART is an extensive language model with 406 million parameters. We found that outputs are detailed, generated meta-reviews manifest polarity, and highlight merits and demerits. *Our model S-MRG,* does a reasonable job of capturing the polarity (see Table 6), and also the generated meta-review is in the third person. However, we notice that some irrelevant text from other papers' common primary keywords is present in generated review, which is eventually noise in the output.

---

[3] https://huggingface.co/.

Table 6. Ground truths and automatically generated meta-review for a given paper.

Original Meta-Review
https://openreview.net/forum?id=B1liraVYwr

This paper tackles neural response generation with Generative Adversarial Nets (GANs), and to address the training instability problem with GANs, it proposes a local distribution oriented objective. The new objective is combined with the original objective, and used as a hybrid loss for the adversarial training of response generation models, named as LocalGAN. Authors responded with concerns about reviewer 3's comments, and I agree with the authors explanation, so I am disregarding review 3, and am relying on my read through of the latest version of the paper. The other reviewers think the paper has good contributions, however they are not convinced about the clarity of the presentations and made many suggestions (even after the responses from the authors). I suggest a reject, as the paper should include a clear presentation of the approach and technical formulation (as also suggested by the reviewers)

PEGASUS [30]

ICLR 2018 Conference Acceptance Decision. The reviewers have unanimously expressed strong concerns about the novelty of the paper.. Reject

BART [21]

This paper proposes a new method for training a generative model that is robust to adversarial perturbations. The reviewers and AC note the critical limitation of novelty of the paper to meet the high standard of ICLR. AC thinks the proposed method has potential and is interesting, but decided that the authors need more works to publish

Simple MRG

This paper proposes a novel application of generative adversarial networks to model neural network generation with arbitrary conditional autoencoders. While the reviewers initially some concerns regarding the motivation of the work, they unanimously agree that the paper was a quite ready for publication in its current form. In particular, the paper is hard to follow and understand the use of GANs, and the contributions is unclear

MRG Decision [18]

The paper proposes a novel method for improving generative properties of GAN training. The reviewers unanimously agree that this paper is not ready to be published, particularly being concerned about the unclear objective and potentially misleading claims of the paper. Multiple reviewers pointed out about incorrect claims and statements without theoretical or empirical justification. The reviewers also mention that the paper does not provide new insights about applicability of the method

Seq to seq decision-aware meta-review generation

This paper proposes a method to train a neural network that uses the weights of a generative model, which can be used to generate the input. The method is evaluated on several datasets. The reviewers and AC agree that the paper is not well written. However, there are some concerns about the novelty of the proposed method and the experimental results are not convincing

Decision-aware MRG [18] model writes the meta-review in the third person/as meta-reviewer in coherence with the existing peer reviews. The decision prediction module has an accuracy of 63%. **Our proposed seq to seq decision-aware MRG model** outputs are detailed and write the meta-review in the third person/as meta-reviewer in coherence with the existing peer reviews and brings out the merits and demerits of the paper. Generated meta-review also manifests polarity. The decision prediction module has an accuracy of 84%, which can be further improved by augmenting review-paper interaction as additional information channels to the model.

5.2   Error Analysis

We perform initial error analysis on our generated output. The automatically generated meta-review sometimes contains repeating texts. We also found that for a few papers, the ground truth decision is a reject. However, the generated meta-review by the model recommends accepting the paper. Sometimes meta-reviewers write from outside the context of the reviews or one-liners with a positive connotation (example: *The work brings little novelty compared to existing literature.*), but the final decision is negative. In such cases, our model fails, probably due to the lack of proper context. We would look forward to doing a more in-depth analysis of our errors.

6   Conclusion

In this preliminary investigation, we propose a new way to incorporate decision awareness for automatic meta-review generation in peer reviews. With the incorporation of several intermediate sub-tasks, we can see the improvement (almost by 21%) in decision prediction, which is crucial to meta-review generation. Our proposed approach significantly outperforms the earlier works and performs comparably with BART, which is a large complex neural architecture with 12 encoders and 12 decoders. However, we agree that only text summarization does not simulate a complex task such as automatically writing meta-reviews. As our immediate next step, we would like to deeply investigate fine-tuning of the specific sub-tasks, use the final-layer representations of the sub-tasks instead of the predictions, and perform a sensitivity analysis of each sub-task on the main task. We would also like to explore a multi-tasking framework for meta-review generation in the future.

Acknowledgements. Tirthankar Ghosal is funded by Cactus Communications, India (Award # CAC-2021-01) to carry out this research. Asif Ekbal receives the Visvesvaraya Young Faculty Award, thanks to the Digital India Corporation, Ministry of Electronics and Information Technology, Government of India for funding him in this research.

References

1. Bharti, P.K., Ghosal, T., Agrawal, M., Ekbal, A.: BetterPR: a dataset for estimating the constructiveness of peer review comments. In: Silvello, G., et al. (eds.) Linking Theory and Practice of Digital Libraries, TPDL 2022. LNCS, vol. 13541, pp. xx–yy. Springer, Cham (2022)
2. Bharti, P.K., Ghosal, T., Agrawal, M., Ekbal, A.: How confident was your reviewer? Estimating reviewer confidence from peer review texts. In: Uchida, S., Barney, E., Eglin, V. (eds.) Document Analysis Systems, pp. 126–139. Springer, Cham (2022). https://doi.org/10.1007/978-3-031-06555-2_9
3. Bharti, P.K., Kumar, A., Ghosal, T., Agrawal, M., Ekbal, A.: Can a machine generate a meta-review? How far are we? In: Text, Speech, and Dialogue (TSD). Springer, Cham (2022)
4. Bharti, P.K., Ranjan, S., Ghosal, T., Agrawal, M., Ekbal, A.: PEERAssist: leveraging on paper-review interactions to predict peer review decisions. In: Ke, H.-R., Lee, C.S., Sugiyama, K. (eds.) ICADL 2021. LNCS, vol. 13133, pp. 421–435. Springer, Cham (2021). https://doi.org/10.1007/978-3-030-91669-5_33
5. Bhatia, C., Pradhan, T., Pal, S.: MetaGen: an academic meta-review generation system. In: Proceedings of the 43rd International ACM SIGIR Conference on Research and Development in Information Retrieval, pp. 1653–1656 (2020)
6. Britto, B.K., Khandelwal, A.: Resolving the scope of speculation and negation using transformer-based architectures. CoRR abs/2001.02885 (2020). http://arxiv.org/abs/2001.02885
7. Devlin, J., Chang, M., Lee, K., Toutanova, K.: BERT: pre-training of deep bidirectional transformers for language understanding. In: Burstein, J., Doran, C., Solorio, T. (eds.) Proceedings of the 2019 Conference of the North American Chapter of the Association for Computational Linguistics: Human Language Technologies, NAACL-HLT 2019, Minneapolis, MN, USA, 2–7 June 2019, (Long and Short Papers), vol. 1, pp. 4171–4186. Association for Computational Linguistics (2019). https://doi.org/10.18653/v1/n19-1423
8. Dong, L., et al.: Unified language model pre-training for natural language understanding and generation. In: Wallach, H.M., Larochelle, H., Beygelzimer, A., d'Alché-Buc, F., Fox, E.B., Garnett, R. (eds.) Advances in Neural Information Processing Systems 32: Annual Conference on Neural Information Processing Systems 2019, NeurIPS 2019, Vancouver, BC, Canada, 8–14 December 2019, pp. 13042–13054 (2019). https://proceedings.neurips.cc/paper/2019/hash/c20bb2d9a50d5ac1f713f8b34d9aac5a-Abstract.html
9. Ghosal, T.: Exploring the implications of artificial intelligence in various aspects of scholarly peer review. Bull. IEEE Tech. Comm. Digit. Libr. 15 (2019)
10. Ghosal, T., Kumar, S., Bharti, P.K., Ekbal, A.: Peer review analyze: a novel benchmark resource for computational analysis of peer reviews. PLoS ONE 17(1), e0259238 (2022). https://doi.org/10.1371/journal.pone.0259238
11. Ghosal, T., Varanasi, K.K., Kordoni, V.: HedgePeer: a dataset for uncertainty detection in peer reviews. In: Proceedings of the 22nd ACM/IEEE Joint Conference on Digital Libraries, JCDL 2022. Association for Computing Machinery, New York (2022). https://doi.org/10.1145/3529372.3533300
12. Ghosal, T., Verma, R., Ekbal, A., Bhattacharyya, P.: DeepSentiPeer: harnessing sentiment in review texts to recommend peer review decisions. In: Proceedings of the 57th Annual Meeting of the Association for Computational Linguistics, pp. 1120–1130 (2019)

13. Ghosal, T., Verma, R., Ekbal, A., Bhattacharyya, P.: A sentiment augmented deep architecture to predict peer review outcomes. In: 2019 ACM/IEEE Joint Conference on Digital Libraries (JCDL), pp. 414–415 (2019). https://doi.org/10.1109/JCDL.2019.00096

14. Hutto, C.J., Gilbert, E.: VADER: a parsimonious rule-based model for sentiment analysis of social media text. In: Adar, E., Resnick, P., Choudhury, M.D., Hogan, B., Oh, A. (eds.) Proceedings of the Eighth International Conference on Weblogs and Social Media, ICWSM 2014, Ann Arbor, Michigan, USA, 1–4 June 2014. The AAAI Press (2014). http://www.aaai.org/ocs/index.php/ICWSM/ICWSM14/paper/view/8109

15. Joshi, D.J., Kulkarni, A., Pande, R., Kulkarni, I., Patil, S., Saini, N.: Conference paper acceptance prediction: using machine learning. In: Swain, D., Pattnaik, P.K., Athawale, T. (eds.) Machine Learning and Information Processing. AISC, vol. 1311, pp. 143–152. Springer, Singapore (2021). https://doi.org/10.1007/978-981-33-4859-2_14

16. Kang, D., et al.: A dataset of peer reviews (PeerRead): collection, insights and NLP applications. In: Walker, M.A., Ji, H., Stent, A. (eds.) Proceedings of the 2018 Conference of the North American Chapter of the Association for Computational Linguistics: Human Language Technologies, NAACL-HLT 2018, New Orleans, Louisiana, USA, 1–6 June 2018, (Long Papers), vol. 1, pp. 1647–1661. Association for Computational Linguistics (2018). https://doi.org/10.18653/v1/n18-1149

17. Konstantinova, N., de Sousa, S.C.M., Díaz, N.P.C., López, M.J.M., Taboada, M., Mitkov, R.: A review corpus annotated for negation, speculation and their scope. In: Calzolari, N., et al. (eds.) Proceedings of the Eighth International Conference on Language Resources and Evaluation, LREC 2012, Istanbul, Turkey, 23–25 May 2012, pp. 3190–3195. European Language Resources Association (ELRA) (2012). http://www.lrec-conf.org/proceedings/lrec2012/summaries/533.html

18. Kumar, A., Ghosal, T., Ekbal, A.: A deep neural architecture for decision-aware meta-review generation. In: 2021 ACM/IEEE Joint Conference on Digital Libraries (JCDL), pp. 222–225. IEEE (2021)

19. Kumar, S., Arora, H., Ghosal, T., Ekbal, A.: DeepASPeer: towards an aspect-level sentiment controllable framework for decision prediction from academic peer reviews. In: Proceedings of the 22nd ACM/IEEE Joint Conference on Digital Libraries, JCDL 2022. Association for Computing Machinery, New York (2022). https://doi.org/10.1145/3529372.3530937

20. Kumar, S., Ghosal, T., Bharti, P.K., Ekbal, A.: Sharing is caring! joint multitask learning helps aspect-category extraction and sentiment detection in scientific peer reviews. In: 2021 ACM/IEEE Joint Conference on Digital Libraries (JCDL), pp. 270–273 (2021). https://doi.org/10.1109/JCDL52503.2021.00081

21. Lewis, M., et al.: BART: denoising sequence-to-sequence pre-training for natural language generation, translation, and comprehension. In: Jurafsky, D., Chai, J., Schluter, N., Tetreault, J.R. (eds.) Proceedings of the 58th Annual Meeting of the Association for Computational Linguistics, ACL 2020, 5–10 July 2020, pp. 7871–7880. Association for Computational Linguistics (2020). https://doi.org/10.18653/v1/2020.acl-main.703

22. Libovický, J., Helcl, J., Marecek, D.: Input combination strategies for multi-source transformer decoder. In: Bojar, O., et al. (eds.) Proceedings of the Third Conference on Machine Translation: Research Papers, WMT 2018, Belgium, Brussels, 31

October–1 November 2018, pp. 253–260. Association for Computational Linguistics (2018). https://doi.org/10.18653/v1/w18-6326

23. Lin, C.Y.: ROUGE: a package for automatic evaluation of summaries. In: Text Summarization Branches Out, Barcelona, Spain, pp. 74–81. Association for Computational Linguistics (2004). https://aclanthology.org/W04-1013

24. Liu, Y., et al.: Roberta: a robustly optimized BERT pretraining approach. CoRR abs/1907.11692 (2019). http://arxiv.org/abs/1907.11692

25. Papineni, K., Roukos, S., Ward, T., Zhu, W.J.: Bleu: a method for automatic evaluation of machine translation. In: Proceedings of the 40th Annual Meeting of the Association for Computational Linguistics, pp. 311–318 (2002)

26. Peyrard, M., Botschen, T., Gurevych, I.: Learning to score system summaries for better content selection evaluation. In: Proceedings of the Workshop on New Frontiers in Summarization, pp. 74–84 (2017)

27. Szarvas, G., Vincze, V., Farkas, R., Csirik, J.: The bioscope corpus: annotation for negation, uncertainty and their scope in biomedical texts. In: Proceedings of the Workshop on Current Trends in Biomedical Natural Language Processing, pp. 38–45 (2008)

28. Verma, R., Shinde, K., Arora, H., Ghosal, T.: *Attend to Your Review*: a deep neural network to extract aspects from peer reviews. In: Mantoro, T., Lee, M., Ayu, M.A., Wong, K.W., Hidayanto, A.N. (eds.) ICONIP 2021. CCIS, vol. 1517, pp. 761–768. Springer, Cham (2021). https://doi.org/10.1007/978-3-030-92310-5_88

29. Yang, Z., Dai, Z., Yang, Y., Carbonell, J., Salakhutdinov, R.R., Le, Q.V.: XLNet: generalized autoregressive pretraining for language understanding. In: Advances in Neural Information Processing Systems, vol. 32 (2019)

30. Zhang, J., Zhao, Y., Saleh, M., Liu, P.: Pegasus: pre-training with extracted gap-sentences for abstractive summarization. In: International Conference on Machine Learning, pp. 11328–11339. PMLR (2020)

31. Zhang, T., Kishore, V., Wu, F., Weinberger, K.Q., Artzi, Y.: BERTScore: evaluating text generation with BERT. In: 8th International Conference on Learning Representations, ICLR 2020, Addis Ababa, Ethiopia, 26–30 April 2020. OpenReview.net (2020). https://openreview.net/forum?id=SkeHuCVFDr

Improving Accessibility to Arabic ETDs Using Automatic Classification

Eman Abdelrahman$^{(\boxtimes)}$ and Edward Fox

Department of Computer Science, Virginia Tech, Blacksburg, USA
fox@vt.edu

Abstract. Electronic Theses and Dissertations (ETDs) are documents rich in research information that provide many benefits to students and future generations of scholars in various disciplines. Therefore, research is taking place to extract data from ETDs and make them more accessible. However, much of the related research involved ETDs in the English language, while Arabic ETDs remain an untapped source of data, although the number of Arabic ETDs available digitally is growing. Therefore, the need to make them more browsable and accessible increases. Some ways to achieve this need include data annotation, indexing, translation, and classification. As the size of the data increases, manual subject classification becomes less feasible. Accordingly, automatic subject classification becomes essential for the searchability and management of data. There are two main roadblocks to performing automatic subject classification of Arabic ETDs. The first is the lack of a large public corpus of Arabic ETDs for training purposes, while the second is the Arabic language's linguistic complexity, especially in academic documents. This research aims to collect key metadata of Arabic ETDs, and apply different automatic subject classification methodologies. The first goal is aided by scraping data from the AskZad Digital Library. The second goal is achieved by exploring different machine learning and deep learning techniques. The experiments' results show that deep learning using pretrained language models yielded the highest accuracy of approximately 0.83, while classical machine learning techniques yielded approximately 0.41 and 0.70 for multiclass classification one-vs-all classification respectively. This indicates that using pretrained language models assists in understanding languages which is essential for the classification of text.

Keywords: Digital libraries · Arabic Electronic Theses and Dissertations (Arabic ETDs) · Natural Language Processing (NLP) · Automatic subject classification · Pretrained language models

1 Introduction

Electronic Theses and Dissertations (ETDs) constitute one of the genres of data that is highly rich in information. Therefore, researchers have recently started researching ways of extracting and mining data from ETDs. However, little has been done with Arabic ETDs despite their growing number being made available

© Springer Nature Switzerland AG 2022
G. Silvello et al. (Eds.): TPDL 2022, LNCS 13541, pp. 230–242, 2022.
https://doi.org/10.1007/978-3-031-16802-4_18

digitally. This is mainly due to two roadblocks: (1) Arabic is a low-resourced language compared to English. Therefore a public corpus of Arabic ETDs to use for research is not readily available for data mining research, and (2) The linguistic complexity of the formal standard Arabic language compared to Colloquial Arabic. The latter places a heavy strain on the data preprocessing and applying common machine learning and deep learning techniques effectively.

Several universities in the Middle East have started to require an Arabic version of students' ETDs or at least an Arabic version of their abstracts and other metadata. Accordingly, the number of Arabic ETDs is growing significantly over time, as shown in Fig. 1. One of the ways to improve the accessibility of digital text data is through automatic subject classification, primarily when works are not cataloged by librarians or domain experts.

The main contribution of this research work is applying existing classification methodologies to an untapped genre of data. This is achieved by first collecting and curating metadata of Arabic ETDs from the AskZad Digital Library, which is a component of the Saudi Digital Library (SDL)[1]. The dataset collected consists of two versions of key metadata of Arabic ETDs, such as abstracts, titles, and keywords in both English and Arabic languages. Second is by leveraging research on the automatic subject classification of Arabic text to provide a methodology for the automatic subject classification of Arabic ETDs based on their metadata. This involved exploring machine learning and pretrained deep learning language models for the automatic classification task.

This is expected to make digitalizing a considerable amount of Arabic ETDs, especially those that are not born digital, more efficient and make them more accessible and searchable. The dataset and code for this research are available on GitHub at https://github.com/Eman-Abdelrahman/Otrouha.

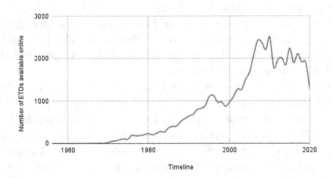

Fig. 1. Number of ETDs available at AskZad [5] digital library across the last 60 years.

---

[1] https://sdl.edu.sa.

2   Related Work

The amount of textual data available online is growing rapidly in the digital age, making text classification essential to access, browse, and preserve that data efficiently. Applying this to Arabic text classification is a challenging research area. This is due to Arabic's complex linguistic characteristics, limited studies on it, and limited open access data available. Therefore, most previous research on text classification has been conducted on English datasets [1]. To the best of our knowledge, there has been no previous research on automatic text classification of Arabic Electronic Theses and Dissertations (ETDs). All of the earlier studies are on different genres of data, such as Arabic tweets and news articles [12,15, 16,18,25].

2.1   Classical Machine Learning Approaches

An automated tool for Arabic text classification has been presented in [3]. One goal of this paper was to build a representative training dataset covering different types of text categories, which can be used for further research. This was done by collecting seven different dataset genres that contained 17,658 text documents with more than 11,500,000 words as their corpus. The corpus included newswire stories, discussion forums, Arabic poems, etc. A second goal was performance comparison between the Support Vector Machine (SVM) [8] and C5.0 algorithms. C5.0 algorithm is a successor of C4.5 algorithm [21], which is used in Data Mining as a Decision Tree classifier. It generates a decision based on a certain sample of data (univariate or multivariate predictors). The study found that the C5.0 algorithm outperformed the SVM algorithm by approximately 10%.

For Arabic text categorization in [12], preprocessing techniques include stop-word removal, root extraction, and stemming for dimensionality reduction. A performance comparison has been made between different classification techniques such as Naïve Bayes [22], k-Nearest Neighbor (k-NN) [14], and distance-based classification methods [11], using an Arabic dataset of 1,000 documents consisting of magazines and newspapers.

The authors' experiment showed that Naïve Bayes outperformed the k-NN and distance-based methods.

An Arabic document categorization tool was developed using the Naïve Bayes algorithm [18]. Non-vocalized Arabic web documents were classified according to five predefined categories using 300 web documents of news. A cross-validation experiment using 2,000 terms/roots showed an average accuracy over all categories of 68.78%, where the best categorization performance was 92.8%.

Experimenting on a large Arabic newswire corpus without preprocessing took place in [25]. The authors posited that statistical methods are powerful for Arabic text classification and clustering (maximum entropy). The results show 89.5%, 31.5%, and 46.61% for recall, precision, and F-measure, respectively. This would generally be viewed as unacceptable; the cause may be the lack of morphological analysis.

Developing a classifier for Arabic text is difficult due to the complexity of Arabic morphological analysis [13]. The Arabic language has high inflectional and derivational morphology, which makes NLP (Natural Language Processing) tasks nontrivial. They used the maximum entropy framework to build a system (ArabCat) that works as a classifier for Arabic documents. Their dataset was collected from Arabic websites. Their results show that ArabCat gave 80.48%, 80.34%, and 80.41% for recall, precision, and F-measure, respectively, while the Sakhr categorizer [24] shows 73.78%, 47.35%, and 57.68%, respectively.

2.2   Deep Learning Approach

One of the ways to better understand languages and relationships between words is through language models. Using Pretrained Language Models (PLMs) has become a dominant approach, improving performance on many NLP tasks such as sentiment analysis, text classification, and machine translation [26], where using them offloads the very costly burden of training from scratch. One of the state-of-the-art models is **B**idirectional **E**ncoder **R**epresentations from Transformers (BERT) [10], which applies the bidirectional training of a transformer, a popular attention model, to language modeling. A bidirectionally trained language model can have a more profound sense of language context and flow than single-direction language models, which is beneficial for Arabic language as it is very context-dependent. The following BERT-based pretrained language models were explored and fine-tuned using our ETD data. BERT

SciBERT   [6] *(for English data):* is a PLM to address the lack of high-quality, large-scale labeled scientific data. It leverages unsupervised pretraining on a large multi-domain corpus of scientific publications to improve the performance on downstream scientific NLP tasks. There are four versions of the SciBERT model, based on: (i) Cased or Uncased, (ii) BASEVOCAB or SCIVOCAB. The two models using BASEVOCAB are fine-tuned from the corresponding BERT-base models. The other two models which use SCIVOCAB are trained from scratch. Our experiments were done using SciBERT (*scibert_scivocab_uncased*) on the English version of our dataset.

AraBERT   [4] *(for Arabic data):* is a PLM specifically for the Arabic language. The aim is to achieve the same success that BERT did for the English language. The performance of AraBERT is compared to multilingual BERT from Google and other state-of-the-art approaches. Their model is pretrained on data from Open Source International Arabic News Corpus (OSIAN), Open Super-large Crawled Aggregated coRpus (OSCAR) and other resources. Their results showed that the newly developed AraBERT achieved state-of-the-art performance on most tested Arabic NLP tasks.

Asafaya   [23] *(for Arabic data):* is another PLM for the Arabic language. The training corpus contains some non-Arabic words inline, which the authors did not remove from sentences since that would affect some tasks like Named Entity Recognition (NER). The model is not restricted to Modern Standard Arabic; the sentences contain some dialectical Arabic too.

A brief comparison of the three aforementioned models is shown in Table 1.

Table 1. Comparison between BERT-based models.

Model	SciBERT	AraBERT	Asafaya
Size of corpus	123 MB	24 GB of text	95 GB of text
Number of tokens/sentences	3.1 billion tokens	70 million sentences	8.2 billion words
Type of data	Papers from semanticscholar.org	• Arabic Wikipedia dump • 1.5B words Arabic corpus • OSIAN • Asafir news articles • OSCAR	• Arabic version of OSCAR • Recent dump of Arabic Wikipedia • Other Arabic resources

3 Dataset

The dataset collected for this research was obtained by searching the AskZad Digital library [5]. When the data was collected, their categorization system consisted of 16 distinct categories, where the number of ETDs in each category varies largely. The AskZad digital library categorization system keeps evolving, which opens the possibility for more extensive research to take place in the future. The distribution of the number of records in each category of the data collected is shown in Table 2.

Table 2. Distribution of documents in each category.

Category	No. of documents
Education	632
Administration	632
Pure & Natural Science	625
Agriculture	626
Psychology	601
Applied Science & Technology	619
Economics	615
Law	600
Sport	610
History	588
Press & Media	599
Politics	603
Environmental Science	236
Philosophy	105
Art	95
Culture	126

3.1   Mapping of AskZad Categories to ProQuest Categories

One of the reasons that makes AskZad digital library suitable source of data for this project is its taxonomy, as shown in Fig. 2. This taxonomy is found to be simple and compatible with ProQuest's high-level taxonomy, which has the largest commercial multidisciplinary full-text ETD database.

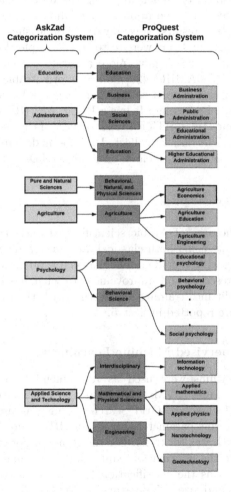

Fig. 2. Mapping AskZad's categories to ProQuest's categories.

For example, the *Law* category in AskZad is mapped to the high-level category *Law and Legal Studies* and its sub-categories in ProQuest. All categories in AskZad have been mapped to one or more corresponding categories in ProQuest, which ensures future consistency in categorization among different digital libraries of Arabic ETDs. This can also assist in improving the granularity of the categories in the future to be more specific.

3.2   Data Preprocessing

To reduce the dimensionality of data, preprocessing techniques were used which included stopword removal as a first step. The average number of words in a raw abstract originally was 204 words; after stopword removal, it was 168 words. Thus, approximately 17% of the raw data was removed for dimensionality reduction and better classification. Then, to bring the root of each word, stemming or lemmatizations needed to be applied. According to the literature, lemmatization provides better results, specially for Arabic since words are context dependent. Different lemmatizers were tested on a sample abstract. It was found that the Farasa lemmatizer [2] gave more accurate output and outperformed the state-of-the-art MADAMIRA [20] and Stanford Arabic Segmenter [19] for Arabic segmentation and lemmatization. Farasa is a full-stack package to deal with Arabic Language Processing. It has a REST API (REpresentational State Transfer) that responds to an HTTP POST request of the raw text, by returning the lemmatized text. The dataset collected will be made publicly available upon acceptance to encourage more research on Arabic ETDs.

4   Methodology

Since research in the area of Arabic scientific text classification is scarce, we conducted experiments using both classical machine learning and deep learning techniques. The code will be made publicly available on github upon acceptance to encourage more research and improvement to what has been started in this research. Data is split into training and testing with the ratio of 70:30 respectively. The results are reported in Sect. 5.

4.1   Classical Supervised Machine Learning

The following algorithms were used as recommended in previous research: Support Vector Machines (SVMs), Decision Trees (DT), and Random Forest (RF). For the SVM classifier, Grid Search tuning was used to compute the optimum values of Kernel parameter (Linear and RBF). For Decision Trees classifier, maximum depth was set to 20. For the Random Forest classifier, entropy criterion to calculate the information gain. Their performance depends on several parameters, such as the classification task (multiclass vs. binary) as well as the dataset type and size. The feature set of the data was extracted using the TF-IDF (Term Frequency-Inverse Document Frequency) Vectorizer in the SciKit-learn library [7] to convert the text to a matrix with TF-IDF features. We adopted both multiclass and binary (one-vs-all) classification techniques to compare the performance of these techniques and get a deeper understanding of the performance of classification per category. We wanted to determine whether using abstracts, titles, and keywords together would result in better performance than using only abstracts. Therefore, both ways were conducted to determine the effect of adding more metadata to the abstracts.

4.2   Deep Learning Using Pretrained Language Models

To benefit from deep learning, which offloads the challenge of feature engineering, and overcome the need for large-scale datasets to train the model, pretrained language models were used. The BERT-based models were pretrained on a large dataset, then adapted to the ETD dataset. SciBERT was adapted to the English version of the dataset, while AraBERT and Asafaya were adapted to the Arabic version of the dataset. There are two main paradigms for adaptation: feature extraction and fine-tuning. In feature extraction, the model's weights are frozen, and the pretrained representations are used in a downstream model similar to classic feature-based approaches [17]. Alternatively, a pretrained model's parameters can be unfrozen and fine-tuned on a new task [9]. We adopted the first paradigm in this research.

BertForSequenceClassification is used, which is a model transformer with a sequence classification head on top (a linear layer on top of the pooled output). We used NVIDIA Tesla K80 GPU available at Google Colab for training and evaluation.

5   Results and Discussion

5.1   Classical Supervised Machine Learning

The performance of SVM, Random Forest, and Decision Trees classifiers yielded an overall accuracy ranging between 0.41–0.45 and 0.19, respectively. This is still higher than random guessing (0.06 in our case) but not reliable enough.

The results of multiclass classification are presented in Table 3.

Table 3. Results of using multiclass classification.

Classifier	Accuracy
Support Vector Machines (SVM)	0.45
Decision Trees	0.19
Random Forest (RF)	0.41

In order to understand more about the classification per category, binary classification experiments were run using Random Forest. The baseline performance is 0.50, which is random guessing. Binary classification resulted in better performance than multiclass classification, giving average accuracy of 0.70. Also, more evaluation metrics were taken into consideration since the dataset is imbalanced such as precision, recall, and F1-score as shown in Table 4. Although some categories had relatively the same number of records, their performance varied, such as *Administration* and *Agriculture*. This is expected to be due to the nature of each category. Categories in Table 4 are sorted alphabetically.

Table 4. Results of using binary classification (One-vs-all).

Category	Precision	Recall	F1	Accuracy	No. docs
Administration	0.83	0.83	0.83	0.83	605
Agriculture	0.70	0.72	0.69	0.69	599
Applied Science & Technology	0.52	0.52	0.52	0.52	592
Art	0.65	0.65	0.65	0.65	95
Culture	0.80	0.80	0.80	0.80	126
Economics	0.65	0.65	0.65	0.65	588
Education	0.85	0.85	0.85	0.85	605
Environmental Science	0.74	0.75	0.75	0.74	236
History	0.53	0.53	0.53	0.53	570
Law	0.86	0.87	0.86	0.86	573
Philosophy	0.62	0.62	0.62	0.62	105
Politics	0.77	0.79	0.77	0.76	585
Press & Media	0.70	0.73	0.70	0.68	581
Psychology	0.58	0.58	0.68	0.68	583
Pure & Natural Science	0.52	0.51	0.51	0.51	598
Sport	0.88	0.88	0.88	0.88	591

5.2 Deep Learning Using Pretrained Language Models

The SciBERT pretrained language model was tried using the English version of the data, then the AraBERT and Asafya models were tried on the Arabic version. Table 5 shows the precision, recall, and F1 scores for each model. Also, in order to take a closer look at the performance, confusion matrices were generated for each of the models, as shown in Fig. 3. The total number of each row is the total of testing data (30% of the total data). A confusion matrix allows visualization of the performance of an algorithm and illustrates if a certain class is usually misclassified as another class; this can help guide future fine-tuning. For example, using SciBERT, the *Culture* class has 42 records in the test set; 20 of them were correctly classified, while 12 of them were misclassified as *Press and Media*. This can give an idea of which classes' features are relatively close to others.

Table 5. Results of using BERT-based language models on English and Arabic versions of data (Abstracts, Titles, and Keywords).

Model	Precision	Recall	F1	Accuracy
SciBERT (En)	0.92	0.92	0.92	0.91
AraBERT (Ar)	0.84	0.83	0.83	0.84
Asafaya (Ar)	0.83	0.83	0.82	0.83

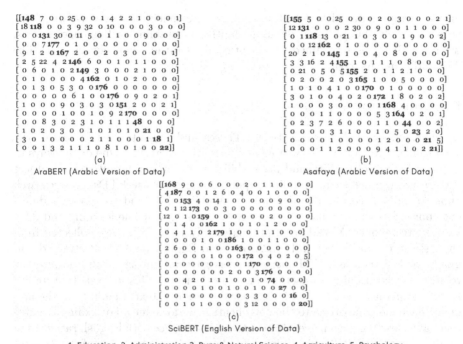

```
[[148  7  0  0 25  0  0  1  4  2  2  1  0  0  0  1]          [[155  5  0  0 25  0  0  0  2  0  3  0  0  0  2  1]
 [ 18 118  0  0  3  9 32  0 10  0  0  0  3  0  0  0]          [ 12 131  0  0  0  2 30  0  9  0  0  1  1  0  0  0]
 [  0  0 131 30  0 11  5  0  1  1  0  0  9  0  0  0]          [  0  1 118 13  0 21  1  0  3  0  0  1  9  0  0  2]
 [  0  0  7 177  0  1  0  0  0  0  0  0  0  0  0  0]          [  0  0  0 12 162  0  1  0  0  0  0  0  0  0  0  0]
 [  9  1  2  0 167  2  0  0  2  0  3  0  0  0  0  1]          [ 20  2  1  0 145  1  0  0  4  0  8  0  0  0  0  0]
 [  2  5 22  4  2 146  6  0  0  1  0  1  1  0  0  0]          [  3  3 16  2  4 155  1  0  1  1  1  0  8  0  0  0]
 [  0  6  0  1  0  2 149  3  0  0  2  1  0  0  0]          [  0 21  0  5  0  5 155  2  0  1  1  2  1  0  0  0]
 [  0  1  0  0  0  0  4 162  0  1  0  2  0  0  0  0]          [  0  2  0  0  2  0  3 165  1  0  0  5  0  0  0  0]
 [  0  1  3  0  5  3  0  0 176  0  0  0  0  0  0  0]          [  1  0  1  0  4  1  0  0 170  0  1  0  0  0  0  0]
 [  0  0  0  0  0  6  1  0  0 176  0  9  0  2  0  1]          [  3  0  1  0  0  4  0  2  0 172  1  8  0  2  0  2]
 [  1  0  0  0  9  0  3  0  3  0 151  2  0  0  2  1]          [  1  0  0  0  3  0  0  0  0  0 168  4  0  0  0  0]
 [  0  0  0  0  1  0  0  1  0  9  2 170  0  0  0  0]          [  0  0  0  1  1  0  0  0  0  5  3 164  0  2  0  1]
 [  0  0  8  3  0  2  3  1  0  1  1  1  48  0  0  0]          [  0  2  3  7  2  6  0  0  0  1  1  0  44  0  0  2]
 [  1  0  2  0  3  0  0  1  0  1  0  1  0  21  0  0]          [  0  0  0  0  3  1  1  0  0  1  0  5  0  23  2  0]
 [  3  0  1  0  0  0  0  2  1  1  0  0  0  1 18  1]          [  0  0  0  0  1  0  0  0  0  1  2  0  0  0 21  5]
 [  0  0  1  3  2  1  1  1  0  8  1  0  1  0  0  22]]          [  0  0  0  1  1  2  0  0  0  9  4  1  1  0  2 21]]
            (a)                                                          (b)
   AraBERT (Arabic Version of Data)                          Asafaya (Arabic Version of Data)
```

```
[[168  9  0  0  6  0  0  0  2  0  1  1  0  0  0  0]
 [  4 187  0  0  1  2  6  0  4  0  0  1  0  0  0  0]
 [  0  0 153  4  0 14  1  0  0  0  0  0  9  0  0  0]
 [  0  1 12 173  0  0  3  0  0  0  0  0  0  0  0  0]
 [ 12  0  1  0 159  0  0  0  0  0  0  2  0  0  0  0]
 [  0  1  4  0  0 162  1  0  0  1  0  1  2  0  0  0]
 [  0  4  1  1  0  2 179  1  0  0  1  1  1  0  0  0]
 [  0  0  0  0  1  0  0 186  1  0  0  1  1  0  0  0]
 [  2  6  0  0  1  1  0  0 163  0  0  0  0  0  0  0]
 [  0  0  0  0  0  1  0  0  0 172  0  4  0  2  0  5]
 [  0  1  0  0  0  0  1  0  0  1 170  0  0  0  0  0]
 [  0  0  0  0  0  0  0  2  0  0  3 176  0  0  0  0]
 [  0  0  4  2  0  1  1  1  0  0  1  0  74  0  0  0]
 [  0  0  0  0  1  0  0  1  0  0  1  0  0 27  0  0]
 [  0  0  1  0  0  0  0  0  0  3  3  0  0  0 16  0]
 [  0  0  1  0  1  0  0  0  0  3 12  0  0  0  0 20]]
                          (c)
            SciBERT (English Version of Data)

1. Education 2. Administration 3. Pure & Natural Science 4. Agriculture 5. Psychology
  6. Applied Science & Technology 7. Economics 8. Law 9. Sport 10. History
 11. Press & Media 12. Politics 13. Environmental Science 14. Philosophy 15. Art 16. Culture
```

Fig. 3. Confusion matrices when using different pretrained language models on the testing dataset.

The observations suggest that deep learning using generic pretrained language models outperforms classical machine learning techniques. The data imbalance persisted even after enlarging the dataset, where the number of records in four categories was much smaller than the other twelve categories. However, using pretrained language models aided in overcoming this problem for the underrepresented categories, such as *Philosophy*, *Art*, *Culture*, and *Sport*. This is due to using the representations generated by the previously trained network to extract meaning from the ETD dataset. For example, *Philosophy* has 68 records in the test set, where 48 of them were classified correctly. Using pretrained language models leads to overcoming the lack of large-scale data needed for deep learning training and reduces the time needed for training from scratch. BERT-based language models are designed to pretrain deep bidirectional representations from the unlabeled text by jointly conditioning on both the left and right context in all layers. Since the Arabic language is written from right to left, conditioning on both left and right context in all layers improved the classification results. Moreover, the results show that using SciBERT on the English version of data yielded higher performance than using AraBERT and Asafaya on the Arabic data, although it is trained on a much smaller data size. This is highly likely due to using domain-adaptive pretraining of language models, where SciBERT is pretrained on scientific data rather than generic data like AraBERT and Asafaya.

6   Conclusions

As the number of Arabic Electronic Theses and Dissertations increases, the need to make them more browsable and accessible increases. One of the ways to improve their browsability and accessibility is by providing automatic subject classification. Since there is limited open access to Arabic ETDs, this research aims to build a corpus of metadata of Arabic ETDs and to research different approaches to automatically classify them using machine learning and deep learning techniques. Metadata of approximately 7600 ETDs was collected from the AskZad digital library in both Arabic and English versions. Pretrained language models such as BERT-based models gave promising results despite the relatively small training dataset used for deep learning. This suggests that understanding languages is essential for the classification of text. In addition, the language itself can contribute to the classification performance. For example, automatically classifying would result in better performance with English rather than Arabic, since SciBERT, which was adapted on the English version of the dataset, gave higher performance than AraBERT and Asafaya, which were adapted on the Arabic version of the dataset. Moreover, domain-specific pretrained language models can significantly improve the classification performance. The corpus built as part of this project is expected to encourage more research on Arabic ETDs, which is a rich genre of data.

7   Future Work

This research, along with the experiments and results, provided good insights to guide future work.

Collecting more Arabic ETDs is essential for improving the machine learning process. This can include collecting more metadata and full-text of ETDs. A challenge will be that not all ETDs are born digital, but rather were captured as a scanned version. This can open more research to extract the text using OCR (Optical Character Recognition) techniques and convert the text into a machine-readable form.

Also, multilabel classification can be considered, but expert annotation will be needed to fine-tune AskZad categories.

Researching how can the categorization system be improved to include a deeper hierarchy and not only basic high-level categories is also important.

Pretrained language models, such as BERT, improved the automatic subject classification of Arabic ETDs. Future work would includes more fine-tuning to models pretrained on Arabic data to yield higher classification accuracy. Also, an Arabic equivalent to SciBERT can be developed to help enhance the browsability of academic work in Arabic. SciBERT has its vocabulary (SCIVOCAB) trained on cased and uncased versions, but this is not needed for Arabic since it lacks uppercase and lowercase versions of alphabets.

This study is expected to encourage researchers to work on Arabic ETDs for further investigation and bench-marking in NLP.

Acknowledgements. Special thanks go to Dr. Wu Jian from Old Dominion University, Dr. Bill Ingram from Virginia Tech, and the team working on the Institute of Museum and Library Services grant LG-37-19-0078-19. Thanks go to the AskZad Digital Library, which is part of the Saudi Digital Library, from which the dataset was collected. Thanks also go to Fatimah Alotaibi for her support during the project.

References

1. Abdeen, M.A., AlBouq, S., Elmahalawy, A., Shehata, S.: A closer look at Arabic text classification. Int. J. Adv. Comput. Sci. Appl. **10**(11), 677–688 (2019)
2. Abdelali, A., Darwish, K., Durrani, N., Mubarak, H.: Farasa: a fast and furious segmenter for Arabic. In: Proceedings of the 2016 Conference of the North American Chapter of the Association for Computational Linguistics, pp. 11–16 (2016)
3. Al-Harbi, S., Almuhareb, A., Al-Thubaity, A., Khorsheed, M., Al-Rajeh, A.: Automatic Arabic text classification. In: 9th International Conference on the Statistical Analysis of Textual Data (JADT 2008) (2008)
4. Antoun, W., Baly, F., Hajj, H.: AraBERT: transformer-based model for Arabic language understanding. arXiv preprint arXiv:2003.00104 (2020)
5. AskZad: AskZad: The World's First and Largest Arabic Digital Library (2020). http://askzad.com. Accessed 14 Jan 2022
6. Beltagy, I., Lo, K., Cohan, A.: SciBERT: a pretrained language model for scientific text. arXiv preprint arXiv:1903.10676 (2019)
7. Buitinck, L., et al.: API design for machine learning software: experiences from the scikit-learn project. In: ECML PKDD Workshop: Languages for Data Mining and Machine Learning, pp. 108–122 (2013)
8. Cristianini, N., Ricci, E.: Support vector machines. In: Kao, M.Y. (ed.) Encyclopedia of Algorithms. Springer, Boston (2008). https://doi.org/10.1007/978-0-387-30162-4_415
9. Dai, A.M., Le, Q.V.: Semi-supervised sequence learning. In: Advances in Neural Information Processing Systems, vol. 28, pp. 3079–3087 (2015)
10. Devlin, J., Chang, M.W., Lee, K., Toutanova, K.: BERT: pre-training of deep bidirectional transformers for language understanding. arXiv preprint arXiv:1810.04805 (2018)
11. Duwairi, R.M.: A distance-based classifier for Arabic text categorization. In: DMIN, pp. 187–192 (2005)
12. Duwairi, R.M.: Arabic text categorization. Int. Arab J. Inf. Technol. **4**(2), 125–131 (2007)
13. El-Halees, A.M.: Arabic text classification using maximum entropy. IUG J. Nat. Stud. **15**, 157–167 (2007)
14. Fix, E., Hodges, J.L., Jr.: Discriminatory analysis-nonparametric discrimination: small sample performance. Technical report, University of California Berkeley (1952)

15. Gharib, T.F., Habib, M.B., Fayed, Z.T.: Arabic text classification using support vector machines. Int. J. Comput. Their Appl. **16**, 192–199 (2009)
16. Khreisat, L.: Arabic text classification using N-gram frequency statistics: a comparative study. In: DMIN 2006, pp. 78–82 (2006)
17. Koehn, P., Och, F.J., Marcu, D.: Statistical phrase-based translation. Technical report, University of Southern California Marina Del Rey Information Sciences Institute (2003)
18. Kourdi, M.E., Bensaid, A., Rachidi, T.: Automatic Arabic document categorization based on the Naïve Bayes algorithm. In: Proceedings of the Workshop on Computational Approaches to Arabic Script-Based Languages, pp. 51–58 (2004)
19. Monroe, W., Green, S., Manning, C.D.: Word segmentation of informal Arabic with domain adaptation. In: Proceedings of the 52nd Annual Meeting of the Association for Computational Linguistics (Volume 2: Short Papers), pp. 206–211 (2014)
20. Pasha, A., et al.: MADAMIRA: a fast, comprehensive tool for morphological analysis and disambiguation of Arabic. In: Calzolari, N., et al. (eds.) Proceedings of the Ninth International Conference on Language Resources and Evaluation (LREC 2014), pp. 26–31. European Language Resources Association (ELRA), Reykjavik, Iceland (2014)
21. Quinlan, J.: C4. 5: Programs for Machine Learning. Elsevier (2014)
22. Rish, I., et al.: An empirical study of the Naive Bayes classifier. In: IJCAI 2001 Workshop on Empirical Methods in Artificial Intelligence, vol. 3, pp. 41–46 (2001)
23. Safaya, A., Abdullatif, M., Yuret, D.: BERT-CNN for offensive speech identification in social media. In: Proceedings of the Fourteenth Workshop on Semantic Evaluation, KUISAIL at SemEval-2020 Task 12, pp. 2054–2059. International Committee for Computational Linguistics, Barcelona (2020). https://www.aclweb.org/anthology/2020.semeval-1.271
24. SakhrSoftware: Sakhr Software: Arabic language technology (Sakhr Solutions: Ranked Number 1 in Accuracy and Performance, Powered by the World's Leading Research in Arabic Natural Language Processing (NLP)) (2022). http://www.sakhr.com. Accessed 6 Jan 2022
25. Sawaf, H., Zaplo, J., Ney, H.: Statistical classification methods for Arabic news articles. In: Third Arabic Natural Language Processing Workshop, in ACL 2001 (2001)
26. Sun, C., Qiu, X., Xu, Y., Huang, X.: How to fine-tune BERT for text classification? In: Sun, M., Huang, X., Ji, H., Liu, Z., Liu, Y. (eds.) CCL 2019. LNCS (LNAI), vol. 11856, pp. 194–206. Springer, Cham (2019). https://doi.org/10.1007/978-3-030-32381-3_16

Short Papers

Robots Still Outnumber Humans in Web Archives, But Less Than Before

Himarsha R. Jayanetti[1]([✉]) [iD], Kritika Garg[1] [iD], Sawood Alam[2] [iD],
Michael L. Nelson[1] [iD], and Michele C. Weigle[1] [iD]

[1] Old Dominion University, Norfolk, VA 23529, USA
{hjaya002,kgarg001}@odu.edu, {mln,mweigle}@cs.odu.edu
[2] Wayback Machine, Internet Archive, San Francisco, CA 94118, USA
sawood@archive.org

Abstract. To identify robots and humans and analyze their respective
access patterns, we used the Internet Archive's (IA) Wayback Machine
access logs from 2012 and 2019, as well as Arquivo.pt's (Portuguese Web
Archive) access logs from 2019. We identified user sessions in the access
logs and classified those sessions as human or robot based on their browsing behavior. To better understand how users navigate through the web
archives, we evaluated these sessions to discover user access patterns.
Based on the two archives and between the two years of IA access logs
(2012 vs. 2019), we present a comparison of detected robots vs. humans
and their user access patterns and temporal preferences. The total number of robots detected in IA 2012 is greater than in IA 2019 (21% more in
requests and 18% more in sessions). Robots account for 98% of requests
(97% of sessions) in Arquivo.pt (2019). We found that the robots are
almost entirely limited to "Dip" and "Skim" access patterns in IA 2012,
but exhibit all the patterns and their combinations in IA 2019. Both
humans and robots show a preference for web pages archived in the near
past.

Keywords: Web archiving · User access patterns · Web server logs ·
Web usage mining · Web robot detection

1 Introduction

With over 686 billion web pages archived [25] dating back to 1996, the Internet
Archive (IA) is the largest and oldest of the web archives. The Wayback Machine,
which can replay past versions of websites, is a public service provided by IA.
Arquivo.pt [15,20], the Portuguese web archive, has been archiving millions of
files from the Internet since 1996. Both web archives contain information in a
variety of languages and provide public search capabilities for historical content.

Our study is an extension of a previous study by AlNoamany et al. [7] that
examined access patterns for robots and humans in web archives based on a web
server log sample (2 million requests, ≈30 min) from 2012 from the Wayback

© Springer Nature Switzerland AG 2022
G. Silvello et al. (Eds.): TPDL 2022, LNCS 13541, pp. 245–259, 2022.
https://doi.org/10.1007/978-3-031-16802-4_19

Machine. By using several heuristics including browsing speed, image to HTML ratio, requests for robots.txt, and User-Agent strings to differentiate between a robot and human sessions, AlNoamany et al. determined that in the IA access logs in 2012, humans were outnumbered by robots 10:1 in terms of sessions, 5:4 in terms of raw HTTP accesses, and 4:1 in terms of megabytes transferred. The four web archive user access patterns defined in the previous study are **Dip** (single access), **Slide** (the same page at different archive times), **Dive** (different pages at roughly the same archive time), and **Skim** (lists of what pages are archived, i.e., TimeMaps).

We revisit the work of AlNoamany et al. by examining user accesses to web archives using three different datasets from anonymized server access logs: 2012 Wayback Machine (**IA2012**), 2019 Wayback Machine (**IA2019**), and 2019 Arquivo.pt (**PT2019**). Using these datasets, we identify human and robot accesses, identify important web archive access patterns, and discover the temporal preference for web archive access. We add to the previous study's criteria for distinguishing robots from humans by making a few adjustments. We used a full day's worth of three web archive access logs datasets (IA2012, IA2019, PT2019) to distinguish between human and robot access. The total number of robots detected in IA2012 is greater than IA2019 (21% more in requests and 18% more in sessions). Robots account for 98% of requests (97% of sessions) in PT2019.

In this paper, we are attempting to understand who accesses the web archives. To be clear, we are not making any value judgments about robots because we recognize that not all bots are bad. For example, there are services like Internet Archive Scholar [41], ArchiveReady [9], TMVis [35], and MemGator [3] which are built on top of web archives that benefit users.

2 Background and Related Work

Extracting useful data from web server logs and analyzing user navigation activity is referred to as web usage mining [40,46,50]. Numerous studies have been conducted for analyzing different web usage mining techniques as well as to identify user access patterns on the Internet [34,37,47]. Web usage mining is used to increase the personalization of web-based applications [39,42]. Mobasher et al. [38] developed an automatic personalization technique using multiple web usage mining approaches. Web usage mining is also applied in user profiling [14,22], web marketing initiatives [10], and enhancing learning management systems [51,51].

In this work, we look at web archive server access logs and perform web usage mining in the context of web archives. There has been past work in how users utilize and behave in web archives [6,16,17,19,21,24], including the 2013 study [7] that we revisit. Web archives maintain their web server access logs as plain text files that record each request to the web archive. Most HTTP servers use the standard Common Log Format or the extended Combined Log Format to record their server access logs [8]. An example access log entry from

Arquivo.pt web archive is shown in Fig. 1. A single log entry consists of the IP address of the client, user identity, authenticated user's ID, date and time, HTTP method, request path, HTTP version, HTTP status code, and size of the response in bytes, referrer, and User-Agent (left to right). The client IP address is anonymized in the access log datasets for privacy reasons. Alam has implemented an HTTP access log parser [1], with exclusive features for web archive access logs, which can be used to process such web archive access logs.

Web servers usually operate on the Hypertext Transfer Protocol (HTTP) [18]. Web clients (such as a web browser or web crawler) make HTTP requests to web servers using a set of defined methods, such as GET, HEAD, POST, etc. to interact with resources [2]. Web servers respond using a set of defined HTTP status codes, headers, and payload (if any).

128.82.7.3 - - [07/Jul/2019:04:44:14 +0100] "GET/wayback/20091223043049/ht
tp://www.cs.odu.edu/ HTTP/1.1" 200 9593 "-" "Mozilla/5.0 (X11; Ubuntu; Linux
x86_64; rv:48.0) Gecko/20100101 Firefox/48.0"

Fig. 1. A sample access log entry from the PT2019 dataset (Fields: IP address of the client, user identity, authenticated user's ID, date and time, HTTP method, request path, HTTP version, HTTP status code, size of the response in bytes, referrer, and User-Agent)

The goal of web archives is to capture and preserve original web resources (URI-Rs). Each capture, or memento (URI-M), is a version of a URI-R that comes from a fixed moment in time (Memento-Datetime). The list of mementos for a particular URI-R is called a TimeMap (URI-T). All of these notions are outlined in the Memento Protocol [49].

AlNoamany et al.'s previous work [7] in 2013 set the groundwork for this study. In addition to their analysis of the prevalence of robot and human users in the Internet Archive, they also proposed a set of basic user access patterns for users of web archives:

Dip - The user accesses only one URI (URI-M or URI-T).
Slide - The user accesses the same URI-R at different Memento-Datetimes.
Dive - The user accesses different URI-Rs at nearly the same Memento-Datetime (i.e., dives deeply into a memento by browsing links of URI-Ms).
Skim - The user accesses different TimeMaps (URI-T).

In a separate study, AlNoamany et al. looked into the Wayback Machine's access logs to understand who created links to URI-Ms and why [5,6]. They found that web archives were used to visit pages no longer on the live web (as opposed to prior versions of pages still on the web), and much of the traffic came from sites like Wikipedia.

Alam et al. [4] describe archival voids or portions of URI spaces that are not present in a web archive. They created multiple Archival Void profiles using

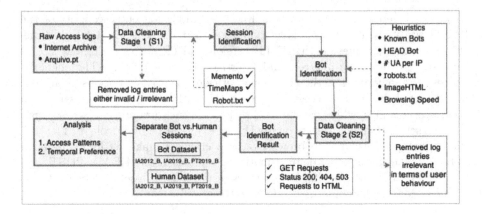

Fig. 2. A chart illustrating the phases in our analytical procedure

Arquivo.pt access logs, and while doing so, they identified and reported access patterns, status code distributions, and issues such as Soft-404 (when a web server responds with an HTTP 200 OK status code for pages that are actually error pages [36]) through Arquivo.pt server logs. While their research is very similar to ours, the mentioned access patterns differ from ours. Their study looks at which users are accessing the archive and what they request, whereas we explain how a user (robot or human) might traverse through an archive.

3   Methodology

In this work, we leverage cleaned access logs after pre-processing raw access logs to identify user sessions, detect robots, assess distinct access patterns used by web archive visitors, and finally check for any temporal preferences in user accesses. The steps of our analysis are shown in Fig. 2. The code [27] and visualizations [26] are published and each step is explained in detail in this section.

3.1   Dataset

In this study, we are using three **full-day** access log datasets from two different web archives: February 2, 2012 access logs from the Internet Archive (IA2012) and February 7, 2019 access logs from Internet Archive (IA2019) and Arquivo.pt (PT2019). We chose the first Thursday of February for our datasets to align with the prior analysis performed on a much smaller sample (2 million requests representing about 30 min) from the Wayback access logs from February 2, 2012 [7].

The characteristics of the raw datasets are listed in Table 1. We show the frequency of HTTP request methods and HTTP response codes, among other features. HTTP GET is the most prevalent request method (>98%) present in all three datasets, while the HTTP HEAD method accounts for less than 1% of requests.

Due to the practice of web archives redirecting from the requested Memento-Datetime to the nearest available memento, IA2012 and IA2019 have numerous 3xx requests. About 20% of requests are 3xx in PT2019, due to the same behavior. IA2019 has the highest number of requests to embedded resources (63%) followed by IA2012 (44%) whereas PT2019 has only 20%. From IA2012 to IA2019, the number of requests with a null referrer field has decreased by more than half. There is an increase in self-identified robots (SI robots) from IA2012 to IA2019. The percentage of SI robots in PT2019 is as twice that in IA2019. We used some of these features (HEAD requests, embedded resources, and SI robots) in the bot identification process (covered in Sect. 3.4).

Table 1. Features for each dataset: February 2, 2012 from IA (IA2012), February 7, 2019 from IA (IA2019), and February 7, 2019 from Arquivo.pt (PT2019).

Feature	IA2012	IA2019	PT2019
	February 2, 2012	February 7, 2019	February 7, 2019
No. of Requests	99,173,542 *(100.00%)*	308,194,916 *(100.00%)*	1,046,855 *(100.00%)*
GET	97,987,295 *(98.80%)*	304,125,661 *(98.68%)*	1,025,132 *(97.92%)*
HEAD	1,109,810 *(1.12%)*	2,578,735 *(0.84%)*	14,330 *(1.37%)*
PROPFIND	2,092 *(0.00%)*	27,896 *(0.01%)*	0 *(0.00%)*
POST	32,557 *(0.03%)*	1,368,941 *(0.44%)*	222 *(0.02%)*
OPTIONS	1,925 *(0.00%)*	7,982 *(0.00%)*	0 *(0.00%)*
Status Code 2xx	32,460,590 *(32.73%)*	148,742,768 *(48.26%)*	272,467 *(26.03%)*
Status Code 3xx	52,131,835 *(52.57%)*	131,729,104 *(42.74%)*	211,709 *(20.22%)*
Status Code 4xx	11,614,387 *(11.71%)*	27,099,599 *(8.79%)*	560,913 *(53.58%)*
Status Code 5xx	2,964,146 *(2.99%)*	614,502 *(0.20%)*	1,764 *(0.17%)*
Embedded Resources	43,260,926 *(43.62%)*	195,287,060 *(63.36%)*	205,976 *(19.68%)*
Null Referrer	47,625,026 *(48.02%)*	60,935,472 *(19.77%)*	265,515 *(25.36%)*
SI Robots	8,867 *(0.01%)*	476,367 *(0.15%)*	3,602 *(0.34%)*

3.2   Data Cleaning

An overview of our data cleaning process is shown in Fig. 2. In the Stage 1 data cleaning (S1), we removed the log entries that were either invalid or irrelevant to the analysis. We only kept legitimate requests to web archive content (mementos and TimeMaps) and requests to the web archive's robots.txt at the end of S1 data cleaning. The robots.txt requests were preserved since they will be utilized as a bot detection heuristic later on in our process.

After S1 data cleaning, we identified user sessions in each of our three datasets (Sect. 3.3) and conducted bot identification (Sect. 3.4). Stage 2 data cleaning (S2) takes place only after the requests were flagged as human or robot. Our study's ultimate goal was to detect user access patterns of robots and humans in our datasets, and to do so, we must ensure that the refined datasets only included requests that a user would make. As a result, in S2 we purged log items that were unrelated in terms of user behavior. This includes the browser's automatic requests for embedded resources, any requests using a method other than HTTP GET, and requests generating responses with status codes other than 200, 404, and 503. Several of these requests, including embedded resources and HEAD requests, were necessary during the bot detection phase. Thus, we had to follow a two-step data cleaning approach.

Table 2 shows the number of requests for each dataset after each cleaning stage. The percentages are based on the raw dataset's initial number of requests. PT2019 had a higher percentage of requests remaining after S2 compared to IA2012 and IA2019. This could be related to the raw dataset's low percentage of embedded resources (20%) in the PT2019 dataset (Table 1).

Table 2. The number of requests in each of the three datasets (IA2012, IA2019, and PT2019): Initial raw data, after stage 1 cleaning, and after stage 2 cleaning.

Dataset	Raw dataset	Stage 1 cleaning	Stage 2 cleaning
IA2012	99,173,542	84,512,394 *(85.22%)*	18,432,398 *(18.58%)*
IA2019	308,194,916	237,901,926 *(77.19%)*	35,015,776 *(11.36%)*
PT2019	1,046,855	904,515 *(86.40%)*	604,762 *(57.77%)*

3.3   Session Identification

A session can be defined as a set of interactions by a particular user with the web server within a given time frame. We split the requests into different user sessions after S1 data cleaning. First, we sorted all of the requests by IP and User-Agent, then identified the user sessions based on a 10-minute timeout threshold similar to the prior study's process [7]. That is, if the interval between two consecutive requests with the same IP and User-Agent is longer than 10 min, the second request is considered as the start of the next session for that user.

3.4   Bot Identification

As the next step in our process, we employed a heuristic-based strategy to identify robot requests (Fig. 2). We incorporated a few new adjustments to the original heuristics used in prior work [7] to improve the performance of the robot detection. The following sub-sections will go through each heuristic in detail.

Known Bots. We created a list of User-Agents that are known to be used by bots. We first constructed UA_l, a list of all User-Agent strings from our three datasets. From this list, we compiled UA_m by filtering for User-Agent strings that contained robot keywords, such as "bot", "crawler", "spider", etc. We compiled a separate bot User-Agent list UA_d by running our full list UA_l through DeviceDetector [12], a parser that filters on known bot User-Agent strings. Our final list [28] of bot User-Agents UA_{K_b} was constructed by combining UA_d with our keyword set UA_m. Any request with a User-Agent found in UA_{K_b} was classified as a robot.

Type of HTTP Request Method. Web browsers, which are assumed to be humans, send GET requests for web pages. As a result, we used HEAD requests as an indication of robot behavior. If the request made is a HEAD request, it is considered a robot request, and the session to which it belongs is counted as a robot session.

Number of User-Agent per IP (UA/IP). There are robots that repeatedly change their User-Agent (UA) between requests to avoid being detected. The previous study [7] found that a threshold of 20 UAs per IP was effective in distinguishing robots from humans. This allows for some human requests behind a proxy or NAT that may have the same IP address but different User-Agents, representing different users sharing a single IP. As discussed in Sect. 3.3, we sorted the access logs from the three datasets based on IP first and then User-Agent. We marked any requests from IPs that update their User-Agent field more than 20 times as robots.

Requests to robots.txt File. A robots.txt [31,52] file contains information on how to crawl pages on a website. It helps web crawlers control their actions so that they do not overburden the web server or crawl web pages that are not intended for public viewing. As a result, a request for the robots.txt file can be considered an indication of a robot request. We identified any user who made a request for robots.txt (including query strings) as a robot.

Browsing Speed (BS). We used browsing speed as a criterion to distinguish robots from humans. Robots can navigate the web far faster than humans. Castellano et al. [13] found that a human would only make a maximum of one request for a new web page every two seconds. Similar to the previous study [7], we classified any session with a browsing speed faster than one HTML request every two seconds (or, $BS \geq 0.5$ requests per second) as a robot.

Image-to-HTML Ratio (IH). Robots tend to retrieve only HTML pages, therefore requests for images can be regarded as a sign of a human user. A ratio of 1:10 images to HTML was proposed by Stassopoulou and Dikaiakos [48] and used in the prior study [7] as a threshold for distinguishing robots from humans. We flagged a session requesting less than one image file for every 10 HTML files as a robot session. IH was found to have the largest effect in detecting robots in the prior study's dataset, and this holds true for our three datasets as well.

We used the aforementioned heuristics on our three datasets to classify each request as human or robot. If a request/session has been marked as a robot at least by one of the heuristics, we have classified it as a robot. After bot identification but before reporting the final results, we performed S2 as described in Sect. 3.2.

4   Results and Analysis

In order to investigate the data further after S2 data cleaning, we divided the dataset into two subsets, human sessions, and bot sessions. For each dataset, we used these two subsets to determine user access patterns and compare them to robot access patterns. Finally, we conducted a temporal analysis of the requests in both subsets for each dataset.

4.1   Robots vs. Humans

Table 3 reports the number of detected robots for each dataset based on the total number of sessions and the total number of requests. We counted the number of requests classified as robots based on each heuristic independently (as mentioned earlier, the heuristics are not mutually exclusive, so these numbers across a column do not need to add to exactly 100%). The final row in the table represents the total number of sessions and requests that are marked as robots after applying all the heuristics together.

Table 3. Bot identification results based on the total number of sessions and the total number of requests for each dataset: IA2012, IA2019, and PT2019 (the header for each column displays the total number of sessions and requests). The heuristics are not mutually exclusive.

Heuristics	IA2012		IA2019		PT2019	
	Sessions	Requests	Sessions	Requests	Sessions	Requests
	1,527,340	22,302,090	2,658,637	42,868,048	3,680	613,672
Known Bots	21,423	398,053	322,379	4,969,187	884	67,453
	(1.40%)	(1.78%)	(12.13%)	(11.59%)	(24.02%)	(10.99%)
#UA per IP	5,050	756,801	5,475	1,442,574	3	2,636
	(0.33%)	(3.39%)	(0.21%)	(3.37%)	(0.08%)	(0.43%)
robots.txt	1,958	11,074	9,296	31,452	404	4,236
	(0.13%)	(0.05%)	(0.35%)	(0.07%)	(10.98%)	(0.69%)
IH Ratio	1,327,896	19,893,394	1,746,989	24,056,112	2,916	589,363
	(86.94%)	(89.20%)	(65.71%)	(56.12%)	(79.24%)	(96.04%)
Browsing Speed	237,271	4,563,851	514,878	21,176,163	1,694	162,068
	(15.53%)	(20.46%)	(19.37%)	(49.40%)	(46.03%)	(26.41%)
Total Robots	**1,340,318**	**20,281,301**	**1,854,282**	**29,968,059**	**3,584**	**603,654**
	(87.76%)	(90.94%)	(69.75%)	(69.91%)	(97.39%)	(98.37%)

The Image-to-HTML ratio (IH) had the largest effect on detecting robots across all three datasets. The impact of IH was ≈85–90% in IA2012 but only around ≈55–65% in IA2019. In PT2019, ≈80–96% of robots were detected using the IH ratio, which is higher compared to IA2019. In PT2019, we were able to detect almost all the robots through this one heuristic, IH. We found that ≈90% of requests were robots in IA2012, ≈70% of requests were robots in IA2019, and ≈98% of requests were robots in PT2019.

The reason for this increase in human sessions in 2019 than in 2012 could be the increase in awareness of web archives among human users. In addition, headless browsers, such as Headless Chromium [11], PhantomJS [23], and Selenium [44], that provide automated web page control have become popular in recent years. Their functionality simulates a more human-like behavior that may not be caught easily by bot detection techniques. For instance, applications like the work of Ayala [43] and tools like the oldweb.today [32,33], DSA Toolkit [29,30], TMVis [35], and Memento-Damage service [45] that replicate human behavior make things challenging for detection algorithms. Between IA2019 and PT2019, PT2019 has ≈30% more robots present. Based on our PT2019 dataset, only 2% of all requests coming into the Arquivo.pt are potential human requests.

4.2 Discovering Access Patterns

Upon distinguishing robots from humans, we divided all three of our datasets into human and bot subdatasets (IA2012_H, IA2012_B, IA2019_H, IA2019_B, PT2019_H, PT2019_B). We used these datasets to identify different access patterns that are followed by both human and robot sessions. Upon distinguishing robots from humans, we divided all three of our datasets into human and bot subdatasets (IA2012_H, IA2012_B, IA2019_H, IA2019_B, PT2019_H, PT2019_B). As introduced in Sect. 2, there were four different user access patterns established by AlNoamany et al. [7]. We looked into each of these patterns and identified their prevalence in our three datasets. We discovered the prevalence of sessions that followed each of the four patterns (Dip, Dive, Slide, Skim), as well as sessions that followed a hybrid of those patterns ("Dive and Slide", "Dive and Skim", "Skim and Slide", and "Dive, Slide, and Skim"). We categorized requests that do not fall into any pattern as **Unknown**.

Figure 3 shows a chart for each subdataset. The horizontal (x) axis represents the different patterns or a hybrid of patterns and the vertical (y) axis represents the percentage of the number of requests. The percentages are based on the total number of requests for each subdataset. According to AlNoamany et al.'s findings based on the IA2012 dataset, **Dips** were the most common pattern in both human and robot sessions. However in our IA2012 dataset (full-day), **Dive** and **Dip** account for about the same percentage of human sessions, although **Skim** is the most common pattern among robot sessions. **Dip** is the most common pattern in IA2019, followed by **Dive, Slide** for both human and robot sessions. The human **Dips** have more than doubled from IA2012 (22%) to IA2019 (50%) indicating that more humans are accessing web archives to access a single URI-M or URI-T. There are a high number of robot **Skims** in IA2012 compared to

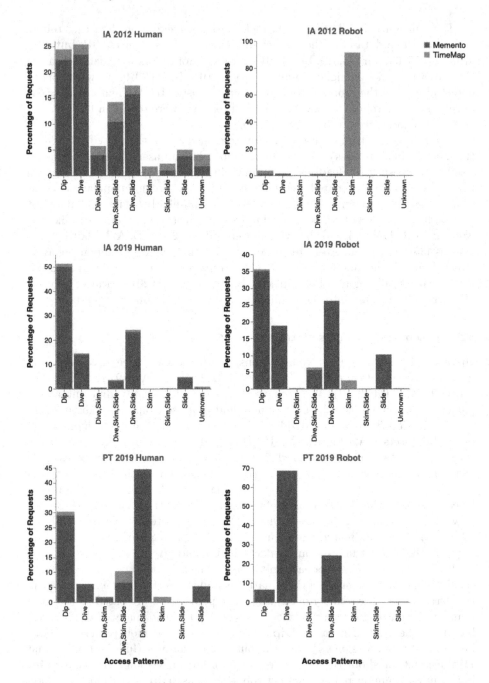

Fig. 3. Access patterns of robots and humans in our subdatasets (IA2012_H, IA2012_B, IA2019_H, IA2019_B, PT2019_H, PT2019_B). The color of the stacked bar distinguishes between requests for mementos (URI-Ms) and TimeMaps (URI-Ts). Note that the y axes in the charts are not the same. (Color figure online)

IA2019. In IA2012 robot sessions, it is over 90% **Skims**. We could see that the long-running robot sessions that request URI-Ts account for most of the **Skim** percentage. In contrast to IA2019, PT2019 humans exhibit a higher percentage of **Dive** and **Slide** (45%) than **Dips** (29%). Even in robot sessions, **Dive** (70%) and **Dive** and **Slide** (24%) percentage is higher than **Dip** (6%).

In IA2012, robots almost always access TimeMaps (95%) and humans access mementos (82%). However, in IA2019, humans and robots almost always access mementos (96%), whereas only 4% of those accesses are to TimeMaps. When looking at the hybrid patterns, PT2019 bot sessions only have a maximum of two patterns while the rest have a small percentage of all three patterns (**Dive, Skim, and Slide**). For each dataset in IA, there is a very small percentage of requests (4.22% in IA2019, 0.97% in IA2012) that do not belong to any of the patterns. We were able to identify all the different patterns in the PT2019 dataset. The percentage of human requests falling under the **Unknown** category in IA2012 (4.02%) is higher compared to the IA2012 robot requests (0.2%), IA2019 human requests (0.85%), and IA2019 robot requests (0.12%).

4.3   Identifying Temporal Preferences

We also explored the requested Memento-Datetime in our subdatasets to see if there was any temporal preference by web archive users. Figure 4 illustrates the temporal preference of robots and humans in our datasets. The x-axis represents the number of years prior, meaning the number of years passed relative to the datetime of the access logs (e.g., for IA2012, 2 years prior is 2010) and the y-axis represents the number of requests. Note that the y-axis in each chart is different.

It is evident that the majority of the requests are for mementos that are close to the datetime of each access log sample and gradually diminish as we go further back in time. There is no significant difference in temporal preference in IA2012 and IA2019. IA2019 humans, IA2019 bots, and PT2019 bots exhibit the same trend however, it is difficult to see a trend in PT2019 humans due to the fewer number of humans in the dataset. For PT2019 humans, there is a spike around 4–5 years prior which implies PT human accesses were mostly for mementos around 2015–2016. There is an advantage to knowing the temporal preferences of web archive users. Web archives can prioritize or store data in memory for the most recent years to speed up disk access.

5   Future Work

AlNoamany et al. [7] observed four different user access patterns in 2013. In our datasets combined, 0.35% of requests were outside of any of these patterns or their combinations. One may look into if the percentage of requests that fell into the **Unknown** category have any other generally applicable patterns, or if they are completely random.

The overall number of robots identified in IA2019 is much lower than in IA2012. We would like to repeat this study on more distinct full-day datasets to

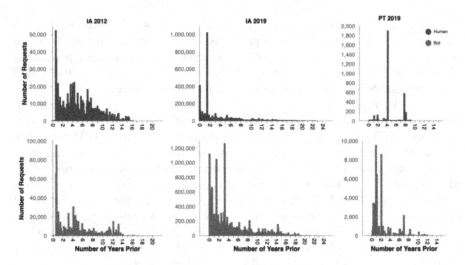

Fig. 4. Temporal preference of bots and humans in IA2012, IA2019, PT2019 datasets.

see if the reduction in robots is a general behavior from 2012 to 2019 or specific to the day we chose. Additionally, the IH [48] and BS thresholds [13] in our bot identification heuristics are based on the behavior of conventional web servers; however, it remains to be determined if the same thresholds apply to web archival replay systems, as the dynamics of web archival replay systems differ (e.g., the Wayback Machine is typically slower than a typical web server).

6   Conclusions

We used a full-day access logs sample of Internet Archive's (IA) Wayback Machine from 2012 and 2019, as well as Arquivo.pt's from 2019, to distinguish between robot and human users in web archives. In IA2012, the overall number of robots discovered was higher than in IA2019 (21% more in requests and 18%t more in sessions). We discovered that robot accesses account for 98% of requests (97% of sessions) based on 2019 server logs from Arquivo.pt. We also discovered that in IA2012, the robots were almost exclusively limited to Dip and Skim, but that in IA2019, they exhibit all of the patterns and their combinations. Regardless of whether it is a robot or a human user, the majority of requests were for mementos that are close to the date-time of each access log dataset, demonstrating a preference for the recent past.

Acknowledgements. We thank Mark Graham, director of the Wayback Machine, for sharing access log data from the Wayback Machine at the Internet Archive. We are grateful to Daniel Gomes and Fernando Melo of Arquivo.pt for sharing access log data from the Arquivo.pt web archive with us.

References

1. Alam, S.: AccessLog Parser and CLI (2019). https://github.com/oduwsdl/accesslog-parser
2. Alam, S., Cartledge, C.L., Nelson, M.L.: Support for various HTTP methods on the web. Technical report. arXiv:1405.2330 (2014)
3. Alam, S., Nelson, M.L.: MemGator - a portable concurrent Memento aggregator: cross-platform CLI and server binaries in Go. In: Proceedings of the 16th ACM/IEEE-CS Joint Conference on Digital Libraries, JCDL 2016, pp. 243–244 (2016)
4. Alam, S., Weigle, M.C., Nelson, M.L.: Profiling web archival voids for memento routing. In: Proceedings of the 21st ACM/IEEE-CS Joint Conference on Digital Libraries, JCDL 2021, pp. 150–159 (2021). https://doi.org/10.1109/JCDL52503.2021.00027
5. AlNoamany, Y., AlSum, A., Weigle, M.C., Nelson, M.L.: Who and what links to the Internet Archive. In: Proceedings of Theory and Practice of Digital Libraries (TPDL), pp. 346–357 (2013)
6. AlNoamany, Y., AlSum, A., Weigle, M.C., Nelson, M.L.: Who and what links to the Internet Archive. Int. J. Digit. Libr. **14**(3), 101–115 (2014)
7. AlNoamany, Y., Weigle, M.C., Nelson, M.L.: Access patterns for robots and humans in web archives. In: Proceedings of the 13th ACM/IEEE-CS Joint Conference on Digital Libraries, JCDL 2013, pp. 339–348 (2013)
8. Apache HTTP Server: Common Log Format and Combined Log Format (2013). https://httpd.apache.org/docs/trunk/logs.html
9. Banos, V., Manolopoulos, Y.: A quantitative approach to evaluate Website Archivability using the CLEAR+ method. **17**, 119–141 (2016). https://doi.org/10.1007/s00799-015-0144-4
10. Berendt, B., Mobasher, B., Spiliopoulou, M., Wiltshire, J.: Measuring the accuracy of sessionizers for web usage analysis. In: Workshop on Web Mining at the First SIAM International Conference on Data Mining, pp. 7–14. SIAM, Philadelphia (2001)
11. Bidelman, E.: Getting Started with Headless Chrome (2018). https://developer.chrome.com/blog/headless-chrome/
12. Burkholder, D.: DeviceDetector (2022). https://github.com/thinkwelltwd/device_detector
13. Castellano, G., Fanelli, A.M., Torsello, M.A.: LODAP: a LOg DAta preprocessor for mining web browsing patterns. In: Proceedings of the 6th WSEAS International Conference on Artificial Intelligence, Knowledge Engineering and Data Bases, pp. 12–17 (2007)
14. Castellano, G., Mesto, F., Minunno, M., Torsello, M.A.: Web user profiling using fuzzy clustering. In: Masulli, F., Mitra, S., Pasi, G. (eds.) WILF 2007. LNCS (LNAI), vol. 4578, pp. 94–101. Springer, Heidelberg (2007). https://doi.org/10.1007/978-3-540-73400-0_12
15. Costa, M., Gomes, D., Couto, F.M., Silva, M.J.: A survey of web archive search architectures. In: Proceedings of the Temporal Web Analytics Workshop, TempWeb 2013, pp. 1045–1050 (2013). https://doi.org/10.1145/2487788.2488116
16. Costa, M., Miranda, J., Cruz, D., Gomes, D.: Query suggestion for web archive search. In: iPRES (2013)
17. Costa, M., Silva, M.J.: Characterizing search behavior in web archives. In: TWAW (2011)

18. Fielding, R.T., Reschke, J.F.: Hypertext Transfer Protocol (HTTP/1.1): Message Syntax and Routing (2014). https://tools.ietf.org/html/rfc7230
19. Gomes, D., Costa, M.: The importance of web archives for humanities. Int. J. Hum. Arts Comput. **8**(1), 106–123 (2014)
20. Gomes, D., Costa, M., Cruz, D., Miranda, J., Fontes, S.: Creating a billion-scale searchable web archive. In: Proceedings of the Temporal Web Analytics Workshop, TempWeb 2013, pp. 1059–1066 (2013). https://doi.org/10.1145/2487788.2488118
21. Gomes, D., Cruz, D., Miranda, J., Costa, M., Fontes, S.: Search the past with the Portuguese web archive. In: Proceedings of the 22nd International Conference on World Wide Web, pp. 321–324 (2013)
22. Grcar, M.: User profiling: web usage mining. In: Proceedings of the 7th International Multiconference Information Society IS (2004)
23. Hidayat, A.: PhantomJS (2011). https://phantomjs.org/
24. Hockx-Yu, H.: Access and scholarly use of web archives. Alexandria **25**(1–2), 113–127 (2014)
25. Internet Archive: Wayback Machine (2022). https://web.archive.org/web/20220527205606/web.archive.org/
26. Jayanetti, H.: Visualizations for Web Archive Access Log Datasets (2022). https://observablehq.com/@himarshaj/visualizations-for-web-archive-access-log-datasets
27. Jayanetti, H., Garg, K.: Access Patterns (2022). https://github.com/oduwsdl/access-patterns/
28. Jayanetti, H., Garg, K.: Known Bot List (2022). https://github.com/oduwsdl/access-patterns/tree/main/Known_Bot_List
29. Jones, S.M.: Improving collection understanding for web archives with storytelling: shining light into dark and stormy archives. Ph.D. thesis, Old Dominion University (2021). https://doi.org/10.25777/zts6-v512
30. Jones, S.M., et al.: The DSA toolkit shines light into dark and stormy archives. Code4Lib J. (2022). https://journal.code4lib.org/articles/16441
31. Koster, M., Illyes, G., Zeller, H., Sassman, L.: Robots Exclusion Protocol (2022). https://datatracker.ietf.org/doc/html/draft-koster-rep-08
32. Kreymer, I., Rosenthal, D.S.H.: Guest Post: Ilya Kreymer on oldweb.today (2016). https://blog.dshr.org/2016/01/guest-post-ilya-kreymer-on-oldwebtoday.html
33. Kreymer, I., Rosenthal, D.S.H.: Announcing the New OldWeb.today (2020). https://webrecorder.net/2020/12/23/new-oldweb-today.html
34. Liu, B.: Web Data Mining: Exploring Hyperlinks, Contents, and Usage Data, vol. 1. Springer, Cham (2011). https://doi.org/10.1007/978-3-642-19460-3
35. Mabe, A., et al.: Visualizing Webpage Changes Over Time (2020). http://arxiv.org/abs/2006.02487
36. Meneses, L., Furuta, R., Shipman, F.: Identifying "Soft 404" error pages: analyzing the lexical signatures of documents in distributed collections. In: Zaphiris, P., Buchanan, G., Rasmussen, E., Loizides, F. (eds.) TPDL 2012. LNCS, vol. 7489, pp. 197–208. Springer, Heidelberg (2012). https://doi.org/10.1007/978-3-642-33290-6_22
37. Mobasher, B.: Web usage mining. In: Encyclopedia of Data Warehousing and Mining, pp. 1216–1220. IGI Global (2005)
38. Mobasher, B., Cooley, R., Srivastava, J.: Automatic personalization based on web usage mining. Commun. ACM **43**(8), 142–151 (2000)
39. Mobasher, B., Dai, H., Luo, T., Sun, Y., Zhu, J.: Integrating web usage and content mining for more effective personalization. In: Bauknecht, K., Madria, S.K., Pernul, G. (eds.) EC-Web 2000. LNCS, vol. 1875, pp. 165–176. Springer, Heidelberg (2000). https://doi.org/10.1007/3-540-44463-7_15

40. Mughal, M.J.H.: Data mining: web data mining techniques, tools and algorithms: an overview. Int. J. Adv. Comput. Sci. Appl. **9**(6) (2018)
41. Newbold, B.: Search Scholarly Materials Preserved in the Internet Archive (2021). https://blog.archive.org/2021/03/09/search-scholarly-materials-preserved-in-the-internet-archive/
42. Pierrakos, D., Paliouras, G., Papatheodorou, C., Spyropoulos, C.D.: Web usage mining as a tool for personalization: a survey. User Model. User-Adap. Inter. **13**(4), 311–372 (2003)
43. Reyes Ayala, B.: Correspondence as the primary measure of information quality for web archives: a human-centered grounded theory study. Int. J. Digit. Libr. **23**(1), 19–31 (2022)
44. Selenium: Selenium Client Driver (2018). https://selenium.dev/selenium/docs/api/py/
45. Siregar, E.: Deploying the Memento-Damage Service (2017). https://ws-dl.blogspot.com/2017/11/2017-11-22-deploying-memento-damage.html
46. Srivastava, J., Cooley, R., Deshpande, M., Tan, P.N.: Web usage mining: discovery and applications of usage patterns from web data. SIGKDD Explor. Newsl. **1**(2), 12–23 (2000). https://doi.org/10.1145/846183.846188
47. Srivastava, J., Cooley, R., Deshpande, M., Tan, P.: Web usage mining: discovery and applications of usage patterns from web data. SIGKDD Explor. **1**(2), 12–23 (2000)
48. Stassopoulou, A., Dikaiakos, M.D.: Web robot detection: a probabilistic reasoning approach. Comput. Netw. **53**(3), 265–278 (2009)
49. Van de Sompel, H., Nelson, M.L., Sanderson, R.: HTTP Framework for Time-Based Access to Resource States - Memento (2013). http://tools.ietf.org/html/rfc7089
50. Varnagar, C.R., Madhak, N.N., Kodinariya, T.M., Rathod, J.N.: Web usage mining: a review on process, methods and techniques. In: 2013 International Conference on Information Communication and Embedded Systems (ICICES), pp. 40–46. IEEE (2013)
51. Zaiane, O.: Web usage mining for a better web-based learning environment. Technical report. TR01-05, University of Alberta (2001). https://doi.org/10.7939/R3736M20P
52. Zeller, H., Harvey, L., Illyes, G.: Formalizing the Robots Exclusion Protocol Specification (2019). https://webmasters.googleblog.com/2019/07/rep-id.html

Cui Bono? Cumulative Advantage in Open Access Publishing

David Pride$^{(\boxtimes)}$, Matteo Cancellieri, and Petr Knoth

The Knowledge Media Institute, The Open University, Milton Keynes, UK
{david.pride,matteo.cancellieri,petr.knoth}@open.ac.uk

Abstract. This study examines the differences in production and consumption of Open Access (OA) literature across institutional prestige variables and examines who is gaining the most benefit from the adoption of current OA publishing practices. In this approach we define production as the publication of OA literature (as a proportion of all research literature produced) by an entity (author, institution, country, continent). We define consumption as evidence of using OA literature as measured by citations to OA literature. Using data points for over 24,000 institutions we examine the role of institutional prestige in the Open Access landscape. Overall, we find medium to strong correlations between OA production and OA consumption. We find that higher ranked institutes are both greater producers and consumers of Open Access literature. Importantly, we find a stronger correlation for higher ranked institutions compared to lower ranked ones when using ranking data from the Times Higher Education (THE) World University Rankings. This indicates that it is the higher ranked and more prosperous institutes that are best placed to benefit from current Open Science and Open Access publishing structures.

1 Introduction

We approach our initial study with the use of two paradigms, production and consumption. In this approach we define production as the publication of OA literature (as a proportion of all research literature produced) by an entity (author, institution, country, continent). We define consumption as evidence of using OA literature by an entity as measured by citation to OA literature.

Using the production and consumption framework, it is possible to measure production and consumption in multiple ways. In this study, we focus on measuring the OA Production Rate, i.e. the proportion of all papers produced by an entity that are OA. While OA production is somewhat straightforward to measure, there are multiple ways in which OA Consumption could be measured. For instance, one option would be to measure the proportion of OA paper downloads by an entity. However, such data are not currently publicly available. As a result, we estimate the OA Consumption Rate as the proportion of OA references an entity (authors, institution, country, etc.) cited in the research papers this entity produced (as a proportion of total references) (Table 1).

© Springer Nature Switzerland AG 2022
G. Silvello et al. (Eds.): TPDL 2022, LNCS 13541, pp. 260–265, 2022.
https://doi.org/10.1007/978-3-031-16802-4_20

Table 1. Terminology used in this study

Terminology	Description
Production	The publication of research papers by an entity (continent, country, institute)
OA Production	Research papers produced by an entity. We use Unpaywall data to distinguish between OA and non-OA literature
OA Production Rate	The proportion of OA research papers produced by an entity
Consumption	The use of a research paper by an entity as measured by citations in that entity's publications
OA Consumption	The use of an OA research paper as measured by citations in that entity's publications
OA Consumption Rate	The proportion of OA research papers used by an entity. In our work, we use as evidence of use the act of citing OA research literature in manuscripts produced by an entity

The subsequent analyses of OA consumption take as a basic assumption that one can only cite what one has read. We understand this is a somewhat imperfect assumption due to two potential confounding factors: (1) that people may indeed often cite articles that they have in fact not read, and (2) "shadow library" websites (most prominently Sci-Hub). As for the former point, we acknowledge that it has been shown that authors sometimes cite research that they have not read (Ball 2002; Bornmann and Daniel 2008). Given our quantitative methods, we are unable to take account of this factor here. We hence treat this as a limitation of our study.

2   Related Work

Recent work by [1] investigated the production of OA literature around the globe based on institutions present in the THE rankings. They found that, in 2017, the 100 top-ranked universities made 80–90% of their research publications available as Open Access. In 2017, [2] undertook a comparison of institutional performance using data from the Leiden Ranking and found that research performance differences among universities mainly stem from size, disciplinary orientation and country location. The authors state that this result underlines, yet again, that larger universities systematically over-perform in citation rankings. However, the exact cause remains under-researched [3]. Regarding citation behaviours, most studies conclude that OA articles receive more citations than articles that are behind paywalls [4–6].

3   Data Sources

Data regarding institutions, authors and articles for these experiments come from the Microsoft Academic Graph (MAG) dataset [7] which as of June 2021 contains 260,423,032 papers. We use the university ranking data from THE World University Rankings and from the Leiden Rankings [8] which we derive our performance/prestige metrics when undertaking comparisons of individual institutions. We used the Unpaywall API to ascertain the OA status of each paper in the dataset.

4   Methodology

In this study we investigate the level of production and consumption of OA literature at an institutional level. We first examine the levels of OA production and consumption (measured as a proportion of all production). We then correlate this at the institutional level, and also measure this using THE ranking and Leiden Ranking data.

We used MAG data to collate all papers with complete metadata to the publishing institution. This methodology identifies 219m paper/institute pairs, representing 84% of the total MAG corpus. We then collated metadata and all known citations for all papers where the institution and author data were complete. From the complete MAG data, we were able to collate identifiers for 219m papers by 44m authors from 24,000 individual institutions (all figures are close approximations). We then use the Unpaywall API[1] to ascertain the OA status of each paper.

5   Results

5.1   Institutional Ranking and OA Consumption

This study was undertaken to determine whether there was a link between the prestige of an institution, using a range of different ranking methodologies, and the levels of OA consumption at these institutes.

When using ranking data from the THE rankings, we find a statistically significant difference in the amount of OA content cited by differently ranked institutions. Institutions ranked in the top third on average cite 13% more open access content than those in the bottom third (Fig. 1).

Figure 2 uses the same dataset of papers, authors, institutions and citations but uses the ranking taken from the Leiden Rankings. The Leiden Ranking are based on bibliometric data. The THE rankings use a proprietary ranking system, the exact calculations for which are not publicly available. It is therefore an interesting result that we only observe a difference in citation rates when using the THE data. The results obtained using the THE ranking data would suggest that lower ranked institutes tend to cite a smaller percentage of OA research papers than their higher ranked counterparts which seems counter-intuitive.

---

[1] https://unpaywall.org/products/api.

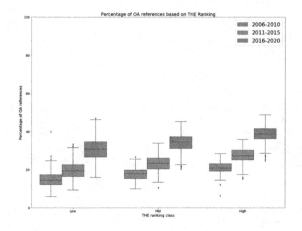

Fig. 1. Percentage of OA references over time (2006–2020) by THE Ranking

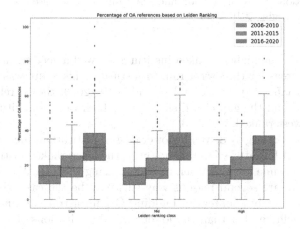

Fig. 2. Percentage of OA references over time (2006–2020) by Leiden Ranking

5.2 Correlation Between Production/Consumption and Institutional Ranking

We examined the correlation between the production and consumption of OA literature for institutions in the THE World University Rankings using Pearson's Correlation Coefficient.

Figure 3 shows the correlation between OA production and OA consumption at the institutional level for two different time periods.

Each dot is a single institution and covers all institutes in THE rankings. The dots are coloured and sized according to the institutions' ranking. It can been seen from these results that during both time periods, there was a far stronger correlation between the production and consumption of OA literature for institutes ranked in the top third of institutes using the THE rankings. For the

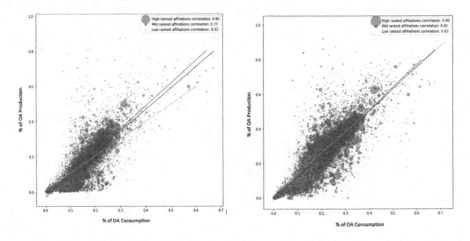

Fig. 3. Correlation of OA production and OA Consumption based on THE ranking.
Left: 2011–2015, Right: 2016–2020

period 2011–215, the highest ranked institutes showed a very strong correlation of $r = 0.86$ whereas for the lowest ranked institutes this figure was significantly weaker at $r = 0.52$. For the second period, 2016–2020, the correlation for all ranks increased and the gap closed slightly; for high ranked institutes $r = 0.90$ and for the lowest ranked, $r = 0.63$.

This change was largely driven by lower ranked institutions increasing rates of production of OA literature. Overall, however, the lower ranked institutions both produce and consume less OA when measured using the THE World University Rankings. There are several reasons why this may be the case. Higher ranked institutions were early adopters in building OA infrastructure and potentially realised its benefits earlier than the lower ranked institutions. The size, wealth or location of the institution in question are all potential confounding factors here and these differences remain to be investigated in future work.

6   Conclusion

The narrative that has formed throughout this study is that the production and consumption of OA literature is highly correlated at the institutional level. We observe the more highly ranked institutions, when using THE rankings, are both greater producers and greater consumers of OA than lower-ranked institutions. One explanation for this phenomenon might be that higher ranked institutions had the resources to invest in OA, that they became the first movers, advocates and adopters of OA, and that their strategy is being followed by the lower ranked institutions. A recent study by Siler et al. (2018) showed that, for the field of Global Health, lower-ranked institutions are more likely to publish in closed outlets. Their rationale here is that this is due to the cost of Article Processing Charges (APCs) levied by the publishers. This study shows some early indications that it is the higher ranked, better funded institutes which are best placed to capitalise on the Open Access movement.

Acknowledgements. The research leading to these results has received funding from the European Union's Horizon 2020 Research and Innovation Programme, under Grant Agreement no 824612 related to the Observing and Negating Matthew Effects in Responsible Research and Innovation Transition (ON-MERRIT) project.

References

1. Neylon, C., et al.: Evaluating the impact of open access policies on research institutions. eLife (2020)
2. Frenken, K., Heimeriks, G.J., Hoekman, J.: What drives university research performance? An analysis using the CWTS Leiden Ranking data. J. Informet. **11**(3), 859–872 (2017)
3. Bornmann, L., Mutz, R., Daniel, H.D.: Multilevel-statistical reformulation of citation-based university rankings: the Leiden ranking 2011/2012. J. Am. Soc. Inform. Sci. Technol. **64**(8), 1649–1658 (2013)
4. Holmberg, K., Hedman, J., Bowman, T.D., Didegah, F., Laakso, M.: Do articles in open access journals have more frequent altmetric activity than articles in subscription-based journals? An investigation of the research output of Finnish universities. Scientometrics **122**(1), 645–659 (2019). https://doi.org/10.1007/s11192-019-03301-x
5. Hajjem, C., Harnad, S., Gingras, Y.: Ten-year cross-disciplinary comparison of the growth of open access and how it increases research citation impact. arXiv preprint cs/0606079 (2006)
6. Kousha, K., Abdoli, M.: The citation impact of Open Access agricultural research: a comparison between OA and non-OA publications. Online Information Review (2010)
7. Sinha, A., et al.: An overview of Microsoft academic service (MAS) and applications. In: Proceedings of the 24th International Conference on World Wide Web, pp. 243–246 (2015)
8. Waltman, L., et al.: The Leiden Ranking 2011/2012: data collection, indicators, and interpretation. J. Am. Soc. Inform. Sci. Technol. **63**(12), 2419–2432 (2012)

Overview Visualizations for Large Digitized Correspondence Collections: A Design Study

Laura Swietlicki and Pierre Cubaud[✉]

Centre d'étude et de Recherche en Informatique et Communication (CEDRIC), Conservatoire National des Arts et Métiers (CNAM), Paris, France
cubaud@cnam.fr

Abstract. Overview visualization is a useful alternative to search engines in digital libraries. We describe such a tool in the context of a large correspondence collection: the Godin-Moret archive (20,000 letters). After a review of previous works, we describe our interface design and how it has been derived with the help of an online co-creation workshop. The interface is organized with a specific representation called the correspondence matrix, coordinated with more standard visualizations like tag clouds, maps and bar graphs.

Keywords: Digital libraries · Cultural heritage · Data visualization · UX design

1 Introduction

Data visualization is recognized nowadays as an essential tool for digital libraries. One of the most important feature of visualization is the capability to provide for the users an overview of the data under study [1]. Designing an overview interface is however a difficult task in the context of digital libraries, because each category of digitized documents (books, photos, music, software, etc.) implies specific browsing and searching practices. We study in this paper the case of correspondence collections.

Correspondence archives are a very important source for a wide spectrum of academic researches in history and sociology. Many correspondence archives have already been digitalized, generally through a joint scholar effort (see for instance a list of over 50 recent projects in [2]). However, as we shall see further, only a few of these projects have developed specific visualization tools. The *FamiliLettres* project gave us an opportunity for such a study. FamiliLettres is the ongoing publishing project for the private correspondence of Jean-Baptiste Godin (1817–1888) and Marie Moret (1840–1908), Godin's collaborator and companion. Godin was a French industrialist, creator of social experimentation inspired by Fourierism that was the Familistère, located at Guise in the north of France. The collection includes more than 20,000 copies of letters[1] archived at CNAM and the Familistère, accounting for about 3,000 correspondents. The digitized collection is hosted by EMAN, a national research platform for digital humanities [3]. It will be available for public use in 2023.

---

[1] As was customary at their time, Godin and Moret kept copies of their letters. These copies were produced using a special mechanical press, then bound together in registers and archived. The collection also includes a thousand original letters received by Godin and Moret.

G. Silvello et al. (Eds.): TPDL 2022, LNCS 13541, pp. 266–273, 2022.
https://doi.org/10.1007/978-3-031-16802-4_21

2   Related Work

One can find in [4] a general review of works dated from 2004 to 2018 on visualization for cultural heritage (CH) collections, but only one of the 166 selected references addresses correspondences specifically (i.e. [5]). The taxonomies of usage and tasks derived by the authors, ranging from casual browsing to specialized scholar research, are however fully relevant to our subject of study. The authors also identify some important challenges for digital libraries design: we need alternatives to search tools that support accidental discovery (serendipity) and help the user's understanding of the collections. Designing "generous" overview interfaces can help to fulfill these challenges [6].

Correspondence letters do have specificities as textual documents. They are most of the time rather short, hand written, signed and dated documents, written for specific addressee(s). Formal metadata grammars have been defined: see for instance the work of the TEI Correspondence SIG [7]. The richness of these metadata impacts upon the visualization tools that must be provided for the digitalized collections. The "social network" identified by the letters needs to be represented as such. Locations of actors ask for maps. Timelines can be used for analyzing the flow of writings.

Table 1 summarizes, in chronological order of publication, theh only papers we found that specifically address interactive visualization for correspondence collections. All of them are based on specific data sets, of very different sizes. The more recent works have benefited from the global progress of computer graphics. One can also note the great variety of the visualization tools, without consensus for any overview organization.

Table 1. Works on visualization for correspondence collections

Project, date and ref.	Collection description	Visualizations
Compus, 2000 [8]	100 TEI-encoded manuscript letters, XVIth century	Text mining oriented, space filing, color for letter structure, bar charts
Emily dickinson, 2006 [9]	300 XML-encoded letters, XIXth century	Text mining oriented, color for letter topics, scatterplots
Mapping the republic of letters, 2008–17 [5]	Six sub projects on Franklin, Kircher, Locke, etc. ±3000 letters each?	Specific interactive views for each project: networks, bar graphs, maps (online)
Emigrant letters, 2014 [10]	4000 TEI-encoded letters, 1740–2010	Multiple (uncoordinated) views: scatterplots, maps, networks, timelines
Diggers diaries, 2016 [11]	337 authors, 688 diaries and letters, 81763 pages, WW1 period	Page grid, facetted view, color for letter topics, timeline, bar graphs (online)

(*continued*)

Table 1. (*continued*)

Project, date and ref.	Collection description	Visualizations
Tudor networks, 2019 [12]	37101 unique names, 132747 letters, XVI-XVIIth century	Interactive tool for network exploration, maps (online)
Raoul hausmann sammlung, 2019 [13]	1400 documents (4500 images) including letters	Multiple coordinated view: thumbnails within timelines, network (online)

3   Collaborative Design

In order to define our own visualization overview for FamiliLettres, we choose to rely at first on co-creation sessions with its stakeholders. We have invited 8 persons with different level of implication in the project (4 historians and 4 curators). All are proficient users of digital libraries and 5 have expert knowledge of Godin's life and work. Unfortunately, meetings were forbidden at this period of time (spring 2021) due to the COVID-19 crisis in France. Two sessions were organized online with collaborative tools, organized the same day. Both had a scheduled duration of 90 min.

For the first session, the panel was asked to analyze a selection of 8 websites with overview interfaces that are representative of CH visualization's current state of art. Work was divided in 4 groups, for 2 sites each, in the order given in Table 2. The analysis was guided by a short usability questionnaire. We asked the groups to designate up to 3 noteworthy visualizations for each site, and to evaluate their relevance for FamiliLettres. The session ended with a debrief of each team and a general discussion. It was found that 7 over 8 sites were considered useful, with variations summarized in Table 2. Every group found at least one reusable visualization tool. Coordinated views within the visualizations were the most noted feature during the debrief.

The purpose of this first phase was also to fuel a creative session for our overview definition. Because of the online situation, we had to rely on whiteboards (Miro). Drawing activities of the panel were simplified to the extreme, focusing on collage of screenshots of selected elements from the sites studied in the first phase (Fig. 1). Two equal groups were formed, tutored by each of us. They were instructed to test as many collage combinations as necessary in order to reach a satisfactory overview definition. The session lasted 1 h and was followed by a collective debrief. The two groups finally produced quite different overviews, but all were organized as coordinated views using tag clouds, maps and the timeline made with thumbnails of [16]. Network visualizations were used only in one group. It was agreed in the debrief that such representation would be of minor use for the FamiliLettres archive because of the great difference of size between active and passive correspondence.

Table 2. Sites studied during the workshop. URLs are in the reference section.

Projects for each group	Noted component(s)	Relevance
Tudor networks [12]	Direct access to the correspondents network Geographic section	Maybe Yes
Raoul hausmann sammlung [13]	Timeline with access to document detail Keywords search section Correspondance section (network)	Yes Definitely yes Definitely yes
Reading traces [14]	Continuous zoom from collection viz. to pages	Maybe
Speculative W@nderverse [15]	Multiple coordinated views Expert and casual navigation Many stackable filters	Yes Definitely yes Yes
Past visions [16]	Timeline and keywords coord. With thumbnails Commentated timeline	Definitely yes Yes
Atlante calvino [17]	None (but "very interesting visual impact")	No
Deutsche digitale bib. [18]	Timeline coordinated with network Places and sectors section	Yes Yes
Diggers diaries [11]	Explore by time and Explore by diary sections	Yes

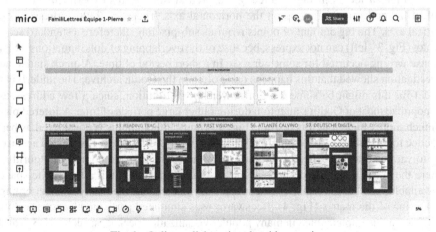

Fig. 1. Online collaborative sketching session.

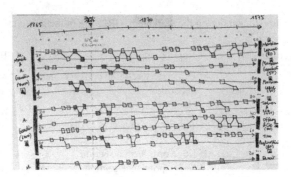

Fig. 2. Early sketch of the correspondence overview.

4 The Correspondence Matrix

The co-creation workshop was followed by other design iterations. We reproduce Fig. 2 one of the first sketches that were produced for the overview representation. We chose to arrange the letters chronologically on an horizontal axis with their respective sender and addressee on the vertical axis. The letters are represented by a small selectable square, possibly colored to convey extra metadata. However, when applied to the Godin-Moret archive, it appeared clearly that this representation couldn't scale to the real amount of letters or would require noticeable user's scrolling. As E. Tufte eloquently demonstrated, dense representations can only be obtained through massive decrease of the "ink/data ratio" in the drawings [19]. So we investigated some more abstract representations like matrix plots.

Figure 3 show the resulting matrix for 8836 letters sent by Godin from 1840 to 1890 (the amount of letters metadata already prepared at time of this experiment, roughly half of the collection). Time is on the horizontal axis. There are 2496 addressees on vertical axis. The big amount of points requires sub-pixeling, therefore a standard scatterplot (Fig. 3 - left) can not express, because of the overlapping of dots, situations when intense writing occurred for some adressee in a short period of time. A quick statistical investigation showed that this happens quite often in the Godin archive. The underlying model for this might be some kind of power-law distribution, since a few addressees monopolize most of Godin's attention during rather large periods of time. A jittered plot is much more efficient in this respect (Fig. 3 - right), although this is considered as bad practice for distribution representation [20]. The jittering effect can be produced according to various drawing schemes. We have used here a recursive randomized algorithm where the dot is randomly pushed around its original position until a free white space is available. The "beeswarm" scheme is also very interesting, especially when zooming into a line of the matrix (Fig. 4). Beeswarm uses simulated particule physics for dots positions and is implemented in many popular visualization packages, such as D3.js and Rawgraphs. It has also been used in the *Atlante Calvino* project [17].

The correspondence matrix cannot be used alone. Figure 4 shows the general organization of the visualization interface[2]. In this wireframe view, all shapes and colors are

---

[2] A video mockup is also available at https://youtu.be/_130fXdQ35k.

arbitrarily defined. Currently selected items by the user are colored in purple. Following our workshop conclusions, we have completed the matrix with: 1) a list of keywords, arranged as a tag-cloud 2) a map of the addressees locations 3) a bar graph summarizing the yearly number of letters 4) idem for each adressee 5) thumbnails views of the letters. These five elements are coordinated: the impact of a user's selection within one of them is computed for the others. Selections can be repeated by the user to narrow her/his search, this can be reset. The matrix can be zoomed by the user, down to the level of each letter (Fig. 5).

This design has been validated by the FamiliLettres stakeholders, but two issues remain to be clarified until the end of the project. How can we represent the letters having unknown date or addressee? Should we integrate further the visualizations of passive and active correspondence? At present, they are only considered as separated views, triggered by switches.

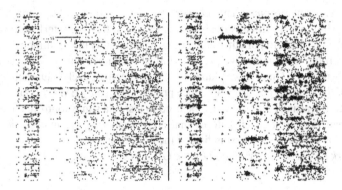

Fig. 3. Correspondence matrix. Left: standard plot. Right: jittered plot revealing activity.

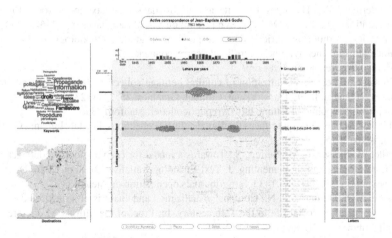

Fig. 4. The overview interface (wireframe). Left: tag-cloud for the collection's keywords and map of letters destinations. Center: correspondence matrix. Right: letters thumbnails.

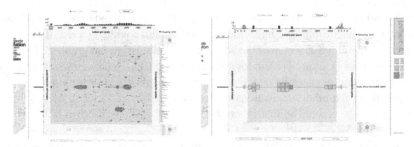

Fig. 5. Zoom in the correspondence matrix. Left: the first level of zooming also reveals a group of correspondents names. Right: zooming further for direct access to the letters thumbnails.

5   Conclusion

We have presented in this paper a novel overview visualization for large correspondence collections. Although specifically designed for FamiliLettres, the interface can certainly be used for the visualization of other collections with possibly bigger dimensions. Before that, the wireframe design that we presented must be implemented as a user interface. Since EMAN relies on Omeka, we plan to prepare a specific Omeka plugin that would be re-usable for the other large correspondence projects hosted by EMAN. Data from other open collections (as in [12]) could also be used to test, via some controlled experiment, our hypothesis concerning the patterns that are revealed by the matrix view, and its effectiveness for the users understanding of the collections.

This work has been partly funded by the GIS CollEx-Persée.

References

1. Shneiderman, B.: The eyes have it: a task by data type taxonomy for information visualizations. In: Proc. 1996 IEEE Symposium on Visual Languages, pp. 336–343 (1996)
2. Walter, R.: L'édition numérique de correspondances: guide méthodologique. Consortium Cahier. https://cahier.hypotheses.org/guide-correspondance (2018)
3. EMAN: https://eman-archives.org/
4. Windhager, F., et al.: Visualization of cultural heritage collection data: state of the art and future challenges. IEEE Trans. Visual. Comput. Graphics. **25**, 2311–2330 (2019)
5. Mapping the republic of letters: https://republicofletters.stanford.edu/
6. Whitelaw, M.: Generous interfaces for digital cultural collections. Digital Humanit. Q. (DHQ) **9**(1), 1–16 (2015)
7. Stadler, P., Illetschko, M., Seifert, S.: Towards a model for encoding correspondence in the TEI: developing and implementing. J. Text Encoding Initiative (9), Sept. 2016–Dec. 2017. https://doi.org/10.4000/jtei.1433. http://journals.openedition.org/jtei/1433
8. Fekete, J.-D., Dufournaud, N.: Compus: visualization and analysis of structured documents for understanding social life in the 16th century. In: Proc. of the fifth ACM conference on Digital libraries - DL'00, pp. 47–55 (2000)
9. Plaisant, C., Rose, J., Yu, B., Auvil, L., Kirschenbaum, M.G., Smith, M.N., Clement, T., Lord, G.: Exploring erotics in Emily Dickinson's correspondence with text mining and visual interfaces. In: Proc. of the 6th ACM/IEEE-CS joint conference on Digital libraries - JCDL'06, pp. 141–150 (2006)

10. Moreton, E., O'Leary, N., O'Sullivan, P.: Visualising the emigrant letter. Rev. Eur. Migr. Int. **30**, 49–69 (2014)

11. Nualart Vilaplana, J., Pérez-Montoro, M.: Diggersdiaries: Using text analysis to support exploration and reading in a large document collection. In: Proc. Eurographics Conf. on Visualization (EuroVis), Posters Track. http://diggersdiaries.org (2017)

12. Ahnert, R., Ahnert, S.E.: Metadata, Surveillance and the Tudor State. History Workshop J. **87**, 27–51 (2019). https://doi.org/10.1093/hwj/dby033

13. Bludau, M.J., Dörk, M., Heidmann, F.: Relational perspectives as situated visualizations of art collections. In: Proc. ADHO Conf. on Digital Humanities (DH'2019) (2019). https://uclab. fh-potsdam.de/hausmann/

14. Bludau, M.-J., Brüggemann, V., Busch, A., Dörk, M.: Reading traces: scalable exploration in elastic visualizations of cultural heritage data. Comput. Graphics Forum **39**, 77–87 (2020). https://uclab.fh-potsdam.de/ff/

15. Hinrichs, U., Forlini, S., Moynihan, B.: Speculative practices: utilizing InfoVis to explore untapped literary collections. IEEE Trans. Vis. Comput. Graph. **22**, 429–438 (2015). https:// vimeo.com/236169311

16. Glinka, K., Pietsch, C., Dörk, M.: Past Visions and Reconciling Views: Visualizing Time, Texture and Themes in Cultural Collections. Digit. Humanit. Quat. **11** (2017). https://uclab. fh-potsdam.de/fw4/en/

17. Atlante Calvino: literature and visualization: http://atlantecalvino.unige.ch/?lang=en (2020)

18. Dörk, M., Pietsch, C., Credico, G.: One view is not enough: high-level visualizations of a large cultural collection. Inform. Des. J. **23**, 39–47 (2022). https://uclab.fh-potsdam.de/ddb/

19. Tufte, E.: The visual display of quantitative information. Graphics Press (2001)

20. Wilkinson, L.: Dot plots. Am. Stat. **53**-**3**, 276–281 (1999)

Developing the EOSC-Pillar RDM Training and Support Catalogue

Paula Oset Garcia[1]([✉]) [iD], Lisana Berberi[2] [iD], Leonardo Candela[3] [iD],
Inge Van Nieuwerburgh[1] [iD], Emma Lazzeri[4] [iD], and Marie Czuray[5] [iD]

[1] Ghent University, Ghent University Library, Rozier 9, 9000 Ghent, Belgium
`Paula.OsetGarcia@UGent.be`
[2] Steinbuch Centre for Computing (SCC), Karlsruhe Institute of Technology, 76128 Karlsruhe,
Germany
[3] Institute of Information Science and Technologies "Alessandro Faedo", via G. Moruzzi 1,
56124 Pisa, Italy
[4] Consortium GARR, Via dei Tizii, 6, 00185 Roma, Italy
[5] Vienna University, Vienna University Library and Archive Services, Universitätsring 1,
1010 Wien, Austria

Abstract. Today's many research infrastructures and European projects offer training catalogues to store and list multiple forms of learning materials. In EOSC-Pillar project we propose a web application catalogue, which consists of training materials as well as day-to-day operational resources with the aim to support data stewards and other RDM (research data management), FAIR data (findable, accessible, interoperable, reusable) and open science actors. In this paper we briefly describe the scope and technical implementation of the EOSC-Pillar RDM Training and Support Catalogue and how we are addressing current challenges such as metadata standards, controlled vocabularies, curation, quality checking and sustainability.

Keywords: EOSC · Open science · Research data management · FAIR · Training material · Catalogue · Virtual research environment

1 Introduction

The EOSC-Pillar project [1] aims to coordinate national open science efforts in Austria, Belgium, France, Germany and Italy, building on each countries' specificities to ensure a well organised contribution to the European Open Science Cloud (EOSC) [2]. The goal is to facilitate the process of becoming EOSC service providers and contribute to the population of EOSC with useful services of wider European interest, based on the real needs and interests of the European scientific communities.

Some of the challenges addressed by the EOSC-Pillar project are narrowing the existing skills gap [3, 4] and promoting the cultural changes that are needed to realize the EOSC and the European Commission's vision for open science to become the 'modus operandi' within the European research community [5]. Moreover, the project seeks

G. Silvello et al. (Eds.): TPDL 2022, LNCS 13541, pp. 274–281, 2022.
https://doi.org/10.1007/978-3-031-16802-4_22

to promote FAIR (findable, accessible, interoperable, reusable) [6] data culture and practices with specific tasks that tackle training and skills development. To this end, the EOSC-Pillar project has developed an online catalogue [7] with a curated selection of searchable training and support resources about FAIR, open science and research data management (RDM).

1.1 Defining the Scope of the Catalogue

Since the EOSC-Pillar project was proposed, an increasing number of institutions have appointed data stewards or similar roles to support researchers with their growing (FAIR) data management and open science requirements, and the need to professionalize such support roles has been recognized [8]. The number of projects and initiatives which promote and support the uptake of the FAIR data principles and open science practices has also increased (e.g. FAIRsFAIR [9], the EOSC Regional Projects, the European Research Infrastructures, etc.). These different teams and initiatives have made available an immense wealth of material to train and help data stewards in their role of supporting researchers with open science and good data management practices all along the research data lifecycle. However, these resources are scattered across different institutional or project websites. The added value by EOSC-Pillar is in curating and cataloguing these materials, and in increasing their visibility by making them findable through a central point by means of interoperable metadata.

The catalogue is aimed at teams of data stewards as well as other RDM support professionals in the first place (both new and consolidated teams), providing them with easy to find, readily available tools and solutions. However, the resources will likely be useful for other types of professionals with an active role in RDM, including researchers. The catalogue consists of conventional training materials as well as day-to-day operational resources and readily applicable tools that can be used by data stewards to support researchers. Therefore, a great diversity of resource types are considered: courses and course modules, tools, checklists, decision trees, audio-visual material, games, etc. Items in the EOSC-Pillar RDM Training and Support catalogue are both discipline agnostic as well as discipline-specific.

Catalogue records are added and managed by a small group of curators within the EOSC-Pillar project. The catalogue is integrated within the EOSC-Pillar virtual research environment (VRE) [10] which includes a social networking platform. For each item published in the catalogue, an automatic post is generated in the social networking area. This collaborative platform can be used by the catalogue members to suggest new records, to provide feedback or updates on existing items, to announce relevant training or events, etc.

1.2 Accessing the EOSC-Pillar RDM Training and Support Catalogue

The catalogue is publicly accessible via the EOSC-Pillar website under the "Resources" menu and the "RDM Training and Support catalogue" submenu. A landing page [11] has been created to provide contextual information about the catalogue as well as a link to access it. There are two ways to access and use the RDM Training and Support catalogue:

– Non-registered users can access metadata for all catalogue items by using the URL:
https://eosc-pillar.d4science.org/web/eoscpillartrainingandsupport/catalogue.
– "Members" can browse metadata and access the resources behind each item, rate
catalogue items and make use of the social networking area to suggest new resources
or to comment on existing entries. To become members of the catalogue space, users
can either register or sign in with an existing academic or social networking account,
by simply clicking on the "Access the VRE" button that can be found on the URL
above-mentioned. Signed-in users will be then redirected to the URL: https://eosc-pil
lar.d4science.org/group/eoscpillartrainingandsupport/home.

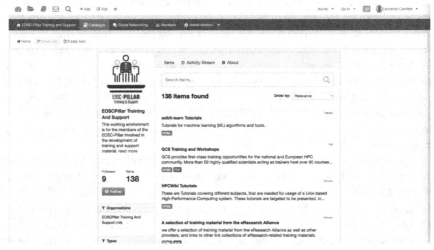

Fig. 1. A screenshot of the EOSC-Pillar RDM Training and Support catalogue search interface
within the EOSC-Pillar VRE (admin user view). From this page, a catalogue member can browse
the catalogue, access the social networking area and other services of the EOSC-Pillar VRE.

Through the catalogue interface (Fig. 1) the search bar allows to look for different
resources. The left side panel contains a series of filters based on item metadata which
can also be used to browse catalogue content or to fine-tune the search results. For each
record, the title and a snapshot of the resource description, together with the resource
format(s) are given. The full metadata record can be accessed by clicking on the resource
title.

2   Catalogue Technical Specifications

2.1   Technology

The catalogue has been developed and operated by the D4Science infrastructure [12].
Actually, a dedicated VRE has been deployed to support the needs of the community
of practice focusing around the catalogue. The catalogue service is also a component

of the EOSC-Pillar Federated Fair Data Space (F2DS) [13] tool set. It relies on CKAN [14] technology, an open source software that allows to develop and manage open data catalogues. The advantage of this technology is that it can be extended to support specific communities with the definition of custom metadata profiles [15]. The approach to define the community-specific metadata elements is explained in Sect. 2.2.

The technology behind the catalogue offers a series of services that facilitate open science and FAIRness. Each item in the catalogue gets a persistent identifier (namely a persistent uniform resource locator or PURL) and is described with rich and open metadata. The content in the catalogue is accessible via a graphical user interface (GUI), a programming interface based on representational state transfer (RESTful API) and it is also interoperable with other systems (e.g. DCAT and OAI-PMH). Adding new records to the catalogue is possible by harvesting items from other data sources, by using web APIs or by publishing items using a GUI.

2.2 Metadata Profile

When the EOSC-Pillar project started, we researched a series of initiatives which were working to define a minimum and recommended set of metadata elements for training resources. We adopted the proposed specifications set in the then recent outputs from the FAIRsFAIR project [16]. Additional details on the metadata profile initially adopted can be consulted on the EOSC-Pillar project Deliverable 5.4 [17].

Throughout the course of the project, some of these initiatives have reached a more developed state of maturity and become accepted by the community. In particular, we highlight the work of the Research Data Alliance (RDA) Interest Group on Education and Training on Handling of Research Data (IG ETHRD) [18]. This group defined a minimal metadata set [19] to aid harmonised discovery of learning resources that has been recently adopted by the EOSC Future project [20] for the prospective EOSC training catalogue. To maximise interoperability, we are currently reviewing the metadata profile of the EOSC-Pillar RDM Training and Support catalogue, aligning it to the current specifications set by the EOSC Future project. A simple mapping between the EOSC-Pillar metadata profile and EOSC Future is presented in Table 1. As can be observed, not all elements in the EOSC-Pillar RDM Training and Support catalogue have a direct equivalent in the EOSC Future specification and vice-versa. We will work to expand the current metadata profile to include these elements and populate them to the extent possible, so this information can eventually flow to the EOSC catalogue.

Table 1. Table showing the mapping between the metadata fields in the EOSC-Pillar RDM Training and support catalogue and the EOSC Future specification, based in the RDA Minimal Metadata for Learning Resources. When an element is not present in one of the two specifications, this is indicated by the letters "NP" in the first and second columns.

EOSC-Pillar RDM Training and support catalogue	EOSC Future (RDA Minimal Metadata for Learning Resources customized for the EOSC training resources)		
Property	Property	Metadata for existing resources	Metadata for new resources
Title	Title	Mandatory	Mandatory
Description	Abstract/Description	Recommended	Recommended
PID	NP		
Resource Name	NP		
Resource URL	URL to Resource	Mandatory	Mandatory
Resource format	NP		
NP	Resource URL Type	Optional	Optional
Resource description	NP		
Author	Author(s)	Mandatory	Mandatory
Data Type	Learning Resource Type	Optional	Recommended
Tags	Keyword(s)	Recommended	Recommended
License	License	Recommended	Recommended
NP	Access Rights	Recommended	Mandatory
NP	Version Date	Recommended	Mandatory
Skills group	NP		
Domain	NP		
Level	Expertise Level	Recommended	Mandatory
Target group	Target Group (Audience)	Recommended	Mandatory
Language	Primary Language	Recommended	Mandatory
Country	NP		
NP	Learning Outcome(s)	Recommended	Mandatory

3   Outcomes and Future Work

Since the EOSC-Pillar RDM Training and Support catalogue was launched, the number of published items and users has increasingly grown. At the time of writing, the EOSC-Pillar RDM Training and Support catalogue lists over 130 records. Since the beginning of 2021, the number of registered users (VRE members) has grown from 54 to 141, and there have been 150 monthly average accesses to the EOSC-Pillar RDM Training and Support VRE. Significant efforts have been undertaken to give visibility to our work, by presenting and demonstrating the catalogue at different events and training courses. Examples of such user engagement activities are the Open Access Belgium week [21], the EOSC-Pillar RDM Training and Support Catalogue webinar [22], the FAIRsFAIR, EOSC-Pillar, EOSC-Synergy and Ghent University Instructor Training Workshop [23], or the recording of an episode for the Stories of Data podcast [24]. Both catalogue content curation and addition as well as promotion are ongoing activities.

In recent years, many European funded projects and European Research Infrastructures have developed training catalogues or are planning to do so. These different projects regularly engage with each other through different platforms such as the OpenAIRE Community of Practice for Training Coordinators (CoP) [25] or the EOSC Training and Skills Working Group [26]. Through a series of meetings and events [27–29], existing or under development catalogues have exchanged knowledge and experiences and discussed common challenges.

A prevailing issue affecting training catalogues is that suitable controlled vocabularies to richly describe data stewardship learning resources are lacking, still under development or have not been agreed upon by the community. In the EOSC-Pillar RDM Training and Support catalogue, it is possible to define controlled vocabularies for each custom (profile) metadata field. Some vocabularies currently used are the FAIR4S framework [30] for "Target group" or the re3data.orgsubject classification [31] for "Domain". The project is aware of alternative possibilities for these and other metadata values (e.g. terms4FAIRskills [32], FAIRSharing Subject Resource Application Ontology SRAO [33], Learning Object Metadata Standard [34]). We will closely follow the evolution of relevant projects, and pay particular attention to decisions made by EOSC Future, to implement the necessary changes and be in line with community agreements and enhance the semantic interoperability of the catalogue.

Another challenge that is common to training catalogues is related to the curation and quality checking of the catalogue items. Some related projects (e.g. SSHOC [35]) organize yearly sprints to review the catalogue content and have developed internal guidelines and documentation. EOSC-Pillar has an embedded user rating system which allows us to gather information about the usefulness of a resource. But, in general, there is a lack of a systematic approach for curation and quality checking of catalogues for training materials. Besides, these tasks are often performed by smaller teams within the project, often without visibility or recognition, leaving the process to a great degree of subjectivity. Efforts are now being started in order to address this challenge by setting a working group on quality assurance of training materials within the OpenAIRE CoP, which aims to co-create guidelines and checklists for the curation and quality checking of training materials.

Finally, the long term sustainability of the results presented is a common challenge arising from the intrinsic time duration and funding availability of the project. In the case of the RDM Training and support catalogue, it will remain accessible to the catalogue administrators and users for at least two years after the project ends. Besides, significant efforts have been put into ensuring syntactic and semantic interoperability, since enabling the machine-to-machine exchange of the catalogue content is the best way to facilitate its future availability.

Acknowledgments. This work has received funding from the European Union's Horizon 2020 research and innovation programme under EOSC-Pillar project (grant agreement No. 857650).

References

1. EOSC-Pillar Project [Online]. Available: https://www.eosc-pillar.eu/
2. What the European Open Science Cloud (EOSC) is [Online]. Available: https://ec.europa.eu/info/research-and-innovation/strategy/strategy-2020-2024/our-digital-future/open-science/european-open-science-cloud-eosc_en
3. European Commission, Directorate-General for Research and Innovation. Digital skills for FAIR and Open Science: Report from the EOSC Executive Board Skills and Training Working Group. Publications Office (2021)
4. European Commission, Directorate-General for Research and Innovation. Realising the European Open Science Cloud: First Report and Recommendations of the Commission High Level Expert Group on the European Open Science Cloud. Publications Office (2016)
5. European Commission, Directorate-General for Research and Innovation. Horizon Europe, Open Science: Early Knowledge and Data Sharing, and Open Collaboration (2021)
6. Wilkinson, M.D., et al.: The FAIR Guiding Principles for scientific data management and stewardship. Sci. Data **3**, 160018 (2016)
7. EOSC-Pillar RDM Training and Support catalogue [Online]. Available: https://eosc-pillar.d4science.org/web/eoscpillartrainingandsupport/catalogue
8. European Commission, Directorate-General for Research and Innovation. Turning FAIR into Reality: Final Report and Action Plan From the European Commission Expert Group on FAIR Data. Publications Office (2018)
9. FAIRsFAIR Project [Online]. Available: https://www.fairsfair.eu/
10. Candela, L., Castelli, D., Pagano, P.: Virtual research environments: an overview and a research agenda. Data Sci. J. **12**, 175 (2013)
11. EOSC-Pillar RDM Training and Support Catalogue Landing Page [Online]. Available: https://www.eosc-pillar.eu/rdm-training-and-support-catalogue
12. Assante, M., et al.: Enacting open science by D4Science. Futur. Gener. Comput. Syst. **101**, 555–563 (2019)
13. Cazenave, N., Candela, L., Berberi, L., van Wezel, J., Hashibon, A., Le Franc, Y.: EOSC-Pillar D5.1 FAIR Research Data Management Tool Set, Zenodo (2020)
14. CKAN Homepage [Online]. Available: https://ckan.org/
15. Candela, L., Frosini, L., Le Franc, Y., Mangiacrapa, F., Cazenave, N.: EOSC-Pillar D5.2 FAIR Research Data Management Workbench Operation Report, Zenodo (2021)
16. Newbold, E., et al.: D6.2 Initial Core Competence Centre Structures, Zenodo (2020)
17. Oset Garcia, P., Lazzeri, E., Van Nieuwerburgh, I., von Hartrott, P., Geistberger, J.: EOSC-Pillar D5.4 FAIR-Oriented Research Data Management Support Training And Assessment Activity Report, Zenodo (2021)
18. Research Data Alliance (RDA) Education and Training on Handling of Research Data Interest Group (IG ETHRD) Homepage [Online]. Available: https://www.rd-alliance.org/groups/education-and-training-handling-research-data.html
19. Hoebelheinrich, N.: Recommendations for a minimal metadata set to aid harmonised discovery of learning resources, RD Alliance (2022)

20. EOSC Future wiki page (Training Catalogue – Minimal Metadata for Learning Resources) [Online]. Available: https://wiki.eoscfuture.eu/display/PUBLIC/Training+Catalogue+-+Min imal+Metadata+for+Learning+Resources

21. Open Access Belgium week (2020) [Online]. Available: https://www.eosc-pillar.eu/events/ eosc-pillar-open-access-week-belgium

22. EOSC-Pillar RDM Training and Support Catalogue webinar [Online]. Available: https://www. eosc-pillar.eu/events/webinar-eosc-pillar-rdm-training-and-support-catalogue

23. FAIRsFAIR, EOSC-Pillar, EOSC-Synergy and Ghent University Instructor Training Workshop [Online]. Available: https://www.eosc-pillar.eu/events/instructor-training-online-wor kshop.

24. Stories of Data Podcast [Online]. Available: https://www.eosc-pillar.eu/stories-data-open-sci ence-podcast

25. OpenAIRE Community of Practice for Training Coordinators (CoP) Homepage [Online]. Available: https://www.openaire.eu/cop-training

26. EOSC Training and Skills Working Group Homepage [Online]. Available: https://eoscsecre tariat.eu/working-groups/skills-training-working-group.

27. Leenarts, E.: OSF Workshop Resources RDM Training and Support Catalogues (21 September 2021), Zenodo (2021)

28. Newbold, E., Kayumbi, G., Whyte, A., Lazzeri, E.: Summary Report: Workshop on Harmonising Training Resource Metadata for EOSC Communities, Zenodo (2021)

29. EOSC5b-TF/FAIRsFAIR Training Resource Catalogue Interoperability Workshop Event Page [Online]. Available: https://www.fairsfair.eu/events/training-resource-catalogue-intero perability-workshop

30. Whyte, A.: D7.3: Skills and Capability Framework (2018)

31. The re3data.org Subject Classification [Online]. Available: https://www.re3data.org/browse/ by-subject/

32. terms4FAIRskills GitHub Repository [Online]. Available: https://terms4fairskills.github.io/

33. FAIRSharing Subject Resource Application Ontology (SRAO) GitHub Repository [Online]. Available: https://github.com/FAIRsharing/subject-ontology

34. Learning Object Metadata, Wikipedia, Wikimedia Foundation

35. SSHOC Project [Online]. Available: https://sshopencloud.eu/

Automatic Generation of Coherent Image Galleries in Virtual Reality

Simon Peterhans$^{(\boxtimes)}$ ⓘ, Loris Sauter$^{(\boxtimes)}$ ⓘ, Florian Spiess$^{(\boxtimes)}$ ⓘ,
and Heiko Schuldt$^{(\boxtimes)}$ ⓘ

University of Basel, Basel, Switzerland
{simon.peterhans,loris.sauter,florian.spiess,heiko.schuldt}@unibas.ch

Abstract. With the rapidly increasing size of digitized and born-digital multimedia collections in archives, museums and private collections, manually curating collections becomes a nearly impossible task without disregarding large parts of the collection. In this paper, we propose the use of Self-Organizing Maps (SOMs) to automatically generate coherent image galleries that allow intuitive, user-driven exploration of large multimedia collections in virtual reality (VR). We extend the open-source VR museum VIRTUE to support such exhibitions and apply it on different collections using various image features. A successful pilot test took place at the Basel Historical Museum with more than 300 participants.

Keywords: Virtual reality · Self-Organizing Maps · Automatic collection curation

1 Introduction

Digital multimedia collections have been growing rapidly over the past decades, both due to the increasing availability and affordability of devices for digital capture, and the growing efforts to digitize existing multimedia collections, especially in the cultural heritage domain. While the size and number of such digital collections is increasing at a rapid pace, methods to organize, manage and explore such collections struggle to keep up with the size and diversity of these data. Especially in the context of museums and archives, manually curating such collections for exhibitions or presentations becomes infeasible very quickly with growing size. Moreover, such digital collections are often far too large to be viewed by a person within reasonable time, much less to be displayed within the physical space available to a museum or archive, leading to only a small subset of the collection being shown and some artifacts never being included at all.

To allow large multimedia collections to be displayed even in small physical spaces, a number of digital-only exhibition solutions have been developed, some, such as the VIRTUE [4] virtual museum, in virtual reality (VR). In this work, we extend the VIRTUE project with the functionality to automatically and interactively generate galleries of coherent images using Self-Organizing Maps (SOMs) [7] for exploration in VR. In May 2022, the VIRTUE system presented

© Springer Nature Switzerland AG 2022
G. Silvello et al. (Eds.): TPDL 2022, LNCS 13541, pp. 282–288, 2022.
https://doi.org/10.1007/978-3-031-16802-4_23

here was successfully trialed by the general public in a large-scale deployment at the Basel Historical Museum[1] at the Basel Museum Night[2]. Furthermore, it was featured at Fantasy Basel 2021[3], one of Europe's largest conventions for popular culture. The contribution of this paper is twofold: first, we show how SOMs can be leveraged to automatically create thematic exhibition rooms and second, we report on a practical deployment of the system in a real museum.

2   Related Work

Virtual museums and even museums in VR, such as [5] and the open-source VR museum VIRTUE [4] on which our approach is based, have been developed and investigated for many years. Recent advances in machine learning have allowed for the extraction of content-based semantic feature representations. While there is no existing work on the application of such methods in the realm of virtual museums, such methods have already been used in the context of archives and museums. One such application is described in [1]. This work uses a semantic feature extraction to cluster images and visualize them through a scatterplot and an image path through the feature space.

3   System Architecture

The open-source system VIRTUE[4] [4], consists of a VR-frontend, Virtual Reality Exhibition Presenter (VREP), an admin frontend, Virtual Reality Exhibition Manager User Interface (VREM-UI) and the backend, Virtual Reality Exhibition Manager (VREM). In order to support content-based automatic exhibition generation, we rely on the open-source content-based multimedia retrieval system *vitrivr* [8]. More specifically, we employ its retrieval engine Cineast [3] and the storage layer Cottontail DB [2].

As illustrated in Fig. 1, Cineast and Cottontail DB expand the existing backend. VIRTUE's frontend VREP and its backend VREM communicate over a REST API provided by VREM using Javalin[5]. The REST API of VREM, likewise the one of Cineast, provide OpenAPI specifications in order to easily generate corresponding clients. Connections to the storage layers of VREM and Cineast are provided over a dedicated MongoDB Java Driver and gRPC respectively. VREP receives exhibition information from VREM and builds the VR experience on the fly. Previously, VIRTUE only supported static exhibitions, which had to be manually created by users using VREM-UI. In this work, we expand the capabilities of VIRTUE to support dynamically generated exhibitions as well. Storage and management of exhibitions is performed in VREM, as well as the interface to Cineast for dynamically generated exhibitions using the means outlined in the following sections.

---

[1] https://www.hmb.ch/en/.
[2] https://museumsnacht.ch/en/.
[3] https://www.fantasybasel.ch/en.
[4] https://github.com/VIRTUE-DBIS.
[5] https://github.com/tipsy/javalin.

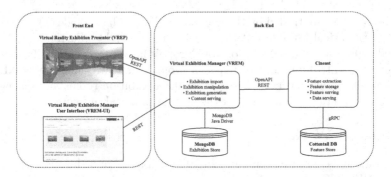

Fig. 1. The architecture of VIRTUE including the extension allowing automatic image gallery generation. Notable interfaces are the two OpenAPI powered REST APIs provided by Cineast and VREM. While the former enables automatic exhibition generation the latter is required in order to display the generated exhibition in VR.

4   Automatic Collection Generation

VIRTUE allows the automatic generation of subsets from an image collection in the form of virtual museum rooms with images being represented by framed exhibits. Much like in an actual museum, the images are not randomly chosen and arranged, but placed in a coherent fashion based on the parameters and features chosen by the user. In order to dynamically generate exhibitions and exhibition rooms, VIRTUE relies on features previously extracted by Cineast and a simple form of the Self-Organizing Map (SOM) algorithm [7].

4.1   Self-Organizing Maps

The SOM, as described by [7], is a type of unsupervised artificial neural network used for dimensionality reduction while maintaining the topological structure of the training data. When trained, it can be used for clustering and data visualization, with samples assigned to nodes in close proximity on the grid being closer in their original vector space than samples assigned to distant nodes. Every node of a SOM grid contains a weight vector of the same dimensionality as the input data, in our case a feature vector of an image. We denote these weights for the i-th node n_i in the grid with m_i. The grid is presented with one sample x at each distinct time step t during the training phase and nodes compete for each sample. The winning node holds the weight vector with the smallest Euclidean distance to the sample. Its index c in the grid can thus be determined as follows:

$$c = \operatorname*{argmin}_i \|x(t) - m_i(t)\| \tag{1}$$

Once the winning node has been declared, the weights of all nodes are updated prior to the next time step $t + 1$ by adjusting a node's weight by a fraction of its difference to the sample. The respective fraction is determined by a neighborhood function h_{ci}, which assigns a scalar to node n_i based on its distance to the winning node n_c on the grid. The further away a node n_i is from the winning node n_c, the smaller the value returned by h_{ci} is. Nodes with larger distances that are not in the neighborhood of the winning node are thus affected less by the current sample and may not have their weight updated at all. Using the neighborhood function, the weights of each node can the be updated prior to the next iteration $t + 1$:

$$\boldsymbol{m}_i(t + 1) = \boldsymbol{m}_i(t) + h_{ci}(t)\left[\boldsymbol{x}(t) - \boldsymbol{m}_i(t)\right] \tag{2}$$

The number of iterations required for convergence depends on the feature vectors, the grid size, and the neighborhood function at hand. When trained, the map can be used for classification and clustering by letting the nodes compete and assigning the sample to the winning node, similar to the process in the training phase. The grid topology of the SOM is chosen based on the desired dimensionality reduction of the input data.

4.2   From SOM to Exhibition

VIRTUE currently generates quadratic and rectangular rooms, consisting of four walls, a floor, and a ceiling. The pictures featured in each room are, by default, arranged in a single row on each wall. To obtain a clustering that is coherent within this room architecture, we arrive at an evenly spaced, circular, one dimensional grid projected onto a cylinder, which defines the topology of the SOM to be trained to cluster and arrange the image collection. To respect these constraints, a two-dimensional toroidal grid that wraps on the vertical axis, essentially representing a bottom- and top-less cylinder, is used by choosing an appropriate neighborhood function. When trained, all images in the collection are clustered on the grid, such that each image is assigned to the closest grid node. For each node the closest image is chosen as representative image for the respective cluster and is displayed in the generated exhibition room. Ultimately, in doing so, the coherent representation of the collection is established, as close images are topically related while images across the exhibition room are only related in so far, as they belong to the same collection.

To illustrate this approach, Fig. 2 shows a SOM trained on a simple color feature from a collection of beach images[6] generated using the method presented in [6]. This 1×16 grid was trained with a wrapping neighborhood function and shows the layout of the 16 nodes and their representative images on the walls in a single exhibition room. As all images that were used in the generation process have been assigned to one of the nodes and are thus represented by a node's representative image, additional SOMs can be recursively generated for each node. This results in users being able to select one of the images in the room and generate a sub-room with images that were also assigned to this node to further explore the collection.

---

[6] https://thisbeachdoesnotexist.com/.

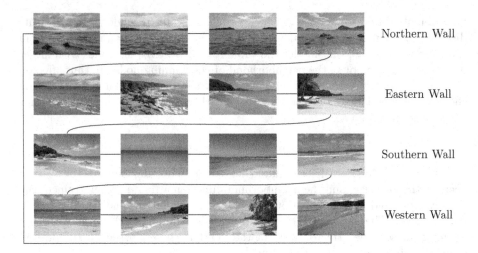

Fig. 2. An example of a 1 × 16 SOM grid trained on color features of beach images and mapped to the exhibition room with four images per wall. Images close to each other exhibit similar color regions and a smooth transition around the room occurs, e.g., with the beach and forest being on the left side on the eastern wall and slowly shifting over to the right side on the Southern and Western wall.

4.3 Features

We have tested our method on a number of different combinations of image collection and feature vector. The features we have found to work best for the purpose of automatic coherent collection generation are an average color grid feature and a deep learning based semantic image content feature.

The average color grid feature consists of a vector containing the average color values sampled from an image in an 8 × 8 grid. Despite being rather simple, it results in visually coherent exhibitions (cf. Fig. 2), especially for collections of images containing diverse and saturated colors. This feature is not suitable to generate coherent exhibitions for all collections, in particular collections of cultural heritage collections (e.g., the ones from the Swiss Society for Folk Studies[7] used in our evaluations), where images only have muted color or no color at all.

As a deep learning based semantic image feature, we use the visual-text co-embedding originally developed for multimedia retrieval, which is described in more detail in [9]. Trained to embed images and associated text descriptions into a common vector space such that semantically similar inputs are close together, this feature extracts a semantic representation from the content of an image. Using this feature, the generated exhibitions exhibit a coherence based on semantic image content, which lends itself well also to gray scale image collections and those with muted colors. As seen in Fig. 3, this feature allows for a clustering more focused on the semantic content of the images and, as a result, allows users to explore the collection based on thematic rather than purely visual similarity.

---

[7] https://archiv.sgv-sstp.ch.

Fig. 3. A generated room for the SGV_10 collection of digitized cultural heritage images provided by the Swiss Society for Folk Studies. Portraits, pictures of multiple people and images featuring landscapes are coherently grouped together.

5   Discussion and Conclusion

In this paper, we proposed the use of SOMs to automatically generate coherent image galleries in VR, that allow for hierarchical exploration of an image collection, and extended the open-source VR museum VIRTUE to support dynamically generated coherent image galleries. Using a simple color feature and a semantic image feature based on deep learning, the approach has been applied to two converse image collections featuring thousands of images. With the topology-preserving nature of the SOM, visually and semantically coherent exhibition rooms were generated in both cases.

The implementation was tested with two image collections, one consisting of 10'000 computer generated images and the other consisting of 6'461 digitized cultural heritage photographs. Our experiments show that while exhibitions can be pre-generated using this method, our implementation is powerful enough to be used for real-time generation, even for large collections. At the Basel Museum Night 2022, we successfully presented the virtual museum to the general public in the premises of a real museum, the Basel Historical Museum, with digitized artworks from this museum. During the event, more than 300 participants had the chance to explore the SOM-generated thematic exhibition rooms.

While our findings are very promising, further research is necessary to develop better methods to generate dynamic and interactive exhibitions from large image corpora and to make them appropriately accessible in VR. Further work is needed especially for personalizing generated exhibitions based on user preferences.

Acknowledgements. This work was partly supported by the Swiss National Science Foundation (project "Participatory Knowledge Practices in Analogue and Digital Image Archives", contract no. CRSII5_193788).

References

1. Bönisch, D.: The curator's machine: clustering of museum collection data through annotation of hidden connection patterns between artworks. Int. J. Digit. Art Hist. **5**, 5–20 (2020)
2. Gasser, R., Rossetto, L., Heller, S., Schuldt, H.: Cottontail DB: an open source database system for multimedia retrieval and analysis. In: Chen, C.W., et al. (eds.) MM 2020: The 28th ACM International Conference on Multimedia, Virtual Event/Seattle, WA, USA, 12–16 October 2020, pp. 4465–4468. ACM (2020). https://doi.org/10.1145/3394171.3414538
3. Gasser, R., Rossetto, L., Schuldt, H.: Multimodal multimedia retrieval with vitrivr. In: El-Saddik, A., et al. (eds.) Proceedings of the 2019 on International Conference on Multimedia Retrieval, ICMR 2019, Ottawa, ON, Canada, 10–13 June 2019, pp. 391–394. ACM (2019). https://doi.org/10.1145/3323873.3326921
4. Giangreco, I., et al.: Virtue: a virtual reality museum experience. In: Proceedings of the 24th International Conference on Intelligent User Interfaces: Companion, pp. 119–120 (2019)
5. Hirose, M.: Virtual reality technology and museum exhibit. In: Subsol, G. (ed.) ICVS 2005. LNCS, vol. 3805, pp. 3–11. Springer, Heidelberg (2005). https://doi.org/10.1007/11590361_1
6. Karras, T., Aittala, M., Hellsten, J., Laine, S., Lehtinen, J., Aila, T.: Training generative adversarial networks with limited data. In: Larochelle, H., Ranzato, M., Hadsell, R., Balcan, M., Lin, H. (eds.) Advances in Neural Information Processing Systems, vol. 33, pp. 12104–12114. Curran Associates, Inc. (2020)
7. Kohonen, T.: Automatic formation of topological maps of patterns in a self-organizing system. In: Proceedings of 2SCIA, Scandinavian Conference on Image Analysis, pp. 214–220 (1981)
8. Rossetto, L., Giangreco, I., Tanase, C., Schuldt, H.: vitrivr: a flexible retrieval stack supporting multiple query modes for searching in multimedia collections. In: Hanjalic, A., et al. (eds.) Proceedings of the 2016 ACM Conference on Multimedia Conference, MM 2016, Amsterdam, The Netherlands, 15–19 October 2016, pp. 1183–1186. ACM (2016). https://doi.org/10.1145/2964284.2973797
9. Spiess, F., et al.: Multi-modal video retrieval in virtual reality with vitrivr-VR. In: Þór Jónsson, B., et al. (eds.) MMM 2022. LNCS, vol. 13142, pp. 499–504. Springer, Cham (2022). https://doi.org/10.1007/978-3-030-98355-0_45

Extracting Funder Information from Scientific Papers - Experiences with Question Answering

Timo Borst[1], Jonas Mielck[2], Matthias Nannt[2], and Wolfgang Riese[1]([envelope])

[1] Leibniz Information Center for Economics, Kiel, Germany
w.riese@zbw.eu
[2] stackOcean GmbH, Kiel, Germany

Abstract. This paper is about automatic recognition of entities that funded a research work in economics as being expressed in a publication. While many works apply rules and/or regular expressions to candidate sections within the text, we follow a question answering (QA) based approach to identify those passages that are most likely to inform us about funding. With regard to a digital library scenario, we are dealing with three more challenges: confirming that our approach at least outperforms manual indexing, disambiguation of funding organizations by linking their names to authority data, and integrating the generated metadata into a digital library application. Our computational results by means of machine learning techniques show that our QA performs similar to a previous work (AckNER), although we operated on rather small sets of training and test data. While manual indexing is still needed for a gold standard of reliable metadata, the identification of funding entities only worked for a subset of funder names.

Keywords: Funder recognition · Question answering · Metadata

1 Introduction

Named-entity recognition (NER) has become one of the most important fields of research in text analysis that has yielded some impressive results with regard to identifying almost any kind of 'thing' or entity a text is about [12]. However, despite of some undisputed progress in adopting and fine-tuning linguistic and computational methods for extracting entities, we still rarely see those techniques being adopted within digital library scenarios and applications. This may be symptomatic: first, it still might mean quite a step even for digital libraries and their workflows to build trust in automatic metadata extraction [7], and secondly it requires some long-term commitment and technical expertise not only to engage with these approaches, but also to support and maintain them in a productive setting.

This paper is about automatic and trained recognition of research funding agencies (FA) that are explicitly mentioned in parts or sections of scientific

© The Author(s) 2022
G. Silvello et al. (Eds.): TPDL 2022, LNCS 13541, pp. 289–296, 2022.
https://doi.org/10.1007/978-3-031-16802-4_24

publications, which are commonly known as acknowledgement phrase (AP) or acknowledgement text (AT). While this might appear as a simple and straight-forward task to be perfectly handled by some NER framework or (pre-)trained language model, we were more curious about finding if recent question answering approaches can be applied to meet three basic requirements: first, we aim at performing as automatically as possible by generating metadata that looked particularly suited for that purpose by implying an essentially binary decision ('funder/grant no. or not?'). Automatic text mining of funder information generally outperforms manual curation particularly with respect to recent papers that are to be indexed yet, with 90% of grants (almost correctly, according to the authors) found by text mining [4]. Taking this for granted, although a text mining approach will miss around 10% recall, it suggests providing information much more timely than a manual indexing process. Secondly, by becoming productive we require the generated metadata to be as flawless as possible, in particular by preventing false-positives. And thirdly, we strive for a productive setting in terms of an existing search application indexing the funding information, e.g. as a metadata facet.

In the following section, we discuss some related work treating NER. In section three, we depict our corpus and textual data together with some subsidiary data sets to accomplish our own NER approach. We explain our technical approach and framework more into detail including different language models and parameters we used. In section four, we delineate and compare the results of our test runs. We conclude by relating the main outcomes to our three basic requirements.

2   Related Work

In recent years, the analysis and extraction of FAs and/or grant numbers (GN) has become subject of both experimental data analyses and retrieval applications. Many works rely on the assumption that acknowledgements are a broader concept in scientific communication, e.g. by distinguishing between moral, financial, editorial, presentational, instrumental, technical, and conceptual support [5]. Therefore, most approaches follow a two-stage process by first identifying a potential textual area, before analysing this 'candidate section' more into detail by distinguishing between FAs represented by their names or acronyms and grants represented by their numbers or codes [1,3,4,6,8,13]. During the second stage, these two metadata are constitutive for extracting FAs. Some works differ in applying either regular expressions, rule-based and/or machine learning based approaches, or a combination of them. While [5] and [10] use regular expressions to identify name variations of selected FAs they are interested in, more inclusive approaches such as [4] or [13] apply a 'rule-based section tagger' to identify the most significant parts of an acknowledgement phrase including candidates for funding entities. Classifiers for calculating and weighing the acknowledgement phrase and its constituents rely on popular language models, such as Stanford-CRF [6], spaCy [1] or SVMs [1,5,13]. Despite benefiting from these pre-trained models, only [13] and [3] made active use of supervised machine learning by organizing and tuning their runs with different training data and continuously adapted classifiers. Only a few works tackle the challenge of normalizing a FA's name by mapping it to a canonical notation [10] or an authority record from a funder database, such as the funder registry from Crossref [6].

Apart from providing manually indexed funding data with databases such as Web of Science[1] or information portals[2], some works at least temporarily integrated the results of their runs into productive bibliographic online databases, e.g. PMCEurope [4] or DBLP[3]. Even if these information services are not propagating the retrieval of FAs, stakeholders such as research funders may find them as a valuable source for assessing the impact of their fundings, as suggested and depicted in [3].

3   Approach

3.1   Processing Pipeline

We decided to use Haystack[3], a framework written in Python, for NLP based QA through transformer-based models (e.g., RoBERTa [9], MiniLM [11]). To our advantage there already exist several pre-trained models for QA with Haystack on Hugging Face[4], so that there was no need to train a model on our own.

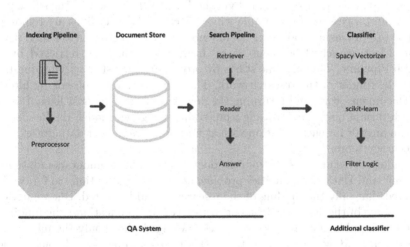

Fig. 1. Processing pipeline

---

[1] https://www.webofscience.com.
[2] https://explore.openaire.eu/.
[3] https://github.com/deepset-ai/haystack.
[4] https://huggingface.co/models?dataset=dataset:squad_v2&pipeline_tag=question-answering.

By manually going through different papers and analysing the wording in which the funder information is presented, we came up with the following questions we provided to the QA system:

Table 1. Question overview: The questions in bold text are the ones that perform best according to their F-score measures, cf. Table 2.

Number	Question
1	Who funded the article?
2	Who funded the work?
3	Who gives financial support?
4	**By whom was the study funded?**
5	Whose financial support do you acknowledge?
6	**Who provided funding?**
7	Who provided financial support?
8	**By which grant was this research supported?**

In the processing pipeline we first extracted the plain text from a PDF document, before we enriched it with various metadata from the repository and its language, the latter determined via the PYCLD2[5] library. In the subsequent step of pre-processing, for example white spaces and empty lines are removed.

The pre-processed plain-text documents and their metadata are then placed in the Elasticsearch 'Document Store' from where they are retrieved by the 'Search Pipeline'. This pipeline starts by processing the list of varying questions about the funder of the research work. Then the retriever proceeds by filtering the 'Document Store' and returning the documents that are most likely relevant for each variant question. By using a pre-trained language model, the Reader predicts an answer for each question variant and provides further data, for example an accuracy score.

While processing the APs from the documents and the funder metadata from Crossref[6] and DataCite[7], another problem came to our attention. So far, we had expected that only the funding of the research would be stated. But we noticed, that in some of the acknowledgement sections of the publications, the funding of open access publishing had also been acknowledged. Since only the information on research funding was relevant to us, this posed an unexpected complication, because now we also needed an automatic detection/filtering of these unwanted findings.

To filter them and to lower the number of false positives, we came up with an additional classifier. The complete pipeline including classifier is shown in Fig. 1.

---

[5] https://pypi.org/project/pycld2/.

[6] https://github.com/CrossRef/rest-api-doc.

[7] https://support.datacite.org/docs/api.

The classifier receives a prediction from the QA model and checks whether it is really a funder. For this purpose, the classifier was trained with the context information found by Haystack in the previous steps. We balanced the dataset before training by splitting it into 80% training data and 20% test data that is unknown to the model. The contexts are then trained in a support vector machine with the support of grid search for hyperparameter tuning.

In the final step of our approach we looked up the preferred labels of the extracted funding information with the help of the authority file of the Crossref Funder Registry v1.34[8] structured in RDF. It is important to note that we set up our pipeline as asynchronous process in order to be more independent from a just-in-time metadata generation probably demanding more powerful hardware.

3.2 Data

For our test sample we first extracted about 7100 open access documents, with a license that would allow us text and data mining, from the EconStor[9] repository, a publication server for scholarly economic literature. In a second step we identified 653 documents - most of them in English - with an associated DOI in that sample. For these documents we extracted the funder information via the Crossref and DataCite APIs. But a quick checkup revealed that not all funders mentioned in the metadata associated with the DOIs could be confirmed in the documents. Therefore we had the APs manually labelled from these 653 documents, so that we had a list with the complete AP for each document that indeed contained such a statement. All this data is combined into a single spreadsheet containing information about all papers including the manually labelled statement whether the paper was funded or not, according to our definition. This definition excludes open access funding which was the case for four of these papers. However, the following attributes have been stored: local repository id, DOI, funder by Crossref API (DOI), funder by Crossref API (plain text) and the manually extracted AP. In order to identify the funders, we used the authority file from the Crossref Funder Registry structured in RDF with 27953 funders and 46390 alternative labels. During our analysis we identified 83 papers to have not been published in English.

4 Results

The F-score relates true positive (TP), false positive (FP) and false negative (FN) values and is commonly used for measuring the quality of NER, cf. [1] or [2]. In this paper, the following formula is used for calculation:

$$F = \frac{TP}{TP + \frac{1}{2}(FP + FN)} \tag{1}$$

---

[8] https://gitlab.com/crossref/open_funder_registry/-/commits/v1.34.
[9] https://www.econstor.eu.

Table 2. F-score comparison of the different language models and three best performing questions. If there is no F-score shown, the accuracy was below benchmark in data pipeline and the language model was therefore dropped.

Question	RoBERTa	ELECTRA	albert-xxl-v2	minilm	XLM-RoBERTa
Question 4	0.6807	0.6721	0.6867	–	0.6015
Question 6	0.6135	**0.6729**	**0.6868**	–	**0.6248**
Question 8	**0.7836**	–	–	**0.7996**	–

Two of the language models used achieve F-scores of close to 0.8 which is equal to what [1] find.

The F-scores of the examination including the classifier differ slightly from the results without classifier. However, the deviation is not large enough to draw conclusions from it. In order to compare the results with and without classifier, the test data of the model without classifier must be reduced to the test data of the model with classifier. This results in a data set split to about 400 papers for training and about 100 papers for testing. We found the test set too small to make any statements about model performance. To put things into perspective, [1] use 321 articles for testing, [3] train on 800 and test on two data sets of 600 documents and [13] train on 2100 documents which they add up iterative and test iterative up to 1100 papers. But this overview suggests that the F-scores shown in Table 2, based on the 653 papers calculated without the classifier, are calculated from a sample size that is similar to what other researchers have. Hence, the presented results appear to be robust from that perspective. As additional analysis, we looked up the preferred label for the funder names with the help of the Crossref Funder Registry. Our algorithm utilized RapidFuzz[10] text comparison and was able to identify 126 funding entities from the 367 funder names correctly found with question 8 "By which grant was this research supported?" and the "RoBERTa" model. The algorithm identified 17 funders incorrectly.

5 Discussion and Outlook

Our results demonstrate the feasibility to automatically extract funding entities, basically confirming the results from AckNER. Our sample size was too small to evaluate the quality of the self-trained classifier model, to this end we would need a larger corpus. Moreover, we still require a gold standard of manually checked funder information, as the reference data provided through Crossref metadata turned out to be inaccurate. In particular, we could not train our classifier for identifying and excluding open access acknowledgements, which are becoming more frequent. With respect to transfering our results into a service environment in terms of a digital library, we could set up an asychronous data processing pipeline for regular metadata generation that demands maintenance of its components, such as Haystack and some Python libraries.

---

[10] https://github.com/maxbachmann/RapidFuzz/tree/v1.4.1.

The code and data underlying this paper is available on Github at https://github.com/zbw/Funder-NER.

References

1. Alexander, D., de Vries, A.P.: This research is funded by...: named entity recognition of financial information in research papers (2021). http://ceur-ws.org/Vol-2847/paper-10.pdf, https://repository.ubn.ru.nl/handle/2066/236372
2. Bian, J., Huang, L., Huang, X., Zhou, H., Zhu, S.: Grantrel: grant information extraction via joint entity and relation extraction. In: Findings of the Association for Computational Linguistics: ACL-IJCNLP 2021, pp. 2674–2685 (2021). https://doi.org/10.18653/v1/2021.findings-acl.236
3. Councill, I.G., Giles, C.L., Han, H., Manavoglu, E.: Automatic acknowledgement indexing: expanding the semantics of contribution in the CiteSeer digital library. In: Proceedings of the 3rd International Conference on Knowledge Capture, pp. 19–26. K-CAP 2005, Association for Computing Machinery, New York, NY, USA (2005). https://doi.org/10.1145/1088622.1088627
4. Europe PMC Consortium: Extracting funding statements from full text research articles in the life sciences (2014). https://cordis.europa.eu/project/id/637529/results
5. Giles, C.L., Councill, I.G.: Who gets acknowledged: measuring scientific contributions through automatic acknowledgment indexing. Proc. Natl. Acad. Sci. **101**(51), 17599–17604 (2004). https://doi.org/10.1073/pnas.0407743101
6. Gregory, M., Kayal, S., Tsatsaronis, G., Afzal, Z.: Systems and methods for extracting funder information from text (2019). https://patents.google.com/patent/US20190005020A1/en
7. Irvin, K.M.: Comparing information retrieval effectiveness of different metadata generation methods (2003). https://doi.org/10.17615/grff-0v98
8. Liu, W., Tang, L., Hu, G.: Funding information in web of science: an updated overview. arXiv:2001.04697 [cs] (2020). http://arxiv.org/abs/2001.04697
9. Liu, Y., et al.: Roberta: a robustly optimized BERT pretraining approach (2019). http://arxiv.org/abs/1907.11692
10. Sirtes, D., Riechert, M.: A fully automated method for the unification of funding organizations in the web of knowledge (2014). https://doi.org/10.13140/2.1.3086.5285
11. Wang, W., Wei, F., Dong, L., Bao, H., Yang, N., Zhou, M.: Minilm: deep self-attention distillation for task-agnostic compression of pre-trained transformers (2020). https://doi.org/10.48550/ARXIV.2002.10957
12. Yadav, V., Bethard, S.: A survey on recent advances in named entity recognition from deep learning models (2019). https://doi.org/10.48550/arXiv.1910.11470
13. Zhang, X., Zou, J., Le, D.X., Thoma, G.: A semi-supervised learning method to classify grant support zone in web-based medical articles. In: Berkner, K., Likforman-Sulem, L. (eds.) Document Recognition and Retrieval XVI, vol. 7247, pp. 286–293. International Society for Optics and Photonics, SPIE (2009). https://doi.org/10.1117/12.806076

CDX Summary: Web Archival Collection Insights

Sawood Alam$^{(\boxtimes)}$ and Mark Graham

Wayback Machine, Internet Archive, San Francisco, CA 94118, USA
{sawood,mark}@archive.org

Abstract. Large web archival collections are often opaque about their holdings. We created an open-source tool called, CDX Summary, to generate statistical reports based on URIs, hosts, TLDs, paths, query parameters, status codes, media types, date and time, etc. present in the CDX index of a collection of WARC files. Our tool also surfaces a configurable number of potentially good random memento samples from the collection for visual inspection, quality assurance, representative thumbnails generation, etc. The tool generates both human and machine readable reports with varying levels of details for different use cases. Furthermore, we implemented a Web Component that can render generated JSON summaries in HTML documents. Early exploration of CDX insights on Wayback Machine collections helped us improve our crawl operations.

Keywords: Web archiving · Summarization · Collection summary · CLI · WARC · CDX Index · Internet Archive · Wayback Machine · Petabox

1 Introduction

Items in the Internet Archive (IA) collections of various media types like image, video, audio, book, etc. often have rich metadata, representative thumbnails, meaningful titles, and interactive hero elements. However, web collections, primarily containing an arbitrary number of Web Archive (WARC) files [3,19] and their corresponding Capture Index (CDX) files [18], often look opaque with a generic thumbnail for each item, similar titles, and limited metadata (Fig. 1).

Opacity of web archival collections is not an IA-specific problem [20]. Since the emergence of the Memento protocol [24,27,28], there have been numerous efforts to explore web archival holdings for use cases such as efficient memento routing [1,4,9–16,21,26] by memento aggregators [2,8] and collection understanding or scholarly access [17,22,25].

To address this issue we created an open-source Command Line Interface (CLI) tool called *CDX Summary* to process sorted CDX files and generate statistical reports [5]. These summary reports give insights on various dimensions of CDX records/captures, such as, total number of mementos, number of unique original resources, distribution of various media types and their HTTP status codes, path and query segment counts, temporal spread, and capture frequencies of top TLDs,

© Springer Nature Switzerland AG 2022
G. Silvello et al. (Eds.): TPDL 2022, LNCS 13541, pp. 297–305, 2022.
https://doi.org/10.1007/978-3-031-16802-4_25

(a) WARC Items Listing   (b) Collection Metadata

Fig. 1. A Petabox Web Collection of the Internet Archive

hosts, and URIs. We also implemented a uniform sampling algorithm to select a given number of random memento URIs (i.e., URI-Ms) with *200 OK* HTML responses that can be utilized for quality assurance purposes or as a representative sample for the collection of WARC files. Our tool can generate both comprehensive and brief reports in JSON format as well as human readable textual representation. We ran our tool on a selected set of public web collections in IA, stored resulting JSON files in their corresponding collections, and made them public. Furthermore, we implemented a custom Web Component [7] that can load CDX Summary report JSON files and render them in interactive HTML representations. Finally, we integrated this Web Component into the collection/item views of the main site of the IA, so that patrons can access rich and interactive information when they visit a web collection/item in Petabox. We also found our tool useful for crawl operators as it helped us identify numerous issues in some of our crawls that would have otherwise gone unnoticed.

2   Implementation

CDX Summary is a Python package [6] that ships with a CLI tool to process sorted stream of CDX files via *STDIN* or as a file/URI argument and generate a compact or detailed report in human or machine readable formats. It has some IA-specific features, but can be used against any local or remote CDX files or CDX APIs. Figure 2 shows installation instructions and available CLI options. Below are some feature highlights of the tool:

- Summarizes local CDX files or remote ones over HTTP
- Handles `.gz` and `.bz2` compression seamlessly
- Handles CDX data input to *STDIN*, allowing any filtering or slicing of input
- Supports Petabox web item summarization using item identifier or URI
- Supports Wayback Machine CDX Server API summarization
- Seamless authorization from IA accounts via the `ia` CLI tool
- Human-friendly summary by default, but supports JSON reports too
- Self-aware, as the input can alternatively be a previously generated JSON

```
$ pip install cdxsummary

$ cdxsummary --help
usage: cdxsummary [-h] [-a [QUERY]] [-i] [-j] [-l] [-o [FILE]] [-r] [-s [N]] [-t [N]] [-v] [input]

Summarize web archive capture index (CDX) files.

positional arguments:
  input                 CDX file path/URL (plain/gz/bz2) or an IA item ID to process (reads from the STDIN, if empty or '-')

optional arguments:
  -h, --help            show this help message and exit
  -a [QUERY], --api [QUERY]
                        CDX API query parameters (default: 'matchType=exact'), treats the last argument as the lookup URL
  -i, --item            Treat the input argument as a Petabox item identifier instead of a file path
  -j, --json            Generate summary in JSON format
  -l, --load            Load JSON report instead of CDX
  -o [FILE], --out [FILE]
                        Write output to the given file (default: STDOUT)
  -r, --report          Generate non-summarized JSON report
  -s [N], --samples [N]
                        Number of sample memento URLs in summary (default: 10)
  -t [N], --tophosts [N]
                        Number of hosts with maximum captures in summary (default: 10)
  -v, --version         Show version number
```

Fig. 2. CDX Summary CLI Installation and Help

From Sect. 2.1 to Sect. 2.6 we describe various reports generated by the tool. Numbers reported in Table 1 through Table 5 are not evaluations, but illustrations of the CLI output based on the collection-level CDX file generated on February 2, 2022, for the *mediacloud* collection[1].

2.1 Collection Overview

Table 1 shows a high-level overview of the collection CDX. It includes reports like the number of mementos/captures, number of unique original URIs and hosts, accumulated WARC record sizes, and the dates of first and last mementos.

Table 1. Collection overview

Total Captures in CDX	3,221,758,919
Consecutive Unique URLs	2,381,208,479
Consecutive Unique Hosts	5,366,007
Total WARC Records Size	172.0 TB
First Memento Date	Jun 09, 2016
Last Memento Date	Feb 02, 2022

2.2 Media Types and Status Codes

Table 2 shows statistics for HTTP status code groups of captures of various media types for the collection. The *Revisit* records do not represent an independent media type, instead, they reflect an unchanged state of representations of resources from some of their prior observations (i.e., the same content digest for the same URI). The *TOTAL* column shows combined counts for each media type irrespective of their HTTP status code and the *TOTAL* row (displayed only if

---

[1] https://archive.org/download/mediacloud.

Table 2. MIME type and status code distribution

MIME	2XX	3XX	4XX	5XX	Other	TOTAL
HTML	965,411,367	276,575,748	125,142,922	10,774,370	254,055	1,378,158,462
Image	595,129,981	1,848,252	1,176,862	110,163	6	598,265,264
CSS	34,916,375	7,815	35,193	658	0	34,960,041
JavaScript	54,437,714	14,160	139,220	1,478	3	54,592,575
JSON	72,073,766	378,508	6,435,865	182,669	0	79,070,808
XML	123,611,319	474,681	8,382,386	265,499	0	132,733,885
Text	9,717,016	4,989,191	5,825,931	89,757	7	20,621,902
PDF	907,503	1,743	297	12	0	909,555
Font	1,348,879	208	5,827	21	0	1,354,935
Audio	1,655,064	7,847	4,701	9	0	1,667,621
Video	2,081,368	14,928	20,936	5	0	2,117,237
Revisit	0	0	0	0	790,098,238	790,098,238
Other	34,327,496	87,943,703	4,302,731	629,212	5,254	127,208,396
TOTAL	1,895,617,848	372,256,784	151,472,871	12,053,853	790,357,563	3,221,758,919

there are more than one media types listed) shows the combined counts of each HTTP status code group irrespective of their media types. When generating the detailed JSON report (i.e., using --report CLI flag), original media types and status codes are preserved instead of being grouped.

2.3 Path and Query Segments

Table 3 shows statistics for the number of path segments and the number of query parameters of various URIs in the collection. For example, the cell *P0* and *Q0* shows the number of captures of homepages of various hosts with zero path segments and zero query parameters. The *TOTAL* column shows combined counts for URIs with a specific number of path segments irrespective of their number of query parameters and the *TOTAL* row (displayed only if there are URIs with a varying number of path segments) shows the combined counts for URIs with a specific number of query parameters irrespective of their number of path segments. When generating the detailed JSON report (i.e., using --report CLI flag), original path segments and query parameter counts are preserved instead of being rolled up under the *Other* key.

Table 3. Path and query segments

Path	Q0	Q1	Q2	Q3	Q4	Other	TOTAL
P0	10,137,110	75,096,506	5,222,175	1,422,227	736,628	2,345,905	94,960,551
P1	322,542,556	43,841,147	27,014,507	29,103,774	7,100,402	41,134,623	470,737,009
P2	370,206,924	55,247,724	28,783,611	31,029,789	9,766,427	26,319,078	521,353,553
P3	367,658,614	61,591,011	17,508,660	15,919,708	5,806,691	13,254,728	481,739,412
P4	310,543,626	140,279,203	80,114,245	7,705,491	2,250,744	6,257,513	547,150,822
Other	881,020,001	157,916,352	26,846,263	18,521,368	6,848,796	14,664,792	1,105,817,572
TOTAL	2,262,108,831	533,971,943	185,489,461	103,702,357	32,509,688	103,976,639	3,221,758,919

2.4 Temporal Distribution

Table 4 shows the number of captures of the collection observed in different calendar years and months. The *TOTAL* column shows combined counts for corresponding years and the *TOTAL* row (displayed only if the captures were observed across multiple calendar years) shows the combined number of captures observed in the corresponding calendar months irrespective of their years.

Table 4. Year and month distribution

Year	Jan	Feb	Mar	Apr	May	Jun
2016	0	0	0	0	0	710,753
2018	0	0	0	0	18,409,894	20,138,119
2019	19,598,526	162,402,131	65,102,242	88,210,019	10,937,609	79,065,196
2020	80,033,841	76,467,578	84,829,936	176,568,383	195,626,716	227,839,303
2021	56,130,245	38,882,332	55,665,115	45,999,374	45,209,593	43,396,066
2022	40,104,802	1,623,012	0	0	0	0
TOTAL	195,867,414	279,375,053	205,597,293	310,777,776	270,183,812	371,149,437

Jul	Aug	Sep	Oct	Nov	Dec	TOTAL
0	0	0	0	0	0	710,753
63,997,290	82,864,370	101,464,239	52,569,004	170,693,250	112,690,671	622,826,837
83,674,051	33,172,213	78,516,813	87,399,023	73,646,742	84,030,203	865,754,768
55,837,610	48,706,314	44,075,057	43,451,655	62,242,880	58,438,537	1,154,117,810
46,897,574	45,611,165	20,527,175	45,615,260	42,424,841	50,262,197	536,620,937
0	0	0	0	0	0	41,727,814
250,406,525	210,354,062	244,583,284	229,034,942	349,007,713	305,421,608	3,221,758,919

2.5 Top Hosts

Table 5 shows configurable top-k hosts of the collection based on the number of captures of URIs from each host. The *OTHERS* row, if present, is the sum

Table 5. Top 10 out of 5,366,007 hosts

Host	Captures
wp.me	11,457,705
upload.wikimedia.org	10,667,921
designtaxi.com	10,639,524
indiewire.com	10,341,593
public-api.wordpress.com	9,176,593
youtube.com	7,301,589
facebook.com	6,414,589
elfagr.com	6,122,678
secure.gravatar.com	6,095,165
googletagmanager.com	5,627,624
OTHERS (5,365,997 Hosts)	3,137,913,938

of the longtail of hosts. When generating the detailed JSON report (i.e., using --report CLI flag), counts for all the hosts are included instead of only top-k.

2.6   Random Memento Samples

Table 6 shows a list of configurable N random sample of captured URIs linked to their corresponding Wayback Machine playback URIs (this is configurable) from the collection. The sample is chosen only from mementos that were observed with the text/html media type and 200 OK HTTP status code. Any unexpected URIs in the list (e.g., with a .png/.jpg/.pdf file extension) are likely a result of the Soft-404 issue [23] from the origin server. These random samples with uniform distribution across the stream are dynamically selected by a single-pass algorithm as illustrated in Fig. 3.

Table 6. Random sample of 100 OK HTML mementos

```
https://web.archive.org/web/20200429135903/https://mcuoneclipse.com/2017/07/09/karwendel/
https://web.archive.org/web/20200529190909/http://www.viralnewslatest.com/2020/01/
https://web.archive.org/web/20210609022051/https://www.towleroad.com/2020/09/canadas-drag-race-queen/
https://web.archive.org/web/20200312232938/https://www.albawabhnews.com/service/nc.aspx?id=3934368
https://web.archive.org/web/20210705095335/https://collingswood.umcommunities.org/events/
https://web.archive.org/web/20220104124729/https://marvamedia.wufoo.com/embed/z9zjza1mpvn62/
https://web.archive.org/web/20211116112557/https://www.urbanet.info/streets-cape-town/
https://web.archive.org/web/20200607204252/https://www.diariopuntual.com/node/40007
https://web.archive.org/web/20200616034412/https://okwave.jp/amp/qa/q388029.html
https://web.archive.org/web/20220103002118/https://www.diarioahora.pe/tag/cc-vulnerables/
```

```
SIZE = <desired_sample_size>
sample = List[SIZE]
processed = 0

def toss(item):
    quotient, remainder = divmod(processed, SIZE)
    if random() < 1 / (quotient + 1):
        sample[remainder] = item
    processed++

def main():
    for item in stream:
        if is_valid_candidate(item):
            toss(item)
    return sample
```

Fig. 3. Uniform Random Stream Sampler Algorithm

2.7   CDX Summary Web Component

At IA we are adopting Web Components[2] for various UI elements. To incorporate collection and item level summaries in the web UI of Petabox for web items we have created and open-sourced the CDX Summary Web Component [7]. To render an interactive HTML element from a CDX Summary JSON file or a Petabox item/collection use the Custom HTML Element as illustrated in Fig. 4.

```
<script src="https://unpkg.com/@internetarchive/cdxsummary"></script>

<cdx-summary src="CDX_SUMMARY_JSON_URL"></cdx-summary>
<!-- OR -->
<cdx-summary item="PETABOX_ITEM_OR_COLLECTION_ID"></cdx-summary>
```

Fig. 4. CDX Summary Web Component

3   Conclusions and Future Work

In this work we implemented a generic CDX Summarization CLI tool to summarize any web archival collection or CDX API. We added some IA-specific features for seamless integration with Petabox. The tool generates both human and machine friendly reports with varying levels of details. For easier HTML rendering of generated summaries we implemented a Web Component and made both the CLI and the Web Component open-source. We implemented a single-pass uniform random stream sample algorithm to efficiently sample mementos for testing, quality assurance, or collection representation.

In the future, we would like to report various statistics based on unique URIs, not just the number of mementos. We would also like to identify and highlight some takeaway points based on heuristics (such as reporting just a few URIs being archived too many times or unusual HTML to page requisites ratio).

Acknowledgements. We thank various IA staff members for their help. Brewster Kahle for testing the CLI, Kenji Nagahashi for feedback on the web UI text, Brenton Cheng and Isa Herico Velasco for main site integration, Jason Buckner for Web Component help, and Jim Shelton for UX feedback.

References

1. Alam, S.: Archive profiler: scripts to generate profiles of various web archives (2014). https://github.com/oduwsdl/archive_profiler
2. Alam, S.: MemGator: A memento aggregator CLI and server in go (2015). https://github.com/oduwsdl/MemGator

---

[2] https://www.webcomponents.org/.

3. Alam, S.: Web ARChive (WARC) file format (2018). https://www.slideshare.net/ibnesayeed/web-archive-warc-file-format

4. Alam, S.: MementoMap: a tool to summarize web archive holdings (2019). https://github.com/oduwsdl/MementoMap

5. Alam, S.: CDX summary (2021). https://github.com/internetarchive/cdx-summary

6. Alam, S.: CDX summary in PyPI (2022). https://pypi.org/project/cdxsummary/

7. Alam, S.: CDX summary web component (2022). https://www.npmjs.com/package/@internetarchive/cdxsummary

8. Alam, S., Nelson, M.L.: MemGator - a portable concurrent memento aggregator: cross-platform CLI and server binaries in go. In: Proceedings of the 16th ACM/IEEE-CS Joint Conference on Digital Libraries, pp. 243–244. JCDL 2016 (2016). https://doi.org/10.1145/2910896.2925452

9. Alam, S., Nelson, M.L., Van de Sompel, H., Balakireva, L.L., Shankar, H., Rosenthal, D.S.H.: Web archive profiling through CDX summarization. In: Proceedings of the 19th International Conference on Theory and Practice of Digital Libraries, pp. 3–14. TPDL 2015 (2015). https://doi.org/10.1007/978-3-319-24592-8_1

10. Alam, S., Nelson, M.L., Van de Sompel, H., Balakireva, L.L., Shankar, H., Rosenthal, D.S.H.: Web archive profiling through CDX summarization. Int. J. Digit. Libr. **17**(3), 223–238 (2016). https://doi.org/10.1007/s00799-016-0184-4

11. Alam, S., Nelson, M.L., Van de Sompel, H., Rosenthal, D.S.H.: Web archive profiling through fulltext search. In: Proceedings of the 20th International Conference on Theory and Practice of Digital Libraries, pp. 121–132. TPDL 2016 (2016). https://doi.org/10.1007/978-3-319-43997-6_10

12. Alam, S., Weigle, M.C., Nelson, M.L.: Profiling web archival voids for memento routing. In: Proceedings of the 21st ACM/IEEE-CS Joint Conference on Digital Libraries, pp. 150–159. JCDL 2021 (2021). https://doi.org/10.1109/JCDL52503.2021.00027

13. Alam, S., Weigle, M.C., Nelson, M.L., Melo, F., Bicho, D., Gomes, D.: MementoMap framework for flexible and adaptive web archive profiling. In: Proceedings of the 19th ACM/IEEE-CS Joint Conference on Digital Libraries, pp. 172–181. JCDL 2019 (2019). https://doi.org/10.1109/JCDL.2019.00033

14. AlSum, A., Weigle, M.C., Nelson, M.L., Van de Sompel, H.: Profiling web archive coverage for top-level domain and content language. In: Proceedings of the 17th International Conference on Theory and Practice of Digital Libraries, pp. 60–71. TPDL 2013 (2013). https://doi.org/10.1007/978-3-642-40501-3_7

15. AlSum, A., Weigle, M.C., Nelson, M.L., Van de Sompel, H.: Profiling web archive coverage for top-level domain and content language. Int. J. Digital Lib. **14**(3–4), 149–166 (2014). https://doi.org/10.1007/s00799-014-0118-y

16. Bornand, N., Balakireva, L., Van de Sompel, H.: Routing memento requests using binary classifiers. In: Proceedings of the 16th ACM/IEEE-CS Joint Conference on Digital Libraries, pp. 63–72. JCDL 2016 (2016). https://doi.org/10.1145/2910896.2910899

17. Holzmann, H., Goel, V., Anand, A.: ArchiveSpark: efficient web archive access, extraction and derivation. In: Proceedings of the 16th ACM/IEEE-CS on Joint Conference on Digital Libraries, pp. 83–92. JCDL 2016 (2016). https://doi.org/10.1145/2910896.2910902

18. Internet archive: CDX file format (2003). http://archive.org/web/researcher/cdx_file_format.php

19. ISO 28500:2017: WARC file format (2017). https://iso.org/standard/68004.html

20. Jackson, A.: Messy web archive collections (2014). https://twitter.com/anjacks0n/status/466690812269846528
21. Klein, M., Balakireva, L., Shankar, H.: Evaluating memento service optimizations. In: Proceedings of the 19th ACM/IEEE-CS Joint Conference on Digital Libraries, pp. 182–185. JCDL 2019 (2019). https://doi.org/10.1109/JCDL.2019.00034
22. Maurer, Y.: Summarize CDX(J) files for MIME analysis per 2nd-level domain (2021). https://github.com/ymaurer/cdx-summarize
23. Meneses, L., Furuta, R., Shipman, F.: Identifying "Soft 404" error pages: analyzing the lexical signatures of documents in distributed collections. In: Zaphiris, P., Buchanan, G., Rasmussen, E., Loizides, F. (eds.) TPDL 2012. LNCS, vol. 7489, pp. 197–208. Springer, Heidelberg (2012). https://doi.org/10.1007/978-3-642-33290-6_22
24. Nelson, M.L., Van de Sompel, H.: Adding the Dimension of Time to HTTP. SAGE Handb. Web Hist. (2018)
25. Ruest, N., Lin, J., Milligan, I., Fritz, S.: The archives unleashed project: technology, process, and community to improve scholarly access to web archives. In: Proceedings of the 20th ACM/IEEE Joint Conference on Digital Libraries, pp. 157–166. JCDL 2020 (2020). https://doi.org/10.1145/3383583.3398513
26. Sanderson, R., Van de Sompel, H., Nelson, M.L.: IIPC Memento Aggregator Experiment (2012). http://www.netpreserve.org/sites/default/files/resources/Sanderson.pdf
27. Van de Sompel, H., Nelson, M.L., Sanderson, R.: HTTP framework for time-based access to resource states - memento. RFC 7089 (2013)
28. Van de Sompel, H., Nelson, M.L., Sanderson, R., Balakireva, L.L., Ainsworth, S., Shankar, H.: Memento: time travel for the web. Technical report arXiv:0911.1112 (2009). https://arxiv.org/abs/0911.1112

"Knock Knock! Who's There?" A Study on Scholarly Repositories' Availability

Andrea Mannocci[1]([envelope]) [iD], Miriam Baglioni[1] [iD], and Paolo Manghi[1,2] [iD]

[1] CNR-ISTI – National Research Council, Institute of Information Science
and Technologies "Alessandro Faedo", 56124 Pisa, Italy
{andrea.mannocci,miriam.baglioni,paolo.manghi}@isti.cnr.it
[2] OpenAIRE AMKE, Athens, Greece

Abstract. Scholarly repositories are the cornerstone of modern open science, and their availability is vital for enacting its practices. To this end, scholarly registries such as FAIRsharing, re3data, OpenDOAR and ROAR give them presence and visibility across different research communities, disciplines, and applications by assigning an identifier and persisting their profiles with summary metadata. Alas, like any other resource available on the Web, scholarly repositories, be they tailored for literature, software or data, are quite dynamic and can be frequently changed, moved, merged or discontinued. Therefore, their references are prone to link rot over time, and their availability often boils down to whether the homepage URLs indicated in authoritative repository profiles within scholarly registries respond or not.

For this study, we harvested the content of four prominent scholarly registries and resolved over 13 thousand unique repository URLs. By performing a quantitative analysis on such an extensive collection of repositories, this paper aims to provide a global snapshot of their availability, which bewilderingly is far from granted.

Keywords: Scholarly repositories · Availability · HTTP resolution · Scholarly communication · Open science

1 Introduction

Scholarly repositories are a vital part of the scholarly infrastructure and therefore are a cornerstone of modern open science practices. Scholarly registries, such as FAIRsharing[1] [12], re3data[2] [11], OpenDOAR[3], and ROAR[4], facilitate the discovery and referencing of scholarly repositories by assigning them an identifier (either local or persistent, as for FAIRsharing and re3data) and maintaining

---

[1] FAIRsharing – https://fairsharing.org.
[2] re3data – https://re3data.org.
[3] OpenDOAR – https://v2.sherpa.ac.uk/opendoar.
[4] ROAR – http://roar.eprints.org/information.html.

© Springer Nature Switzerland AG 2022
G. Silvello et al. (Eds.): TPDL 2022, LNCS 13541, pp. 306–312, 2022.
https://doi.org/10.1007/978-3-031-16802-4_26

a public profile displaying summary metadata, as in https://fairsharing.org/ FAIRsharing.wy4egf.

However, like any other resource on the Web [1,2], scholarly repositories as well, be they tailored for literature, software or data, are dynamic and often changed, moved, merged or discontinued. Indeed, as scholars soon got to understand, referencing consistently scholarly resources is far from straightforward [4,5,8,9]. Therefore, references to repositories are vulnerable to link rot over time, and their availability often boils down, especially for research infrastructures and scholarly communication services aggregating content from registries, to whether their homepages are live and able to respond or not.

In this paper, we harvested the content of four prominent scholarly registries, namely FAIRsharing, re3data, OpenDOAR, and ROAR, and distilled a comprehensive, longitudinal, repository-type-agnostic collection of over 13 thousand unique URLs pointing to scholarly repositories worldwide. Then, each URL has been requested via HTTP with multiple methods and the response codes, redirection lists and ultimately resolved URLs have been tracked, thus providing a global snapshot of the availability of scholarly repositories.

The analysis highlights that about the 25% of repository URLs and homepages registered in scholarly registries are problematic. Even more so, the requests terminating successfully from a syntactical standpoint can still be incorrect semantically, as the content served has nothing to relate with the original scope of the repository. In our opinion, such results are bewildering, as the URLs considered in this analysis are those available in official repository profiles maintained by scholarly registries and not "vanilla" repository references parsed "in the wild" from the research literature.

2 Related Work

Web reference and link rot inside and outside the scholarly domain have been extensively studied over the years [1,2,4–6,8,9]. However, to the best of our knowledge, no prior study focused on the availability of scholarly repositories by examining the URLs contained in repository profiles registered by repository managers into scholarly registries.

Despite registries are aware of such issues, and they best-effort notify their users (e.g., https://fairsharing.org/1724 or https://www.re3data.org/ repository/r3d100011299), in several cases, repository profiles could be not yet flagged as problematic. Furthermore, the authoritative nature of such URLs can open to implications regarding repository management (and not just referencing) that are worth investigating.

In this work, we took inspiration from the methodology introduced in [5] for studying the persistence of DOIs, which we adapted to the peculiarities of the case study at hand.

Table 1. Overview of the four registries considered in this analysis.

Registry	Dump date	Dump method	Registry Licence	# repos
FAIRsharing	Feb 2022	JSON (rest API)	CC-BY-SA	1,853
re3data	Feb 2022	OpenAIRE	CC-BY	2,793
OpenDOAR	Feb 2022	OpenAIRE	CC-BY-NC-ND	5,811
ROAR	Feb 2022	CSV (website)	CC-BY	5,444

3   Data and Methods

For this analysis, we selected four major scholarly repository registries, namely FAIRsharing, re3data, OpenDOAR and ROAR, whose details are briefly summarised in Table 1. The content of the four registries was dumped by various means in February 2022. Each repository profile in the four registries was processed, and its homepage accrued in a list of 13,356 unique URLs.

Each URL was requested via HTTP transactions, as documented in RFC 7231 [3], comprehending a client issuing an HTTP request consisting of a request method and request headers, and a server replying to such request with response headers and (optionally) a response body. In this study, the HTTP requests adhere to the two most common HTTP request methods, i.e., GET and HEAD. As documented in the RFC, the main difference between HEAD and GET is that the server returns a resource representation in the response body for GET requests, which is instead omitted for HEAD requests. As per RFC 7231, we expect identical results for the two request methods, except for negligible differences in latency. HTTP requests were issued via Python, were allowed to follow a maximum of 30 redirects, and had a timeout set to 30 s. For each HTTP request successfully concluded, a number of response headers was tracked, namely *(i)* original URL; *(ii)* final URL (same as the original or redirected); *(iii)* final status code; *(iv)* redirection chain (in case of redirects); *(v)* redirection status codes (in case of redirects); *(vi)* latency. If the server instead could not respond within this interval, the request was marked as unsuccessful, and the error message (e.g., timeout, connection refused) was noted. It is worth mentioning that we did not alter the protocol in any way, be it `http://` or `https://`, nor did we alter any other part of the original URLs such as ports, as doing so could alter the perceived error rate, despite reducing further the URLs space to process.

For the sake of open science and reproducibility, the content of the registries, the URL list, the code issuing the requests, the collected data, and the Jupyter notebooks for the analysis of the results are available on Zenodo [10].

4   Results

We start our analysis by examining the last HTTP status code returned by the last accessible link in the redirection chain. If no redirection takes place, only one status code is returned. We aggregated the returned status codes in Table 2,

Table 2. Final HTTP status codes.

Method	2xx	4xx	5xx	Err
HEAD	74.83% (9,995)	6.11% (816)	0.86% (115)	18.2% (2,431)
GET	76.05% (10,158)	5.19% (694)	0.76% (102)	18% (2,403)

where rows indicate HTTP request methods, while columns indicate the number of status code occurrences aggregated per response classes (i.e., 2xx for successful requests, 4xx for client errors, and 5xx for server errors).

The largest part of the performed HTTP requests returned 2xx-class status codes (74.83% and 76.05% for HEAD and GET, respectively), while the remaining requests exhibited issues of various kinds. More specifically, about 18% of HEAD and GET requests failed due to time out, excessive retries or redirects, connection reset by peer, malformed URLs, and so on. Furthermore, a considerable amount of 4xx-class status codes was returned (i.e., 6.11% for HEAD, 5.19% for GET), while a much smaller yet non-negligible quantity of 5xx-class status codes was collected (i.e., 0.86% for HEAD, 0.76% for GET). Please notice that the 3xx-class is relative to redirection, and therefore no final HTTP status code is expected to belong to this class as all redirections were followed, eventually resolving into a non-3xx status code or an error (e.g., for maxing out the number of redirects allowed, or for a timeout). A significant divergence across the two request methods cannot be observed, even though the slight difference suggests that requests were served differently based on the method used, which infringes the RFC recommendations. Indeed, https://idr.openmicroscopy.org triggers an error due to an exceeding number of redirects for HEAD while returning a 200 OK for GET requests.

In total, it is safe to say that about one-quarter of the performed HTTP requests failed to hit their target and resolve successfully, a result that we found bewildering. This is particularly true, especially if we consider that HTTP requests resolving into 2xx-class status codes, despite being syntactically correct from the protocol perspective, can still be semantically wrong in relation to the content of the web page served. Indeed, on manual inspection of randomly sampled URLs, we verified that, despite the syntactic correctness, the page resolved had nothing to do with academia or with the repository/project anymore. For example, http://www.dlese.org/library/ (https://v2.sherpa.ac.uk/id/repository/425) resolves, without further redirects, to a web page suggesting that the domain has not been renewed for its original purposes and that someone else put it back onto the market. Similarly, http://ejournal.windeng.net (http://roar.eprints.org/1530/), together with five more URLs, redirects to http://survey-smiles.com via HEAD, which ostensibly has nothing to do with the initial purpose of the repository.

This event led us to investigate redirections further, which *per se* do not signal a sure malfunction (e.g., redirect from `http://` to `https://`) while can still contribute to semantic incorrectness as they could serve an unrelated page (e.g., the repository has been moved somewhere else and the original URL redirects to an error page). Redirection happens in about 32% of the requests, i.e., 4,330 and 4,359 for HEAD and GET requests, respectively. We also noticed that 378 redirection chains for HEAD requests ended up with a status code other than 2xx-class status codes (338 in the 4xx-class, 40 in the 5xx-class), while, for GET requests, 344 redirections chains shared a similar epilogue (307 in the 4xx-class, 37 in the 5xx-class).

No redirection chain longer than five was observed, except for those maxing out the number of redirections allowed. This was observed sporadically, eight times for HEAD and once for GET, leaving little room for further speculations. Most redirections resolved in one hop, and the number of N-long redirection chains quickly decreases as N increases. We experimentally verified that the most frequent reason for one-hop-long redirection chains was to switch from `http://` to `https://`, prepend `www`, append a trailing slash, or combinations of such and similar alterations.

Incidentally, we noticed that the URL space dramatically shrinks, i.e., from the over 13 thousand unique URLs we started with, excluding the errors, 10,926 of them resolved to 9,331 unique URLs via HEAD (-14.59%), while 10,954 of them resolved to 9,353 unique URLs via GET (-14.61%). More specifically, for HEAD requests, a pool of 3,051 unique repository URLs redirected at least twice onto the same URL, for a total of 1,456 unique URLs after redirection. For GET requests, we registered similar numbers: 3,060 unique repository URLs redirected at least twice onto one of 1,459 unique URLs after redirection. As it can be noticed, there is no substantial difference between the two methods, yet the behaviour is not identical as it should be expected as per RFC recommendations. This is also confirmed by 146 unique URLs for which HEAD and GET returned two different locations.

By aggregating the final URLs after redirections and counting the number of conflated original URLs, we discovered something interesting. In several cases, for which unfortunately do not exist systematic identification criteria, redirections hid issues worth commenting on. For example, 16 distinct URLs[5] redirected to https://www.unit.no/ugyldig-lenke-til-dokument-i-vitenarkiv. The latter alerts about the incorrectness of the (original) URLs (i.e., "You are trying to reach a document via a link that is not valid") and leaves the user with no further indication of the repository's actual location.

Similarly, 6 distinct URLs[6] conflated onto https://www.nlm.nih.gov/toxnet/index.html, where a note claims that "most of NLM's toxicology information services have been integrated into other NLM products and services", thus leaving no trace of the previous databases and relative information about the

---

[5] http://brage.bibsys.no/hia/ {ks, hig, hiak, politihs, hsf, hive, misjon, hinesna, hvo, hibo, histm, dhh, hint, hibu, bdh}.

[6] https://toxnet.nlm.nih.gov/cgi-bin/sis/htmlgen?CCRIS,   https://toxnet.nlm.nih.gov/cgi-bin/sis/htmlgen?HSDB,   https://www.nlm.nih.gov/toxnet/index.html, https://toxmap.nlm.nih.gov/toxmap/,   https://toxnet.nlm.nih.gov/newtoxnet/tri.htm, https://toxnet.nlm.nih.gov/newtoxnet/cpdb.htm.

content. Similarly, http://csdb.glycoscience.ru/help/migrate.html indicates that two original databases redirecting here have been merged into a new one.

On a slightly different note, 7 distinct and seemingly unrelated, URLs[7] all redirected to https://www.oclc.org/url/notfound, whose domain is held by a company positioned in the digital libraries & services market segment.

Alas, such problems can manifest for any number of conflated URLs, and making a comprehensive list of such cases would equate to examining all the URLs by hand, which quickly grows unfeasible.

5 Discussion

The current study suffers from a few limitations. Firstly, a one-shot resolution provides a snapshot that institution-wide or nationwide infrastructure outages could temporarily distort. As of June 2022, we tested this hypothesis by checking Ukrainian repositories (i.e., .ua domain) and verified that 36 out of 146 (24.6%) were unreachable, of which several are in Kharkiv, east Ukraine. Similarly, other repositories can have downtime for technical reasons. Therefore, repeating the experiment over an extended timeframe would help recover from spurious transients, provide a better overview of the actual situation, and put scholarly repositories' availability in a long-term perspective.

Furthermore, we resolved the URLs in this analysis via HEAD and GET only. However, we empirically noticed that in some cases, URLs behave differently when accessed via browser, a behaviour already observed in [7]. Therefore, we could extend the study by including HTTP parameters (e.g., user agent, accepted cookies) and by simulating human-like browser interactions via Selenium[8].

Nonetheless, the results show that about one out of four URLs from repository profiles in scholarly registries is problematic. Moreover, this result is a lower bound, as problems could be related to the content served after a successfully served request. In fact, as we came to realise, many HTTP requests returned, both with and without redirection, a web page unrelated to the repository pertaining to the original URL. The methodology described in [4] could help to assess the occurrence of such events; however, this would apply only to the cases for which pre- and post- repository registration snapshots exist. Unfortunately, an exhaustive estimation of content drift would entail a fully manual inspection of repository URLs and the relevant entries on the registries.

As a final remark, repository and IT infrastructure managers have a role in such dysfunctions and should be aware that changes in the infrastructure or, by any means, in the repository lifecycle should be notified and reflected onto registries to strive for accountability and that an incorrect metadata description of a repository can have an impact on reproducibility and open science practices.

---

[7] http://content.wsulibs.wsu.edu/cdm/,   http://idahohistory.cdmhost.com/cdm/, http://ccdl.libraries.claremont.edu/collection.php?alias=irw, http://gettysburg.cd mhost.com, http://cdm16378.contentdm.oclc.org, http://content.wsulibs.wsu.edu/, http://trinity.cdmhost.com/index.php.

[8] Selenium WebDriver – https://www.selenium.dev.

Acknowledgements. This work was partially funded by the EC H2020 OpenAIRE-Nexus (Grant agreement 101017452).

References

1. Bar-Yossef, Z., Broder, A.Z., Kumar, R., Tomkins, A.: Sic transit gloria telae: Towards an understanding of the web's decay. In: Proceedings of the 13th Conference on World Wide Web - WWW 2004, p. 328. ACM Press, New York, NY, USA (2004). https://doi.org/10.1145/988672.988716
2. Cho, J., Garcia-Molina, H.: Estimating frequency of change. ACM Trans. Internet Technol. **3**(3), 256–290 (2003). https://doi.org/10.1145/857166.857170
3. Fielding, R., Reschke, J.: Hypertext transfer protocol (HTTP/1.1): semantics and content (2014)
4. Jones, S.M., de Sompel, H.V., Shankar, H., Klein, M., Tobin, R., Grover, C.: Scholarly context adrift: three out of four URI references lead to changed content. PLoS One **11**(12), e0167475 (2016). https://doi.org/10.1371/journal.pone.0167475
5. Klein, Martin, Balakireva, Lyudmila: On the persistence of persistent identifiers of the scholarly web. In: Hall, Mark, Merčun, Tanja, Risse, Thomas, Duchateau, Fabien (eds.) TPDL 2020. LNCS, vol. 12246, pp. 102–115. Springer, Cham (2020). https://doi.org/10.1007/978-3-030-54956-5_8
6. Klein, M., Balakireva, L.: An extended analysis of the persistence of persistent identifiers of the scholarly web. Int. J. Digit. Libr. **23**(1), 5–17 (2021). https://doi.org/10.1007/s00799-021-00315-w
7. Klein, M., Balakireva, L., Shankar, H.: Who is asking? humans and machines experience a different scholarly web. In: 16th International Conference on Digital Preservation. Open Science Framework, Amsterdam (2019). https://doi.org/10.17605/OSF.IO/SMCY2
8. Klein, M., et al.: Scholarly context not found: one in five articles suffers from reference rot. PLoS One **9**(12), e115253 (2014). https://doi.org/10.1371/journal.pone.0115253
9. Lawrence, S., et al.: Persistence of web references in scientific research. Computer **34**(2), 26–31 (2001). https://doi.org/10.1109/2.901164
10. Mannocci, A.: Analysis of scholarly repositories' availability. Data and notebooks (2022). https://doi.org/10.5281/zenodo.6906885
11. Pampel, H., et al.: Making research data repositories visible: the re3data.org registry. PLOS One **8**(11), e78080 (2013). https://doi.org/10.1371/journal.pone.0078080
12. Sansone, S.A., et al.: FAIRsharing as a community approach to standards, repositories and policies. Nat. Biotechnol. **37**(4), 358–367 (2019). https://doi.org/10.1038/s41587-019-0080-8

Exploring Research Fields Through Institutional Contributions to Academic Journals

Tove Faber Frandsen[1]([⊠]) [iD] and Jeppe Nicolaisen[2] [iD]

[1] University of Southern Denmark, Kolding, Denmark
t.faber@sdu.dk
[2] Copenhagen University, Copenhagen, Denmark

Abstract. Academic journals are vehicles for the dissemination and sharing of science. They can form the basis in digital libraries for an exploration of a research field. Bibliometric journal studies have frequently taken the author as the focus of study when researching the activity of research in a field, and more seldom the affiliation (research institutions, universities, etc.). In this study, institutional contributions to ten library and information journals are explored using measures that have previously been employed in author studies. The so-called continuants, movers, newcomers and transients are used to analyse the data. The results show that there are great differences across journals when it comes to the distribution of institutions and their contributions to the journals under study. Some journals have many institutions contributing regularly. Others are characterized by many institutions contributing infrequently or rarely. The implications for exploring research fields in digital libraries are considered.

Keywords: Bibliometrics · Institutions as contributors · Library and information science journals

1 Introduction

Journals are essential for sharing and disseminating science and thus the subject of many analyses. A review from 2009 identifies as many as 82 bibliometric studies using single journals as unit of analysis [1]. Journals are studied since "[a]nalyzing journals can provide a solid grasp of research trends, their main applications and the emerging technologies" [2, p. 549]. The bibliometric studies of journals typically analyze a set of journals considered significant within a field and thus reflect the activity of research in the field [1]. According to Jokić [3] it is a common method of exploring the development in library and information science to perform bibliometric analyses of journal articles. Kim, Feng and Zhu [2] consider these studies domain analyses. It has been argued that analyses of a single journal can represent a field [4], however extrapolations from a single journal to an entire field can be problematic [5]. Therefore, extrapolations from journal to field are strengthened by comparative analyses of other journals in the field [5]. Many different aspects of journals have been studied bibliometrically including analyses of countries, publication venues, authors and keywords to understand the target

© Springer Nature Switzerland AG 2022
G. Silvello et al. (Eds.): TPDL 2022, LNCS 13541, pp. 313–319, 2022.
https://doi.org/10.1007/978-3-031-16802-4_27

disciplines [2, 5]. Anyi, Zainab and Anuar [1] list the following groups of bibliometric measures used to study single journals which can be further specified into more than 40 measures: (a) article productivity, (b) author characteristics, (c) author's productivity, (d) co-authorship pattern, (e) content analysis, (f) citation analysis, (g) characteristics of the editorial board.

Journals can be considered aggregates of authors as well as documents [6] allowing for a wide range of analyses. In this study, we are focusing on journals as aggregates of authors, which can be studied using three different types of measures (author characteristics, institutions and geography). Apart from characteristics of the individual (e.g. gender, profession), authors can also be characterized by their affiliations and geographical location [1].

Geographical location is particularly well-studied. Several researchers have studied how foreign authors contribute to library and information science journals [e.g. 4, 7–11]. There are also studies of institutional affiliations although not as many, probably because the analyses are time-consuming and involve many manual processes to uniquely identify institutions [12]. The existing studies of institutions as producers of journal articles typically focus on the most productive institutions [12–14]. Other studies have focused on the type of institution e.g. academic or non-academic [15].

There are a few studies analyzing the distribution of institutions as contributors to journals in further detail. In a study of *American Documentation* and the *Journal of the American Society for Information Science*, Koehler [16] finds a major reorientation over fifty years in terms of type of contributing institutions. Furner notes institutional frequencies of publication follow a power-law distribution characterized by a small group of institutions contributing with many of the articles and with many institutions contributing with just one article [12]. Similarly, the strongly skewed distribution of contributions is also found in a study of LIS journals from 2007 to 2012 demonstrating that the most productive institutions account for 20% of the articles and more than 90% of the departments contributed five articles or fewer [17]. Consequently, it seems that the level of institutional commitment to journals can vary as in the case of author commitment to journals [18] and commitment to journals are tied to journals and their level of specialization. In this study we explore the development over time in institutions as contributors to journals. We draw on methods used to analyze recurring authors to measure institutional journal commitment to a selection of Library and Information Science journals. We aim to explore to what extent institutional contributions to Library and Information Science journals are stable over time and if there are differences across journals. The patterns of contribution in and the concentration of institutions can provide us with valuable perspectives to further our understanding of the contributors of journals.

2   Methods

We measure institutional contributions to journals using concepts and measures from studies of authors suggested by De Solla Price [19] and used by e.g. Moed, Aisati and Plume [20]. We are operating with four types of institutions in relation to a journal:

- Continuants in year Y are defined as institutions publishing in year Y who had at least one paper during a period of three years preceding Y and at least one paper in the three years following Y.
- Movers in year Y are defined as institutions with a paper in the three preceding years but no publications during the three subsequent years.
- Newcomers in year Y are defined as institutions in year Y were defined as authors with no papers in the preceding three years and at least one paper in the three subsequent years.
- Transients in year Y are defined as institutions who in year Y had only published papers in Y and no papers in the three preceding or subsequent years.

For each journal, contributing institutions are matched with contributing institutions in the three preceding and following years to identify these four types of institutions in that set of journals. The indicator is binary and therefore only counts whether institution has contributed publications in the same journal although institutions may have contributed with several publications in the time period analyzed. Ten Library and Information Science journals were included in the study: Data Technologies and Applications; Electronic Library; Information Processing & Management; Information Technology and Libraries; Journal of Documentation; Journal of Information Science; Journal of the Association for Information Science and Technology; Library and Information Science Research; Library Resources and Technical Services; Scientometrics. The ten core journals were taken from an existing list of core journals in Library and Information Science categorizing them as either information science journals or library automation [21]. We have adjusted according to title changes and discontinued titles. This list of core journals has formed the basis of several studies of library and information science in its original version as well as revised versions [recent examples include 22–24].

Publication data from these journals were collected from 1997 to 2020 using Scopus. Three document types were included: article, review and note. The institution matching in this study relies on Scopus Affiliation Identifier that assigns an 8-digit AFID to each institution and links variants to the main AFID. Institutional disambiguation is very difficult and up to one in five publications can have discrepancies in author affiliations between the major bibliographic databases [25]. Scopus definitely has room for improvement as is the case for other bibliographic databases [25, 26]. In a study of this size, we cannot manually check every AFID but we will have to take the limitations of the tool in to account before making conclusions. The analyses in the study are based on publication data from the ten journals. For each publication the AFIDs of all authors are extracted and matched to the AFIDs of the previous and following three years. The distribution of institution types (continuants, movers, newcomers and transients) is calculated as percentages of the contributing institutions each year for all journals. The results are presented using graphical overviews.

3   Results

In the results we are going to focus on the continuants. In this study, we are measuring institutional journal commitment to a selection of Library and Information Science journals and explore the concentration of institutions and the continuants allow us to analyze the contributions of the institutions that contribute in year Y but also within three years before as well as three years after year Y. These are the most committed institutions to the journals. At the other end of the scale, we find the transients that contribute in year Y but not in the three preceding or subsequent years. These are the less committed institutions to a specific journal and results on these are therefore not presented in this paper.

The institutional continuants in the ten LIS journals from 2004 to 2018 are illustrated in Fig. 1. The library automation journals are marked with a dotted line. In the figure we see that the information science journals have more continuant institutions than the library automation journals. However, there huge differences across journals. The information science journal with the highest mean share of continuants is Journal of the Association for Information Science and Technology (41%) whereas Journal of Information Science has the lowest (22%). For the library automation journals the highest mean share of continuants is found in Electronic Library (21%) and the lowest mean share is found in Information Technology and Libraries (9%). Consequently, for some journals only around 10% of the contributing institutions have contributed to the journal in the last three years and will again within the next three years. At the other end of the scale, we find three information science journals with an average of over a third of the contributing institutions being continuants.

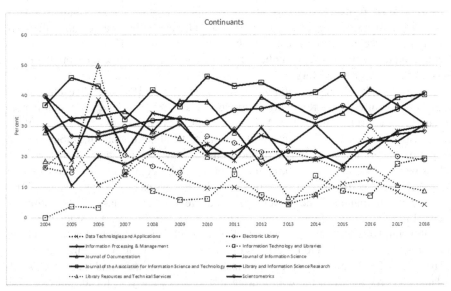

Fig. 1. Institutional continuants from 2004 to 2018 in percentages. Library automation journals are marked with dotted lines.

We find little indication of a tendency over time to increasing or decreasing shares of continuant institutions. Some of the journals publish few articles, reviews and notes every year which tends to make the numbers more unstable and thus make it more difficult to detect possible tendencies over time. Therefore, we have done analyses of the data set as two groups of journals as well, but it did not provide statistically significant results. Therefore, in this study we will not argue that there is development over time in the percentages of continuant institutions for these journals, individually or as groups.

We find that the six information science journals have more institutions contributing regularly to the journals whereas the library automation journals are characterized by a higher number of transient contributing institutions. The higher degree of institutions contributing regularly to some journals corresponds with previous studies of these ten journals. A previous study finds a higher frequency of returning authors in especially the six information science journals than others, consequently showing a larger degree of community commitment [24]. The library automation journals generally publish more papers by less experienced researchers [27]. The results of this study as well as previous studies indicate that author characteristics and thus maybe also institution characteristics are somewhat different in the information science and library automation journals. Reputation of the journal may also play a role here although it is beyond the scope of this paper. Selecting a journals to publish in can be seen as a reward seeking process implying that authors will choose the most prestigious journal among the journals they believe will accept their papers [24].

Consequently, if the share of institutional continuants is high, the contributing institutions can be used to depict a richer picture of a research field, and this can be used for explorative purposes in digital libraries.

4 Discussion and Conclusion

First, we need to consider limitations, especially, the use of the AFIF to determine the identity of institutions. We expect reduced accuracy at the institutional level and future works involve additional data cleaning for disambiguating affiliation data as recommended [28]. In the present study, we should be careful making conclusions based on small variations in the data set as the data quality does not allow for it.

Our results are important for the understanding of institutions as contributors to journals. Existing studies find a power-law distribution characterized by a small group of institutions contributing with many of the articles [12] although the type of contributing institutions can change gradually over time [16]. Our results support these findings but also suggest that some journals publish more contributions from continuants whereas other journals have more transients. Some journals appear to be characterized by a higher degree of concentration of contributing institutions. Specialization may be a contributing factor as more specialized journals would attract more contributions from fewer, more specialized institutions. Some of the journals in our data set are more applied and thus attracting contributions from practitioners and they may not have time for publishing regularly. Furthermore, non-faculty authors have traditionally contributed considerably to the LIS literature including more than two-thirds of the articles in the practice-oriented journals [17]. However, the share of articles written by practicing librarians have declined steadily over the past decades and thus resulting in less contributions by libraries. However, the journals need to reach a broader audience and focus more on the science and practice of information science. High concentration of institutions may thus not be desirable [29]. Interdisciplinarity may also be contributing to the distribution of contributing institutions. Journals publishing more interdisciplinary studies may attract authors from many different disciplines and they would to a greater extent become transients in those journals. Again, a high share of transient could be valuable when addressing challenges associated with the global information crises. The development of solutions to future information crises depends on interdisciplinary collaborations with a variety of perspectives and fields [29].

Furthermore, Institutions contributing to journals can form the basis for an exploration of a research field. Making these patterns of contributing institutions available in digital libraries allows the users to explore a research field as defined by the contributing institutions. Some journals have a high percentage of continuants and a low degree of transients. The contributing institutions thus characterize the journal and can be used to explore the organization of the journal and the research field.

Summing up, there seems to be great variation in the distribution of institutions contributing to journals. Some journals have many institutions contributing regularly while others have a large number contributing sparingly. Exploring the concentration of institutions may add valuable perspectives to this research and adding some of the variables explaining the distributions would allow for more in-depth analyses. In order for information science to be shared and disseminated, journals are vital and our understanding of the contributors of them would benefit from being strengthened. The contributors of journals can form the basis for an exploration of a research field.

References

1. Anyi, K.W.U., Zainab, A.N., Anuar, N.B.: Bibliometric studies on single journals: a review. Malays. J. Libr. Inf. Sci. **14**, 17–55 (2009)
2. Kim, M.C., Feng, Y., Zhu, Y.: Mapping scientific profile and knowledge diffusion of Library Hi Tech. Libr. Hi Tech **39**, 549–573 (2020)
3. Jokić, M.: Productivity, visibility, authorship, and collaboration in library and information science journals: central and eastern European authors. Scientometrics **122**(2), 1189–1219 (2019). https://doi.org/10.1007/s11192-019-03308-4
4. Lipetz, B.-A.: Aspects of JASIS authorship through five decades. J. Am. Soc. Inf. Sci. **50**, 994–1003 (1999)
5. Harter, S.P., Hooten, P.A.: Information science and scientists: JASIS, 1972–1990. J. Am. Soc. Inf. Sci. **43**, 583–593 (1992)
6. Larivière, V., Sugimoto, C.R., Cronin, B.: A bibliometric chronicling of library and information science's first hundred years. J. Am. Soc. Inf. Sci. Technol. **63**, 997–1016 (2012)
7. He, S., Spink, A.: A comparison of foreign authorship distribution in JASIST and the Journal of Documentation. J. Am. Soc. Inf. Sci. Technol. **53**, 953–959 (2002)
8. Uzun, A.: Assessing internationality of scholarly journals through foreign authorship patterns: the case of major journals in information science, and scientometrics. Scientometrics **61**, 457–465 (2004)
9. Barik, N., Jena, P.: Authorship distribution and collaboration in LIS open access journals: a scopus based analysis during 2001 to 2015. Libr. Philos. Pract. (2019)
10. Nebelong-Bonnevie, E., Frandsen, T.F.: Journal citation identity and journal citation image: a portrait of the Journal of Documentation. J. Doc. **62**, 30–57 (2006)

11. Bharvi, D., Garg, K., Bali, A.: Scientometrics of the international journal scientometrics. Scientometrics **56**, 81–93 (2003)

12. Furner, J.: Forty years of the Journal of Librarianship and Information Science: a quantitative analysis, Part I. J. Librariansh. Inf. Sci. **41**, 149–172 (2009)

13. Sethi, B.B., Maharana, B., Mohanty, B.K.: Periodical literature bibliometric analysis: a case study of four international journals. Libr. Philos. Pract. **2016**, 1–25 (2016)

14. Willett, P.: Library review 1989–2017: publication and citation statistics. Glob. Knowl. Mem. Commun. **70**, 272–281 (2020)

15. Davarpanah, M.R., Aslekia, S.: A scientometric analysis of international LIS journals: productivity and characteristics. Scientometrics **77**, 21–39 (2008)

16. Koehler, W.: A profile in statistics of journal articles: fifty years of American Documentation and the Journal of the American Society for Information Science. Cybermetrics Int. J. Sci. Inf. Bibliometr. **3** (2000)

17. Walters, W.H., Wilder, E.I.: Disciplinary, national, and departmental contributions to the literature of library and information science, 2007–2012. J. Assoc. Inf. Sci. Technol. **67**, 1487–1506 (2016)

18. Nicolaisen, J., Frandsen, T.F.: Epistemic community formation: a bibliometric study of recurring authors in medical journals. Scientometrics **127**(7), 4167–4189 (2022)

19. De Solla Price, D.: The Citation Cycle. Key Papers in Information Science (1980)

20. Moed, H.F., Aisati, M.H., Plume, A.: Studying scientific migration in Scopus. Scientometrics **94**, 929–942 (2013)

21. White, H.D., McCain, K.W.: Visualizing a discipline: an author co-citation analysis of information science, 1972–1995. J. Am. Soc. Inf. Sci. **49**, 327–355 (1998)

22. Zhao, D., Strotmann, A.: Intellectual structure of information science 2011–2020: an author co-citation analysis. J. Doc. **78**, 728–744 (2021)

23. Hou, J., Yang, X., Chen, C.: Emerging trends and new developments in information science: a document co-citation analysis (2009–2016). Scientometrics **115**, 869–892 (2018)

24. Nicolaisen, J., Frandsen, T.F.: Journals as communities: a case study of core journals in LIS. Proc. Assoc. Inf. Sci. Technol. **58**, 510–514 (2021)

25. Purnell, P.J.: The prevalence and impact of university affiliation discrepancies between four bibliographic databases – scopus, web of science, dimensions, and microsoft academic. Quant. Sci. Stud. 1–47 (2022)

26. Schmidt, C.M., Cox, R., Fial, A.V., Hartman, T.L., Magee, M.L.: Gaps in affiliation indexing in Scopus and PubMed. J. Med. Libr. Assoc. **104**, 138–142 (2016)

27. Frandsen, T.F., Nicolaisen, J.: Publishing in library and information science journals: the success of less experienced researchers. J. Inf. Sci. (2022)

28. Donner, P., Rimmert, C., van Eck, N.J.: Comparing institutional-level bibliometric research performance indicator values based on different affiliation disambiguation systems. Quant. Sci. Stud. **1**, 150–170 (2020)

29. Xie, B., et al.: Global health crises are also information crises: a call to action. J. Assoc. Inf. Sci. Technol. **71**, 1419–1423 (2020)

Implementation Issues for a Highly Structured Research Report

Robert B. Allen(✉) [ID]

New York, NY, USA
rba@boballen.info

Abstract. We have proposed that scientific research reports should be constructed entirely of structured knowledge rather than text. In an earlier paper, we emphasized Research Designs as a framework for structured research reports and described how a structured implementation might be applied to Pasteur's classic swan-neck flask experiment. In this paper, we examine some of the issues encountered in developing that implementation using dynamic models. For instance, we consider issues associated with modeling state transitions.

Keywords: Declarative programming · Direct representation · Hypothesis Model · Pasteur · Research Designs

1 Semantic Modeling for Research Reports

Over time scientific research reports have become increasingly structured. That trend has accelerated with automated and flexible data management and description. Among these are [8, 12] (see [11] for an overview). However, we have found no attempts to structure all aspects of research reports as our approach proposes [1–7].

Structured scientific research reports are arguments for the research claims. They are complex digital objects and should be implemented with comprehensive, standard vocabularies, based on general world knowledge, and previous research results. Potentially, the structured reports will become the foundation for a knowledge-based scientific digital library. The heart of a research report is interwoven sequences of transitions. In [6], transitions are described as state changes with rules or triggers that activate when given conditions are met. One sequence of transitions is the Research Procedure which is based on the Research Design [7]. For experimental Research Procedures, the triggers (manipulations) are the actions of the researcher. The other sequence comprises causal Hypothesis Models for the phenomenon under investigation. Potentially, Research Procedures will cause a sequence of transitions in the research environment (microworld) as predicted by one or another of the hypotheses. In [7] we described these two types of sequences as "yoked" in experiments.

Goal and Roadmap: There are many advantages to highly structured research reports. They would facilitate research claims validation, inferences, and interactive tutorial

© The Author(s) 2022
G. Silvello et al. (Eds.): TPDL 2022, LNCS 13541, pp. 320–327, 2022.
https://doi.org/10.1007/978-3-031-16802-4_28

explanations. This paper extends our initial proposal for a structured report of Pasteur's swan-neck flask experiment [7] by examining implementation issues. We focus on developing robust representations and dynamic models. Our approach is related to object-oriented modeling; we model the interaction of objects as a dynamic simulation across time, with the research set in a microworld. In our implementation, the classes are based on the SUMO ontology [17] extended to cover the vocabulary required for the specific research domain. We do not focus on text mining. Nor do we focus on inference across large knowledgebases, and we do not at this point emphasize machine learning or the cognition of discovery [19].

Section 2 explores general issues for developing structured research reports. Section 3 focuses on developing a structured report for a somewhat simplified version of Pasteur's Model swan neck flask experiment. This includes a software implementation of a Hypothesis Model. Section 4 discusses the potential for a broad knowledgebase of research reports and related materials.

2 Highly Structured Research Reports

A typical research report is a structured argumentation document. It has a Goal, Question, Strategy, Hypothesis, Procedures, Results, and Claim. The strength of the argument is measured by accepted standards of evidence given different research designs and methods. Together they provide a "warrant" for further acceptance of the Claim.

The Research Goal is the motivation for the research. It is often based on human needs and values such as extending the human lifespan or improving the human food supply. In most cases, the Research Question addresses a specific issue related to the Research Goal. Because determining causation is one of the central goals of science [9], the Research Question may be framed as finding rules for considers causal transitions. A variety of Research Designs has been explored for structuring the relationship between the hypotheses and the procedures [18]. Different designs (e.g., experimental, quasi-experimental, observational) support different strengths of inferences about the results based on the internal and external validity. Construct validity, which considers whether the constructs being examined match reality, is closely related to ontology. A paradigm shift is the result of the realignment of several related constructs [21].

The Hypothesis is a simple causal transition (e.g., "biogenesis") while the Hypothesis Models a causal sequence. Typically, Hypothesis Models are not standard mechanisms [6] but ad hoc sequences applied to the specific research environment. The Procedure is the actions taken by the researcher. Because the Procedure and Hypothesis Models in experiments are interdependent, we say they are yoked [7]. Since experiments often require a highly controlled environment, the Procedure may include presets to the state of objects in the microworld.

Figure 1 and Fig. 2 illustrate the Procedure (red) and the Hypothesis Model (blue) in two contexts, experimental and observational. In both cases, the causal path of the Hypotheses Model moves from the independent variable (IVhyp) to the dependent variable (DVhyp). For experiments (Fig. 1), the manipulation by the researcher (IV$manip$) is intended to trigger the IVhyp that might not be directly observed; there is a causal sequence between IV*manip* and IV*hyp* (also blue). Similarly, DV*hyp* may not be observed directly but only as reflected in DV*obs*.

In observational studies (Fig. 2) there is a Procedure for the observations, but no specific manipulation. Rather, the focus is on the selection of conditions and variables and the interaction with other models. In some cases, observational research may examine specific IV*obs* and DV*obs* as shown in Fig. 2. In other cases, there may not be à priori expectations of the causal pathways. Here, we concentrate on experimental research; we plan to address observational research in later papers.

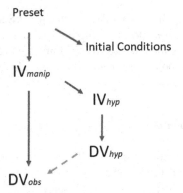
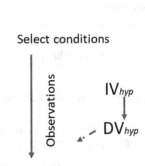

Fig. 1. Experimental research procedures (red) include a manipulation (IV*manip*). This affects the Hypothesis Model (vertical blue). (Color figure online)

Fig. 2. Observational research may also explore Hypothesis Models but there is no manipulation thus, weakly yoked. (Color figure online)

In addition to the framework described above for the Procedures and Hypothesis Models, the obtained results need to be modeled. Planned comparisons apply specific tests to the observations to evaluate the hypotheses [4]. Other comparisons may be developed as appropriate. In most cases, the Claim reflects the initial research question and hypothesis although extended Questions and the Claims can be asserted at different levels of generality (see "Structured Annotations" below).

The myExperiment project [10] is a collection of community-deposited workflows based on Taverna. Our approach extends that project's approach by pairing structured workflows with structured hypothesis (outcome) models along with adding structured Goals, Questions, Results, and Claims.

3   Pasteur's Swan-Neck Flask Experiment

Background and Framework: Aristotle proposed that life can arise from nonliving matter; he believed that air contains vital heat, which causes the development of new organisms. This process is known as Spontaneous Generation. By comparison, Germ Theory was based on biogenesis, that is that "life is required for the creation of life". There was an extended debate and several studies between proponents of Spontaneous Generation and Germ Theory. Around 1859, Pasteur [16] effectively settled the debate with the elegant swan-neck flask experiment. The curved swan neck traps microbes and heavier particles but allows air to pass into the flask holding nutrient broth. Later, the flask is tilted so that the broth reaches the curve with the trapped microbes. Pasteur found that microbes grew in the broth only after the flask had been tilted. In [7], we outlined a framework for describing the swan-neck flask experiment; here, we examine issues in implementing that framework.

Ultimately the Research Goal is related to improving human health and food production by understanding more about microbes. While desirable microbes can produce wine and dairy products, undesirable microbes can create spoilage. Similarly, microbes can be beneficial or adverse to human health. By understanding the lifecycle of microbes, potentially spoilage could be minimized and health improved. Based on the Goal, the Research Question could be framed as whether Spontaneous Generation or Biogenesis accounts for the origin of microbes.

Representations: Dynamic models require transitions that may involve changes in an attribute, in a process state, or in the relationship to other objects. For detailed models, the transition must be defined in combination with a specific object. In our approach, an object is defined as a Python class for the transition and the transition as a function within that class that is applied to the object.

The greatest challenges are in the representation of complex objects that change through time. For example, for multi-granular objects and their transitions. It is not feasible to model each molecule of air or broth or each microbe and its behavior. Rather, we model them as groups and maintain a general characterization of their properties. Representing small changes in the count of numerous objects (such as due to the reproduction of microbes) remains a challenge for qualitative modeling. Thus, we used pseudo counts for attributes such as the number of microbes (also for intervals of time).

The more granular level is not implemented although it may be acknowledged as part of an explanation. This is implemented as a declarative model but not strictly object modeling. Perhaps, the details could be implemented with multi-granular models (e.g., [15]). Or perhaps limited object models could be introduced as examples or scenarios for the more general process. For example, microbes are carried by air currents. When air is still, as it is in the neck of the flask, gravity dominates and microbes fall to the bottom of the neck. We model this competition of forces with qualitative force dynamics, a concept adapted from linguistics [20].

A second major set of challenges relates to representing locations in a microworld. We implemented subRegions within which compound entities (e.g., collections of microbes) could have their own state. The regions can be dynamic as the objects change Moreover, there are nuanced interactions between the regions and the objects. For instance, as the flask is tilted and a portion of broth flows into the neck, do we need to reduce the broth spatial subRegion in the body of the flask? Because it was not significant for our purposes, we did not implement a change in the flaskBody microworld. A notation could be developed to address these modeling issues.

Hypothesis Models, Procedure, Results, Comparisons, and Claims: Pasteur's experiment had two conditions; one in which the flasks are tilted to allow microbes to enter broth and one in which they are not tilted. Because there are two Hypotheses (biogenesis and spontaneous generation), there are four (2 × 2) Hypothesis Models. Here, we focus on only one of the four in detail because of space limitations but the others are analogous. The short version of the Hypothesis Model is that the introduction of microbes to the sterile broth causes fermentation of that broth. That can be extended by more specifics about the transitions of the objects as the experiment progresses. In other words, the Hypothesis Model is a causal chain.

In addition to the initial models, the full report needs to include the actual results as well as comparisons and claims based on them. For the swan-neck flask experiment, there could be comparisons across conditions [3, 7] and across time (before tilting versus after). The results support biogenesis and not the spontaneous generation (vital heat) hypothesis. In most cases, the Claim is based on one of the hypotheses. When unexpected results are obtained, a different claim could be developed. If we believe that the microbes in Pasteur's research environment are typical of other types of microbes, based on induction [13], we could assert the broad Claim that:

The reproduction of microbes is a necessary condition for the development of new microbes.

Our willingness to accept generalizations depends on factors such as the strength of the research results, whether we know of counter-examples, and whether there is a plausible mechanism to account for the results. These are issues of external validity. For Pasteur's experiment, we could ask how typical the microbes in Pasteur's flasks are of the broader population of microbes, which is an external validity challenge due to the "Interaction of the Causal Relationship of Units" (Table 3.2 [18]). Disputes about the claims can be represented with structured Toulmin-style argumentation.

Structured Annotations: The components described above form a framework for the research report. That framework can be extended for annotations that could include metadata and reasons for choices and explanations. Because we are developing dynamic models there are transitions with many nuances. While under normal circumstances, a given transition may be triggered across a range of conditions, for a given research scenario, those conditions may be greatly restricted. As the details of the models are refined, those conditions can be sharpened. A structured annotation for a transition typically would include: (a) associated objects and case roles [7], (b) necessary conditions (e.g., triggers, input rules), inputs, outputs, and side-effects, (c) purpose, and (d) potential sub-processes and more finely-grained representation.

Claims could be associated with different levels of confidence and include structured annotations for or against internal and external validity. For instance, the researcher might use a "check on the manipulation" to strengthen the case for internal validity. Internal validity errors occur when the researcher's action does not have the intended effect, see Table 2.4 in [18]. This check would compare the intended state of the microworld with its actual observed state following the manipulation. Tables 2.4, 3.1, and 3.2 in [18] can be used as an initial categorization for criticisms of the research.

Software Implementation: We developed a Python implementation for the Hypothesis Model described above. Specifically, for the condition where tilting the flask results in microbe growth. The first step is establishing the microworld and objects such as the flask located in it. These objects are initialized to the states needed for the research. For instance, the flasks are filled with broth, that broth is boiled, and the swan neck on the flask is created. Subregions include parts of the flask such as the flask-body broth, the air in the upper portion of the flask body, and parts of the flask neck. Potentially, spatial partitioning with scene graphs used in computer graphics worlds such as in computer games could be applied as a data structure. Next, the ongoing processes associated with the microworld are initiated. There are air currents that carry the microbes from the external air into the flask neck. However, inside the neck, the air is mostly still; gravity is the dominant force on the microbes so they settle to the floor of the neck [20].

Many of the objects in the simulation are complex; they change state and interact with other objects at different points. To keep track of the current state each object class has its own copy of a Python list of relationships that are replicated down the inheritance tree and updated when there is a state change. As shown below, when a generic flask class is specialized as a glass flask, "we add a tuple that specifies the "madeOf" attribute to the Python list of relationships".

RelList.append([["attribute"],["always"],["madeOf"],["cGlass"],["comment"]])

Hypothesis Models are causal sequences, of events that are triggered by changes in the states of objects in the environment. This suggests programming asynchronous events with declarative programming (cf., [14]). While a declarative program might have been implemented with a blackboard and scheduler or with threading, we used a clock-tick-based rotation through the subregions of the microworld where the current state of the objects is evaluated and updated if the trigger conditions are satisfied. The program runs to completion and generates the expected response for the biogenesis hypothesis under the flask-tilt condition.

4   Discussion and Conclusion

Knowledgebase: While we have focused on individual research reports, we envision digital-library-like collections of reports that could be annotated, indexed, and cross-linked. As suggested in [3], traditional document citations could be replaced by linking claims along with structured justifications for the relevance of the claim links (categories of citations). Moreover, there could be structured review-style documents discussing the reliability (replicability) of the effects, integrating and comparing the claims from multiple studies, and discussing the development of theories based on the studies.

The repository would be associated with a rich ontology and other types of world knowledge. For instance, the rule that "boiling kills microbes" is common knowledge, although if needed it could be derived from principles such as the biochemistry of microbes and the effect of heat and cached in the knowledgebase. In addition, the knowledgebase would also include structured research methods as well specialization and applications.

Summary: Highly structured research reports would have several advantages over traditional text reports. They could provide rich linking and be the basis of text generation and tutoring at varying levels of detail. In addition, interactive interfaces could be developed for exploring the research reports. These interfaces could allow users to get overviews and drill down into details as desired. While models of scientific phenomena are often idealized [22], our models should extend previous approaches by allowing exploration across different levels of granularity.

There are many open questions about how best to structure research reports. We have focused on relatively simple qualitative models but richer quantitative modeling techniques could eventually be incorporated [15]. Model operators will need to be developed for these extensions to the techniques described above.

References

1. Allen, R.B.: Highly structured scientific publications. In: JCDL, pp. 472 (2007). https://doi.org/10.1145/1255175.1255271
2. Allen, R.B.: Model-oriented scientific research reports. D-Lib. Mag. (2011). https://doi.org/10.1045/may2011-allen
3. Allen, R.B.: Supporting structured browsing of research reports (2012). arXiv: 1209.0036
4. Allen, R.B.: Rich linking in a digital library of full-text scientific research reports. In: Columbia University Research Data Symposium (2013), PDF. https://doi.org/10.7916/D8J M2JZ4
5. Allen, R.B.: Rich semantic models and knowledgebases for highly-structured scientific communication (2017). arXiv: 1708.08423
6. Allen, R.B.: Issues for using semantic modeling to represent mechanisms, 2018, arXiv: 1812.11431
7. Allen, R.B.: Yoked flows for direct representation of scientific research. In: Digital Infrastructures for Scholarly Content Objects (DISCO) (2021), CEUR, pp. 2976–2983
8. Bechhofer, S., DeRoure, D., Gamble, M., Goble, C., Buchan, I.: Research objects: towards exchange and reuse of digital knowledge. Nat. Proc. **1** (2010). https://doi.org/10.1038/npre. 2010.4626.1
9. Ben-Menahem, Y: Causation in Science. Princeton University Press (2018)
10. de Roure, D., Goble, C., Stevens, R.: The design and realisation of the MyExperiment virtual research environment for social sharing of workflows. Future Generation Comput. Syst. **25**, 561–567 (2009). https://doi.org/10.1016/j.future.2008.06.010
11. de Waard, A., Kircz, J.: Modeling scientific research articles – Shifting perspectives and persistent issues. In: ELPUB, Conference on Electronic Publishing, Toronto (2008). CiteSeer: 10.1.1.578.6751
12. de Waard, A., Tel, G.: The ABCDE format enabling semantic conference proceedings, SemWiki, Workshop on Semantic Wikis, Budva, Montenegro, CEUR: 206/paper8.pdf (2006)
13. Holland, J., Holyoak, K, Nisbett, R.E., Thagard, P.: Induction: Processes of Inference, Learning, and Discovery. MIT Press (1986)
14. Kuipers, B.J.: Qualitative simulation. Artificial Intell. **29**, 289–338 (1986)
15. Park, M., Fishwick, P.A., Lee, J.: Multimodeling. In: Fishwick, P.A. (ed.) Handbook of Dynamic System Modeling, Chapman, pp. 14.1–14.28 (2007)
16. Pasteur, L.: Sur les corpuscules organisés qui existent dans l'atmosphère: Examen de la doctrine des générations spontanées: Leçon Professée À la Sociéte Chimique de Paris le 19 Mai 1861.

17. Pease, A.: Ontology: A Practical Guide. Articulate (2011)
18. Shadish, W.R., Cook, T.D., Campbell, D.T.: Experimental and Quasi-experiment Designs for Generalized Causal Inference. Houghton, Boston (2002)
19. Shrager, J., Langley, P. (eds.): Computational Models of Scientific Discovery and Theory Formation. Morgan-Kaufmann (1990)
20. Talmy, L.: Force dynamics in language and cognition. In: Talmy, L. (ed.), Toward a Cognitive Semantics. MIT Press, Cambridge (Cambridge)
21. Thagard, P.: Conceptual Revolutions. Princeton University Press (1992)
22. Weisberg, M.: Three kinds of idealization. J. Philos. 639–659 (2007). https://doi.org/10.5840/jphil20071041240

MINE – Workspace as a Service for Text Analysis

Triet Ho Anh Doan[✉][ID], Péter Király[ID], and Sven Bingert[ID]

Gesellschaft für wissenschaftliche Datenverarbeitung mbH Göttingen,
Burckhardtweg 4, 37077 Göttingen, Germany
{triet.doan,peter.kiraly,sven.bingert}@gwdg.de
https://www.gwdg.de

Abstract. This paper introduces the MINE platform, which aims to help scientists overcome the difficulties in data acquisition and text analysis in a large scale. Foremost, MINE provides a search portal, which facilitates the data acquisition process by allowing users to search and download data across multiple repositories. After investigating other state-of-the-art systems on the market at the moment, we realize that they cannot satisfy the complexity of a text analysis workflow. Therefore, a text analysis workspace was created in MINE. This workspace gives users not only a chance to build their own analysis workflows, but also to execute them on a powerful and reliable infrastructure. Although this workspace is a promising feature, there are still some works to be done. However, we strongly believe that it will be released for public use in this year.

Keywords: Text analysis · Workspace · Workflow · Infrastructure

1 Introduction

1.1 Problems

Digital Humanity (DH) is an intersection of digital technologies and the study of humanities [4]. Since the printed work is no longer the main material, the aim of DH is to bring tools and methods to the study of humanities [2]. There are different projects in DH, such as digital archives, cultural analytics, online publishing, and so on. The focus of our work is on text analysis in DH.

There are two problems that we want to solve within our work. The first one is data access. To do text analysis, the very first step is to obtain the data. However, data acquisition is not an easy task for scientists. They need to know where the data is by visiting different websites and using various types of search engines. After the data is found, how can it be downloaded? And even when the data is already at hand by any means, license is also an issue.

The second problem that we recognize is the scale of analyses. From what we observe, many DH scientists are still running their analyses on their local setup. Unlike image or video processing, text analysis has an advantage in data size, since text does not occupy so much space like other media. However, in the era of big data and the rapid increasing in complexity of models, scalability in text analysis is becoming an unavoidable obstacle.

© Springer Nature Switzerland AG 2022
G. Silvello et al. (Eds.): TPDL 2022, LNCS 13541, pp. 328–334, 2022.
https://doi.org/10.1007/978-3-031-16802-4_29

1.2 Our Background

Göttingen University Library, founded in 1734, is one of the five largest libraries in Germany [6]. This means that there is a huge amount of textual data to offer to scientists. However, these data are located in different repositories, such as GDZ [12], GRO [11], and Textgrid [24]. Due to this data scattering, it is challenging for scientists to find and get them.

The second partner in this project is the Gesellschaft für wissenschaftliche Datenverarbeitung mbH Göttingen (GWDG) in Göttingen. GWDG is a data center, which is currently hosting Emmy, the 47th fastest computer in the world and the fastest computer in Northern Germany [7]. Having both data and infrastructure at hand, we develop a platform, called MINE, to facilitate the textual data acquisition and allow scientists to execute their data analysis workflows on our infrastructure.

This paper is structured as follows: Sect. 1 gives an overview of the problems and our background. State of the Art and detailed description of MINE are presented in Sects. 2 and 3 respectively. Finally, Sect. 4 is for the conclusion.

2 State of the Art

2.1 HathiTrust

Founded in 2008 in Michigan, USA, HathiTrust is a "not-for-profit collaborative of academic and research libraries" [16]. It offers access to more than seventeen million digitized items at the moment. From the homepage, users can search for data in the HathiTrust Digital Library using its search engine or browse collections. Additionally, there is an integrated viewer, which allows users to view the digitized items online. As a guest user, one can only download one page at a time. To download the whole book, institutional login is required.

Besides offering data access, HathiTrust also has a platform called HathiTrust Research Center (HTRC), which is a text analysis workspace. Data found in the HathiTrust Digital Library can be analyzed in the HTRC. According to its description [14], there are three featured services in HTRC. The first one is called Extracted Feature. It is a dataset containing metadata and word counts for every page of books in their database. The second service is Text Analysis Algorithms, which is a web-based tool that performs text analysis on chosen dataset. HTRC provides a list of off-the-shelf algorithms for users to select and run so that programming skill is not required. Data Capsules is the third service. By using this service, users can have Ubuntu virtual machines running and access them via either a VNC client or SSH. To be able to use HTRC, one has to log in with an institutional account.

Although HathiTrust is a feature-rich platform with a lot of data, most of its features require institutional login. One cannot register as a single user to get an account, but his or her institute must be a partner with HathiTrust. To obtain the partnership, an institute has to pay annual fee according to their cost model [15]. Besides, most of the work from HathiTrust are in English. Only 8.6%, which is around 800,000 works, are in German [13]. Among them, most have unknown copyright status [1]. Regarding HTRC, users can only choose algorithms offered by the platform. Customization or creating their own algorithms is not well-supported. Lastly, if users want to analyze their own datasets, there is no option to upload data to HTRC.

2.2 IBM Watson, Google Cloud NLP, and Microsoft Azure NLP

For a quick Google search with the term "NLP services", one can find many Natural Language Processing (NLP) services available on the Internet to use. Although these services come from different companies, they have a lot of features in common. We investigate three services from three famous companies: IBM Watson, Google Cloud NLP, and Microsoft Azure NLP.

The very first impression is that they are very easy to start with. Users can simply create an account for free, then they can try out many features of a service. There are various types of text analyses which can be done using these services such as named-entity recognition, sentiment analysis, relationship extraction, and so on [8,17]. Furthermore, it is not only the type of analysis, but the domain is also diversified, ranging from insurance, finance [18], to health care [10,21], and many more. If pre-trained models do not meet users' need, they can upload their own dataset and train a new model.

Although an account can always be created for free, a free account always comes with a lot of limitations. Since the business model used by these services is "pay as you go", resources which are consumed by a free account are limited [9, 19,20]. The resource can be the number of requests, the length of text, or units which are defined by the service owner. Another obstacle of these services for scientists is the ability to customize the models. Despite the fact that users can re-train the models with their own data, it is not possible to fine-tune the models' hyperparameters. Besides, they do not provide any possibility for users to pre-process the data (e.g., data cleaning) on their platform. Since the aim of these services is to provide NLP-as-a-Service, they have high availability, easy to begin with and quick results can be obtained with minimum effort. However, as scientists working in research, they need a platform where they can process their data and fine-tune their models, which these services cannot satisfy.

3   The MINE System

3.1   A Search Portal

To overcome the difficulties in data acquisition mentioned in Sect. 1, a unified search portal was developed in the first phase of the MINE project[1]. The motivation comes from the fact that data of the Göttingen University Library are stored in different repositories, which makes it difficult for scientists to discover and access them. The whole architecture of this portal is illustrated in Fig. 1.

---

[1] https://mine-graph.de/.

There are three main components in this architecture: connector, knowledge extractor, and web server.

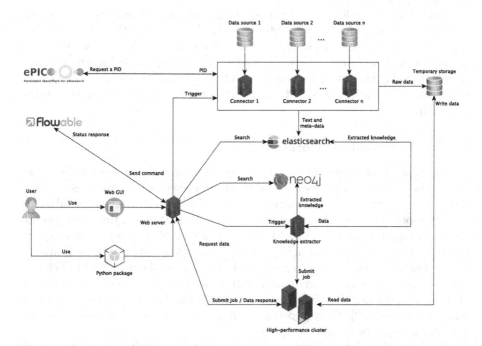

Fig. 1. The architecture of the MINE system. It shows different components of the system and how they interact with each other.

Connectors, as the name suggests, connect data sources with MINE. Since data sources offer their contents in various ways, it is impossible to have only one connector which can handle all sources. For that reason, whenever we want to add a new data source to the system, usually a new connector is built. The tasks of a connector include authenticating against the data source, getting the metadata and raw data, standardizing metadata, requesting Persistent Identifiers (PIDs), indexing data into Elasticsearch, and keeping data up-to-date.

After connectors finished indexing data, the knowledge extractor is triggered. This component is responsible for data analytics. We are currently running different analyses here, ranging from the simple one, like word count, to the more complicated ones, such as Named-Entity Recognition (NER) and topic modelling. The information gained from these analyses does not only give us more insight about our data, but they are also indexed back in Elasticsearch to enhance the search capability. Furthermore, as shown in Figure 1, the information extracted by NER and topic modelling is pushed to Neo4j to create a knowledge graph, which is an added value to the search functionality and data exploration. The connection between the knowledge extractor and the High-Performance Cluster

(HPC) indicates that these analyses might be executed on the HPC. The decision is made by the knowledge extractor depending on the size of the dataset and the type of the analysis.

From the client side, all communication must go through the web server. There are two ways for users to interact with the system, either using the web user interface, or the Python package. Additionally, the web server also plays the role of a coordinator, which can trigger other components by sending commands to them. The command comes from Flowable [5], a workflow management platform. The detailed usage of Flowable in MINE was presented in another paper [3].

3.2   A Data Analysis Workspace

The purpose of this phase is to offer a data analysis workspace as a service. After logging in, users will have the possibility to run either built-in analyses, or their data analysis workflows on our infrastructure. For the first case, some endpoints are developed to provide pre-trained models to users. By using the search portal, users can pipe the search results to the analytic endpoints. Since a search query might return a huge amount of data, these analyses usually take a long time to finish. Therefore, users have to come back later to see the results of the chosen analyses. Regarding the analytic endpoints, to avoid wasting resources by having them up and running the whole time, we take the Function-as-a-Service approach using OpenFaaS [22]. Since a container is spawned when a request comes, no resource is consumed during idle time.

Realizing that data analysis is not only about the analysis itself, but other steps, such as data exploration or pre-processing, also play an important role, MINE offers users an environment to build and execute data analysis workflows. This workspace is mainly built using Orchest [23]. Although it is new on the market, Orchest is a feature-rich open-source program with a large and active community. It is very easy to set up a running instance for testing. However, deploying it as a service is another story, since Orchest itself is quite complicated with many components involved, such as Jupyter Notebook, web UI, or queuing system. To build a data analysis workflow, many steps must be created. Each step is a source code file written in Python, R, Julia or Bash. Users can upload their own code, or create the files directly via Jupyter Notebook integrated in the system. These steps can be connected using the visual workflow editor to form a workflow, as shown in Fig. 2. Additionally, each workflow can have one or many services. A service is a Docker container which starts when the workflow starts and is destroyed when the workflow finishes. This feature proves to be very handy in various use cases. For example, a step in a workflow needs to extract text from PDF using Apache Tika. It would be cumbersome to keep an Apache Tika server running somewhere for this workflow. Instead, a cleaner approach is to use the service feature and have the Apache Tika server run only when the workflow is executed.

A workflow is not a static object. One can create a dynamic workflow by giving it an ability to receive parameters. For example, a user wants to build

Fig. 2. A named-entity recognition workflow in orchest

different models using the same workflow but with different hyperparameters. Another interesting feature is to run a workflow at every fixed time interval, e.g., once a day. This feature is not only useful for users, but we also utilize it to keep our data up-to-date with the data sources. Last but not least, virtual environment for workflows is also supported. The idea is the same as virtual environments for Python projects, but this time is for workflows.

Since there are still some developments need to be done, this Workspace-as-a-Service feature from MINE is currently available for internal use only. Since we already have a Jupyter Notebook running as a service at GWDG, it makes more sense to connect this service to MINE than running another one. One disadvantage of Orchest is that it does not offer authorization at the moment. Therefore, solving this problem is in high priority. Once these two issues are solved, the workspace will be offered for external users as well.

4   Conclusion

As we can see, MINE is a platform which is different from others currently on the market. It does not only offer a search portal, but also a workspace, on which users have the freedom to analyze their data on a powerful infrastructure. Although this workspace feature is not yet available for public use, we strongly believe that this feature will be released in this year. Furthermore, by running the knowledge extraction process on every dataset in MINE, it gives us the insight of the data and at the same time enhance the search capability with every knowledge we learn from our data.

References

1. Behnk, R., Georgi, K., Granzow, R., Atze, L.: Testing the HathiTrust copyright search protocol in germany: a pilot project on procedures and resources. D-lib Mag. **20**(9/10) (2014)
2. Burdick, A., Drucker, J., Lunenfeld, P., Presner, T., Schnapp, J.: Digital_Humanities. MIT Press, Cambridge (2016)
3. Doan, T.H.A., Bingert, S., Yahyapour, R.: Using a workflow management platform in textual data management. Data Intell. **4**(2), 398–408 (2022)
4. Drucker, J., Kim, D., Salehian, I., Bushong, A.: Introduction to Digital Humanities Course Book. Methods, and Tutorials for Students and Instructors, Concepts (2014)

5. Flowable: open source. https://www.flowable.com/open-source/. Accessed 18 July 2022

6. Georg-August-Universität Göttingen - Öffentlichkeitsarbeit: Goettingen State and University Library. https://www.uni-goettingen.de/en/about+the+goettingen+state+and+university+library/56613.html. Accessed 16 May 2022

7. Georg-August-Universität Göttingen - Öffentlichkeitsarbeit: Press release: Northern Germany's fastest computer. https://www.uni-goettingen.de/en/3240.html?id=6091 (2020). Accessed 16 May 2022

8. Google cloud: features. https://cloud.google.com/natural-language#section-6. Accessed 16 May 2022

9. Google cloud: pricing. https://cloud.google.com/natural-language#section-7. Accessed 16 May 2022

10. Google cloud: using the healthcare natural language API. https://cloud.google.com/healthcare-api/docs/how-tos/nlp. Accessed 16 May 2022

11. GRO.publications: Göttingen Research Online Publications. https://publications.goettingen-research-online.de/. Accessed 23 Feb 2022

12. Göttinger Digitalisierungszentrum: Ein Service der SUB Göttingen. https://gdz.sub.uni-goettingen.de/. Accessed 23 Feb 2022

13. HathiTrust: HathiTrust Languages. https://www.hathitrust.org/visualizations_languages. Accessed 16 May 2022

14. HathiTrust: HathiTrust Research Center Analytics. https://analytics.hathitrust.org/. Accessed 16 May 2022

15. HathiTrust: Overview of HathiTrust Cost Model and Annual Fees. https://www.hathitrust.org/Cost. Accessed 16 May 2022

16. HathiTrust: welcome to HathiTrust! https://www.hathitrust.org/about. Accessed 16 May 2022

17. IBM Watson: features. https://www.ibm.com/cloud/watson-natural-language-understanding/details. Accessed 16 May 2022

18. IBM Watson: IBM Watson discovery. https://www.ibm.com/cloud/watson-discovery. Accessed 16 May 2022

19. IBM Watson: pricing. https://www.ibm.com/cloud/watson-natural-language-understanding/pricing. Accessed 16 May 2022

20. Microsoft: cognitive service for language pricing. https://azure.microsoft.com/en-us/pricing/details/cognitive-services/language-service/. Accessed 16 May 2022

21. Microsoft: what is the text analytics for health in azure cognitive service for language? https://docs.microsoft.com/en-us/azure/cognitive-services/language-service/text-analytics-for-health/overview?tabs=ner. Accessed 16 May 2022

22. OpenFaas: serverless functions, made simple. https://www.openfaas.com/. Accessed 18 Jul 2022

23. Orchest: build data pipelines, the easy way. https://www.orchest.io/. Accessed 18 Jul 2022

24. TextGrid: TextGrid. https://textgridrep.org/. Accessed 23 Feb 2022

Conducting the Opera: The Evolution of the RDA Work to the Share-VDE Opus and BIBFRAME Hub

Ian Bigelow(✉) 🆔

University of Alberta, Edmonton, AB, Canada
bigelow@ualberta.ca

Abstract. This paper examines recent developments in the use of Resource Description and Access Work, BIBFRAME Hub, and Share-VDE Opus (referred to collectively as Opera) in bibliographic description. These Opera will be discussed to capture the current state of developments in this area, but also make recommendations for a path forward as we reach a confluence with these parallel developments. With a new version of the Official RDA, and many libraries working towards BIBFRAME implementation this is a good point of reflection, where scientific analysis of conceptions of Opera have been further developed through initiatives at the Library of Congress (LC), and Share-VDE. Past discussions comparing the RDA and BIBFRAME models have focused on compatibility issues, but this paper will attempt at framing the differences as part of a developmental trajectory.

Keywords: BIBFRAME · Bibliographic entities · Cataloguing · FRBR · Library reference model · Linked data · Metadata · Opus · RDA · RDF

1 Introduction

1.1 The Work at Hand

This paper examines recent developments in the use of Resource Description and Access (RDA) Work, bf: Hub, and Share-VDE Opus (referred to collectively as Opera) in bibliographic description. These Opera will be discussed to capture the current state of developments in this area, but also make recommendations for a path forward as we reach a confluence with these parallel developments. With a new version of the Official RDA, and many libraries working towards BIBFRAME implementation this is a good point of reflection, where scientific analysis of conceptions of Opera have been further developed through initiatives at the Library of Congress (LC), and Share-VDE. Past discussions comparing the RDA and BIBFRAME models have focused on compatibility issues, but this paper will attempt at framing the differences as part of a developmental trajectory.

© Springer Nature Switzerland AG 2022
G. Silvello et al. (Eds.): TPDL 2022, LNCS 13541, pp. 335–343, 2022.
https://doi.org/10.1007/978-3-031-16802-4_30

2   Works in Context

As captured by Sally McCallum in *Collocation and Hubs: Fundamental and New Version* (2022):

> Collocation of information items has been a primary purpose of rules for bibliographic descriptions for a very long time …The traditional library collocation is attained by clustering item descriptions by agent names (e.g., authors) and titles – enabling this collocation is a major contribution of the Library cataloger [1].

With the development of FRBR [2] however, the Work, Expression, Manifestation, Item (WEMI) structure present in RDA today emerged [3], and the WEMI stack was further developed with the IFLA Library Reference Model (LRM) in 2017 [4]. The WEMI structure was then incorporated into RDA, with the RDA Work defined as "A distinct intellectual or artistic creation, that is, the intellectual or artistic content." [3] Yet, from the very beginning of RDA in 2010 it was known that an alternative to MARC was needed to support RDA [5–7]. MARC remains flat, resisting the potential for aggregation and clustering for the WEMI stack and based on Opera types. Following closely after RDA though, work on BIBFRAME began in 2011, with a goal of allowing libraries to use RDA beyond MARC.

As outlined by Bigelow and Sparling (2022) [32], modelling choices for RDA and BIBFRAME have raised questions about how one can work with the other [8–16]. In part this was the result of a different approach taken by LC for BIBFRAME early on such that "BIBFRAME took a slightly simplified approach to FRBR and combined work and expression." [1] The outcome from this was the split between the RDA WEMI model and the BIBFRAME Work, Instance, Item (WII) model for some time.

MARC, BIBFRAME, and RDA

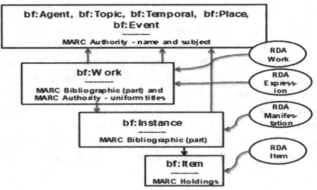

Fig. 1. MARC, BIBFRAME, and RDA (McCallum, Sally, 2017). [17]

This state of differentiation is well summarized by Fig. 1, highlighting the WEMI vs WII models of RDA and BIBFRAME respectively.

From the initial work on BIBFRAME in 2011 to approximately the time of the creation of the diagram in Fig. 1 in 2017 debate needed to largely focus on the theoretical and conceptual models. Continued work in MARC did not support the surfacing of these entities and posed little resistance to the differences in definition.

By the time we come to 2017 though, LC was underway with the first BIBFRAME pilot [18], and also released open tools and specifications for use by the wider community [19]. Similarly, and in relation to this work picked up with the PCC [20] and projects such as LD4P [21] and Share-VDE [22]. Acknowledging and explosion of work at a number of institutions and organizations, focus here will be on LC and Share-VDE given the scale of data conversion and thus refinement in practice.

So, from 2017–2022, work was carried out by dozens of libraries in Share-VDE along with LC, generating 10s of billions of triples/quads of BIBFRAME data (24 billion quads in Share-VDE as of 2019) [23], evaluating and refining data, models, and best practice. What happened here with respect to the RDA and bf: Work is critical to review because in both cases the output for the data model was updated based on working with real world data at scale and adapting theory and modelling to represent what works in practice. In the case of LC the bf: Hub emerged, and for Share-VDE the Opus was created, but what is quite striking is that each of these was developed in parallel and both came to a very close result.

3   New Opera Entities: The Opus and Hub

3.1   Opus

Following initial work on conversion from MARC to BIBFRAME, in 2018 the Share-VDE community identified the need to aggregate like works, and the Share-VDE Opus was created [24].

The Share-VDE Opus is a type of bf: Work [26] and is defined as "an entity that permits the grouping of works that are considered functional or near equivalents. The opus is defined by a constellation of elements that form the shared content of BIBFRAME works." [27].

A more detailed outline of the Opus in the Share-VDE model can be found in the Share-VDE Model Outline [26], but Fig. 2 captures the extension of the BIBFRAME model to include the Opus. In this diagram the Hub has not yet been added, but for Share-VDE the bf: Work remains, with a further layer added for the Opus as a type of bf: Work equivalent to the RDA Work. The bf: Work then takes the place of the RDA Expression, but also includes properties from the RDA Work/Share-VDE Opus. The result is a more complete entity for bf: Work (as opposed to the RDA Expression) to support discovery, while allowing for said bf: Works to be aggregated by the Opus by leveraging shared properties across like bf: Works. This model has been applied within the Share-VDE Portal, and had ongoing user experience testing by the UX/UI Working Group [28] and Share-VDE member libraries [29].

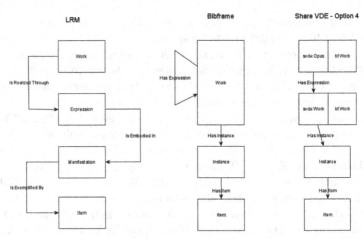

Fig. 2. LRM, BIBFRAME and Share-VDE model comparison. (Ford, Kevin 2020b. [Share-VDE - Option 4]. Created for the Share-VDE Sapientia Entity Identification Working Group) [25]

3.2 Hub

Based on a similar recognition for the need for collocation of bf: Work, LC developed the Hub at approximately the same time as the Share-VDE Opus. Again, the Hub is a type of bf: Work and is defined as "An abstract resource that functions as a bridge between two Works." [30] Sally McCallum provides further context that.

> The expanded hub contains data that would have resided in a MARC title authority. It contains the title variations, author/title labels when there are multiple creators, and cataloger notes that support the hub content. And it has some characteristics of a work description. But it will not contain subject information allocated to the FRBR work, which will remain in the BIBFRAME work description, thus avoiding the merger issue [1].

The result is a set of highly related equivalent models where RDA and WEMI have evolved through BIBFRAME with the Hub (from WII to HWII), and to Share-VDE with the Opus (OWII) [31].

3.3 Opus and Hub

While the similarities of the Opus and Hub are striking, and validating for the RDA Work, there are also key differences to consider. In developing the Opus, Share-VDE utilized differentiation between RDA elements for Work and Expression along with core element sets from LC/PCC to define the boundaries of the Share-VDE Opus and Share-VDE Work [32]. In contrast, the Hub was "Pursued because [they] realized [they] were trying to do too much with bf: Work" [33]. For the Hub the conceptualization focused on being "Intentionally brief. Intentionally abstracted. Designed to ensure they are lightweight and maximally (re)usable" [33].

As a result, despite the similarities there are key differences in processing in the conversion and clustering of data for the Hub and Opus. The Hub for instance, focuses on name/title access point information and equivalent MARC field usage [34], while the Opus tried to map out conversion and clustering based on MARC fields relating to RDA core element sets (Distinctions between Work and Expression) [35, 36]. As interoperability of BIBFRAME data is further tested, this will need to be looked at more closely to determine whether the Hub and Opus should be reconciled, or if the differences should be embraced, but more clearly defined to support interchange and data sharing.

4 Findings

What seems clear though is that theory and conceptual modelling has progressed to research, experimentation, development of best practices, and adaptation of the models outlined with FRBR in 1998. If we look at the progression from the FRBR model to the existing one in Share-VDE as developments in the field rather than incompatibilities then we should consider several key findings.

4.1 RDA Constraints and Conformance

As noted in *Control or Chaos* the emphasis on constrained elements and conformance by RDA creates a barrier to reuse and interchange [32]. This was referenced as a concern early in the development of RDA [37], and has now manifested by the PCC (including LC) not utilizing RDA constrained elements [38]. To provide an example of this for Works, consider a library implementing BIBFRAME in the Share-VDE community. The Opus could be utilized as an equivalent to the RDA Work, but currently this data would be considered non-conformant and present barriers for interchange. Work in the Share-VDE community has shown that BIBFRAME can support RDA as an implementation scenario and that RDA and BIBFRAME can be used in the same data set provided that RDA unconstrained elements are utilized [26]. Utilizing a less constrained approach would both reduce interchange issues from RDA to BIBFRAME, and also support connections to other conceptualizations of the same entities for discovery purposes, as demonstrated by work in Share-VDE with Wikidata [39], and the recent organization for common entity definitions for WEMI in the Dublin Core community (OpenWEMI) [40]. Linked data for libraries should support the connection between digital library collections and enable inferencing, not create further silos.

4.2 Work & Expression vs. Opus & Work

Looking at similarities between Opera, an important remaining difference is in the next level of description or the next entity to relate to the Opus and Hub. With the Opus and Hub, the bf: Work is preserved as an entity (really both are a type of bf: Work), a construct of RDA Work and Expression. This is a result of the expression not making sense as a standalone entity (without utilizing properties from the Work level).

One approach to solving this has been presented by Hahn and Dousa, who suggest the application of a set-theoretical approach to map from bf:Work to RDA Work and

Expression [16]. While an excellent technical solution though, it is also worth reviewing fundamental theory and modelling. If libraries were to repeat the same experimentation and work on data at scale accomplished by LC and Share-VDE with RDA RDF the Expression level would present the same challenges and need redefinition as an equivalent to the bf:Work entity. Movement in this direction is already occurring for RDA with the Representative Expression [42, 43]. This is to say again that the focus here should be less on incompatibilities between RDA and BIBFRAME, and more on updating standards to reflect the nature of these entities when implemented in real world settings. Particularly for Share-VDE, where large volumes of data from varied institutions needed to be brought to a production level, one of the key successes was in identifying the need to cluster and aggregate at the Opus, Work, and instance levels of description. This was functionally important for the data, but also to support dis-covery.

5 Summary and Conclusions

The WEMI model has only recently been tested at scale through work on BIBFRAME implementation. This work on BIBFRAME at LC and Share-VDE has moved our under-standing of the data, and the models themselves forward considerably and supported implementation scenarios for RDA and BIBFRAME. This work has provided crucial updates to conceptual models which should be incorporated into library standards.

Based on these arguments the following actions should be taken: Eliminate con-formance barriers in RDA to support metadata exchange and enhance discovery by supporting connections between myriad data sources; Openly define the Opera (RDA Work, bf: Hub, and Share-VDE Opus) equivalencies and reconcile each as appropriate; Update RDA to include the equivalent to the bf: Work to replace the RDA Expres-sion, and to utilize the Opus in place of the RDA Work; Generally update RDA and IFLA LRM models to reflect the developments of the Opus-Work-Instance-Item model currently being implemented by libraries worldwide with BIBFRAME.

Differentiation is natural in the evolution of a concept and where research confirms how theory should be operationalized there needs to be a feedback loop. While there are issues to overcome, generally we have a development trajectory rather than compatibility problems between RDA and BIBFRAME. I would also argue that LRM and RDA should be revised to recognize the feedback loop from the testing and implementation of said theories with real world data at scale. Action plans for the RSC related to BIBFRAME focus on starting mappings from RDA to BIBFRAME from 2022–2023 [41]. This is important work, but beyond mappings work is required to adapt standards based on current research and development. The Opera need a conductor.

References

1. McCallum, S.H.: Collocation and hubs. fundamental and new version. JLIS.it, Italian J. Libr. Arch. Inf. Sci. **13**(1), 45–52 (2022). https://doi.org/10.4403/jlis.it-12760
2. IFLA Study Group on the Functional Requirements for Bibliographic Records, and Standing Committee of the IFLA Section on Cataloguing. Functional Requirements for Bibliographic Records Final Report. Berlin: De Gruyter (1998). https://doi.org/10.1515/9783110962451

3. RDA: resource description and access. Chicago: American Library Association (2010)
4. Riva, P., Le Bœuf, P, Žumer, M.: IFLA Library Reference Model: a conceptual model for bibliographic information (2017). https://www.ifla.org/files/assets/cataloguing/frbr-lrm/ifla-lrm-august-2017.pdf
5. Samples, J.: Will RDA mean the death of MARC? In: Presentation at the American Library Association Midwinter Meeting, San Diego, CA (2011). https://connect.ala.org/HigherLogic/Sys-tem/DownloadDocumentFile.ashx?DocumentFileKey=0ca55eba-615b-4aa0-aa84-1fba223483d5
6. McGrath, K.: Will RDA kill MARC? In: Presentation at the American Library Association Midwinter Meeting, San Diego, CA (2011). https://pages.uoregon.edu/kelleym/publications/McGrath_Will_RDA_Kill_MARC.pdf
7. Cronin, C.: Will RDA mean the death Of MARC?: the need for transformational change to our metadata infrastructures. In: Presentation at the American Library Association Midwinter Meeting, San Diego, CA (2011). https://www.academia.edu/1679819/Will_RDA_Mean_the_Death_of_MARC_The_Need_for_Transformational_Change_to_our_Metadata_Infrastructures
8. Zapounidou, S., Sfakakis, M., Papatheodorou, C.: Mapping derivative relationships from RDA to BIBFRAME 2. Cat. Classif. Q. 57(5), 278–308 (2019). https://doi.org/10.1080/01639374.2019.1650152
9. Taniguchi, S.: Examining BIBFRAME 2.0 from the viewpoint of RDA metadata schema. Cat. Classif. Q. 55(6), 387– 412 (2017). https://doi.org/10.1080/01639374.2017.1322161
10. Baker, T., Coyle, K., Petiya, S.: Multi-entity models of resource descrip-tion in the semantic web: a comparison of FRBR RDA and BIBFRAME. . Libr. Hi Tech 32(4), 562–582 (2014). https://doi.org/10.1108/LHT-08-2014-0081
11. Guerrini, M., Possemato, T.: From record management to data management: RDA and new application models BIBFRAME, RIMMF, and OliSuite/WeCat. Cat. Classif. Q. 54(3), 179–199 (2016). https://doi.org/10.1080/01639374.2016.1144667
12. Seikel, M., Steele, T.: Comparison of key entities within bibliographic con-ceptual models and implementations: definitions, evolution, and relationships. Libr. Resour. Tech. Serv. 64(2), 62–71 (2020). https://doi.org/10.5860/lrts.64n2.62
13. Taniguchi, S.: Mapping and merging of IFLA library reference model and BIB-FRAME 2.0. Cat. Classif. Q. 56(5–6), 427–454 (2018). https://doi.org/10.1080/01639374.2018
14. El-Sherbini, M.: RDA implementation and the emergence of BIBFRAME. JLIS.It 9(1), 66–82 (2018). https://doi.org/10.4403/jlis.it-12443
15. Zapounidou, S.: Study of library data models in the semantic web environment. Ionian University, Department of Archives, Library Science and Museology PhD Thesis (2020). https://zenodo.org/record/4018523
16. Hahn, J., Dousa, T.M.: Mapping bf: work to lrm: Work and lrm:Expression: Towards a set-theoretical approach. Proc. Assoc. Inf. Sci. Technol. 57(1), 1–3 (2020). https://doi.org/10.1002/pra2.408
17. McCallum, S.H.: Focus for BIBFRAME. In: 2017 European BIBFRAME Workshop. https://wiki.dnb.de/download/attachments/125433008/Denmark-Focus_for_BIBFRAME.pdf
18. Library of Congress. n.d.a. BIBFRAME Training at the Library of Congress. Library of Congress. Last modified October 2020.Accessed 4 June 2022. https://www.loc.gov/catworkshop/bibframe/
19. Library of Congress. n.d.a. BIBFRAME Framework Initiative. Library of Congress. Last modified June 2022, accessed July 22, 2022. https://www.loc.gov/bibframe/
20. Program for Cooperative Cataloging. n.d.a. BIBFRAME and the PCC. Last modified July 2022, Accessed 22 July 2022. https://www.loc.gov/aba/pcc/bibframe/bibframe-and-pcc.html

21. Branan, B., Futornick, M.: n.d.a. Linked data for production: closing the loop (LD4P3). Linked Data for Production. Last modified July 2022. Accessed 22 July 2022. https://wiki. lyrasis.org/display/LD4P3

22. Lionetti, A.: n.d.a. Share-VDE: linked data for libraries. Share-VDE. Last modified February 2022. Accessed 22 July 2022. https://wiki.share-vde.org/wiki/Main_Page

23. Share-VDE. Share-VDE major achievements in 2019 (2019). https://drive.google.com/drive/ search?q=share%20vde%20major%20achievements

24. Samples, J., Bigelow, I.: MARC to BIBFRAME: converting the PCC to linked data. Cat. Classif. Q. **58**(3/4), 403–417 (2020). https://doi.org/10.1080/01639374.2020.1751764

25. Ford, K.: Share-VDE - Option 4. Share-VDE Sapientia Entity Identification Working Group (2020)

26. Hahn, J., Bigelow, I., Possemato, T.: Share-VDE model overview. In: Share-VDE Virtual Workshop (2021). https://docs.google.com/presentation/d/116PwHecnqooEjW3c4Eks 77Ah6RilpiOpAfCe61K4UoI/edit#slide=id.gbfe20d43fa_0_0

27. Bigelow, I.: Modus operandi: creating the superwork in share-VDE and the opus level of description. In: ALA MidWinter ALCTS Bibliographic Conceptual Models Interest Group, Philadelphia, PA, 26 January 2020. https://connect.ala.org/HigherLogic/System/DownloadD ocumentFile.ashx?DocumentFileKey=17ecd7b2-6867-2732-56e3-f03ac3d7c43c&forceD ialog=0

28. Lionetti, A.: n.d.a. Share-VDE and Share Family working groups outline. Share-VDE. Last modified June 2022. Accessed 22 July 2022. https://wiki.share-vde.org/wiki/ShareVDE: Members/Share-VDE_working_groups#SVDE-AC_User_Experience.2FUser_Interface_ working_group_.28UX-UI.29

29. Hahn, J., Camden, B., Ahnberg, K.A: Comparative evaluation of linked data discovery in the Share-VDE 2.0 catalog. ALA Annual Conference, Washington DC, 25 June 2022. https:// wiki.share-vde.org/w/images/c/ce/Penn_SVDE_Evaluation_Presentation_2022-06-25.pdf

30. Library of Congress. n.d.a. BIBFRAME List View: Hub. Library of Congress. last modified n.d.a. Accessed 4 June 2022. https://id.loc.gov/ontologies/bibframe.html#c_Hub

31. Share-VDE. IFLA-LRM vs. BIBFRAME vs. Share-VDE: Comparison between entity models (2019). https://docs.google.com/presentation/d/15NQUC1lGLZ56S136IHkeeZBkgSiGZ 2U9gPcBArR_bJg/edit#slide=id.g419a8327d6_0_0

32. Bigelow, I., Sparling, A.: Control or chaos: embracing change and harnessing innovation in an ecosystem of shared bibliographic data. JLIS.It **13**(1), 67–85 (2022). https://doi.org/10. 4403/jlis.it-12735

33. Ford, K.: On Bibframe Hubs. In: Presentation at the American Library Association Mid-winter Meeting, Philadelphia, PA (2020). https://wiki.share-vde.org/w/images/7/7b/ALA2020_M idwinter_BCMIG_On_BIBFRAME_Hubs.pdf

34. Library of Congress. lcnetdev/marc2bibframe2: Hub. Accessed 4 June 2022. https://github. com/lcnetdev/marc2bibframe2/search?p=2&q=Hub&type=code

35. BIBCO Mapping BSR to BIBFRAME 2.0 Group. Final Report to the PCC Oversight Group (2017). https://www.loc.gov/aba/pcc/bibframe/TaskGroups/BSR-PDF/FinalReportB IBCO-BIBFRAME-TG.pdf

36. Balster, K., Rendall, R., Shrader, T.: Linked serial data: mapping the CONSER standard record to BIBFRAME. Cat. Classif. Q. **56**(2–3), 251–261 (2018). https://doi.org/10.1080/ 01639374.2017.1364316

37. Danskin, A.: Linked and open data: rda and bibliographic control. JLIS. It **4**(1), 147–160 (2013). https://doi.org/10.4403/jlis.it-5463

38. Program for Cooperative Cataloging Policy Committee. PCC's Position Statement on RDA (2019). https://www.loc.gov/aba/pcc/rda/PCC%20RDA%20guidelines/PCC-Position-Statement-on-RDA.docx

39. Camden, B., Danskin, A., Sparling, A., Delle Donne, R. The Share Family: one project, many tenants. LD4 Conference 2022, 15 July 2022. https://wiki.share-vde.org/w/images/d/d5/The_ Share_Family%E2%80%94One_Project%2C_Many_Tenants.pdf

40. Coyl, K.: n.d.a. OpenWEMI. Dublin Core Metadata Initiative. Last modified July 19 2022. Accessed 22 July 2022. https://www.dublincore.org/groups/openwemi/

41. Andresen, L.: BIBFRAME: Report from the European BIBFRAME Meeting. In: EURIG – Members' Business Meeting (2022). http://www.rda-rsc.org/sites/all/files/BIBFRAME.pdf

42. Lorimer, N.: RDA works in BIBFRAME & sinopia profiles. In: BIBFRAME Workshop in Europe Conference, Stockholm, Sweden, 17 Sept 2019. https://www.kb.se/download/18.d0e 4d5b16cd18f600eac7/1569246613471/BF%20RDA%20Works.pdf

43. Glennan, K.: Representative expressions. In: RDA Preconference: RDA Toolkit Redesign Up-date and Preview, ALA Midwinter Conference, Denver, Colorado, 9 Feb 2018. http:// www.rda-rsc.org/sites/all/files/representative%20expressions.pdf

PH-Remix Prototype

A Non Relational Approach for Exploring AI-Generated Content in Audiovisual Archives

Chiara Mannari[1], Davide Italo Serramazza[2]([✉]), and Enrica Salvatori[3]

[1] Dipartimento di Filologia, Letteratura e Linguistica, Università di Pisa, Pisa, Italy
chiara.mannari@fileli.unipi.it
[2] Dipartimento di Informatica, Università di Pisa, Pisa, Italy
davide.serramazza@fileli.unipi.it
[3] Dipartimento di Civiltà e Forme del Sapere, Università di Pisa, Pisa, Italy
enrica.salvatori@unipi.it

Abstract. Born in the complex and interdisciplinary scenario of digital culture, PH-Remix is a prototype of a web platform granting access and reuse of a vast amount of clips extracted from videos through AI techniques. The paper focuses both on the contribution of AI with the use of multiple machine learning algorithms specialized in the extraction of information from videos and on the possibilities derived from the use of a NoSQL database that plays a key role in the microservices architecture developed.

Keywords: Multimedia archive · Non relational database · Machine learning · Video remix · Public history · Film heritage

1 Introduction

PH-Remix is a prototype platform[1] based on artificial intelligence developed in the context of a two year research project led by the Laboratory of Digital Culture of the University of Pisa, in collaboration with Festival dei Popoli (FdP), Mediateca Toscana and Fondazione Sistema Toscana. The platform enables the uploading, cataloguing, search, consultation, extraction and remix [2,11,12] of primary filmic sources. A search engine provides access to a vast index of clips extracted from the documentaries of FdP archive and a video editor allows final users to preview them and create video remixes. The platform is conceived as a tool for public history [13] and can be useful for both academics and public. It aims to help archives and other institutions devoted to video preservation to enhance the cataloging of their film heritage and promote it through the study of history and new collaborative ways to make history with the public [3].

The FdP documentary archive is the case study for the development of the prototype. The data management is based both on traditional cataloguing techniques, assigning standard metadata to the films, and on the use of AI techniques

---

[1] Public History remix 2020–2022. http://www.labcd.unipi.it/ph-remix.

© Springer Nature Switzerland AG 2022
G. Silvello et al. (Eds.): TPDL 2022, LNCS 13541, pp. 344–350, 2022.
https://doi.org/10.1007/978-3-031-16802-4_31

to automatically extract the clips, i.e. significant video segments with different duration. For the development of the prototype a sample consisting of 400 films (about 400 h of contents) was selected extracting more than 1 million of clips through AI processors.

The aim of the project PH-Remix is to design and develop a first prototype for exploring the possibilities that arise from the introduction of AI and remix practice in audiovisual archives. In expectation of future works with the objective to host the whole FdP archive and other collections, a flexible structure capable of supporting large amount of data has been developed. In the following chapters the technical solutions behind the project are presented focusing on the non relational approach experimented for data management and the microservices software architecture as possible alternatives to monolithic software and relational databases [1,7].

2   Platform Architecture and Database

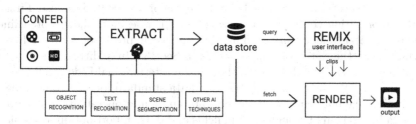

Fig. 1. Platform architecture based on microservices: the box *Other AI techniques* refers to the ease of adding other processors thanks to the architecture adopted

The architecture of the platform is shown in Fig. 1: it is made up of several microservice components, connected each other through rest APIs. The main components are:

- Confer: a web platform allowing to upload new films to be analysed and to insert the related metadata;
- Extract: once a video is uploaded, the extractor is in charge of its analysis: it calls different machine learning algorithms extracting *clips*, i.e. sub-segments of the whole video. They aim to detect specific features in the video portion and isolate them (more information about these algorithms are in Sect. 3). We later refer to these algorithms as *processors*. Once the algorithms terminate their job, the Extract module collects the information about the extracted clips and stores them in the data store;
- Data store: the database of the platform described later in this section;
- Remix: a web application in which users can query *clips*, remix them and watch a preview of the built remix. It is described in Sect. 4;

– Render: once a user is satisfied of their creation, they can request the final remix which is a video file made up of an intro, the remix itself, credits about the films from which the used clips were extracted from and an outro.

In this platform a key component is the *Data store* since each other components either store or read data from it. More in detail it is a MongoDB database, thus a NoSQL one, containing the following collections:

– Users: it stores the list of users allowed to upload films to the platform;
– Video: in this collection the metadata of the uploaded videos are stored, e.g. bit rates, aspects, audio/video codecs, etc.
– Films: it contains information about the same video present in the previous collection. In this case the information concerns the artwork as for instance title, director, nationality, production, etc.
– Segments: a collection containing information about the extracted clips from the uploaded videos. Each element contains a reference to the video which it was extracted from, the starting point and the duration of the clip, the detected information from the machine learning algorithms, etc.

There are several motivations behind the use of a NoSQL database. First of all, the information contained in these collections does not follow a predefined schema: the items in *Segments* differ because each processor stores different information in the database (more details in Sect. 3). In addition, the items in *Films* collection may be different: although the International Federation of Film Archives (FIAF)[2] was adopted as the metadata standard for the cataloguing of FdP archive, the platform was designed to promote interoperability and support any metadata schema through custom fields and data import option available in the back-end. The policy adopted was to add as much metadata as possible in order to perform a full text search across the whole index of clips, in a way similar to search engines (more detail in Sect. 4). Other motivations are the higher performances in retrieving documents that a NoSQL database can guarantee [6,9] and lastly, the way in which the data are stored in a NoSQL database, namely key-value pairs, i.e. the data structure required from the rest API.

3   Use of Artificial Intelligence

In this section the three *processors* developed so far will be described.

The first one, *Object recognition* relies on *RetinaNet* [10] to perform predictions on the frames making up a film. The adopted version uses as backbone *ResNet152* [4] trained using the *Open Images* dataset [8], arguably the one with the highest number and wider diversity of target classes. The developed processor uses the predictions made on consecutive frames to compose a segment lasting from the first time to the last time in which an object O is detected. In addition to the common information listed in Sect. 2, this processor stores in the

---

[2] https://www.fiafnet.org/images/tinyUpload/E-Resources/Commission-And-PIP-Resources/CDC-resources/20160920%20Fiaf%20Manual-WEB.pdf.

data store the information about the detected object along with the rectangle coordinates surrounding the detected object and the related confidences. This score is used for sorting the results in decreasing order: the score of a segment of this processor is the average of the single predictions score. A future development of the platform will be to have similar scores $s \in [0,1]$ also for the other two processors in order to have results fully sorted according to this metadata.

The second processor *Text Recognition*, also analyses all the Film frames. It relies on the concatenation of two algorithms: EAST [17] which detects the frame portions in which text is present and the popular utility *Tesseract* to retrieve the texts from these areas. This processor aims to analyse just the subtitles that were impressed in the film frames thus it processes only the lower half of the frames. To build a segment starting from the single frame predictions a similarity score among the text extracted from the frame f_i and the frame f_{i+1} is used: if the Normalized *Levenshtein distance* [16] falls under the value 0.5, i.e. the two sets of characters share less than 50% of the elements, the subtitles are considered to be different. The beginning and ending times of a segment are the ones corresponding to the first and the last time a subtitle s is shown. The label in this case is the extracted subtitle.

A future development will be to take into account other information present in these segments to evolve the platform with a semantic approach. They contain results of a master thesis which aimed at analysing the extracted transcripts applying NLP algorithms on them. Some examples are keep only relevant items (eliminating the stop words), lemmatization or detecting Named Entity.

The last processor *Scene Segmentation* is based on *Trans Net v2* [14]. Differently from the previous two, this processor works directly on the video rather than on the frames composing it. It analyses the video and detects the shots within it, labeling them with their dominant colour.

The labels that are assigned at each segment from the different processors are used in the remix platform to search for segments, fitting the users needs to build their own remix. In order to allow users to perform queries in different languages, the segments generated from the first and third processors contain in the labels also the wikidata entry [15] related to the detected object/colour.

4   Remix Platform

The platform architecture and the extraction processes described above have been designed with the aim to support the access of final users to the remix service: the front-end application for video remix.

Represented in Fig. 2, the remix tool is a single page application with a rich user interface divided into three areas:

- an area at the top right corner of the screen for searching and browsing clips;
- a video editor at the bottom to remix clips and perform basic video editing operations through drag and drop. This area includes also a button for launching the server side task to export remixes in the final mp4 format;
- a video player at the top left for the local preview of single clips and remixes.

Fig. 2. Remix application

The core of the remix application is the search engine of clips that is still in an early version. Through the interaction with a simple text field it is possible to build queries at different level of complexity, then send the request to the server through the search API (as illustrated in Fig. 1). The query is processed by a server side script in NodeJS which performs searches in the MongoDB database.

In simple searches the algorithm queries directly in the collection of clips performing a proximity search (i.e. the result may be the exact string, a substring or a similar string according to MongoDB text search). Clips to be returned are subsequently ordered following criteria similar to search engines and IR models: first are provided results more similar to the value searched, then are returned the more different. The score associated to the clips extracted by the object detection processor (see Sect. 3) is particularly relevant for ordering such clips.

On the other hand, in complex searches users can use filters to narrow the search to particular films with specific values. This kind of search is developed both at client and at server side. At client side, a query-text component provides a list of suggestions that appear when the user types in a prefix. Prefixes used in the prototype refer to common entities that are of interest to the users: people, places, film titles and countries of production. Results originate from an index generated from the extraction of single or multiple field values in the collection Films of the data store. As shown in Fig. 3, by typing "@" followed by at least three characters, the prefix for people is activated and a list of names which aggregates values from multiple fields of the collection Films appears. These fields store person entities, e.g. film director, producers, technicians, staff members but also anthroponyms, i.e. people or characters mentioned in the film's plot. When the server receives a request for a filtered search, the script performs a two-level search in the MongoDB database. First, the films matching the specified criteria are selected, then the query is limited only on these films. As described in Sect. 2, the reference that each segment has to the film which it was extracted from is essential both for this kind of search and for the Render microservice that generates credits for the films used in the current remix.

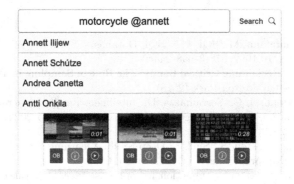

Fig. 3. Advanced search with filter for people active

The search could be further improved developing an extended query language and a more complex IR system to facilitate users in their searches. The structure of the collections in the database supports extensions such as language independent searches based on wikidata, entity based searches or a system to manage licenses for copyrighted materials. Eventually, the use of a NoSQL database to manage archival data stimulates additional evaluations on the use of different approaches to explore catalogues. The full-text search based on entities and autocompletion proper of IR systems is a user friendly solution spread over the internet thanks to search engines and social networks [5] and future tests could contribute to the evaluation of this approach as an alternative solution to the traditional grid interfaces provided by catalogues based on relational databases.

5   Conclusions

The microservice architecture facilitates the evolution of the platform through the improvement of existing modules and the development of new ones. The FdP archive is the case study for the development of the prototype but in a future more archives could be added to the platform. As described in the previous sections, the flexibility of the NoSQL database and the APIs developed allow to easily add new contents coming from different archives. The support of different schemas promotes interoperability between archives and the platform.

The availability of a tool capable to perform searches within large quantities of data provided both by machine learning algorithms and by human cataloguing leads the way to new approaches for the exploration of audiovisual cultural heritage. The prototype developed is now an essential tool for directly evaluating the possibilities offered by the information extraction from videos by AI.

Automatic video analysis and segmentation is particularly challenging nowadays with the huge amount of data produced and spread through the internet. For this reason, PH-Remix platform, including searchable index of clips and editor for video remix aims to be an innovative tool to be experimented in different scenarios: research, dissemination of cultural heritage, users engagement.

References

1. Meier, A., Kaufmann, M.: SQL & NoSQL Databases. Springer, Wiesbaden (2019). https://doi.org/10.1007/978-3-658-24549-8
2. Gallagher, O.: Reclaiming Critical Remix: The Role of Sampling in Transformative Works. Routledge, Milton Park (2018)
3. Grasso, G., Mannari, C., Serramazza, D.: Intelligenza artificiale e archivi audiovisivi: potenzialità e sfide del progetto "ph-remix". In: AIUCD 2022 - Proceedings, pp. 141–144 (2022)
4. He, K., Zhang, X., Ren, S., Sun, J.: Deep residual learning for image recognition. arxiv 2015. arXiv preprint arXiv:1512.03385 (2015)
5. Hu, S.: Efficient text autocompletion for online services. In: Takeda, K., Ide, I., Muhandiki, V. (eds.) Frontiers of Digital Transformation: Applications of the Real-World Data Circulation Paradigm, pp. 171–185. Springer, Singapore (2021). https://doi.org/10.1007/978-981-15-1358-9_11
6. Jose, B., Abraham, S.: Performance analysis of NoSQL and relational databases with MongoDB and MySQL. Mater. Today: Proc. **24**, 2036–2043 (2020)
7. Kalske, M., Mäkitalo, N., Mikkonen, T.: Challenges when moving from monolith to microservice architecture. In: Garrigós, I., Wimmer, M. (eds.) Current Trends in Web Engineering, pp. 32–47. Springer International Publishing, Cham (2018)
8. Kuznetsova, A., et al.: The open images dataset v4. Int. J. Comput. Vis. **128**(7), 1956–1981 (2020)
9. Li, Y., Manoharan, S.: A performance comparison of SQL and NoSQL databases. In: 2013 IEEE Pacific Rim Conference on Communications, Computers and Signal Processing (PACRIM), pp. 15–19. IEEE (2013)
10. Lin, T.Y., Goyal, P., Girshick, R., He, K., Dollár, P.: Focal loss for dense object detection. In: Proceedings of the IEEE International Conference on Computer Vision, pp. 2980–2988 (2017)
11. Navas, E.: Remix Theory. The Aesthetics of Sampling. Springer, Heidelberg (2012). https://doi.org/10.1007/978-3-7091-1263-2
12. Navas, E., Gallagher, O., Burrough, X.: The Routledge Handbook of Remix Studies and Digital Humanities. Routledge, Milton Park (2021)
13. Salvatori, E.: Digital (public) history: the new road of an ancient discipline. RiMe - Rivista dell'Istituto di Storia dell'Europa Mediterranea **1**(1), 57–94 (2017)
14. Souček, T., Lokoč, J.: Transnet v2: an effective deep network architecture for fast shot transition detection. arXiv preprint arXiv:2008.04838 (2020)
15. Vrandečić, D., Krötzsch, M.: Wikidata: a free collaborative knowledgebase. Commun. ACM **57**(10), 78–85 (2014)
16. Yujian, L., Bo, L.: A normalized levenshtein distance metric. IEEE Trans. Pattern Anal. Mach. Intell. **29**(6), 1091–1095 (2007)
17. Zhou, X., et al.: East: an efficient and accurate scene text detector. In: Proceedings of the IEEE Conference on Computer Vision and Pattern Recognition, pp. 5551–5560 (2017)

The SSH Data Citation Service, A Tool to Explore and Collect Citation Metadata

Cesare Concordia[1]([✉]) [ID], Nicolas Larrousse[2] [ID], and Edward Gray[2] [ID]

[1] Institute of Information Science and Technology – CNR, Pisa, Italy
cesare.concordia@isti.cnr.it
[2] Huma-Num CNRS, Paris, France
{nicolas.larrousse,edward.gray}@huma-num.fr

Abstract. This paper presents the SSH Data Citation Service (DCS), a software tool that provides functionalities to find, collect and analyse metadata related to digital objects, in particular datasets, referred to in citation strings. Starting from the citation string of a dataset, the DCS aggregates metadata related to the data from different sources: the repository hosting the dataset, PID Registration Agencies and Knowledge Graphs and gives a unified view of information about datasets coming from these sources. The DCS has been designed and developed in the Social Sciences & Humanities Open Cloud (SSHOC) project. It has been used in a project activity as a tool to help investigate approaches adopted for data citation by Social Sciences and Humanities organisations managing data repositories, and as an utility to help data managers to create citation metadata. The paper presents motivations underlying the creation of the tool, the design principles adopted, an overall description of the functionalities of the current release and a summary of ongoing activities.

Keywords: Data citation · Social Sciences and Humanities · Data repositories and archives

1 Introduction

This paper presents a software tool, designed and developed in the Social Sciences & Humanities Open Cloud (SSHOC) project[1], that finds, collects and analyses metadata related to a data citation string. One of the activities carried out in the SSHOC project has been to investigate approaches adopted by organisations and research groups publishing data in the Social Science and Humanities (SSH) domains, to implement standards and recommendations on data citation. The investigation started by making an inventory of citation practices and analysing the approaches followed by main communities in SSH domains. The result of this phase is described in detail in Deliverable 3.2 of the project[2], essentially in the communities investigated, practices were seldom standardised and were very diverse. The second part of the activity has been to define a set

---

[1] https://sshopencloud.eu.
[2] https://doi.org/10.5281/zenodo.4436736.

© Springer Nature Switzerland AG 2022
G. Silvello et al. (Eds.): TPDL 2022, LNCS 13541, pp. 351–356, 2022.
https://doi.org/10.1007/978-3-031-16802-4_32

of recommendations[3] to build citations for SSH data, based on principles defined by Force11 [7]. These recommendations have been discussed and validated by a committee of experts during several internal events and in a public round table[4]. The final part of this activity has been to analyse 85 repositories identified during the project, to check which of the defined recommendations are implemented by each of them, results of this survey[5] are encouraging - even if there is room for improvement, particularly in the use of Persistent Identifiers (PID). The SSH Data Citation Service (DCS) is a software tool developed during this activity. Starting from the citation string of a dataset, the DCS aggregates related metadata from different sources: the repository hosting the dataset, PID Registration Agencies[6] and a number of Knowledge Graphs. Thus the DCS gives a unified view of metadata related to datasets coming from different sources. It provides some functionalities to analyse the metadata, in particular actionability and interoperability metadata. This paper presents main motivations underlying the creation of the tool, the design principles adopted and an overall description of its functionalities. At the time when this paper is written a prototype of the DCS is published and activities are in progress to release a stable version.

2 The Citation Metadata

The great heterogeneity of scientific data, and the variety of data management systems adopted to publish it, has outlined the importance of creating specific practices and guidelines for 'data citation' [1]. There are several recommendations and best practices that describe the information that a citation string should include, typically the citation should identify the data source, the authors, the publisher, the terms of use of data etc. According to FORCE11 principles [7], data citations should [also] facilitate access to the data themselves and to associated metadata, documentation, code, and other materials, as are necessary for both humans and machines to make informed use of the referenced data. We can say that the role of data citation does not end with the ability to attribute credits, just as important is the ability to enable the reuse of the cited data. However the information needed to reuse data [2, 5], especially those needed by automatic agents, are not present in the citation string (which typically includes information to attribute the data); this information is usually published in metadata records associated with the data. This is due to the changeability and the impermanence of digital data: a dataset could be migrated to new formats and stored in a different management system, data in a repository may be deleted, completely or partly, for instance due to modification in licences. Furthermore, datasets having complex structures could require a reorganisation that may affect this information. There is a need to ensure that a citation remains consistent despite these potential changes: the use of a PID Persistent Identifier (PID) could be a first step but it's not enough. The set of metadata associated with a dataset is defined in the data management and stewardship plan adopted by a publisher; there are good practices and guidelines for creating these plans, however there are several

---

[3] https://doi.org/10.5281/zenodo.5361717.

[4] https://www.sshopencloud.eu/news/roundtable-experts-data-citation.

[5] https://doi.org/10.5281/zenodo.5603306.

[6] https://pidservices.org/.

different metadata models (in some cases domain specific) and the metadata published may not contain enough information to facilitate the access to the data. The SSH Data Citation Service has been designed to help investigate this specific aspect of the data citation in SSH domains: it enables researchers to discover, collect and analyse the meta-data associated with published datasets and it may help to *enrich* the citation with the metadata records collected.

3 The SSH Data Citation Service

The SSH Data Citation Service is a software tool designed and developed to retrieve and analyse metadata related to the digital object referred in a citation string, the collected metadata may be visualised in a web based GUI, stored as JSON objects and possibly processed by software agents. The DCS is designed according to the classical client server architecture: the backend implements the discovering, the management and the persistence of metadata, the client, called Citation Metadata Viewer, shows the metadata and provide actionability functionalities; a REST API implements the interaction protocol between client and server components, and can also be used also as the integration layer with third party systems and agents. The connection of the DCS with an Authentication, Authorization, and Accounting Infrastructure (AAAI) is not yet completely implemented; currently a token authentication mechanism is used. Web based technologies have been used for the implementation: Angular JS framework for the frontend, Java language and technology framework for the backend, the source code of the DCS current release is available.

3.1 Getting the Metadata

The DCS uses the data citation infrastructure [4] to retrieve metadata related to a dataset. The data citation infrastructure is the technological infrastructure that implements referring to data in a unique and persistent manner, it is built upon existing scholar infrastructures and provides functionalities for not just referring to data, but also to making data reusable [3]. Technically speaking it is an heterogeneous infrastructure whose key components are servers resolving identifiers of digital objects and frameworks managing repositories. The citation metadata are published by the components of this infrastructure, however mechanisms and protocols to retrieve this information are very diverse and depend on the components used to publish them. The DCS uses the citation string to find the metadata; it parses the string, extracts the identifier, and retrieve the metadata using different mechanisms:

- **Getting metadata from PID Registration Agencies (RA).** The PID RAs are crucial components of the citation infrastructure, their role is to provide services that enable organisations to create a Persistent ID for digital objects and to implement the association of the PID with the link of the digital object. Some of the RAs, in particular those managing Digital Object Identifiers (DOI), also provide services for hosting and publishing metadata describing digital objects; these metadata are created by organisations when registering persistent identifiers for their digital objects. The metadata models provided for datasets usually include many of the information required to access the data. If the identifier of the data is a DOI the DCS try to retrieve metadata using RA API[7] and or content negotiation[8].

- **Getting metadata from landing pages**. The DCS checks if the identifier refers to a web page, web pages linked by identifiers contained in citations are called landing pages. They are human readable documents describing the cited resource, that also provide links and information for accessing the actual data. This information may also be present in the landing page as machine readable metadata; the DCS parses the source code of landing pages to extract the metadata.
- **Getting metadata using repositories API**. Many repositories provide an API to access the data, the DCS in these cases try to extract metadata using the API. To do this it uses information stored in the R3Data registry[9]. The R3Data registry contain information about repositories and, if the repository provides API, this information includes the type of the API provided and the API entry string. The DCS identifies the repository by dereferencing the identifier; if the repository is registered in R3Data and has an API, the DCS uses the API to try to obtain metadata. Currently it is implemented for the OAI-PMH API.
- **Getting metadata from knowledge graphs**. A Knowledge Graph (KG) is a collection of research objects interlinked by semantic relationships. A number of knowledge graphs containing information about SSH datasets exist, among there: the FREYA PID graph[10], the ResearchGraph built by the ResearchGraph Foundation[11], the Research Graph built in OpenAIRE[12]. The KGs do not merely contain bibliographic metadata, they also provide semantic descriptions of scholarly knowledge in the form of actionable statements. The semantic statements and their models may be defined by computational logic-based ontology languages. Knowledge graphs may contain significant information to help implement data citation accessibility and an activity is in progress to implement a module in the DCS to extract metadata from KGs (Fig. 1).

The metadata collected by the DCS is shown to a user by the Citation Metadata Viewer and can be stored locally as a JSON object.

3.2 Data Citation and Machine Actionability

The machine actionable citation metadata is the subset of the metadata that may enable a software agent to automatically identify the structure of the cited data and in some cases process it. The DCS provides a functionality to individuate this kind of information in the collected metadata and to enrich the metadata with information that could be used

---

[7] Crossref: https://github.com/CrossRef/rest-api-doc, DataCite: https://support.datacite.org/reference/introduction, mEDRA: https://api.medra.org/, EIDR: https://www.eidr.org/technical-documentation/.

[8] https://data.datacite.org/, http://data.medra.org/.

[9] https://www.re3data.org/.

[10] https://www.project-freya.eu/en/pid-graph/the-pid-graph.

[11] https://researchgraph.org/.

[12] https://graph.openaire.eu/.

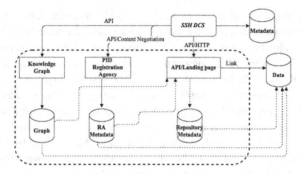

Fig. 1. DCS and citation infrastructure

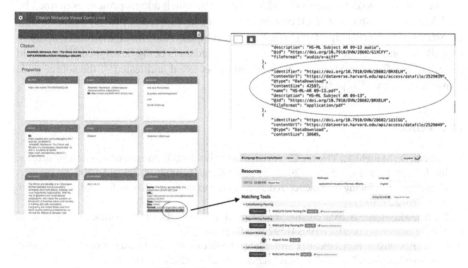

Fig. 2. Citation metadata viewer

by an automatic agent. An example of this functionality is shown in Fig. 2: the metadata associated to the dataset referred by an identifier includes metadata values that can be used for actionability. The DCS recognizes it and the Citation Metadata Viewer displays a button that activates an external application to process the data. In this example the external application is the CLARIN Language Resource Switchboard[13] (LRS), a tool registry that identifies and presents in a GUI a set of tools that can process a resource; by clicking on the button of the Citation Metadata Viewer the data is automatically uploaded on the LRS and eventually processed by the selected tool.

4 Conclusions and Ongoing Activities

The SSH Data Citation Service has been built within the SSHOC project to support investigating the data citation approaches adopted in SSH domains. The DCS provides

---

[13] https://switchboard.clarin.eu.

functionalities to discover, analyse and render data citation metadata, i.e. the metadata used to describe dataset referred in a citation, in particular the metadata enabling access and reuse of data. It has been designed and developed from scratch and is composed of two main parts: the Citation Metadata Viewer that implements the visualisation logic, and the back end that implements the business logic and the persistence layer. A prototype of DCS has been presented in a number of public events[14], during these events many suggestions and remarks have been collected about its functionalities and possible improvements. The current activity of the DCS development team is mainly focused on integrating an AAAI and on building a stable release of the tool. An investigation is in place to verify the possibility to extend the DCS software modules that implements the machine actionability of citation metadata to interoperate with the technical solutions created inside two interesting SSH projects: an implementation of CMDI-based Signposting [6], and the "Digital Object Gateway"[15] (DOG) project, which adopts principles defined by the FAIR Digital Objects (FDO) community[16]. Furthermore, a SPARQL-based module to interact with Knowledge Graphs is being developed. Additionally, a functionality to partially automate error detection in collected metadata is being developed. The current release of the Citation Metadata Viewer can be accessed and tested[17], the source code is available in a GIT repository[18].

References

1. Castelli, D., Manghi, P., Thanos, C.: A vision towards scientific communication infrastructures. Int. J. Digit. Libr. **13**, 155–169 (2013). https://doi.org/10.1007/s00799-013-0106-7
2. Hourclé, J.: Advancing the practice of data citation: a to-do list. Bull. Am. Soc. Inf. Sci. Technol. **38**(5), 20–22 (2012)
3. Fenner, M., et al.: A data citation roadmap for scholarly data repositories. Sci. Data **6**, 28 (2019). https://doi.org/10.1038/s41597-019-0031-8
4. Groth, P., Cousijn, H., Clark, T.: Carole Goble; FAIR data reuse – the path through data citation. Data Intell. **2**(1–2), 78–86 (2020). https://doi.org/10.1162/dint_a_00030
5. Silvello, G.: Theory and practice of data citation. J. Assoc. Inf. Sci. Technol. **69**(1), 6–20 (2018). https://doi.org/10.1002/asi.23917
6. Arnold, D., Fisseni, B., Trippel, T. Signposts for CLARIN. In: Selected Papers from the CLARIN Annual Conference 2020 (2021). https://doi.org/10.3384/ecp1803
7. Data Citation Synthesis Group: Joint Declaration of Data Citation Principles. In: Martone, M. (ed.) FORCE11, San Diego CA (2014) https://doi.org/10.25490/a97f-egyk

---

[14] https://www.sshopencloud.eu/events/fair-ssh-data-citation-practical-guide.

[15] https://www.clarin.eu/sites/default/files/20210610-Dieter_Van_Uytvanck-DOG.pdf.

[16] https://fairdo.org.

[17] https://v4e-lab.isti.cnr.it/citview/demo/index.html.

[18] https://gitea-s2i2s.isti.cnr.it/concordia/sshoc-citationservice.

B!SON: A Tool for Open Access Journal Recommendation

Elias Entrup[1] , Anita Eppelin[1] , Ralph Ewerth[1,3] , Josephine Hartwig[2] ,
Marco Tullney[1] , Michael Wohlgemuth[2] , and Anett Hoppe[1,3(✉)]

[1] TIB - Leibniz Information Centre for Science and Technology, Hannover, Germany
{bison,anett.hoppe}@tib.eu
[2] Saxon State and University Library, Dresden, Germany
[3] L3S Research Center, Leibniz University Hannover, Hannover, Germany

Abstract. Finding a suitable open access journal to publish scientific
work is a complex task: Researchers have to navigate a constantly growing number of journals, institutional agreements with publishers, funders'
conditions and the risk of Predatory Publishers. To help with these challenges, we introduce a web-based journal recommendation system called
B!SON. It is developed based on a systematic requirements analysis, built
on open data, gives publisher-independent recommendations and works
across domains. It suggests open access journals based on title, abstract
and references provided by the user. The recommendation quality has
been evaluated using a large test set of 10,000 articles. Development by
two German scientific libraries ensures the longevity of the project.

Keywords: Recommendation system · Open access · Paper
submission · Publishing

1 Introduction

The open access landscape keeps growing, making it harder and harder to choose
a suitable journal to publish research findings. There is an increasing number of
journals: The Directory of Open Access Journals (DOAJ), an online directory of
peer-reviewed open access journals, added over 5,000 journals in the last three
years. All of these journals offer a variety of publishing conditions, including
different peer-review schemes, publication costs and waivers, copyright and rights
retention clauses. But there is also growing support for researchers to facilitate
open access publishing: The recent years brought on various agreements formed
between academic institutions and publishers, which determine publication costs
and conditions; scientific libraries increasingly offer support services. Also, more
funding agencies expect scientists to use open access options and specify clear
conditions with respect to how funded work is to be published. This adds to the
overall workload of researchers: They have to assess the open access landscape
while taking into account factors such as newly established journals, predatory
publishing schemes, quality measures, and, finally, individual publication costs.

© The Author(s) 2022
G. Silvello et al. (Eds.): TPDL 2022, LNCS 13541, pp. 357–364, 2022.
https://doi.org/10.1007/978-3-031-16802-4_33

In this paper, we present B!SON, a web-based recommendation system which aims to alleviate these problems. Open access journals are recommended based on content similarity (using title, abstract and keywords) and the cited references. User requirements were systematically collected in a survey [9], focusing primarily on researchers, but also addressing libraries, publishers and editors of scholar-led journals. Findings from these surveys have been discussed in depth with a user community and were incorporated into the system specification accordingly. The quality of B!SON's recommendation is evaluated on a large test set of 10,000 articles. The rest of the paper describes the B!SON prototype by first reviewing existing work on scientific recommendation (Sect. 2), then describing the B!SON service, its data sources, algorithm and functionality (Sect. 3), and concluding in Sect. 4.

2   Related Work

Scientific recommendation tasks span the search for potential collaborators [17] and reviewers [18], of papers to read [1] and to cite [2,5]. With more and more ways of publishing scientific articles, the recommendation of scientific publication outlets (journals/conferences) is a task which is on the rise (e.g. [22,25]).

Prototypical approaches explore diverse data sources to provide recommendations. A major source of information is the article to be published: The text's title, abstract or keywords are used to compare against papers that previously appeared in an outlet [14,25] . Other systems exploit the literature cited by the article, and try to determine the best publication venue using bibliometric metrics [7,20]. An alternative stream of research focuses more on the article authors, exploring their publication history [24] and co-publication networks [16,23].

While there is a number of active journal recommender sites, they all come with limitations. Several publishers offer services limited to their own journals like Elsevier's Journalfinder[1] [10] or Springer's Journal suggester[2]. Others, like Journal Guide[3] are closed-source and do not provide transparent information on their recommendation approach. Several collect user and usage data , e.g. Web of Science's manuscript matcher[4]. Notably, some open recommenders exist, e.g. Open Journal Matcher[5], Pubmender[6] [4] and Jane[7] [21], the latter two being limited to medical journals. All of these open services provide little information on journals, are limited to abstract input and do not offer advanced filter options.

---

[1] https://journalfinder.elsevier.com/.
[2] https://journalsuggester.springer.com/.
[3] https://www.journalguide.com/.
[4] https://mjl.clarivate.com/manuscript-matcher.
[5] https://ojm.ocert.at/.
[6] https://www.keaml.cn/abc/.
[7] https://jane.biosemantics.org/.

3   B!SON – The Open Access Journal Recommender

B!SON is the abbreviation for *Bibliometric and Semantic Open Access Recommender Network*. It combines several available data sources (see Sect. 3.1 for details) to provide authors and publication support services at libraries with recommendations of suitable open access journals, based on the entered title, abstract and reference list of the paper to be published.

3.1   Data Sources

The B!SON service is built on top of several open data sources with strong reputation in the open access community:

DOAJ: The Directory of Open Access Journals (DOAJ)[8] collects information on open access journals which fulfill a set of quality criteria (available full text, dedicated article URLs, at least one ISSN, etc.). The dataset includes basic information on the journal itself, but also metadata of the published articles (title, abstract, year, DOI, ISSN of journal, etc.). The DOAJ currently contains 17,669 journals and 7,489,975 articles. The data is available for download in JSON format under CC0 for articles and CC BY-SA for journal data [3].

OpenCitations: The OpenCitations initiative[9] collects (amongst other) the CC0-licensed COCI data set for citation data. It is based on Crossref data and contains over 72,268,850 publications and 1,294,283,603 citations [15]. The information is available in the form of DOI-to-DOI relations and it covers 44% of citations in Scopus and 51% of the citations in Dimensions [13]. COCI lacks citations in comparison to commercial products, but can be used to check which articles published in DOAJ journals cite the references given by the user (details in Sect. 3.2). As open access journals are incentivized to submit their articles' metadata, we can assume that the coverage of COCI in this regard is better.

Journal Checker Tool: The cOAlition S initiative (a group of funding agencies that agreed on a set of principles for the transition to open access) provides the Journal Checker Tool[10]. A user can enter journal ISSN, funder and institution to check whether a journal is open access according to Plan S, if the journal is a transformative journal or has a transformative agreement with the user's institution, or whether there is a self-archiving option [8]. An API allows to fetch this information automatically. Since B!SON does not retrieve data on funder or institution, we use the funder information of the European Commission to check if a journal is Plan-S compliant.

Other data sources: There are many other projects whose data might be used in B!SON's future to supplement the currently used data sets. Crossref would allow us to extend the article data of the DOAJ which are occasionally incomplete. OpenAlex (by OurResearch) could add e.g. author information.

---

8 https://doaj.org.
9 https://opencitations.net.
10 https://journalcheckertool.org/.

Table 1. Top@N accuracy for the different search methods.

Method	top@1	top@5	top@10	top@15
Bibliometric search	0.2048	0.3789	0.4185	0.4342
Title search	0.2102	0.4481	0.5489	0.5989
Abstract search	0.2501	0.5148	0.6160	0.6621
Combined search	0.2770	0.5644	0.6716	0.7229

3.2 Technology

B!SON consists of a Django backend[11] and a Vue.js[12] frontend.

Data Integration: PostgreSQL and Elasticsearch are used as databases. Data from DOAJ and OpenCitations' COCI index are bulk downloaded and inserted into PostgreSQL and Elasticsearch. The information on Plan-S compliance stems from Journal Checker Tool and is fetched from their API using "European Commission Horizon Europe Framework Programme" as the funder.

All developed software will be published open source in the upcoming weeks[13].

Recommendation: The recommendation is based on similarity measures with regard to the entered text data (title, abstract and keywords) and reference list.

Text similarity: Elasticsearch has a built-in functionality for text similarity search based on the Okapi BM 25 algorithm [19]. This is used to determine those articles already indexed in the DOAJ which are similar to the entered information. Stop word removal is performed as a pre-processing step. As the DOAJ contains articles in several languages, we combine the stop word lists from Apache Lucene for this purpose.

Bibliographic coupling: Additionally to textual data, the user can enter the list of cited articles, allowing to match journals based on bibliometric coupling [11]. For this, we extract the DOIs from the input list using regular expressions, then rely on the OpenCitations' COCI index to find existing articles citing the same sources. The current solution is in a prototypical state: The number of matching citations is divided by the highest number of matching citations of the compared articles; if the normalized value is higher than a threshold (which is currently manually defined), the article is considered similar. We are currently working on integrating more sophisticated normalisation methods (e.g. [12]) and exploring options on how to dynamically define the threshold value.

Combination of text-based and bibliographic similarity: Similar articles are matched with their journal and the total score is calculated as a sum. Refined aggregation methods are currently explored and will be available soon.

---

[11] https://www.djangoproject.com/.

[12] https://vuejs.org/.

[13] https://gitlab.com/TIBHannover/bison/.

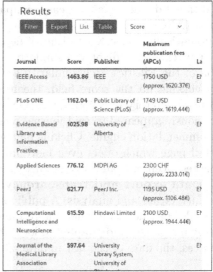

Fig. 1. Screenshot of B!SON prototype with an exemplary query.

Recommendation Evaluation: The algorithm is evaluated on a separate test data set of 10,000 DOAJ articles. To ensure realistic input data, all articles in the test set have a minimal abstract length of 100 characters and a minimal title length of 30 characters. As the references are not part of the DOAJ data, the COCI index was used to fetch references via the article DOI. Only articles with at least one reference were included. We assume that the articles were published in a suitable journal to begin with, counting a positive result if the originating journal appears in the top-n results of the recommendation. While this may not be correct for each individual article, we rely on the assumption that the overall journal scope is defined by the articles published in a journal. This current recommendation algorithm reaches the top@N accuracy shown in Table 1 when tested on a test set of 10,000 DOAJ articles.

3.3   User Interface and Functionality

The current state of the B!SON prototype is available for testing[14]. The user interface has been designed deliberately simple, a screenshot is shown in Fig. 1.

Data entry: The start page directly allows the user to enter title, abstract and references or fill them out automatically by fetching the information from Crossref with a DOI so that open access publication venues can be found based on previously published research.

Result page: To inspect the search results, the user has the choice of representing them as a simple list or a table which offers a structured account of

---

[14] https://service.tib.eu/bison/.

additional details, enabling easy comparison of the journals. Author publishing costs (APCs) are displayed based on the information available in DOAJ, and automatically converted to Euro if necessary.

Currently, the displayed similarity score is calculated based on simple addition of the Elasticsearch similarity score and the bibliometric similarity score. By clicking on the score field, the user has the option to display a pop-over with explanatory information: B!SON will then display the list of articles which previously appeared in said journal which were determined to be similar by the recommendation engine. Clicking on a journal name leads the users to a separate detail page which offers even more information including keywords, publishing charges, license, Plan-S compliance, and more.

Data export and transparency: Search results can be exported as CSV for further use and analysis. A public API is available for programmatic access. It is also planned to provide the recommendation functionality in a form that is easily integrated and adapted to local library systems. For transparency on data sources, the date of the last update of the data is shown on the "About Page".

4   Conclusion

In this paper, we have presented a novel prototypical recommendation system for open access journals. The system combines semantic and bibliometric information to calculate a similarity score to the journals' existing contents, and provides the user with a ranked list of candidate venues.

The B!SON prototype is available online for beta-testing. Based on the community feedback received so far, we are currently working on further optimisations. This concerns, for instance, the computation of the similarity score which is, to date, a simple addition of semantic and bibliometric similarity results. More sophisticated aggregation methods will allow optimised weighting of both components and, perspectively, better interpretability of the resulting score. Furthermore, we are currently exploring embedding-based text (used by e.g. Pubmender [4]) and citation graph representations [6] to further improve the recommendation results. Several remarks also concern the user interface. The community's wishlist includes more sophisticated methods for the exploration of the result list, e.g. graph-based visualisations, an extension of the filtering options and an improved representation of the similarity score.

Going beyond the scope of the B!SON project, it could be interesting to extend recommendations to other venues which offer open access publication such as conferences. Moreover, the integration of person-centred information, such as prior publication history and frequent co-authors seems promising.

Acknowledgements. B!SON is funded by the German Federal Ministry of Education and Research (BMBF) for a period of two years (funding reference: 16TOA034A) and partners with DOAJ and OpenCitations. The publication was funded by the Open Access Fund of the TIB - Leibniz Information Centre for Science and Technology.

References

1. Beel, J., Gipp, B., Langer, S., Breitinger, C.: Research-paper recommender systems: a literature survey. Int. J. Digit. Libr. **17**(4), 305–338 (2015). https://doi.org/10.1007/s00799-015-0156-0
2. Brack, A., Hoppe, A., Ewerth, R.: Citation recommendation for research papers via knowledge graphs. In: Berget, G., Hall, M.M., Brenn, D., Kumpulainen, S. (eds.) TPDL 2021. LNCS, vol. 12866, pp. 165–174. Springer, Cham (2021). https://doi.org/10.1007/978-3-030-86324-1_20
3. Directory of Open Access Journals. https://doaj.org/. Accessed 25 May 2022
4. Feng, X., et al.: The deep learning-based recommender system "Pubmender" for choosing a biomedical publication venue: development and validation study. J. Med. Internet Res. **21**(5), e12957 (2019). https://doi.org/10.2196/12957
5. Färber, M., Sampath, A.: HybridCite: a hybrid model for context-aware citation recommendation. In: Proceedings of the ACM/IEEE Joint Conference on Digital Libraries in 2020, pp. 117–126. Association for Computing Machinery, New York, NY, USA (2020). https://doi.org/10.1145/3383583.3398534
6. Ganguly, S., Pudi, V.: Paper2vec: combining graph and text information for scientific paper representation. In: Jose, J.M., et al. (eds.) ECIR 2017. LNCS, vol. 10193, pp. 383–395. Springer, Cham (2017). https://doi.org/10.1007/978-3-319-56608-5_30
7. Ghosal, T., Chakraborty, A., Sonam, R., Ekbal, A., Saha, S., Bhattacharyya, P.: Incorporating full text and bibliographic features to improve scholarly journal recommendation. In: 2019 ACM/IEEE Joint Conference on Digital Libraries (JCDL), pp. 374–375. IEEE, Champaign, IL, USA (2019). https://doi.org/10.1109/JCDL.2019.00077
8. Hannah Hope: Unboxing the Journal Checker Tool | Plan S. https://www.coalition-s.org/blog/unboxing-the-journal-checker-tool/. Accessed 01 June 2022
9. Hartwig, J., Eppelin, A.: Which journal characteristics are crucial for scientists when selecting journals for their publications? Results tables of an online survey (2021). https://doi.org/10.5281/zenodo.5728148. Type: dataset
10. Kang, N., Doornenbal, M.A., Schijvenaars, R.J.: Elsevier journal finder: recommending journals for your paper. In: Proceedings of the 9th ACM Conference on Recommender Systems, pp. 261–264. RecSys 2015, Association for Computing Machinery, New York, NY, USA (2015). https://doi.org/10.1145/2792838.2799663
11. Kessler, M.M.: Bibliographic coupling between scientific papers. Am. Doc. **14**(1), 10–25 (1963). https://doi.org/10.1002/asi.5090140103
12. Leydesdorff, L.: On the normalization and visualization of author co-citation data: Salton's cosine versus the Jaccard index. J. Assoc. Inf. Sci. Technol. **59**(1), 77–85 (2008). https://doi.org/10.1002/asi.20732
13. Martín-Martín, A., Thelwall, M., Orduna-Malea, E., Delgado López-Cózar, E.: Google Scholar, Microsoft Academic, Scopus, Dimensions, Web of Science, and OpenCitations' COCI: a multidisciplinary comparison of coverage via citations. Scientometrics **126**(1), 871–906 (2021). https://doi.org/10.1007/s11192-020-03690-4
14. Nguyen, D., Huynh, S., Huynh, P., Dinh, C.V., Nguyen, B.T.: S2CFT: a new approach for paper submission recommendation. In: Bureš, T., et al. (eds.) SOFSEM 2021. LNCS, vol. 12607, pp. 563–573. Springer, Cham (2021). https://doi.org/10.1007/978-3-030-67731-2_41

15. OpenCitations: COCI CSV dataset of all the citation data (2022). https://doi.org/10.6084/m9.figshare.6741422.v14

16. Pradhan, T., Pal, S.: A hybrid personalized scholarly venue recommender system integrating social network analysis and contextual similarity. Futur. Gener. Comput. Syst. **110**, 1139–1166 (2020). https://doi.org/10.1016/j.future.2019.11.017

17. Pradhan, T., Pal, S.: A multi-level fusion based decision support system for academic collaborator recommendation. Knowl.-Based Syst. **197**, 105784 (2020). https://doi.org/10.1016/j.knosys.2020.105784

18. Pradhan, T., Sahoo, S., Singh, U., Pal, S.: A proactive decision support system for reviewer recommendation in academia. Expert Syst. Appl. **169**, 114331 (2021). https://doi.org/10.1016/j.eswa.2020.114331

19. Robertson, S.E., Zaragoza, H.: The probabilistic relevance framework: BM25 and beyond. Found. Trends Inf. Retr. **3**(4), 333–389 (2009). https://doi.org/10.1561/1500000019

20. Rollins, J., McCusker, M., Carlson, J., Stroll, J.: Manuscript matcher: a content and bibliometrics-based scholarly journal recommendation system. In: Proceedings of the Fifth Workshop on Bibliometric-enhanced Information Retrieval (BIR) colocated with the 39th European Conference on Information Retrieval (ECIR 2017), Aberdeen, UK, 9th April 2017. http://ceur-ws.org/Vol-1823/paper2.pdf

21. Schuemie, M.J., Kors, J.A.: Jane: suggesting journals, finding experts. Bioinformatics (Oxford, England) **24**(5), 727–728 (2008). https://doi.org/10.1093/bioinformatics/btn006

22. Schäfermeier, B., Stumme, G., Hanika, T.: Towards Explainable Scientific Venue Recommendations. arXiv:2109.11343 (2021). http://arxiv.org/abs/2109.11343

23. Yu, S., et al.: PAVE: personalized academic venue recommendation exploiting co-publication networks. J. Netw. Comput. Appl. **104**, 38–47 (2018). https://doi.org/10.1016/j.jnca.2017.12.004

24. Zawali, A., Boukhris, I.: Academic venue recommendation based on refined cross domain. In: Abraham, A., Gandhi, N., Hanne, T., Hong, T.-P., Nogueira Rios, T., Ding, W. (eds.) ISDA 2021. LNNS, vol. 418, pp. 1188–1197. Springer, Cham (2022). https://doi.org/10.1007/978-3-030-96308-8_110

25. ZhengWei, H., JinTao, M., YanNi, Y., Jin, H., Ye, T.: Recommendation method for academic journal submission based on doc2vec and XGBoost. Scientometrics **127**(5), 2381–2394 (2022). https://doi.org/10.1007/s11192-022-04354-1

Visual Web Archive Quality Assessment

Theresa Elstner[1]([✉]), Johannes Kiesel[2], Lars Meyer[2], Max Martius[1],
Sebastian Schmidt[1], Benno Stein[2], and Martin Potthast[1]

[1] Leipzig University, Leipzig, Germany
theresa.elstner@uni-leipzig.de
[2] Bauhaus-Universität Weimar, Weimar, Germany

Abstract. The large size of today's web archives makes it impossible
to manually assess the quality of each archived web page, i.e., to check
whether a page can be reproduced faithfully from an archive. For automated web archive quality assessment, previous work proposed to measure the pixel difference between a screenshot of the original page and a
screenshot of the same page when reproduced from the archive. However,
when categorizing types of reproduction errors (we introduce a respective taxonomy in this paper) one finds that some errors cause high pixel
differences between the screenshots, but lead to only a negligible degra-
dation in the user experience of the reproduced web page. Therefore,
we propose to visually align page segments in such cases before measuring the pixel differences. Since the diversity of reproduction error types
precludes a one-size-fits-all solution for visual alignment, we focus on
one common type (translated segments) and investigate the usefulness
of video compression algorithms for this task.

Keywords: Web archiving · Automatic quality assessment · Visual
web page alignment

1 Introduction

Web archives are created for posterity and they already serve researchers in social
sciences, history, linguistics, humanities, and—not least—computer science. The
diversity of web technologies and the way users interact with web pages are the
main challenges for web archiving. In fact, creating high-quality archives that
reliably reproduce layout, content, and behavior of web pages from archived
data is a largely unsolved problem: An estimated 44% of archived web pages
have minor to major defects due to reproduction errors, while as many as 4% of
them are unusable [3]. These are significant portions of the 685 billion web pages
archived by the Internet Archive's Wayback Machine at the time of writing [2].

Reproduction errors are parts of a web page that do not look the same
when reproduced from a web archive as they did when archived. In this regard,
Fig. 1 (left) illustrates three common reproduction errors: A missing video causes
the translation of underneath content, and the addition of white space or the

© Springer Nature Switzerland AG 2022
G. Silvello et al. (Eds.): TPDL 2022, LNCS 13541, pp. 365–371, 2022.
https://doi.org/10.1007/978-3-031-16802-4_34

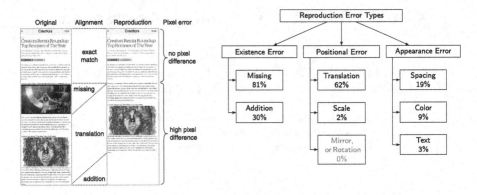

Fig. 1. *Left:* Screenshots of a web page in its original form and when reproduced from an archive with reproduction errors: A missing video causes a vertical translation of content. *Right:* Reproduction error types and the respective percentage of affected pages (i.e., pages with at least one such error) in a web archive sample.

reduction of screen height. Only the missing video (if relevant to the web page author's intended message) affects the archive quality, not the translation. The example illustrates why it is difficult to identify web pages with low archive quality, even if a screenshot of the original web page is available for reference. Therefore, evaluating the quality of web archives requires a user-oriented (semantic) analysis that takes into account the usefulness of an archived page for specific purposes. However, no significant progress has been made in this regard since the task was first proposed along with a benchmark dataset (see Sect. 2). This paper makes three contributions to take the next steps: (1) a taxonomy of reproduction errors and an empirical assessment of the error frequencies, (2) a proposal for a normalization task (visual segment alignment) to improve automatic web archive quality assessment, and (3) an analysis of the applicability of video compression algorithms for this task. Our code and data is publicly available.[1,2]

2   Related Work

While a considerable amount of research addresses web archive quality, little work has been done on its automatic assessment using visual information. The Internet Archive's Archive-It suggests to "Browse through your archived site(s), clicking links and activating dynamic media players in order to make sure that they were archived in accordance with your expectations" [1]. Reyes Ayala et al. [4–6] outline the need for an automated solution using screenshots based on an analysis of Archive-It's support tickets. The degree of similarity between screenshots of the original and archived versions of a page contributes significantly to manual evaluation. Reyes Ayala et al. [6] study image similarity measures in

---

[1] Code https://github.com/webis-de/TPDL-22.
[2] Data https://zenodo.org/record/6881335.

terms of their ability to detect such differences. Kiesel et al. [3] have created a large benchmark dataset of 10,000 archived pages for this task. They introduce the root-mean-square error (RMSE), which is calculated from the pixel difference of original and archive screenshots, as a well-performing measure, yet conclude that "[...] a single missing advertisement banner at the top of the page can shift up the entire web page, causing the RMSE to become unjustifiably high."

3   A Taxonomy of Web Archive Reproduction Errors

Figure 1 (right) shows a taxonomy of reproduction error types identified when comparing screenshots of an original web page with its archived version (original–archive screenshots). Relative frequencies were determined manually using a random sample of 100 original–archive screenshots with pixel differences from our dataset.[3] Each frequency estimates the proportion of archived pages for which a given reproduction error is expected, i.e., a pair may contain multiple errors. Each of the three branches in the taxonomy describes the way in which a segment in the archive screenshot may look different compared to the corresponding segment in the original screenshot: (1) existence errors indicate elements that are present in the original but not in the archive screenshot or vice versa; (2) position errors indicate where a segment appears in the archive screenshot and how its position differs from the corresponding segment in the original screenshot; and (3) appearance errors indicate differences in the content or layout of an archived item compared to its original, including color differences.

A reproduction error can affect either the whole or a part of a segment. One segment may also be affected by multiple reproduction errors. Existence errors occur most frequently, followed by translation and spacing errors, and they can even cause a number of other errors. For example, a missing segment may cause translation errors affecting segments further down the page (as in Fig. 1), which may result in additional segments (content) at the bottom.

Beyond visual reproduction error types, a web page's interactive content (audio, animation, or any functional elements triggered by interaction, including hyperlinks) may also contain errors. These errors cannot be identified using screenshots. Furthermore, some seemingly erroneous differences may only affect its screenshot, not the archived web page itself: 41% of the 100 manually annotated web pages were affected by this, with many of them being timing issues, e.g. showing different parts of a GIF animation.

4   Visual Alignment of Original–Archive Screenshot Pairs

We present a generic framework for web archive quality assessment with three steps: (1) visual segment alignment, where original–archive screenshots with reproduction errors that do not affect the quality of an archived web page are

---

[3] The fraction of screenshots without pixel differences (no reproduction errors) in our dataset is 12.9% (845/6531).

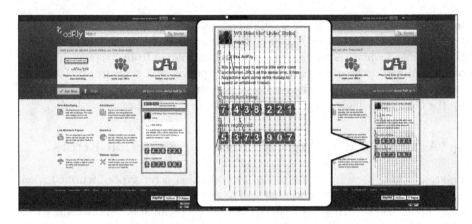

Fig. 2. Original and archive screenshot as two frames of a H.264-encoded video. The element marked by a pink border in the original screenshot is missing in the archive screenshot, so the element below (marked by a green border) is translated upwards as indicated by the motion vectors (black arrows). (Color figure online)

aligned (in our prototype translated DOM elements are returned to their original position), (2) visual edit distance calculation, and (3) quality prediction, where machine learning is used to predict human quality annotations based on the visual edit distance. Our experiments are based on a sample of original screenshots from the Webis-Web-Archive-17 [3], supplemented by new reproductions and a corresponding description of structure. To ensure the validity of the human annotations from Webis-Web-Archive-17 for this dataset, it does not contain web pages whose reproductions differ by more than 5% of the corresponding pixels.

Visual Segment Alignment. Our visual segment alignment method moves translated DOM elements in archive screenshots to their respective positions in the original screenshot. The positions of elements in the archive screenshots are derived from the available page structure descriptions. As these are unavailable for the screenshots of the original web pages, we derive the original positions using motion estimation algorithms from video encoding software as follows.

We use the media conversion framework ffmpeg [7] to encode original–archive screenshots into an H.264 video. From this video, we obtain motion vectors containing information about the translation of pixel blocks in the archive screenshot compared to the original screenshot. Figure 2 shows a corresponding example. Together with the position information of the elements from the page structure description, we can recover the positions of the moved elements according to the motion vectors. It should be noted that motion vectors for an element do not always indicate the same original position, so we use majority voting to decide whether to perform a move. This may lead to errors (e.g., large translated child elements cause translations of their parents).

Calculating the Visual Edit Distance. The second component is implemented as a visual edit distance. It compares each pixel in the aligned and archive screenshot with the pixel at the same position in the original screenshot. This results in two

Table 1. *Left:* Confusion matrix Δ from baseline to aligned regression, with correct classifications (i.e., on the main diagonal) highlighted. *Right:* Precision, recall, and F_1-score for detecting pages with low reproduction quality (per targeted "low quality") per aligned regression, including delta from baseline to aligned regression.

Truth	\multicolumn Predicted quality					Target	Precision (Δ)	Recall (Δ)	F_1 (Δ)
	1	2	3	4	5	2–5	0.850 (+0.008)	0.770 (+0.045)	0.808 (+0.029)
1	+1	+4	−6	+1	±0	3–5	0.644 (+0.053)	0.186 (+0.012)	0.289 (+0.020)
2	−108	+115	−8	±0	+1	4–5	0.518 (−0.035)	0.101 (−0.007)	0.169 (−0.011)
3	+2	−7	+4	±0	+1	5	0.185 (−0.019)	0.049 (±0.000)	0.077 (−0.002)
4	−10	+7	+3	−3	+3				
5	−7	+7	+3	−3	±0				

visual edit distances: *aligned* and *baseline*. Both of them count the minimum number of applications of the substitution, insertion, and deletion operations.

In a pilot study, we evaluated three methods for coloring gaps created when translating elements: (1) using duplicates of translated elements, which leaves no gaps; as well as coloring the gap in the most frequent color (2) around the edges of the translated element; and (3) in the archive screenshot. Method 3 achieved the least visual edit distance. Hence it was considered in the following step.

Predicting Web Archive Quality. We implement a linear regression model evaluated with a 10-fold cross-validation to predict the quality of archived web pages on a 5-point scale as per the used benchmark dataset's human annotation [3]. As an input to this model, we test features from three categories. *Unaligned features* are: (u1) the size difference of the unaligned archive and original screenshots in pixels due to different screenshot heights; (u2) the baseline visual edit distance as described above, which includes u1; (u3) the baseline visual edit distance normalized by the original screenshot size; and (u4) the pixel size of the original screenshot to put u1 and u2 into context. *Aligned features* (a1–a3) correspond to u1–u3 for the aligned archive screenshot. *Translation features* count the DOM elements translated between original and archive as per the visual alignment: (t1) all translated elements; (t2–t9) elements translated into a particular direction as per the motion vectors, namely towards the top, top right, right, bottom right, etc.; (t10, t11) elements translated by a large or small distance, the latter being too small to indicate a missing content element;[4] (t12–t27) the same as t2–t9, but once counting only large and once counting only small translations like for t10 and t11; and (t28) all elements from the archived page, again for context.

---

[4] Based on a frequency analysis, we set the threshold for small to be 5 or fewer pixels vertically and 8 or fewer pixels horizontally.

5   Evaluation

Table 1 shows the improvement of an aligned regression over a baseline regression restricted to unaligned features (u1–u4). We tested each feature combination for the baseline regression and multiple inter- and intra-group combinations of the three groups of features (u,a,t) for the aligned regression. Δ describes the change in the respective value from the best-performing baseline regression system (which uses the size difference u1 and visual edit distance u3) to the best-performing alignment regression system (which uses only the aligned visual edit distance a3). For the confusion matrix on the left of Table 1, we find that the number of correct classifications increases, indicating small classification improvements despite the very prototypical nature of our approach and features. As the table shows, the main improvement of the aligned regression lies in a better differentiation between quality 1 ("not affecting the visitor" per [3]) and 2 ("small effect on a few visitors"). Following Kiesel et al. [3], the right hand side of Table 1 shows the achieved precision, recall, and F_1 score for detecting pages of low reproduction quality. Across all three scores, our prototypical approach yields some improvements for identifying reproductions of quality 2–5 and 3–5. If the targeted low quality includes only 4 ("affect, but page can still be used") and 5 ("unusable page"), the prototypical alignment slightly reduces the scores. However, we assume that a quality of 3 ("small effect on many or all visitors") is already a cause for concern for web archivists worth detecting.

Limitations. Our approach considers translation errors only. However, also other types of reproduction errors lead to a higher visual edit distance than warranted for the associated decrease in reproduction quality. While the selected translation features (t) could not improve the regression in our prototypical study, more elaborate features that go beyond counting translated DOM elements may be able do so. Similarly, other algorithms than linear regression might improve the quality assessment. For example, one could also integrate our alignment into a convolutional neural network [3].

Our study employs only a single approach for the critical task of detecting translated elements. But other approaches, not based on video encoding, might also be suited for web pages. Indeed, we found that the video encoding misses some translations. We manually annotated translations in 80 randomly sampled web pages from the dataset: Our annotation identified 148 million translated pixels, but only 28 million of them (about 1/5) were found automatically. Although many translations were detected correctly, we noticed that especially translations of large areas are sometimes missed. This suggests that more work on tuning the video encoding as well as alternative approaches are needed.

6   Conclusion

We explore a novel approach to automatic quality assessment of archived web pages based on visual alignment. To this end, we categorized visually perceivable reproduction error types, proposed a three-step framework for automatic quality assessment, and implemented and tested a prototypical implementation based on detecting translated elements from motion vectors. Our implementation shifts translated elements in the archive screenshot back to their original position, thereby bringing the pixel difference between original and archive screenshot closer to the human perception of reproduction quality. A comparison of two linear regression models, using features from unaligned and aligned screenshots respectively, shows small improvements over the baseline when using aligned screenshots even for our prototypical implementation. However, the design space for archive quality assessment algorithms is vast, and a more thorough exploration is necessary to develop reliable assessment technology—potentially based on our generalizable framework of normalization through visual segment alignment.

References

1. Internet archive: quality assurance overview (2022). https://support.archive-it.org/hc/en-us/articles/208333833-Quality-Assurance-Overview
2. Internet archive: wayback machine size as displayed on its front page (2022). https://web.archive.org/web/20220531094827/
3. Kiesel, J., Kneist, F., Alshomary, M., Stein, B., Hagen, M., Potthast, M.: Reproducible web corpora: interactive archiving with automatic quality assessment. J. Data Inf. Qual. (JDIQ) **10**(4), 17:1–17:25 (2018). https://doi.org/10.1145/3239574
4. Reyes Ayala, B., Phillips, M., Ko, L.: Current quality assurance practices in web archiving. UNT Digital Library, pp. 1–34, August 2014
5. Ayala, B.R.: Correspondence as the primary measure of quality for web archives: a grounded theory study. In: Hall, M., Merčun, T., Risse, T., Duchateau, F. (eds.) TPDL 2020. LNCS, vol. 12246, pp. 73–86. Springer, Cham (2020). https://doi.org/10.1007/978-3-030-54956-5_6
6. Ayala, B.R., Hitchcock, E., Sun, J.: Using image similarity metrics to measure visual quality in web archives. In: JCDL 2019: Web Archiving and Digital Libraries (WADL) Workshop, pp. 11–13. ACM (2019). https://doi.org/10.7939/r3-yh2n-rx10
7. Tomar, S.: Converting video formats with FFmpeg. Linux J. **2006**(146), 10 (2006)

The Knowledge Trust: A Proposal for a Blockchain Consortium for Digital Archives

Harry Halpin[✉]

American University of Beirut, P.O. Box 11-0236, Riad El-Solh,
Beirut 1107 2020, Lebanon
hhalpin@ibiblio.org

Abstract. We present a modest proposal for a blockchain-based consortium to preserve and provide a consistent view of the global integrity of digital information currently scattered across various archives. Based on a number of real-world threats to centralized archives, our design provides increased and frequent integrity checks that can help detect and ameliorate data loss in digital archives.

Keywords: Digital libraries · Integrity · Blockchain

1 Introduction

In our proposal called *The Knowledge Trust*, existing digital libraries can use blockchain technology to leverage the benefits of their own expertise in curation while gaining increased resilience via decentralization of missing or corrupted digital objects.[1] A permissioned blockchain run by digital libraries can quickly audit the global integrity of every digital object in the archives of its members, helping preserve our collective digital memory in the face of increasing threats from misinformation and censorship. Prior work such as LOCKSS (Lots of Copies Keep Stuff Safe) uses a peer-to-peer network to repair backups of digital objects [11], and thus helps solve the problem of availability. However, it does not store the hashes of the digital object like a blockchain but instead focuses on using hashes of available content in a peer-to-peer network to detect and repair broken content, and so does not solve the problem of integrity. Using hash functions for integrity has been proposed within the context of web page preservation [2], but not in a general purpose or decentralized environment. We systematize the threat model facing digital libraries in Sect. 2 in lieu of prior research and then present the design of the Knowledge Trust in Sect. 3. We discuss the trade-offs between performance and decentralization in terms of blockchain-based integrity archiving in Sect. 4. We conclude this proposal with next steps for the Knowledge Trust in Sect. 5.

---

[1] There is a copyright on "The Knowledge Trust" name held by the University of North Carolina at Chapel Hill. Thanks to Gary Marchionini for permission for its use in this proposal.

© Springer Nature Switzerland AG 2022
G. Silvello et al. (Eds.): TPDL 2022, LNCS 13541, pp. 372–378, 2022.
https://doi.org/10.1007/978-3-031-16802-4_35

2   Threat Model and Properties

The most comprehensive threat model to digital libraries was presented in the context of LOCKSS [12]. Namely, threats are separated into 1) *failures* in media, hardware, software (including the format), organizational, economic, and network failures (such as network service failure like the failure of a URL to resolve or communication failures such as the bits lost in transit when transferring a large file), 2) *errors* such as operator error (for example, when a librarian makes an unintentional mistake in ingesting or categorizing a digital object) 3) *attacks* including both internal attacks by insiders (such as a librarian destroying a record on government order) and external attacks by malicious actors (like the "hacking" of a digital library), 4) obsolescence of media, software, and hardware (such as lacking the ability to render a digital object due to loss of the software or hardware to read the media) and 5) natural disaster [12].

We propose that the following properties are necessary to confront above threat model of digital libraries and archives [12], building from earlier work in risk assessment for digital libraries [15]:

- **Availability**: A digital object is available for use.
  - *Identity*: Each digital object is referenceable and distinguishable from others.
  - *Persistence*: The bit sequences of each digital object are usable and so can be retrieved from the media on which they are stored.
  - *Renderability*: The "significant characteristics" of the digital object are maintained for future users [15].
  - *Understandability*: The metadata associated with the digital object allow it to be "appropriately interpreted" by users [15].
  - *Reliability*: The digital object is available over long periods of time.
- **Integrity**: The bits of the digital object are preserved against errors. This is also called "fixity" in the field of long-term digital preservation.
  - *Authenticity*: The digital object "is what it purports to be" [15].
  - *Provenance*: Changes to and custody of the digital object can be traced over time.

Furthermore, can these properties be achieved *globally* across *all* archived digital objects across institutions? The only operational large-scale decentralized system for digital objects is LOCKSS, based on peer-to-peer *replication* of the content, with copies of each artifact stored between many peers who then may check each other's copies for integrity against a randomly selected number of peers (at least two), where a majority vote determines the canonical version of the digital object [8]. However, LOCKSS provides only *local availability* in case of a copy being corrupted or destroyed. Integrity is also only *local integrity* and so created on ingestion but not necessarily regularly audited across the network for each object, and so there is no *global integrity* of all artifacts across all participants in LOCKSS. In addition, LOCKSS does not easily provision *provenance* for changing objects, although there is now prototype support Memento [13].

Lastly, if a LOCKSS-style network is open to participation without a clear "vetting" process for new actors, like all other peer-to-peer system, LOCKSS could suffer a *sybil* attack where a malicious insider may add their own nodes and so corrupt the integrity of the replication [14]. A "peer-in-the-middle" sybil attack could corrupt the sampling procedure used by LOCKSS [11]. While randomized periodic sampling may prevent these attacks over time [7], it does not absolutely prevent these attacks. These threats hold also true to the aforementioned fully decentralized alternatives to LOCKSS such as Filecoin[2] and Arweave.[3]

In contrast, blockchain systems are a type of decentralized system, composed of two components: 1) A chain of hashes that maintains the global integrity and a total ordering of all items of interest over time (i.e. provenance) and a 2) consensus algorithm that maintains the same replicated state across many computers [9]. Thus blockchains provide availability of the state of the entire system via a consensus algorithm from distributed systems research, and global integrity of the system's state via the use of cryptography. This could be a potential game-changing technology for digital archives as it allows an easy way to track the current and historical state of the integrity of digital objects and so provide a "source of ground truth" for regular audits. This is important because previous work has estimated the mean time to data loss in an archive without an audit is only 64 days, but with an audit every two weeks, this time to data loss increases to twelve years [3]. With regular audits running every hour or day in a decentralized manner, the archives would be able to reduce data loss by byzantine faults over their collection of objects. Regular audits by a global blockchain system could help systematize local audits to cover all the digital objects stored globally anywhere.

3   Design of the Knowledge Trust

Our novel proposal for *The Knowledge Trust* combines blockchain technology and curation in order to create regular checks for the global integrity of digital objects in a decentralized manner. The Knowledge Trust is a proposed consortium of digital archives and libraries, where each institution runs a piece of software called a *validator*. The core concept of the Knowledge Trust is straightforward: A digital library may register digital objects via submitting a cryptographic hash (created locally) and metadata to a validator. The object itself is not stored like in LOCKSS, as the digital object is stored on one or more "off-chain" locations that are pointed to by its block. Each institution that is part of the Knowledge Trust uses its private cryptographic key to sign the hash of the digital object and its metadata, and this new "block" is proposed to the blockchain. A group of validators then reach consensus using a standard consensus algorithm to add the new block to the Knowledge Trust blockchain.

Note there is no cryptocurrency attached to the Knowledge Trust and thus the Knowledge Trust neither incurs any fees in cryptocurrency to insert a block

---

[2] https://filecoin.io/.

[3] https://www.arweave.org/.

into the blockchain by any member nor offers any reward for institutions for participating, other than regular audits of the integrity of their archive. As there is no "proof of work" algorithm used, energy costs should be the same as any distributed database and other complaints against typical cryptocurrency systems should likely be rendered moot. The group of validators can be determined by a human-centric democratic governance process, where members may apply to join and vote for other members to run a validator. The Knowledge Trust would qualify as a *proof of authority* system ran in a democratic manner. The Knowledge Trust includes the following components:

Curators are users who are trained in digital curation and run software (such as BitCurator [6] with a Knowledge Trust plug-in) on their local client or on a server remotely. The curator submits a *digital object* (*O*) – web-pages, photos, videos, scanned text, or any other form of media – to the Knowledge Trust validator run by their local institution, which runs the cryptographic hash (*H*) of the digital object and adds to it a (non-hashed) copy of the metadata, so preparing block for insertion in the chain. The *metadata* (*M*) can use standardized format such as MARC (AARC2), OAI, RDA, DCMI, etc. and should include the time of submission to the Knowledge Trust as well as links to one or more copies of the digital object stored locally. Older metadata can be overwritten by newer edits and missing metadata may be completed, but this would require a new hash being created as well as the block with the new hash being linked to the previous block with the incomplete or incorrect metadata. The identity of the curator should always be included in every block of metadata *M* with the signature of their institution or their own self-signed signature.

Validators are run by a group of institutions such as libraries and archives. In our current proposal, the validators are a permissioned set which use a clear social governance structure (one that is voting or consensus as has been used by groups like the W3C or the LOCKSS Alliance) to add and remove members. Each validator maintains at least one cryptographic key to sign its contribution. The Knowledge Trust uses the Tendermint consensus algorithm, a PBFT algorithm that requires $\frac{2}{3} + 1$ consensus amongst validators (block producers) in order to add a new block and reach finality [1]. Note that adding an individual digital object's hash to the blockchain does not require the validators to run the hash function themselves to check it, as a particular digital object may be held by a minority or even a single institution and so not all validators need to create the hash. The usage of large enough and thus redundant set of validators should address concerns that integrity data would be centralized and so easily attacked, as such an attack would have to effect the majority of validators to be successful.

The Knowledge Trust Blockchain is a linked list of blocks ($B = b_1, b_2..b_x$) where each block contains a Merkle Tree (T) of cryptographic hashes of digital objects and its associated metadata ($b_i = T(H(O_i)|M_i, ...)$), where consensus on the blocks are maintained by the validators. The digital object itself is not stored on the blockchain. Each leaf of the Merkle Tree is the hash of a curated digital object. As a strong cryptographic hash function is used, each digital object should have a unique hash for identity and an associated metadata file.

If "over decade- or century-long timespans" the hash function starts to produce cryptographic collisions,[4] then it is relatively straightforward to simply upgrade the hash function to the newest version, such as from SHA-2 to SHA-3 or from SHA-3 to a not-yet-existent SHA-4. This is done by a simple software upgrade by the validators and has no effect on future block production, other than rendering pre-upgrade blocks less useful due to the possibility of a collusion.

Operations: When a new digital object is added, the algorithm checks the Merkle Tree of the latest block against all the previous blocks to determine if the hash of the object is already in the Knowledge Trust. If it is not, the metadata is also checked to see if another file with related metadata yet a different hash is already in the Knowledge Trust using a more expensive linear text search, although this would require manual intervention. If the digital object is identified as being in the blockchain already and there are conflicts, then the metadata conflicts are resolved manually as well, via import of metadata repositories such as OCLC and then manual discussion afterwards until consensus is reached.[5] If there is a conflict over the hash and the consensus threshold is not reached, there has been a corruption and the institution is notified to retrieve a new copy from another participating institution. If the hash of the object is not in the Knowledge Trust already, then it is automatically added and the validators are alerted to import the metadata from OCLC and determine if they also have a copy of the digital object. If the metadata has changed, the object's hash is linked to its previous hash and metadata.

4   Scalability

One question is whether or not it is possible to decentralize the operations needed for global integrity constraints. As shown by Fig. 1 [5], there is a approximately linear scaling to the number of validators, taking from 10 s. at 7 validators up to 300 s. for 100 validators to reach consensus. This adds therefore up to a few minutes for changes to resources to be propagated through the system. Ingesting a new archive will take days: For example, the *ibiblio.org* archive of a size of 1,660,329 unique files (64 GB) at the present moment would require approximately a week to ingest due to the time needed to hash every file. However, regular global integrity checks should be possible after ingestion at intervals of every hour to incorporate updates to the archive and audits of the integrity of a collection taking place at weekly intervals. Importantly, to add and search the Merkle Tree (including for errors, but also for duplicate artifacts) should remain nearly constant time (3–5 s.) on the order of a few seconds.

---

[4] https://blog.dshr.org/2018/09/blockchain-solves-preservation.html.
[5] https://www.oclc.org/en/home.html.

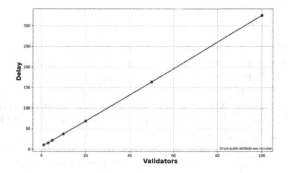

Fig. 1. Number of validators vs. delay in consensus time (s.)

5   Conclusion

Rather than attempt to build a decentralized repository with trust depending on a single institution, the Knowledge Trust distributes trust so that the components both map to traditional trusted institutions such as libraries, letting them take advantage of the global provenance and integrity provided by blockchain technology while building on their existing infrastructure. As only the hashes of the digital object and metadata are stored on the blockchain, members of the Knowledge Trust could provide access within the legal rules of their local jurisdiction. Additionally, the Knowledge Trust could host its validators across multiple jurisdictions to prevent legal attacks as well and increase redundancy. The Knowledge Trust would resist sybil attacks due to the Tendermint consensus algorithm, so these attacks would be more difficult and easy to detect used than in pure peer-to-peer system that only guaranteed local integrity like LOCKSS. Unlike previous proposals [4], the Knowledge Trust would also not have unfortunate financial repercussions on users and institutions, instead building on top of existing curation workflows and institutional norms to increase the integrity of digital objects. Future work needs a complete evaluation including both the ingestion and periodic updates of real-world archives. Participants should be given approximate hardware requirements for participants (including tests on heterogeneous nodes with less-than-ideal connection speeds and disks). Future work should also include duplication and corruption detection in artifacts on members, and a more detailed governance structure. In order to reduce the probability of false alarms of corrupted data, locality sensitive hashing could be investigated as well [10]. Very important questions have not been tackled such as how the manual resolving of metadata conflicts works in the case of conflict. Availability is the goal, but the first step should be global consensus on the integrity of our common global digital heritage.

References

1. Amoussou-Guenou, Y., Del Pozzo, A., Potop-Butucaru, M., Tucci-Piergiovanni, S.: Dissecting Tendermint. In: Atig, M.F., Schwarzmann, A.A. (eds.) NETYS 2019. LNCS, vol. 11704, pp. 166–182. Springer, Cham (2019). https://doi.org/10.1007/978-3-030-31277-0_11
2. Aturban, M., Alam, S., Nelson, M.L., Weigle, M.C.: Archive assisted archival fixity verification framework. In: 2019 ACM/IEEE Joint Conference on Digital Libraries (JCDL), pp. 162–171. IEEE (2019)
3. Baker, M., et al.: A fresh look at the reliability of long-term digital storage. In: Proceedings of the 1st ACM SIGOPS/EuroSys European Conference on Computer Systems 2006, pp. 221–234 (2006)
4. Collomosse, J., et al.: Archangel: trusted archives of digital public documents. In: Proceedings of the ACM Symposium on Document Engineering 2018, pp. 1–4 (2018)
5. Halpin, H.: Nym credentials: Privacy-preserving decentralized identity with blockchains. In: 2020 Crypto Valley Conference on Blockchain Technology (CVCBT), pp. 56–67. IEEE (2020)
6. Lee, C.A., Kirschenbaum, M., Chassanoff, A., Olsen, P., Woods, K.: Bitcurator: tools and techniques for digital forensics in collecting institutions. D-Lib Mag. 18(5/6), 14–21 (2012)
7. Maniatis, P., Rosenthal, D.S., Roussopoulos, M., Baker, M., Giuli, T.J., Muliadi, Y.: Preserving peer replicas by rate-limited sampled voting. In: Proceedings of the Nineteenth ACM Symposium on Operating Systems Principles, pp. 44–59 (2003)
8. Maniatis, P., Roussopoulos, M., Giuli, T.J., Rosenthal, D.S., Baker, M.: The LOCKSS peer-to-peer digital preservation system. ACM Trans. Comput. Syst. (TOCS) 23(1), 2–50 (2005)
9. Narayanan, A., Bonneau, J., Felten, E., Miller, A., Goldfeder, S.: Bitcoin and Cryptocurrency Technologies: a Comprehensive Introduction. Princeton University Press, Princeton (2016)
10. Paulevé, L., Jégou, H., Amsaleg, L.: Locality sensitive hashing: A comparison of hash function types and querying mechanisms. Pattern Recogn. Lett. 31(11), 1348–1358 (2010)
11. Reich, V., Rosenthal, D.S.: LOCKSS (lots of copies keep stuff safe). New Rev. Acad. Librariansh. 6(1), 155–161 (2000)
12. Rosenthal, D.S., Robertson, T.S., Lipkis, T., Reich, V., Morabito, S.: Requirements for digital preservation systems: a bottom-up approach. arXiv preprint cs/0509018 (2005)
13. Van de Sompel, H., Nelson, M.L., Sanderson, R., Balakireva, L.L., Ainsworth, S., Shankar, H.: Memento: time travel for the web. arXiv preprint arXiv:0911.1112 (2009)
14. Troncoso, C., Isaakidis, M., Danezis, G., Halpin, H.: Systematizing decentralization and privacy: lessons from 15 years of research and deployments. Proc. Priv. Enhancing Technol. 4, 307–329 (2017)
15. Vermaaten, S., Lavoie, B., Caplan, P.: Identifying threats to successful digital preservation: the SPOT model for risk assessment. D-lib Mag. 18(9), 1–21 (2012)

Enabling Portability and Reusability
of Open Science Infrastructures

Giuseppe Grieco⬤, Ivan Heibi(✉)⬤, Arcangelo Massari⬤, Arianna Moretti⬤,
and Silvio Peroni⬤

Research Centre for Open Scholarly Metadata, Department of Classical Philology
and Italian Studies, University of Bologna, Bologna, Italy
{ivan.heibi2,arcangelo.massari,arianna.moretti4,silvio.peroni}@unibo.it

Abstract. This paper presents a methodology for designing a container-ized and distributed open science infrastructure to simplify its reusability, replicability, and portability in different environments. The methodology is depicted in a step-by-step schema based on four main phases: (1) Analysis, (2) Design, (3) Definition, and (4) Managing and provisioning. We accompany the description of each step with existing technologies and concrete examples of application.

Keywords: Open Science Infrastructures · OpenCitations · FAIR · POSI

1 Introduction

Open Science Infrastructures (OSInfras) are resources and services that the scholarly ecosystem depends upon to foster research and "to support open science and serve the needs of different communities" [19]. According to a survey published in 2020 [10], there are 120 OSInfras in Europe, heterogeneous by domain and objectives. In recent years, several founders – including the European Union with its financial support towards building the European Open Science Cloud (EOSC, https://eosc-portal.eu/about/eosc) – and institutions, such as UNESCO with its Open Science recommendations [19], have strongly emphasised how the survival of OSInfras is crucial for enabling Open (i.e. good) Science.

An OSInfra is made by several complementary pillars that concern (a) technological aspects (i.e. "software, hardware, and technical services" [15]), (b) social (i.e. the people behind the infrastructures) and (c) economic endeavours (i.e. their sustainability in the long term). Several guidelines, such as [3,8,18], have been published to help the scholarly community running, monitoring, and maintaining OSInfras in all these aspects.

Focusing on technological concerns, several of these guidelines agree on adopting open source software for running OSInfras' services. Indeed, both the *Principles for Open Scholarly Infrastructures* [3] and another recent report by the Knowledge Future Group about the values and principles for an OSInfra [18]

G. Silvello et al. (Eds.): TPDL 2022, LNCS 13541, pp. 379–385, 2022.
https://doi.org/10.1007/978-3-031-16802-4_36

mention using open software, technologies, standards, and protocols. Such principles are essential for ensuring that the OSInfra can be reusable and portable into new organisations if the original maintainer is not capable anymore of handling it. These aspects concerning the reusability (in the FAIR sense [7,11,14,20]) and portability of OSInfras are crucial values to guarantee. Indeed, in [18], the authors stress that an OSInfra should enable and encourage the reuse of code, and ensure the portability and durability of the content (including software and services) that it hosts. Others explicitly ask to enable easy migration of such content to another platform if needed [8], guaranteeing that all the ongoing assets can be "archived and preserved when passed to a successor organisation" [3].

An OSInfra is a complex system providing several services that can be either tied up into a monolithic container or distributed in distinct locations federated via APIs, and even if the software for replicating the OSInfra is released with open source licenses, this is not enough to guarantee reusability, portability, and redistribution of the OSInfra. Indeed, specific documentation and tools should be considered to allow an easy reuse and deployment in a different environment.

In this paper, to address the issues mentioned above, we present a methodology in four steps that proposes the adoption of existing technologies to enable the isolation, federation and distribution of the services of individual OSInfras to simplify their reusability, replicability and portability. The solution we propose is tied with the *infrastructure-as-code* (IaC) practice [1], where we use a standard language to design an infrastructure, including aspects related to scripting, automation, configuration, models, required dependencies, and parameters. This approach is combined with methods based on containers for separation and isolation of services to foster a more interoperable application packaging [16], platform-as-a-service (PaaS) runtimes [2], and a better scalability and reliability [9] of services, so that the software modification could be done directly on the desired service without impacting the other ones provided by the OSInfra [9].

All the steps of the methodology, introduced in Sect. 2, are accompanied by examples of (future) applications on OpenCitations (https://opencitations.net) [17], i.e. an existing OSInfra dedicated to the publication of open bibliographic metadata and citation data. Finally, in Sect. 3, we conclude the paper sketching out some future works.

2 Methodology

As summarised in Fig. 1, our methodology is based on four steps: (1) Analysis, (2) Design, (3) Definition, and (4) Managing and provisioning, that are detailed in the following subsections. The workflow of the methodology is bidirectional: in clockwise, the output of each step becomes the input of the following one; in counterclockwise, it enables a backward step (an explanation on when it is needed is discussed in the following subsections) to re-process and refine the output returned previously. In addition, the methodology is not entirely connected in a closed circle since the output of step 4 *is not* given as input to step 1 – and, thus, any counterclockwise move from step 1 to step 4 is prohibited.

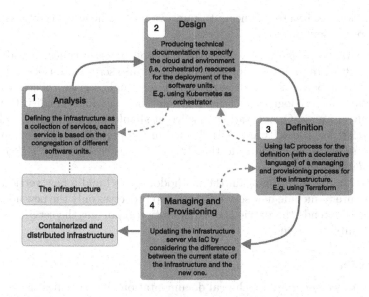

Fig. 1. The workflow summarising the steps of the proposed methodology.

2.1 Analysis

The aim of this step is to define a new organization to the infrastructure as a collection of separated services, each of them defined as a composition of different software units. This step is structured in two sub-steps.

First Sub-step: Software Units. We analyze the software units (e.g. specific libraries and applications) used by the infrastructure. This process should be done with the calculation of a trade-off between *decoupling* and *cohesion* [5], that are crucial aspects to consider for determining how well components communicate with each other and with the end-user. Decoupling avoids situations where highly coupled components cause intensive intra-infrastructure traffic and are logically codependent. Instead, when components are highly cohesive, managing the overall load balancing is challenging since it could be hard to isolate the components for which more resources are needed. In addition, a wise choice of the trade-off between these two aspects permits the integration of other third party components (e.g. software) inside the infrastructure. This aspect is particularly relevant to support a federated infrastructure.

If any problem arises during the definition of the software units, then a document should be produced highlighting how to improve the cohesion and decoupling trade-off with respect to infrastructure requirements. Issues detected in this phase do not concern system efficiency but rather the evaluation of relevant factors that might impact the logical design of a distributed infrastructure.

For example, OpenCitations (as of 5 June 2022) handles everything through one service, which is highly cohesive since it is the main hub in charge of several other sub-services, such as the website, the APIs, and the access to the stored collections. Therefore, in this case, a document should be produced to guide

OpenCitations' software engineers to improve such a huge cohesiveness before moving to the next sub-step.

Second Sub-step: Services. Once the trade-off between cohesion and decoupling is verified, the software units are organized into services to isolate the work of the different parts of the infrastructure. Each single service collects the software units which are logically related and relevant to its functionality. Considering the current main OpenCitations service, it should be split into several other services (that use the software units defined in the previous step). For instance, such new services should include the OpenCitations *website*, the *REST APIs*, and the *database access*.

In case we are iterating again the methodology to build a new version of the infrastructure to include new services, this step processes only the new additional services and extends the previous documentation reporting the services and the software units managed.

2.2   Design

In this step, we generate a technical documentation that specifies the resources needed by the software units composing the services provided by the infrastructure. The documentation describes the resources to be created in the cloud, e.g. virtual machines with specific computational and storage capacities provided to cloud users by particular cloud provider such as the Amazon Web Services, and in an environment managed by the *orchestrator*, i.e. a software agent that defines how to select, deploy, monitor, and dynamically control the configuration of multi-container packaged applications [6]. A popular orchestrator tool is Kubernetes [12]. In Kubernetes, an object is a *record of intent*: once it is created, Kubernetes constantly works to ensure that such object keeps working. In other words, creating an object tells Kubernetes how we want its workload to be handled in terms of usage of resources, including hardware resources and behaving policies (e.g., upgrades and fault-tolerance).

In OpenCitations, Kubernetes should be used to specify a *pod* (the smallest deployable unit of computing in Kubernetes) and its deployment specifications (e.g. load balancing) for each individual service, e.g. the *website* and *REST APIs*. Each pod groups all the containers needed to run a corresponding software unit needed by a particular service – for instance, in case of the OpenCitations *website*, we might use a pod for the database used for *authentication* and another for the *HTTP web server*. It should also be necessary to specify the hardware resources and network requirements for each pod, e.g. deciding to accept or not incoming requests external to the Kubernetes cluster – For example, for the *website*, we can grant to accept HTTP GET requests since it needs to be exposed externally.

The output of this step is a documentation which groups the containers and the cloud resources needed by each service, and defines the overall design of the infrastructure. Of course, we can go back to the previous step in case we find out that the services partitioning is not satisfying/correct, e.g., due to the inclusion of unrelated software units or if we think there are services that incorporate too many software units.

2.3 Definition

In this step, we define the design of the infrastructure using infrastructure-as-a-code (IaC) - a process for managing and provisioning an infrastructure by defining it through declarative language instead of using classical tools based on configuration files, CLI, and control panels [13]. In IaC, the declarative language specifies the desired state of the infrastructure, and lets the actions to achieve it be automatically inferred. One of the possible tools to adopt for declarative IaC is Terraform [4], a software for defining, launching, and managing IaC across a variety of cloud and virtualization platforms.

Using IaC gives us several advantages. It enables the unification of all resource definitions using a standard language, thus facilitating both maintenance and understanding by external adopters. In addition, specifying all the parameters for deployment in appropriate configuration files simplifies the infrastructure migration process, which is of particular relevance for supporting portability of the OSInfra, in case the organization decides to no longer maintain its services. Indeed, these aspects of IaC favor the organizations willing to reuse the infrastructure's services and preserve its heritage [3], ensure the development of a highly maintainable and sustainable software product [7], and foster reproducibility and reusability by facilitating OSInfra understanding and trust [20].

In this step, the resources (i.e. cloud and environment ones) are coded following the requirements established during the design phase. It might be necessary to return to the design phase if we realize that the infrastructure model does not provide sufficient detail on the resources needed, or in case some necessary resources are not included. In OpenCitations, we can use Terraform to declare the resources needed by each of the services following the documentation provided in the previous phase – for instance, the pods and the network configurations needed by OpenCitations *website* service.

2.4 Managing and Provisioning

This is the final step of the methodology, it takes in input the state of the infrastructure defined via IaC and updates the remote state of the server with respect to such definitions. This operation is accomplished again via IaC. Depending on the IaC technology used, the state of the infrastructure could be updated using two different strategies: push strategy—the state is sent to the recipient servers, or pull strategy—the state is pulled by the recipient servers. In case this is not the first iteration of the methodology, the state of the infrastructure is updated considering the delta between the current state of the infrastructure and the new one.

To evaluate the result of this phase and decide whether to go back to the previous step or not, benchmarks on the infrastructure are needed to assess the infrastructure efficiency from a technical point of view. It is worth mentioning that it is difficult to obtain the optimal infrastructure after one iteration, therefore it is highly expected to step backwards to previous steps and refine the results until we finally obtain the *desired* output.

The term *desired* is deliberately ambiguous, because the constraints might not be purely technical, e.g. the number of users to be supported or the financial limitations to respect. Therefore, a benchmark strategy for this step should test the infrastructure considering all these constraints.

In OpenCitations, concerning this step, we should design benchmarks for all the services, e.g. the *website*, the *REST APIs* and the *database access*, for instance through the application of massive stress tests on the services.

3   Discussion and Conclusions

Re-engineering an OSInfra from one single monolithic to a containerized and distributed model increases the scalability and reliability of its services. A continuous benchmark analysis of the system is essential to achieve the desired result, since the performances of the infrastructure components may vary with a large degree of unpredictability considering the new factors involved in the new distributed model.

One of the crucial aspects of this methodology concerns the use of IaC as a mean to promote the reproducibility and reusability of the infrastructure. IaC has been applied in literature for the research software. However, in this paper, we have abstracted this approach to involve the technical organisation of an OSInfra.

It is necessary that the implementation of each phase of the methodology is followed by software engineers and software developers. In addition, from an administrative point of view, the maintenance and management of this architectural model requires a continuous configuration, monitoring, and optimization of the components composing the infrastructure.

Finally, the methodology has been designed to be flexible and adaptable to specific use cases. Therefore, it is possible to integrate additional in-between sub-steps to address specific requirements, e.g. to refine the output of a step or to add other technical output required by a next step. Our upcoming plan is to apply the methodology to re-engineer the current OpenCitations technical infrastructure.

Acknowledgements. The work has been partially funded by the European Union's Horizon 2020 research and innovation program under grant agreement No 101017452 (OpenAIRE-Nexus).

References

1. Artac, M., Borovssak, T., Di Nitto, E., Guerriero, M., Tamburri, D.A.: DevOps: introducing infrastructure-as-code. In: 2017 IEEE/ACM 39th International Conference on Software Engineering Companion (ICSE-C), pp. 497–498 (2017). https://doi.org/10.1109/ICSE-C.2017.162
2. Bernstein, D.: Containers and cloud: From LXC to docker to Kubernetes. IEEE Cloud Comput. 1(3), 81–84 (2014). https://doi.org/10.1109/MCC.2014.51

3. Bilder, G., Lin, J., Neylon, C.: The principles of Open Scholarly Infrastructure (2020). https://doi.org/10.24343/C34W2H

4. Brikman, Y.: Terraform: Up and Running Writing Infrastructure as Code. O'Reilly Media Inc, 1st edn. (2017)

5. Candela, I., Bavota, G., Russo, B., Oliveto, R.: Using cohesion and coupling for software remodularization. ACM Trans. Softw. Eng. Methodol. 25(3), 1–28 (2016). https://doi.org/10.1145/2928268

6. Casalicchio, E.: Container orchestration: a survey. In: Puliafito, A., Trivedi, K.S. (eds.) Systems Modeling: Methodologies and Tools. EICC, pp. 221–235. Springer, Cham (2019). https://doi.org/10.1007/978-3-319-92378-9_14

7. Hong, N.P.C., et al.: FAIR principles for research software (FAIR4RS principles). In: Recommendations with RDA Endorsement in Process, Research Data Alliance (2022). https://doi.org/10.15497/RDA00068

8. Confederation of open access repositories, SPARC*: good practice principles for scholarly communication services. Technical report, Confederation Of Open Access Repositories and SPARC* (2019). https://sparcopen.org/our-work/good-practice-principles-for-scholarly-communication-services/

9. Fazio, M., Celesti, A., Ranjan, R., Liu, C., Chen, L., Villari, M.: Open issues in scheduling microservices in the cloud. IEEE Cloud Comput. 3(5), 81–88 (2016). https://doi.org/10.1109/MCC.2016.112

10. Ficarra, V., Fosci, M., Chiarelli, A., Kramer, B., Proudman, V.: Scoping the open science infrastructure landscape in Europe, October 2020. https://doi.org/10.5281/zenodo.4159838

11. Hasselbring, W., Carr, L., Hettrick, S., Packer, H., Tiropanis, T.: From FAIR research data toward fair and open research software. it-Inf. Technol. 62(1), 39–47 (2020). https://doi.org/10.1515/itit-2019-0040

12. Hightower, K., Burns, B., Beda, J.: Kubernetes: Up and Running Dive into the Future of Infrastructure. O'Reilly Media Inc, 1st edn. (2017)

13. Johann, S.: Kief Morris on infrastructure as code. IEEE Softw. 34(1), 117–120 (2017). https://doi.org/10.1109/MS.2017.13

14. Lamprecht, A.L., et al.: Towards FAIR principles for research software. Data sci. 3(1), 37–59 (2020). https://doi.org/10.3233/DS-190026

15. Lin, D., et al.: The TRUST principles for digital repositories. Sci. Data 7(1), 144 (2020). https://doi.org/10.1038/s41597-020-0486-7, http://www.nature.com/articles/s41597-020-0486-7

16. Morabito, R., Kjällman, J., Komu, M.: Hypervisors vs. lightweight virtualization: a performance comparison. In: 2015 IEEE International Conference on Cloud Engineering, pp. 386–393 (2015). https://doi.org/10.1109/IC2E.2015.74

17. Peroni, S., Shotton, D.: OpenCitations, an infrastructure organization for open scholarship. Quant. Sci. Stud. 1(1), 428–444 (2020). https://doi.org/10.1162/qss_a_00023

18. Skinner, K., Lippincott, S.: Values and principles framework and assessment checklist. Technical report, Knowledge Futures Group, July 2020. https://doi.org/10.21428/6ffd8432.5175bab1

19. UNESCO: UNESCO Recommendation on Open Science. Programme and meeting document SC-PCB-SPP/2021/OS/UROS, UNESCO (2021). https://unesdoc.unesco.org/ark:/48223/pf0000379949

20. Wilkinson, M.D., et al.: The FAIR guiding principles for scientific data management and stewardship. Sci. Data 3(1), 160018 (2016). https://doi.org/10.1038/sdata.2016.18

Simulating User Querying Behavior Using Embedding Space Alignment

Saber Zerhoudi[(⊠)] and Michael Granitzer

University of Passau, Passau, Germany
{saber.zerhoudi,michael.granitzer}@uni-passau.de

Abstract. Simulation is used as a cost-efficient and repeatable means of experimentation to support Information Retrieval (IR) systems and digital libraries with more realistic directives when user interaction data is lacking. While simulation has been mainly used for the study of user search behaviours, we argue that the potential of using it for generating querying behavior is in its infancy. In this paper, we describe a pilot study to simulate query sessions via embedding alignment techniques and assess its capability of transferring knowledge from one source to the other. Besides, we validate the simulated query sessions using a cost and benefit evaluation task and investigate whether they can reproduce properties of real query sessions. We found that Skip-thought vectors are well suited for query embedding. In particular, using Skip-thought with vocabulary expansion as a support for embedding alignment techniques is effective in transferring contextualized embeddings that represent a user querying behavior. While the results of the performance evaluation are encouraging and comparable to related research, it is still challenging to simulate interactive query reformulations.

Keywords: Query simulation · Embeddings alignment · Query embedding · User querying behavior

1 Introduction

Originally, the Cranfield paradigm [10] is considered to be the leading methodology for evaluating Information Retrieval (IR) systems and platforms such as digital libraries. It standardizes the notion of test collections and introduces a series of implicit and explicit assumptions about the retrieval systems and their users. These assumptions can lead to a highly abstracted and simplified understanding of users representation which does not reflect the complexity of real search behavior. To compensate for this shortcoming, the use of the history log of user interactions has been introduced in the evaluation process. However, due to privacy concerns, log data is usually achieved on the cost of the confidentiality of users' personal information. TREC Session Track [7] and Dynamic Test Collections [6] are two important attempts to address the lack of user interactions in the evaluation process. They expand Test Collections with sequences of simulated interactions (i.e., simulation of queries, clicks, stopping, dwell).

© Springer Nature Switzerland AG 2022
G. Silvello et al. (Eds.): TPDL 2022, LNCS 13541, pp. 386–394, 2022.
https://doi.org/10.1007/978-3-031-16802-4_37

There has been growing interest in the generation of simulated query behavior, and in particular how to develop more realistic query variants [5,18], for multiple reasons: First, query simulation offers a way to overcome the lack of experimental real-world data, especially when the acquisition of such data is costly or challenging (e.g., academic search engines). Second, it helps studying the robustness of ranking models when faced with query variations [25]. While most related studies focus on query generation strategies (i.e., user query variants), few studies have investigated the utility of simulating user querying behavior. To the best of our knowledge, the degree to which querying simulators reproduce real user query sessions has not yet been analyzed with TREC test collections.

The query formulation is one of the first user interactions with the search system and serves as a critical component for any subsequent simulated interactions like clicks. As opposed to previous work in this regard, it is not our primary goal to generate the most effective queries but rather to simulate and evaluate if simulated query sessions represent a better approximation of the original ones.

To summarise, the main contributions of our work are as follows: (1) We investigate the use of Skip-thought as an encoder-decoder model to generate query embedding, (2) we expand our query model's vocabulary using alignment embedding and sent2vec, we then learn a mapping function to simulate new query pairs, (3) we evaluate the performance of our approaches using Cost and Benefit evaluation tasks.

2   Approach

In this study, our goal is not to simulate query strings using query variant generation techniques. Instead, we seek to model and simulate user querying behavior, and evaluate to which extend simulated query sessions can replace or complement sample-based ones.

2.1   Querying Behavior Simulation

In the following, we first outline the Skip-thought model that we used for query representation. We then describe how we explored supervised sentence to sentence embedding alignment to (1) expand our model's vocabulary and (2) develop a querying behavior model.

Query Embedding Model: We propose investigating the use of Skip-thought as an encoder-decoder model [16] to generate query embeddings. The encoder outputs a fixed-dimension vector as the representation z_i for the input query q_i. Then, conditioned on the representation z_i, two separate decoders are trained to minimise the reconstruction error of the surrounding queries (i.e., preceding query q_{i-1} and succeeding query q_{i+1} given the embedding z_i in a search session).

This reconstruction error is back-propagated to the encoder which maps the input query to its surrounding queries in the context of a search session. After training, we discard the decoders and only keep the trained encoder as it captures both syntactic and semantic properties. We implemented the Skip-thought model under the same settings and encoder design according to Kiros et al. [16].[1] Since the comparison among different recurrent neural networks is not our main focus, we decide to work with gated recurrent unit (GRU) [8], which is fast and stable while dealing with language modeling tasks [9].

Instead of learning to compose a query representation solely from the token (i.e., word) representations, the Skip-thought model utilizes the structure and relationship of the adjacent queries in the context of user search sessions. Similarly to the original Skip-thought model, our model depends on having a training corpus of contiguous text. We chose to use a collection of query log sessions, namely the user query variations (UQV) dataset [3] (Sect. 2.3).

Query Vocabulary Expansion: In order to generalize the Skip-thought model trained with relatively small, fixed queries' vocabulary to a large amount unseen queries, Kiros et al. [16] proposed a word expansion method that learns a linear mapping between the pretrained word embeddings *word2vec* and learned RNN word embeddings [20]. In our approach, we extend their method and use sent2vec [22] to induce query representations. Thus, the model benefits from the generalization ability of the pretrained Skip-thought query embeddings.

Let $\mathcal{V}_{ST}$ denote the Skip-thought query embedding space and $\mathcal{V}_{s2v}$ the query embedding space of a dataset containing a list of single queries. Such a dataset can either be found in the literature (i.e., TREC 2019 Deep Learning Track [11])[2] or put together using state-of-the-art query variant generation techniques [5].

We assume the vocabulary of $\mathcal{V}_{s2v}$ is much larger than that of $\mathcal{V}_{ST}$. Our goal is to construct a mapping $f : \mathcal{V}_{s2v} \rightarrow \mathcal{V}_{ST}$ parameterized by a matrix W such that $v\prime = Wv$, where $v \in \mathcal{V}_{s2v}$ and $v\prime \in \mathcal{V}_{ST}$. Inspired by Mikolov et al. [20], we solve an unregularized L2 linear regression loss for the matrix W by learning linear mappings between both query spaces. Thus, any query from $\mathcal{V}_{s2v}$ can now be mapped into $\mathcal{V}_{ST}$.

Query Embedding Alignment: A user query session can be divided into pairs of consecutive queries (q_i, q_{i+1}). Let D_1 and D_2 be two subdatasets, originating from the same query session dataset D. D_1 contains only the set of source queries q_i and D_2 the set of target queries q_{i+1} available in D across all query sessions. The functions $f_1 : D_1 \rightarrow \mathbb{R}^{d_1}$ and $f_2 : D_2 \rightarrow \mathbb{R}^{d_2}$ represent two mappings from the two subdatasets to their associated vector embedding spaces.

Given source query embedding v_{q_i} and target query embedding $v_{q_{i+1}}$ acquired using our Skip-thought model described above, the relationship between these two vector spaces represents the query reformulation and can be captured by a linear mapping function $A : \mathbb{R}^{d_1} \rightarrow \mathbb{R}^{d_2}$ such that $A(f_1(q_i)) \approx f_2(q_{i+1})$. Following

---

[1] The skip-thought code is available at https://github.com/ryankiros/skip-thoughts.
[2] https://microsoft.github.io/msmarco/TREC-Deep-Learning-2019.

Mikolov et al. [20]'s findings, we use their linear regression model and find a transformation matrix W such that Wv_{q_i} approximates $v_{q_{i+1}}$.

This mapping can then be applied to simulate new query pairs. Particularly, for any given new source query q_j and its continuous vector representation v_{q_j}, we can map it to the target space by computing $v_{q_{j+1}} = Wv_{q_j}$. Then we find the query whose representation is closest to $v_{q_{j+1}}$ in the target query space, using cosine similarity as the distance metric.

2.2 Evaluation

We evaluate the performance of our approaches for Cost and Benefit tasks. State-of-the-art methods often evaluate **only single queries**, on several evaluation tasks. It includes semantic relatedness (SICK) [19], paraphrase detection (MSRP) [12], question type classification (TREC) [17], and 4 benchmark datasets [14,23,24,26]. However, in order to account for a more user-oriented evaluation, we simulate and evaluate instead query sessions with regards to the cost (number of submitted queries) and the resulting benefit (cumulated gain).

We first simulate query sessions of ten queries and an increasing number of documents per query. Then we evaluate the results using the sDCG measure [15] as the cumulated gain is discounted for each result and query. Furthermore, we explore Azzopardi's economic theory [1] to evaluate the closeness between isoquants (i.e., for a fix level of cumulated gain, query reformulations can be compensated by browsing depth and vice versa) of simulated and real queries by the Mean Squared Logarithmic Error (MSLE).

2.3 Datasets and Implementation Details

In our experimental setup, we simulate query sessions using two approaches: (1) Skip-thought model and query vocabulary expansion which we denote ST_{s2v}, (2) Skip-thought model, query vocabulary expansion, and query embedding alignment which we denote ST_{EA}.

To model query embeddings, we use the user query variations (UQV) dataset provided by Benham et al. [3][3]. For each topic texts, users formulated at least one query for each topic, and the fifth user (denoted as $(UQV)^5$) formulated ten queries for each topic. More details about the query collection process are provided by Bailey et al. [2]. In addition, to evaluate the performance of our approaches for Cost and Benefit tasks, we use Anserini [27] to index the topics of TREC Common Core 2017 (Core17) [4] test collection using The New York Times Annotated Corpus [21] and retrieve the initial ranking list using a BM25 ranker and Anserini's default parameters (b = 0.4, k = 0.9).

According to Breuer et al. [5], to achieve a better approximation of user queries, they should be simulated using methods that allow parameterizing the query reformulation behavior. Authors introduced some state-of-the-art query

---

[3] Dataset is available at https://culpepper.io/publications/robust-uqv.txt.gz and http://dx.doi.org/10.4225/49/5726E597B8376.

generation strategies which provide better approximations of real query effectiveness. In this study, we compare our methods to their two best strategies (i.e., TTS_{S4} and $TTS_{S4''}$) using the same experimental setup. In both strategies, searchers consider every possible combination of 4-grams made from a term set composed of the topic's title, description and narrative. TTS_{S4} searchers tend to prefer topic terms and mostly keep terms of previous queries while $TTS_{S4''}$ searchers stick to the topic terms without necessarily keeping terms of previous queries. In the following we denote TTS_{S4} and $TTS_{S4''}$ strategies as B_{S1} and B_{S2} respectively and use them as a strong baseline to evaluate our approaches.

To expand our query model vocabulary, we use B_{S1} and B_{S2} strategies to simulate single queries from all the Core17 test collection topic's title, description and narrative. Let D_{c17} be the resulting dataset. Thus, our goal is to learn linear mappings $f : \mathcal{V}_{c17} \rightarrow \mathcal{V}_{UQV}$ between both query spaces.

3   Experimental Results

We aim to investigate whether simulated query sessions can replace or complement sample-based ones. Therefore, we simulate query sessions of ten queries each using the following approaches: ST_{s2v}, ST_{EA}, B_{S1} and B_{S2}, and evaluate them using the sDCG measure (instantiated with b = 2, bq = 4). Figure 1 (top) reports the results for sessions with 3, 5, or 10 queries and an increasing number of documents per query, and compares the original queries of $(UQV)^5$ [2] to the simulated query sessions using above-mentioned approaches. We note that the cumulative gain is correlated with the number of queries per session, which indicates that the cumulative gain grows rapidly when more queries per session are used. Moreover, we notice a similarity between the cumulative gains by the $(UQV)^5$ and ST_{EA} queries. This shows that it is possible to reproduce a cumulative gain close to that of real queries using the ST_{EA} approach.

Figure 1 (bottom) illustrates the trade-off between querying and documents assessing of a simulated user to reach predefined levels of nDCG $(0.2, 0.4)$. As the browsing depth increases, the number of submitted queries decreases and vice versa. This phenomena is similar for all the approaches, although the least amount of assessed documents is achieved with B_{S1} queries (i.e., lower bound limits) and the most with ST_{s2v} queries (i.e., upper bound limits) which can be explained by the poorer retrieval performance. To gain further insights, we evaluate the closeness between isoquants (i.e., the minimum amount of inputs required to produce a specified level of gain) of simulated and real queries using MSLE measure. As shown by the MSLE table, the B_{S1} isoquant has the lowest error for all values of nDCG. In particular, we notice a better approximation of the $(UQV)^5$ isoquant with the ST_{EA} method and that it is possible to reproduce economic properties through mapping the query reformulation behavior.

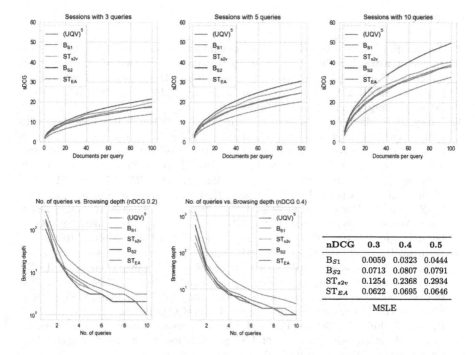

Fig. 1. Top: simulations with 3, 5, or 10 queries per session evaluated by sDCG, and bottom: Isoquants and MSLE across simulations and UQV^5 with fixed nDCG.

4 Conclusion

This paper explores the possibility to simulate querying behavior using embedding space alignment with an auxiliary Skip-thought embedding representation of queries. We showed that the resulting method named ST_{EA} obtains consistently better approximation of real query sessions using the Cost and Benefit evaluation tasks. Moreover, it models the user querying behavior on a dataset and utilizes it to better simulate query sessions on another. One limitation of our approach is that it excludes the relevance feedback from previous search results - as users normally include terms of documents or snippets they consider as relevant [13] in their query reformulations - and neglect of click simulations. In future, this work aims to be applied for complementing user search behavior simulation, and exploring more advanced alignment techniques.

The proposed approach represents a theoretical foundation for experimental studies of alignment techniques and opens up many opportunities to leverage query log data to generate various realistic query simulators especially for search sessions datasets lacking query logs.

Acknowledgments. This work has been partially supported by the DFG (German Research Foundation) through the project 408022022 "SINIR – Simulating INteractive Information Retrieval".

References

1. Azzopardi, L.: The economics in interactive information retrieval. In: Ma, W., Nie, J., Baeza-Yates, R., Chua, T., Croft, W.B. (eds.) Proceeding of the 34th International ACM SIGIR Conference on Research and Development in Information Retrieval, SIGIR 2011, Beijing, China, 25–29 July 2011, pp. 15–24. ACM (2011). https://doi.org/10.1145/2009916.2009923
2. Bailey, P., Moffat, A., Scholer, F., Thomas, P.: UQV100: a test collection with query variability. In: Perego, R., Sebastiani, F., Aslam, J.A., Ruthven, I., Zobel, J. (eds.) Proceedings of the 39th International ACM SIGIR Conference on Research and Development in Information Retrieval, SIGIR 2016, Pisa, Italy, 17–21 July 2016, pp. 725–728. ACM (2016). https://doi.org/10.1145/2911451.2914671
3. Benham, R., Culpepper, J.S.: Risk-reward trade-offs in rank fusion. In: Koopman, B., Zuccon, G., Carman, M.J. (eds.) Proceedings of the 22nd Australasian Document Computing Symposium, ADCS 2017, Brisbane, QLD, Australia, 7–8 December 2017, pp. 1:1–1:8. ACM (2017). https://doi.org/10.1145/3166072.3166084
4. Benham, R., et al.: RMIT at the 2017 TREC CORE track. In: Voorhees, E.M., Ellis, A. (eds.) Proceedings of The Twenty-Sixth Text Retrieval Conference, TREC 2017, Gaithersburg, Maryland, USA, 15–17 November 2017. NIST Special Publication, vol. 500–324. National Institute of Standards and Technology (NIST) (2017). https://trec.nist.gov/pubs/trec26/papers/RMIT-CC.pdf
5. Breuer, T., Fuhr, N., Schaer, P.: Validating simulations of user query variants. In: Hagen, M., et al. (eds.) ECIR 2022. LNCS, vol. 13185, pp. 80–94. Springer, Cham (2022). https://doi.org/10.1007/978-3-030-99736-6_6
6. Carterette, B., Bah, A., Zengin, M.: Dynamic test collections for retrieval evaluation. In: Allan, J., Croft, W.B., de Vries, A.P., Zhai, C. (eds.) Proceedings of the 2015 International Conference on The Theory of Information Retrieval, ICTIR 2015, Northampton, Massachusetts, USA, 27–30 September 2015, pp. 91–100. ACM (2015). https://doi.org/10.1145/2808194.2809470
7. Carterette, B., Kanoulas, E., Hall, M.M., Clough, P.D.: Overview of the TREC 2014 session track. In: Voorhees, E.M., Ellis, A. (eds.) Proceedings of The Twenty-Third Text REtrieval Conference, TREC 2014, Gaithersburg, Maryland, USA, 19–21 November 2014. NIST Special Publication, vol. 500–308. National Institute of Standards and Technology (NIST) (2014). http://trec.nist.gov/pubs/trec23/papers/overview-session.pdf
8. Cho, K., van Merrienboer, B., Bahdanau, D., Bengio, Y.: On the properties of neural machine translation: encoder-decoder approaches. In: Wu, D., Carpuat, M., Carreras, X., Vecchi, E.M. (eds.) Proceedings of SSST@EMNLP 2014, Eighth Workshop on Syntax, Semantics and Structure in Statistical Translation, Doha, Qatar, 25 October 2014, pp. 103–111. Association for Computational Linguistics (2014). https://doi.org/10.3115/v1/W14-4012
9. Chung, J., Gülçehre, Ç., Cho, K., Bengio, Y.: Empirical evaluation of gated recurrent neural networks on sequence modeling. CoRR abs/1412.3555 (2014), http://arxiv.org/abs/1412.3555
10. Cleverdon, C., Mills, J., Keen, M.: Factors Determining the Performance of Indexing Systems (1966)
11. Craswell, N., Mitra, B., Yilmaz, E., Campos, D., Voorhees, E.M.: Overview of the TREC 2019 deep learning track. CoRR abs/2003.07820 (2020), https://arxiv.org/abs/2003.07820

12. Dolan, B., Quirk, C., Brockett, C.: Unsupervised construction of large paraphrase corpora: Exploiting massively parallel news sources. In: COLING 2004, 20th International Conference on Computational Linguistics, Proceedings of the Conference, 23–27 August 2004, Geneva, Switzerland (2004). https://aclanthology.org/C04-1051/

13. Eickhoff, C., Teevan, J., White, R., Dumais, S.T.: Lessons from the journey: a query log analysis of within-session learning. In: Carterette, B., Diaz, F., Castillo, C., Metzler, D. (eds.) Seventh ACM International Conference on Web Search and Data Mining, WSDM 2014, New York, NY, USA, 24–28 February 2014, pp. 223–232. ACM (2014). https://doi.org/10.1145/2556195.2556217

14. Hu, M., Liu, B.: Mining and summarizing customer reviews. In: Kim, W., Kohavi, R., Gehrke, J., DuMouchel, W. (eds.) Proceedings of the Tenth ACM SIGKDD International Conference on Knowledge Discovery and Data Mining, Seattle, Washington, USA, 22–25 August 2004, pp. 168–177. ACM (2004). https://doi.org/10.1145/1014052.1014073

15. Järvelin, K., Price, S.L., Delcambre, L.M.L., Nielsen, M.L.: Discounted cumulated gain based evaluation of multiple-query IR sessions. In: Macdonald, C., Ounis, I., Plachouras, V., Ruthven, I., White, R.W. (eds.) ECIR 2008. LNCS, vol. 4956, pp. 4–15. Springer, Heidelberg (2008). https://doi.org/10.1007/978-3-540-78646-7_4

16. Kiros, R., et al.: Skip-thought vectors. CoRR abs/1506.06726 (2015), http://arxiv.org/abs/1506.06726

17. Li, X., Roth, D.: Learning question classifiers. In: 19th International Conference on Computational Linguistics, COLING 2002, Howard International House and Academia Sinica, Taipei, Taiwan, 24 August–1 September 2002. https://aclanthology.org/C02-1150/

18. Mackenzie, J., Moffat, A.: Modality effects when simulating user querying tasks. In: Hasibi, F., Fang, Y., Aizawa, A. (eds.) ICTIR 2021: The 2021 ACM SIGIR International Conference on the Theory of Information Retrieval, Virtual Event, Canada, 11 July 2021, pp. 197–201. ACM (2021). https://doi.org/10.1145/3471158.3472244

19. Marelli, M., Menini, S., Baroni, M., Bentivogli, L., Bernardi, R., Zamparelli, R.: A SICK cure for the evaluation of compositional distributional semantic models. In: Calzolari, N., et al. (eds.) Proceedings of the Ninth International Conference on Language Resources and Evaluation, LREC 2014, Reykjavik, Iceland, 26–31 May 2014, pp. 216–223. European Language Resources Association (ELRA) (2014). http://www.lrec-conf.org/proceedings/lrec2014/summaries/363.html

20. Mikolov, T., Le, Q.V., Sutskever, I.: Exploiting similarities among languages for machine translation. CoRR abs/1309.4168 (2013). http://arxiv.org/abs/1309.4168

21. Mozzherina, E.: An approach to improving the classification of the New York times annotated corpus. In: Klinov, P., Mouromtsev, D. (eds.) KESW 2013. CCIS, vol. 394, pp. 83–91. Springer, Heidelberg (2013). https://doi.org/10.1007/978-3-642-41360-5_7

22. Pagliardini, M., Gupta, P., Jaggi, M.: Unsupervised learning of sentence embeddings using compositional n-gram features. In: Walker, M.A., Ji, H., Stent, A. (eds.) Proceedings of the 2018 Conference of the North American Chapter of the Association for Computational Linguistics: Human Language Technologies, NAACL-HLT 2018, New Orleans, Louisiana, USA, 1–6 June 2018, Volume 1 (Long Papers), pp. 528–540. Association for Computational Linguistics (2018). https://doi.org/10.18653/v1/n18-1049

23. Pang, B., Lee, L.: A sentimental education: sentiment analysis using subjectivity summarization based on minimum cuts. In: Scott, D., Daelemans, W., Walker, M.A. (eds.) Proceedings of the 42nd Annual Meeting of the Association for Computational Linguistics, 21–26 July, 2004, Barcelona, Spain, pp. 271–278. ACL (2004). https://doi.org/10.3115/1218955.1218990

24. Pang, B., Lee, L.: Seeing stars: exploiting class relationships for sentiment categorization with respect to rating scales. In: Knight, K., Ng, H.T., Oflazer, K. (eds.) ACL 2005, 43rd Annual Meeting of the Association for Computational Linguistics, Proceedings of the Conference, 25–30 June 2005, University of Michigan, USA, pp. 115–124. The Association for Computer Linguistics (2005). https://doi.org/10.3115/1219840.1219855

25. Penha, G., Câmara, A., Hauff, C.: Evaluating the robustness of retrieval pipelines with query variation generators. In: Hagen, M., et al. (eds.) ECIR 2022. LNCS, vol. 13185, pp. 397–412. Springer, Cham (2022). https://doi.org/10.1007/978-3-030-99736-6_27

26. Wiebe, J., Wilson, T., Cardie, C.: Annotating expressions of opinions and emotions in language. Lang. Resour. Evaluation **39**(2–3), 165–210 (2005). https://doi.org/10.1007/s10579-005-7880-9

27. Yang, P., Fang, H., Lin, J.: Anserini: reproducible ranking baselines using Lucene. ACM J. Data Inf. Qual. **10**(4), 16:1–16:20 (2018). https://doi.org/10.1145/3239571

A Closer Look into Collaborative Publishing at Software-Engineering Conferences

Rand Alchokr[1]([✉])[iD], Jacob Krüger[2][iD], Yusra Shakeel[1,3][iD], Gunter Saake[1][iD], and Thomas Leich[4][iD]

[1] Otto-von-Guericke University, Magdeburg, Germany
{rand.alchokr,saake}@ovgu.de
[2] Ruhr-University, Bochum, Germany
jacob.krueger@rub.de
[3] Karlsruhe Institute of Technology, Karlsruhe, Germany
yusra.shakeel@kit.edu
[4] Harz University and METOP GmbH, Wernigerode, Germany
tleich@hs-harz.de

Abstract. Computer science and particularly software engineering is a rapidly evolving research discipline increasingly conducted by large, collaborative teams. Unfortunately, there is little research on the underlying publication activity and collaboration patterns in software engineering. To address this gap, we study two properties of research collaborations in software engineering: the number of collaborators (i.e., authors of a paper) and their academic age (i.e., their experience of working in research). More precisely, we investigate collaborations for papers published at all main tracks of three top-level software-engineering conferences (i.e., ASE, ESEC/FSE, ICSE) and one top-level reference conference (i.e., JCDL), including a total of 5,188 papers and the corresponding 8,730 unique authors. Our results indicate that collaboration is more prevalent now than ever before, with a decline in the proportion of researchers who contribute single-author papers. Moreover, our analysis revealed that the ideal team size seems to range from two to four researchers, and that junior researchers seem to need the support of more experienced co-authors to get published at such top-level conferences. Ultimately, our goal is to understand how collaborations in software engineering have evolved and impact different researchers (e.g., newcomers, juniors), helping to highlight potential impediments and consequent improvements regarding the quality of research, collaborations, and mentoring.

Keywords: Software engineering · Publications · Scientific collaboration · Junior researchers

1 Introduction

Collaboration is key in research to cope with the complex nature and rapidly evolving corpus of scientific work—specifically in computer-science-related

© Springer Nature Switzerland AG 2022
G. Silvello et al. (Eds.): TPDL 2022, LNCS 13541, pp. 395–402, 2022.
https://doi.org/10.1007/978-3-031-16802-4_38

disciplines with their high pace of advancements. Consequently, there has been an increased emphasis on collaboration as a tool of science [20]. Scientific collaboration refers to a number of individuals (e.g., researchers, students, practitioners) working together on a research problem that leads to a co-authored research paper. Collaboration is a complex task that depends on the involved researchers' attitude towards it and involves numerous social factors that may impede or facilitate its cooperative aspects. Most studies build on the underlying assumption that collaborative activity increases research productivity [11,25]. Still, other studies revealed contribution challenges that certain groups of researchers face, for instance, new researchers (e.g., juniors, newcomers) [1,3,9,19]. As a consequence, it is particularly important to understand how different groups of researchers are involved in and impacted by scientific collaborations.

For our work, we consider the activity of writing and publishing papers to reflect on the interaction between researchers. In this paper, we take a step towards understanding how junior researchers are involved in scientific collaborations by quantitatively analyzing their publishing activity, co-authors, and evolutionary patterns. For this purpose, we elicited data from digital libraries with *the goal of understanding scientific collaborations' impact on publication productivity inside the software-engineering (SE) community over time with a focus on the involvement of junior researchers.* To address this goal, we defined two research questions (RQs):

RQ1. *Are collaboration patterns in software-engineering stable over time?*
RQ2. *What are frequent collaboration patterns for software-engineering juniors?*

Precisely, we tracked the collaborations of authors at the following three top-level software-engineering conferences (1, 2, 3) and one reference conference (4), each of which involves more junior researchers as active participants over the past years: 1) IEEE/ACM International Conference on Automated Software Engineering (ASE), 2) ACM Joint European Software Engineering Conference and Symposium on the Foundations of Software Engineering (ESEC/FSE), 3) IEEE/ACM International Conference on Software Engineering (ICSE), and 4) ACM/IEEE Joint Conference on Digital Libraries (JCDL). These conferences have a high reputation, which is why most researchers of any academic age and reputation aim to publish at them.

We report the results of our quantitative analysis involving 5,188 main-track papers written by 8,730 authors over a time period of 43 years, from 1975 to 2020. Our complete dataset is available as an open-access repository.[1] Unfortunately, it is not possible to study the papers that were rejected at each conference, which is why we have to be careful with interpreting our results since they build only on accepted and published papers. Still, the results of our analysis reveal important insights concerning SE research, collaboration patterns, and the involvement of junior researchers. Our findings uncover a changing trend in each of the selected conferences from papers with few or single authors towards multi-authored papers, indicating an ideal team size of two to four researchers. The analysis also indicates juniors' needs for collaboration to be successful in

---

[1] https://doi.org/10.5281/zenodo.6824306.

getting their papers accepted at such conferences. Ultimately, we hope that the results of our study provide a better understanding of scientific collaboration and serve as a foundation for further research to understand whether certain groups of researchers are over- or underrepresented.

2 Background and Related Work

Collaboration is key for advancing science and creating new knowledge; generally defined by two elements: working together for a common goal and sharing knowledge [12]. Researchers tend to collaborate due to different factors, such as their different specializations and the growth of interdisciplinary fields [4]. Their different skills and expertise benefit the development of research projects and corresponding papers, which is why multi-authored papers are common in science [4,12]. Eventually, research on scientific collaborations has aimed to understand collaboration patterns to better comprehend the scientific process [17,18]. For instance, Costas and Bordons [8] present results regarding collaborations between members from more than one group. The results indicate a constantly increasing number and frequency of collaborations over time. Related bibliometrics study [10,13] focus on authorship trends in software engineering, and found that the number of authors is increasing on average with around 0.40 authors/decade until 1980. Other studies concentrate on more specific collaboration aspect, such as co-authorships (e.g., author order in multi-authored papers), that are critical components for successful collaborations.

Since most research teams comprise both early and later career scientists, studies concerning these two groups have been conducted. For example, Zhou et al. [24] found that newcomers tend to collaborate more with existing group members than with other newcomers to gain more experience and reputation. Similarly, juniors (i.e., researchers that have worked up to three years in academia [1,14]) were the focal point of several studies due to their essential role in providing innovative ideas, and broadening the scope of collaborations [16] as well as their high motivation that can inspire others and improve the work atmosphere [1–3]. While most of such studies report interesting findings, the datasets used are old and they do not investigate collaboration over time, specifically between authors with different levels of expertise. Out study in this paper fills this gap by extracting recent papers and analyzing evolution trends.

3 Methodology

We extracted data for four top-level conferences, because computer-science (and particularly software-engineering) research is generally more focused on those instead of journals [7,15,22]. Namely, we studied the main research tracks of these conferences from their first edition (in parentheses) until 2020, with three software-engineering ones (ASE 1991; ESEC/FSE 1987; ICSE 1976) and one partially software-engineering related (JCDL 2001). We chose JCDL because it is more general than the other conferences, and thus serves as a reference to comparing software engineering to other computer-science fields.

Table 1. Overview of our dataset.

Conference	Period	# Papers	# Authors	# Unique authors
ASE	1991–2020	1,069	3,740	2,482
ESEC/FSE	1987–2020	1,239	4,264	2,614
ICSE	1976–2020	2,300	7,434	4,380
JCDL	2001–2020	580	2,087	1,393
Total		5,188	17,525	8,730

For our analysis, we collected data by automatically crawling *dblp*,[2] which provides structured bibliographic data and distinguishes authors with identical names. To improve the quality of our data, we studied only main research-track papers and manually compared the session information in dblp to official information in the ACM Digital Library[3] to identify mislabeled papers. However, some older conferences did not clearly label their papers, which us why we excluded a paper if it comprised fewer than seven pages. Overall, our analysis resulted in a total of 5,188 main-track papers, which we summarize in Table 1. Note that the total number of unique authors (8,730) is not the sum of the last column, since we counted each author only once across all conferences. For each extracted paper, we additionally crawled and extracted the corresponding authors' bibliographic data from dblp.

4   RQ1: Collaboration Patterns

Measurements. To understand how collaboration patterns between researchers changed over time (**RQ1**), we measured for each conference individually the total number of single-authored papers, the single-junior-authored papers, the number of multi-authored papers, and the number of papers written by multiple authors where a junior author is the first author. We distinguish junior authors from other authors based on the academic age of each author using the authors' first publication year ($Year_{firstPaper}$) and a paper's publishing year ($Year_{paper}$), extracted from dblp individually for each (author, paper) pair. The academic age is the time span for which a researcher has actively published papers, which we computed as follows:

$$Age_{academic} = Year_{paper} - Year_{firstPaper} + 1 \qquad (1)$$

Junior researchers have an academic age that ranges from one up to three years.

Results. The average number of authors for the papers during the observation period increases on average (year/average):

- ASE: 1991/2,0 – 2000/2,8 – 2010/3,7 – 2015/4,1 – 2020/4,8
- ESEC/FSE: 1987/2,2 – 2000/2,5 – 2010/3,3 – 2015/3,8 – 2020/4,6

---

[2] https://dblp.uni-trier.de/.
[3] https://dl.acm.org/proceedings.

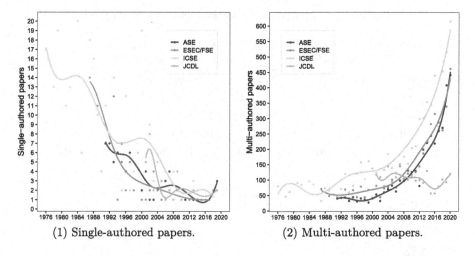

(1) Single-authored papers.   (2) Multi-authored papers.

Fig. 1. Authorship trends at the four conferences.

- ICSE: 1978/1,8 – 2000/2,5 – 2010/3,7 – 2015/4,1 – 2020/4,8
- JCDL: 2001/3,0 – 2010/3,7 – 2015/3,2 – 2020/3,6

The average increases and seeing that the changing number of authors does not fully align with the number of accepted papers (e.g., ICSE'12: 87; '13: 85; '14: 99; '15: 82; '16: 101) [5], it seems that the continuous increase is caused by more collaboration [6]. This is a widely acknowledged pattern caused by the number of authors on papers increasing over time [23].

We display the number of papers written by single and multiple authors in Fig. 1. Here, we can see that collaboration has been trending upwards. The high variance particularly in the earlier years may have various reasons, such as the number of active researchers at that time or the popularity of the computer-science domain and software engineering. Moving to juniors' contributions and the level of collaboration they need to reach top-level conferences, we display in Table 2 the number of single-authored papers and single-junior-authored papers—in addition to the papers where a junior is the first/lead author. It is clear that juniors tend to participate at a higher rate in multi-authored papers in subsequent positions. These findings are not surprising, because juniors are less experienced and knowledge is a cumulative process that needs time. So, a senior is more likely to have better abilities to write papers [21]. Our data may also signalizes that the reputation and quality of the conferences could have a negative impact on juniors, since they may be discouraged to submit alone.

Table 2. Overview of author collaborations and juniors' involvement.

Conference	Single-authored papers/juniors	%	Multi-authored papers/ juniors as 1st author	%
ASE	81/17	21	3,659/397	10.8
ESEC/FSE	85/24	28.2	4,179/395	9.4
ICSE	281/96	34.1	7,153/665	9.2
JCDL	34/3	8.8	2,053/189	9.2
All	481/140	29.1%	17,044/1,646	9.6%

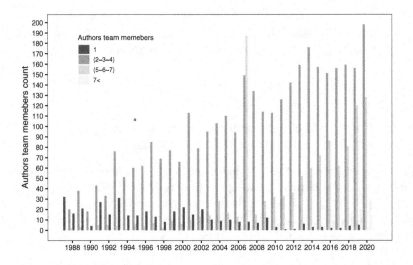

Fig. 2. Collaborating author teams' members count of the four conferences.

5   RQ2: Frequent Collaboration Patterns

Measurements. To discover the most frequent number of authors collaborating together to publish a paper, we analyzed all papers' authors for each year. Specifically, we measured for each conference individually and combined the number of authors participating in a paper (multi-authored paper). We categorized the results into four groups: single-authored, (2-3-4) authors, (5-6-7) authors, more than 7 authors.

Results. We can see in Fig. 2 that most authors' team sizes is within the (2-3-4) category, whereas papers written by more than seven authors represent the lowest over all years. So, the most frequent combination are two to four authors, and as we are focusing on accepted papers at top-level conferences, we can consider this combination as the most successful team size for collaborations. The exact numbers for ASE and ICSE are two authors, while it is three authors for ESEC/FSE and JCDL.

6   Conclusion

In this paper, we studied researchers' collaborations at four top-level conferences. By analyzing 5,188 main-track papers and their 8,730 authors, we observed a rise in the average number of co-authors that does not fully align with the number of published papers. More precisely, the results indicate an increasing level of collaboration and decreasing number of single-author papers. This illustrates potential challenges certain groups of researchers may encounter, since juniors comprise approximately 29% of the authors of single-authors papers, whereas their chances as first authors decline to 9.6% in multi-authors papers. The results reveal that the most frequent collaboration pattern ranges from two to four authors. In the future, we plan to expand on these findings to improve our understanding of juniors' impediments.

References

1. Alchokr, R., Krüger, J., Shakeel, Y., Saake, G., Leich, T.: Understanding the contributions of junior researchers at software-engineering conferences. In: Joint Conference on Digital Libraries (JCDL). IEEE (2021)
2. Alchokr, R., Krüger, J., Shakeel, Y., Saake, G., Leich, T.: On academic age aspect and discovering the golden age in software engineering. In: International Conference on Cooperative and Human Aspects of Software Engineering (CHASE). ACM (2022)
3. Alchokr, R., Krüger, J., Shakeel, Y., Saake, G., Leich, T.: Peer-reviewing and submission dynamics around top software-engineering venues: a juniors' perspective. In: International Conference on Evaluation and Assessment in Software Engineering (EASE). ACM (2022)
4. Bordons, M., Gomez, I.: Collaboration networks in science. In: The Web of Knowledge: A Festschrift in Honor of Eugene Garfield (2000)
5. Bultan, T., Whittle, J.: ICSE 2019 PC Chairs Report (2019)
6. Casadevall, A., Semenza, G., Jackson, S., Tomaselli, G., Ahima, R.: Reducing bias: accounting for the order of co-first authors. J. Clin. Investig. **129**(6), 2167–2168 (2019)
7. Chen, J., Konstan, J.A.: Conference paper selectivity and impact. Commun. ACM **53**(6), 79–83 (2010)
8. Costas, R., Bordons, M.: Do age and professional rank influence the order of authorship in scientific publications? Some evidence from a micro-level perspective. Scientometrics **88**, 145–161 (2011)
9. Diem, A., Wolter, S.: The use of bibliometrics to measure research performance in education sciences. Res. High. Educ. **54**(1), 86–114 (2013)
10. Fernandes, J.M.: Authorship trends in software engineering. Scientometrics **101**(1), 257–271 (2014). https://doi.org/10.1007/s11192-014-1331-6
11. Godin, B., Gingras, Y.: Impact of collaborative research on academic science. Sci. Public Policy **27**(1), 65–73 (2000)
12. Hara, N., Solomon, P., Kim, S.L., Sonnenwald, D.H.: An emerging view of scientific collaboration: scientists' perspectives on collaboration and factors that impact collaboration. J. Am. Soc. Inf. Sci. Technol. **54**(10), 952–965 (2003)

13. Laurance, W.: Second thoughts on who goes where in author lists. Nature **442**, 26 (2006)
14. Li, W., Aste, T., Caccioli, F., Livan, G.: Early coauthorship with top scientists predicts success in academic careers. Nat. Commun. **10**, 1–9 (2019)
15. Meyer, B., Choppy, C., Staunstrup, J., van Leeuwen, J.: Viewpoint research evaluation for computer science. ACM **52**(4), 31–34 (2009)
16. Perretti, F., Negro, G.: Mixing genres and matching people: a study in innovation and team composition in hollywood. J. Organ. Behav. **28**, 563–586 (2007)
17. Qi, M., Zeng, A., Li, M., Fan, Y., Di, Z.: Standing on the shoulders of giants: the effect of outstanding scientists on young collaborators' careers. Scientometrics **111**, 1839–1850 (2017)
18. Regalado, A.: Multiauthor papers on the rise. Science **268**, 25 (1995)
19. Rørstad, K., Aksnes, D.: Publication rate expressed by age, gender and academic position - a large-scale analysis of Norwegian academic staff. J. Informetr. **9**(2), 317–333 (2015)
20. Simonin, B.L.: The importance of collaborative know-how: an empirical test of the learning organization. Acad. Manag. J. **40**(5), 1150–1174 (1997)
21. Tien, F., Blackburn, R.: Faculty rank system, research motivation, and faculty research productivity: measure refinement and theory testing. J. High. Educ. **67**(1), 2–22 (1996). Cited By 108
22. Tran, H., Cabanac, G., Hubert, G.: Expert suggestion for conference program committees,pp. 221–232, May 2017
23. Wren, J.D., Kozak, K.Z., Johnson, K.R., Deakyne, S.J., Schilling, L.M., Dellavalle, R.P.: The write position. EMBO Rep. **8**(11), 988–991 (2007)
24. Zhou, M., Mockus, A.: What make long term contributors: willingness and opportunity in OSS community. In: International Conference on Software Engineering (ICSE), pp. 518–528 (2012)
25. Zuckerman, H.: Nobel laureates in science: patterns of productivity, collaboration, and authorship. Am. Sociol. Rev. **32**(3), 391–403 (1967)

Design and Evaluation of a Mobile Application for an Italian UNESCO Site: *Padova Urbs Picta*

Daniel Zilio[(✉)] and Nicola Orio[(✉)]

Department of Cultural Heritage, University of Padua,
Piazza Capitaniato 7, Padua, Italy
{daniel.zilio,nicola.orio}@unipd.it

Abstract. This paper presents the design, development and a first evaluation of a smartphone application aimed at promoting a cultural heritage site, Padua's fourteenth-century fresco cycle, which has been registered in the UNESCO World Heritage List under the lettering Padua Urbs Picta. The evaluation have been realized through a questionnaire submitted to a number of master students.

Keywords: Mobile application · Cultural heritage · User experience · Usability · UNESCO

1 Introduction

Since the introduction of the first audioguides in 1952 [1], cultural sites – museums, archaeological sites, ancient civic and religious – have been proposing novel methods to increase visitors' interaction in addition to typical tools such as paper brochures and text panels. The fast technological evolution of mobile devices and their ubiquitous presence suggest that the "bring your own device" paradigm can be applied also to the enjoyment of cultural heritage, as can be stated by analyzing the state of the art.

An overview of mobile applications for cultural heritage is presented in [2], with a focus on user experience in a specific environment: the Palatine Chapel in Palermo. A prototype of a guide app for the Athens Numismatic Museum is described in [5], while in [4], the authors examine the experience of producing and distributing an iPhone web application to promote Maltese cultural heritage, including analysis of the benefits of developing a mobile application instead of a website. The paper also contains practical information to consider during the design process, concerning text management, social features, and so forth. The design of an interactive and dynamic user interface made for the collection of Australian paintings in the National Gallery of Australia is presented in [8], where authors evaluated the application through a set of tasks created for both users and curators. Starting from a set of user apps and classification requirements in [7], the design of a user-friendly, reliable mobile system prototype

© Springer Nature Switzerland AG 2022
G. Silvello et al. (Eds.): TPDL 2022, LNCS 13541, pp. 403–409, 2022.
https://doi.org/10.1007/978-3-031-16802-4_39

suitable for museums was realized. The authors established a set of parameters relating to educational environment, usefulness, type of application and ease of use and they created a database architecture in support to the system. The aim was to enhance the visiting experience for end-users and to facilitate management and preservation activities for museum personnel. User experience and satisfaction have also been addressed in [10] and in [9].

This paper presents the design and initial evaluation of an application aimed at promoting a UNESCO site: "Padua's fourteenth-century fresco cycles". The aim of this work is to introduce the main design choices of the application and to analyze the impact of its elements on the overall user experience. Our main interest is on usability, which can be defined as "the extent to which a product can be used by specific users to achieve specified goals with effectiveness, efficiency, and satisfaction in a specified context of use" [6].

2   Design and Development of *Padova Urbs Picta*

2.1   Motivation

During the 4° extended session of the World Heritage Committee, held in Fuzhou, China, "Padua's fourteenth-century fresco cycles" were registered in the UNESCO World Heritage List. Recognized with the lettering *Padova Urbs picta*[1] it includes a set of eight complexes of buildings of the Italian city of Padua: Cappella degli Scrovegni, Chiesa dei Santi Filippo e Giacomo agli Eremitani, Palazzo della Ragione, Cappella della Reggia Carrarese, Battistero della Cattedrale, Basilica and Convento di Sant'Antonio, Oratorio di San Giorgio and Oratorio di San Michele. All buildings are characterized by fourteenth-century frescoes. One of the activities undertaken by the municipality to facilitate the promotion and understanding of this heritage was the development of a smartphone application. The main aims were to make this cultural heritage accessible to a lay audience and provide tourists with a tool to obtain the necessary information about the sites. In this way, both tourists and locals could be easily engaged and more conscientious about this unique heritage.

The app *Padova Urbs picta* was created as a tool to discover the eight places and the origins of the Padua's fourteenth-century fresco cycles project. It has been developed as a native application for both Google Android[2] and iOS systems[3]. The available languages are English and Italian, and we are currently working on German, French and Spanish versions.

2.2   App Structure

After the initial boot, which shows short presentation slideshow, the application starts on the *Home* screen depicted in Fig. 1. There is a brief motto and a

---

[1] *Urbs picta* means "painted city".
[2] https://play.google.com/store/apps/details?id=com.meeple.padovaurbspicta.
[3] https://apps.apple.com/it/app/padova-urbs-picta/id1612607171.

greeting on this screen, which automatically changes depending on the time of day. This is the first gamification element because, on some specific days, the applications shows a specific message about historical events related to the city, the characters of the epoch and so forth. There is no way to discover this fact unless the user opens the application on those days and the user is not informed about how many special mottoes have been added. The middle part of the screen contains buttons directing toward the main elements, like the historical parts, the Map, etc. At the bottom, there are two elements: the audio player and the menu.

2.2.1   Content Elements

The smallest unit of information inside the app is the *activity*. Each activity describes a single subject, and it is represented using a text, a set of images, and a short audio recording. The content creation work is structured as follows: for each of the eight places on the site a domain expert gathered a list of essential information, split into several activities. Two of the most important requisites concerned length and complexity level of each activity. We asked the content creator to avoid complex terminology and focus each activity on single historical episodes, topics, fresco descriptions, and so forth. This was done to reduce the cognitive payload required to the user. In simple terms, we can say that each activity is an informative morsel.

There are 85 total activities, subdivided into nine parts. The average number of words for single activities is 55. With these texts, an audio was recorded by a professional speaker, processing the text so that each audio stayed inside a short time length: the average duration of a single audio item is 40 s, and the entire duration of the audio narrative is 57 min. An example of screen activities is shown in Fig. 2. The numbers in the upper-right corner represent the progress of that activity inside the overall set of a block.

By activating the Autoplay function, the app automatically starts the next activity at the conclusion of the active audio, allowing for progressive fruition. There are two buttons in the bottom navigator bar to move between the activities and the Reader button, allowing users to choose from a Light or Dark Reading Mode and increase or decrease the font size. These preferences are stored inside the phone, so the application is set each time it is launched.

2.2.2   Informative Elements

One of the tasks of the app is to provide users with all the information needed to plan the visit. To accomplish this, some areas have been dedicated to introduce this information in different ways. Firstly, there is the *Map*, where each of the eight places is depicted by a marker on a digital map (Google Maps for Android, Maps for iOS). By clicking on a marker, users can open a direct link to the dedicated navigating smartphone app or the list of related activities inside the app. In addition, we designed a specific section for each place where users can find tourist information (address, opening hours, etc.) and send an email, open the website and place a phone call by clicking on the buttons located on the

Fig. 1. Home   **Fig. 2.** Activity   **Fig. 3.** Diary

button navigation bar. There is also a link to the official web portal to reserve a ticket.

Other elements include *Team*, a section with all information involved in the app's development. An area in which users can contact the development team, and view the privacy policies and conditions of use. We also added a button to allow a user to share the app with friends.

2.2.3   Gamification Elements

In order to engage users and encourage them to explore all the activities and features of the app we developed a specific section, the *Diary*, which is shown in Fig. 3. The idea was inspired by the Google Fit system, transforming the aim of walking into one of reading and/or listening to the activities. When users open one of them, a set of usage information, like date and time spent, is saved in the smartphone's memory. Through these data, users can analyze their progress. In addition, the app keeps score and displays the amount of *Culture Points*, earned by using the app, and the number of minutes spent reading or listening to the activities. Users have to stay on the activity screen for at least six seconds to be tallied, so it is not possible to increase progress points by just an open-close action.

In addition, there is also a badge collection system. The goal is to encourage users to take a look at the credits, and discover tourist information and the position of the buildings by visiting the sites. A number of panels with QR Codes have been placed in close proximity of the buildings, thus the user can prove of having visited the building by scanning its QR Code.

All the features described above have been designed to encourage users to discover all the app contents, both cultural and tourist. However users obtain a further reward if they play with the app. Following three progressive steps concerning the activities completed and the obtained badges users can unlock a hidden part of the app: the *Beast*. The first time it is selected, there is a personality test where users have to answer a set of questions related to events and situations in the Middle Ages. For example, manage a siege conducted by the feudal lord Ezzelino III da Romano, or choose food from a list of ancient recipes. After this test, a fantasy "Beast" is assigned to the user, with its associated story. In the first stage, users can only see one sketch of that beast and read only a piece of its tale. After two further stages, the last one being unlockable only after obtaining four badges and accessing 100% of the activities, the picture will be completed and the tale concluded. The choice of this theme is taken from frescoes preserved in the sites, examples of medieval bestiaries.

3   First Evaluation

The initial evaluation of the app has been carried our through a on-line questionnaire sharing the URL on an e-Learning platform of the University of Padua. It comprises seven different modules, each on a single web page, for a total of thirty-five questions. The respondents must answer each module statement in order to move forward. Except for two open questions, we consistently used a 5-point Likert scale, with the "Strongly Agree" choice shown to the right. The language used was English and participants were anonymous. Questions and statements concerns the usability, gamification elements, aesthetics and interface, and so forth. Regarding to the usability we asked the ten statements forming the System Usability Scale (SUS).

There were ten participants in the questionnaire, five used the Apple iOS version and five the Google Android. The average age was about 23 years old, and all of theme came from the master course on Tourism, Culture, Sustainability of the University of Padua. Four of them decided to use both the Reading and Listening mode, while three the Reading and three the Listening. The score given by the System Usability Scale was 78.3, so quite good overall. Table 1 reports the average score for each statement. In general, the results are good, and we had better values than the average presented in [3]. For positive statements, the lowest score was given to statement 1 about the intentions to use the app frequently, with an average score of 3.2. We suspect this was because the statement was not well understood in our specific situation, because students in general did not behave like actual tourists. Considering statements in negative form, there are no specific problems, although the app might appear a bit more complex than we expected because statement 2 about the app being unnecessarily complex had an average score of 1.8.

Concerning the time of usage, which was an open question, participants reported an average app usage of about twenty minutes. The app was mainly used at home, while in three cases it was used during a visit. Texts appear easy

Table 1. The adapted ten statements of the System Usability Scale

Statement	μ
1. I think that I would like to use this app frequently	3.2
2. I found the app unnecessarily complex	1.8
3. I found the app was easy to use	4.3
4. I think that I would need the support of a technical person to be able to use this app	1.3
5. I found the various functions in this app were well integrated	3.9
6. I thought there was too much inconsistency in this app	1.7
7. I would imagine that most people would learn to use this app very quickly	4.0
8. I found the app very cumbersome to use	1.8
9. I felt very confident using the app	4.0
10. I needed to learn a lot of things before I could get going with this app	1.5

to read and understand, but we expected this from these particular participants who have a bachelor degree in humanities. The app proved suitable for both art experts and non-experts, which is a significant result considering the efforts to design the texts to reach a wide range of user.

As regards the gamification section of the app, seven participants declared they opened the Diary section, but only one of them unlocked the Beast. The values show that this part, despite not presenting negative elements, still did not report such high values. The interface proved easy to use, some improvements could be made with the graphics. In the open statements, we received three pointers towards similar apps and a number of suggestions related to making the app more visually pleasant with more color variations and concerning some difficulty in understanding the voices. However, the overall comments are positive.

4   Conclusions and Future Work

In general, the usability and satisfaction responses are encouraging. The good System Usability Score values we obtained – and the associated statements that confirmed it – indicate that the choices made in the application's design make it relatively easy to learn and use. Furthermore, the interface was appreciated by the testers, although some improvements could be made to facilitate its use. We are not completely satisfied with the values obtained from the access measurements given by the users' interactions with some parts of the application, and we believe some modifications will be necessary to improve the amount of time spent with the app. In a future version, we must study how to improve user engagement through the gamification features, perhaps by facilitating access to the Beast. We are also considering allowing users to collect all the Beasts created, and not only one. We are developing a version of the app reserved for testers where we will track each single interaction. In this way, we aim to obtain detailed information about how users interact with the app and what actions could be done to improve overall user satisfaction. The next updates relative to the integration of other languages could improve the spread of the app and its impact on the promotion of Italian cultural heritage.

Acknowledgments. The authors thank the City of Padua for their support and the choice to develop an app dedicated to the UNESCO site of "Padua's fourteenth-century fresco cycles". The authors also thank everyone who has contributed to the development of the application.

References

1. Alexander, E., Alexander, M.: American Association for State and Local History: Museums in Motion: An Introduction to the History and Functions of Museums. American Association for State and Local History Book Series. AltaMira Press (2008). https://books.google.it/books?id=owHSEk96qxQC
2. Andolina, S., Pirrone, D., Russo, G., Sorce, S., Gentile, A.: Exploitation of mobile access to context-based information in cultural heritage fruition. In: 2012 Seventh International Conference on Broadband, Wireless Computing, Communication and Applications, Victoria, BC, Canada, 12–14 November 2012, pp. 322–328. IEEE (2012). https://doi.org/10.1109/BWCCA.2012.60
3. Bangor, A., Kortum, P.T., Miller, J.T.: An empirical evaluation of the System Usability Scale. Int. J. Hum. Comput. Interact. **24**(6), 574–594 (2008). https://doi.org/10.1080/10447310802205776
4. Boiano, S., Bowen, J.P., Gaia, G.: Usability, design and content issues of mobile apps for cultural heritage promotion: the Malta Culture guide experience. CoRR abs/1207.3422 (2012). http://arxiv.org/abs/1207.3422
5. Chasapis, P., Mitropoulos, S., Douligeris, C.: A prototype mobile application for the Athens numismatic museum. Appl. Comput. Inform. (2019)
6. ISO/IEC-9241: Ergonomics requirements for office with visual display terminals (VDTs). International Organization for Standardization, Geneva, Switzerland (1992)
7. Koukoulis, K., Koukopoulos, D.: Towards the design of a user-friendly and trustworthy mobile system for museums. In: Ioannides, M., et al. (eds.) EuroMed 2016. LNCS, vol. 10058, pp. 792–802. Springer, Cham (2016). https://doi.org/10.1007/978-3-319-48496-9_63
8. Li, R.Y.C., Liew, A.W.C.: An interactive user interface prototype design for enhancing on-site museum and art gallery experience through digital technology. Museum Manag. Curatorship **30**(3), 208–229 (2015). https://doi.org/10.1080/09647775.2015.1042509
9. Rossi, S., Barile, F., Galdi, C., Russo, L.: Recommendation in museums: paths, sequences, and group satisfaction maximization. Multimedia Tools Appl. **76**(24), 26031–26055 (2017). https://doi.org/10.1007/s11042-017-4869-5
10. Tesoriero, R., Gallud, J.A., Lozano, M., Penichet, V.M.R.: Enhancing visitors' experience in art museums using mobile technologies. Inf. Syst. Front. **16**(2), 303–327 (2012). https://doi.org/10.1007/s10796-012-9345-1

Ontology-Based Metadata Integration for Oral History Interviews

Maria Vrachliotou[1] and Christos Papatheodorou[2(✉)]

[1] Department of Archives, Library Science and Museology, Ionian University, Corfu, Greece
119vrac@ionio.gr
[2] Department of History and Philosophy of Science, National and Kapodistrian University of Athens, Athens, Greece
papatheodor@phs.uoa.gr

Abstract. There is a burgeoning discussion on creating a new schema for Oral History, an Oral History Core. In this paper we present the characteristics of Oral History collections and the problems users might face when attempting to access this type of material. As a solution, we propose an integration model. From the cultural heritage milieu, we have chosen CIDOC CRM that acts as a mediating schema, while from the European audiovisual community, we have selected EBUcore ontology. By taking into consideration their strengths and their characteristics, we form a mapping methodology from EBUcore to CIDOC CRM and we present the issues that might rise. The goal of this research is to generate a model of describing Oral History interviews, in order to facilitate exchange of information between existing collection management systems of audiovisual and cultural heritage collections and to meliorate the searching experience for users.

Keywords: Oral history · CIDOC CRM · EBUcore · Mapping · Semantic integration · Ontology-based metadata integration

1 Introduction

When it comes to accessing Oral History (OH) collections, users might face various challenges. One of the main characteristics of these collections is the thematic diversity and the heterogeneity of documents that come in different forms and types. Interconnection between them is not always the case. Each interview is unique and may generate any or all of the following: audio/video file(s) in a number of formats (wav, MP3, MPEG-4 etc.), transcripts, notebooks, text summaries and keywords, interview logs, the interviewer's questions and notes, various forms, personal information about the interviewee and information about access restrictions, material donated by the interviewee (photos, notebooks, even 3D objects) [1, 2].

Due to the thematic diversity, metadata schemas and good quality metadata play a vital role towards the discovery of digital objects [3]. There is not an ontology or metadata model describing the audiovisual content of Oral History interviews, although it is important to collect metadata from the first stages of the interviewing process [4]. Occasionally, institutions with OH collections have adopted various metadata schemas.

© Springer Nature Switzerland AG 2022
G. Silvello et al. (Eds.): TPDL 2022, LNCS 13541, pp. 410–416, 2022.
https://doi.org/10.1007/978-3-031-16802-4_40

The aim of this research is to develop a metadata model for describing, managing and retrieving OH resources, which are actually interviews. We present a model for the semantic representation of the activities and the produced information resources during the stages of OH interviews. By taking into consideration the peculiarities of OH Collections and the needs of users for meaningful, simultaneous access, we consider that the proposed model should be based on EBU Core ontology and CIDOC CRM.

From the field of audiovisual content, we have chosen EBUcore ontology (henceforth EBUcore) because it is user friendly, easy, flexible, customizable [5] and currently curators of OH collections consider it as an alternative to PBcore. It is an ontology created by the PBcore and EBUcore communities, available in RDF/OWL and used by several European projects such as EUSCreen [6]. EBUCore offers an adaptable solution to the mapping of different metadata schemas into a common format. In audiovisual industry there might be various identifiers and titles, descriptions or rights in different languages. OH video or audio recordings also share these characteristics. EBUcore provides also some additional classes that could be useful in oral history interviews, like the *Rating* for parental or user rating, the *Publication history* for describing when, in what format and under which rights it is publicly available. The class *Part* is also useful as it supports description of parts (segments) that might be helpful in describing parts of an interview at a very low level of granularity. It can also generate timelines of technical characteristics, to define a playlist of different files, or simply to split and organize groups of related metadata. It also provides the class *Textline* that allows to line text to parts/segments, scenes or timestamps. This class could be used in OH interviews at synchronizing segments with transcription text or summaries. Events are important in OH, which is built upon the need of the representation of the people participation to activities and events that take place in places during time periods [7].

Nevertheless, OH interviews carry rich information about history, ethnography, cultural heritage artifacts, personal views and feelings. Though EBUcore ontology exhibits several advantages, it is not designed to describe historical or cultural heritage content. In order to represent the semantics of such content, we have Cultural Heritage, the CIDOC Conceptual Reference Model (CIDOC CRM), a formal ontology for integration and exchange of heterogeneous cultural heritage information that constitutes the international standard ISO21127 [8, 9]. One of its strengths is that it is a high level ontology that could play the role of the mediated schema in information integration of cultural heritage data and their correlation with library and archive information [9]. In CIDOC CRM concepts like agents, location and dates of an object are always connected and represented with an Event or an Activity. One of its weaknesses is its inability to describe digital objects such as digital audiovisual material. Technical attributes like encoding, storage, system requirements for digital images, audio, video, text and multimedia are not supported. Physical features can be described but not visual or audio features such as volume (a trait that is necessary for users with a hearing impairment). Hierarchical or sequential summaries of audiovisual content, which specify keyframes, scene changes or key videoclips, are not supported [10].

The proposed model integrates CIDOC CRM and EBUcore, providing a mapping between these two ontologies, that will support interconnection of the existing repositories and meaningful access to OH resources.

2   Modeling OH Interviews

The main entities and procedures that describe an OH interview have been firstly represented by CIDOC CRM and then by EBUCore ontology. According to Oral History Association there are four key elements of OH: Preparation, Interviewing, Preservation and Access [11]. In order to conform to these four elements, we've divided the interview process in three stages: (a) The pre-interview, preparatory stage, (b) the interview stage and (c) the post- interview stage. These stages produce metadata that we had to collect based on guidelines, schemas, systems and publications and with respect to the digital curation lifecycle for preserving and adding value to the OH interviews. For instance, for the metadata of the pre-interview and interview stages there exist the recommendations of the 'Principles and Best Practices' of the Oral History Association [11], while for the post-interview stage there exist the OH cataloguing manual [12]. We have also taken into consideration the Oral History Metadata Synchronizer (OHMS) which is recognized as a pioneer in the collection and preservation of oral histories [13]. Regarding the description of audiovisual material we have adopted essential elements, such as provenance information and rights, restrictions and legal information, preservation, technical and structural metadata [14], while regarding audio or video indexing and segmentation, we have utilized the articles of 'Oral History in the Digital Age'.[1]

The identified entities that participate in the activities of the mentioned stages for planning, implementing and post-processing an OH interview and the relationships between the entities are represented as CIDOC CRM paths revealing in detail the events and produced resources of the interview and post interview stages. A path is defined as a sequence of triples domain-property-range (d - p - r), where d and r are the domain and the range of the property p respectively (Figs. 1 and 2 present in detail the parts of an interview. The rectangles in the figures correspond to the CIDOC CRM classes (the upper boxes) and their instances (the lower boxes), while the arrows correspond to CIDOC CRM properties).[2]

Regarding the second stage, the implementation of an interview (Fig. 1),[2] it all begins with an idea, a project (represented by an instance of the class *E28 Conceptual Object*) that has a theme, even a title (instance of the class *E35 Title*) and a small description (E62 String). According to this idea we have the event of the interview (*E5 Event*). This event has two participants: an interviewer (instance of the class *E39 Actor*, because it might be an organization) and an interviewee (instance of the class *E21 Person*) -that might be more than one. The interviewer has a name (instance of the class *E41 Appellation*) and might be a researcher affiliated to an institution (*E74 Group*) with contact info (*E41 Appellation*). Moreover, the interviewer keeps a record of information about the interviewee: Name (*E41 Appellation*), Date of Birth (represented by the path *E67 Birth-P4 has time span of- E52 Time-Span*), Place of Birth (path *E67 Birth-P7 took place at (witnessed)-E53 Place*), etc. The interviewee might offer a 3D object (modeled as an instance of the class *E22 Human made Object*, or even *E18 Physical Thing*) or a photograph (*E73 Information Object*) that might have a relation to the narration. During the recording (modeled by *E7 Activity*) the interviewer might keep notes (modeled by

---

[1] OHDA, https://www.oralhistory.org/oral-history-in-the-digital-age/.

[2] All the figures are available at: http://users.uoa.gr/~papatheodor/tpdl2022.html.

an event *E65 Creation*) and might transfer the custody of the recording (modeled by the class *E10 Transfer of Custody*). The result of the recording is considered as an instance of *E33 Linguistic Object*. Furthermore, for the activity of recording (*E7 Activity*) a specific equipment might be used (instance of the class *E70 Thing*). By the end of the recording the interviewer prepares the final outcome of the interview (represented by the path *E39 Actor - E65 Creation- E33 Linguistic Object*), probably by excluding any sensitive, confidential information enabling the recording to be online accessible. The recording activity produces a video (modeled by both the classes *E33 Linguistic Object* and *E73 Information Object*) or an audio (*E33 Linguistic Object*) having technical characteristics and transfer medium (modeled by the class *E22 Human Made Object*).

The post-interview stage is represented by CIDOC CRM paths, using a similar procedure (Fig. 2)[2]. Furthermore, the same stages their entities and relationships are represented utilizing concepts and paths of EBUcore[2]. The difference is the absence of events.

In the next phase, the alignment of the paths of each model is held by creating a table with two columns. In each column the paths of each model (EBUcore and CIDOC CRM) are placed, each path in a row. In each row the paths of each model with the same meaning are placed.[3]

3   Mapping EBUCore to CIDOC CRM

There have been some previous works on mapping to CIDOC CRM [15, 16]. Regarding multimedia, there have been works on mapping MPEG-7 to CIDOC CRM proposing a mapping that allows the use of multimedia content annotation to the cultural heritage digital libraries [17]. Hunter proposes a combination of the CIDOC CRM with the MPEG-7, in order to describe Multimedia in museums. In particular, an extension of the CIDOC CRM, where she uses as an attachment point the E73 *Information Object* class, where she adds the subclass *MultimediaContent* of the MPEG-7 [10].

In our mapping the source schema is EBUcore, while the target schema is CIDOC CRM. Our main goal is to map the entities and properties of the source schema to the target schema, so as the meaning of data of the source schema to be preserved. For instance, in EBUCore the person in front of the camera is considered a contributor. According to this condition, an interview in EBUcore is an *Editorial object* provided by the interviewee who is the contributor. This statement is modeled by the path: *ebucore: Editorial Object - ebucore: hasContributor- ebucore: Person*. In CIDOC CRM, the same information is modeled by two paths having in common the same event: (a) *E28 Conceptual Object - P94 has created - E5 Event* and (b) *E5 Event - P14 carried out by-performed – E21 Person* (Fig. 4)[2].

Another example comes from the post interview stage, that includes all the necessary activities for the preservation and curation of the produced recordings (video or audio). As already mentioned, in long lasting interviews it is crucial for the user to have the ability to access the exact points of interest. Indexing and description of segments could help towards a most efficient access. Those segments have a duration, a starting and

---

[3] The full version of Table 1 is available at: http://users.uoa.gr/~papatheodor/tpdl2022.html.

an ending point represented in timecodes. These characteristics are expressed by the following EBUcore paths: (a) for the starting point: *ebucore: Part - ebucore: startTimcode - ebucore: string*, (b) for the ending point: *ebucore: Part - ebucore: EndTimecode - ebucore: string* and (c) for the duration of the segment: *ebucore: Part - ebucore: TimelinePartDurationTimecode - ebucore:string*. In CIDOC CRM the interview segments are considered as instances of the class E90 Symbolic Object. Moreover, the main attributes of a segment are its start point and its duration. This information is expressed by the following CIDOC CRM paths: (a) for the starting point *E90 Symbolic object - P140 was attributed by - E13 Attribute Assignment - P141 assigned - E52 Time- span- P79 beginning is qualified by - E62 String*, (b) for the ending point point *E90 Symbolic object - P140 was attributed by - E13 Attribute Assignment - P141 assigned - E52 Time- span- P80 end is qualified by - E62 String* and (c) for the duration: *E90 Symbolic object - P140 was attributed by - E13 Attribute Assignment - P141 assigned - E52 Time- span - P191 had duration -was duration of - E54 Dimension - P81 ongoing throughout - E61Time Primitive* (Fig. 5)[2].

The mapping of EBUcore to CIDOC CRM presented various challenges due to differences in their approach. One of the strengths of CIDOC CRM is the ability to represent these stages as events or activities that occur in the lifecycle of the interview. EBUcore cannot represent the events and procedures occurred during the interview; its class Events represents the events narrated by the interviewee. CIDOC CRM is flexible and can represent events that are part of other events or activities or events that have relationships with other events. In EBUcore there is the property *ebucore: has Event Related Event* that defines relations between events, without defining the semantics of the relationship (e.g. an event precedes another event). Moreover, the CIDOC CRM event *E10 Transfer of Custody* cannot be mapped to any class of EBUcore.

In CIDOC CRM the discrimination between video and audio recordings is not clear. We represent a video recording as instance of both the classes *E33 Linguistic* and *E73 Information Object*, while an audio recording as an instance of the Class *E33 Linguistic Object*. In EBUcore there is the class *ebucore: Audio object* for audio recordings, but there is not a similar class for video. There used to have the class *ebucore: Video object* that disappears after the EBUcore version 1.4. For video recordings we have used the general class *ebucore: Media Resource*.

Another issue derives from the fact that Oral History interviews are considered unpublished video or audio recordings and treated as such, according to the policies of each cultural institution. CIDOC CRM is flexible enough to depict either published or unpublished Cultural Heritage Objects, while EBUcore offers only the classes *ebucore: Publication Channel, ebucore: Publication Channel Type, ebucore: Publication Event*, etc., due to its origination from the Mass Media and Audiovisual communities.

In the field of accessing long-lasting interviews the EBUcore class *ebucore: Part*, proves to be really versatile. This class was originally introduced to identify 'editorial' segments of content within a media resource and has been extended to allow any form of partitioned description, editorial or technical, optionally bound to a specific timeline. In CIDOC CRM these segments are represented by the class *E90 Symbolic Object* a class that comprises, among the others, multimedia objects. Furthermore, in CIDOC CRM it is possible to define sections of physical objects using spatial measurements and the temporal location of events or periods but there are no properties to define directly temporal, spatial or spatio-temporal locations within digital media [10]. In general, technical features like versions of files, mediums, formats, codecs, checksums, which should be documented for the handling and preservation of audiovisual material, cannot be expressed in detail in CIDOC CRM. In EBUcore there is a variety of classes on technical attributes.

4 Conclusions

In this paper we analyzed the characteristics of OH interviews and their metadata. We have found out that there is not a core standard that suits the needs for their descriptions. The need for interconnection and integration of information between Cultural Institutions has led us to choose two ontologies: CIDOC CRM from the cultural heritage field and EBUcore from the audiovisual European Community. These two ontologies produce rich semantics and could be used to model adequately an OH interview. Thus, we proposed a mapping of EBUcore to CIDOC CRM, using a path-oriented methodology. Having CIDOC CRM as the target schema in our mappings, offers a rich and explicit expression of semantics of the concepts that are present in OH interviews. The outcome of this work is the creation of a machine-understandable model, which can be used to semantically describe OH interviews. The scope of this research is to test this model on existing OH collections, in order to see how to manage them in practice.

References

1. Mazé, E.A.: Metadata: Best Practices for Oral History Access and Preservation. Oral History in the Digital Age. http://ohda.matrix.msu.edu/2012/06/metadata/ (2012). Last accessed 15 October 2018
2. Boyd, D.: Informed accessioning: questions to ask after the interview. Oral History in the Digital Age. http://ohda.matrix.msu.edu/2015/03/informed-accessioning-questions-to-ask-after-the-interview/ (2015). Last accessed 8 October 2018
3. Nelson, C.: Oral History in your library. Libraries Unlimited, Santa Barbara (2018)
4. Boyd, D.: Interviewer-Generated Metadata – Oral History in the Digital Age. http://ohda.mat rix.msu.edu/2012/06/interviewer-generated-metadata/. Last accessed 6 December 2018
5. EBU: tech3293v1_10:EBU CORE METADATA SET. https://tech.ebu.ch/docs/tech/tec h3293.pdf (2020)
6. Evain, J.-P.: EBUcore Ontology. https://www.ebu.ch/metadata/ontologies/ebucore/. Last accessed 28 May 2020
7. Shaw, R.B.: Events and Periods as Concepts for Organizing Historical Knowledge. https://aeshin.org/static/shaw-2010-events-and-periods.pdf (2010). Last accessed 21 May 2021
8. Theodoridou, M., Bruseker, G., Daskalaki, M., Doerr, M.: Methodological Tips For Mappings To CIDOC-CRM. https://www.slideshare.net/ariadnenetwork/methodological-tips-for-mappings-to-cidoc-crm (2016)
9. Doerr, M., Bruseker, G., Bekiari, C., Ore, C.E., Velios, T., Stead, S.: Volume A: Definition of the CIDOC Conceptual Reference Model. https://www.cidoc-crm.org/sites/default/files/cidoc_crm_version_7.1.2.pdf (2021)

10. Hunter, J.: Combining the CIDOC CRM and MPEG7 to Describe Multimedia in Museums. Researchgate. https://www.researchgate.net/publication/245699474_Combining_the_CIDOC_CRM_and_MPEG7_to_Describe_Multimedia_in_Museums (2011). Last accessed 4 May 2019

11. O.H.A.: Principles and Best Practices | Oral History Association. http://www.oralhistory.org/about/principles-and-practices/. Last accessed 9 October 2018

12. Matters, M.E.: Oral history cataloging manual. Society of American Archivists, Chicago, Illinois. http://hdl.handle.net/2027/mdp.39015034027618 (1995). Last accessed 6 April 2018

13. Boyd, D.: OHMS: enhancing access to oral history for free. Oral Hist. Rev. **40**, 95–106 (2013). https://www.tandfonline.com/doi/full/10.1093/ohr/oht031. Last accessed 8 October 2018

14. Griesinger, P.: A Brief Overview of Metadata for Audiovisual Materials. https://ndsr.nyc digital.org/a-brief-overview-of-metadata-for-audiovisual-materials/. Last accessed 7 January 2021

15. Lourdi, I., Papatheodorou, C., Doerr, M.: Semantic integration of collection description: Combining CIDOC/CRM and dublin core collections application profile. D-Lib Mag. **15** (2009). https://doi.org/10.1045/july2009-papatheodorou. Last accessed 21 October 2020

16. Gergatsoulis, M., Bountouri, L., Gaitanou, G., Papatheodorou, C.: Query transformation in a CIDOC CRM based cultural metadata integration environment. In: 14th Eur. Conf. Digit. Libr. ECDL 2010, Glasgow, Scotland, UK, Sept. 2010, pp. 38–45 (2010)

17. Angelopoulou, A., Tsinaraki, C., Christodoulakis, S.: Mapping MPEG-7 to CIDOC / CRM. In: Int. Conf. Theory Pract. Digit. Libr. TPDL 2011, Berlin, Ger. Sept. 26–28, 2011, pp. 40–51 (2011)

Making FAIR Practices Accessible and Attractive

Lyudmila Balakireva$^{(\boxtimes)}$ (ID) and Fedor Balakirev (ID)

Los Alamos National Laboratory, Los Alamos, NM 87545, USA
ludab@lanl.gov

Abstract. Facing rapidly growing volumes of research datasets, scientists and research funding agencies are putting forward new principles of data management, such as data Findability, Accessibility, Interoperability, and Reusability (FAIR). To this end, data science experts are developing FAIR data policies, methods, protocols, and repositories, while actual research practices are lagging behind because FAIR compliance remains a burden for many researchers. Here we present a prototype data management infrastructure deployed at the National High Magnetic Field Laboratory (NHMFL/MagLab) aimed at helping scientists efficiently annotate and manage experimental data produced by their MagLab projects and making FAIR practices accessible and attractive. The infrastructure incorporates the Open Science Framework (OSF) data repository platform. We will describe infrastructure elements such as the data formats, the metadata schema, the repository integration, the naming conventions, the templates to organize the data, and the automated data pipeline from measurement stations to the FAIR repository objects.

Keywords: FAIR data · Open science · Repository · Dataset publishing

1 Introduction

With the advances in machine learning technology and the availability of vast quantities of digital information, data are becoming more usable and valuable than ever. At the same time, only properly annotated data objects can be reused by humans and machines to gain viable scientific output [34]. Alongside the persistence and accessibly of the data object, the information that puts it in a context of a research field and outlines its purpose is equally important. Many of the ideas in the FAIR principles gear towards enabling "machine actionability", or automatic knowledge extraction, where data object identifying information plays a significant role. Can we also automate collecting of the data and metadata into data objects which are FAIR-ready and immediately useful? Can we build

Supported by the Department of Energy, the National Science Foundation Cooperative Agreement No. DMR-1644779, and the State of Florida.

G. Silvello et al. (Eds.): TPDL 2022, LNCS 13541, pp. 417–424, 2022.
https://doi.org/10.1007/978-3-031-16802-4_41

upon established research tools and practices instead of forcing scientists to start from scratch in order to comply with FAIR standards?

While major sponsors of research strongly encourage the implementation of the FAIR data management principles [35], data acquired in a laboratory is often not annotated in an informative way, e.g. handwritten rather than electronic lab notebooks, or poorly described and widely varying data file formats. Even if made public, such datasets are often cannot be utilized without some extrinsic contextual knowledge, such as a separate scholarly communication. According to a prior MagLab study [31] of data management problems in the condensed matter physics community, the most often noted problem is the lack of file naming conventions (52%), followed by the difficulties in interpreting data due to poor or lost documentation (50%); the lack of version control (36%); and the inability to access data due to obsolescence, proprietary formats, expired software licenses, or other issues (35%). It is clear that FAIR compliance will require major changes in the research culture and the implementation and normalization of data management technologies and practices [28,30,35].

The MagLab Pulsed Field Facility at the Los Alamos National Laboratory [27] attracts hundreds of researchers from around the world to conduct fundamental and applied science experiments at the highest possible magnetic field intensity. The diverse environment of the MagLab user program allows for a comprehensive study how the practices and methods of motivating scientists to engage with the FAIR principles might be changed for the better. We studied all the stages of the dataset lifecycle, and we demonstrate how FAIR practices and automatic data object creation could be introduced in such an environment in an approachable and efficient fashion.

In this paper, we will describe the research data management infrastructure devised and implemented at the MagLab, as outlined on Fig. 1. We propose the data object creation process which links the description of the research project with the metadata-rich experimental results. The project description provides scientific context and purpose of the data object, while the proposed hierarchical data format allows for data organization and for metadata to be included at different layers of the composite object. The resulting dataset files are encapsulated into FAIR-ready data object with sufficient information for its reuse. We also show how to increase the degree of automation for the collection, aggregation, and repository submission of the scientific data that is ready for sharing, where the repository project itself can become FAIR data object and actionable knowledge unit.

2   Related Work

Because experimental science needs flexibility to change the methodology and the parameters, automating data management workflows at the time of creation can assure that FAIR principles are upheld from the outset [29], keeping data objects stable. Several scientific communities started designing and implementing solutions in this direction such as in climate modelling [7], language data and

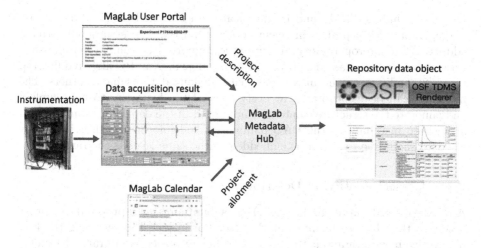

Fig. 1. Architecture of the FAIR-ready data management framework across heterogeneous systems. Data recorded during the user experiment is automatically uploaded to the corresponding OSF project in FAIR-ready format.

technologies [5] and material science [21]. Online FAIR data repositories [6] help facilitate the adoption of FAIR standards by providing frameworks for storage, access, search, Application Programming Interface (API), and other features that create organized hubs of scientific data. One needs to distinguish between the notions of FAIR data, open data access, and data management. While data management is about the stewardship of data from the cradle onwards, open data focus on access, and FAIR goes beyond with promotion of truly reusable data [13]. For example, the FAIR repository standards can even be adhered to in the restricted environments [4,9] with locally installed OSF [23] as secure internal data management and collaboration space for LANL research. Switching to electronic and open lab books can also ease FAIR transition, where publicizing the details of the experimental dataset creation can help establish its context and purpose [21,29].

3 Results

3.1 Experimental Data Set Acquisition, Formats, and Metadata Descriptors

MagLab implements a uniform data acquisition (DAQ) infrastructure to record experimental data at each of the MagLab DAQ stations [12]. The DAQ infrastructure utilizes National Instruments LabVIEW software [1,15] incorporating a wide variety of DAQ instruments. Technical Data Management Streaming (TDMS) format [32] was selected as the primary standard for the data records. TDMS is an industry-standard structured open data format with flexible metadata options to describe the data at each level of the hierarchy. Structured data formats, including TDMS and Hierarchical Data Format Five (HDF5) [11] are finding broader acceptance in scientific communities. The structured formats address FAIR interoperability because it is supported by many scientific software packages, such as MATLAB [20], Origin [24], NumPy [22], IGOR [14], Excel [8], and it can contain rich metadata, making data usable to others. The metadata can be incorporated at every level of the hierarchy to help explain and annotate the structure, contents, and format of the data. For example, such acquisition metadata as the DAQ parameters and information describing how the data should be read can be embedded at the same level as the raw data.

3.2   Dataset-Identifying Descriptors

Any external or local researcher (user) can submit a research proposal to request access to the MagLab facilities at the User Portal [17], thus creating the first descriptive metadata about the project, including project and grant identifiers, experiment purpose and description, primary investigator (PI), DAQ station, and the dates of the experiment. This type of the "administrative" metadata addresses contextual questions such as "who", "when", "where" and "why". The administrative metadata is important to preserve together with the acquisition metadata, which describes "how" the data was generated.

The metadata that identifies the proposal exists as a separate administrative record kept by the MagLab headquarters [17], which was not accessible to the DAQ software. To address this gap, we developed a Metadata Hub [19] that serves as a linking element to collect proposal metadata from existing administrative sources and provide Representational State Transfer (REST) back-end API with easily parsable JavaScript Object Notation (JSON) format [3]. Each DAQ station can now request information about the scheduled experiment from Metadata Hub. We also developed a web-based front-end to aid local administrators and support staff scientists in tracking MagLab proposals and their corresponding metadata.

We enhanced the DAQ software with a Project Metadata dashboard describing the experiment (see Fig. 2). The dashboard displays the key proposal identifiers, such as the PI and the proposal title. If the displayed proposal does not match the actual one (e.g. researcher's experiment was relocated to a different DAQ station), the user can select the correct proposal from the list.

3.3   FAIR Data Repository Integration

MagLab scientists survey pointed out that while most scientists do not use repositories, there is an occasional usage of inconsistent sharing solutions. A common repository platform for MagLab users and uniform data curation standards will facilitate data accessibility and reuse. Standardization also allows for automation of dataset archiving and retrieval. An online repository provides additional benefit for a dispersed team, where an efficient data pipeline and shared repository space shorten the time from data production to analysis.

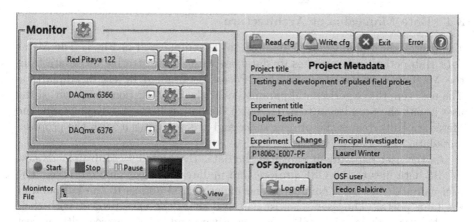

Fig. 2. Fragment of MagLab DAQ Software interface with new Project Metadata dashboard with the project identification information and OSF Synchronization section.

Repositories must earn the trust of the communities they intend to serve [16], while providing persistent and dependable services. OSF [10] is a data repository that seeks to facilitate open collaboration in scientific research by combining many attractive features including structured projects, ample data storage, and integration with third-party services. To streamline data sharing and access, as well as eventual publication of the datasets, the MagLab has selected the Open Science Framework as the repository standard.

The users willing to publicize their experiment as a persistent data object can accomplish the task with a push of the OSF login button. Once the user authenticates to OSF via OAuth2 mechanism [19,25,33], the Metadata Hub automatically creates a project at the OSF repository and pre-populates it with the proposal metadata that was harvested from the User Portal. The Metadata Hub also assigns several common tags to the OSF projects, such as "maglab" and project identifier. The use of common tags to find the MagLab projects also facilitates discoverability and has the potential to showcase all achievements of the MagLab to the public. We created a web TDMS renderer tool as OSF plug-in [2]. By bringing this user-friendly tool to a popular FAIR data repository, we hope that we have helped to foster a FAIR-ready environment for scientists.

The data recorded during the user experiment is automatically uploaded to the corresponding OSF project via HTTP protocol. For each uploaded TDMS binary file, we create a companion ASCII markup file which lists the metadata extracted from the TDMS file to enhance the data findability. We also provide an "electronic lab book" functionality as part of the dataset synchronization, where a wiki-based OSF electronic lab book is pre-populated with the file metadata to help users track, contextualize, and share the experimental details using OSF file-sharing capabilities.

3.4   Data Management Architecture

The overall data management architecture is summarized in Fig. 1. The Metadata Hub periodically updates its database with administrative metadata from the MagLab calendar [18] and User Portal maintained by the headquarters. The user sets the experimental parameters at the DAQ station computer. If the user grants the permission to synchronize the data collection with the OSF, the Metadata Hub creates the project space and pre-populates it with the proposal metadata.

As the user experiment captures the data, the Metadata Hub uploads new TDMS data files to the OSF project, and updates the electronic lab book. The user can add their own comments and experimental details to the lab book at the OSF portal. The user scientist can also share the OSF project with their collaborators. The initial OSF project is private and is only shared with project collaborators. The user can publicize the project and create its persistent digital object identifier (DOI).

3.5   Discussion and Future Work

The adoption of FAIR standards remains a challenge, where the largest obstacle is the diversity and complexity of research techniques. The vocabulary of basic measurement units in e.g. material science is universally understood and accepted, but the research context is rapidly evolving and hard to track. Some of these obstacles can be ameliorated by incorporating contextual metadata at the moment of data creation by automatic means.

The proposed uniform data acquisition infrastructure supports a modern electronic lab book and augments the datasets with the project context and the author identification information. Uploading the data to the repository immediately after the data is collected makes data ready for collaboration and sharing. The repository project can thus become a FAIR data object on its own merit. Since deployment, researchers enthusiastically using the framework, and we already see 30+ OSF projects generated by the MagLab users.

The metadata can be further expanded with supporting information such as the sample description and the provenance info, measurement instrumentation identifiers, probe schematic data and design files, the software versions, the user Open Researcher and Contributor ID (ORCID) information, and even the role of each researcher in data collection. Linking researchers' names and ORCIDs with the datasets will help build an incentive system for propelling data sharing by better crediting researchers for datasets creation [26].

3.6   Conclusion

We showcase a FAIR-ready data management framework which non-disruptively integrates existing practices at the user facility. Using today's advances in information technology, we were able to automate data management and reduce the FAIR-compliance burden, making FAIR attractive and beneficial to every researcher. We open-sourced our data acquisition and metadata hub software, along with APIs to synchronize data to OSF, so other laboratories can build upon the ideas presented here. We believe that our project will inspire other experimental sciences laboratories to carve the pathway to the FAIR-ready data.

References

1. Actor framework. https://labviewwiki.org/wiki/Actor_Framework. Accessed 30 Apr 2022
2. Bailey, C.B., Balakirev, F.F., Balakireva, L.L.: Closing the gap between FAIR data repositories and hierarchical data formats. Code4Lib (2021)
3. Bray, T.: The JavaScript Object Notation (JSON) data interchange format (2017). https://datatracker.ietf.org/doc/html/rfc8259
4. Cain, B., Klein, M., Finnell, J.: Nucleus - deploying research data management infrastructure at the Los Alamos national laboratory. In: 2019 ACM/IEEE Joint Conference on Digital Libraries (JCDL), pp. 396–397 (2019). https://doi.org/10.1109/JCDL.2019.00087
5. The research infrastructure for language as social and cultural data. http://www.clarin.eu/. Accessed 30 Apr 2022
6. Data repository guidance. https://www.nature.com/sdata/policies/repositories. Accessed 30 Apr 2022
7. Infrastructure for the European network for earth system modelling. https://is.enes.org/. Accessed 30 Apr 2022
8. excel. https://www.microsoft.com/en-us/microsoft-365/excel
9. Finnell, J., Klein, M., Cain, B.J.: Nucleus: a pilot project. https://arxiv.org/ftp/arxiv/papers/1705/1705.07862.pdf. Accessed 30 Apr 2022
10. General repository comparison. https://doi.org/10.5281/zenodo.3946720. Accessed 30 Apr 2022
11. Hdf5 file format description and documentation from HDF group. https://portal.hdfgroup.org/display/HDF5/HDF5. Accessed 30 Apr 2022
12. High magnetic field science toolset. https://github.com/ffb-LANL/High-Magnetic-Field-Science-Toolset. Accessed 30 Apr 2022
13. Higman, R., Bangert, D., Jones, S.: Three camps, one destination: the intersections of research data management, FAIR and open. Insights **32**(1) (2019)
14. IGOR. https://en.wikipedia.org/wiki/IGOR_Pro
15. Labview. https://www.ni.com/en-us/shop/labview.html. Accessed 30 Apr 2022
16. Lin, D., et al.: The trust principles for digital repositories. Sci. Data **7**(1), 144 (2020). https://doi.org/10.1038/s41597-020-0486-7
17. Maglab. https://nationalmaglab.org/. Accessed 30 Apr 2022
18. Maglab calendar. https://users.magnet.fsu.edu/Experiments/Calendar.aspx. Accessed 30 Apr 2022
19. Maglab metadata hub. https://github.com/luda171/Maglab-Metadata-Hub. Accessed 30 Apr 2022
20. MATLAB. https://www.mathworks.com/products/matlab.html
21. The novel materials discovery (nomad) centre of excellence. https://nomad-coe.eu/. Accessed 30 Apr 2022
22. numpy. https://numpy.org/
23. Open science framework. https://osf.io/. Accessed 30 Apr 2022
24. Origin. https://www.originlab.com/

25. Osf apiv2 documentation. https://developer.osf.io/. Accessed 30 Apr 2022

26. Pierce, H.H., Dev, A., Statham, E., Bierer, B.E.: Credit data generators for data reuse (2019). https://www.nature.com/articles/d41586-019-01715-4, https://doi.org/10.1038/d41586-019-01715-4

27. Pulsed field facility. https://nationalmaglab.org/user-facilities/pulsed-field-facility. Accessed 30 Apr 2022

28. National Academies of Sciences, E., Medicine: open science by design: realizing a vision for 21st century research. The National Academies Press, Washington, DC (2018). https://doi.org/10.17226/25116, https://nap.nationalacademies.org/catalog/25116/open-science-by-design-realizing-a-vision-for-21st-century

29. Solle, D.: Be FAIR to your data. Anal. Bioanal. Chem. **412**(17), 3961–3965 (2020). https://doi.org/10.1007/s00216-020-02526-7

30. Stall, S., et al.: Make scientific data fair. https://doi.org/10.1038/d41586-019-01720-7. Accessed 30 Apr 2022

31. Stvilia, B., et al.: Research project tasks, data, and perceptions of data quality in a condensed matter physics community. J. Am. Soc. Inf. Sci. **66**, 246–263 (2015)

32. Tdms file format description and documentation from national instruments. https://www.ni.com/en-us/support/documentation/supplemental/06/the-ni-tdms-file-format.html. Accessed 30 Apr 2022

33. The OAuth 2.0 authorization framework. https://datatracker.ietf.org/doc/html/rfc6749. Accessed 30 Apr 2022

34. Turning fair into reality. https://op.europa.eu/en/publication-detail/-/publication/7769a148-f1f6-11e8-9982-01aa75ed71a1/language-en. Accessed 30 Apr 2022

35. Wilkinson, M.D., et al.: The fair guiding principles for scientific data management and stewardship. Sci. Data **3**(1), 160018 (2016). https://doi.org/10.1038/sdata.2016.18

Structured References from PDF Articles: Assessing the Tools for Bibliographic Reference Extraction and Parsing

Alessia Cioffi[1] and Silvio Peroni[2,3]

[1] Digital Humanities and Digital Knowledge, Department of Classical Philology and Italian Studies, University of Bologna, Bologna, Italy
alessia.cioffi@studio.unibo.it

[2] Research Centre for Open Scholarly Metadata, Department of Classical Philology and Italian Studies, University of Bologna, Bologna, Italy
silvio.peroni@unibo.it

[3] Digital Humanities Advanced Research Centre (/DH.arc), Department of Classical Philology and Italian Studies, University of Bologna, Bologna, Italy

Abstract. Many solutions have been provided to extract bibliographic references from PDF papers. Machine learning, rule-based and regular expressions approaches were among the most used methods adopted in tools for addressing this task. This work aims to identify and evaluate all and only the tools which, given a full-text paper in PDF format, can recognise, extract and parse bibliographic references. We identified seven tools: Anystyle, Cermine, ExCite, Grobid, Pdfssa4met, Scholarcy and Science Parse. We compared and evaluated them against a corpus of 56 PDF articles published in 27 subject areas. Indeed, Anystyle obtained the best overall score, followed by Cermine. However, in some subject areas, other tools had better results for specific tasks.

Keywords: References extraction · References parsing · Structured citation data

1 Introduction

In past decades, the academic publishing world has needed to face an exponential increase in the volume of scientific literature materials [13, 29]. The necessity to handle such a vast amount of information has been one of the drivers of the digitalisation of literature materials. The conversion of academic knowledge to structured and machine-readable formats revealed positive effects also in the searchability and availability of such information, thanks to services like search engines [19]. At the same time, the structured format allowed us to valorise the citation graph connecting the scientific literature [7]. Also, in the past 50 years, bibliographic references have assumed a more prominent role in the scientific community, not only for tracking evolution in science but also for measuring impact [14].

In the past five years, the Initiative for Open Citations (I4OC, https://i4oc.org) has emphasised the importance of making citation data public. One of the main challenges

G. Silvello et al. (Eds.): TPDL 2022, LNCS 13541, pp. 425–432, 2022.
https://doi.org/10.1007/978-3-031-16802-4_42

to address for reaching this goal concerns extracting them from unstructured documents, like PDFs, and converting them into structured data in specific formats (e.g. JSON, XML, RDF). However, such extraction is made even more complex by the variety of (either standard or ad hoc) reference styles [15].

In the past, several tools have been proposed to address this task. Our work aims to analyse the current availability of these tools to identify which outperforms the others in extracting and parsing bibliographic references of academic papers.

The rest of the paper is structured as follows. In Sect. 2, we introduce the methodology adopted for identifying relevant tools and analyse their performance against a gold standard. The outcomes of the tools are shown in Sect. 3 and are discussed in more detail in Sect. 4. In Sect. 5, we introduce some of the essential related works in reference extraction approaches and tools. Finally, Sect. 6 concludes the work by sketching out some future developments.

2   Materials and Methods

We devised a methodology for the identification and evaluation of the reference extraction tools, which is based on four steps: (a) systematic literature review, (b) creation of a dataset, (c) creation of translation scripts, and (d) evaluation scripts. Following [31], a specific procedure was implemented and formalised in a protocol fully described in [5] – which is not reported entirely here for page constraints. Such a protocol is based on a citation-based search strategy [30] and uses seed papers for starting the search process [18]. In the first step (a), we decided to consider only papers written in English and dated after 2005. Once relevant articles were chosen in the literature, the focus moved to identify the reference extraction tools described in such documents. We decided to consider, in the analysis, only the tools that can parse full-text PDF papers, retrieve singularly tagged references, retrieve the metadata of each reference, and be either a standalone application or a programming language library, including APIs. At the end of this step, we have identified the following tools: Anystyle (https://github.com/inukshuk/anystyle-cli), CERMINE [26], EXCITE [17], GROBID [20], PDFSSA4MET (https://github.com/eliask/pdfssa4met), Scholarcy [8], and Science Parse (https://github.com/allenai/science-parse).

The next step (b) concerned preparing the data to use to test the tools identified. An initial dataset of papers in PDF format was selected to be processed by the reference extraction tools to obtain these data. This dataset included academic papers from different research fields from a corpus of selected articles used in a complementary study [24]. The dataset comprised 2,538 bibliographic references referring to almost 1,000 different journals, extracted from two articles for each one of the following 27 subject areas: Agricultural and Biological Sciences (AGR-BIO-SCI), Arts and Humanities (ART-HUM), Biochemistry, Genetics and Molecular Biology (BIO-GEN-MOL), Business, Management and Accounting (BUS-MAN-ACC), Chemical Engineering (CHE-ENG), Chemistry (CHEM), Computer Science (COM-SCI), Decision Sciences (DEC-SCI), Dentistry (DEN), Earth and Planetary Sciences (EAR-PLA-SCI), Economics, Econometrics and Finance (ECO-ECO-FIN), Energy (ENE), Engineering (ENG), Environmental Science

(ENV-SCI), Health Professions (HEA-PRO), Immunology and Microbiology (IMM-MIC), Materials Science (MAT-SCI), Mathematics (MAT), Medicine (MED), Multi-disciplinary (MUL), Neuroscience (NEU), Nursing (NUR), Pharmacology, Toxicology and Pharmaceutics (PHA-TOX-PHA), Physics and Astronomy (PHY-AST), Psychology (PSY), Social Sciences (SOC-SCI), Veterinary (VET). These were complemented with additional two articles having bibliographic references not introduced in a 'References' or 'Literature' section (Z-NOTES-TEST). We created a gold standard for comparing the outcomes of the reference extraction tools from these papers. We used the common metadata defining bibliographic references according to the analysis run in [24] as a base-line to understand which metadata must be identified and marked in each bibliographic reference depending on the type of the cited object.

The following step (c) consisted of translating the output of the reference extraction tools into the same format (TEI was chosen) to enable automatic comparison of such output with the gold standard. Finally, we evaluated (d) the tools using precision, recall and f-score, according to the following dimensions (based on prior studies [12, 27]):

1. *Correctly identified references.* The software's ability to distinguish each reference from the surrounding text and other references. The aim is to determine how many references are correctly identified by each parser.
2. *Correctly identified fields per reference.* The number of correctly tagged metadata, independently from content correctness. This analysis allows us to check the tools' quality of the markers' usage.
3. *Correctly identified contents per reference.* How many parts of the bibliographic reference have been correctly parsed and tagged for verifying if the text inside a correctly identified metadata is correct.

The software and all the data used for the experiment are available in [3] and [4].

3   Results

The overall results of the tools' assessment, introduced in Table 1, showed that Anystyle had the best performance. Nonetheless, it is possible to see a different distribution of the values between references, metadata and contents. As expected, the lowest f-score was retrieved in the correct identification of references since it was derived from the correct identification of the metadata elements and their content. Cermine showed its lowest f-score in the references dimension and its highest f-score in the metadata element identification. Overall, the dimension related to metadata contents showed that, even if the metadata element was correctly identified, the content it contained was prone to parsing errors.

The results per subject area, summarised in Fig. 1, differed slightly from the overall ones. Indeed, Anystyle showed coherent results, with all f-values above 0.5 and the highest value registered at 0.97 (BUS-MAN-ACC in Fig. 1). Another noticeable aspect is the high quality of the identification of references in the set of files which included bibliographic references in a section not labelled as "References" or "Literature" (Z-NOTES-TEST), whose p-value lay above 0.85.

Table 1. Precision (P), recall (R) and f-score (F1) of each dimension analysed per tool.

Tools	References			Metadata			Content		
	P	R	F1	P	R	F1	P	R	F1
Anystyle	**0.81**	0.74	**0.77**	0.93	**0.97**	**0.95**	0.87	0.91	**0.89**
Cermine	0.75	0.67	0.71	0.94	0.94	0.94	0.86	0.87	0.86
ExCite	0.59	0.53	0.56	0.93	0.92	0.92	0.79	0.79	0.79
Grobid	0.54	0.55	0.54	0.86	**0.97**	0.91	0.81	**0.92**	0.86
Pdfssa4met	0.01	0.14	0.07	0.01	0.29	0.14	0.01	0.19	0.09
Scholarcy	0.62	**0.78**	0.69	**0.96**	0.70	0.81	0.90	0.65	0.75
Science Parse	0.43	0.32	0.37	1.00	0.55	0.71	**0.94**	0.51	0.66

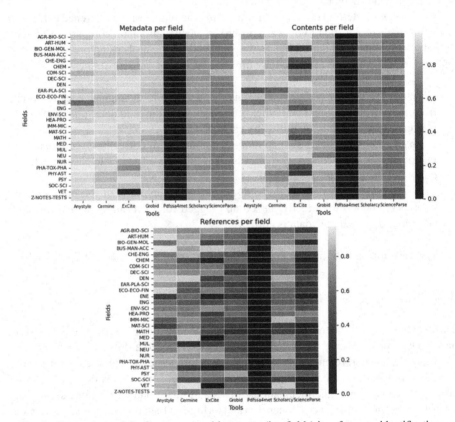

Fig. 1. Comparison of the f-scores per subject areas (i.e. fields) in references identification.

Also, Cermine showed a high precision in reference identification, with a maximum score of 0.96 and a minimum of 0.23. The values were distributed among the fields so that, while only a few fields presented high values above 0.9, many of the fields were close to slightly lower values ranging between 0.6 and 0.8.

ExCite showed high f-scores for reference identification (e.g. 0.91 in BUS-MAN-ACC), with related high f-scores in metadata and content identification (e.g. 0.98

and 0.97, respectively, for the same subject area). However, it could not identify any bibliographic reference in the articles in VET.

The f-scores gathered using GROBID varied a lot in assessing reference identification (from 0.28 to 0.85), but they showed a smaller range in identifying contents (from 0.71 to 0.93). Pdfssa4met, instead, was the tool showing the worst performances. It was able to identify a few references (and related metadata) only in seven subject areas and showed a very low precision (from 0.01 to 0.03).

Scholarcy's f-scores highlighted the excellent performances of the tool in the main part of the subject areas, where the f-scores for the identification of references, metadata element and related content were greater than 0.58, 0.87 and 0.75, respectively. Finally, Science Parse had 0.78 as the maximum f-score in the task of reference identification (in the BUS-MAN-ACC subject area). It is worth mentioning that the precision was 1.0 in all the fields. This was not unexpected since this tool could identify only four metadata elements in each reference (i.e. author, title, source and year), thus reducing the chances of mismatching different elements.

4 Discussion

The comparison between tools' output and the gold standard showed a complex scenario in which a tool, Anystyle, outperformed the others. Indeed, Anystyle obtained the best score in all three dimensions of the analysis, i.e. references, metadata and contents, followed by Cermine. The remaining tools showed good performances on average, except Pdfssa4met.

It is worth mentioning that other factors that affected the reference extraction by the tools were the citation practice of particular subject areas since it affected the results mainly due to the different writing and collecting references practices. Indeed, reference identification was very effective in some subject areas, but other areas (e.g. ENE) showed low performance in all the tools. Thus, it came out that the tools' performances are affected by the practices in the subject areas and that none of the tools was good per se in all the subject areas.

This work presents three major limitations. First, the input dataset was small, even if appropriate to run initial experiments on the topic. Indeed, even if providing a vast number of research fields, each subject area included only two papers, enough to provide a preliminary insight rather than a definitive view on the topic. Second, the tools have been used off-the-shelf, without any training. For the CRF-based tools, this lack of training could have resulted in a loss in performance for some of the tools [28]. Finally, we adopted the Levenshtein distance as a unique metric to compute the similarity of the metadata content in the bibliographic references. Nonetheless, other works have identified other measures, e.g. the soft TF-IDF [6], to outperform the Levenshtein distance in measuring the similarity between two names in text retrieval tasks.

5 Related Works

Apart from the tools identified and used in our analysis, we took notes about other theoretical approaches and workflows presented in other articles when we identified the tools to use in our study. This section presents some of the most important ones, organised in three categories.

Single Reference Parsing. This category of tools represents a set of tools which can parse a single reference and returns the metadata it is composed of in a structured format. The tools can be different depending on the approach they are based on, the input data they accept, the focus on different types of citation, e.g. academic or generic references, or the ability to extract a different number of metadata from the reference strings. Some of these tools are based on machine learning techniques, e.g. [33], while others use Hidden Markov Model [9, 32, 22], rule-based methods [25] and frame-based approaches [10] to address the same tasks.

Parsers for Reference Lists. This is a category of tools that extract and parse references from files in different formats, but not from full-text pdf files. Indeed, in most cases, they can, given a text file with a list of references (one line per reference), extract single references, parse them and return the metadata of each reference, such as Neural Parscit (https://github.com/WING-NUS/Neural-ParsCit).

Frameworks for Parsing Bibliographic References in PDF Full Text. In [23], the authors describe a machine-learning-based framework that outperforms the results obtained on the same input dataset by an HMM-based method. Similarly, in [26], the authors explore a composed tool based on simple HMM and rules thought to be easily modifiable by the user. Other solutions are based on rules, e.g. [1, 11, 16], ontologies [21], or deep pully convolutional networks [2].

6   Conclusions

This work aimed to retrieve from the available literature all the tools able to extract the bibliographic references from full-text PDF papers and evaluate them. Seven tools have been selected: Anystyle, Cermine, ExCite, Grobid, Pdfssa4met, Scholarcy and Science Parse. Three dimensions have been analysed for each: the correctly extracted metadata, the related correctly extracted contents, and the correctly extracted references.

Anystyle outperformed the others in all the three dimensions considered in the analysis. Nonetheless, the results for the analysis per subject area showed that, in some cases, Anystyle was outperformed by other tools. Thus, while Anystyle is the best tool for bibliographic reference extraction and parsing, cooperation between the tools based on the specific subtasks may be relevant to obtaining the best possible results.

In future developments, extending the current corpus of input PDF documents could be appropriate to consolidate the results obtained in this research.

Acknowledgements. The work of Silvio Peroni has been partially funded by the European Union's Horizon 2020 research and innovation program under grant agreement No 101017452 (OpenAIRE-Nexus).

References

1. Azimjonov, J., Alikhanov, J.: Rule based metadata extraction framework from academic articles. arXiv:1807.09009 [Cs] (2018)
2. Bhardwaj, A., Mercier, D., Dengel, A., Ahmed, S.: DeepBIBX: deep learning for image based bibliographic data extraction. In: Liu, D., Xie, S., Li, Y., Zhao, D., El-Alfy, E.-S. M. (eds.) Neural Information Processing, pp. 286–293. Springer International Publishing, Cham (2017). https://doi.org/10.1007/978-3-319-70096-0_30
3. Cioffi, A.: Code for converting different formats to TEI XML and evaluation of the results. Zenodo (2022).https://doi.org/10.5281/zenodo.6182128
4. Cioffi, A.: Data for testing and evaluating references extraction and parsing tools. Zenodo (2022).https://doi.org/10.5281/zenodo.6182066
5. Cioffi, A.: Systematic literature review about software for references extraction. protocols.io (2022). https://doi.org/10.17504/protocols.io.buz9nx96
6. Cohen, W.W., Ravikumar, P., Fienberg, S.E.: A comparison of string distance metrics for name-matching tasks. In: IIWEB 2003: Proceedings of the 2003 International Conference on Information Integration on the Web (2003). https://doi.org/10.5555/3104278.3104293
7. Fortunato, S., et al.: Science of science. Science **359**(6379), aao0185 (2018). https://doi.org/10.1126/science.aao0185
8. Gooch, P.: How Scholarcy contributes to and makes use of open citations. Scholarcy (2021). https://www.scholarcy.com/how-scholarcy-contributes-to-and-makes-use-of-opencitations/
9. Hetzner, E.: A simple method for citation metadata extraction using hidden Markov models. In: Proceedings of the 8th ACM/IEEE-CS Joint Conference on Digital Libraries - JCDL 2008, p. 280. Pittsburgh PA, PA, USA: ACM Press (2008)
10. Hsieh, Y.L., et al.: A frame-based approach for reference metadata extraction. In: Cheng, S.M., Day, M.Y. (eds.) Technologies and Applications of Artificial Intelligence. LNCS, vol. 8916, pp. 154–163. Springer, Cham (2014). https://doi.org/10.1007/978-3-319-13987-6_15
11. Huynh, T., Hoang, K.: GATE framework based metadata extraction from scientific papers. In: 2010 International Conference on Education and Management Technology, pp. 188–191. Cairo, Egypt. IEEE (2010). https://doi.org/10.1109/ICEMT.2010.5657675
12. Indrawati, A., Yoganingrum, A., Yuwono, P.: Evaluating the quality of the indonesian scientific journal references using ParsCit, CERMINE and GROBID. Lib. Philos. Pract. (2019)
13. Khabsa, M., Giles, C.L.: The number of scholarly documents on the public web. PLoS ONE **9**(5), e93949 (2014). https://doi.org/10.1371/journal.pone.0093949
14. Kim, K., Chung, Y.: Overview of Journal Metrics. Sci. Editing **5**(1), 16–20 (2018). https://doi.org/10.6087/kcse.112
15. King, D., Jérome, D., Van Allen, M., Shepherd, P., Bollen, J.: Tools and metrics: keynote speech. Inf. Serv. Use **28**(3–4), 215–28 (2009). https://doi.org/10.3233/ISU-2008-0579
16. Kluegl, P., Hotho, A., Puppe, F.: Local adaptive extraction of references. In: Dillmann, R., Beyerer, J., Hanebeck, U.D., Schultz, T. (eds.) KI 2010. LNCS (LNAI), vol. 6359, pp. 40–47. Springer, Heidelberg (2010). https://doi.org/10.1007/978-3-642-16111-7_4
17. Körner, M., Ghavimi, B., Mayr, P., Hartmann, H., Staab, S.: Evaluating reference string extraction using line-based conditional random fields: a case study with German language publications. In: Kirikova, M., et al. (eds.) ADBIS 2017. CCIS, vol. 767, pp. 137–145. Springer, Cham (2017). https://doi.org/10.1007/978-3-319-67162-8_15
18. Lecy, J.D., Kate, E.: Beatty: representative literature reviews using constrained snowball sampling and citation network analysis. SSRN Electron. J. (2012)https://doi.org/10.2139/ssrn.1992601
19. Levene, M.: An Introduction to Search Engines and Web Navigation, 2nd edn. John Wiley, Hoboken (2010)

20. Lopez, P.: GROBID: combining automatic bibliographic data recognition and term extraction for scholarship publications. In: Agosti, M., Borbinha, J., Kapidakis, S., Papatheodorou, C., Tsakonas, G. (eds.) Research and Advanced Technology for Digital Libraries. Lecture Notes in Computer Science, vol. 5714, pp. 473–474. Springer, Berlin (2009). https://doi.org/10.1007/978-3-642-04346-8_62

21. Ning, X., Jin, H., Wu, H.: SemreX: towards large-scale literature information retrieval and browsing with semantic association. In: 2006 IEEE International Conference on E-Business Engineering (ICEBE 2006), pp. 602–609. Shanghai, China. IEEE (2006). https://doi.org/10.1109/ICEBE.2006.87

22. Ojokoh, B., Zhang, M., Tang, J.: A Trigram hidden Markov model for metadata extraction from heterogeneous references. Inf. Sci. **181**(9), 1538–1551 (2011). https://doi.org/10.1016/j.ins.2011.01.014

23. Peng, F., Andrew M.: Accurate information extraction from research papers using conditional random fields. In: NAACL (2004)

24. Santos, E.A.D., Peroni, S., Mucheroni, M.L.: The way we cite: common metadata used across disciplines for defining bibliographic references. In: Proceedings of the 26th International Conference on Theory and Practice of Digital Libraries (TPDL 2022). arXiv.org (2022, to appear). https://doi.org/10.48550/arXiv.2202.08469

25. Suryawati, E., Widyantoro, D.H.: Combination of heuristic, rule-based and machine learning for bibliography extraction. In: 2017 5th International Conference on Instrumentation, Communications, Information Technology, and Biomedical Engineering (ICICI-BME), pp. 276–81, Bandung. IEEE (2017). https://doi.org/10.1109/ICICI-BME.2017.8537772

26. Tkaczyk, D., Szostek, P., Dendek, P.J., Fedoryszak, M., Bolikowski, L.: CERMINE -- automatic extraction of metadata and references from scientific literature. In: 2014 11th IAPR International Workshop on Document Analysis Systems, pp. 217– 21. IEEE (2014).https://doi.org/10.1109/DAS.2014.63

27. Tkaczyk, D., Collins, A., Sheridan, P., Beel, J.: Evaluation and comparison of open source bibliographic reference parsers: a business use case. arXiv:1802.01168 (2018)

28. Tkaczyk, D., Collins, A., Sheridan, P., Beel, J.: Machine learning vs. rules and out-of-the-box vs. retrained: an evaluation of open-source bibliographic reference and citation parsers. In: Proceedings of the 18th ACM/IEEE on Joint Conference on Digital Libraries, pp. 99–108. Fort Worth Texas USA. ACM (2018)

29. Van Noorden, R.: Global scientific output doubles every nine years. nature news blog (2014). http://blogs.nature.com/news/2014/05/global-scientific-output-doublesevery-nine-years.html

30. Wohlin, C.: Guidelines for snowballing in systematic literature studies and a replication in software engineering. In: Proceedings of the 18th International Conference on Evaluation and Assessment in Software Engineering - EASE 2014 (2014)

31. Xiao, Y., Watson, M.: Guidance on conducting a systematic literature review. J. Plan. Educ. Res. **39**(1), 93–112 (2019)

32. Yin, P., Zhang, M., Deng, Z., Yang, D.: Metadata extraction from bibliographies using bigram HMM. In: Chen, Z., Chen, H., Miao, Q., Fu, Y., Fox, E., Lim, E.-P. (eds.) ICADL 2004. LNCS, vol. 3334, pp. 310–319. Springer, Heidelberg (2004). https://doi.org/10.1007/978-3-540-30544-6_33

33. Zhang, X., Zou, J., Le, D.X., Thoma, G.R.: A structural SVM approach for reference parsing. BMC Bioinform. **12**(S3), S7 (2011). https://doi.org/10.1186/1471-2105-12-S3-S7

On Dimensions of Plausibility
for Narrative Information Access
to Digital Libraries

Hermann Kroll[(✉)] [iD], Niklas Mainzer, and Wolf-Tilo Balke [iD]

Institute for Information Systems, TU Braunschweig, Braunschweig, Germany
{kroll,balke}@ifis.cs.tu-bs.de, n.mainzer@tu-bs.de

Abstract. Designing keyword-based access paths is a common practice in digital libraries. They are easy to use and accepted by users and come with moderate costs for content providers. However, users usually have to break down the search into pieces if they search for stories of interest that are more complex than searching for a few keywords. After searching for every piece one by one, information must then be reassembled manually. In previous work we recommended narrative information access, i.e., users can precisely state their information needs as graph patterns called narratives. Then a system takes a narrative and searches for evidence for each of its parts. If the whole query, i.e., every part, can be bound against data, the narrative is considered plausible and, thus, the query is answered. But is it as easy as that? In this work we perform case studies to analyze the process of making a given narrative plausible. Therefore, we summarize conceptual problems and challenges to face. Moreover, we contribute a set of dimensions that must be considered when realizing narrative information access in digital libraries.

Keywords: Narrative information access · Plausibility · Dimensions

1 Introduction

Digital libraries are large-scale repositories containing a plethora of heterogeneous but well-curated data: texts, images, videos, research data, and many more. Today, keyword-based search (on texts or respective metadata) forms the primary access path for collections: It is easy to use and thus a commonly accepted interface, and implementing a respective search index comes with acceptable costs for content providers. In addition, keyword queries can be evaluated against different data representations; See keyword-based searches in literature and books, in knowledge bases [10,15], and data set repositories [8]. Although the advantage of keyword-based search is apparent, moving towards alternative access paths is heavily investigated, e.g., the biomedical database SemMedDB [21] on top of Medline, the Open Knowledge Research Graph [18], or the Europeana as Linked Open Data [16] and DBpedia [2]. A good example is the current trend towards structured knowledge graphs: Here users can formulate their information needs as structured queries (e.g., via SPARQL interfaces)

© Springer Nature Switzerland AG 2022
G. Silvello et al. (Eds.): TPDL 2022, LNCS 13541, pp. 433–441, 2022.
https://doi.org/10.1007/978-3-031-16802-4_43

asking for a combination of knowledge particles (i.e., automatically joining pieces of information).

However, integrating different and heterogeneous sources into a single knowledge representation comes with new problems, such as the validity of fused information [22], identifying and canonicalizing pieces of information (entity linkage), and practical extraction problems when mining knowledge from different sources; See [33] for a good overview. A remedy might be the use of *narrative information access* to bypass the necessary integration of different sources. In [23], **narratives** are defined by directed edge-labeled graph patterns involving entities (things and concepts), events (state or state changes), literals (values), and their respective relationships (properties, temporal, and causal predicates, etc.).

Since the individual information particles within a narrative form proper subgraphs, narratives can be understood as forming a logical overlay on top of different knowledge repositories. A narrative query is then successfully answered if evidence for every single relationship of the narrative can be found in some collection's data. This evidence forms so-called **narrative bindings** connecting each relationship against a concrete piece of information stated in some knowledge repository, i.e., any form of data storage (e.g., relational databases, knowledge graphs, data sets, etc.). In previous works we formulated a conceptual model [23] for narrative information access, discussed the binding process from a technical perspective [24], showed how queries can be processed over collections of scientific publications [25], and discussed conceptual problems like context compatibility when answering queries over independent knowledge bases [26].

In contrast to fact-checking, where the task refers to deciding whether some statement is indeed a fact (and thus true) or is rejected because it has no evidence [14,32], narrative structures may be composed out of several statements. Moreover, we do not require a universally valid decision, i.e., based on a given ground truth (a theory in physics for example), we can make a narrative plausible, whereas we cannot make the narrative plausible on a different ground truth. While question answering and its methods [19,20,35,35] are related to narrative information access, we see significant differences in the evaluation: Narrative information access considers contexts [22,26], i.e., we do not fuse information from different contexts. For a good example, consider claims from the biomedical domain: Combining claims made when treating mice with claims when treating humans can be a serious threat to the overall validity because no one guarantees that these claims should also be valid for humans then.

In summary, the key advantage of narrative information access is to make user-formulated graph patterns *plausible* in valid contexts. But beyond apparent technical problems and the problem of context compatibility in narrative information access, the notion of *plausibility* has yet to be discussed in detail. Our current model considers a narrative as plausible if evidence for every of its claims can be found. But is it as easy as that? In this paper we summarize the conceptual problems of our narrative query model. Therefore, we perform case studies in different domains to find the basic building blocks for an actionable notion of plausibility. Moreover, we open up a design space and discuss our

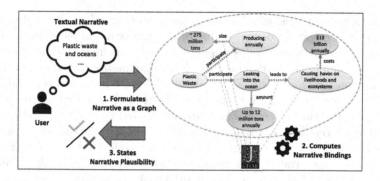

Fig. 1. Making narratives plausible by computing bindings against knowledge repositories. Here our example Narrative 1 is bound against the digital library JSTOR.

notion of plausibility in detail by arguing on different evaluation semantics, the trustworthiness of sources, and the quality of bindings.

2 Case Studying Narrative Plausibility

In brief, a user models a narrative of interest as a graph structure. Then, a process searches for evidence for each relationship in a set of given knowledge repositories. If we can find evidence for the whole narrative, i.e., every narrative's relationship, we consider it plausible [23]. The process is shown in Fig. 1. Note that we may build different plausibility validation processes, which can vary in their included and excluded knowledge repositories for the binding computation, e.g., peer-reviewed scientific papers, fact-checked sources, or arbitrary websites. Due to the lack of existing implementations for such a process, we performed manual case studies, i.e., we searched for evidence through keyword queries in knowledge repositories and evaluated the results manually.

Narrative 1. *Of the approximately 275 million metric tons of plastic waste produced annually, up to 12 million tons leak into oceans, wreaking havoc on livelihoods and ecosystems (CIEL, 2020). The result is an estimated $13 billion in annual environmental damage to marine ecosystems. [1] (See Fig. 1).*

The central entity of our example is *plastic waste*, around which the rest of the narrative revolves. The narrative states two events directly relating to plastic waste, its *annual production*, and that *plastic waste is leaking into the ocean*. The *havoc on livelihoods and ecosystems* is a direct consequence of *ocean plastic* and represents the third event of our example. Each event that we described is further connected to a literal: There are approximately *275 million tons* of annual plastic waste production, up to *twelve million tons* leak into the ocean, and the havoc on livelihoods and ecosystems costs around *13 billion dollars per year*. Note that we may extract different graph representations of the same textual narrative but we discuss this transformation ambiguity in the next section.

We next present a plausibility validation process based on the digital library JSTOR (https://www.jstor.org/). One of the problems we faced in the beginning was that some relationships require more context from the narrative itself, e.g., *Producing annually an amount of 275 million metric tons* does not include that it is about *plastic waste*. Either the model must include this detail in the event *Producing annually*, or we must verify that the context of the production must match plastic waste. Therefore, we started by evaluating that *around 275 million metric tons of plastic waste are annually produced*. We formulated different keyword queries to search for the given relationship. We retrieved a source that claimed the 275 million metric ton estimation [17]. We found two more sources, one of which reported an annual plastic production of 381 million metric tons in 2015, of which 79% are considered waste [34]. We performed the calculation ourselves, and the result was around 300 million tonnes of plastic waste per annum [34] or respectively 321 million metric tonnes per year [30].

We then evaluated that *up to 12 million tons of plastic waste are annually leaking into the ocean*. [30] reported that in 2010, approximately nine million tons of plastic were added to the ocean. [34] estimated that around 4.8 to 12.7 million tons of plastic entered the ocean in 2010. The plausibility validation seemed to confirm the narrative claim in this way. We moved to the next relationship: *The leaking of plastic into the ocean leads to havoc on livelihoods and ecosystems*. Even in 1987, [3] already reported an endangerment of marine environments caused by plastic in the ocean. A more recent article described dangers to the marine animal and plant life due to microplastic as well as the economic dangers [9]. For the last relation we searched evidence that the impact of plastic waste in oceans costs 13 billion dollars annually. [30] reported 75 billion Dollar annual environmental costs originating from plastics. However, the source did not state how much of the total costs are connected to plastic waste in the ocean. Apart from [30], we could not find any other sources stating the actual costs.

2.1 Summary of Other Case Studies

We performed the plausibility validation for three additional narratives: 1. Deforestation of the Amazonian Rainforest and forests in general, 2. Claims about the connection between government measures during the Covid-19 pandemic and the number of Covid-related deaths, and 3. Global warming and the effects of carbon dioxide emissions on the climate. For 3. we only considered fact-checked articles, whereas we allowed every website on the first result page of our Google Search for the 1. and 2. narrative.

An interesting finding of the deforestation narrative occurred when we evaluated the percentage of the Earth's landmass covered by forests. The narrative stated a value of 30%. One of our retrieved sources confirmed this narrative claim by stating a value of 30.7% [4]. Another source, however, stated that forests cover 38% of the habitable land area [31]. These values greatly differ and could be classified as counter-evidence because 30% could not be verified precisely. However, we noticed that [4] base their value on the total land area, while [31] makes this calculation based on the habitable land area, explaining the difference in these values.

We performed a selection of our approaches multiple times over a period of several weeks to observe how the results would change over time. We retrieved the global warming narrative from [28]. When we initially accessed this source, the narrative reported an average surface temperature of 1.18 °C on Earth. However, over time this value has been changed to one degree Celsius, which is less specific than the initial estimate. While performing the initial plausibility validation, we noticed various factors determining Earth's average surface temperature changes, such as the data collection methods and the point in time used as a reference. Various sources described warming of around one degree, but we could not precisely confirm the 1.18 °C. The fact that NASA changed that value confirms our assumption that there is too much uncertainty about the data to state such a specific temperature change.

3   Concluding Discussion on Narrative Plausibility

In the following we summarize the main findings from our previous case studies.

Confirmation Bias. Confirmation bias describes "the seeking or interpreting of evidence in ways that are partial to existing beliefs, expectations, or a hypothesis at hand" [29]. As this definition suggests, bias can already occur in the search for information, and its effects highly depend on how the plausibility validation process searches for evidence. For instance, evaluating *plastic waste causes 13 billion dollars annually in environmental costs by leaking into the ocean* could lead to other results than searching without a concrete cost value.

Narrative's Context. The narrative itself spans a context that must be considered when binding its relationships individually. For instance, searching for *an amount of leakage* without *plastic waste* may result invalid results. Similarly, evaluating the *average surface temperature* without a concrete year may also yield results that do not match the user's indented context.

Finding the Narrative's Source. Imagine a narrative extracted from a study reports scientifically disputed findings. We would assume such a narrative to be evaluated as implausible in a plausibility validation process. However, the process will likely find the study's sources again – even if they are disputed.

Ambiguity of Narrative Extraction. Narratives can be interpreted differently since they make various claims, usually without explaining exactly how everything is meant. Without an objective understanding of what the narrative is exactly stating, this will affect the narrative model extracted from the actual textual narrative. Consequently, the plausibility validation process computes narrative bindings for a selected instance of the possible interpretations, making the conclusion about narrative plausibility dependent on the chosen narrative model and, therefore, on the chosen interpretation of the narrative. A plausibility validation process based on another interpretation of the same narrative might result in a different conclusion about the narrative's plausibility.

Evidence. We observed three issues when searching for evidence: 1. Indirect Evidence: The process may not find direct but rather indirect evidence (e.g., a certain percentage of the annual plastic production), which requires further computations. 2. Counter-Evidence: We may find counter-evidence, i.e., evidence that contradicts a narrative's relationship. 3. Absence of Evidence: Not finding evidence is always connected to uncertainty since we cannot be sure if evidence does not exist or if we simply did not find it. All issues are especially relevant if we utilize error-prone NLP and retrieval methods [6,12].

Trustworthiness of Sources. When computing bindings against different types of sources, the credibility of sources must be considered. On the one hand, we may utilize Provenance information that has already been curated [7,13,27]. Provenance allows knowledge curators to precisely describe how a certain piece of information was created or obtained. If we bind against that certain piece, we can then utilize its Provenance. On the other hand, we may integrate tests like the CRAAP test [5] or automated heuristics, e.g., scientific publications before websites, highly influential over low cited publications, etc. Note that we are aware of highly influential papers that have been retracted but handling such cases in digital libraries is a research field on its own [11]. But if we do not have curated information available, we must think about alternatives here.

3.1   Dimensions of Narrative Plausibility

The contribution of this work is the introduction of **dimensions** influencing narrative plausibility. When implementing a validation process in a digital library, the designers must decide how the following criteria should be handled.

Narrative Structure. We have seen that transforming a story of interest (a user's query) into a graph representation can be challenging and may yield several different representations. Moreover, each representation might end up in a different result (plausible/not plausible) which could confuse users. Do we consider the exact narrative, or do we allow a few derivations (e.g., relaxing the query a bit)? What can users then expect if a narrative is considered plausible?

Validation Approach. Which knowledge repositories are considered for the binding computation? Which methods are used to compute the actual bindings? What do these methods guarantee? And thus, what could a user then expect?

Types of Evidence. Beyond suitable evidence we may face the *indirect, missing,* and *counter-evidence* in practice. What should we do if we cannot find evidence for all of a narrative's relationships? Is the narrative simply considered as *not plausible*? Or should we instead show the user how much of the narrative is plausible and which parts lack evidence? Do we consider counter-evidence? And if we do, what does the existence of counter-evidence then mean, e.g., that the narrative is not plausible? As we have argued before, there is a fine line between evidence not exactly confirming a relationship and counter-evidence.

Confidence of Bindings. How trustworthy do the sources have to be? How should this trustworthiness be determined or measured? How is the quality of the actual bindings from a technical perspective, e.g., the confidence of a retrieval process or similarity measures for values? Should we use thresholds to consider trustworthy sources and high-quality bindings only? Which evaluation strategy do we select, e.g., the trustworthiness of sources over binding quality? Do we average both *values* into an overall confidence?

References

1. Plastics and the Environment. https://www.genevaenvironmentnetwork.org/resources/updates/plastics-and-the-environment/. Accessed May 2022
2. Auer, S., Bizer, C., Kobilarov, G., Lehmann, J., Cyganiak, R., Ives, Z.: DBpedia: a nucleus for a web of open data. In: Aberer, K., et al. (eds.) ASWC/ISWC -2007. LNCS, vol. 4825, pp. 722–735. Springer, Heidelberg (2007). https://doi.org/10.1007/978-3-540-76298-0_52
3. Azzarello, M.Y., Vleet, E.S.V.: Marine birds and plastic pollution. Mar. Ecol. Prog. Ser. **37**(2/3), 295–303 (1987). http://www.jstor.org/stable/24824704
4. Bank, W.: Forest area (% of land area). https://data.worldbank.org/indicator/AG.LND.FRST.ZS. Accessed 25 May 2022
5. Blakeskee, S.: The CRAAP test. LOEX Quart. **31**, 4(2004). https://commons.emich.edu/loexquarterly/vol31/iss3/4
6. Blatz, J., et al.: Confidence estimation for machine translation. In: COLING 2004: Proceedings of the 20th International Conference on Computational Linguistics, pp. 315–321. COLING, Geneva, Switzerland, 23–27 August 2004. https://aclanthology.org/C04-1046
7. Carroll, J.J., Bizer, C., Hayes, P.J., Stickler, P.: Named graphs. J. Web Semant. **3**(4), 247–267 (2005). https://doi.org/10.1016/j.websem.2005.09.001
8. Chapman, A., et al.: Dataset search: a survey. VLDB J. **29**(1), 251–272 (2019). https://doi.org/10.1007/s00778-019-00564-x
9. Clark, J.R., et al.: Marine microplastic debris: a targeted plan for understanding and quantifying interactions with marine life. Front. Ecol. Environ. **14**(6), 317–324 (2016). http://www.jstor.org/stable/44001167
10. Elbassuoni, S., Blanco, R.: Keyword search over RDF graphs. In: Proceedings of the 20th ACM International Conference on Information and Knowledge Management, pp. 237–242. CIKM 2011. Association for Computing Machinery, New York, NY, USA (2011). https://doi.org/10.1145/2063576.2063615
11. Fu, Y., Schneider, J.: Towards knowledge maintenance in scientific digital libraries with the keystone framework. In: Huang, R., Wu, D., Marchionini, G., He, D., Cunningham, S.J., Hansen, P. (eds.) JCDL 2020: Proceedings of the ACM/IEEE Joint Conference on Digital Libraries in 2020, Virtual Event, China, 1–5 August 2020, pp. 217–226. ACM (2020). https://doi.org/10.1145/3383583.3398514
12. Gandrabur, S., Foster, G.F., Lapalme, G.: Confidence estimation for NLP applications. ACM Trans. Speech Lang. Process. **3**(3), 1–29 (2006). https://doi.org/10.1145/1177055.1177057
13. Group, W.W.: PROV-overview. an overview of the PROV family of documents (2013). https://www.w3.org/TR/prov-overview/
14. Guo, Z., Schlichtkrull, M., Vlachos, A.: A survey on automated fact-checking. Trans. Assoc. Comp Linguist. (TACL) **10**, 178–206 (2022)

15. Han, S., Zou, L., Yu, J.X., Zhao, D.: Keyword search on RDF graphs - a query graph assembly approach. In: Proceedings of the 2017 ACM on Conference on Information and Knowledge Management, pp. 227–236. CIKM 2017. Association for Computing Machinery, New York, NY, USA (2017). https://doi.org/10.1145/3132847.3132957

16. Haslhofer, B., Isaac, A.: data.europeana.eu: the Europeana linked open data pilot. In: Baker, T., Hillmann, D.I., Isaac, A. (eds.) Proceedings of the 2011 International Conference on Dublin Core and Metadata Applications, DC 2011, The Hague, The Netherlands, 21–23 September 2011, pp. 94–104. Dublin Core Metadata Initiative (2011). http://dcpapers.dublincore.org/pubs/article/view/3625

17. Jambeck, J.R., et al.: Plastic waste inputs from land into the ocean. Science 347(6223), 768–771 (2015). https://doi.org/10.1126/science.1260352

18. Jaradeh, M.Y., et al.: Open research knowledge graph: Next generation infrastructure for semantic scholarly knowledge. In: Kejriwal, M., Szekely, P.A., Troncy, R. (eds.) Proceedings of the 10th International Conference on Knowledge Capture, K-CAP 2019, Marina Del Rey, CA, USA, 19–21 November 2019, pp. 243–246. ACM (2019). https://doi.org/10.1145/3360901.3364435

19. Jin, Q., et al.: Biomedical question answering: a survey of approaches and challenges. ACM Comput. Surv. 55(2), 1–36 (2022). https://doi.org/10.1145/3490238

20. Khot, T., Sabharwal, A., Clark, P.: Answering complex questions using open information extraction. In: Barzilay, R., Kan, M. (eds.) Proceedings of the 55th Annual Meeting of the Association for Computational Linguistics, ACL 2017, Vancouver, Canada, 30 July – 4 August, Volume 2: Short Papers, pp. 311–316. Association for Computational Linguistics (2017). https://doi.org/10.18653/v1/P17-2049

21. Kilicoglu, H., Shin, D., Fiszman, M., Rosemblat, G., Rindflesch, T.C.: SemMedDB: a PubMed-scale repository of biomedical semantic predications. Bioinformatics 28(23), 3158–3160 (2012). https://doi.org/10.1093/bioinformatics/bts591

22. Kroll, H., Kalo, J.-C., Nagel, D., Mennicke, S., Balke, W.-T.: Context-compatible information fusion for scientific knowledge graphs. In: Hall, M., Merčun, T., Risse, T., Duchateau, F. (eds.) TPDL 2020. LNCS, vol. 12246, pp. 33–47. Springer, Cham (2020). https://doi.org/10.1007/978-3-030-54956-5_3

23. Kroll, H., Nagel, D., Balke, W.-T.: Modeling narrative structures in logical overlays on top of knowledge repositories. In: Dobbie, G., Frank, U., Kappel, G., Liddle, S.W., Mayr, H.C. (eds.) ER 2020. LNCS, vol. 12400, pp. 250–260. Springer, Cham (2020). https://doi.org/10.1007/978-3-030-62522-1_18

24. Kroll, H., Nagel, D., Kunz, M., Balke, W.: Demonstrating narrative bindings: linking discourses to knowledge repositories. In: Campos, R., Jorge, A.M., Jatowt, A., Bhatia, S., Finlayson, M.A. (eds.) Proceedings of Text2Story - Fourth Workshop on Narrative Extraction From Texts held in conjunction with the 43rd European Conference on Information Retrieval (ECIR 2021), Lucca, Italy, 1 April 2021 (online event due to COVID-19 outbreak). CEUR Workshop Proceedings, vol. 2860, pp. 57–63. CEUR-WS.org (2021). http://ceur-ws.org/Vol-2860/paper7.pdf

25. Kroll, H., Pirklbauer, J., Kalo, J.-C., Kunz, M., Ruthmann, J., Balke, W.-T.: Narrative query graphs for entity-interaction-aware document retrieval. In: Ke, H.-R., Lee, C.S., Sugiyama, K. (eds.) ICADL 2021. LNCS, vol. 13133, pp. 80–95. Springer, Cham (2021). https://doi.org/10.1007/978-3-030-91669-5_7

26. Kroll, H., Plötzky, F., Pirklbauer, J., Balke, W.: What a publication tells you - benefits of narrative information access in digital libraries. CoRR (Accepted to JCDL2022) abs/2205.00718 (2022). https://doi.org/10.48550/arXiv.2205.00718

27. Lebo, T., Sahoo, S., McGuinness, D.: PROV-O: The PROV Ontology (2013). https://www.w3.org/TR/prov-o/

28. NASA: Global Temperature — Vital Signs - NASA Climate Change. https://
    climate.nasa.gov/evidence/. Accessed 25 May 2022
29. Nickerson, R.S.: Confirmation bias: a ubiquitous phenomenon in many guises. Rev.
    Gen. Psychol. **2**(2), 175–220 (1998). https://doi.org/10.1037/1089-2680.2.2.175
30. Rhodes, C.J.: Plastic pollution and potential solutions. Sci. Prog. **101**, 207–260
    (2018)
31. Ritchie, H., Roser, M.: Forests and deforestation. Our World in Data (2021).
    https://ourworldindata.org/forests-and-deforestation
32. Uscinski, J.E., Butler, R.W.: The epistemology of fact checking. Crit. Rev. **25**(2),
    162–180 (2013)
33. Weikum, G., Dong, X.L., Razniewski, S., Suchanek, F.M.: Machine knowledge:
    creation and curation of comprehensive knowledge bases. Found. Trends Databases
    10(2–4), 108–490 (2021). https://doi.org/10.1561/1900000064
34. Williams, A., Rangel-Buitrago, N.: Marine litter: solutions for a major environ-
    mental problem. J. Coast. Res. **35**(3), 648–663 (2019). https://doi.org/10.2112/
    JCOASTRES-D-18-00096.1
35. Zhao, C., Xiong, C., Qian, X., Boyd-Graber, J.L.: Complex factoid question
    answering with a free-text knowledge graph. In: Huang, Y., King, I., Liu, T., van
    Steen, M. (eds.) WWW 2020: The Web Conference 2020, Taipei, Taiwan, 20–24
    April 2020, pp. 1205–1216. ACM/IW3C2 (2020). https://doi.org/10.1145/3366423.
    3380197

Early Experiments on Automatic Annotation of Portuguese Medieval Texts

Maria Inês Bico[1,2]([✉]) [iD], Jorge Baptista[3,4] [iD], Fernando Batista[4,5] [iD], and Esperança Cardeira[1,2] [iD]

[1] Univ. Lisboa - Fac. Letras, Lisbon, Portugal
{mariainesb1,ecardeira}@campus.ul.pt
[2] Centro de Linguística da Universidade de Lisboa, Lisbon, Portugal
[3] Univ. Algarve - Fac. Ciências Humanas e Sociais, Faro, Portugal
jbaptis@ualg.pt
[4] INESC-ID Lisboa - Human Language Technology Lab, Lisbon, Portugal
[5] ISCTE - Instituto Universitário de Lisboa, Lisbon, Portugal
fernando.batista@iscte-iul.pt

Abstract. This paper presents the challenges and solutions adopted to the lemmatization and part-of-speech (PoS) tagging of a corpus of Old Portuguese texts (up to 1525), to pave the way to the implementation of an automatic annotation of these Medieval texts. A highly granular tagset, previously devised for Modern Portuguese, was adapted to this end. A large text (~155 thousand words) was manually annotated for PoS and lemmata and used to train an initial PoS-tagger model. When applied to two other texts, the resulting model attained 91.2% precision with a textual variant of the same text, and 67.4% with a new, unseen text. A second model was then trained with the data provided by the previous three texts and applied to two other unseen texts. The new model achieved a precision of 77.3% and 82.4%, respectively.

Keywords: Automatic annotation · Lemmatization · Part-of-speech tagging · Old portuguese

1 Introduction

For a long time, researchers in historical linguistics handpick the traces of the phenomena they choose to study. It is laborious and slow work, and the pressure of time and deadlines usually meant that the scope of the investigation has to be restricted, whether in terms of the phenomena or in the quantity of the data perused. In addition, though the availability of old texts on the web is

Research for this paper was partially funded by public funds through Fundação para a Ciência e a Tecnologia: J. Baptista and F. Batista (INESC-ID Lisboa, proj.ref UIDB/50021/2020), E. Cardeira (School of Arts and Humanities, Center of Linguistics, University of Lisbon, proj.ref. UIDP/00214/2020) and M.I. Bico by Ph.D grant (proj.ref. UI/BD/152806/2022).

G. Silvello et al. (Eds.): TPDL 2022, LNCS 13541, pp. 442–449, 2022.
https://doi.org/10.1007/978-3-031-16802-4_44

larger than ever before [1,3,5,11,12,19,22], most of the times they are produced only as a facsimile or, even if transcribed and edited, they are not linguistically annotated, at least for the words' parts-of-speech (PoS), i.e. morphosyntactic categories (noun, verb, adjective, etc.) and their inflection, as well as the words' *lemmata* [8,13]. This presents a challenge to those researchers focused on studying the history of a language. When looking for phenomena that rely on the written word to know how the language was at a particular time, picking up the data manually can both be an valuable asset and a kryptonite. Thus, having texts' words annotated for their lemmas and PoS allows for further linguistic processing, namely automatic syntactic analysis (parsing) and the modelling of former stages of language by way of treebanks [16] and texts' collation [2]. For this reason, Natural Language Processing (NLP) tools and techniques [10] can be very useful to Historical Linguistics [5,6,18]. Not only do they allow new and different kinds of research questions, but they also introduce new research tools and methods regarding the collection of data and speed up its analysis.

This paper is part of a larger project that aims to use NLP methods on the investigation of Old Portuguese, particularly on the texts that make up the *Corpus de Textos Antigos* 'Old Texts Corpus' (CTA)[1], a project started in 2015 by the Center of Linguistics of the University of Lisbon (CLUL)[2]. As a repository of transcribed and edited texts in Old Portuguese, dated up to 1525, this corpus can be a helpful resource to researchers interested in the older stages of the language. Nevertheless, the CTA's texts are not yet annotated neither for their PoS nor for their lemmas. Manual annotation of the entire corpus is a very time-consuming, highly-skilled and costly task, hence a machine-learning approach would better suit these goals. In fact, even if the automatic annotation produced by this language models is not completely accurate, it goes a long way in preparing the textual material for a manual revision and correction, speeding up the human annotation effort. This paper, then, will present some early results of the automatic annotation of a subset of the corpus whose data was prepared for a machine-learning PoS and lemmatization tasks.

2   Corpus of Ancient Texts (CTA)

The *Corpus de Textos Antigos* is a project developed by CLUL's Philology group, which aims to publish all hagiographic, spiritual and didactic texts written in or translated to Portuguese up to 1525 (this is a flexible date, deliberately chosen to allow the inclusion of *incunabula* and also texts that, despite dating from the first quarter of the 16th century, transmit older manuscripts). The main purpose of this project is to offer editions that reproduce the texts with high fidelity to the manuscript (ms.) or incunable[3]. Following this principle, there is little or no editorial intervention when it comes to the correction of errors, the restitution

---

[1] http://teitok.clul.ul.pt/teitok/cta/ (last access: September 12, 2022). All the remaining URL in this paper were check on this date.

[2] http://www.clul.ulisboa.pt/grupo/filologia.

[3] http://teitok.clul.ul.pt/teitok/cta/index.php?action=criterios.

of lacunae or orthographic variation. This is why a simple string search would almost never capture all the instances of a word occurring within the corpus, so that lemmatization is an essential previous step towards efficient lexical queries. The corpus uses the web-based framework TEITOK [9,20], an online tool which combines both textually annotated texts with linguistic annotations. With a modular design and the granular customization it allows, TEITOK can be used with very different corpora.

As of April 2022, the corpus consists of 31 editions of 26 different texts. There are three texts with more than one edition: *Horto do Esposo* has two edited manuscripts from the late 14th century; *Vida de Santa Maria Egipcia*, with two mss. from the 15th century; and *Vida e Milagres de Santa Senhorinha de Bastos*, written in the second half of 13th century, has four edited witnesses that date from the early 17th century to the 19th century. The texts differ in extension, from a couple hundreds to more than 150,000 words. As shown, texts also vary both in the date of redaction and in date of production. The oldest text (and manuscript) is the ms. A of *Horto do Esposo*[4] and it dates between 1390–1437. The most recent text (not necessarily the most recent manuscript or edition) is *Memorial da Infanta Santa Joana*[5] and dates between 1513–1525. The most recent manuscript comes from the end of the 18th century, the ms. P of *Vida e Milagres de Santa Senhorinha de Bastos*[6].

3   Text Selection, Preparation and Annotation

In this section, the text selection, preparation and annotation process are described. For the manual annotation, the ms. A of *Horto do Esposo* (henceforward, *HdE-A*), whose both the manuscript and the text date from about the same time (c. 1390–1437), was chosen. For testing, the ms. G1 of *Vida e Milagre de Santa Senhorinha de Basto* (henceforward, *VMSSB-G1*)[7] was chosen. This is a text dated between 1248–1284 and whose manuscript has been dated from 1620–1645. As the corpus has three others, albeit fragmented, witnesses of *Horto do Esposo* (henceforaward, *HdE-DCE*)[8], the testing was also done on this witness. The HdE-DCE ms. was chosen for testing the POS-tagger because of its natural likeness to HdE-A, while the choice of VMSSB-G1 is due to the fact that, being both HdE-A and VMSSB-G1 hagiographic in genre, a greater similarity between their respective lexicons is expected. For another experiment, a second model was trained on these 3 texts, and 2 other texts were selected from the corpus for testing: the *História do mui nobre Vespasiano* (henceforward, *Vespasiano*)[9], printed in Lisbon in 1496, and the text of *Memorial da Infanta Santa*

---

[4] Biblioteca Nacional (Portugal), Alc.198, fls. 1r–155r.

[5] Biblioteca do Museu de Aveiro, ms. 1 [33/CD], fls. 48a–110b.

[6] Biblioteca Mun. Porto, Safe n. 527 (Cat. n. 683), ff. 196v–208v.

[7] Arq. Mun. Alfredo Pimenta (Guimarães), Ms. da Colegiada 793, fls. 211r–236r.

[8] Arq. Nac. Torre do Tombo. Fragm., Cx. 21, n.26 (Casa Forte). Lorvão, Livro 10, fl. 13r. Fragm., Cx. 21, n.23a (Casa Forte).

[9] Lisboa, Valentim Fernandes, [1496?]. Biblioteca Nacional (Portugal), Inc. 571.

Joana (henceforward, *MISJ*)[10], in a manuscript later than 1525, although it is thought to have been first written between 1513 and 1525. Table 1 presents the contents of the texts selected from the CTA corpus for the experiments in this paper. The selected texts are indicated by a conventional code with their respective date (see details below). Information on the number of tokens, words, different word forms (case sensitive) and punctuation signs is provided.

Table 1. Texts from Old Portuguese Corpus

Corpus (date)	tokens	words	diff.	punct
HdE-A (1390–1437)	154,952	137,710	14,333	17,174
HdE-DCE (1391–1450)	2,694	1,841	722	849
VMSSB-G1 (1248–1284)	13,948	12,403	2,352	1,541
MISJ (1513–1525)	51,680	46,517	7,007	5,162
Vespasiano (1496?)	19,141	17,893	2,759	1,241
Total	242,415	216,364	21,595	25,967

The manual annotation task consisted in attributing to each token the corresponding lemma and the part-of-speech (PoS) tag. A set of guidelines for this task were produced to define the criteria for attributing the *lemmata*, to describe the tagset, and to explicitly guide the PoS-tag attribution, especially in more complex cases. For the lemmatization of the word forms, the modern lemma was adopted whenever possible, in order to ensure an efficient way to query the corpus. The traditional criterion for lemma attribution was generally adopted: the impersonal infinitive for the verbs, the masculine-singular form for the adjectives, the singular form for nouns (masculine or feminine, depending on its gender), and so on. Each PoS-tag consists of a morphosyntactic *category* (v.g. adjective, adverb, conjunction, determiner, interjection, noun, preposition, pronoun or verb) and, if applicable, an *inflection* code indicating the morphological categories relevant to that category (i.e., tense-mood and person-number, for verbs; gender and number for nouns; etc.). We adopt a highly granular tagset, adapting one already developed for Modern Portuguese and presented in [4,14,15]. The formalism here used is generically the same that was originally developed by [7]. Three annotators participated in the task, all linguists familiar with Old Portuguese texts and its grammar. At the end of the process, a set of procedures was put in place to verify and correct eventual inconsistencies.

4   Experiments and Results

Having all words present in *Horto do Esposo* (HdE-A) initially annotated with lemmas and PoS-tag, a thorough revision was made, not only regarding the

---

[10] Biblioteca do Museu de Aveiro, ms. 1 [33/CD], fls. 48a-110b.

correctness of the lemmas attribution but also considering the formal consistency of the annotation. Errors and inconsistencies, due to manual annotation, were detected and corrected. A PoS-tagging model was then trained with the TREETAGGER [17] and applied to both HdE-DCE and VMSSB-G1. Then, after correcting the annotations produced for these two texts, a new model was trained and applied to both the MISJ and Vespasiano. Table 2 shows the results of the different experiments in automatically PoS-tagging the corpus' texts.

Table 2. Experiments in PoS-tagging. Preliminary results: Precision and error analysis

Corpus	TP	P	L-t	L-z	T-p	T-t	T-z	U-p	U-t	U-z	punct
HdE-CDE	2,458	91,24%	14	1	6	1	26	70	29	84	5
VMSSB-G1	9,401	67,40%	170	43	24	22	257	1,233	357	1,015	1,426
MISJ	39,956	77,31%	93	1	44	316	442	5,198	1,171	4458	12
Vespasiano	15,768	82,38%	280	30	9	17	254	1,259	652	866	0

A preliminary, manual inspection of the results and the corresponding error analysis was then carried out. Entirely correct matches (lemma, PoS and morphosyntactic tag) are marked as true-positives (**TP**) and precision (**P**) is provided. Then, lemma attribution was considered, either correctly (**L-**), or incorrectly (**T-**) attributed, or, else, not given (unknown, **U-**). Within each of these lemma attributions, the correcteness of the PoS and the morphosyntactic tag were also distinguished: **-p** indicates when both PoS and morphosyntactic tag were correctly given; **-t** indicates that the correctly marked PoS was, but not the morphosyntactic tag; **-z** indicates that neither PoS nor tag were correct. Punctuation (**punct**) marks were often marked by the system as unknown lemmas instead of the conventional notation adopted. Often, these were incorrectly given a PoS and a morphosyntactic tag.

Concerning the first experiment, the better performance of the model on HdE-DCE (precision: 91,24%) could be explained by the fact that it is another witness of *Horto do Esposo*. Both manuscripts (HdE-A and HdE-DCE) thus have the same lexicon and the same syntactical structures. The proximity in the dates of the manuscripts may also have played a role in this results. Several aspects may explain the worst performance of the model on VMSSB-G1 (precision: 67,4%). The ms. VMSSB-G1 dates from the 17th century, which is much later than the date of HdE-A (c.1390–1437). Though some older traces of the language are preserved, VMSSB1-G1 shows some linguistic changes that happened between the two periods. For example, the program did not recognize the form *nao* (adverb 'no') as HdE-A only presents the forms *nõ, non, nom*, and *nã* This new graphic form *nao* signals the changes in the nasal word endings, converging into the diphthong <ão>. On the other hand, many lemmas could not be ascribed due to graphic differences found in this manuscript, even if the same word appears in both. Also, VMSSB-G1 makes use of the comma 1,426 times, whereas HdE-A only uses the full stop, which explains the punctuation errors signaled in the Table.

The model built upon the data of HdE-A, HdE-DCE and VMSSB-G1 was then applied on the MISJ and Vespasiano. Results show that the new model produced better results on Vespasiano (precision: 82.38%) than in MISJ (precision: 77.31%), though it still fails to recognize a large number of lemmas, especially in the latter. Again, many words show a spelling different from the one used to learn the model.

As for the incorrect annotations (false-positives), there are two types of errors, based on whether the model attributes a lemma to a word (column **T-z**) or not (column **U-z**). A large number of words with unknown lemmas (**U-**) are still adequately tagged as for their PoS (**U-p**) or their morphosyntactic values (**U-t**). This case corresponds to the PoS-tagger being able to correctly guess those values from the surrounding words. Many cases in **T-z** correspond to the typical situation of PoS ambiguity. For example the word *nos* may correspond to different inflections of the personal pronoun (*nós/nos*, 'we,us') but also to the contraction of preposition and a definite article (*em_os* 'in_the-masc.pl.'). As for the cases with unknown lemmas and where the system also fails the PoS and morphosyntactic tags (**U-z**), this may hint at the natural limitations of the machine-learning approach here adopted.

5 Conclusion and Future Work

This paper presents the preliminary steps taken towards the automatic annotation of the Portuguese *Corpus de Textos Antigos*. This annotation consists in attributing lemmas and PoS-tags to their word forms, both the morphosyntactic categories and their inflection values. An initial annotation task was manually carried out on HdE-A, containing almost 150 thousand tokens. Such data was then used to train a Machine Learning model, and then used to automatically annotate two other smaller documents: another ms. (HdE-CDE) of the same text used for training; and another text, different but of a similar genre (VMSSB-G1). As expected, the second ms. of the HdE text achieved a very high precision (91.24%). With the unrelated text of VMSSB-G1, the model only produced a modest precision (67.4%), mostly because many word forms (8.84%) had not been previously seen by the model, so that their *lemmata* were labelled as *unknown*. Still, the model was able to correctly assign the PoS and the inflection values to most of them.

The preliminary results of the automatic annotation show how the model improves the more data it receives. The performance of the second model on Vespasiano is better than the outcome of the first experiment on VMSSB-G1. Whereas the latter was annotated with a model with the data from only one text, the former had the model trained with three different texts. As for the errors, whenever the tagger inaccurately attributes a lemma, it is often due to the ambiguous nature of the word.

The use of NLP methods on the corpus will allow for new questions to be asked in new approaches to this linguistic data. Based on the lexically annotated corpus, it will now be possible to analyse the irregularity of the forms and linguistic changes. The use of an annotated corpus could also be helpful in determining the affiliation between different witnesses of the same text [2], using automatic collation tools, such as Collatex [21][11].

References

1. Britto, H., Finger, M.: Constructing a parsed corpus of historical Portuguese. In: Proceedings of International Humanities Computing Conference, University of Virginia, Charlottesville. ACH/ALLC (1999)
2. Camps, J.B., Ing, L., Spadini, E.: Collating medieval vernacular texts. aligning witnesses, classifying variants. In: Digital Humanities Conference (DHC) 2019. Utrecht, Netherlands (2019). https://hal.archives-ouvertes.fr/hal-02268348
3. Davies, M.: New directions in Spanish and Portuguese corpus linguistics. Stud. Hisp. Lusophone Linguist. 1(1), 149–186 (2008)
4. Eleutério, S., Ranchhod, E., Freire, H., Baptista, J.: A system of electronic dictionaries of Portuguese. Linguisticae Investigationes 19(1), 57–82 (1995)
5. Gamallo, P., Pichel, J.R., Santalha, J.M.M., Neves, M.: Uso de tecnologias linguísticas para estudar a evolução dos sufixos -çom e -vel no galego-português medieval a partir de corpora históricos. Linguamática 13(2), 3–17 (2021)
6. Gonçalves, M.F., Banza, A.P.: Da antiga à nova Filologia: o Projecto MEP-BPEDig. In: Actas del XXVI Congreso Internacional de Lingüística y de Filología Románicas. Tome VII, vol. 7, pp. 205–210. Walter de Gruyter (2013)
7. Gross, M.: La construction de dictionnaires électroniques. Ann. Télécommun. 44, 4–19 (1989). https://doi.org/10.1007/BF02999875
8. Hendrickx, I., Marquilhas, R.: From old texts to modern spellings: an experiment in automatic normalisation. J. Lang. Technol. Comput. Linguist. 26(2), 65–76 (2011)
9. Janssen, M.: TEITOK: text-faithful annotated corpora. In: Proceedings of the 10th International Conference on Language Resources and Evaluation (LREC 2016), pp. 4037–4043. European Language Resources Association (ELRA), Portorož, Slovenia (2016). https://aclanthology.org/L16-1637
10. Jurafsky, D., Martin, J.H.: Speech and language processing (draft) (2021). https://web.stanford.edu/jurafsky/slp3/
11. Lopes, J., Rocio, V., Xaxier, M.F., Vicente, G.: Criação automática de uma colecção de textos de português medieval parcialmente anotados sintacticamente. In: Actas del Segundo Seminário de Escuela Interlatina de Altos Estudios en Lingüística Aplicada, pp. 203–220 (2002)
12. Mendes, A.: Linguística de corpus e outros usos dos corpora em linguística. In: Martins, A.M., Carrilho, E. (eds.) Manual de linguística portuguesa, vol. 16, pp. 224–251. Walter de Gruyter GmbH & Co KG (2016)
13. Parkinson, S.R., Emiliano, A.H.: Encoding medieval abbreviations for computer analysis (from Latin-Portuguese and Portuguese non-literary sources). Literary Linguist. Comput. 17(3), 345–360 (2002)
14. Ranchhod, E., Mota, C., Baptista, J.: A computational lexicon of Portuguese for automatic text parsing. In: Standardizing Lexical Resources (SIGLEX 1999), pp. 74–80. ACL/SIGLEX, Maryland, USA (1999)

---

[11] https://collatex.net/.

15. Ranchhod, E.M.: O uso de dicionários e de autómatos finitos na representação lexical. In: Ranchhod, E.M. (ed.) Tratamento das Línguas por Computador. Uma introdução à Linguística Computacional e suas aplicações, pp. 13–47. Caminho (2001)

16. Rocio, V., Alves, M.A., Lopes, J.G.P., Xavier, M.F., Vicente, G.: Automated creation of a medieval Portuguese partial treebank. In: Abeillé, A. (ed.) Treebanks: Building and Using Parsed Corpora, vol. 20, pp. 211–227. Springer, Dordrecht (2003)

17. Schmid, H.: Probabilistic part-of-speech tagging using decision trees. In: Proceedings of International Conference on New Methods in Language Processing, pp. 154–163 (1994)

18. Schmid, H.: Deep learning-based morphological taggers and lemmatizers for annotating historical texts. In: Proceedings of the 3rd International Conference on Digital Access to Textual Cultural Heritage, pp. 133–137 (2019)

19. de Sousa, M.C.P.: O corpus Tycho Brahe: Contribuições para as Humanidades Digitais no Brasil. Filologia e linguística portuguesa 16(esp.), 53–93 (2014)

20. Vaamonde, G., Janssen, M.: Da edición dixital á análise lingüística. A creación de corpus históricos na plataforma TEITOK, pp. 271–292 (01 2020). https://doi.org/ 10.17075/cbfc.2020.008

21. van Zundert, J., Haentjens Dekker, R., Van Hulle, D., Neyt, V., Middell, G.: Computer-supported collation of modern manuscripts: CollateX and the Beckett digital manuscript project. Literary and Linguistics Computing 30(3), 452–470 (2014). https://doi.org/10.1093/llc/fqu007

22. Xavier, M.F.: O CIPM - Corpus Informatizado do Português Medieval, fonte de um dicionário exaustivo. In: Lingüística de corpus y lingüística histórica iberor-románica, pp. 137–156. De Gruyter (2016)

Creating Structure in Web Archives with Collections: Different Concepts from Web Archivists

Himarsha R. Jayanetti[1]([⊠]), Shawn M. Jones[2], Martin Klein[2],
Alex Osbourne[3], Paul Koerbin[3], Michael L. Nelson[1],
and Michele C. Weigle[1]

[1] Old Dominion University, Norfolk, VA, USA
hjaya002@odu.edu, {mln,mweigle}@cs.odu.edu
[2] Los Alamos National Laboratory, New Mexico, USA
{smjones,mklein}@lanl.gov
[3] National Library of Australia, Canberra, Australia
{aosborne,pkoerbin}@nla.gov.au

Abstract. As web archives' holdings grow, archivists subdivide them
into collections so they are easier to understand and manage. In this
work, we review the collection structures of eight web archive platforms. We note a plethora of different approaches to web archive collection structures. Some web archive collections support sub-collections
and some permit embargoes. Curatorial decisions may be attributed to
a single organization or many. Archived web pages are known by many
names: mementos, copies, captures, or snapshots. Some platforms restrict
a memento to a single collection and others allow mementos to cross collections. Knowledge of collection structures has implications for many
different applications and users. Visitors will need to understand how
to navigate collections. Future archivists will need to understand what
options are available for designing collections. Platform designers need
it to know what possibilities exist. The developers of tools that consume
collections need to understand collection structures so they can meet the
needs of their users.

Keywords: Web archives · Collections · Information organization ·
Memento

1 Introduction

Researchers, including journalists [4,38], social scientists [3,6], and historians
[22], are increasingly applying web archives to their work. Web archives preserve
the content of web pages as they were at a specific point in time as **mementos**. Web archives are vast, the largest consisting of billions of documents [18].
Collections are a common organizational technique employed to bring order to
this vastness. Using collections simplifies management for archivists and allows

G. Silvello et al. (Eds.): TPDL 2022, LNCS 13541, pp. 450–458, 2022.
https://doi.org/10.1007/978-3-031-16802-4_45

them to showcase content, making patrons aware of the collection as well as their web archiving organization as a whole. Patrons benefit from collections because they have an intelligently selected set of mementos to review that supports their topic of interest. In the scope of this paper, we define **collection** based on a web archive platform's front-end presentation of a set of mementos that are grouped by topic. We differentiate collections from the **greater web archive** – the web archiving platform as a whole.

Here we document the **collection structures** of eight different web archive platforms: Archive-It [2], Conifer [30], the Croatian Web Archive (HAW) [24], the Internet Archive's user account web archives [10], Library of Congress (LC) [20], PANDORA [36], Trove [37], and the UK Web Archive (UKWA) [35]. While the collection structure of each platform may vary depending on their organization's requirements and design choices, each structure shares some basic elements. In this work, we define and standardize nomenclature to discuss these elements. Our goal is not to prescribe how a collection should be designed, but rather to understand the different collection structures already in existence. For example, if a memento is created in an Archive-It collection, it is not shared between collections, whereas, with PANDORA, this is possible. Trove supports sub-collections, while Archive-It does not. Vistors to LC first visit the landing page to view a set of page titles and then decide among mementos for that page whereas at UKWA the collection directly presents links to mementos. Design decisions like these represent different collection structures that serve as models for how an archivist or platform designer might thematically organize their mementos. Collection structures also present different challenges to authors of third-party tools that consume and analyze these collections as part of Big Data efforts.

Through this summarized review (a more detailed review is available [11]), we address the following research questions:

- RQ1: What different collection structures exist?
- RQ2: What do these distinct collection structure approaches have in common?

Existing work has focused on the nature of digital collections [8], user behavior when curating personal collections [23,39], the behavior of archivists [28], the capabilities of web archive platforms [25], and the challenges of building collections with Archive-It [7,32]. Our work augments this work by focusing on web archive collection structures for the benefit of future archivists as well as web archive platform and analytics tool designers.

2   Background

When building a web archive collection, an archivist selects a set of URIs as **seeds**. Each seed is an **original resource** that reflects the current state of the web resource. Each memento is an observation of that resource at a particular point in time, its **memento-datetime**. Each original resource is identified by its URI-R (e.g., https://www.cnn.com) and each of its mementos is identified by

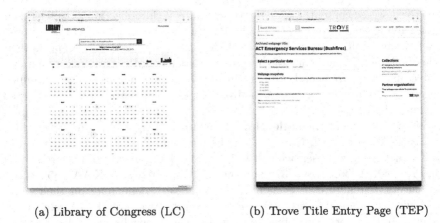

(a) Library of Congress (LC)   (b) Trove Title Entry Page (TEP)

Fig. 1. Screenshots showing examples of human-readable TimeMaps.

a URI-M (e.g., https://wayback.archive-it.org/7678/20190319204514/ https://www.cnn.com/). A **TimeMap** is a listing of the mementos created for an original resource, including the URI-M of each memento and its memento-datetime. **Human-readable** TimeMaps are rendered as a list or calendar with links to each URI-M. Some examples of human-readable TimeMaps are shown in Fig. 1. **Machine-readable** TimeMaps can take a variety of formats, such as JSON. Many web archives are compliant with the Memento Protocol [33], which formalizes these concepts and provides standardized methods of linking mementos, original resources, and TimeMaps.

Not all original resources are seeds. An archivist can instruct the web archiving platform to follow links from a seed to other original resources and capture those as well. **Seed mementos** are mementos that the archivist directly asked the platform to capture. **Deep mementos** are mementos captured by crawling a seed memento's links. We make this distinction because a visitor can immediately discover the seed mementos through a web archive collection's user interface, but may need to click links from seed mementos to discover deep mementos. Tools attempting to capture information about a collection are also limited by this distinction because seed mementos are advertised through the user interface while deep mementos must be crawled to be discovered. Archive-It is an example of a platform that requires this distinction.

3   Related Work

Fenlon's work [8] has inspired our technical analysis of collection structures. Mull and Lee [23], and later Wang et al. [39] applied the Users and Gratifications model [34] to understand why Pinterest users select certain items for their collections. We study the structures that result from such decisions.

Several studies focused on creating and curating web archive collections, or understanding archivists' motivations for doing so [19,26–28]. Our work analyzes what is present already and the behavior of platform designers as revealed through collection structures. Studies exist on the design and consumption of collection [5,7,9,21,25,31,32]. We analyze the capabilities of different web archives, but, unlike others' work, we focus on the subset of web archives that offer themed collections, and we provide a model of their different collection structures.

Other research examined the fundamental properties of web archive collections. Padia et al. [29] created several visualization techniques to help users better grasp collection characteristics. AlNoamany et al. [1] pioneered the concept of combining social media stories with web archive collections to provide user-friendly corpus summaries. Hypercane [15,17] and the Off-Topic Memento Toolkit (OTMT) [16] summarize and filter web archive collections. Both rely on AIU [13] to discover seeds within Archive-It, PANDORA, and Trove collections. These platforms have adopted Memento [33], but have no standard method for clients to discover seeds and metadata. These tools belong to the Dark and Stormy Archives (DSA) project [12,14] which summarizes web archive collections. Our work exists to help efforts like the DSA that consume and analyze web archive collections.

4   Web Archive Collection Structures

In December 2021, we chose eight web archive platforms with thematic collections that specifically contain mementos. Table 1 shows the collection structures of the different platforms we analyzed, addressing RQ1. Here we see several different behaviors representing the needs of different archiving platforms. Below we will address RQ2, highlighting the similarities and differences in collection structures between platforms.

We see different names for mementos. The term *memento* was formally established in RFC 7089 [33] in 2013. Many platforms predate that formality, thus different terms used exist for mementos. Developers will need to understand the nomenclature of the platform and how these are synonymous. Most platforms support sub-collections, allowing an archivist to further narrow a collection's topic. These sub-collections have a variety of names, such as sub-collection (Trove, PANDORA), subject (PANDORA), or subcategory (HAW, PANDORA). Tools that encounter sub-collections must handle this hierarchy.

The UKWA, LC, and HAW all attribute the selection of their mementos to the greater web archive, meaning that the projects of the archiving organization as a whole led to the creation of these mementos. In contrast, PANDORA and Trove collections attribute memento selection to one or more organizations who requested their capture. Archive-It and Conifer, however, support individual accounts, thus memento selection is done by the person or organization that maintains that account. As account-based services, they support private collections for those users who are not ready to share their mementos. The collections on these platforms are separate from each other. Archive-It supports an `/all/`

Table 1. Details on different web archive platform collection structures.

Collection platform	Name for mementos	Sub-collections?	Attribution	Private collections supported?	Mementos are accessible from more than one collection?	Deep mementos accessible from within the collection?	Human-readable TimeMap membership	Embargoed resources?	Navigational hierarchy
Archive-It	Captures	No	Single account	Yes	No*	Yes	Collection	No	Type 1
Conifer	Captures	Yes	Single account	Yes	No	Yes	No human-readable TimeMap	No	Type 2
HAW	Archived copies	Yes	Greater web archive projects	No	Yes	No	Greater web archive	No	Type 1
Internet Archive (IA) user account web archives	Captures	No	Single account	No	Yes	No	Greater web archive	No	Type 2
LC	Captures	No	Greater web archive projects	No	Yes	No	Greater web archive	Yes	Type 1
PANDORA Subject/Collection	Webpage snapshots	Yes	Organizational collaborators	No	Yes	No	Greater web archive	No	Type 1
Trove Collection	Webpage snapshots	Yes	Organizational collaborators	No	Yes	No	Greater web archive	No	Type 2
UKWA	Captures	Yes	Greater web archive projects	No	Yes	No	Greater web archive	Yes	Type 2

* – the /all/ collection is an exception containing all mementos on Archive-It

collection containing mementos from every collection, but it is not advertised through the user interface. With this exception, a memento from an Archive-It collection is not accessible from another collection. If two archivists create two Archive-It mementos from the same original resource at the same memento-datetime, but for different collections, then the mementos are distinct. This holds true for Conifer as well. Likewise, any deep mementos created from the crawls in these collections are only accessible to a user or tool browsing within the collection. Archive-It takes this a step further, with human-readable TimeMaps that only apply to an original resource as captured within the collection. LC and UKWA embargo resources. In both cases, some mementos are only available to patrons who physically visit their library campus. This creates challenges for Internet-based collection analysis tools because some mementos are hidden.

We also identified two different **navigational hierarchies**. These navigational hierarchies help us understand how a visitor or crawler navigates each collection for information. Type 1 (example in Fig. 2a) allows the visitor to review a TimeMap before choosing a memento from the collection, thus an original resource supports the collection's theme. Type 2 (example in Fig. 2b) gives visitors direct access to mementos in a collection without having to go through a TimeMap, thus the memento supports the collection's theme.

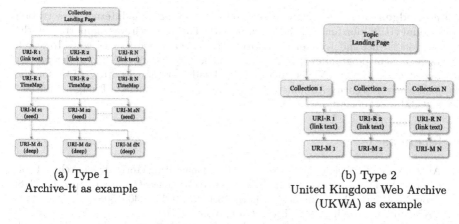

(a) Type 1
Archive-It as example

(b) Type 2
United Kingdom Web Archive
(UKWA) as example

Fig. 2. The navigational hierarchies of different web archive collection platforms.

5   Conclusion

As web archives grow, archivists eventually create collections to make their archives easier to understand and manage. Collections help visitors narrow the number of documents they need to review for a specific topic. Web archive collections are also targets for different data management and analysis tools. Each collection's structure influences how it meets these different use cases.

We have addressed RQ1 by reviewing the collection structures of eight web archive platforms. Through this analysis we discovered a diversity of capabilities for potential new web archiving platforms and tools. For RQ2 we sought similarities in these collection structures to better understand their current state. Some are account-centric, meaning that an individual user or organization cares for the collection separately from the archiving platform itself. Others are general web archives that created collections from their vast holdings. Some collections restrict a memento to a single collection while others share mementos between collections. Some attribute curation to a single entity while other cite different organizational collaborators. Most offer sub-collections and a few embargo resources. We discovered two types of navigational hierarchies for collections. In Type 1, an original resource supports the collection's theme. In Type 2, a memento supports the collection's theme. These different structures reflect different decisions on resource membership among collections.

We did not attempt to prescribe how a web archive collection should be designed but rather analyzed existing platforms. Such information is helpful to future archivists, platform designers, and software developers. With an understanding of collection structures, these parties will know how to ensure that researchers acquire the metadata and mementos they seek.

Acknowledgements. Our many thanks go to the International Internet Preservation Consortium (IIPC) for funding this work in part. This research was supported by the Information Science and Technology Institute and by the Laboratory Directed Research and Development program of Los Alamos National Laboratory (LANL) under project number 20210529CR. LANL is operated by Triad National Security, LLC, for the National Nuclear Security Administration of the U.S. Department of Energy (Contract No. 89233218CNA000001).

References

1. AlNoamany, Y., Weigle, M.C., Nelson, M.L.: Generating stories from archived collections. In: Proceedings of the 2017 ACM on Web Science Conference, pp. 309–318. Troy, New York (2017). https://doi.org/10.1145/3091478.3091508
2. Archive-It: archive-it (2022). https://archive-it.org
3. Arms, W.Y., Aya, S., Dmitriev, P., Kot, B., Mitchell, R., Walle, L.: A research library based on the historical collections of the internet archive. D-Lib Mag. **12**(2), (2006). http://www.dlib.org/dlib/february06/arms/02arms.html
4. Brodkin, J.: US edits National Stockpile website after Kushner claims it's not for states. Ars Technica (2020). https://arstechnica.com/tech-policy/2020/04/us-edits-national-stockpile-website-after-kushner-claims-its-not-for-states/
5. Crook, E.: Web archiving in a web 2.0 world. Electron. Libr. **27**(5), 831–836 (2009). https://doi.org/10.1108/02640470910998542
6. Curty, R.G., Zhang, P.: Social commerce: looking back and forward. In: Proceedings of the 2011 Meeting of the American Society for Information Science and Technology, vol. 48, pp. 1–10. New Orleans, Louisiana (2011). https://doi.org/10.1002/meet.2011.14504801096
7. Deutch, S., McKay, S.: The future of artist files: here today, gone tomorrow. Art Documentation J. Art Libr. Soc. N. Am. **35**(1), 27–42 (2016). https://doi.org/10.1086/685975
8. Fenlon, K.: Toward a characterization of digital humanities research collections: A contrastive analysis of technical designs. In: Proceedings of the 2017 Annual Meeting of the Association for Information Science and Technology, pp. 82–92. Washington, DC (2017). https://doi.org/10.1002/pra2.2017.14505401010
9. Gossen, G., Demidova, E., Risse, T.: Analyzing web archives through topic and event focused sub-collections. In: Proceedings of the 2016 ACM Conference on Web Science, pp. 291–295. Hannover, Germany (2016). https://doi.org/10.1145/2908131.2908175
10. Graham, M.: The Wayback machine's save page now is new and improved (2019). https://blog.archive.org/2019/10/23/the-wayback-machines-save-page-now-is-new-and-improved/
11. Jayanetti, H.R., et al.: Creating structure in web archives with collections: different concepts from web archivists. Technical report arXiv (2022)
12. Jones, S.M.: Improving collection understanding for web archives with storytelling: shining light into dark and stormy archives. Ph.D. thesis, Old Dominion University (2021). https://doi.org/10.25777/zts6-v512
13. Jones, S.M., Jayanetti, H., Kelly, M.: GitHub - oduwsdl/aiu: a library for interacting with web archive collections at Archive-It, Trove, PANDORA, and more. https://github.com/oduwsdl/aiu. Accessed 25 May 2021
14. Jones, S.M., et al.: The DSA toolkit shines light into dark and stormy archives. Code4Lib J. (2022). https://journal.code4lib.org/articles/16441

15. Jones, S.M., Weigle, M.C., Klein, M., Nelson, M.L.: Hypercane: intelligent sampling for web archive collections. In: 2021 ACM/IEEE Joint Conference on Digital Libraries (JCDL), pp. 316–317 (2021). https://doi.org/10.1109/JCDL52503.2021. 00049
16. Jones, S.M., Weigle, M.C., Nelson, M.L.: The off-topic memento toolkit. In: Proceedings of the 15th International Conference on Digital Preservation, pp. 1–10. Boston, Massachusetts, USA (2018). https://doi.org/10.17605/OSF.IO/UBW87
17. Jones, S.M., Weigle, M.C., Nelson, M.L.: Hypercane: toolkit for summarizing large collections of archived webpages. ACM SIGWEB Newsl. (Summer), 1–14 (2021). https://doi.org/10.1145/3473044.3473047
18. Kahle, B.: Wayback machine now has 898,570,440,000 URL's (2020). https:// twitter.com/brewster_kahle/status/1225167435399036939
19. Klein, M., Balakireva, L., Van de Sompel, H.: Focused crawl of web archives to build event collections. In: Proceedings of the 2018 ACM Conference on Web Science, pp. 333–342. Amsterdam, Netherlands (2018). https://doi.org/10.1145/3201064. 3201085
20. Library of congress: library of congress web archive (2022). https://www.loc.gov/ web-archives/collections/
21. Milligan, I.: Lost in the infinite archive: the promise and pitfalls of web archives. Int. J. Hum. Arts Comput. 10(1), 78–94 (2016). https://doi.org/10.3366/ijhac. 2016.0161
22. Milligan, I.: History in the Age of Abundance: How the Web Is Transforming Historical Research. McGill-Queen's Unversity Press, Montreal (2019)
23. Mull, I.R., Lee, S.E.: PIN pointing the motivational dimensions behind Pinterest. Comput. Hum. Behav. 33, 192–200 (2014). https://doi.org/10.1016/j.chb.2014.01. 011
24. National and University Library in Zagreb: Croatian Web Archive (2022). https:// haw.nsk.hr/
25. Niu, J.: Functionalities of web archives. D-Lib 18(3/4) (2012). https://doi.org/10. 1045/march2012-niu2
26. Nwala, A.C., Weigle, M.C., Nelson, M.L.: Bootstrapping web archive collections from social media. In: Proceedings of the 2018 ACM Conference on Hypertext and Social Media, pp. 64–72. Baltimore, Maryland, USA (2018). https://doi.org/10. 1145/3209542.3209560
27. Nwala, A.C., Weigle, M.C., Nelson, M.L.: Scraping SERPs for archival seeds: it matters where you start. In: Proceedings of the 2018 ACM/IEEE Joint Conference on Digital Libraries, pp. 263–272. ACM, Fort Worth, Texas (2018). https://doi. org/10.1145/3197026.3197056
28. Ogden, J., Halford, S., Carr, L.: Observing web archives: the case for an ethnographic study of web archiving. In: Proceedings of the 2017 ACM on Web Science Conference, pp. 299–308 (2017). https://doi.org/10.1145/3091478.3091506
29. Padia, K., AlNoamany, Y., Weigle, M.C.: Visualizing digital collections at archive-it. In: Proceedings of the 2012 ACM/IEEE-CS Joint Conference on Digital Libraries, pp. 15–18. Washington, DC, USA (2012). https://doi.org/10.1145/ 2232817.2232821
30. Rhizome: Conifer (2022). https://conifer.rhizome.org/
31. Risse, T., Demidova, E., Gossen, G.: What do you want to collect from the web. In: Proceedings of the Building Web Observatories Workshop (BWOW). Seoul, Korea (2014). http://www.l3s.de/risse/pub/bwow2014.pdf

32. Slania, H.: Online art ephemera: web archiving at the national museum of women in the arts. Art Documentation J. Art Libr. Soc. North Am. **32**(1), 112–126 (2013). https://doi.org/10.1086/669993

33. Van de Sompel, H., Nelson, M., Sanderson, R.: RFC 7089 - HTTP Framework for Time-Based Access to Resource States - Memento (2013). https://tools.ietf.org/html/rfc7089

34. Stafford, T.F., Stafford, M.R., Schkade, L.L.: Determining uses and gratifications for the Internet. Decis. Sci. **35**(2), 259–288 (2004). https://doi.org/10.1111/j.00117315.2004.02524.x

35. The British Library, Bodleian Libraries, The National Library of Wales, The National Library of Scotland, Cambridge University Library, Trinity College Dublin: United Kingdom Web Archive (2022). https://www.webarchive.org.uk/

36. The national library of Australia: PANDORA web archive (2022). http://pandora.nla.gov.au/

37. The national library of Australia and others: trove (2022). https://trove.nla.gov.au/

38. Tolliver, J.: Buffalo Mass Shooting Livestream Reached Millions Even After Twitch Removed Footage. HuffPost (2022). https://www.huffpost.com/entry/buffalo-mass-shooting-video-reached-millions-due-to-reuploads_n_628417f4e4b0c2dce65605b3

39. Wang, R., Yang, F., Zheng, S., Sundar, S.S.: Why do we pin? new gratifications explain unique activities in Pinterest. Soc. Media+Soc. **2**(3), 2056305116662173 (2016). https://doi.org/10.1177/2056305116662173

Weighted Altmetric Scores to Facilitate Literature Analyses

Yusra Shakeel[1,2]([✉]), Abhisar Bharti[2], Thomas Leich[3,4], and Gunter Saake[2]

[1] Karlsruhe Institute of Technology, Karlsruhe, Germany
yusra.shakeel@kit.edu
[2] Otto-von-Guericke University, Magdeburg, Germany
abhisar.bharti007@gmail.com, saake@ovgu.de
[3] Harz University of Applied Sciences, Wernigerode, Germany
tleich@hs-harz.de
[4] METOP GmbH, Magdeburg, Germany

Abstract. With a rapidly increasing corpus of published papers, assessing their scientific impact has become increasingly challenging. Particularly, for analysts performing systematic literature analysis, such as a systematic literature review or systematic mapping study, the problem of manually assessing a large data set has now become quite evident. Thus, the research community is actively involved in developing techniques relying on different methods to determine impact of a paper with reduced manual effort, for example, using bibliometrics, and the more recently introduced, altmetrics. Therefore, in this work we extend the ongoing investigation and propose weighted altmetric scores for a more fair and reliable analysis of papers, eventually supporting the literature analysis process. Our findings show that weighted altmetrics perform well and achieve an accuracy of 69.81% considerably reducing the time and effort required for a manual literature analysis.

Keywords: Altmetrics · Literature analyses · Study selection · PlumX

1 Introduction

A literature analysis, particularly systematic literature review has become a key methodology for enabling evidence-based researchers to concatenate and critically evaluate the existing evidence regarding a research topic [7,14]. Being an established method in the medicine domain, systematic literature reviews are emerging as an effective technique in other disciplines as well, such as, social sciences, business, and computer science. The execution process of systematic literature reviews follows a well-defined and focused plan, that makes it transparent and up to a certain degree, repeatable [2,8]. Generally, the first step is to define the research questions and search strategy to outline the framework of the review. The relevant studies are retrieved and the extracted information is structured appropriately to represent the findings from the study. Since,

© Springer Nature Switzerland AG 2022
G. Silvello et al. (Eds.): TPDL 2022, LNCS 13541, pp. 459–465, 2022.
https://doi.org/10.1007/978-3-031-16802-4_46

the number of published papers is constantly increasing, systematic literature reviews usually involve large data sets to be analyzed for retrieving the most relevant primary studies. Thus, performing a systematic literature review entirely manually becomes very time consuming and difficult.

Unfortunately, as explicitly explained by Hassler et al. [4] and Shakeel et al. [12], the tool support available for analysts to select and assess papers seem to be of limited capability and require further improvements. Eventually, encouraging researchers to actively involve in developing techniques that can support an analyst. Meanwhile, bibliometrics also emerged as a means of deducing importance of papers, established metrics, such as citation counts, impact factor, and author h-index, are some of the most popular metrics within the scientific community [1]. More recently, altmetrics have also gained popularity as a potential means of reflecting on the impact and importance of scientific papers [3]. These metrics provide information differently from the traditional bibliometrics, focusing on web interactions and social impact of papers, immediately after being published online. Thus, in this paper, we critically investigate whether altmetrics can complement the traditional means of assessing impact of papers. Particularly, focusing on determining whether weighted altmetrics can be useful for developing a metrics-based technique to assess papers, thus supporting an analyst while performing a literature analysis.

2   Data

2.1   Selected Metrics

The development of altmetrics has provided new possibilities to determine scientific impact, and its increasing popularity has led, one of the largest multidisciplinary database, Elsevier to partner with one of the major almetircs tool, i.e., the Plum Analytics.[1] This helps an analyst to obtain the altmetrics data directly from their automatic searches on Scopus[2] and Science Direct.[3] Therefore, for our analysis, we consider PlumX as an Application Programming Interface (API) to gather the data, including:

- five categories of PlumX, namely, *captures, usage, mentions, social media, citations*, and
- three venue metrics from Scopus, including, *SNIP* (Source Normalized Impact per Paper), *SJR* (Scimago Journal Rank) and *CiteScore*.

We investigate the aforementioned metrics to determine the weighted scores within our analysis. Once we acquire the data set, our analysis follows testing two feature weight learning methods.

---

[1] http://www.plumanalytics.com/about.html.

[2] https://www.scopus.com/sources.uri.

[3] http://www.sciencedirect.com.

2.2   Data Acquisition

For our analysis, we gather all the papers published during 2015–2021 within the software engineering subject area, comprised in the Scopus database. The extracted data set includes 76,346 papers, out of which 70,542 comprise at least one non-zero numerical value for a PlumX category (either of the five categories, i.e., usage, citations, captures, mentions or social media).[4] To tackle with missing data, we replace all missing values by zero, since any other way of replacing these values, for example, by median or mean, most frequent, etc., would have incorrectly influenced the importance of a paper. For extracting altmetrics, the Digital Object Identifiers (DOIs) for each paper must be acquired. Thus, we design a Python workflow to extract, transform and model the retrieved data to proceed further. To acquire the bibliometric data, we use Scopus APIs in combination with *Pybibliometrics*, allowing multiple GET requests and to store the results in a structured tabular format. To extract PlumX data, we use a combination of Scopus PlumX Metrics API,[5] and *Pybibliometrics* API to construct our data set.

3   Methodology

3.1   Learning Feature Weights

Once the data is gathered, we use it to calculate the contributions of each metric. We test two different, most commonly used methods for learning feature weights, namely *Principal Component Analysis (PCA)* and *Laplacian Score*. Based on the outcome of this comparative experimental analysis, we select the best performing method to define the weight of each metric to replicate two different case studies for evaluation.

Principal Component Analysis (PCA). PCA is a multivariate statistical technique that enables understanding of the contribution of each component [6]. For our data set of 70,542 papers, each paper is represented as a vector of 8 dimensions corresponding to each of the metrics. Formally, the Eq. 1 is used, where α_1 is a vector of p constants ranging from α_{11} till α_{1p}. We find $\alpha_2^T x$, which should be uncorrelated to the first one and has a maximum variance in the next step. We repeat this process until we reach the p_{th} element, to find all the p principal components of the data. As a result, the learned importance is normalized to obtain values between 0 and 1 to be interpreted as a feature weight for each dimension.

$$\alpha_1^T x = \alpha_{11}^T x_1 + \alpha_{12}^T x_2 + ... + \alpha_{1p}^T x_p = \sum_{j=1}^{p} \alpha_{1j} x_j \qquad (1)$$

---

[4] Complete dataset is available here: https://doi.org/10.5281/zenodo.6905592.
[5] https://dev.elsevier.com/documentation/PlumXMetricsAPI.wadl.

Laplacian Score. As an alternate method, we use the Laplacian Score, an unsupervised feature selection method, based on the concepts of Laplacian Eigenmap and locality preserving projection, as explained by He at al. [5]. Laplacian scores, as calculated using Eq. 2, determines features within the defined geometry of the graph and weight matrix. For N observations, f_r is the $f_r = [f_{r1}, f_{r2}, f_{r3}..., f_{rN}]$ r-th feature vector, and Laplacian score selects important features by minimizing the objective function. w_{ij} represents the matrix, and $Var(f_r)$ individual elements represent the rth feature's variance. We use the *skfeature* (python package) to calculate the Laplacian score. Based on the defined objective function, features with lower scores are given higher rankings, hence features with strong local preservation capability are selected.

$$L_r = \frac{\sum_{i,j=1}^{N} (f_{ri} - f_{rj})^2 w_{ij}}{Var(f_r)} \tag{2}$$

Table 1. Learned feature weights and the Pearson correlation efficient (r) for the selected methods.

Method	Captures	Usage	Mentions	Social media	Citations	SNIP	SJR	Scopus citation	r
PCA	0.937	5.28E−06	0.005	0.002	0.057	0.019	0.972	0.009	0.85
Laplacian	3.97E−06	2E−07	0.003	4.76E−05	4.04E−05	0.016	0.010	0.001	0.42

The results from our experiment, including the learned feature weights for both methods is shown in Table 1. A variation can be observed for all metrics' weightage across the two methods we tested. Based on our comparative experimental analysis, we deduce that PCA performs better for our data set. We compute Pearson's correlation coefficient (r) to determine the association of each method with citation count (cf. Table 1). Our results show that PCA exhibits the strongest correlation, with metrics, namely, SJR and captures being the prominent features, which can be due to the approach being a linear dimensional reduction algorithm, while Laplacian method being a non-linear one, considering that the data exists in the lower dimension manifold.

3.2   Checklist

Traditionally, the checklist-based approach is applied to manually analyse quality of scientific papers [8]. Although, being an effective method to evaluate scientific papers, and retrieve important primary studies, there still remains a possibility of errors. For example, some potential primary studies can be rejected if they only partially satisfy the analysis to answer the quality assessment questions, thus resulting in a loss of evidence. To overcome this problem, for our analysis, we define a more granular checklist using the *MOOSE* [13] and *PRISMA* [10] guidelines. As a result, we define nineteen different questions, as listed in Table 2, covering all significant aspects of a paper, including methods, evaluation, and results section. We design the questions so that they should only result in either "Yes" or "No" as an answer. The checklist we propose contains detailed aspects to consider while evaluating a paper, mainly addressing the approach adopted for search strategies, queries formulation, explanation of the proposed method, and presentation of the study outcomes.

Table 2. Overview of the proposed checklist comprising quality assessment questions.

Questions	Yes	No
General overview		
Q1: Does Abstract specifies the name of the applied method?		
Q2: Does Introduction highlights the problem?		
Study overview		
Q3: Is the design of study explained?		
Q4: Is the search strategy explained?		
Q5: Has different approach to paper collection mentioned for restricted papers explained?		
Q6: Is Inclusion criteria/Exclusion criteria explained?		
Q7: Inclusion criteria/Exclusion criteria includes approach to handle papers in different languages?		
Q8: Is data collection strategy explained?		
Q9: Is risk associated with bias addressed?		
Q10: Is approach to filter article yet to published addressed?		
Method		
Q11: Is the applied method justify the research aim?		
Q12: Are there any tests to validate the robustness of method?		
Results		
Q13: Are any statistical approach applied to validate methods?		
Q14: Are sufficient and suitable graphs and table provided to convey the results?		
Q15: Are any possible assumptions and considerations explained?		
Discussion		
Q16: Are limitations explained?		
Q17: Is any possible use of outcome for practical use discussed?		
Conclusion		
Q18: Are the outcome generalized?		
Q19: Is scope for future use discussed?		

Table 3. Summary of the evaluation results: confusion matrix and performance measures.

ID	Confusion matrix				Performance measures			
	TP	FN	FP	TN	Accuracy	Precision	Recall	F1-Score
CS 1	2	3	16	21	0.55	0.11	0.40	0.17
CS 2	7	1	15	30	0.70	0.32	0.88	0.47

TP: true positive; TN: true negative; FP: false positive; FN: false negative.

4   Results and Discussion

Based on our experimental analysis, we found PCA to exhibit the strongest correlation with citation, thus we use their feature weights to determine the performance of weighted altmetric scores. For that, we perform an initial small scale experiment based on two existing case studies, namely: Nuñez et al. [9] (case study 1) and Salinas et al. [11] (case study 2). The main idea is to replicate these two manually performed case studies, selected within computer science, using the obtained weighted scores for the features. We derive a confusion matrix based on the results for both case studies, that is provided in Table 3, to compute the accuracy, precision, recall, and F1-scores. For each case study, we perform the same search strategy as described originally and obtain their respective results, which forms the input to proceed with the analysis. Then the obtained results are manually scored using the checklist (cf. Table 2) and also, analysed by the implemented prototype with weighted altmetric scores. The papers that scored above or equal to the average altmetric scores for the respective case studies are considered as potential primary studies. This result is later compared with original case study results to establish the performance metrics. We present our results in Table 3, the low performance values for precision and F1 scores can be expected due to the missing data for altmetrics. Overall, our results seem to be promising, however, there must be further research performed in this regard to fully understand the feasibility of weighted altmetric scores. With this work, we believe to have provided the building block towards weighted altmetrics analysis and intend to continue with further extensive investigations in this research area.

5   Conclusion

In this paper, we propose weighted altmetric scores for reflecting on the scientific impact of papers. We suggest models for determining the scores and thus ranking the quality of papers to suggest the most important ones within a specific field. Our analysis is based on a dataset comprising literature from the computer science domain, however, it can be applied to other different domains as well. This work is a first step towards further evaluation and investigative research to determine the usability of weighted altmetric scores. However, based on our

understanding and current work, there seems a potential in improving the reliability of altmetrics by defining weightage scores, which must be proved by further
experiments.

Acknowledgements. This research is funded by the German DFG-MatWerk, NFDI
38/1, project # 460247524 and supported by the Helmholtz Metadata Collaboration
Platform & the German National Research Data Infrastructure.

References

1. Aksnes, D.W., Langfeldt, L., Wouters, P.: Citations, citation indicators, and
   research quality: an overview of basic concepts and theories. SAGE Open **9**(1),
   1–17 (2019)
2. Biolchini, J., Mian, P.G., Natali, A.C.C., Travassos, G.H.: Systematic review in
   software engineering. Technical report, RT-ES 679/05, Systems Engineering and
   Computer Science Department, COPPE/UFRJ (2005)
3. Crotty, D.: Altmetrics: finding meaningful needles in the data haystack. Serials
   Rev. **40**, 141–146 (2014)
4. Hassler, E., Carver, J.C., Hale, D., Al-Zubidy, A.: Identification of SLR tool needs
   - results of a community workshop. IST **70**, 122–129 (2016)
5. He, X., Cai, D., Niyogi, P.: Laplacian score for feature selection. In: Advances in
   Neural Information Processing Systems 18 (2005)
6. Jolliffe, I.T.: Principal Component Analysis. Springer Series in Statistics, p. 29.
   Springer, New York (2002). https://doi.org/10.1007/b98835
7. Kitchenham, B.A., Budgen, D., Brereton, P.: Evidence-Based Software Engineering
   and Systematic Reviews. CRC Press, Boca Raton (2015)
8. Kitchenham, B.A., Charters, S.: Guidelines for performing systematic literature
   reviews in software engineering. Technical report, EBSE-2007-01 (2007)
9. Nuñez, A., Moquillaza, A., Paz, F.: Web accessibility evaluation methods: a systematic review. In: Marcus, A., Wang, W. (eds.) HCII 2019. LNCS, vol. 11586, pp.
   226–237. Springer, Cham (2019). https://doi.org/10.1007/978-3-030-23535-2_17
10. Page, M.J., et al.: The PRISMA 2020 statement: an updated guideline for reporting
    systematic reviews. BMJ 372 (2021)
11. Salinas, E., Cueva, R., Paz, F.: A systematic review of user-centered design tech-
    niques. In: Marcus, A., Rosenzweig, E. (eds.) HCII 2020. LNCS, vol. 12200, pp.
    253–267. Springer, Cham (2020). https://doi.org/10.1007/978-3-030-49713-2_18
12. Shakeel, Y., Krüger, J., Nostitz-Wallwitz, I.V., Saake, G., Leich, T.: Automated
    selection and quality assessment of primary studies: a systematic literature review.
    JDIQ **12**, 1–26 (2019)
13. Stroup, D.F., et al.: Meta-analysis of observational studies in epidemiology: a pro-
    posal for reporting. Jama **283**(15), 2008–2012 (2000)
14. Webster, J., Watson, R.T.: Analyzing the past to prepare for the future: writing a
    literature review. MIS Q. **26**(2), xiii–xxiii (2002)

Accelerating Innovation Papers

Exploring LSTMs for Simulating Search Sessions in Digital Libraries

Sebastian Günther[✉], Paul Göttert, and Matthias Hagen

Martin-Luther-Universität Halle-Wittenberg, Halle (Saale), Germany
{sebastian.gunther,paul.goettert,matthias.hagen}@informatik.uni-halle.de

Abstract. We explore the application of long short-term memory models (LSTM) to simulate search behavior in a digital library. Like web search engines, digital libraries update the retrieval backend or the user interface. However, with the typically rather small user base, evaluating the changes based on user behavior analysis is difficult. To improve this process, we explore whether an LSTM-based model can generate realistic user behavior data. Trained on a cleaned version of the SUSS dataset (555,008 search sessions), the LSTM model uses the whole session history to predict the next interaction. Our preliminary experiments show that this approach can generate realistic sessions.

Keywords: Simulation · Search behavior · User modeling · LSTM

1 Introduction

Web search engines like Google are able to evaluate and improve their retrieval backend via A/B tests on millions of daily user sessions. Most digital libraries, however, have considerably less traffic—making reliable evaluations via A/B tests much more difficult. Thus, several previous studies suggested to simulate digital library sessions via Markov models or other "classic" machine learning-based approaches. In our study, for the first time, we explore recurrent neural networks (RNN) with a long short-term memory architecture (LSTM) for session simulation. We start by cleaning an existing digital library session log on which we then use Keras and Tensorflow to train and tune LSTM models.

Instead of creating individual simulation models for specific aspects like query reformulation, stopping behavior, or dwell time, we want to evaluate whether a combination of features can be used to directly simulate complex behavior. Our focus is on simulating realistic interaction sequences while abstracting from fine-grained details like, for instance, the exact strings of possibly submitted queries. Besides the LSTM-based simulation approach, we also present and analyze metrics for session similarity and the quality of whole session logs.[1] Our study highlights the importance of not "overfitting" the simulated sessions to be too similar to the original data, but to enable the creation of also somewhat different sessions when utilizing machine learning for simulation.

---

[1] Code and data: https://github.com/webis-de/tpdl22-lstm-session-simulation.

© Springer Nature Switzerland AG 2022
G. Silvello et al. (Eds.): TPDL 2022, LNCS 13541, pp. 469–473, 2022.
https://doi.org/10.1007/978-3-031-16802-4_47

2   Related Work

Search interactions usually fall into a few key types (i.e., query formulation, snippet and document examination, etc.) that Maxwell et al. [5] captured in the Complex Searcher Model (CSM) and implemented in the SimIIR framework [4]. For realistic simulations, past interactions can play an important role as demonstrated by Cheng et al. [2] who used session history in their LSTM-based LostNet model for re-ranking and query prediction. In our study, we will thus try LSTMs to simulate whole sessions of interactions. However, predicting future interactions from historic data is difficult. Kinley et al. [3] run a user study with 50 participants on search tasks and show that the same searcher is likely to have a high variation in behavior for different tasks that a machine learning model without knowledge of the task types might miss.

Besides simulating realistic search behavior, analyzing optimal strategies can also be interesting. Baskaya et al. [1] studied the impact of user behavior factors on the retrieval effectiveness. They concluded that there is no single best strategy for every task type, and that simulated ideal user behavior is not realistic.

An important aspect of realistic or optimal search simulation also is the temporal dimension—with reading as a major factor (snippets, documents). Weller et al. [7] analyzed reading time for different text characteristics (e.g., font type, topic, length). On data of 1,000 study participants, they found that a simplistic text length-based model works very well to predict reading time. We will use regression models to simulate interaction times.

3   Search Session Dataset and Data Preparation

For our study, we use the Sowiport User Search Sessions dataset (SUSS)[2] with 558,008 sessions collected over a 1-year period in 2014. Sowiport [6] was a digital library for the field of social science and was operated until 2017. To prepare the data for LSTM simulation model training and evaluation, we filter out sessions with no search-related interactions, and we detect and remove anomalous interactions from within sessions, as removing the entire sessions would reduce the dataset size substantially. We also identify a small subset of systematic irregularities caused by the logging process (e.g., no duration for the last action of a session), which we "fix" by extrapolating from respective interactions with time information. Lastly, sessions are split after 30 min without interaction.

4   Model Training

We train LSTM models on 80% of the data using the open-source library Keras. Each input vector consists of at least two interaction steps from the training data. We initially test two variants: one with five features (action length, action, subaction, origin action, response) and one with six additional features (search

---

[2] https://data.gesis.org/sharing/#!Detail/10.7802/1380.

Table 1. Basic characteristics of real sessions (test data) and simulated sessions.

Data	Interaction duration		Query length		Page number		Number of results	
	avg	sd	avg	sd	avg	sd	avg	sd
SUSS test data	46.95	354.18	12.52	8.02	1.24	0.59	11.71	5.28
LSTM-simulated	46.82	331.63	12.80	7.88	1.21	0.62	11.68	5.22

term type, search term length, search term complexity, sorted, page, information type). We choose the latter for its slightly improved prediction accuracy.

We normalize continuous values (removing 5% upper outliers) and one-hot encode categorical features. Our rather simple models have two hidden layers with 128 and 64 nodes, sigmoid as the activation function, cross-entropy as the loss function, a learning rate of 0.001, and a batch size of 128. We also set class weights to boost interactions classes that are rare in our training data and conclude training after 20 epochs, as the prediction accuracy does not further improve. The simulation uses regression models to "predict" continuous values (e.g., interaction duration, query length). However, the SUSS data does not contain all the data needed for predictions. An example is interaction time for reading: without document content, it can only be guessed with some randomness. More accurate predictions of reading time or query length require more knowledge about the search intent, the result documents, or the shown snippets.

5 Experiments

Assessing simulated sessions is a difficult task, as there are no established measures and the task is further complicated by the multidimensional nature of the session data. We therefore use three different approaches to assess the simulated sessions, with each approach covering different aspects.

Comparing Basic Session Characteristics. The results in Table 1 show that, on average, the basic characteristics of real SUSS sessions from the test data and of 1,000 LSTM-simulated sessions are very similar. From that perspective, LSTM-based simulation is promising.

Human Assessment. In our second assessment, we conduct a manual pilot annotation to evaluate the sessions' "look and feel" from a human perspective. We sample 20 real and 20 simulated sessions each containing a sequence of interactions with durations, number of results, and the usage of pagination or sorting. In random order, one annotator familiar with the SUSS data labeled each session as 'real' or 'simulated'. Afterwards, our annotator told us that their assessments were mostly based on three properties and possible issues of simulated sessions.

(1) Interaction Sequence. Search sessions usually follow a cycle of submitting queries and examining results (comparable to the CSM [5]), interleaved with changing parameters like sorting or pagination. Any deviation is an indicator for either a malformed or a multi-browser-tab session.

472   S. Günther et al.

(2) Interaction Duration. Some interactions' duration can indicate abnormal behavior (e.g., assessing a document as relevant after zero seconds). Still, this might also occur when using multiple tabs, refreshing the page, or by misclicks.

(3) Parameters. While most parameter values are plausible, impossible combinations may occur (e.g., examining a result from a zero-result SERP).

Obviously, some of the above properties exploited by our annotator can occur legitimately and may have led to some wrong assessments. In our small pilot annotation, from the 20 real sessions, 16 were correctly identified as real, while 4 were falsely judged as simulated. From the simulated sessions, 8 were correctly identified as simulated, while 12 were convincing enough to be judged as real.

Session Novelty. Search session simulation usually has two somewhat conflicting goals: realism (i.e., the sessions should be similar to real ones) but also not just memorization (i.e., not just sampling from the training data). Like Google's reported daily 15% of unseen queries,[3] simulated sessions should also contain "new" interaction sequences. We thus focus on novelty for our third assessment.

Using a new similarity measure for "almost exact matches" (i.e., sessions with the same interactions, in the same order, that take about the same time), we mark sessions as novel that have no match in the SUSS training data in two scenarios. In the first scenario, the LSTM model is trained on the first 80% of the SUSS sessions and the remaining 20% are simulated, while in the second scenario the ratio is 90% to 10%. For both scenarios, we compare the ratio of novel simulated sessions to that of the respectively remaining test data. While in the 80% scenario, about 5.46% of the real SUSS sessions are novel (5.18% @ 90%), the ratio is slightly higher for the simulated sessions at 5.91% (5.74% @ 90%). Also from that perspective, LSTM-based simulation thus is promising.

6   Conclusion and Future Work

We have shown some preliminary results on using LSTM models to simulate search sessions in a digital library. For our study, we filtered and transformed the SUSS dataset to extract suitable search sessions. The interaction histories were compiled into short time series datasets that we used to train models for the predictions. In an experimental analysis, we analyzed basic statistical characteristics of the simulated sessions, manually assessed their plausibility by trying to distinguish real from simulated sessions, and analyzed session novelty compared to the training data. Our results indicate that LSTM-based session simulation is very promising from all three evaluation angles.

In future work, we want to generalize our small-scale experiments by comparing LSTM-based session simulation to other approaches like Markov modeling or the rather simpler approaches implemented in the SimIIR simulation framework.

Acknowledgments. This work has been partially supported by the DFG (German Research Foundation) through the project 408022022 "SINIR – Simulating INteractive Information Retrieval".

[3] https://blog.google/products/search/our-latest-quality-improvements-search/.

References

1. Baskaya, F., Keskustalo, H., Järvelin, K.: Modeling behavioral factors in interactive information retrieval. In: He, Q., Iyengar, A., Nejdl, W., Pei, J., Rastogi, R. (eds.) Proceedings of the 22nd ACM International Conference on Information and Knowledge Management (CIKM 2013), San Francisco, CA, USA, 27 October–1 November 2013, pp. 2297–2302. ACM (2013)
2. Cheng, Q., et al.: Long short-term session search: joint personalized reranking and next query prediction. In: Proceedings of the Web Conference 2021 (WWW 2021), Virtual Event/Ljubljana, Slovenia, 19–23 April 2021, pp. 239–248. ACM/IW3C2 (2021)
3. Kinley, K., Tjondronegoro, D., Partridge, H., Edwards, S.L.: Relationship between the nature of the search task types and query reformulation behaviour. In: Trotman, A., Cunningham, S.J., Sitbon, L. (eds.) The Seventeenth Australasian Document Computing Symposium (ADCS 2012), Dunedin, New Zealand, 5–6 December 2012, pp. 39–46. ACM (2012)
4. Maxwell, D., Azzopardi, L.: Simulating interactive information retrieval: SimIIR: a framework for the simulation of interaction. In: Proceedings of the 39th International ACM SIGIR Conference on Research and Development in Information Retrieval (SIGIR 2016), Pisa, Italy, 17–21 July 2016, pp. 1141–1144. ACM (2016)
5. Maxwell, D., Azzopardi, L., Järvelin, K., Keskustalo, H.: Searching and stopping: an analysis of stopping rules and strategies. In: Proceedings of the 24th ACM International Conference on Information and Knowledge Management (CIKM 2015), Melbourne, VIC, Australia, 19–23 October 2015, pp. 313–322. ACM (2015)
6. Mayr, P.: Sowiport User Search Sessions data set (SUSS) (Version: 1.0.0) (2016)
7. Weller, O., et al.: You don't have time to read this: an exploration of document reading time prediction. In: Jurafsky, D., Chai, J., Schluter, N., Tetreault, J.R. (eds.) Proceedings of the 58th Annual Meeting of the Association for Computational Linguistics (ACL 2020), 5–10 July 2020, pp. 1789–1794. Association for Computational Linguistics (2020)

Got 404s? Crawling and Analyzing an Institution's Web Domain

Martin Klein$^{(\boxtimes)}$ and Lyudmila Balakireva

Los Alamos National Laboratory, Los Alamos, NM, USA
{mklein,ludab}@lanl.gov

Abstract. Link rot - disappearance of web resources - is detrimental to an institution's web presence, which is commonly used to communicate, for example, research highlights and organizational news. Organizations, especially taxpayer-funded ones such as the Los Alamos National Laboratory (LANL), therefore put emphasis on the availability and authenticity of their institutional record on the web. We conducted a web crawl of the lanl.gov domain and investigated the scale of missing resources and the ratio of resources recovered from public web archives. We found a noticeable number of special cases of link rot (soft404s) and transient errors, and had little success in recovering resources from web archives. We argue that, as an institution, we could become a better steward of our web content by establishing an institutional web archive to improve the availability and authenticity of web resources.

Keywords: Institutional web archiving · Link rot · Domain crawl

1   Introduction and Motivation

Los Alamos National Laboratory (LANL) is a US Department of Energy federally-funded research and development center with more than 12 thousand employees and an annual operating budget of around three billion US dollars. LANL is host to a broad spectrum of research efforts such as national security, nuclear non-proliferation, space exploration, and renewable energy. The laboratory's website [10] serves as an important medium to communicate organizational news, research accomplishments, as well as policy changes to its staff and the public. The availability and authenticity of this digital record, shared via the lanl.gov domain, but also circulated via various social media channels, is therefore of utmost importance to the institution, the taxpayer, and the government.

While browsing the institutional web, we noticed instances of broken links. The link rot phenomenon is not new and has been studied in the past [23] but two specific arguments set this case apart and motivated us to further investigate our observations. First, as a taxpayer-funded laboratory, LANL holds, in our view, a particular responsibility to maintain access to its public content. In the age of mis- and disinformation, government agencies should play a primary role in informing the public. Secondly, instead of the standard "404 - page not found"

© Springer Nature Switzerland AG 2022
G. Silvello et al. (Eds.): TPDL 2022, LNCS 13541, pp. 474–479, 2022.
https://doi.org/10.1007/978-3-031-16802-4_48

missing page scenario, we observed cases of what is known as "soft404s" [14]. The original URL, e.g. [6] does not resolve anymore and instead of responding with the proper 404 HTTP response code, the server redirects to a generic URL that shows the message "Unavailable Service" and responds with a 200 "OK" code, indicating no error had occurred.

With our prior experience of web crawling [19,22] we decided to conduct a web crawl of the entire lanl.gov domain to further investigate and quantify the scale of link rot. No sitemap of the entire domain is available, so we had no prior knowledge regarding the number of URLs we were about to crawl. We are able to provide an informed estimate of the size of the institutional lanl.gov domain, quantify the scale of link rot, including soft404s, and determine the ratio of missing LANL URLs that we can and can not recover from web archives. Link rot and soft404s are not unique to LANL. However, we hope that this work can contribute to highlighting the status quo for institutional websites and help inform decision making for organizational stewardship of digital content going forward. We outline our methodology that can serve as a blueprint for such experiments, and detail the highlights of our results in the following sections.

2   Related Work and Methodology

Given the dynamic nature of the web [15], the phenomenon of link rot has effected web resources, for example in the scholarly communication [21,24,26]. McCown et al. [25] highlighted a number of common reasons for web pages to disappear, including lapsed domain registrations. Link rot can be mitigated proactively by creating archival copies of linked web resources in the publicly available web archiving infrastructure and adding additional HTML attributes to web links to allow for various fallback mechanisms in case the original URL is missing (or its content has drifted [17]) as introduced in [18]. More popular web content has a higher probability of being archived as confirmed in [13]. Jones et al. [16] identified four semantic categories of archival collections: subject-based, time bounded for expected and unexpected events, and self-archiving. Institutions archiving their own domain fall into the latter category, so our investigation is most closely aligned with this common type of archival collection.

We devised our plan to crawl the lanl.gov domain, count all observed link rot instances, and check their availability in more than two dozen web archives by using the TimeTravel service [11]. As often done for domain crawls when no complete list of URLs to crawl is available, we used Google's search engine to discover the 20 most popular subdomains in the lanl.gov space and used these URLs as our seeds [20]. To avoid crawler traps we blacklisted several subdomains e.g., search pages of the library catalog where the content's value does not necessarily warrant the required resources to complete the crawl. In addition, we had to modify the crawler software [2] to properly quantify LANL's instances of soft404s, identified by redirects to LANL's generic error page.

We are not able to rely on a simple lookup response to the archives to determine whether a URL has an archival copy in a web archive, as the soft404s are

Table 1. Summary of HTTP response codes

Code	200	301	302	400	401	403	404	500	502	504
Amount	148, 169	174	8, 405	1	101	518	7	6	39, 216	225
Percentage	75.3%	0.1%	4.3%	0.001%	0.1%	0.3%	0.003	0.003%	19.9%	0.1%

now part of the archived record. According to the TimeTravel service, at least nine web archives hold archived versions of the generic error page [12] and the Internet Archive (IA) alone holds more than 33 thousand copies [1]. We therefore implemented additional logic to check archived copies for redirects and their final URL to dismiss cases of archived soft404s. Since we do not know when missing URLs disappeared, we only look for the most recent available copy in the archives. The available archival copy may not accurately represent the live version's last state, but for the purpose of this experiment, we leave it at counting available "proper" archival copies and do not further investigate content drift.

3   Results

In total, we crawled 216, 427 unique URLs, 196, 822 (90.9%) of which are in the lanl.gov domain, leaving roughly 20 thousand non-LANL outlinks dismissed for this analysis. The observed HTTP response codes for all URLs in Table 1 highlight three noticeable observations. First, the large percentage (75.3%) of 200 response codes is positive but also somewhat misleading as this number includes all discovered soft404s. We identified 3, 577 soft440s, which corresponds to 1.82% of all crawled URLs and 2.4% of all 200 responses. While this percentage may not seem that high, it represents a noticeable fraction of URLs that contribute to a detrimental browsing experience, potentially undermine the public's trust in the laboratory's communication. Secondly, we notice almost 20% of URLs return a 502 response code, indicating a server error. This percentage is surprisingly high and may be a function of some web services not responding properly to crawler requests, as we have seen in previous experiments [19]. Lastly, we see 4.3% of URLs responding with a 302 response code. It is possible that our crawler timed out trying to follow too many redirects, or a web server simply stopped responding. In either case, the latter two observations can also be categorized as a detriment to the browsing experience, though these cases may be transient.

We notice that the majority of soft404s are from the www.lanl.gov (1, 412) and lanl.gov (787) domains (Fig. 1). Beyond that, we find a long tail of 46 subdomains, 25 of which have less than ten soft404s. In total, we recovered 404 out of the 3, 577 soft404s, which amounts to 11.3%. The majority of recovered URLs are from the www.lanl.gov domain, which seems to confirm earlier findings of more popular pages being more frequently represented in web archives [13]. We were able to recover most of the URLs from the IA [5], the Library of Congress [9], and the Portuguese [4] web archives. In addition to analyzing the outcome of our crawl, we also built a web archive of all crawled lanl.gov domain resources [7] through which web pages of the domain can be replayed [8].

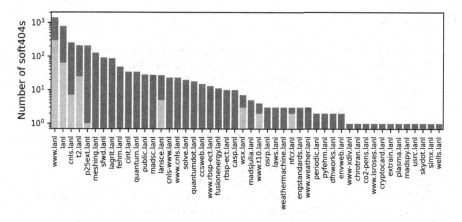

Fig. 1. Distribution of discovered soft404s by LANL domain. Yellow overlay bars indicate the fraction of recovered URLs from web archives. (Color figure online)

4 Discussion and Summary

Institutions are following different approaches to address the link rot problem, to increase the availability of their resources, to build trust, and serve as an exemplary steward of their digital content on the web. While outsourcing archival efforts to a third party such as Archive-It [3] is the common path, in-house initiatives leave an institution in better control over the scale and scope of the effort. Our framework and analysis can help other organizations that are concerned about their institutional footprint on the web, so they can assess the level of link rot within their domain and explore mitigation approaches to the problem.

Soft404s are a special case of link rot that have, as demonstrated, unintended consequences to search engines and web archives and a require special detection methodology during a crawl. With no prior knowledge about the domain, we created a seed list, conducted a domain crawl, optimized our crawler to avoid traps, incorporated logic to detect soft404s, and provided insights into the scale of link rot at the laboratory. We found a noticeable percentage of soft404s and a surprising number of transient errors. We recover 11% of all missing pages from the archived web. We created an archive of the crawled resources that serves as a demonstration of an institutional web archive and provides a source from which the organization can serve resources missing on the live web and provide evidence of the existence of a resource and its state at a point in the past.

There are many reasons why resources disappear from the web, but link rot is avoidable. With this work, we aim to make a step towards assessing an organization's status quo and providing arguments for institutional web archives. In a more perfect world, the answer to the question "Got 404s?" will be a clear "No, not anymore!".

References

1. IA Archival Copies of. http://www.lanl.gov/errors/service-unavailable.php
2. Web crawler for Java. https://github.com/yasserg/crawler4j
3. Archive-it-web archiving services. https://archive-it.org/
4. Arquivo.pt - search pages from the past!. https://arquivo.pt/
5. Internet archive wayback machine. http://web.archive.org/
6. LANL soft404 in a browser https://lanl.gov/discover/news-release-archive/2017/July/0719-ultracold-reactions.php redirects to. https://www.lanl.gov/errors/service-unavailable.php which returns an HTTP 200
7. LANL web archive. http://lanlwebarchive.org/memento/
8. LANL web archive - e.g. Archival copy of. http://www.lanl.gov/library/, http://lanlwebarchive.org/memento/20210213211725/http://www.lanl.gov/library/
9. Library of congress web archives. https://webarchive.loc.gov/
10. Los Alamos national lab: national security science. https://www.lanl.gov/
11. Memento TimeTravel. http://timetravel.mementoweb.org/
12. TimeTravel search results for. http://www.lanl.gov/errors/service-unavailable.php, http://timetravel.mementoweb.org/list/20220506051138/http://www.lanl.gov/errors/service-unavailable.php
13. Ainsworth, S.G., et al.: How much of the web is archived? In: Proceedings of the 11th Annual International ACM/IEEE Joint Conference on Digital Libraries, pp. 133–136 (2011). https://doi.org/10.1145/1998076.1998100
14. Bar-Yossef, Z., et al.: Sic transit Gloria Telae: towards an understanding of the web's decay. In: Proceedings of WWW 2004, pp. 328–337 (2004)
15. Cho, J., Garcia-Molina, H.: Estimating frequency of change. ACM Trans. Internet Technol. **3**(3), 256–290 (2003). https://doi.org/10.1145/857166.857170
16. Jones, S., et al.: 205.3 the many shapes of archive-it. (2019). https://doi.org/10.17605/OSF.IO/EV42P
17. Jones, S.M., et al.: Scholarly context adrift: three out of four URI references lead to changed content. PLoS ONE **11**(12), e0167475 (2016)
18. Jones, S.M., et al.: Robustifying links to combat reference rot. Code4Lib 50 (2021). https://journal.code4lib.org/articles/15509
19. Klein, M., Balakireva, L.: An extended analysis of the persistence of persistent identifiers of the scholarly web. Int. J. Digit. Libr. **23**(1), 5–17 (2021). https://doi.org/10.1007/s00799-021-00315-w
20. Klein, M., Balakireva, L.: LANL domain crawl seed list (2022). https://doi.org/10.6084/m9.figshare.19912459.v1
21. Klein, M., et al.: Scholarly context not found: one in five articles suffers from reference rot. PLoS ONE **9**(12), e115253 (2014)
22. Klein, M., Shankar, H., Balakireva, L., Van de Sompel, H.: The memento tracer framework: balancing quality and scalability for web archiving. In: Doucet, A., Isaac, A., Golub, K., Aalberg, T., Jatowt, A. (eds.) TPDL 2019. LNCS, vol. 11799, pp. 163–176. Springer, Cham (2019). https://doi.org/10.1007/978-3-030-30760-8_15
23. Koehler, W.: Web page change and persistence-a four-year longitudinal study. J. Am. Soc. Inform. Sci. Technol. **53**(2), 162–171 (2002). https://doi.org/10.1002/asi.10018

24. McCown, F., et al.: The availability and persistence of web references in d-lib magazine (2005). https://doi.org/10.48550/ARXIV.CS/0511077
25. McCown, F., et al.: Why web sites are lost (and how they're sometimes found). Commun. ACM **52**(11), 141–145 (2009). https://doi.org/10.1145/1592761.1592794
26. Wren, J.D.: URL decay in MEDLINE-a 4-year follow-up study. Bioinformatics **24**(11), 1381–1385 (2008). https://doi.org/10.1093/bioinformatics/btn127

Automatic Knowledge Extraction from a Digital Library and Collaborative Validation

Eleonora Bernasconi[1]([✉])[iD], Miguel Ceriani[2][iD], Massimo Mecella[1][iD], and Alberto Morvillo[1][iD]

[1] Sapienza Università di Roma, ITA, Rome, Italy
{bernasconi,mecella,morvillo}@diag.uniroma1.it
[2] Università di Bari Aldo Moro, ITA, Bari, Italy
miguel.ceriani@uniba.it

Abstract. The automatic extraction of knowledge from a Digital Library is a crucial task in the world of Digital Humanities by enabling the discovery of information on a scale that is not achievable by human experts alone. However, the automation of information extraction processes brings the typical problems of a fully automated process, namely data quality and explainability of the results. This paper proposes a system that allows domain experts to collaboratively validate information previously automatically extracted from a Digital Library (DL), supporting an incremental data quality improvement approach, specifically through entity linking. Furthermore, rather than seeing just the results of the extraction process, the domain experts can trace the origin of where the AI recognized a specific entity (i.e. a "snippet" of text or an image).

In order to allow the domain experts to contextualize the information they need to validate (i.e. topics, descriptions, etc.) leveraging the Knowledge Graph potential, in the proposed use case, the validation is integrated into the interface designated for the DL semantic exploration.

Keywords: Digital Library · Knowledge Extraction · Data quality · Collaborative validation

1 Introduction

In this work, we propose a system that, in addition to semantically extracting the concepts contained in a Digital Libraries (DL), allows the experts of

This work has been partly supported by projects ARCA (POR FESR Lazio 2014–2020 - Avviso pubblico "Creatività 2020", domanda prot. n. A0128-2017-17189) and SCIBA (Regione Lazio and MIUR - Determinazione n. G07413 del 16/06/2021). Miguel Ceriani acknowledges funding from the Italian Ministry of University and Research (MIUR), within the European program PON R&I 2014–2020 – Attraction and International Mobility (AIM) – project no. COD. AIM1852414, activity 2, line 1.

© Springer Nature Switzerland AG 2022
G. Silvello et al. (Eds.): TPDL 2022, LNCS 13541, pp. 480–484, 2022.
https://doi.org/10.1007/978-3-031-16802-4_49

the domain treated in the library to validate the information extracted. The automatic extraction thus represents a solid basis from which to intervene collaboratively by optimizing the quality of the associations between documents and their respective contents. Numerous researches [1,4,5] show that automatic extractions are insufficient to meet an acceptable quality level by communities of domain experts. At the same time, it would be too expensive in terms of time and cost to semantically annotate information manually. In our approach, the User Interface shows the semantic search result, the trace of the origin from where the information has been automatically extracted, and the history of user validation activities to facilitate the domain experts to validate the consistency of the relationships between automatically extracted concepts and a DL documents.

2 Related Work

Methods to semantically enrich unstructured content can be classified in three main approaches [8]: *manual*, *automatic*, and *semi-automatic*. In the *manual* approach humans are fully in charge with the semantic annotation of content. **Omeka S**[1], for example, is a platform to connect digital cultural heritage collections with other online resources, and **SenTag** [7], which enables tagging a corpus of documents through an intuitive and easy-to-use user interface. In manual systems, quality errors are reduced to human input errors, but the throughput of the process is limited by the amount time knowledgeable people can contribute to the process. Furthermore, the possible divergence in the criteria used for classification by different users needs also be taken into account.

Automatic methods use a variety of techniques (including machine learning algorithms and natural language processing) in order to allow a machine to derive semantic information from the unstructured content, with minimal user intervention. **AnnoTag** [6], for example, provides concise content annotations by employing entity-level analytics in order to derive semantic descriptions in the form of tags. The **Arca/Sciba** [2,3] system, thanks to the automatic association of unstructured content with concepts in a knowledge graph (KG), allow complex queries on data and visualization of semantic associations connecting concepts and documents.

Semi-automatic approaches as the one presented here aim to get the best of both worlds, by providing some form of collaboration between the machine, providing automatic annotation, and the human experts, who are still able to control the final result of the process. An example is the one of **tagtog**[2], which is a collaborative tool to annotate texts. It allows searching for documents and entities, but lacks the capability of visualising relationships between entities.

---

[1] https://omeka.org.
[2] https://tagtog.net.

3   How to Improve Data Quality

Improving the quality of data in a system that manages books, metadata, concepts, and images requires considering each of these entities and their associations.

We decided to start with validating the associations between concepts and books by showing users in what terms the considered concept is described in the considered document, so a large percentage of errors due to completely automatic extractions can be eliminated in a short time.

This validation will be stored in the KG and the Cloud, allowing immediate collaborative work. Validations could improve the search and display of results, and the system keeps track of the history of validations so the user can choose which information he prefers to view.

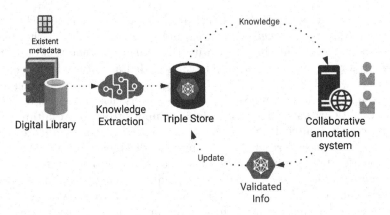

Fig. 1. The platform pipeline. Users can validate or deny the relations between a corpus of texts and their relative concepts in the Knowledge extracted from a Digital Library.

Figure 1 shows the semantic enrichment extraction and information validation processes pipeline. Once the Artificial Intelligence service has extracted the concepts from the text (Named Entity Recognition) and from the images (Object Detection), the Semantic Enrichment Engine connects the identified concepts with the DBpedia Knowledge Base[3]. This mechanism allows visualizing the semantic associations between concepts. The validation process creates new associations between the ID of the user logged into the platform and the validated concept/book pair. These new associations are sent to the KG, which manages the validation versions from the different users of the system. With each new validation, the system updates the relationships, improving the results of the searches and the related visualization of the associations, establishing a process that aims to achieve the optimal quality for domain experts.

---

[3] https://www.dbpedia.org/.

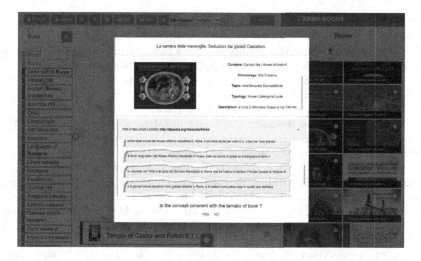

Fig. 2. Example of the UI. The relationships can be reviewed before validation.

Figure 2 represents the tool's screenshot showing the snippets associated with the concept/book couple: "Rome/La Camera delle Meraviglie". Through this window, the user can establish whether the Rome concept is consistent with the theme dealt with in the book. To be guided in the decision, the user sees the book's text snippets (in this case, the sentences) from where the concept was automatically detected.

Automatic semantic extraction includes the disambiguation of concepts, i.e. the choice of the best meaning based on the context of the sentence. For this reason, we believe that showing the text snippets to the user allows it to have all the information available to decide whether or not to validate the association.

4   Conclusion and Future Work

Automatically extracting knowledge from a digital library is a tricky challenge in line with enhancing cultural heritage. Giving life to information hidden in piles of documents in the most efficient, least expensive, and most attractive way possible is a challenge that contemplates various thematic research areas such as Digital Humanities, Knowledge Extraction, Information Visualization, Search Interfaces and Human-Computer Interaction. In this paper, we wanted to tell the evolution of a system that deals with automatically extracting information from a corpus of texts and allows the research, exploration and visualization of semantic connections. We have described the system's ongoing development that allows collaborative validation of automatically extracted associations, founding the high utility of implementing a validation system for associations during user tests and, in future work, we will take care of following and supporting this track.

References

1. Beall, J.: Metadata and data quality problems in the digital library. J. Digit. Inf. **6**(3) (2005). https://journals.tdl.org/jodi/index.php/jodi/article/view/65
2. Bernasconi, E., et al.: SCIBA - a prototype of the computerized cartographic system of an archaeological bibliography. In: Araujo, J., et al. (eds.) Joint Proceedings of RCIS 2022 Workshops and Research Projects Track Co-located with the 16th International Conference on Research Challenges in Information Science (RCIS 2022). ceur-ws.org, May 2022. http://ceur-ws.org/Vol-3144/RP-paper11.pdf
3. Bernasconi, E., Ceriani, M., Mecella, M.: Exploring a text corpus via a knowledge graph. In: Dosso, D., Ferilli, S., Manghi, P., Poggi, A., Serra, G., Silvello, G. (eds.) Proceedings of the 17th Italian Research Conference on Digital Libraries. ceur-ws.org, Feb 2021. http://ircdl2021.dei.unipd.it/static/downloads/paper8.pdf
4. Candela, G., Escobar, P., Carrasco, R.C., Marco-Such, M.: Evaluating the quality of linked open data in digital libraries. J. Inf. Sci. **48**, 21–43 (2022). https://doi.org/10.1177/0165551520930951
5. Hallo, M., Luján-Mora, S., Maté, A., Trujillo, J.: Current state of linked data in digital libraries. J. Inf. Sci. **42**, 117–127 (2016)
6. Kumar, A., Spaniol, M.: AnnoTag: concise content annotation via LOD tags derived from entity-level analytics. In: Berget, G., Hall, M.M., Brenn, D., Kumpulainen, S. (eds.) TPDL 2021. LNCS, vol. 12866, pp. 175–180. Springer, Cham (2021). https://doi.org/10.1007/978-3-030-86324-1_21
7. Loreggia, A., Mosco, S., Zerbinati, A.: Sentag: A web-based tool for semantic annotation of textual documents. In: Berget, G., Hall, M.M., Brenn, D., Kumpulainen, S. (eds.) Thirty-Sixth AAAI Conference on Artificial Intelligence. AAAI Press, Jun 2022. https://doi.org/10.1609/aaai.v36i11.21724
8. Neves, M., Ševa, J.: An extensive review of tools for manual annotation of documents. Briefings Bioinform. **22**(1), 146–163 (2019). https://doi.org/10.1093/bib/bbz130

Holistic Graph-Based Representation and AI for Digital Library Management

Stefano Ferilli$^{(\boxtimes)}$ (iD)

University of Bari, 70125 Bari, BA, Italy
stefano.ferilli@uniba.it
http://lacam.di.uniba.it/people/ferilli.html

Abstract. The traditional record-based approach used in Digital Libraries has gone as far as it could. To support the needs and activities of different kinds of users, we propose a graph-based 'holistic' representation of DL knowledge, describing the documents' metadata, physical aspects, content, context and lifecycle. We also propose its implementation based on a framework in which Formal Ontologies play the role of data schemas for the LPG-based DBs. This enables automated reasoning on the DL data, and we propose the use of multiple inference strategies.

Keywords: Artificial Intelligence · Knowledge Representation · Knowledge Graphs · Digital Libraries

1 Introduction and Motivation

The traditional record-based approach used in Digital Libraries (DLs) has successfully served the need of users, researchers and practitioners for many decades. The enormous growth in production, types and availability of documents, the opening of their use to a wider public (with different background, goals and perspectives), the advent of digital technologies, and the convergence of many different traditionally separate disciplines call for new and advanced organization strategies, and new ways of exploitation, for the documents and the information they carry. This requires a change of paradigm. It is necessary to deconstruct the traditional record-based approach with predefined fields (author, title, etc.), and to move to a reticular description, in which all the entities involved in a description 'live' with their own dignity and can be related to each other, rather than being just field values in the record. Such a new setting is also instrumental to broaden the focus of the descriptions, from a fixed set of formal parameters of the documents in the library to a larger and more variable set including also information concerning their physical support, content, context, and even use. We have called it a *holistic* description approach.

In Artificial Intelligence (AI for short), the networking of data is well-known for being the core of *knowledge*. So, we call for a step up from the Data Base (DB) perspective to the Knowledge Base (KB)—more specifically, Knowledge Graph

© Springer Nature Switzerland AG 2022
G. Silvello et al. (Eds.): TPDL 2022, LNCS 13541, pp. 485–489, 2022.
https://doi.org/10.1007/978-3-031-16802-4_50

(KG)— one. KGs have been thoroughly studied in the Knowledge Representation (KR for short) branch of AI, interested in Ontologies and Automated Reasoning. While research in KR has developed its own solutions for representing and storing knowledge, that have departed from the mainstream solutions for DBs, we believe that DL data representation and storage must still be rooted in DB technology, in order to ensure optimization and efficiency in data storage and handling. However, we also believe that the switch to KBs requires more advanced DB solutions, and some kind of cooperation with the solutions coming from KR, that may boost the effectiveness of DL data management so as to support the needs of different kind of users, providing them new possibilities for data exploitation and unprecedented opportunities to carry out their activities [6].

The rest of this paper will describe our technological proposal to support this vision, an overview of the holistic data schema we envision, and some examples of possible advanced exploitation that are enabled by these proposals.

2   Technological Solution

Research in KR resulted in an established representation standard for formal ontologies (the Ontology Web Language, or OWL) and associated data storage technology, called triplestores. Triplestores adopt the RDF graph model, based on triples *(Subject, Predicate, Object)* of atomic (Uniform Resource Identifiers— URIs— or literal) values. However, these attempts have not met wide acceptance in industrial applications, where significant success among big industrial players has been obtained by a new graph-based NoSQL technology, of which Neo4j is the most outstanding representative. It is based on the Labeled Property Graphs (LPG) model, that allows to associate sets of attribute-value pairs and labels to nodes and arcs. Nodes represent entity instances, arcs represent binary relationships on them, the attribute-value pairs represent properties, and the labels usually represent the type of entity or relationship. Neo4j is schema-less.

So, we propose to adopt LPG-based DBs for data storage and basic handling, and formal ontologies as data schemas. The current solutions in the literature are OWL-centric: they focus on applying OWL solutions to LPGs. Since the LPG model is incompatible with, and more expressive than, the RDF one, such solutions either do not exploit the full power of LPGs or propose non-standard extensions of RDF (see [4] for a more detailed discussion of related works). In contrast, our approach is LPG-centric, based on a specific ontological formalism that leverages the full power of the LPG model features (see [4] for a detailed description of the language). For this purpose, we developed a framework called *GraphBRAIN* [4], and associated tools for schema and instance handling [5], including a Web application[1]. In GraphBRAIN, the ontologies define the data model, expressing what the DB can store and how it is structured, while the graph DB stores the instances. As in standard relational DB, they are kept separate from each other, differently from proposals in the literature in which the schema is represented within the graph. This allows to superimpose different

---

[1] A demo is available at http://193.204.187.73:8088/GraphBRAIN/.

ontologies as schemas on the same graph, representing different views on the same data. A GraphBRAIN API acts as a wrapper for the DB to make it available to to external applications. All accesses to the DB and operations on its content must pass through the API methods, that given a DB instance and a schema/ontology provides access to the DB so as to ensure compliance with the data schema. Functionality is also provided to import OWL ontologies and/or individuals into GraphBRAIN, and to export GraphBRAIN schemas and/or instances to OWL, so that existing Semantic Web tools can be applied on them.

3   Holistic Description

We propose a 'holistic' approach to document representation in DLs, that considers and brings to cooperation many different aspects:

Formal including usual metadata used in library records;
Physical including materials, processing and even mechanics, if applicable;
Content of various kind:
  - *Textual*, at several levels (words, phrases or excerpts) and in any language, also including grammatical information;
  - *Layout*, concerning the visual appearance of documents;
  - *Logical*, dealing with the roles played by the document's components;
  - *Conceptual*, interested in the meaning conveyed by the documents; concepts are represented as instances within the KG, so that they can be linked to other instances of any class in the KB[2];
Context adding information that is external to the documents, but that may be useful or relevant to properly understand it;
Lifecycle including process and usage data, useful for personalization purposes.

Some components (entities, relationships, attributes) of the ontology correspond to the elements in existing DL standards such as the Dublin Core Metadata Initiative (DCMI), the IFLA Functional Requirements for Bibliographic Records (FRBR) report [7], the Open Archives Initiative Object Reuse and Exchange (OAI-ORE) [2], and OpenAIRE [8].

The content and context portions of the graph can be populated interactively by the users, or automatically by ingesting existing resources or applying Natural Language Processing, Image Processing and Information Extraction techniques to the documents in the DL or to other information sources. The resulting graph will allow indirect, non-trivial connections between the represented items.

---

[2] Concepts can be taken from standard taxonomies (e.g., WordNet [9], the Dewey Decimal Classification (DDC) system [3] or the ACM Computing Classification System (CCS) [1]). Several taxonomies can be stored, aligned and merged, also adding user-defined and/or domain-specific items.

4   Data Management

Using ontologies as schemas for the graph DB makes it a fully-fledged KG, and enables reasoning on the data. While OWL-based approaches are specifically oriented toward ontological reasoning, GraphBRAIN is more generic and supports also additional kinds of reasoning, by acting as a middle layer that transparently exports (off-line or on-the-fly) the instances (and ontologies) to the external reasoners in the format they require. We are especially interested in those connected to the Logic Programming setting, which is partially incompatible with those based on Description Logics and thus not available in OWL-based settings.

In particular, we propose to use and mix the following reasoning approaches:

Associative based on graph traversal, naturally supported by graph DBs and their query languages;

Ontological in charge of inheritance handling and consistency checks (the properties guaranteed for this kind of reasoning depend on the chosen export ontological language);

Deductive in the form of rule-based approaches, as in deductive DBs;

Abductive to guess missing information (nodes, arcs, attributes) needed by other kinds of reasoning or to explain the available data;

by Abstraction to ignore data that are irrelevant for a given purpose;

Argumentative to determine consistent portions of an inconsistent DB;

Uncertain to add flexibility to the other inference strategies;

by Similarity to support instance-based processing;

Analogic to identify subgraphs with the same structural pattern, and allow them to expand each other;

Inductive to learn high-level concepts or discover (ir-)regularities on the data (both Machine Learning and Data Mining approaches can be included).

In turn, multistrategy reasoning may support advanced techniques for other relevant DL tasks, such as: (lexical or semantic) Information Retrieval, Recommendation, Personalization, Network Analysis, etc.

5   Conclusion

We proposed a graph-based organization of DL data, based on a technology mixing DBs and ontologies. We also proposed a holistic data schema allowing to store information that is not explicitly present in any of the single documents, but emerges from their direct or indirect relationships. Together with AI techniques based on multistrategy reasoning, we believe that this setting may significantly expand the effectiveness of data processing and may dramatically improve the exploitation possibilities of documents. E.g.: in scholarly research, it might support or even suggest investigation directions; in document clustering ir document classification, it may improve the quality of the outcome by expanding and integrating the information present in the document with related information coming from the background knowledge or from other documents;

in document indexing, it may allow retrieving documents that do not explicitly contain the search parameters set by the user; in query answering, it may allow finding more source documents, indirectly related to the question posed by the user but relevant to answer it; etc.

References

1. https://dl.acm.org/ccs
2. https://www.openarchives.org/ore/
3. Dewey, M.: A Classification and Subject Index for Cataloguing and Arranging the Books and Pamphlets of a Library. Amherst, Massachusetts (1876)
4. Ferilli, S.: Integration strategy and tool between formal ontology and graph database technology. Electronics **10**, 2616 (2021)
5. Ferilli, S., Redavid, D.: The GraphBRAIN system for knowledge graph management and advanced fruition. In: Helic, D., Leitner, G., Stettinger, M., Felfernig, A., Raś, Z.W. (eds.) ISMIS 2020. LNCS (LNAI), vol. 12117, pp. 308–317. Springer, Cham (2020). https://doi.org/10.1007/978-3-030-59491-6_29
6. Ferilli, S., Redavid, D.: An ontology and knowledge graph infrastructure for digital library knowledge representation. In: Ceci, M., Ferilli, S., Poggi, A. (eds.) IRCDL 2020. CCIS, vol. 1177, pp. 47–61. Springer, Cham (2020). https://doi.org/10.1007/978-3-030-39905-4_6
7. IFLA Study Group on the FRBR: functional requirements for bibliographic records - final report. Technical report, International Federation of Library Associations and Institutions (2009)
8. Manghi, P., et al.: The OpenAIRE research graph data model, April 2019. https://doi.org/10.5281/zenodo.2643199
9. Miller, G.: Wordnet: a lexical database for English. Commun. ACM **38**, 39–41 (1995)

Optimizing the Digitization Workflow of Heritage Institutions to Increase Quality of Digitized Texts

Mirjam Cuper$^{(\boxtimes)}$ and Sarah D'Huys

KB, National Library of the Netherlands, Prins Willem-Alexanderhof 5, 2595 BE Den Haag, The Netherlands
{mirjam.cuper,sarah.dHuys}@kb.nl

Abstract. An often used method in digitizing heritage collections is the use of mass digitization. While this leads to a lot of digitized content in a short amount of time, quality control and information about the quality of digitized material is generally lacking. To overcome this problem, we propose a theoretical design of an optimized digitization workflow. It will be designed as a plug-in pipeline where different modules can be added or removed based on organizational needs. By integrating a high level of automation it will be suitable for high-throughput, low-funding settings.

Keywords: Digitization · Data quality management · Digital heritage

1 Introduction

Most heritage institutions use mass digitization to make their heritage collections digitally available [1]. With this method, a lot of content can be made available in a relatively short amount of time. While mass digitization leads to an extensive collection of digitized heritage, there are some drawbacks to this method.

Due to the amount of material that is processed, it is not possible to manually check the quality of each processed document. To ensure some kind of quality check, the KB, for example, uses random samples to check the material. However, due to the variation in, among others, quality and layout of the original material, this random sample is not representative and does not generalize to the whole collection. Regardless of the quality, all digitized text are published online.

This lack of information about quality can lead to several issues for the end users. First of all, the lower the quality of a digitized text, the lower the chance that this text will be found through a standard search interface. As such a search interface is often used by heritage institutions to provided users access to their collections, this can lead to documents that will never be found and can potentially lead to wrong research conclusions.

Furthermore, researchers are often interested in analysing a large number of texts [3] using computational methods. To be able get reliable results after conducting these analyses, a certain quality of digitized texts is needed.

© Springer Nature Switzerland AG 2022
G. Silvello et al. (Eds.): TPDL 2022, LNCS 13541, pp. 490–494, 2022.
https://doi.org/10.1007/978-3-031-16802-4_51

Finally, more and more heritage institutions are interested in complying with the FAIR principles [4]. The FAIR principles are intended to make data findable, accessible, interoperable and reusable. Providing transparency about the quality benefits the compliance to this FAIR principles.

2   Example of a Mass Digitization Workflow

As an example of a mass digitization workflow, we will illustrate the mass digitization workflow that is currently used by the KB, the national library of the Netherlands, for publishing heritage collections on their platform Delpher [5]. Figure 1 shows a (simplified) graphical representation of this workflow.

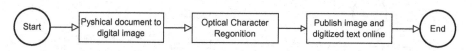

Fig. 1. Graphical representation (simplified) of the current mass digitization workflow of the KB.

As shown in Fig. 1, the workflow is straightforward. First, a digital image of the physical material is created. Then, the digital image is used to perform layout recognition and Optical Character Recognition (OCR). This information is used to create a digital representation with computer readable text. At the KB, both the creation of the scan and the process of transforming a scan into a computer readable text are outsourced.

After the digitization of the text, automatic controls are performed to check the received batches of digitized material on aspects such as validity, correctness of metadata, page numbering and completeness. To determine the quality of the digitized texts itself, random samples are taken from this batches to check the quality of the provided text. When the quality is below a pre-determined cut-off point, the batch is sent back to the supplier to redo the digitization.

As last step, the scanned image and the corresponding text are published online. The layout information is used to locate words on the scanned image and highlight them in the document viewer.

As can be seen in this short description, there is only a small amount of quality checks in the process. Also, the quality of the largest part of the documents is unknown. At the KB, we strive for an improved workflow that provides more information about the quality of our material and what parts can be improved.

3   Optimizing the Digitization Workflow

Our proposed redesign of the digitization workflow is feasible for institutions and can overcome the limitations of current mass digitization workflows. Our redesign focuses on the part after the original material is scanned and ends with a digitized, computer readable documents from which the quality is known.

The main purpose of the optimized workflow is increasing the quality of digitized texts and providing transparency about their quality. The workflow is not only usable for optimizing the digitizing workflow for new materials but is also suitable for improving already existing digital collections.

The proposed workflow is an adaptive plug-in pipeline, where modules can be inserted or excluded based on the requirements and organizational needs. The aim is to create a workflow that is highly automated by using computational methods. At first, manual input will be needed for training and testing. However, after a while there should be less need for human intervention, making the

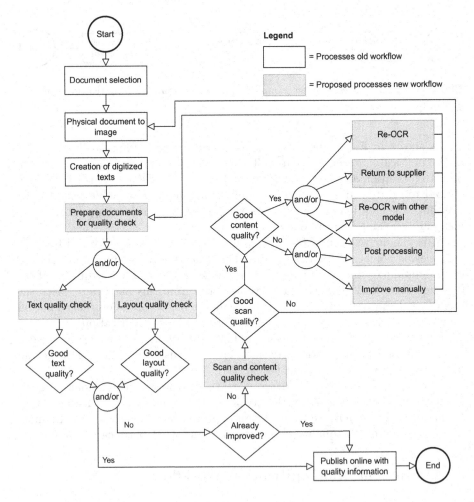

Fig. 2. Graphical representation (simplified) of the proposed workflow.

modules as automated as possible. This will lead to an approach that is feasible for high throughput, low funding settings.

The proposed workflow consists of various steps. The first step is to transform the scanned image of a document into a digitized, computer readable, format. After this format is created, the workflow starts with one or multiple automated quality checks, based on the inserted modules. These quality checks focus on the OCR-ed text, the layout, and the quality of the image (both scan and content). The outcomes of these checks determine the path that a document will follow through the workflow, as shown in Fig. 2.

If there is a chance of improvement, various modules could be implemented, such as modules for re-ocr, post-processing, or an interface for manually correcting. After these improvements, the quality checks are performed again. This can lead to another round of improvements, or to publishing the content online.

Sometimes, it is not possible to improve the quality of a document, for example if the source material is badly damaged. In such a case, the improvements steps will be skipped, and the material can be published online with information regarding the low quality.

4 Benefits of the Improved Digitization Workflow

Our proposed digitization workflow has several benefits, both for the organizations itself and for the end users.

From an organizational point of view, the proposed workflow provides institutions more insight in the quality of their data. When working with an external manufacturer for the digitization of psychical material and/or Optical Character Recognition, various modules in the workflow can support the institution by making sure quality standards are in place and enforced. Furthermore, institutions can make informed decisions about which material to improve and which methods to use. Instead of basing this on a sample and generalized information, institutions can now target their improvements by deciding on a document level if, and how, an improvement is needed.

As the modules can vary, institutions can easily update or improve separate modules without having to put a whole new workflow in use. Also, institutions can exchange updates and improvements of the modules with other institutions or researchers. Due to the highly automated processes, the workflow is suited for a high throughput of material.

When looking from the point of view from the end user, there are also several benefits. Improved material leads to more reliable results in search interfaces. Furthermore, with transparency and knowledge about the quality of the material, researchers can make an informed decision about which documents to include or exclude from their analyses based on this information.

5 Next Steps

We realize that our proposed workflow is theoretical, and additional work is needed to examine if our suggested approach is affordable and feasible for organizations. However, we are convinced that our approach is beneficial. Therefore, the KB has started experimenting with possible methods for the modules [2].

As for a lot of modules specific domain knowledge is needed, we seek collaboration with researchers and experts from other institutions. We think collaborations can accelerate the process and lead to modules of a high quality.

References

1. Dahlström, M., Hansson, J., Kjellman, U.: 'As we may digitize' - institutions and documents reconfigured. LIBER Q. **21**, 455 (2012)
2. Cuper, M.: Examining a multi layered approach for classification of OCR quality without ground truth. DHBenelux J. **4**, 43–59 (2022)
3. Jänicke, S., Franzini, G., Cheema, M.F., Scheuermann, G.: Visual text analysis in digital humanities. Comput. Graph. Forum **36**, 226–250 (2017)
4. FAIR principles. https://www.go-fair.org/fair-principles/. Accessed 16 June 2021
5. Delpher. https://www.delpher.nl. Accessed 16 June 2021

Mapping STI Ecosystems via Open Data: Overcoming the Limitations of Conflicting Taxonomies. A Case Study for Climate Change Research in Denmark

Nicandro Bovenzi⬤, Nicolau Duran-Silva⬤,
Francesco Alessandro Massucci⁽✉⁾⬤, Francesco Multari⬤,
and Josep Pujol-Llatse

SIRIS Lab, Research Division of SIRIS Academic, 08003 Barcelona, Spain
francesco.massucci@sirisacademic.com
https://sirisacademic.com/

Abstract. Science, Technology and Innovation (STI) decision-makers often need to have a clear vision of *what* is researched and by *whom* to design effective policies. Such a vision is provided by effective and comprehensive mappings of the research activities carried out within their institutional boundaries. A major challenge to be faced in this context is the difficulty in accessing the relevant data and in combining information coming from different sources: indeed, traditionally, STI data has been confined within closed data sources and, when available, it is categorised with different taxonomies. Here, we present a proof-of-concept study of the use of Open Resources to map the research landscape on the Sustainable Development Goal (SDG) 13 – Climate Action, for an entire country, Denmark, and we map it on the 25 ERC panels.

Keywords: Science mapping · Deep Learning · Open data repositories · Sustainable development goals

1 Introduction

To inform their decisions, policy-makers in the Science, Technology and Innovation (STI) sector typically need "maps", either at a territorial or at an institutional level, to understand what is researched and by whom. Generally, those maps need to provide information about the research and innovation topics and about the relevant actors linked to them, so that effective policy-actions could be proposed, by covering the right scientific domains and by being catered for the adequate users. These maps need to be comprehensive to extensively cover *i.* the whole STI value chain (from basic research up to industrial innovation), *ii.* the different scientific domains and *iii.* all possible relevant actors. As such, these

This work was partly funded by the European Commission H2020 Programme via the INODE project, under grant agreement No. 863410.

maps should rely on different data sources that could offer the broadest possible view of STI inputs and outputs. Some major challenges faced at a policy level arise because many of those data sources are not openly available (undermining therefore the participatory processes), they are not interoperable in terms of data classification schemes and institutional identification (therefore limiting transversal analyses) and they are hardly manageable by non-expert users [5].

In this paper, we present a proof of concept of merging different open datasets and of analysing them with a common classification scheme specifically designed for the sake of our analyses. To do so, we gather data for the whole Danish[1] STI ecosystem from 4 different data sources, namely: *i.* the CORDIS database[2], through the UNICS [6] platform, for H2020-funded R&D projects, *ii.* the Kohesio linked-data portal[3] for Regional R&D projects funded by the EC Cohesion initiative, and the *iii.* OpenAlex [9] and *iv.* OpenAIRE [10] repositories for publications and other scientific outputs (these last being accessed through their respective APIs). After gathering these records, we use open knowledge-bases [4] and fine tune openly available Deep Learning models [2,12] to: *i.* **Identify STI documents linked with the Sustainable Goal 13**, Climate Action [4], and *ii.* **Categorise** Danish research on Climate Action **within the 25 panels of the European Research Council** (ERC).

In this way, we aim at showcasing how research in emerging fields (such as the SDGs [13]) can be gathered from open data sources and identified by means of modern, openly available AI models [1]. Finally, we demonstrate how gaps in taxonomic classifications across datasets may be filled by means of Deep Learning textual classifiers, by using the ERC panels as a paradigmatic example.

2   Main Results

We gathered, from a series of heterogeneous data sources, a dataset of scientific publications abstracts and R&D projects descriptions for the entire STI ecosystem of Denmark for the 2014–2019 time period. We then tagged each single record by means of a controlled vocabulary for SDG 13 – Climate Action [4] (that is, we identified the vocabulary terms in each single text by applying a series of textual matching rules). This enabled us to identify, within the initial dataset, all textual records linked with SDG 13.

The number of documents that we could identify in each data source as well as those we could link with SDG 13 are reported in Table 1. About 2% of Scientific publications in Denmark between 2014 and 2019, both from OpenAIRE and

---

[1] We choose Denmark as our case study because (i) it is a medium-size country and the size of its scientific production is such that one can practically retrieve all the documents from publications repositories, (ii) Danish R&D ecosystem is internationally visible and competitive and (iii) Denmark is internationally acknowledged as being one of the leading countries in terms of climate action policies and efforts (1st in the world according to the 2022 Environmental Performance Index (EPI)).

[2] https://cordis.europa.eu/.

[3] https://kohesio.ec.europa.eu/.

OpenAlex, are related to our SDG of interest. In contrast, European projects are more linked, in relative terms, to the issue of Climate Action: this comes as no surprise, given the orientation of EU policies towards the sustainability issues.

Table 1. Number of records with at least one author affiliation or beneficiary from Denmark (2014–2019) and relative volume mapped to SDG 13.

Data source	Total records in DK	Records related to SDG 13
OpenAlex	191,399	3,821 (2%)
OpenAIRE	235,906	5,273 (2.2%)
CORDIS	2,196	320 (14.6%)
Kohesio	294	14 (4.8%)

We finally applied Topic Modelling [7,11] and we classified per ERC panels the SDG-related corpus, in order to obtain both a series of topics characterising Climate Action-related research and to gain a "disciplinary" view of such research. In Fig. 1, we show a t-SNE visualisation of the automatically extracted topics [8] from textual data in publications (from OpenAlex and OpenAIRE) and projects (from CORDIS and Kohesio) concerning SDG 13.

Fig. 1. t-SNE visualisation of the 30 topics extracted from the SDG 13 corpus.

In Fig. 1, each dot is a single document: as one can observe, we were able to extract a series of thematically different topics from the SDG 13 corpus, each dealing with a different aspect of climate action. At the centre of the figure, one finds topics related with the environment, while going anti-clockwise from the top, it is possible to encounter topics related with energy, traditional and alternative fuels, emissions and pollution, impact on the biosphere and finally education and policy issues.

As a final pilot exercise, we proceeded to classify the documents linked to SDG 13 per ERC panels. To do so, we trained a Deep Learning textual classifier by fine-tuning [3,12] the BERT-based SPECTER model [2] on a weakly supervised dataset, and we applied it to our Danish SDG 13 corpus. This effort allowed us to obtain a disciplinary classification of the records which is consistent across data sources and which may enable, in turn, a comparison of the Danish STI ecosystem with other geographical perimeters of interest. In Fig. 2, we present the distribution of documents by source and ERC panel. Perhaps surprisingly, the majority of the STI documents analysed were linked to Social Science issues, followed by Earth Sciences. Also, interestingly (and underscoring the importance of cross-platform analyses such as this one), one can see that the various data sources have a different coverage of the panels.

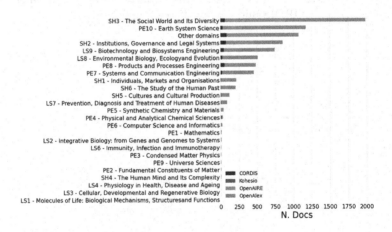

Fig. 2. Number of documents per source and by ERC Panel.

3   Conclusions

In this paper, we presented a proof-of-concept study of the use of Open Resources to map the research landscape on SDG 13 (Climate Action), for an entire country, Denmark. This type of mapping exercise is extremely useful for STI decision-makers, who, to design effective policies within their respective sphere of influence, need to have a clear vision of *what* is researched and by *whom*.

Here, we carried out a study of this sort by relying on Open Data for Research Projects (gathered from CORDIS and the Kohesio platform) and Scientific publications (collected from OpenAIRE and OpenAlex), by using an open vocabulary for mapping STI records on SDG 13 and by using openly available Deep Learning models to classify the corpus in accordance with the 25 ERC panels. The results we obtain are fairly encouraging: the coverage of the data analysed is extensive, both in absolute terms[4] and in terms of scientific disciplines and actors. Interestingly, the data sources analysed offer a complementary view of the research domains, and allow one, when used in combination, to obtain a wide and precise overview of the local STI ecosystem.

References

1. Chesbrough, H.: Open innovation: a new paradigm for understanding industrial innovation. Open Innov. Res. New Paradigm **400**, 1–19 (2006)
2. Cohan, A., Feldman, S., Beltagy, I., Downey, D., Weld, D.S.: Specter: document-level representation learning using citation-informed transformers (2020)
3. Devlin, J., Chang, M.W., Lee, K., Toutanova, K.: BERT: pre-training of deep bidirectional transformers for language understanding. arXiv preprint arXiv:1810.04805 (2018)
4. Duran-Silva, N., Fuster, E., Massucci, F.A., Quinquillà, A.: A controlled vocabulary defining the semantic perimeter of sustainable development goals. Dataset, Zenodo (2019). https://doi.org/10.5281/zenodo.4118028
5. Fuster, E., Massucci, F., Matusiak, M.: Identifying specialisation domains beyond taxonomies: mapping scientific and technological domains of specialisation via semantic analyses. In: Capello, R., Kleibrink, A., Matusiak, M. (eds.) Quantitative Methods for Place-Based Innovation Policy, pp. 195–234, January 2020. https://doi.org/10.4337/9781789905519
6. Gimenez, X., Mosca, A., Roda, F., Rondelli, B., Rull, G.: UNiCS: the open data platform for research and innovation. In: SEMANTiCS Posters & Demos (2018)
7. Griffiths, T.L., Steyvers, M.: Finding scientific topics. Proc. Natl. Acad. Sci. **101**(suppl 1), 5228–5235 (2004)
8. Van der Maaten, L., Hinton, G.: Visualizing data using t-SNE. J. Mach. Learn. Res. **9**(11), 2579–2605 (2008)
9. Priem, J., Piwowar, H., Orr, R.: OpenAlex: a fully-open index of scholarly works, authors, venues, institutions, and concepts (2022). https://doi.org/10.48550/ARXIV.2205.01833. https://arxiv.org/abs/2205.01833
10. Rettberg, N., Schmidt, B.: OpenAIRE-building a collaborative open access infrastructure for European researchers. Liber Q. J. Eur. Res. Libr. **22**(3), 160–175 (2012)
11. Sangaraju, V.R., Bolla, B.K., Nayak, D.K., Kh, J.: Topic modelling on Consumer Financial Protection Bureau data: an approach using BERT based embeddings (2022)
12. Sun, C., Qiu, X., Xu, Y., Huang, X.: How to fine-tune BERT for text classification? In: CCL (2019)
13. UN: Global indicator framework for the sustainable development goals and targets of the 2030 agenda for sustainable development (2017). https://unstats.un.org/sdgs/indicators/indicators-list/

---

[4] We made an overall comparison with results produced by Scopus: the number of records was much lower than what found both in OpenAIRE and OpenAlex, for the same country and time period.

BetterPR: A Dataset for Estimating the Constructiveness of Peer Review Comments

Prabhat Kumar Bharti[1]([✉]), Tirthankar Ghosal[2], Mayank Agarwal[1], and Asif Ekbal[1]

[1] Department of Computer Science and Engineering, Indian Institute of Technology Patna, Patna, India
{prabhat_1921cs32,mayank265,asif}@iitp.ac.in
[2] Faculty of Mathematics and Physics, Institute of Formal and Applied Linguistics, Charles University, Staré Město, Czech Republic
ghosal@ufal.mff.cuni.cz

Abstract. Review comments play an important role in the improvement of scientific articles. There are typically many rounds of review-revision before the different reviewers with varying backgrounds arrive at a consensus on a submission. However, not always the reviews are helpful. Sometimes the reviewers are unnecessarily critical of the work without justifying their comments. Peer reviews are always meant to be critical yet constructive feedback on the scientific merit of a submitted article. However, with the rising number of paper submissions leading to the involvement of novice or less experienced reviewers in the reviewing process, the reviewers tend to spend less expert time on their voluntary reviewing job. This results in lackluster reviews where the authors do not have many takeaways from their reviews. The entire scientific enterprise is heavily dependent on this very human peer-review process. In this paper, we make an attempt to automatically distinguish between *constructive* and *non-constructive* peer reviews. We deem constructive comment to be the one that, despite being critical, is polite and provides feedback to the authors to improve their submissions. To this end, we present *BetterPR*, a manually annotated dataset to estimate the constructiveness of peer review comments. Further, we benchmark *BetterPR* with standard baselines and analyze their performance. We collect the peer reviews from open access forums and design an annotation scheme to label whether a review comment is *constructive* or *non-constructive*. We provide our dataset and codes (https://github.com/PrabhatkrBharti/BetterPR.git) for further exploration by the community.

Keywords: Peer reviews · Review constructiveness · Peer review quality

© Springer Nature Switzerland AG 2022
G. Silvello et al. (Eds.): TPDL 2022, LNCS 13541, pp. 500–505, 2022.
https://doi.org/10.1007/978-3-031-16802-4_53

1   Introduction

Peer review is meant to provide journals and conferences with high-quality science by evaluating manuscripts and making suggestions for improvement. Peer reviews were designed centuries ago [1,3,25] so that scientists can receive critical feedback from their colleagues, a science gets vetted and subsequently improved. Finally, the best of the investigations gets disseminated to the community. However, it is expected that peer reviewers maintain collegiality in their communications with the authors and provide critical yet helpful feedback so that the feedback narrative always appears constructive with the larger goal of improving science. Unfortunately, such is not the case always [4,5,9,10,17,23]. A certain study of over 1106 scientists from 46 countries and 14 disciplines [26] found that despite the anonymity promise, over half of the respondents reported receiving at least one "unprofessional" comment. The study defined a personal attack on a scientist as one that does not provide constructive criticism or is unnecessarily harsh. By constructive comments, we mean those review comments where the reviewer highlights a deficiency in the work under scrutiny in a suggestive tone or respectfully asks questions. Also, a key task for authors is to clearly understand the review comments and determine which comments require action or response and which do not. Hence, an automated mechanism to classify review comments according to the need for further actions would help authors to comprehend the review well. It would also help the reviewers to craft better and constructive reviews. With this goal in mind, we present a dataset of 1496 manually annotated review comments from three independent sources: https://shitmyreviewerssay. tumblr.com, open review platform https://openreview.net and certain other open-access interdisciplinary sources [2,16–18,26]. Our downstream task description is simple: *Given a peer review comment, can we automatically determine whether the review comment is constructive or not?* We envisage our proposed dataset *BetterPR* would propel research to answer this question. Some relevant works on NLP/ML for peer reviews are worthy exploring in this regard [6–8,11–15,19–22,27].

2   Data Procurement and Description

We crawl the peer review comments from: shitmyreviewerssay[1], open review platform[2], and certain other open-access interdisciplinary sources [2,16–18,26]. We focus on negative peer review comments from the data sources mentioned earlier. We store the review comments in plain text and manually annotate the review comments with only two labels: constructive (criticism with feedback) and non-constructive (criticism without feedback) (Table 1).

---

[1] http://shitmyreviewerssay.tumblr.com.
[2] https://openreview.net.

Table 1. Statistics of the proposed *BetterPR* dataset

# No. of total annotated review comments	1496
# No. of constructive comments	749
#No. of non-constructive comments	747
Average length of constructive comments (in terms of words)	21.2109
Average length of non-constructive comments (in terms of words)	17.7207

2.1 Annotation Labels and Guidelines

Table 2 presents our annotation label definitions with examples. The task of our annotators was to read the review comments (sentences) and select a label for each comment. When a review comment does not address a specific label, we leave out the comment. The first two authors in this paper (who are very familiar with the peer review process) performed the annotations and the interrater agreement using Cohen's Kappa [24] turned out to be 0.93, indicating substantial agreement.

Table 2. Annotation Guidelines

Label	Label description	Example
Constructive	A review is constructive if it contributes to the author's work by referencing the paper briefly and indicating the direction the author is taking the paper. Moreover, the review provides direct or indirect feedback regarding possible areas for improvement	*The paper could be considered for acceptance given a rewrite of the paper and a change in the title and abstract*
Non-constructive	Reviews are non-constructive if they criticize a paper without providing any explanation or improvement that needs to be made to improve it. The review does not mention directly or indirectly which part of the paper requires improvement	*I am personally offended that the authors believed that this study had a reasonable chance of being accepted to a serious scientific journal*

3 Experiments

We train binary classifiers to classify constructive and non-constructive review comments. We use hand-crafted feature-based learning instead of neural models because they are easier to interpret and also since our dataset's current size is not adequate to train a deep neural model. We use a set of fifteen features which include TF-IDF (term frequency-inverse document frequency), word count, sentiment features, PoS (Part of Speech), i.e., nouns, adjectives, verbs, and adverbs for constructive and non-constructive comments, and ToxicBERT[3], which gives the harshness of a review comment as scores of six features: toxicity, severe toxicity, obscene, threat, insult and identity attack. Kindly refer to our Github repository for definition and implementation of our full feature set. We use 80% of the data for training and the remaining 20% for evaluation. We implement all the machine learning models using the scikitlearn[4] package. We use different regularization parameters for our classifiers: Support Vector Classifier (SVC), Naive Bayes, and XGBoost (please refer to our Github repository). Finally we report our results on five-fold cross validation (see Table 3). We see XGBoost as the best-performing classifier in our case. We reserve the analysis of our baseline model performance and impact of the different features as a future empirical work.

Table 3. Performance of the classification algorithms on the *BetterPR* dataset with Precision, Recall, Accuracy, and F1-score as metrics.

Model type	Accuracy	Precision	Recall	F1 score
SVC	0.710	0.727	0.683	0.696
Naive Bayes	0.714	0.676	0.801	0.721
XGBoost	0.737	0.715	0.754	0.736

4   Conclusion

In this *Acceleration Innovation Paper*, we introduce *BetterPR*, a dataset to study constructiveness of peer review comments. We also provide baseline experiments to identify if a *peer review comment was constructive or not*. In future work, we would like to expand on this dataset and introduce more fine-grained labels while also studying the linguistic phenomena associated with the downstream task. We would further like to study if the reviewers' backgrounds play a role in the associated task. We envisage that further research would help build a review-moderation tool that would help reviewers and chairs (with varied backgrounds and cultures) write high-quality constructive peer reviews.

Acknowledgement. Prabhat Kumar Bharti acknowledges the Quality Improvement Programme, an initiative of the All India Council for Technical Education (AICTE), Government of India, for fellowship support. Asif Ekbal received the Visvesvaraya Young Faculty Award and extended his thanks to the Digital India Corporation,

---

[3] https://huggingface.co/unitary/toxic-bert.
[4] https://scikit-learn.org/stable/.

Ministry of Electronics and Information Technology, Government of India. Finally, Tirthankar Ghosal acknowledges and extends his thanks to Cactus Communications, India, for funding him in this research.

References

1. A brief history of peer review. https://blog.f1000.com/2020/01/31/a-brief-history-of-peer-review/. Accessed 15 Jul 2022
2. Don't be reviewer 2 Reflections on writing effective peer review comments. https://www.ncbi.nlm.nih.gov/pmc/articles/PMC8505560/ (2022). Accessed 18 Jul 2022
3. Peer Review & #x2013; A Historical Perspective. https://mitcommlab.mit.edu/broad/commkit/peer-review-a-historical-perspective/ (2022). Accessed 29 May 2022
4. This paper is absolutely ridiculous. https://www.humanities.hk/news/this-paper-is-absolutely-ridiculous-ken-hyland (2022). Accessed 15 Jul 2022
5. Beaumont, L.J.: Peer reviewers need a code of conduct too. Nature **572**(7769), 439–440 (2019)
6. Bharti, P.K., Ghosal, T., Agrawal, M., Ekbal, A.: How confident was your reviewer? estimating reviewer confidence from peer review texts. In: Uchida, S., Barney, E., Eglin, V. (eds.) Document Analysis Systems, pp. 126–139. Springer International Publishing, Cham (2022)
7. Bharti, P.K., Kumar, A., Ghosal, T., Agrawal, M., Ekbal, A.: Can a machine generate a meta-review? how far are we? In: Text, Speech, and Dialogue (TSD). Springer International Publishing, Cham (2022)
8. Bharti, P.K., Ranjan, S., Ghosal, T., Agrawal, M., Ekbal, A.: PEERAssist: leveraging on paper-review interactions to predict peer review decisions. In: Ke, H.-R., Lee, C.S., Sugiyama, K. (eds.) ICADL 2021. LNCS, vol. 13133, pp. 421–435. Springer, Cham (2021). https://doi.org/10.1007/978-3-030-91669-5_33
9. Coniam, D.: Exploring reviewer reactions to manuscripts submitted to academic journals. System **40**(4), 544–553 (2012)
10. Gerwing, T.G., Gerwing, A.M.A., Avery-Gomm, S., Choi, C.Y., Clements, J.C., Rash, J.A.: Quantifying professionalism in peer review. Res. Integrity Peer Rev. **5**(1), 1–8 (2020)
11. Ghosal, T.: Exploring the implications of artificial intelligence in various aspects of scholarly peer review. Bull. IEEE Tech. Comm. Digit. Libr. 15 (2019)
12. Ghosal, T., Kumar, S., Bharti, P.K., Ekbal, A.: Peer review analyze: A novel benchmark resource for computational analysis of peer reviews. PLoS ONE **17**(1), e0259238 (2022). https://doi.org/10.1371/journal.pone.0259238
13. Ghosal, T., Varanasi, K.K., Kordoni, V.: Hedgepeer: A dataset for uncertainty detection in peer reviews. In: Proceedings of the 22nd ACM/IEEE Joint Conference on Digital Libraries. JCDL 2022, Association for Computing Machinery, New York, NY, USA (2022). https://doi.org/10.1145/3529372.3533300
14. Ghosal, T., Verma, R., Ekbal, A., Bhattacharyya, P.: DeepSentiPeer: harnessing sentiment in review texts to recommend peer review decisions. In: Proceedings of the 57th Annual Meeting of the Association for Computational Linguistics, pp. 1120–1130 (2019)
15. Ghosal, T., Verma, R., Ekbal, A., Bhattacharyya, P.: A sentiment augmented deep architecture to predict peer review outcomes. In: 2019 ACM/IEEE Joint Conference on Digital Libraries (JCDL), pp. 414–415 (2019). https://doi.org/10.1109/JCDL.2019.00096

16. Gross, D.: The Best Worst Reviewer Comments - MedSci Communications. https://medscicommunications.com/2020/09/30/the-best-worst-reviewer-comments/ (2022). Accessed 18 Jul 2022
17. Hyland, K., Jiang, F.K.: This work is antithetical to the spirit of research: an anatomy of harsh peer reviews. J. Engl. Acad. Purp. **46** (2020)
18. Kostoulas, A.: Peer review: the good, the bad and the ugly. https://achillea skostoulas.com/2018/05/01/peer-review-the-good-the-bad-and-the-ugly/ (2022). Accessed 18 Jul 2022
19. Kumar, A., Ghosal, T., Bhattacharjee, S., Ekbal, A.: Investigations on meta review generation from peer review texts leveraging relevant sub-tasks in the peer review pipeline. In: Silvello, G., et al. (eds.) TPDL 2022. LNCS, vol. 13541, pp. xx–yy. Springer, Cham (2022)
20. Kumar, A., Ghosal, T., Ekbal, A.: A deep neural architecture for decision-aware meta-review generation. In: 2021 ACM/IEEE Joint Conference on Digital Libraries (JCDL), pp. 222–225. IEEE (2021)
21. Kumar, S., Arora, H., Ghosal, T., Ekbal, A.: DeepASPeer: towards an aspect-level sentiment controllable framework for decision prediction from academic peer reviews. In: Proceedings of the 22nd ACM/IEEE Joint Conference on Digital Libraries. JCDL 2022, Association for Computing Machinery, New York, NY, USA (2022). https://doi.org/10.1145/3529372.3530937. https://doi.org/10.1145/3529372.3530937
22. Kumar, S., Ghosal, T., Bharti, P.K., Ekbal, A.: Sharing is caring! joint multitask learning helps aspect-category extraction and sentiment detection in scientific peer reviews. In: 2021 ACM/IEEE Joint Conference on Digital Libraries (JCDL), pp. 270–273 (2021). https://doi.org/10.1109/JCDL52503.2021.00081
23. Mavrogenis, A.F., Quaile, A., Scarlat, M.M.: The good, the bad and the rude peer-review. Int. Orthop. **44**(3), 413–415 (2020). https://doi.org/10.1007/s00264-020-04504-1
24. McHugh, M.L.: Interrater reliability: the kappa statistic. Biochemia medica **22**(3), 276–282 (2012)
25. Shema, H.: The birth of modern peer review. https://blogs.scientificamerican.com/information-culture/the-birth-of-modern-peer-review/ (2022). Accessed 15 Jul 2022
26. Silbiger, N.J., Stubler, A.D.: Unprofessional peer reviews disproportionately harm underrepresented groups in STEM. PeerJ **7**, e8247 (2019)
27. Verma, R., Shinde, K., Arora, H., Ghosal, T.: Attend to your review: a deep neural network to extract aspects from peer reviews. In: Mantoro, T., Lee, M., Ayu, M.A., Wong, K.W., Hidayanto, A.N. (eds.) Neural Information Processing, pp. 761–768. Springer, Cham (2021)

BookSampo Fiction Literature Knowledge Graph Revisited: Building a Faceted Search Interface with Seamlessly Integrated Data-Analytic Tools

Eero Hyvönen[1,2(✉)], Annastiina Ahola[1], and Esko Ikkala[1]

[1] Semantic Computing Research Group (SeCo), Aalto University, Espoo, Finland
{eero.hyvonen,annastiina.ahola,esko.ikkala}@aalto.fi
[2] Helsinki Centre for Digital Humanities (HELDIG), University of Helsinki, Helsinki, Finland
https://seco.cs.aalto.fi

Abstract. *BookSampo – Finnish Fiction Literature on the Semantic Web* is a Linked Data (LD) service and portal deployed in 2011 by the Public Libraries of Finland with nearly 2 million annual users. However, BookSampo's user interface (UI) on top of the underlying knowledge graph (KG) in a SPARQL endpoint has been created using traditional search and data exploration methods, and the full potential of the KG—8.74 million triples today—has not been fully utilized: the data, covers all Finnish fiction literature and beyond and is interesting from a Digital Humanities (DH) research perspective, too. This paper presents first results in creating a new BookSampo UI using faceted semantic search with data-analytic tools for Digital Humanities (DH) research, based on the Sampo Model and Sampo-UI framework.

Keywords: Semantic web · Digital libraries · Linked data · User interfaces · Portals

1 BookSampo Data and Portal: From Research to Practice

BookSampo[1] [11,14] provides information on virtually all fiction literature published in Finland since mid 19th century. Its contents are based on rich semantic descriptions of books and theirs contexts using Linked Data (LD) that originates from multiple heterogeneous data sources. BookSampo is an application instance of the more general "Sampo Model"[2] for LD publishing and series of semantic

---

[1] Portal: http://kirjasampo.fi; research homepage: https://seco.cs.aalto.fi/applications/kirjasampo/.

[2] The model is called "Sampo" according to the Finnish epic Kalevala, where Sampo is a mythical machine giving riches and fortune to its holder, a kind of ancient metaphor of technology according to the most common interpretation of the concept.

© Springer Nature Switzerland AG 2022
G. Silvello et al. (Eds.): TPDL 2022, LNCS 13541, pp. 506–511, 2022.
https://doi.org/10.1007/978-3-031-16802-4_54

portals in use[3] in Finland and beyond [7]. The original Drupal-based UI in use since 2011 provides traditional text search engines for finding records and then related contents as links for data exploration. However, the full potential of the LD for searching, exploring, and for data analytic research has not been used as in other later Sampo systems. This paper presents a case study on developing a semantic UI for BookSampo, based on faceted search and seamlessly integrated data analytic tools, using the Sampo model [7] and Sampo-UI framework[4] [8].

2   Sampo-UI Interface for BookSampo Knowledge Graph

A key idea of Sampo-UI-based UIs is to "standardize" the UI logic so that the portals are easier to us in versatile ways: 1) Different thematic *application perspectives* are provided on the landing page of the Sampo portal by re-using the data service. 2) The perspectives are used by a two-step cycle for research: First the focus of interest, the target group, is filtered out using faceted semantic search [4,15,16]. Second, the target group is visualized or analyzed by using ready-to-use data analytic tools of the application perspectives. The Sampo model and Sampo-UI framework aim not only at data publishing with search and data exploration [12] but also to data analysis and knowledge discovery with seamlessly integrated tooling for finding, analysing, and even solving research problems in interactive ways using methods of Artificial Intelligence [6].

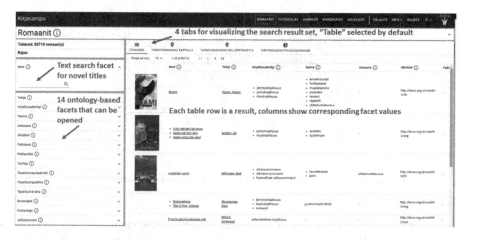

Fig. 1. Application perspective for searching, visualizing, and analyzing novels

---

[3] See https://seco.cs.aalto.fi/applications/sampo/ for Sampos, links, videos, and publications.

[4] Available at Github: https://github.com/SemanticComputing/sampo-ui.

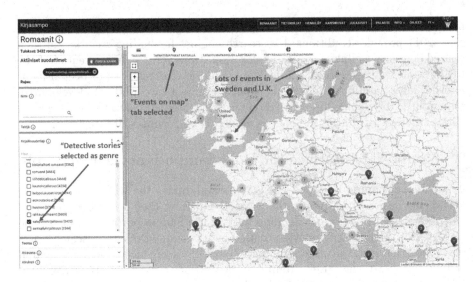

Fig. 2. Detective stories on a map. By clicking a place marker, related novels are found.

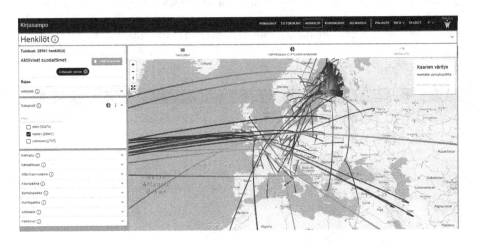

Fig. 3. Migrations of female authors visualized as clickable arcs.

In our case, the UI consists of a landing page with five thematic perspectives for searching and analyzing instances of 1) Novels (807 18 pcs), 2) Nonfiction books (1956), 3) Persons (622 07), 4) Book covers (112 971), and 5) Different manifestations of the books (213 877). Each application perspective includes three parts, as illustrated in Fig. 1 for the Novels application perspective: 1) A faceted search engine on the left, based on the annotation ontologies of the KG; here 15 facets are used: Book title text search, Authors, Genres, Themes, Keywords, Original languages, Prizes, Main persons, Actors, Narrative environments, Places, Times, Number of pages, Publishers, Years of publishing. 2) A paginated results table view on the right, where the search results are shown by default as table rows with facet values as columns. 3) Tabs on the top of the search results for other data-analytic views and visualizations of the results.

In the Novels view there are 4 visualizations: Table of results (default), Events on map, Heat map of places, and Pie charts for data-analysis. In Fig. 2 the user has filtered "detectives stories" using the Genre facet and selected the tab "Events on map". Clicking on a result lets the user to see and navigate the "homepage" of the result instance that aggregates all data, images, and links, both internal and external, regarding the instance. Also instance pages have a set of tabs to be used for data-analytic views of the instances and for data export. The same UI logic is used in the other perspectives, too. For example, in Fig. 3 female authors were selected in the Persons perspective and their migrations from the place of birth (blue end of an arrow) to the place death (red end of an arrow) is visualized. By clicking on an arrow, the homepages of the corresponding persons are found, such as Doris Lessing based on the arrow from Iran to London.

3   Contributions and Related Works

Contributions. The novelty of the BookSampo UI demonstrator lays in the seamless integration of data-analytic tooling for DH research with faceted semantic search and browsing, and the semantic richness of the underlying KG. Our case study suggests that configuring the existing Sampo-UI search components, including the data-analytic tools in application perspective tabs and for visualizations on the instance homepages, is easys: the first version of the demonstrator could be shown to the librarians in two weeks, created by a developer not familiar with the Sampo-UI framework before.

A challenge in using the data for research is that using structured linked data requires new kind data literacy [9] and source criticism[5] from the end user. In many cases, the underlying real world may be too complex to be modelled fully. For example, the place ontology covers centuries of places that change in time; in our case Finland was part of Sweden until 1809, then part of Russia until independent in 1917, and after that some parts of her were annexed to the Soviet Union that became later the modern Russia. What the data means is not always clear and issues of Big Data quality, such as incompleteness, veracity, skewness, uncertainty, fuzziness, and errors of data arise.

Related Work. Linked Data and ontologies have been used in libraries [3], museums and archives [2,17]. [2]. Using LD is advocated by major library organizations, such as IFLA[6] and OCLC[7], and several libraries provide their collec-

---

[5] https://ranke2.uni.lu/define-dsc/#%20,%20Universit%C3%A9%20du %20Luxembourg.

[6] https://www.ifla.org/references/best-practice-for-national-bibliographic-agencies-in-a-digital-age/service-delivery/linked-open-data/.

[7] https://www.oclc.org/research/areas/data-science/linkeddata/linked-data-overview.html.

tions as data in this form [13]. LD has been used in building infrastructures, such as ARIADNEplus[8] for archaeology, Linked Art[9] in the U.S., and in local efforts in Italy [1], the U.K. [10], and Finland [5] to list a few examples. Cultural Heritage and DH have become a major application domain for LD technologies [18]. However, there has been less research on how to use the LD through intelligent UIs [7].

Acknowledgements. Thanks to Matti Sarmela, Kaisa Hypén, and Tuomas Aitonurmi for providing the new version of BookSampo KG and for research collaborations. Our work is related to the EU project InTaVia (https://intavia.eu). CSC – IT Center for Science, Finland, provided computational resources.

References

1. Carriero, V.A., et al.: ArCo: the Italian cultural heritage knowledge graph. In: Ghidini, C., et al. (eds.) ISWC 2019. LNCS, vol. 11779, pp. 36–52. Springer, Cham (2019). https://doi.org/10.1007/978-3-030-30796-7_3
2. Hallo, M., Luján-Mora, S., Maté, A., Trujillo, J.: Current state of linked data in digital libraries. J. Inf. Sci. **42**(2), 117–127 (2016). https://doi.org/10.1177/0165551515594729
3. Haslhofer, B., Isaac, A., Simon, R.: Knowledge graphs in the libraries and digital humanities domain. arXiv preprint arXiv:1803.03198 (2018)
4. Hyvönen, E., Saarela, S., Viljanen, K.: Application of ontology techniques to view-based semantic search and browsing. In: Bussler, C.J., Davies, J., Fensel, D., Studer, R. (eds.) ESWS 2004. LNCS, vol. 3053, pp. 92–106. Springer, Heidelberg (2004). https://doi.org/10.1007/978-3-540-25956-5_7
5. Hyvönen, E., Viljanen, K., Tuominen, J., Seppälä, K.: Building a national semantic web ontology and ontology service infrastructure –the FinnONTO approach. In: Bechhofer, S., Hauswirth, M., Hoffmann, J., Koubarakis, M. (eds.) ESWC 2008. LNCS, vol. 5021, pp. 95–109. Springer, Heidelberg (2008). https://doi.org/10.1007/978-3-540-68234-9_10
6. Hyvönen, E.: Using the semantic web in digital humanities: shift from data publishing to data-analysis and serendipitous knowledge discovery. Semant. Web - Interoperability, Usability, Applicability **11**(1), 187–193 (2020)
7. Hyvönen, E.: Digital humanities on the semantic web: Sampo model and portal series. Semantic Web - Interoperability, Usability, Applicability (2022). http://semantic-web-journal.org/content/digital-humanities-semantic-web-sampo-model-and-portal-series. Accepted
8. Ikkala, E., Hyvönen, E., Rantala, H., Koho, M.: Sampo-UI: a full stack javascript framework for developing semantic portal user interfaces. Semant. Web - Interoperability, Usability, Applicability **13**(1), 69–84 (2022). https://doi.org/10.3233/SW-210428
9. Koltay, T.: Data literacy for researchers and data librarians. J. Librariansh. Inf. Sci. **49**(1), 3–14 (2015). https://doi.org/10.1177/0961000615616450
10. Lei, Y., Lopez, V., Motta, E., Uren, V.: An infrastructure for semantic web portals. J. Web Eng. **6**(4), 283–308 (2007). https://journals.riverpublishers.com/index.php/JWE/article/view/4105

---

[8] https://ariadne-infrastructure.eu/.
[9] https://linked.art/.

11. Mäkelä, E., Hypén, K., Hyvönen, E.: BookSampo—lessons learned in creating a semantic portal for fiction literature. In: Aroyo, L., et al. (eds.) ISWC 2011. LNCS, vol. 7032, pp. 173–188. Springer, Heidelberg (2011). https://doi.org/10.1007/978-3-642-25093-4_12

12. Marchionini, G.: Exploratory search: from finding to understanding. Commun. ACM **49**(4), 41–46 (2006). https://doi.org/10.1145/1121949.1121979

13. Mitchell, E.T.: Library Linked Data: Early Activity and Development. ALA TechSource Chicago, IL (2016)

14. Mäkelä, E., Hypön, K., Hyvénen, E.: Fiction literature as linked open data - the BookSampo dataset (2013). https://doi.org/10.3233/SW-120093

15. Tunkelang, D.: Faceted search. Morgan & Claypool Publishers, CA (2009)

16. Tzitzikas, Y., Manolis, N., Papadakos, P.: Faceted exploration of RDF/S datasets: a survey. J. Intell. Inf. Syst. **48**(2), 329–364 (2016). https://doi.org/10.1007/s10844-016-0413-8

17. Van Hooland, S., Verborgh, R.: Linked Data for Libraries, Archives and Museums: How to Clean, Link and Publish Your Metadata. Facet Publishing, London (2014). https://doi.org/10.1080/00048623.2016.1162277

18. Zeng, M., Sula, C., Gracy, K., Hyvönen, E., Lima, V.M.A.: JASIST special issue on digital humanities (DH). J. Assoc. Inf. Sci. Technol. (JASIST) **73**, 1–5 (2021). https://doi.org/10.1002/asi.24584

Solutions for Data Sharing and Storage: A Comparative Analysis of Data Repositories

Joana Rodrigues[1,2]([⊠]) [iD] and Carla Teixeira Lopes[1,2] [iD]

[1] INESC TEC, Rua Dr. Roberto Frias, 4200-465 Porto, Portugal
`jsrodrigues@fe.up.pt`
[2] Faculty of Engineering, University of Porto,
Rua Dr. Roberto Frias, 4200-465 Porto, Portugal
`ctl@fe.up.pt`

Abstract. Research data management is an essential process in scientific research activities. It includes monitoring data from the moment it is created until it is deposited in a repository so that later it can be accessed and reused by others. Sharing and reuse are the last steps in this process. It is essential to ensure that the data stored in digital repositories is well preserved in the long term and that its adequate interpretation and future reuse is guaranteed. Following this debate, questions arise related to the interoperability of systems and the suitability of platforms. In this study, we study how data management platforms can solve the problems associated with description, preservation, and access in digital media, making their usefulness evident. We identify some of the most relevant repository platforms in the scope of research data management, offering the scientific community an aggregating view of the various solutions and their main characteristics, thus aiming at a better understanding of them for their appropriate choice.

Keywords: Research data management · Data repositories · Sharing

1 Contextualization

Currently, the number of articles and datasets produced in science is increasing [1]. Allied to this, we see a growing awareness of the importance of producing research data. This fact motivated the publication and sharing of data to gain a greater importance for researchers who want to see their data properly organized, stored, and described, in order to promote their sharing, reuse, and citation. The management of these resources has become a concern for researchers and research institutions. A proper data management contributes to the reproducibility of science, the reduction of duplicate efforts in data production, and the possibility of comparing results with those of peers [4,6].

© Springer Nature Switzerland AG 2022
G. Silvello et al. (Eds.): TPDL 2022, LNCS 13541, pp. 512–517, 2022.
https://doi.org/10.1007/978-3-031-16802-4_55

Research data management can be seen as a set of policies and activities, which accompany the entire life cycle of data and which aim to ensure that they fulfill their role in the context of the research activity and, in particular, that they are preserved [1]. One of the main results of this practice is that researchers use platforms to manage their data, share them with the entire research community, and contribute to their preservation over time [1,3]. The diversity of platforms available makes it difficult to choose, as it becomes more complicated to choose the one that specifically meets identified needs. Some of the obstacles are in defining metadata for description and long-term preservation [1].

The abrupt growth of data production is one of the reasons that promote repository platforms to implement functionalities to describe the datasets that are deposited on them [2]. The various stakeholders in this process, whether research institutions, individual researchers, or curators, contribute to the description of the data produced. In this context, the role of curators is intrinsically linked to maintaining the accessibility, quality, and integrity of data over time [1]. Thus, the description that researchers make of their data, combined with the metadata of the datasets themselves, creates the necessary conditions for their future reuse and citation by other researchers. The support of protocols such as OAI-PMH (Open Archives Initiative Protocol for Metadata Harvesting) for retrieving metadata from different sources and creating an interface for displaying indexed resources makes the dissemination of data more effective [5].

2   Repository Analysis

The selection of platforms took into account their relevance in the context in question, recognizing their influence and usefulness in the context of research data management. Based on the Registry of Open Access Repositories (ROAR)[1] statistics, eight software solutions were selected, but this was not the only choice criterion. Priority was given to platforms that support interoperability features and also support repositories of research and government institutions. Issues associated with the description of datasets or the definition of metadata were also taken into account. Thus, the following platforms were considered: CKAN, Dataverse, DSpace, ePrints, EUDAT, Figshare, Zenodo, and Islandora.

We analyze each of the platforms according to six analysis criteria. These criteria were derived from the documentation of the platforms and the experimentation of demo instances. They are divided into six categories whose structure is inspired by the Open Archival Information System (OAIS) model [7] and can be seen in the next subsections.

2.1   Infrastructure

Basic attributes that support the functioning of the platforms (Table 1).

---

[1] http://roar.eprints.org/view/software/.

Table 1. Comparison of platforms for the infrastructure component

	Infrastructure			
	Open source	Storage	Installation	Payment system
CKAN	√	Local or remote	Installation	x
Dataverse	√	Local or remote	Installation or service	x
DSpace	√	Local or remote	Installation or service	x
ePrints	√	Local or remote	Installation or service	x
EUDAT	√	Remote	Service	x
Figshare	x	Remote	Service	x
Zenodo	√	Remote	Service	x
Islandora	√	Local or remote	Installation	x

2.2   Ingestion

Integration and interoperability within the platform itself or with other systems (Table 2).

Table 2. Comparison of platforms for the ingestion component

	Ingestion		
	Interoperability	API of deposit of data	Automatic import of metadata from files
CKAN	OAI-PMH	SWORD	x
Dataverse	OAI-PMH	SWORD	√
DSpace	OAI-PMH	SWORD	√
ePrints	OAI-PMH	x	√
EUDAT	OAI-PMH	SWORD	√
Figshare	OAI-PMH	SWORD	√
Zenodo	OAI-PMH, REST	SWORD	√
Islandora	OAI-PMH	SWORD	√

2.3   Content Organization and Control

Structuring of content and its control within each platform (Table 3).

Table 3. Comparison for the content organization and control component

	Content organization and control					
	Organization of contents	Access granularity	User profile	Authentication	Support of attached documents	Embargo
CKAN	Linear	Grups	✓	✓	✓	✓
Dataverse	Hierarchical	File, User	✓	✓	✓	✓
DSpace	Hierarchical	Groups	✓	✓	✓	✓
ePrints	Hierarchical and linear	User	✓	✓	✓	✓
EUDAT	Linear	User	✓	✓	✓	✓
Figshare	Linear	Institution, Publisher, Researcher	✓	✓	-	✓
Zenodo	Hierarchical	User	✓	✓	✓	✓
Islandora	Hierarchical	User	✓	✓	✓	✓

	Content organization and control					
	Volume and size	Eligibility of depositor	Language	Data maturity	Deposit elimination	Licensing
CKAN	-	All allowed	All allowed	Any state	✓	✓
Dataverse	database: 3 GB, files: 3 GB, records: 1 GB	All allowed	All allowed	Any state	✓	✓
DSpace	-	All allowed	All allowed	Any state	✓	✓
ePrints	-	All allowed	All allowed	Any state	✓	✓
EUDAT	max 20 GB per record, max 10 GB per file	All allowed	All allowed	Any state	✓	✓
Figshare	max 20 GB per record	All allowed	All allowed	Any state	✓	✓
Zenodo	max 50 GB per record	All allowed	All allowed	Any state	✓	✓
Islandora	-	All allowed	All allowed	Any state	✓	✓

2.4 Metadata

Data description and the ways in which it takes place on different platforms (Table 4).

Table 4. Comparison for the metadata component

	Metadata			
	Schema/standard/ model flexibility	Schema export	Validation	License registration
CKAN	✓	x	x	✓
Dataverse	x	DDI, DC	✓	✓
DSpace	✓	QDR, MARC, MODS	✓	✓
ePrints	x	-	✓	✓
EUDAT	✓	DC, MARC, MARCXML	✓	✓
Figshare	x	DC	x	✓
Zenodo	✓	DC, MARC, MARCXML	✓	✓
Islandora	✓	DC, DDI, MODS, METS	✓	✓

DDI: Data Documentation Initiative; DC: Dublin Core; QDR: Qualification Dataset Register; MARC: Machine-Readable Cataloging; MARCXML: Machine-Readable Cataloging XML; MODS: Metadata Object Description Schema; METS: Metadata Encoding and Transmission Standard

2.5 User Interface

Interaction between the user and the software (Table 5).

Table 5. Comparison for the user interface of component

	User interface	
	Customization of design	Design for mobile
CKAN	√	√
Dataverse	√	√
DSpace	√	√
ePrints	√	-
EUDAT	x	-
Figshare	-	-
Zenodo	√	-
Islandora	√	√

2.6 Articulation with Other Services

Possibility of platforms embedding in themselves raw data analysis functionalities, through additional plug-ins (Table 6).

Table 6. Comparison for the articulation with other services component

	Articulation with other services				
	Media viewing and reproduction	Tabular data graph	Georeferenced data analysis	Diverse data types	Data access via API
CKAN	-	√	√	√	-
Dataverse	-	√	√	√	√
DSpace	x	-	√	√	x
ePrints	√	-	-	√	√
EUDAT	√	√	√	√	√
Figshare	√	√	-	√	√
Zenodo	-	√	-	√	√
Islandora	√	√	√	√	√

3   Conclusion and Future Work

The analysis of the repositories proved that the selection of a platform for data management can be a difficult task, as it is necessary to assess the concrete needs in each situation. An important aspect to focus on is the fact that repositories tend to be increasingly prepared to be in line with data interoperability and accessibility guidelines. Of course, data sharing is one of the goals of data repositories, however, it is necessary to ensure that, when accessed, the data are properly interpreted, as this will guarantee their reproducibility. Data reused by third parties guarantee credit to authors, through citations and references.

It is important to emphasize that repositories are not mere guardians of data. The competent description needs to be promoted through varied metadata models and domain-specific vocabularies. It is necessary to guarantee different conditions of access, such as full access to data or only access to metadata, but with the safeguard of the possibility of contacting the authors. Authors must be safeguarded by associating a DOI (Digital Object Identifier) to the data while facilitating the citation and reuse process. There are several challenges, however, the advantages will outweigh all efforts.

Acknowledgements. Joana Rodrigues is supported by research grant from FCT - Fundação para a Ciência e Tecnologia: PD/BD/150288/2019.

References

1. Amorim, R.C., Castro, J.A., Rocha da Silva, J., Ribeiro, C.: A comparison of research data management platforms: architecture, flexible metadata and interoperability. Univ. Access Inf. Soc. **16**(4), 851–862 (2016). https://doi.org/10.1007/s10209-016-0475-y
2. Armbruster, C., Romary, L.: Comparing repository types: challenges and barriers for subject-based repositories, research repositories, national repository systems and institutional repositories in serving scholarly communication. SSRN Electron. J. (2010). https://doi.org/10.2139/ssrn.1506905
3. Guedj, D., Ramjoué, C.: European commission policy on open-access to scientific publications and research data in horizon 2020. Biomed. Data J. **01**, 11–14 (2015). https://doi.org/10.11610/bmdj.01102
4. Heidorn, P.: Shedding light on the dark data in the long tail of science. Libr. Trends **57**, 280–299 (2008). https://doi.org/10.1353/lib.0.0036
5. Lagoze, C., Sompel, H., Nelson, M., Warner, S.: The open archives initiative protocol for metadata harvesting (2002)
6. Lynch, C.A.: Institutional repositories: essential infrastructure for scholarship in the digital age. Portal Libr. Acad. **3**(2), 327–336 (2003). https://doi.org/10.1353/pla.2003.0039
7. Nelson, M.L., Sompel, H.V.d., Warner, S.: Advanced overview of version 2.0 of the open archives initiative protocol for metadata harvesting. In: Proceedings of the 2nd ACM/IEEE-CS Joint Conference on Digital Libraries (2002). https://doi.org/10.1145/544220.544367

LOD that Picture: Leveraging Linked Open Data to Enhance Navigation of the Photographic Archive of the Teatro Comunale of Bologna

Andrea Schimmenti[id] and Paolo Bonora[✉][id]

Department of Classical Philology and Italian Studies, University of Bologna, Bologna, Italy
paolo.bonora@unibo.it

Abstract. The paper presents the adoption of semantic metadata design and domain entity linking to enrich an opera photographic digital collection, proving how to leverage the Semantic Web to get authoritative information to enrich metadata. The ongoing digitisation program of the photographic archive of the Teatro Comunale di Bologna produced so far more than 8 thousand images over a century of opera seasons. During the design of the browsing application, the initial requirement was to access photos by simple and domain related criteria. Given that the cataloguing process produced some very basic metadata, an LD-aided procedure was developed to enrich metadata through the alignment with two external Knowledge Bases (KBs): WikiData and Corago LOD, the KB about the Italian opera. The result is a web application based on the Omeka S platform that enables users to browse the collection by works, events or portrayed artists. The experimentation confirms both the feasibility and benefits resulting from the adoption of Linked Data to organise and enhance archival information in a performing arts case study.

Keywords: Linked open data · Opera · Photographic archives

1 Opera in Pictures

This paper presents the ongoing work for "Scatti d'Opera": the cataloguing and digital archiving project of the photographic collection of the historical archive of the Teatro Comunale di Bologna[1] (TCBo). The theatre, founded in 1763, has produced and hosted opera performances for over 250 years. From the beginning of the twentieth century, sporadic shootings of the productions were taken, which became systematic after World War II. Over time, photographs of performances (opera, ballet, symphonic, jazz and drama), artists, audiences and the theatre's various tours have been collected. This resulted in a rich iconographic collection, but it did not find its way into a proper archive. With the advent of digital filming, this heritage of analogue images has become less and less

---

[1] https://www.tcbo.it/en/.

G. Silvello et al. (Eds.): TPDL 2022, LNCS 13541, pp. 518–522, 2022.
https://doi.org/10.1007/978-3-031-16802-4_56

accessible. In 2021, thanks to funding from the Italian Ministry of Culture,[2] the collection was transferred to the International Museum and Library of Music in Bologna[3] to start the first systematic inventory, description and digitisation. Then a metadata model was needed for describing images and enabling browsing.[4] Instead of referring to generic subject indexing, specific entities from the opera domain were adopted: the event, the work being performed, and the performers portrayed [1]. The chronology of performances, the repertoire and the authority file of artists', musicians', and professionals' names thus become the preferred criteria for accessing the digital collection.

2 "Madamina il Catalogo è Questo"[5]

The cataloguing activity is an essential part of the whole inventorying and conservation process. Given the size of the collection (over 30 thousand photos estimated) and the timeline of the grant, it was not possible to detail the description of subjects beyond the annotations on the back of the prints or information derived from the accompanying documents (folders, side letters, etc.). This led to a very basic description of the event without a controlled reference to the repertoire. This motivated the alignment with external information sources with qualified information to introduce indexes for consultation.

At the same time, starting from back notes carrying information on the identity of the portrayed subject(s), we began with an authority control of interpreters to relate their name to an authority file. The process aimed to normalise and qualify names within the catalogue and then to use this authority information to enrich the description of the entity with data extracted from Linked Open Data (LOD) sources.

Unfortunately, we did not have any reference to a collective authority file. We explored several knowledge bases (KBs), and Wikidata was the one with the highest number of matched entries, but for some less renowned names, we still had very little information. Then, through a Named Entity Recognition (NER) Python library, SpaCy,[6] we extracted personal names from the back notes. The NER recognized names were aligned with the corresponding IDs on Wikidata, to further extract metadata (e.g. place of birth, citizenship, gender...) via API requests through SPARQLWrapper.[7] The WikiData IDs we initially obtained contained several duplicates, which we substantially reduced via progressively more constrained SPARQL queries in order to limit the manual supervision to disambiguate duplicates.

---

[2] The project was granted under the Photography Strategy 2020 programme by the Italian Ministry of Cultural Heritage.

[3] http://www.museibologna.it/musica/.

[4] As of today, the DL requires authentication as copyright terms are under assessment. It is available upon request at: http://astorico-tcbo.it/omeka-s/s/archivio-storico-del-teatro-comunale-di-bologna.

[5] Title of the aria from act I, scene V of "Don Giovanni" by W.A. Mozart, libretto by L. Da Ponte, in which Leporello (bass), Don Giovanni's servant, shows the catalogue he personally edited of his master's amorous conquests.

[6] https://spacy.io/.

[7] https://github.com/RDFLib/sparqlwrapper.

To relate images to the corresponding work, we linked them to the depicted event, which is the link to the performed work. The chosen knowledge base (KB) for the opera repertoire was the Corago LOD KB[8] [2].

The description of the event usually contains the title of the work which is the key we used to identify the corresponding resource in Corago LOD. Once we aligned the Corago URIs, we could import information by querying the Corago SPARQL endpoint obtaining data such as the author of the libretto or the setting of the work, both additional metadata that better contextualise the photograph.

3   Metadata Design

Identification even of "famous" entities, such as actors and singers, had its fair share of issues. Similarly, works that we could neither reconcile to Corago's nor Wikidata's entries were described as simple strings within the event's record to be searched through text queries. Instead, for fully qualified works, disambiguation was almost immediate thanks to contextual information from the TCBo's performance inventory [3]. Then an entry has been created for each work with metadata extracted from the KB. The result is a uniform set of reconciled, domain-specific information supporting both indexing and text searching.

The Omeka S[9] platform was chosen to implement the browsing application as an off-the-shelf web publishing platform supporting the use of ontologies to model metadata: a basic requirement when importing data from LODs. However, it is not a "true" LOD repository as it does not use triples to store data, rather it implements LOD features from a SQL DBMS. This means that the data is not stored as RDF, although Omeka S natively employs some reference ontologies to draft its descriptive model: DCTerms,[10] BIBO[11] and FOAF.[12] Entities from our domain are conceptually representable according to the Functional Requirement for Bibliographic Records (FRBR) model [4]: the repertoire corresponding to the "work" level, performances to the "expression" level and the single photo represents an "item" of its "manifestation". This conceptual hierarchy was translated into the logical model of Omeka S with vertical (ItemSets) and horizontal relationships (resource links). Works, events and documents were represented through items with different metadata sets derived from the ontologies configured on the system.

As many data are derived from WikiData, we adopted, in addition to some Dublin Core properties, other based on those existing on WikiData ontology, creating a set of properties and classes called WikiData Semantic Model for the TCBo, in short WD-TCBO.[13] At the moment, it is just a working draft to serve as an internal model for Omeka S in which vocabulary entries for property domains were mainly derived from WikiData [5]. It will be implemented as a proper ontology towards dataset publication.

---

[8] http://corago.unibo.it/lod.

[9] https://omeka.org/s/.

[10] https://www.dublincore.org/specifications/dublin-core/dcmi-terms/.

[11] https://bibliontology.com/.

[12] http://xmlns.com/foaf/spec/.

[13] https://github.com/aschimmenti/Wikidata-TCBO-SM.git.

Specific ItemSets (functionally similar to classes) were defined for: works, events and documents. Document items (functionally similar to instances), named with the corresponding inventory code, hold the photograph's metadata and associated media: the front and back of the print in JPG format.[14] Records about person carry a set of information, mostly biographic and professional data, as well as the reference to WikiData or VIAF.[15] Events items have the title, the date and location, and the reference to the work being performed, when available. Works are described by a subset of Corago LOD metadata, relying on the external reference to allow users to get more details.

Both the digital acquisition of the photographic collection and the subsequent publication are still in progress and they are expected to be completed by the end of 2022. As of today (May 2022), the digital collection reached the following numbers: total documents: 4182, with 8080 attached images (recto and verso); total people: 266; total works: 17; total performances: 88.

4 Lessons Learned, Future Development and Conclusions

While the development of the DL is still in progress, we can affirm that obtaining qualified information from LOD sources has significantly enriched the information originally available within the catalogue. The extended set of metadata organises the digital repository according to works, events and people, all dimensions that were missing and that became the privileged access keys for the DL. Then, the repertoire constitutes the reference to timeless contents, while the events' chronological sequence highlights the interaction between repertoire and performances, telling the complex relationship between opera, its public and the surrounding society. From this perspective, each image is the vector of specific information explicitly related to both.

Our experimentation confirms the relevance of domain-specific criteria to fulfilling user requirements in DLs design and proves the role that LOD may play when metadata enrichment is required. Data extracted from external KBs let us integrate the set of information from the original cataloguing with a relevant added value. This suggests that LOD can be a starting point and not only an outcome: it can efficiently help to meet functional requirements and enrich information at sustainable costs. Besides, a close collaboration of domain and LOD experts becomes increasingly necessary in each phase of the DL's design.

Further steps will leverage LOD to cross the boundaries of the TCBo's digital repository. This starting with a further alignment with performing art KBs as Specialised Information Service Performing Arts [6] and linking the TCBo's to digital archives of sibling opera theatres such as La Scala in Milan and La Fenice in Venice or editors' such as the Archivio Ricordi. The result would be a photographic meta-archive to tell the story of the Italian opera with a documentary richness that has not been experienced yet. Then the resulting dataset should be published as LOD in order to make it, in turn, a source open to reuse.

---

[14] Original digital images (600 dpi TIFs) have been converted through ImageMagick into JPGs to reduce disk footprint and optimise the uploads via the Omeka S REST APIs and a watermark was added for future copyright management.

[15] http://viaf.org/.

References

1. Bonora, P.: Shots Behind the Scenes of the Teatro Comunale di Bologna. New Directions in Photographic Digital Archives Design. In: DIID. Disegno Industriale Industrial Design - ISSN:1594–8528, vol. 73, pp. 193–201 (2021)
2. Bonora, P., Pompilio, A.: Corago in LOD. The debut of an Opera repository into the Linked Data arena. In: JLIS.IT - ISSN:2038-1026, vol. 12 (2), pp. 54-72 (2021). https://doi.org/10.4403/jlis.it-12699
3. Pirrone, N.: Cronache musicali del teatro comunale di Bologna: Cronologia degli spettacoli 1984–2014. Edizioni Pendragon (2014)
4. IFLA Study Group: Functional Requirements for Bibliographic Records, IFLA Section on Cataloguing. K.G. Saur München (1998)
5. Thalhath, N., Nagamori, M., Sakaguchi, T., Sugimoto, S.: Wikidata Centric Vocabularies and URIs for Linking Data in Semantic Web Driven Digital Curation. In: Garoufallou, E., Ovalle-Perandones, MA. (eds.) Metadata and Semantic Research. MTSR 2020. Communications in Computer and Information Science, vol 1355. Springer, Cham (2021). https://doi.org/10.1007/978-3-030-71903-6_31
6. Beck, J., et al.: Performing Entity Facts. Datenbank Spektrum **17**, 47–52 (2017). https://doi.org/10.1007/s13222-016-0241-6

MedSeer: A Medical Controversial Information Retrieval System Based on Credible Sources

Dina Sayed[1(✉)], Mohamed Noureldin[2], and Heiko Schuldt[1]

[1] DBIS Research Group, University of Basel, Basel, Switzerland
{dina.awad,heiko.schuldt}@unibas.ch
[2] Cairo, Egypt
noureldin@protonmail.com

Abstract. The impact of misinformation on the web is harmful to individuals and society. In healthcare, misinformation can even be life-threatening in extreme cases. Therefore, being able to assess the truthfulness and quality of health-related information is vital. In this paper, we introduce *MedSeer*, an open-source system that helps lay people to assess the quality of health-related statements and thus builds a bridge between individuals and the latest healthcare research. Scientific papers from reputable sources contain rich information that has usually undergone thorough peer review to guarantee the quality of its content. MedSeer uses these sources to harvest knowledge with reliable credibility and exploits the BERT question and answering model to highlight possible answers.

Keywords: Health misinformation · Academic search · Medical search

1 Introduction

The more individuals use the Internet as a source of health information, the more likely they change their health lifestyle [1]. Acquiring fake medical information from unverified sources could be highly damaging. Many influencers, bloggers, or Youtubers on social media are constantly spreading inaccurate health-related information, and some of it can be very risky if applied by their followers, like in the case of methanol poisoning [9]. Therefore, it is essential to involve public health practitioners and professionals in designing and evaluating health-based information systems [3,5]. Such systems need to be domain-specific to acquire more beneficial results [4]. Many medical questions are controversial by nature in the sense that they refer to questions with possible debatable answers. For instance, a simple question like *"Can plasma be effective in Covid-19 treatment?"* [6] could have different answers depending on the sought information sources. MedSeer is a system that aims at countering this trend by providing access to high-quality, peer-reviewed medical content[1]. The contribution of this

---

[1] It should be noted that systems like MedSeer cannot replace a medical consultation.

© Springer Nature Switzerland AG 2022
G. Silvello et al. (Eds.): TPDL 2022, LNCS 13541, pp. 523–527, 2022.
https://doi.org/10.1007/978-3-031-16802-4_57

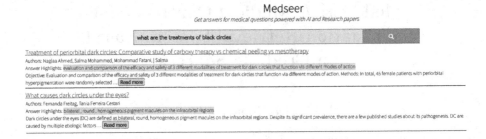

Fig. 1. Sample MedSeer search result.

paper is twofold: i.) we introduce the concept of MedSeer, its architecture and its adaptability to new application domains in Sect. 2, ii.) we present the evaluation strategy and preliminary results in Sect. 3.

2   MedSeer Overview and Architecture

MedSeer[2] is an AI-powered search engine that helps users find trusted sources for health-related questions. MedSeer uses advances in natural language processing and machine learning to extract and highlight answers to users' questions using scientific literature from academic sources at the backend, i.e., sources with reliable credibility. As shown in Fig. 1, users can simply type their question in natural language, and MedSeer will respond with related academic documents and highlight parts of relevant answers. The prototype of MedSeer follows a simplified architecture of Seer-Dock framework [13] and is shared on github[3]. Currently, MedSeer covers literature from dermatology; it is intended, though, to expand it to other health domains. The overall architecture and the entire workflow are shown in Fig. 2. The system is composed of three sequential stages: i.) *Data Preparation & Extraction*, ii.) *Data Ingestion*, and iii.) *Search Workflow*.

Data Preparation & Extraction is implemented by steps 1 and 2 in Fig. 2. To build the dataset, we manually crafted 150 seed questions in the dermatology domain, then expanded these seed questions using the people-also-ask API [10], an API that helps retrieve related questions from Google Featured Snippets. After removing duplicate questions, we generated 2,069 unique questions. To collect and download related academic papers to our generated questions, we used the Google custom search engine API and scoped the search to the websites of the most important publishers in the field of dermatology. This led to harvesting the URLs of 14,344 academic papers. We used scripts and various publisher APIs (e.g., Wiley's TDM API[4]) to download the harvested academic papers, leading to 13,088 academic papers – out of which some documents had size 1K as we were not entitled to download due to access restrictions. Finally, the preparation and extraction phase resulted in 11,822 academic papers. Then,

---

[2] http://seer-dock.dmi.unibas.ch:8880.

[3] https://github.com/dinasayed/MedSeer.

[4] https://onlinelibrary.wiley.com/library-info/resources/text-and-datamining.

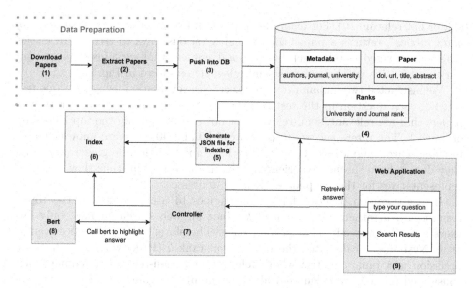

Fig. 2. MedSeer system architecture and workflow.

we used the Grobid extractor [7] to process these academic papers and extract information like paper title, abstract, URL, author names, and organization(s).

Data Ingestion is done in 3, 4, 5, and 6 in Fig. 2. The Grobid extraction output comes in tei.xml format. By using the Django framework, Grobid XMLs were imported, parsed, and inserted into a Postgres database. Some documents failed to be ingested due to the unstructured nature of academic papers, for instance because of a long paper title, missing abstract, missing metadata, unsupported characters, etc. This led to 10,239 academic papers, which were successfully inserted into the database. Using Django, we added a component to extract all ingested abstracts and titles and their corresponding unique ID. This helped in putting these papers in JSON format for indexing using the Pyserini [11].

Search Workflow corresponds to steps 7, 8, and 9 in Fig. 2. Users can type their query and search for results from the web interface. The query is processed by the controller which searches in the index for relevant papers. Getting the IDs of the relevant papers, the controller extracts the corresponding title, author name, and abstract from the database. The controller also uses Distil-BERT [12] to refine and provide highlights for answers in the abstracts of the papers retrieved. As shown in Fig. 1, the search result consists of paper titles and their abstracts. Moreover, the part relevant to the answer is highlighted in the abstract.

3   Evaluation

To assess the retrieval quality of MedSeer, we prepared a test set composed of 300 random questions selected programmatically from a total of 2,069 questions that were initially extracted using the people-also-ask API. For each question, the retrieved documents are characterized as either relevant (score 2), semi-relevant

(1), or not relevant (0). For example, a question like *"what are the treatments of black circles"*, returns a paper that explains various ways to treat dark circles (this will be rated as relevant), but also a document that explains the causes of dark circles (this will be rated as semi-relevant) as shown in Fig. 1.

We instructed two human raters to execute the evaluation using the same test set. For each question in the test set, the raters count the number of retrieved papers that are relevant, semi-relevant, or not relevant among the top 10 results on page 1. The raters age group is between 30 and 40, they are knowledgeable in using search engines like Google, they have good English language skills, and they do not have specific experience in the medical domain; thus they are good representatives for the lay people MedSeer addresses.

It is a common practice for search engines to use precision at the top k results with a rather small value of k, since for web search engines, only few users actually proceed to the second page. Therefore, to test the effectiveness of the system, we calculated the precision-at-rank-k (P@k) with $k = 10$. Since precision is a binary metric where relevant and semi-relevant documents are considered related, we calculated also the cumulative gain (CG) as the sum of the graded relevance values of all results in a search result list for the top 10 retrieved documents. The CG for a particular rank position k is defined as:

$$CG_k = \sum_{n=1}^{k} rel_n$$

where rel_n is the graded relevance of the result at position n. In addition, P@k is defined as follows: where $P@k$ is the precision at the fixed rank k and $tp@k$ the relevant and semi-relevant documents (true positives) while $fp@k$ are the irrelevant (false positive) documents.

The raters average CG values were 4.38 and 5.42, their average precision values 0.31 and 0.37, resp. The preliminary results show low precision values, yet 83% of the questions have at least one relevant or semi-relevant answer.

4   Conclusion and Future Work

We presented MedSeer, a open-source prototypical search engine that helps users find trusted sources for health-related questions using academic papers.

Based on our evaluation, we identify several ways to enhance the results: i.) *Enriching the sources for academic papers:* by adding more publishers in the domain and eliminating unrelated sources. ii.) *Enhance Ingestion:* About 28% of the papers were not ingested thus enhancing the extraction, parsing, and importing features to capture more information (e.g., publishing date or journal rank). iii.) *Enhance Inquiries:* Some inquiries are not clear, too generic, or did not have enough studies. These questions need to be revisited or eliminated. iv.) *Enhancing answer highlights:* Scientific transformer-based methods like SciBERT [2] and BioBERT [8] have proven better results compared to BERT. Similarly, we aim at fine-tuning in the dermatology domain with less consumption of memory and lower latency as in DistilBERT [12].

References

1. Ayers, S.L., Kronenfeld, J.J.: Chronic illness and health-seeking information on the internet. Health **3**, 327–347 (2007)
2. Beltagy, I., Cohan, A., Lo, K.: SciBERT: pretrained contextualized embeddings for scientific text. CoRR (2019). http://arxiv.org/abs/1903.10676
3. Benigeri, M., Pluye, P.: Shortcomings of health information on the internet. Health Promot. Int. **4**, 381–386 (2003)
4. Bhavnani, S.K.: Domain-specific search strategies for the effective retrieval of healthcare and shopping information. In: Extended abstracts of the 2002 Conference on Human Factors in Computing Systems (CHI 2002), pp. 610–611. ACM (2002). https://doi.org/10.1145/506443.506508
5. Bhavnani, S.K., Jacob, R.T., Nardine, J., Peck, F.A.: Exploring the distribution of online healthcare information, pp. 816–817. ACM (2003). https://doi.org/10.1145/765891.766009
6. Understanding the COVID-19 plasma treatment debate. https://healthjournalism.org/blog/2020/08/understanding-the-covid-19-plasma-treatment-debate/. Accessed 5 June 2022
7. GROBID. https://grobid.readthedocs.io/en/latest/Introduction/. Accessed 5 June 2022
8. Lee, J., et al.: BioBERT: a pre-trained biomedical language representation model for biomedical text mining. CoRR (2019). http://arxiv.org/abs/1901.08746
9. Mesquita, C.T., Oliveira, A., Seixas, F.L., Paes, A.: Infodemia, fake news and medicine: science and the quest for truth. Int. J. Cardiovasc. Sci. **33**(3), 203–205 (2020). https://doi.org/10.36660/ijcs.20200073
10. People-Also-Ask API. https://pypi.org/project/people-also-ask/. Accessed 5 June 2022
11. pyserini 0.17.0. https://pypi.org/project/pyserini/. Accessed 5 June 2022
12. Sanh, V., Debut, L., Chaumond, J., Wolf, T.: DistilBERT, a distilled version of BERT: smaller, faster, cheaper and lighter. CoRR (2019). http://arxiv.org/abs/1910.01108
13. Sayed, D., Nour, M., Schuldt, H.: Seer-Dock: a general-purpose dockerized scholarly document collection and management framework. In: Proceedings of the 44th International ACM SIGIR Conference on Research and Development in Information Retrieval (SIGIR 2021), pp. 2485–2490. ACM (2021). https://doi.org/10.1145/3404835.3463251

Referency: Harmonizing Citations in Transdisciplinary Scholarly Literature

Elisa Bastianello[1], Alessandro Adamou[1]([envelope]), and Nikos Minadakis[2]

[1] Bibliotheca Hertziana - Max Planck Institute for Art History, Rome, Italy
alessandro.adamou@biblhertz.it
[2] Advance Services, Heraklion, Greece

Abstract. The digital transformation of research articles that cross contemporary and traditional disciplines faces several common hurdles. The heterogeneous formats of bibliographical references, citations of works that predate DOIs, the inlining of references in notes and the use of co-referencing, diminish the effectiveness of modern-day citation extraction services. We combine structural and syntactic analysis of citations with the incorporation of knowledge bases to detect, extract and link citations and integrate them in structured texts. Its implementation, Referency, currently achieves what is unattainable even by contemporary machine learning-based solutions when dealing with nonstandard citations.

Keywords: Citation extraction · Digital Humanities · Digital curation

1   Introduction

Modern-day digital publishing workflows increasingly prefer structured document formats, like the XML-based JATS[1] and TEI[2], over readily typeset PDF [7]. However, the authors whose contributions are at the basis of such workflows can only be asked for a limited effort to sway from their authoring practices in complying with editorial norms. Citations and references are of particular interest: while authors can be reasonably required to format them according to certain standards, their structural formatting, inclusion in footnotes or in inline text, and the use of reference managers is usually left to their judgment.

Even more incongruities are found in Digital Humanities, due to vague editorial guidelines [11] and even regional patterns [4]. For instance, articles where the references are directly in the footnotes (i.e. Chicago notes), with only their first occurrence fully spelled and no dedicated bibliography section, are not uncommon. Backreferences like *ibid.* or *idem/eadem* require tight cross-referencing within a document. Additionally, much unlike the hard sciences, publications in the Humanities tend to cite historical sources, like Plato or Vitruvius, with

---

[1] Journal Article Tag Suite, http://jats.nlm.nih.gov/.
[2] Text Encoding Initiative, https://tei-c.org/.

© Springer Nature Switzerland AG 2022
G. Silvello et al. (Eds.): TPDL 2022, LNCS 13541, pp. 528–532, 2022.
https://doi.org/10.1007/978-3-031-16802-4_58

a frequency and valence comparable to contemporary sources. To further complicate matters, such sources may be referenced through one of many editions, transcriptions or translations, and these are in turn historical, hence may lack DOIs or other digital resolution methods . Editorial workflows in the Humanities tend not to disrupt the scholarly practices of authors or journals with a long-running publishing history, yet this comes at the price of citations that are hard to recognize, let alone link with OPACs and integrate back into the document. From our experience as curators of digital editions, we postulate that editors and curators avail themselves of decades worth of author submissions in word processor formats like DOC(X), and therefore a wealth of corpora from which citations can be mined more effectively than through their PDF counterparts.

We present an approach to the harmonization of nonstandard citations and references in scholarly literature across disciplines. Though grounded on a structural and linguistics basis, our approach is knowledge-driven, using open datasets for named entity recognition and reference reconciliation with authorities and databases like WorldCat. An open source implementation, Referency, realizes this workflow and generates interoperable citations in RDF format. The goal is to simplify digital editorial workflows in the creation of JATS/TEI-compliant bibliographies from word processor documents, and to contribute the resulting enhancements upon the reference data into bibliographical databases.

1.1 Related Work

Structural and syntactic analysis was integrated with knowledge-based approaches that used ontologies already in the early days of citation mining [2]. With the rise of machine learning and hybrid approaches, citation extraction was widely adopted at the software-as-a-service level: currently maintained state-of-the-art services include the open source GROBID [5] and the proprietary Scholarcy[3]. These, along with other methods that extract bibliographies from PDF [1], are limited by assuming no added value in the availability of sources in word processor format, which causes many references, e.g. in footnotes, to stay undetected.

2   Harmonizing Citations

By harmonizing citations, we mean the process that goes from detecting citations in a scholarly document (e.g. an article), to making them – and the corresponding references – actionable, reusable and integrated with a standardized version of the document. It can be summarized as in Fig. 1, which follows a reasonably standard model. First, (1) the document is parsed from its source format into a structured one; then (2) the result is processed to detect citations and extract references from them; (3) detected references are linked with OPACs and digital libraries, using different sources to refine the result; finally, (4) the citations are integrated with the structured document, and references are exported as RDF.

In what follows, the individual steps will be described in further detail.

---

[3] Scholarcy, https://www.scholarcy.com/.

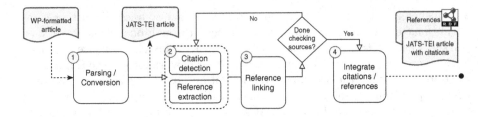

Fig. 1. Basic workflow of citation harmonization.

Document Parsing. A document in word processor format, like OOXML (.docx) or OpenDocument (.odt), must be transformed into a structured one like TEI or JATS. While the choice of either standard is not a requirement in itself, the process needs to preserve structural elements such as notes (endnotes or footnotes), since transdisciplinary literature notes are likely to carry backreferences.

Citation and Reference Extraction. A note is split into sentences to detect multiple citations, and each sentence is processed twice: first through heuristics for detecting standalone references of type author-work, then through heuristics for collective works (edited books or proceedings) complementing the first results.

The heuristics for author-based patterns further break up the sentence into candidate elements of a citation, such as comma-separated combinations of capitalized words and initials for author lists, tolerating stopwords like "de" or "van" and at most one comma . Words are checked against a dataset of given names and surnames, like the one distilled from public Facebook dumps [10]. The first candidate is found through a relaxed version of the search, to take into account that it might not be at the beginning of a sentence . Author naming patterns are cascaded, attempting full-names ones first, then falling back to initials-based ones down to the family name alone. Zero-match is also acceptable, to tackle coreferences that omit authors or titles, as in "De vita solitaria, p. 196" or "Biondo, pp. 163–168"; "*et al.*" and variations are also valid if at least one author pattern is matched. Publication-related patterns follow a similar rationale: look up place names on a dataset, like a gazetteer or GIS, and cascade patterns by preference, e.g. (`location year`) or (`publisher year`) down to location or year alone.

Collective works patterns are, for the most part, cascaded regular expressions, for example to find forms like in `<editors> ed, <booktitle>, <publishing>`, which is progressively relaxed by losing the editors or booktitle. Similar dataset lookups as for authors are performed for editors, translators etc.

Reference Linking. After stripping a citation of its coordinates like page numbers, we take the remainder as a reference and attempt to link it with entries published by OPACs, digital libraries and citation databases. The way such resources are queried depends on how they make themselves available, yet the general strategy is a progressive query relaxation using Ratcliff-Obershelp similarity [9] for author names and titles. Relaxation strategies include (a) trimming author lists if an *et al.* form is present, and (b) using shortened versions of the title .

Up to four different data sources, which can be queried iteratively, are supported for the retrieval of bibliographical references: WorldCat[4] and the art history catalog Kubikat[5] are queried by crawling their user search facility and scraping the results; BVB[6] and OpenCitations[7] are queried in SPARQL by title similarity, retrieving identifiers like DOI, ISBN and OCLC where available.

Structured Text Enrichment. Once there are no more queries left to perform for linking, references and citations are integrated back into the structured document in JATS or TEI format using the tags supported by the respective standards . To ensure reusability of references, these can also be exported to BibTeX format as well as to RDF for inclusion with linked datasets. The ontological model used for the RDF export employs a combination of Bibo[8] and Dublin Core[9].

3   Implementation

Referency is an open source prototype implementation of the described approach[10]. It is a Python Web application that can be deployed standalone or in a Docker container. It inherits from the meTypeset library the ability to convert OOXML, ODT and binary DOC for legacy MSWord into TEI and JATS [3], and uses the X3ML library to convert extracted references to RDF [6].

Anticipating a future evaluation, we report that this tool was able to harmonize loosely-structured citations in our test corpora that neither Scholarcy not GROBID detected. This is partly due to the loss of significant layout information in the transition to PDF that GROBID requires, and to Scholarcy assuming a dedicated bibliography section is always present . While being valuable tools on their own merits, they would at least require bespoke trained models before they can serve use cases like integrated bibliographies, hence our proposed approach.

4   Conclusion

Our approach allows editors of transdisciplinary publication to tackle the problem of curating nonstandard citations. Using a hybrid linguistic and knowledge-driven approach, and despite the bias of knowledge bases like the Facebook names dataset, and heuristics in need of refining, we can already obtain promising results that we could not achieve with machine learning toolkits.

---

[4] WorldCat, https://www.worldcat.org/.

[5] Kubikat, http://aleph.mpg.de/.

[6] B3Kat, Bibliotheksverbund Bayern, https://www.bib-bvb.de/web/b3kat.

[7] OpenCitations, https://opencitations.net/.

[8] The Bibliographic Ontology, http://bibliontology.com.

[9] Dublin Core Metadata Terms, http://dublincore.org/documents/dcmi-terms/.

[10] Code at https://github.com/biblhertz/referency (GPLv3), demo available at https://doi.org/10.48431/res/nxgb-q747.

Future work sees the improvement of citation detection algorithms, implementation of a pipeline for contributing to OpenCitations [8], and a user study on whether the tool simplifies the work of editors in correcting mistaken citations.

References

1. Alves, N.F., Lins, R.D., Lencastre, M.: A strategy for automatically extracting references from PDF documents. In: 2012 10th IAPR International Workshop on Document Analysis Systems, pp. 435–439 (2012). https://doi.org/10.1109/DAS.2012.12
2. Day, M., et al.: A knowledge-based approach to citation extraction. In: Zhang, D., Khoshgoftaar, T.M., Shyu, M. (eds.) Proceedings of the 2005 IEEE International Conference on Information Reuse and Integration, IRI - 2005, Las Vegas, NV, USA, pp. 50–55. IEEE Systems, Man, and Cybernetics Society (2005). https://doi.org/10.1109/IRI-05.2005.1506448
3. Garnett, A., Alperin, J.P., Willinsky, J.: The public knowledge project XML publishing service and meTypeset: don't call it "yet another Word-to-JATS conversion kit". In: Journal Article Tag Suite Conference (JATS-Con) Proceedings 2015 [Internet]. Bethesda (MD). National Center for Biotechnology Information (2015). https://www.ncbi.nlm.nih.gov/books/NBK279666/
4. Kulczycki, E., et al.: Publication patterns in the social sciences and humanities: evidence from eight European countries. Scientometrics **116**(1), 463–486 (2018). https://doi.org/10.1007/s11192-018-2711-0
5. Lopez, P.: GROBID: combining automatic bibliographic data recognition and term extraction for scholarship publications. In: Agosti, M., Borbinha, J., Kapidakis, S., Papatheodorou, C., Tsakonas, G. (eds.) Research and Advanced Technology for Digital Libraries, 13th European Conference, ECDL 2009, Corfu, Greece. Proceedings. Lecture Notes in Computer Science, vol. 5714, pp. 473–474. Springer (2009). https://doi.org/10.1007/978-3-642-04346-8_62
6. Marketakis, Y., et al.: X3ML mapping framework for information integration in cultural heritage and beyond. Int. J. Digit. Libr. **18**(4), 301–319 (2017). https://doi.org/10.1007/s00799-016-0179-1
7. Packer, A.L., et al.: Why XML? (2014). https://blog.scielo.org/en/2014/04/04/why-xml/
8. Peroni, S., Shotton, D.M.: OpenCitations, an infrastructure organization for open scholarship. Quant. Sci. Stud. **1**(1), 428–444 (2020). https://doi.org/10.1162/qss_a_00023
9. Ratcliff, J.W., Metzener, D.E.: Pattern-matching - the Gestalt approach. Dr Dobbs J. **13**(7), 46 (1988)
10. Remy, P.: Name dataset (2021). https://github.com/philipperemy/name-dataset
11. dos Santos, E.A., Peroni, S., Mucheroni, M.L.: An analysis of citing and referencing habits across all scholarly disciplines: approaches and trends in bibliographic metadata errors. CoRR abs/2202.08469 (2022). https://arxiv.org/abs/2202.08469

A Study of the Grammacographical Textual Genre Across Time

Silvia Muzzupappa[1] and Giorgio Maria Di Nunzio[2]([⊠]) [iD]

[1] Department of Linguistic and Literary Studies, Padua, Italy
silvia.muzzupappa@phd.unipd.it
[2] Department of Information Engineering, University of Padua, Padua, Italy
giorgiomaria.dinunzio@unipd.it

Abstract. In this paper, we discuss the problem of the representation of the grammaticographical textual genre across time. The choice to deal with this topic derives from the observation that there are no truly comprehensive studies on this subject, but only analyses of the work of individual authors who, although certainly useful, lack in defining a true common framework of this peculiar textual genre. We focus the attention of our research on Spanish grammars for Italian speakers published between the XVI and XIX centuries. We analyze the research challenges of a methodology to process these types of texts and the requirements of the database that will store both the textual information in the documents and the linguistic hypotheses of the researcher that study those texts.

Keywords: Linguistic databases · Grammaticography · Diachronic Studies

1 Introduction

Grammaticography, the art of writing grammars, is a particular field of linguistics which has been emerging in the last years [1]. Questions related to this new field of study are, for example, what kind of information a reference grammar should contain or how this content could or should be presented. In this paper, we examine a particular corpus of grammars, the Spanish grammars for Italians (i.e., Italians who want to learn Spanish as a second language) and other didactic texts published between the XVI and XIX centuries, in order to highlight the nature and characteristics of the contrastive traits described by the grammarians, as well as parallels and divergences with the Spanish and Italian grammatical tradition. We believe, in fact, that the study and definition of the grammaticographical genre of Spanish grammar for Italian speakers published in those centuries is relevant for at least two reasons: firstly, knowing the choices made by the authors of the past – also analyzed by contrast between the different solutions adopted – can provide useful insights for a further development of the discipline, opening new research frontiers about the methods of teaching Spanish. Secondly, we believe that the results of this project can potentially be extended to further works and different study contexts and languages, especially thanks to the digital cataloging of the common features of the texts.

© Springer Nature Switzerland AG 2022
G. Silvello et al. (Eds.): TPDL 2022, LNCS 13541, pp. 533–537, 2022.
https://doi.org/10.1007/978-3-031-16802-4_59

Our study aims to define the textual genre of these grammars for the study of the second language (or L2 grammars) starting from the identification of: i) their structure, ii) their themes, and iii) the order in which they appear. In addition, we want to describe the diachronic evolution of these pieces of these identified elements – for example, do their placement changes across time? Is there any theme or element that appears at some point in time that was never used in previous grammars? – and compare them with the up-to-date grammars. We consider and examine six texts, all written by as many different authors [2–7]. We will use an Entity-Relationship (ER) diagram [8] to describe the structure and the evolution in time and have both a conceptual description of this problem and a schema ready to be implemented in a database.

2   Research Challenges

One of the most difficult challenges of this research is the definition of the structure of the elements that compose a grammar. We need to decide the granularity of the elements that should be not too general nor too specific. In the first case, it would be difficult to see any significant difference between grammars across time; in the second case, a plethora of very small elements may be hard to follow in a diachronic sense and interfere with the research hypothesis. In this preliminary analysis, we have started to identify the main themes that are common for most (if not all) of the grammars. These main themes are the nine parts of speech (or grammatical categories), as recurring topics to all the authors taken into consideration:

1. Article,
2. Name
3. Adjective,
4. Pronoun,
5. Verb,
6. Adverb,
7. Conjunction,
8. Preposition,
9. Interjection.

The first five are variable parts (articles, names, adjectives, pronouns, and verbs), while the last four are invariable parts (adverbs, conjunctions, prepositions, interjections).

2.1   Naming and Placement issues

A first observation concerns the naming and subdivision and placements of the parts of the speech by the authors of the different grammars.

An example of this kind is the part of speech "adjective". All six authors place adjectives as sort of subcategory, or integral part, of the category "Name". It is not an autonomous category, and it is usually not even mentioned in the index or in the appendices of the book. The most common names are "*Nome Adiettivo*" or simply "*Adiettivo*". This situation deserves adequate attention because it also represents the problem of how to describe the temporal evolution of a category (adjective that is "promoted" to a category after a few centuries) and a change in the meaning of the term that designates the concept of Adjective: *"Nome Adiettivo"* and *"Adiettivo"* indicate different concepts across time.

The action of "merging" grammatical categories into a single "theme" is also an example of diachronic variation. This phenomenon is evident in Alessandri [7] in his "Voci indeclinabili", a bilingual terminology glossary (Italian - Spanish) in which the author does not explicitly specify which category the terms belong, but it is evident from the structure of the glossary that there are four invariable categories (adverbs, conjunctions, prepositions, interjections).

The same work [7] is important for another reason: the titles of the chapters are missing. It is up to the reader to infer the grammatical category the author is referring to. Moreover, Alessandri makes some sporadic references to the concept, for example, of adverb or conjunction, without ever giving a precise and unitary definition. Therefore, it is necessary to model also the absence of an explicit indication of the part of the grammar when studying the evolution of the parts of speech across time.

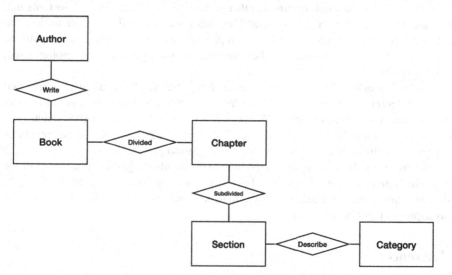

Fig. 1. Entity-Relationship diagram (simplified version, properties have been omitted for readability reasons) of the main entities and the relationships between them.

2.2 Structure vs Macrostructure

Another crucial point is the definition of the macrostructure of these grammars. The macrostructure is the order in which the topics are presented in the book. As a matter of fact, the order and specificity with which grammatical categories are treated are hardly the same for all the grammars under study. The article as a subcategory of name is an example of this kind. Without going into the issue of understanding why this choice was made, if we compare the year of publication of the grammars, it is possible to notice evolution on both the structure (categorization of parts of speech) and macrostructure (detail and order of elements) as we approach the nineteenth century: the texts become more structured, organized, and detailed. Further divisions emerge, such as the separation of the category of the article from the name or the specification of what Alexandri's "Voci indeclinabili" are, and more details are added to the topics covered, such as the introduction of the degrees of comparison of the adjective or the numerals, sporadic references are becoming less, and the precise and unitary definitions of each topic are increasing more and more.

3   Final Remarks and Future Work

In Sect. 2, we have described the challenges that the grammaticographical textual genre poses in terms of the design of a conceptual model for the management and analysis of the grammatical categories across time. In Fig. 1, we show a simplified Entity-Relationship diagram based on the requirements above-mentioned. Despite the linearity of the diagram - an Author writes a Book (grammar) that is divided into Chapters and Sections that contain the description of grammarical Categories – it is already possible to describe relationships between authors, works and topics treated even in those cases of extreme variability of the order of the detailed classification of the arguments, terminology used, definitions, etc.

The relationships between the different categories (and granularities) expressed across different centuries need to be discussed carefully. For example, how to model the fact that the former category "*Nome Adiettivo*" is related to the subsequent (and current) categories "Name" and "Adjective", and how the placement of these categories expresses the different changes of the views of Spanish grammar.

We are currently working on the evaluation of the advantages and drawbacks of the possible implementation of this model as a relational database or a graph database. At the same time, we are analyzing solutions to make this database compliant with the FAIR principles of Open Science [9].[1]

References

1. Mosel Grammaticography, U.: The art and craft of writing grammars. In: Ameka, F.K., Dench, A., Evans, N. (eds.) Catching Language: The Standing Challenge of Grammar Writing, pp. 41–68. De Gruyter Mouton, Berlin, New York (2008). https://doi.org/10.1515/9783110197693.41
2. Chirchmair, M. (ed.) Gramatica spagnuola e italiana. Giuseppe Manni, Firenze (1709)
3. Fabro, A. (ed.) Grammatica per imparare le lingue italiana, francese e spagnola. Gio. Dini, Venezia (1627)
4. Franciosini, L. (ed.) Gramatica spagnola e italiana. Sarzina, Venezia (1624)
5. Miranda, G. (ed.) Osservationi della lingua castigliana. Venezia: Gabriele Giolito. Edizione e studio critico di Castillo Peña, Carmen, Padova, Cleup (2020)
6. Perles y Campos, J.F. (ed.) Gramatica Española, o' modo de entender, leier, y escrivir Spañol. Nápoles: Parrino & Mutii (1689)

---

[1] https://www.go-fair.org/fair-principles/.

7. Polo, A.: La tradición gramatical del español en Italia. «Il Paragone della lingua Toscana e Castigliana» de Giovanni Mario Alessandri d'Urbino. Estudio y edición crítica, Padova: Cleup (2017)
8. Li, Q., Chen, Y.L.: Entity-Relationship Diagram. In: Modeling and Analysis of Enterprise and Information Systems. Springer, Berlin, Heidelberg (2009). https://doi.org/10.1007/978-3-540-89556-5_6
9. Di Nunzio, G.M., Vezzani, F.: One Size Fits All: A Conceptual Data Model for Any Approach to Terminology. ArXiv abs/2112.06562 (2021). https://arxiv.org/abs/2112.06562

A Methodology for the Management of Contact Languages Data. The Case Study of the Jews of Corfu

Georgios Vardakis[1] and Giorgio Maria Di Nunzio[2]($\boxtimes$) (iD)

[1] Department of Linguistic and Literary Studies, University of Padua, Padua, Italy
georgios.vardakis@phd.unipd.it
[2] Department of Information Engineering, University of Padua, Padua, Italy
giorgiomaria.dinunzio@unipd.it

Abstract. Language contact is an actuating force of language change and in certain multilingual settings may lead to the transfer of syntactic features between languages, to the emergence of new grammatical categories or even to the abrupt genesis of new languages. While literature in contact linguistics abounds with case studies in the emergence of 'hybrid' or 'contact' languages, many of them not only remain poorly documented, but also lack digital written corpora and therefore rich representation in the area of computational linguistics. This paper aims at i) presenting the creation of the first annotated corpus of written and oral linguistic data related to the linguistic practices of the Corfiot Jews; ii) producing specific rules on the identification of diachronic and synchronic morphosyntactic features of written and oral linguistic data of Corfioto, the Romance variety of the Jewish community of Corfu; iii) the integration of a text-mining framework for the automatic language recognition of morphosyntactic features of Corfioto.

Keywords: Contact languages · Corpus annotation · Language identification

1 Introduction

Corfioto (autoglossonym) or 'Italián Corfióto', 'Corfiot Italian' [1] 'Italkian' [2], or 'Corfiot(e) Italkian' [3] is a minoritarian Romance variety traditionally spoken by the Jewish community of Corfu, Greece and still spoken today by the very few native Corfiot Jews and their descendants, living in Greece or in the diaspora in Israel, and Italy. The emergence of this variety should be dated to the period of the Venetian rule of Corfu (1387–1797), after the settlement of successive waves of Jews from Spain and southern Italy in Corfu [4].

Previous studies on manuscripts attributed to the Jewish community, although not easy to date, provide us with linguistic evidence supporting the co-presence of different languages within the Jewish community of Corfu [5]. Linguistic descriptions and analyses of oral data [1, 6–9] support the idea of contact-induced language change affecting the lexicon and the morphosyntactic patterns of the linguistic repertoire of Corfiot Jews. Indeed, analyses of oral data collected in fieldwork highlight the etymological relation

© Springer Nature Switzerland AG 2022
G. Silvello et al. (Eds.): TPDL 2022, LNCS 13541, pp. 538–542, 2022.
https://doi.org/10.1007/978-3-031-16802-4_60

of its lexis to Venetian and Italian, while certain syntactic structures, mainly verb complementation shows significant similarities to those of the Romance and Greek varieties spoken in southern Italy and Greece. Interestingly, despite important variation among the speakers in existing oral corpora, analyses of data [8, 9] show that the impact of contact in the morphosyntax of Corfioto as spoken currently by its speakers has been such that Corfioto cannot easily fit in standard classifications of morphosyntactic features of Romance varieties [10].

In this paper, our aim is to present a methodology for i) the creation of the first annotated corpus of written and oral linguistic data related to the linguistic practices of the Corfiot Jews; ii) the production of specific rules on the identification of diachronic and synchronic morphosyntactic features of written and oral linguistic data of Corfioto; iii) the integration of a text-mining framework for the automatic language recognition of morphosyntactic features of Corfioto. The integration of a text-mining analysis of the created corpora serves a twofold purpose: a) fulfilling the need of a highly structured representation of the corpus enabling retrieval of particular morphosyntactic structures, namely complementation structures; b) the possibility to automatically recognize linguistic features in other Corfioto corpora to be added to ours in the future.

The paper is organized as follows: In Sect. 2, we describe a particular linguistic feature that characterizes Corfioto; Sect. 3 presents the methodology of the annotation of oral and written corpora for Corfioto. In Sect. 4, we give our final remarks and discuss the ongoing work.

2 The Linguistic Issue

Reduction or loss of infinitive complementation in Corfioto and replacement by finite complementation structures is the most remarkable and commented feature in all previous linguistic studies on the language [9]. In the following lines, we show an example of a sentence in Venetian, the interlinear glosses,[1] and the translation of the sentence in English.

(1) *El*   *ne*   *vol*   *parl-á-r*   *domán*
    SCL   OCL   want.2/3SG   talk-1V-INF   tomorrow
    'he wants to talk to us tomorrow'.

Unlike Venetian, considered as the primary lexifier language from which Corfioto borrowed most of its lexical and morphological elements, where infinitives, namely nonfinite verb forms, are selected by a series of complement-taking predicates such as modal or aspectual verbs, e.g. *volér* 'want' in subject co-reference, complementation clauses in Corfioto are introduced by a subordinator/complementizer *ke*, followed by a finite verb

---

[1] The glosses used in the paper are the following: SG = Singular; PL = Plural; 1/2/3SG = 1st/2nd/3rd Singular; 1/2/3PL = 1st/2nd/3rd Plural; SCL = Subject Clitic; OCL = Object Clitic; 1 V = 1st Verb inflectional class; INF = Infinitive; PREP = preposition; PRT = Particle; SUBJ = Subjunctive; DEF = Definite Article; INDEF = Indefinite Article; PNP = Perfective Non Past Form; M = Masculine; F = Feminine; PREP = Preposition; NOM = Nominative.

form, showing morphological agreement with the complement-selecting verb form in subject co-reference:

(2) *Vol-émo   ke*   *and-émo a*   *Korfú*
    want-1PL PRT   go-1PL PREP   Corfu
    'We want to go to Corfu'.

Interestingly, the replacement of infinitive by finite complementation is the most attested and eminent feature of Corfioto and the most perspicuous and widely spread morphosyntactic feature of the *Balkan Sprachbund* [11, 12].

Limited but important written and oral data in the scarce literature on the languages of the Corfiot Jews seem to support that infinitival loss in Corfioto might have been triggered by interference of parallel complementation structures in the dialects of southern Italy, the latter being one of the lands of origin of the Apulian Jews of Corfu.

3 Towards an Annotated Digital Corpus of Written and Oral Data of the Corfiot Jews

Major contemporary syntactic approaches to language change concur on the essential role of quantitative approaches to synchronic or diachronic variation in corpora [13–16]. Beyond the significant remarks regarding linguistic features in previous studies of oral data of the Corfiot Jews, building and annotating a corpus that will enable a quantitative analysis of individual and inter-speaker variation remains a desideratum. While our intention is to annotate all data in our disposal, analysis of verb complementation in Corfioto will be based on a quantitative data-driven analysis of relevant structures in utterances coming both from free speech production and elicitation e.g., translation or grammaticality judgments. Annotation of data will be performed using the authoring tool ITE (Interlinear Text Editor),[2] which enables to transcribe, tokenize, gloss and translate the texts while code-switching and borrowings will be tagged directly in the XML file.

In order to verify the existence of patterns of diachronic change exploiting written data attributed to the Corfiot Jews, we intend to compile an annotated corpus of linguistic data transcribed in Latin script coming from multilingual texts seemingly reflecting the oral practices of the Corfiot Jews. These include unedited multilingual broadsides and manuscripts in Greek and Latin, or glossaries created by speakers in Greek, Hebrew or Latin script. Since our analysis does not imply a phonetic transcription of the data, we are going to transcribe using writing conventions. Since the speakers' code switch among Corfioto, Greek and Hebrew, with respect to their linguistic profile, we have decided to fully annotate inter- and intra-sentential code-switching instances. This may lead to statistical findings of the variation of syntactic dependencies, showing co-presence of finite and non-finite complementation structures competing in the speaker's grammar(s).

Following recent proposals in automatic annotation of low resource languages [17, 18] we intend to uptake a basic annotation using a Part-of-Speech Tagging, to be followed by morphological tagging, creating a gold-standard annotation in a sample of the corpus

---

[2] http://michel.jacobson.free.fr/ITE/index_en.html.

considered as representative of Corfioto that may later be used as a test set. Emphasis will be given to the annotation of complementation structures, so as to train the tagger and to eventually expand the annotation to the whole corpus.

4 Final Remarks and Future Work

We presented an ongoing work on constructing an annotated multilingual corpus of Corfioto, based primarily on oral data collected in fieldwork and secondarily on written sources attributed to the Corfiot Jews that will enable a quantitative analysis of variation in the morphosyntactic structure of verb complementation. While an overall meticulous annotation of all data, considering metadata, such as the linguistic profile of all the speakers, given the absence of digital corpora of oral data, the possibility of mapping the annotation and quantitative analysis to concrete computational tasks would allow us to overcome the obstacle of large-scale annotation while providing a quantitative approach to the study of variation across the speakers. Given scarce annotation of oral data, we consider creating gold-standard annotations for a sample of the resource, which will be later used as a test set to finally develop a tagging tool for Corfioto. This attempt will facilitate arriving to conclusions that may enable a formal conception of syntactic change in all data to be included in our multilingual corpus. This study aims to enrich the ever-increasing interest of computational linguistics in language documentation and linguistic analysis and contribute to bringing NLP research closer to the endangered languages.

References

1. Mücke, J.: Infinitive reduction in corfiot italian: a case of areal convergence? In: Balas, A.-M., Giannopoulou, S., Zagoura, A. (eds.) Proceedings of the 5th Patras International Conference of Graduate Students in Linguistics (PICGL5), pp. 214–38. University of Patras, Patras. https://13090d2d-5e38-4d98-93e7-47a01aa1c4b4.filesusr.com/ugd/69b6b1_13334a5abde14258abecb06fa588cc3e.pdf (2019)
2. Salminen, T.: "Europe and North Asia. In: Moseley, C. (ed.) Encyclopedia of the World's Endangered Languages. Routledge Handbooks Online (2007)
3. Moseley, C. (ed.): Atlas of the World's Languages in Danger, 3rd edn. UNESCO Publishing, Paris. http://www.unesco.org/culture/en/endangeredlanguages/atlas (2010)
4. Zeldes, N.: Jewish Settlement in Corfu in the Aftermath of the Expulsions from Spain and Southern Italy, 1492–1541. Mediterr. Hist. Rev. 27(2), 175–188 (2012)
5. Sermoneta, G.: Testimonianze Letterarie Degli Ebrei Pugliesi a Corfù. Medioevo Romanzo 15(1), 139–168 (1990)
6. Nachtmann, J.: Italienisch Als Minderheitensprache: Fallbeispiel Korfu. Unpublished Master's Thesis, University of Freiburg, Freiburg (2002)
7. Vardakis, G.:. Linguistic Variation in Jewish-Romance and Greek Dialects: A Structural Analysis of the Judeo-Italian Dialect of Corfu. Unpublished Master's Thesis, Sorbonne Université, Paris (2019)
8. Vardakis, G.: Documenting corfioto. evidence for contact-induced grammaticalisation in a romance variety in contact with Greek. In: The Naxos Papers. Volume II: On Language Change (forthcoming)

9. Vardakis, G.: A formal analysis of complementation in Corfioto. Master's Thesis, Università degli Studi di Padova, Padua (2021)
10. Ledgeway, A.: The North-South Divide. L'Italia Dialettale, 3, **81**(17), 29–49 (2020)
11. Joseph, B.D.: The synchrony and diachrony of the balkan inifinitive: a study in areal, general, and historical linguistics. Cambridge Studies in Linguistics, Supplementary Volume. Cambridge University Press, Cambridge (1984)
12. Tomić, O.M.: Balkan sprachbund morpho-syntactic features. In: Studies in Natural Language and Linguistic Theory. Springer, Netherlands (2006)
13. Yang, C.: Internal and external forces in language change. Lang Var. Change **12**, 231–250 (2001)
14. Yang, C.D.: Grammar competition and language change. In: Lightfoot, D.W. (ed.) Syntactic Effects of Morphological Change. Oxford Academic, Oxford (2002)
15. Kroch, A.S.: Syntactic change. In: Baltin, M., Collins, C. (eds.) The Handbook of Contemporary Syntactic Theory, pp. 698–729. Blackwell Publishers Ltd, Oxford, UK (2001)
16. Poplack, S.: A variationist perspective on language contact. In: Adamou, E., Matras, Y. (eds.) The Routledge Handbook of Language Contact, pp. 46–62. Routledge, London; New York: Routledge, 2020. | Series: Routledge handbooks in linguistics (2020). https://doi.org/10.4324/9781351109154-5
17. Anastasopoulos, A., Christopher, C., Hilaria, C., Graham, N.: Endangered languages meet modern NLP. In: Proceedings of the 28th International Conference on Computational Linguistics: Tutorial Abstracts, pp. 39–45. Barcelona, Spain (2020)
18. Sira, N., Di Nunzio, G.M., Nosilia, V.: Towards an automatic recognition of mixed languages: the case of ukrainian-russian hybrid language surzhyk. Umanistica Digitale **5**(9), 97–116 (2020). https://doi.org/10.6092/issn.2532-8816/10740

SurvAnnT: Facilitating Community-Led Scientific Surveys and Annotations

Anargiros Tzerefos[1,2]([✉]) [ID], Ilias Kanellos[2] [ID], Serafeim Chatzopoulos[2] [ID],
Theodore Dalamagas[2] [ID], and Thanasis Vergoulis[2] [ID]

[1] University of the Peloponnese, Tripoli, Greece
[2] IMSI-ATHENA RC, Marousi, Greece
{tzerefos,ilias.kanellos,schatz,dalamag,vergoulis}@athenarc.gr

Abstract. A core research activity in many scientific domains concerns gathering data via questionnaire-based surveys. Meanwhile, annotation projects, that require input by field specialists, are invaluable in various research areas. Surveys and annotation projects share inherent similarities, since they both depend on participants who are prompted to answer a set of questions referring to particular artifacts (e.g., text segments). Both tasks are hindered by their dependence on volunteering, often requiring participants of a particular background, thus burdening research conductors to seek suitable ones. In this paper, we present SurvAnnT, a platform that facilitates the creation and management of surveys and annotation projects. SurvAnnT goes beyond existing tools offering customizable gamification aspects to motivate participation, as well as expert finding mechanisms to facilitate the identification of suitable participants.

Keywords: Surveys · Annotation · Expert finding · Gamification

1 Introduction

Designing and running survey campaigns is a core research activity in many scientific domains (e.g., social sciences, psychology), as a means to gather data and reveal important insights. At the same time, annotation tasks also constitute an important part of the daily routine in various scientific disciplines, being instrumental for the effective training and evaluation of Machine Learning models. However, surveys and annotation projects involve similar tasks, such as seeking a set of participants (either field experts or citizen scientists), who are prompted to answer a set of questions, usually referring to a particular artifact (e.g., text-segment, image). Despite being at the core of scientific endeavour, catalysing scientific discovery and/or assisting the creation of useful datasets, both activities are often hindered by their innate dependency on volunteers, thus facing common challenges. For instance, finding and recruiting the required number of participants can be a burden, especially when a particular expertise is required. Furthermore, since it is required to spend significant time on repetitive tasks, participants often become uninterested and avoid participation.

© Springer Nature Switzerland AG 2022
G. Silvello et al. (Eds.): TPDL 2022, LNCS 13541, pp. 543–547, 2022.
https://doi.org/10.1007/978-3-031-16802-4_61

Surprisingly, despite their evident similarities and common challenges, surveys and annotation projects are traditionally managed by different platforms. Motivated by the above, we present SurvAnnT[1] (**Surv**ey and **Ann**otation design **T**ool), an open source[2] Web-based platform to facilitate the creation and management of both surveys and annotation projects. This approach can be useful when running multiple surveys and annotation campaigns in order to leverage common pools of potential participants, and utilise common toolsets (e.g., gamification schemes, analytics), thus reducing the required management effort. In addition, SurvAnnT offers community management functionalities and facilitates the identification of potential expert participants by exploiting VeTo+ [2], an expert recommendation approach. Last but not least, SurvAnnT implements customizable gamification functionalities (e.g., tailored badges, leaderboards) to make the whole activity more attractive and less tiresome.

2   System Overview

SurvAnnT is centered around the notion of a *campaign*, which represents a survey or an annotation project. A campaign consists of sets of *resources* and questions associated with them. Resources can be various types of artifacts, such as images or texts[3] which are the annotation targets (in case of annotation projects) or contain supplementary information for the questions (for surveys).

SurvAnnT's architecture comprises the following set of software components: (*i*) the *Campaign Editor* enables the creation and configuration of campaigns, (*ii*) the *User Manager* is responsible for the creation of new users and the management of their roles and permissions, (*iii*) the *Expert Finder* offers recommendations for new participants for campaigns according to their expertise, (*iv*) the *Campaign Conductor* implements the required data entry procedures and the gamification features for the campaigns, and (*v*) the *Analyser* is responsible for performing basic analytics on the campaign results. All aforementioned components leverage the underlying relational database to store and retrieve data, while users interact with the platform through a Web-based *User Interface*.

The system utilises the VeTo+ [2] academic expert recommendation system, to implement the functionality of the Expert Finder component. Specifically, given a set of academic experts, VeTo+ recommends additional experts based on their similarity, according to the topics of their papers and the venues they choose to publish. To this end, VeTo+ relies on the information encoded in a Scholarly Knowledge Graph, i.e., a graph representing different types of academic entities (e.g., academics, papers, publication venues, topics) as well as the relationships among them. We configured VeTo+ to utilize an open Scholarly Knowledge Graph from DBLP [9], that largely contains Computer Science literature. However, it should be noted that since SurvAnnT is an open source tool, other datasets or even other recommendation systems can be incorporated.

---

[1] SurvAnnT: http://survannt.athenarc.gr.

[2] Source code: https://github.com/athenarc/SurvAnnT.

[3] Simple questionnaires are represented by null resources.

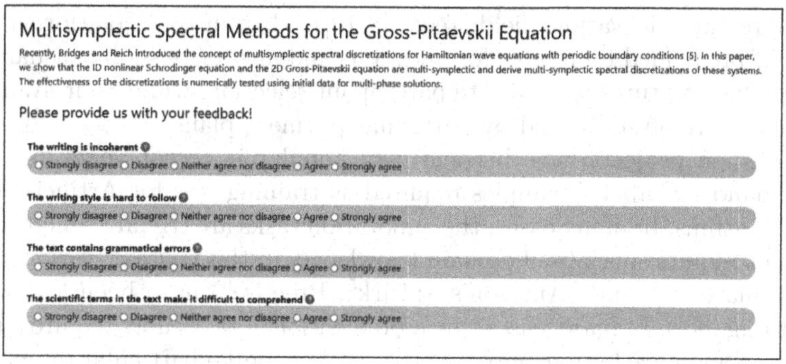

Fig. 1. SurvAnnT's annotation screen.

3   Functionalities

In the following paragraphs, we present the basic functionality of SurvAnnT from the perspective of *Campaign Owners* and *Participants*.

Campaign Owners. SurvAnnT assists campaign owners to create new and edit existing campaigns. In both cases, a set of well-defined steps is followed: first, the user provides basic information about their campaign (e.g., its name, description, active period). Then, the user selects the collection of resources that will be used for the campaign and a set of pre-existing or new questions. Each question comes with a set of possible answers. SurvAnnT supports a list of possible answer types, including free text input and 5-/7-point likert scales (see Fig. 1), which are commonly used in surveys [1].

Participants selection can be benefited from recommendations of specialists with similar expertise to the current participants utilizing VeTo+ [2]. Campaign owners can also create rewards, in the form of badges, awarded to participants reaching a predefined goal (e.g., a number of annotations). This gamification aspect aims to motivate user participation. Finally, another important functionality for campaign creators is the set of analytics provided by the Analyzer.

Participants. From a participant's perspective SurvAnnT offers the ability to participate in the available surveys upon request and a competing rewarding system based on leaderboards. The gamification aspects of SurvAnnT may motivate participants in two levels: at the campaign level based on the badge system defined, as well as at the global level, in the form of leaderboards.

4   Related Work

Traditionally, surveys have been useful tools both in science and in market research. Consequently, a variety of online tools for survey creation and management have been developed. Tools including LimeSurvey, Surveymonkey, Quick-Data [6], Google Forms, and Qualtrics Survey Platform[4] have been employed in

---

[4] Qualtrics Survey: https://www.qualtrics.com/.

scientific research in various fields (e.g., [8,10]). Most of these platforms offer a number of predefined templates for questions and answer types but usually they do not provide features to facilitate participant selection, while their availability and features are often limited by particular payment plans.

Annotation projects have become very popular in recent years due to the large demand for labeled samples required as training sets for Artificial Intelligence algorithms. In many cases, the annotation tasks are trivial ("micro-tasks") and do not require specialised domain knowledge. In this context, various *crowdsourcing* platforms (e.g., Amazon's MTurk[5], Premise[6]) have been leveraged in the past (e.g., [5]). In many cases, the aforementioned tasks may require a particular type of audience for participation (e.g., field experts, particular target demographics, etc.). Hence, platforms such as Prolific[7] focus on recruitment of such participants, who are then redirected to survey/crowdsourcing platforms such as those previously discussed. Other platforms, like Doccano[8], focus on particular annotation tasks (i.e., text annotation for Doccano). While such platforms share common ideas with SurvAnnT, our platform has some key differences. First of all, SurvAnnT does not rely solely on user-provided profiles, but instead leverages Scholarly Knowledge Graphs (e.g., [3,4,9]), which utilise information about scientists and their publications to identify experts from the research community at large, not only those already registered in the platfrom. In addition, SurvAnnT is completely open-source, non-profit, and free to use. Unlike most other platforms, which require fees, its aim is to facilitate the work of scientists by fostering volunteering and citizen science.

Finally, *gamification* techniques (like those implemented in SurvAnnT) have been used in the past to motivate participants for annotation projects. Among the most popular and successful examples of this, is the "Stall catchers" project[9], created with the aim to help acceleration of Alzheimer's research [7]. In general, gamifcation is a major technique that could facilitate and foster citizen science.

5   Conclusion and Future Work

In this work, we presented SurvAnnT, an open source platform that facilitates the creation and management of surveys and annotation projects. that includes configurable gamification features to facilitate participation and incorporates an Expert Recommendation system to facilitate the identification of field experts, if required. In the future, we plan to extend SurvAnnT to support additional types of resources (e.g., sound files) or question types, and to support conditional questions (i.e., branches).

---

[5] Amazon MTurk: https://www.mturk.com.

[6] Premise: https://www.premise.com/.

[7] Prolific: https://www.prolific.co/.

[8] Doccano: https://doccano.herokuapp.com/.

[9] Stall catchers: https://stallcatchers.com/about.

References

1. Allen, I.E., Seaman, C.A.: Likert scales and data analyses. Qual. Prog. **40**(7), 64–65 (2007)
2. Chatzopoulos, S., Vergoulis, T., Dalamagas, T., Tryfonopoulos, C.: VeTo+: improved expert set expansion in academia. Int. J. Digit. Lib. **23**(1), 57–75 (2021). https://doi.org/10.1007/s00799-021-00318-7
3. Jaradeh, M.Y., et al.: Open research knowledge graph: next generation infrastructure for semantic scholarly knowledge. In: Proceedings of the 10th International Conference on Knowledge Capture, K-CAP 2019, Marina Del Rey, CA, USA, 19–21 November 2019, pp. 243–246 (2019). https://doi.org/10.1145/3360901.3364435
4. Manghi, P., Bardi, A., Atzori, C., Baglioni, M., Manola, N., Schirrwagen, J., Principe, P.: The OpenAIRE research graph data model (2019). https://doi.org/10.5281/zenodo.2643199
5. Munro, R., et al.: Crowdsourcing and language studies: the new generation of linguistic data. In: NAACL Workshop on Creating Speech and Language Data With Amazon's Mechanical Turk, pp. 122–130. Association for Computational Linguistics (2010)
6. Nidy, D.R.: QuickData: online survey creation and data collection. In: EdMedia+ Innovate Learning, pp. 3493–3498. Association for the Advancement of Computing in Education (AACE) (2005)
7. Nugent, J.: Game for good with stall catchers citizen science. Sci. Scope **42**(7), 10–13 (2019). https://www.jstor.org/stable/26898936
8. Symonds, E.: A practical application of SurveyMonkey as a remote usability-testing tool. Lib. Hi Tech (2011)
9. Tang, J., Zhang, J., Yao, L., Li, J., Zhang, L., Su, Z.: ArnetMiner: extraction and mining of academic social networks. In: Proceedings of the 14th ACM SIGKDD, pp. 990–998. ACM (2008)
10. Williams, M., Peterson, G.M., Tenni, P.C., Bindoff, I.K.: A clinical knowledge measurement tool to assess the ability of community pharmacists to detect drug-related problems. Int. J. Pharm. Pract. **20**(4), 238–248 (2012)

Author Index

Printed in the United States
by Baker & Taylor Publisher Services